Introduction to Windows® 98 Programming

ISBN 0-13-012202-5

MICROSOFT TECHNOLOGY SERIES

- **Introduction to Windows® 98 Programming**
  Murray/Pappas
- **Core MCSE: Networking Essentials**
  Keogh
- **Building SQL Server Websites**
  Byrne
- **NT Networking Programming Toolkit**
  Murphy
- **Multithreaded Programming with WIN32**
  Pham/Garg
- **Optimizing SQL Server 7, 2nd ed.**
  Schneider/Garbus
- **Windows NT Cluster Server Guidebook**
  Libertone
- **COM-CORBA Interoperability**
  Geraghty/Joyce/Moriarty/Noone
- **Building COM Applications with Internet Explorer**
  Loveman
- **Windows NT Server: Management and Control, 2nd ed.**
  Spencer/Goncalves
- **Windows NT 4.0 Server: Security Guide**
  Goncalves
- **Tuning and Sizing NT Server**
  Aubley
- **Microsoft Technology: Networking, Concepts, Tools**
  Woodward/Gattuccio/Brain
- **Architecturing and Administrating a Microsoft Backoffice**
  Kemp/Goncalves/Kemp
- **Understanding DCOM**
  Rubin/Brain
- **Windows NT Device Driver Book**
  Baker

MICROSOFT TECHNOLOGY SERIES

MURRAY/PAPPAS

Introduction to Windows® 98 Programming

Prentice Hall, Upper Saddle River, NJ 07458
www.phptr.com

Library of Congress Cataloging-in-Publication Data

Murray, William H.,
    Introduction to Windows 98 programming / William H. Murray
  Chris H. Pappas.
       p.   cm.— (Prentice Hall series on Microsoft technologies)
    ISBN 0-13-012202-5
    1. Microsoft Windows (Computer file) 2. Operating systems
  (Computers)   I. Pappas, Chris H.   II. Title.
  III. Series.
  QA76.76.063M8675   1999
  005.4'469—dc21   99-24535
                                                               CIP

Editorial/Production Supervision: *Nicholas Radhuber*
Acquisitions Editor: *Jeffrey Pepper*
Marketing Manager: *Dan Rush*
Manufacturing Manager: *Alexis Heydt*
Cover Design: *Talar Agasyan*
Cover Design Direction: *Jerry Votta*
Series Design: *Gail Cocker-Bogusz*

© 1999 Prentice Hall PTR
Prentice-Hall, Inc.
Upper Saddle River, NJ 07458

Prentice Hall books are widely used by corporations and government agencies for training, marketing, and resale.

The publisher offers discounts on this book when ordered in bulk quantities. For more information, contact Corporate Sales Department, Phone: 800-382-3419; fax: 201-236-714; email: corpsales@prenhall.com or write Corporate Sales Department, Prentice Hall PTR, One Lake Street, Upper Saddle River, NJ 07458.

All rights reserved. No part of this book may be
reproduced, in any form or by any means, without
permission in writing from the publisher.

Printed in the United States of America

10 9 8 7 6 5 4 3 2 1

ISBN 0-13-012202-5

Prentice-Hall International (UK) Limited, *London*
Prentice-Hall of Australia Pty. Limited, *Sydney*
Prentice-Hall Canada Inc., *Toronto*
Prentice-Hall Hispanoamericana, S.A., *Mexico*
Prentice-Hall of India Private Limited, *New Delhi*
Prentice-Hall of Japan, Inc., *Tokyo*
Prentice-Hall (Singapore) Pte. Ltd., *Singapore*
Editora Prentice-Hall do Brasil, Ltda., *Rio de Janeiro*

To Our Friends

Richard and Marie Sternberg

CONTENTS

Preface xix

ONE Understanding Windows Concepts and Terminology 1

Reasons For Developing Windows Applications 1
Objects Are Everything 2

Key Elements of Windows 3
Beginnings: Windows 3
Windows As Operating Systems 3
Common User Interface 4
Preemptive Multitasking 4
Greatly Improved Memory Management 5
Queue-based Input 5
Message-based Communication 6
Hardware Independence 6
Plug and Play 8
Reusable Dynamic Link Libraries 8
Win16 versus Win32 9
Platform Independence 10
All Platform Compatibility with Win32s 10
Multiprocessing 12
Scalability 12
Distributed Computing 13
Security 13
Windows Open Systems Architecture 13
Crash Management 13
Virtual Memory 14
Comparison of Windows 14
Support for New Technologies 16
New Wizards and Utilities 16

Getting Started 16
Required Software 17
System Requirements 17

Windows 98 and NT Concepts and Terminology 17

Windows versus windows 18

Creating the "Look" 19
The Window Border 19
The Window Title Bar 19
The Control Box 19
The System Menu 19
The Minimize Box 20
The Maximize Box 20
The Terminate Box 20
The Vertical Scroll Bar 20
The Horizontal Scroll Bar 20
The Menu Bar 21
The Client or Work Area 21

Object Classes to the Rescue 21

Using Object-Oriented Technology 22
Icon Objects 23
Cursor Objects 23
Caret Objects 23
Message Box Objects 24
Dialog Box Objects 24
Font Objects 24
Bitmap Objects 25
Pen Objects 25
Brush Objects 26

Communication Via Messages 26
Standard Message Formats 27
Who Sends Messages? 28
Processing Messages 29
The Standard Message Loop 29

Standard Windows Resources 30

Standard Windows Functions 31
Calling Convention 31

A First Look at WINDOWS.H 32

Understanding the Style of Windows Code 32

The Seven Fundamental Steps for Developing Windows Programs 34
The Visual C/C++ Compiler 34
The Resource Editor 34
The Resource Compiler 34
Using The Linker 34

In the Next Chapter... 35

Contents ix

TWO Step by Step: Writing Simple Windows Applications 37

Ways to Develop Windows Applications 37
Starting the Visual Studio 38
Starting a New Project 40
Adding Files to a Project 45
Generating the Executable 53
Executing Your First Program 55
Understanding the Simple Windows Template 57
The Comment Block 57
<windows.h> 58
The Callback Function 58
A Brief Word About Handles 59
The **WinMain()** Function 60
Understanding MSG 62
Understanding WNDCLASS 63
swt.cpp WNDCLASS wcApp 65
*Understanding **RegisterClass()** 66*
*Understanding **CreateWindow()** 68*
Showing and Updating a Window 68
Creating a Message Loop 69
*Using **GetMessage()** 69*
*Using **TranslateMessage()** 70*
*Using **DispatchMessage()** 70*
***WinMain()** return 70*
The Required Window Function 71
The WM_PAINT Message 79
The WM_DESTROY Message 81
The **DefWindowProc()** Function 81

The basetsd.h File 81
Using the Workspace Pane 82
Additional ReBuild All... File Entries 83
Additional Rebuild All... Debug File Entries 84
In the Next Chapter 87

THREE Windows Details 89

Accessing the Windows Environment 89

The Coordinate System 90
Basic Mapping Modes 90
Understanding Device Coordinates 92
Understanding Viewports 92
Changing Viewport and Window Extents 93
User-Defined Coordinates 93
Choosing Initial Window Sizes, Position, Icons, Cursors, and Styles 94
Displaying the Window with **ShowWindow()** 112
Changing the Window with **SetClassWord()** or **SetClassLong()** 114
Commonly Used Controls and Dialog Boxes 114
What Is a Static Control? 115
What Is a Push-Button Control? 114
What Is a Radio-Button Control? 115
What Is a Check-Box Control? 115
What Is a List Box? 115
What Is an Edit Box? 116
What Is a Scroll Bar Control? 116
What Is A Virtual Key? 117
What Is A System Timer? 120
What Makes the Timer Tick? 121
Effective Use of Timers 121
MEMORY 122
Memory Allocation via the Operating System 123
Managing Your Memory 123

Changing a Windows Background Color 125
Examining the Application File (backgnd.cpp) 128

Changing a Windows Mapping Mode 130
Examining the Application File (mapper.cpp) 133

Using the System Timer to Control Messages 136
Examining the Application File (systimer.cpp) 139
What's Next? 141

FOUR Using Graphics Device Interface Drawing Primitives 143

The Graphics Device Interface 143

The GDI Environment 144
The Default Pixel Mapping Mode 144
Information on Installed Devices 144
Using the Device Context Handle 149

An Introduction to GDI Drawing Primitives 150
Frequently Used Graphics Primitives 150
*The **Arc()** and **ArcTo()** Functions 151*
*The **Chord()** Function 151*
*The **Ellipse()** (and Circle) Function 152*
*The **LineTo()** Function 153*
*The **MoveToEx()** Function 154*
*The **Pie()** Function 154*
*The **Polygon()** Function 155*
*The **Polyline()** and **PolylineTo()** Functions 156*
*The **Rectangle()** Function 157*
*The **RoundRect()** Function 157*
*The **SetPixel()** and **GetPixel()** Functions 157*
GDI Tools And Techniques 158
Pens 158
Brushes 159
Changing Text Colors 161
Drawing Mode Selection 162
Simple Applications Using GDI Tools and Techniques 163
Drawing a Variety of Shapes 163
Creating a Simple Bar Chart 168
Manipulating Bitmapped Images 175
*The **BitBlt()** Bitmap Function 176*
Loading and Drawing Bitmapped Images 181

Writing GDI Applications 187

FIVE   Taking Control of the Window 189

Understanding Scroll Bars 190
Speaking of Scroll Bars 190
Scroll Bar Constants 191
Scroll Bar Range 192
Scroll Bar Position 192
Two Types of Scroll Bars 192

Adding Scroll Bars to an Application 193
Examining the Application File (scroll.cpp) 199
WM_CREATE 201

WM_SIZE 201
WM_HSCROLL 203
WM_VSCROLL 204
A Word About WM_PAINT 204

Using Scroll Bars and the System Timer 204
Examining the Application File (ticker.cpp) 208
WM_TIMER 209
What's Happening in WM_PAINT 210

Scroll Bars Used to Scroll a Table of Information 211
Examining the Application File (loan.cpp) 218
The WM_PAINT Message Handler 219

Scroll Bars and Graphics 223
Examining the Application File (graphics.cpp) 228
Scrolling Images under WM_PAINT 228

What's Next? 230

SIX   Using Fonts 231

Windows Font Definitions 231
Font Constants 232
The TEXTMETRIC Structure 234
The LOGFONTA Structure 265
The Font Character Cell 237

Font Basics 238
Font Widths 239
Automatic Leading and Kerning 239
OEM Versus ANSI Character Sets 239
Logical versus Physical Fonts 240
Vector, Raster, and TrueType Fonts 240
A Scheme for Mapping Fonts 240

Font Families 241
System Default Fonts 242
Using Printer Fonts 242

Font Change Example Programs 242
The **CreateFont()** Function 242
The CreateFontIndirect Function 244
The CF Application 245
The cf.cpp Application File 247
The CFI Application 250

The cfi.cpp Application File 252
The Count Application 253
The count.cpp Application File 256 Looking Ahead 257

SEVEN   Working with Icons and Cursors 259

Icons and the Resource Editor 257
Icon Sizes 260
Custom or Standard Icons? 261
Working with a Large Custom Icon 262
Working with Large and Small Icons 268
Special Icon Functions 273
*The **LoadIcon()** Function 273*
*The **DrawIcon()** and **DrawIconEx()** Functions 274*
*The **CreateIconIndirect()** Function 274*
*The **DestroyIcon()** Function 275*

Cursors and the Resource Editor 275
Custom or Standard Cursors 276
Working with a Custom Cursor 278
Special Cursor Functions 281
*The **LoadCursor()** Function 282*
*The **LoadCursorFromFile()** Function 283*
*The **SetCursor()** Function 284*
*The **SetCursorPos()** Function 284*
*The **ShowCursor()** Function 285*

What's Next? 285

EIGHT   Adding Multimedia Sound Resources 287

Finding and Making Sound Resources 287
Finding Resources Already on Your Computer 288
Finding Resources on the Internet 292
Making Your Own Sound Resources with the Sound Recorder 294

The sndPlaySound() Function 297

Adding Multimedia Sound Resources to an Application 298

More Resources? 300

NINE Creating and Displaying Bitmaps 301

Images in the Window 301

Important Windows Bitmap Functions 302
The **BitBlt()** Function 302
Working with GDI Images 303
Working with Photographs and Scanned Images 304
The **StretchBlt()** Function 306
The **SetStretchBltMode()** Function 306

Complete Bitmap Examples 309
A GDI Graphics Example 309
Using a Scanned Bitmap Image 312
Working with a Bitmapped Photograph 320

More Resources? 328

TEN Adding Menu and Keyboard Accelerators 329

Menu Concepts 330
What Is a Menu? 330
Designing a Menu 330
Designing Keyboard Accelerators 338
The Resource File 341

Menus—A Variety of Options 345
Using a Menu to Change the Size of Graphics Shapes 345
The Header File (Resource.h) 350
The C++ Source Code File (Menu1.cpp) 351
Changing a Background Color with a Menu 352
The Header File (Resource.h) 357
The Resource File (Menu2.rc) 358
The C++ Source Code File (Menu2.cpp) 359
Determining System Information with a Menu 361
The Header File (Resource.h) 366
The Resource File (Menu3.rc) 366
The C++ Source Code File (Menu3.cpp) 367
Obtaining Directory Listings with a Menu 370
The Header File (resource.h) 377
The Resource File (menu4.rc) 377
The C++ Source Code File (Menu4.cpp) 378

What's Next? 380

Contents **XV**

ELEVEN Adding Dialog Boxes 381

What Is a Dialog Box? 385

The Resource Editor 386
Why Use Resource Editor? 386
Using the Resource Editor 387

Using Controls in a Dialog Box 389
Creating an About Dialog Box 392

Dialog Boxes Solve a Variety of Input Needs 394
An About Dialog Box Application 394
The Application File (AboutDlg.cpp) 399
Using Radio Buttons in a Dialog Box 401
The Application File (ShapeDlg.cpp) 408
Entering Text and Integers in a Dialog Box 411
The Application File (TxtIntDlg.cpp) 418
Entering Real Numbers in a Dialog Box 421
The Application File (RealMessgDlg.cpp) 428

Get Ready 432

TWELVE Special Controls and Dialog Boxes 433

Toolbars and Tooltips 434
Toolbar Bitmaps 435
The resource.h Header File 435
The toolbar.rc Resource Script File 437
The toolbar.cpp Source Code File 438
Unique Source Code 445

Investigating the Spin and Progress Bar Common Controls 448
A Spin or Up-Down Control 448
A Progress Control 453
Project Code 456
Unique Features 463

The Common Font Dialog Box 469
The resource.h Header File 469
The CommFont.rc Resource Script File 470
The CommFont.cpp Source Code 471
Unique Source Code 475

The Common Color Dialog Box 478

The resource.h Header File 480
The CommColor.rc Resource Script File 481
The CommColor.cpp Source Code 482
Unique Source Code 485
What's Coming? 491

THIRTEEN   Developing Complete Applications 493

The Pie Chart 493
 Unique Coding Features 509
WM_CREATE 510
WM_COMMAND 510
WM_SIZE 512
WM_PAINT 513
WM_DESTROY 517

The Bar Chart 517
Unique Coding Features 535
WM_CREATE 535
WM_COMMAND 535
WM_SIZE 538
WM_PAINT 538
WM_DESTROY 544

Charting Variations 544

FOURTEEN   Sketching, Animation, and Video 545

A Mouse Sketching Application 545
The Sketch Files 546
The Sketch.cpp Application Code 556

Flying Saucer Animation Application 559

A Video Player Application 570
The Common File Selection Dialog Box 576
The Code for Playing AVI Files 580

Experiment and Have Fun 581

FIFTEEN   Building Screen Saver Applications 583

A Screen Saver Application 584
Screen Saver Components 584
The ScrSav Screen Saver Project 586
Source Code Details 595
Building the Application 596

Is There More? 599

SIXTEEN   What's Next? 601

A Look at the Microsoft Foundation Class Library 601
Why Do I Need the MFC Library? 602
Design Considerations 602
CObject 603
Important Parent Classes 605

MFC Programming Concepts 610
Creating a Window 610
Using the afxwin.h Header File 611
CTheApp from CWinApp 612
The CFrameWnd Class 613
Using Member Functions 615
The Constructor 615
Executing the MFC Application 615

A Complete MFC Application 616
The SwtMFC.h Header File 618
The Application File 618
Running the SwtMFC Project 619

What's Really Next? 623

Index 625

PREFACE

What an exciting time to be living! Windows® offers an exciting 32-bit passageway into the next generation of graphical applications. Perhaps no other product has been more eagerly anticipated or needed than Windows 98®. Windows 98 frees the programmer and software developer from the constraints of the DOS operating system and the various patches applied to Windows 95®.

Now is the time to learn the programming techniques used in applications that can work across all versions of Windows. Now is the time to prepare yourself for the future.

You have declared, by purchasing this book, your interest in the Windows environment and your need for developing your programming capabilities in this area.

We have assumed that you have Windows installed on your computer and the latest version of Microsoft's Visual C++ compiler and the Windows tools associated with the product. Some programming experience in C and/or C++ is also needed.

There is a plan to the layout of this book. Early chapters get you off the ground by explaining and defining Windows terminology, the operating environment, and various functions. Simple programs illustrate these definitions and concepts. As you progress through later chapters, simple concepts are linked together to form more complex programs.

If you are a beginner at Windows programming, start with the first chapter of this book. Each chapter is a step that builds on the information presented in the previous chapter. Examples in early chapters are kept as short as possible. We want to teach programming concepts without burdening you with excessive programming code. As you progress to later chapters, the programs become more involved, as we use earlier material as building blocks to a more professional design. Stick with us—you will be absolutely amazed at what you can do by the end of this book!

If you are a seasoned C/C++ or Windows programmer, you will be able to move at a more rapid pace through the book, learning about the new features of Windows.

What an exciting time to be programming—you are on the cutting edge of a whole new programming environment!

O N E

Understanding Windows Concepts and Terminology

Except for niche environments, words like UNIX and OS/2 are quickly fading under the all-consuming evolution of Microsoft Windows 95/98 and Windows NT. In today's development environment, it is impossible to avoid coding for, or interacting with, some form of Microsoft Windows. The truth of this statement is why you are reading this!

This text is designed to help you master Windows in all its forms, from the historic 16-bit Windows 2.x and 3.x underpinnings to the user-friendly Windows 95 and its tweaked 98 counterpart to the "Big Brother" of all Microsoft OSs—Windows NT.

Whether you are an experienced Windows 98 developer already or you want to upgrade your programming skills, you'll find accurate and thorough explanations of all Windows concepts, terms, and programming fundamentals right here at your fingertips.

Reasons for Developing Windows Applications

Imagine a future of information interchange that is language-independent, hardware- and software-indifferent, and file-format-transparent. Imagine a future where universal knowledge is virtually at your fingertips; a future free of cryptic protocols, translation algorithms, and inaccessible domains. The operating system of the future will be able to:

- Access information from any source
- Communicate with others
- Easily store, retrieve, and browse information

- Integrate various kinds of information
- Automate everyday business procedures

This almost unbelievable scenario is the goal of the visionary software engineers at Microsoft. Windows 98 already includes many of these features in its document-centric approach, and the next release of Windows NT will include even more. We are on the evolutionary migration path toward tapping vast storehouses of universal knowledge.

Objects Are Everything

The goals for "information at your fingertips" include the creation, use, organization, and finding of information, regardless of what or where it is. This requires a consistent object model representation for application or system information. This scalable, easy-to-use object model gives the user a personal work space that can be customized, controlled, and extremely flexible.

Objects provide a consistent look to all of the controls for the visual interface, regardless of the data source: CD, camcorder, VCR, CD-ROM, or DVD. The object-model representation of information will take into consideration what kind or class of data is being represented. It will also consider where the information is found (the context), independent of the implementation (or provider). For example, a faxed message has certain common characteristics, regardless of whether the fax was simply received over the phone or transferred from an internal message center. However, the object-model would differentiate unique features, or the quality of the service. Design emphasis will shift totally to that of an object-based philosophy, where there will be one model for all interactions, regardless of type (users, processes, documents, or devices).

To fully understand and appreciate Windows, you must start with each product's goals and target audiences. From the user's viewpoint, Windows 98, with its new user interface, is the most updated version of Windows yet! Windows was designed to be a document-centric environment. A document-centric environment means that programs open the applications (type the name of a word processor program and that program will start the word processor automatically), not the more common way of opening Microsoft Word and searching for the file to edit.

Under Windows, the emphasis is on creating, editing, manipulating, storing, and retrieving data. The Windows NT operating system was designed as a 32-bit, high-end, secure computing platform. Windows NT is targeted for the developer, power end user, corporate MIS manager, multihardware platform, and network server implementor.

Current Windows OSs are 32-bit preemptive multitasking OSs that combine the ease of use and proven productivity of the older 16-bit nonpreemptive version of Windows (3.1) with the power and advanced capabilities of a new high-end operating system. Windows also unlocks the potential of a wide range of advanced PC hardware as it runs on Intel-based 80x86 microprocessors and RISC architectures, and it supports symmetric multiprocessing (MIPS). Thus, Windows extends your investment in hardware but not at the expense of previous investments in software. Both Windows run all carefully developed 16-bit applications written for MS-DOS and Windows 3.1. Carefully developed programs are those that follow Microsoft's rules for program development.

Upward compatibility makes Windows a safe platform for future application development. Windows 98 offers the advantages of Plug-and-Play, which frees the user from having to configure applicable hardware items such as modems, printers, pointers, etc. The Windows NT hardware interface enables it to take advantage of all current I/O technologies, from CD audio to real-time video, and to evolve with future developments. The real success for all of the generations of Microsoft Windows can be summed up in one sentence: "It makes people more productive than ever before."

Key Elements of Windows

Many users are so profoundly happy with their Windows 3.x version, that they can't understand the hoopla about Windows 98 or Windows NT. As good as Windows 3.x was, there was still a lot of room for improvement. The following discussion explains the features that make Windows the platform for development well into the next century.

Beginnings: Windows

The Windows NT development group began laying their foundations back in the late 1980s and the Windows 95 development group began in the early 1990s. The Windows NT development team was headed by Dave Cutler and included expert software engineers with experience in designing Windows, UNIX, VMS, and OS/2. The first successful boot of Windows NT took place in late 1989 on an Intel i860. In early 1990, Microsoft made the decision to base the Windows operating systems on a Windows-based 32-bit application program interface (API). Microsoft then focused its design around the Intel and RISC architectures.

Windows As Operating Systems

Compared to the conventional 16-bit MS-DOS operating system with Windows 3.1, the Windows 98 and NT operating systems offer considerable advantages to both users and programmers. Individually, the three primary capabilities (graphics-oriented user interface, multitasking, and hardware independence) are not new. What is innovative is attempting to combine all three of them into a single microcomputer operating system! Windows NT still retains the "look" of earlier versions of Windows, such as Windows 3.x. Windows 98, however, presents an entirely new user interface.

COMMON USER INTERFACE

The most obvious capability provided by Windows is the standardized graphics-oriented user interface. This consistent user interface uses pictures, or *icons,* to represent drives, files, subdirectories, and many of the operating system commands and actions. Most Windows applications make use of both the keyboard and mouse interfaces. Although most functions of Windows applications can be controlled through the keyboard, using the mouse is often easier for many tasks. With a common interface, the user will no longer have to spend long hours learning to use a new application program as all Windows applications have an intuitive feel. This consistent user interface is achieved by using subroutines built directly into Windows to construct menus and dialog boxes. For example, all menus have the same keyboard and mouse interface because Windows, not the application itself, handles the job.

PREEMPTIVE MULTITASKING

A multitasking operating system allows the user to have several applications, or several instances of the same application, running concurrently. At any time, the user can move the windows on the screen, change their size, switch between applications, and exchange information among Windows. One of the main differences between Windows 3.1 (WIN32s), and Windows (Win32) is true preemptive multitasking. Though the visual interface between all Windows versions may appear similar, what is going on in the background is completely different.

With the 16-bit version of Windows 3.1, you could have several applications loaded, but only one of them could actually use the processor at any given time. The distinction between a task that was processing and one that was merely running was important. Under Windows, the processor automatically switches between applications and does not have to wait for the currently executing program to release control of the processor. This is true preemptive multitasking.

Windows also provides a third state called *active.* An active application is the one receiving the user's attention or focus. Just as only one application can be processing at any given instant, so too can only one application be active at a time. However, there can be any number of concurrently running tasks. Partitioning up the microprocessor's time is the responsibility of Windows. It controls the sharing of the microprocessor by using queued input and messages.

Before the advent of true multitasking operating systems, application programs had exclusive control of all the computer's resources, including the input and output devices, memory, video display, and even the CPU itself. Under Windows, however, all of these valuable resources must be shared. For example, a standard C/C++ program no longer has access to all the memory not used by the system or the program itself.

GREATLY IMPROVED MEMORY MANAGEMENT

Next to the microprocessor itself, memory is the second most important shared resource under Windows. With more than one application running at the same time, the applications must cooperate to share memory in order not to exhaust the resource. Additionally, as new programs are started up and old ones are terminated, memory can become fragmented. Windows is capable of consolidating free memory space by moving blocks of code and data in memory. Windows permits applications to "overcommit" memory. That is, an application can contain more code than will actually fit into memory at one time. Windows can discard code from memory and later reload the code from the program's executable (.exe) file.

In addition, Windows allows the user to have several instances, or copies, of the same program running concurrently. To conserve space, Windows shares the same code. Programs running under Windows can even share routines located in other .exe files. The files that contain these shared routines are called *dynamic link libraries* (DLLs). Windows includes the mechanism to link the program with the routines in the DLLs at run time.

QUEUE-BASED INPUT

Under Windows, an application does not make explicit calls to read from the keyboard or mouse input device. Instead, keyboard and mouse input are treated as a shared resource under Windows. No longer can a C/C++ program read directly from the keyboard by means of a **getchar()** function call. Windows itself receives all input from the keyboard, mouse, and timer in the *system queue*. It is the queue's responsibility to redirect the input to the appropriate application by copying it from the system queue into the application queue. When the application is ready to process any input, it reads from its queue and dispatches a message to the appropriate window. This input is provided in a uniform format called an *input message*. All input messages specify the system time, the state of the keyboard, the scan code of any depressed key, the position of the mouse, which mouse button has been pressed (if any), and information specifying which device generated the message.

The good news is that all keyboard, mouse, and timer messages have identical formats and are all processed in the same manner. Additionally, with each message, Windows provides a device-independent virtual key code that identifies the key (it doesn't matter which type of keyboard is used), the device-dependent scan code generated by the keyboard, and the status of other keys on the keyboard, such as NUM LOCK, ALT, SHIFT, and CTRL. Because the keyboard and mouse are a shared resource, one keyboard and one mouse must supply all the input for each program running under Windows. With the keyboard, all input messages go directly to the currently active window. However, mouse messages are handled differently; they are sent to the window that is immediately beneath the mouse cursor.

Windows allows a program to set a timer so that one of its windows receives a message at periodic intervals. Timer messages are very similar to keyboard and mouse messages, in that they go directly into the program's message queue. There are also other messages that get into a program's message queue as a result of the program calling certain Windows functions. These functions will be discussed individually as they occur in example programs in future chapters.

MESSAGE-BASED COMMUNICATION

Windows uses what is called a *message system* to disseminate information in a multitasking environment. From the application's viewpoint, a message can be seen as a notification that some event of interest has occurred, which may or may not require a specific action. These events may be initiated by the user, such as clicking or moving the mouse, changing the size of a window, or making a menu selection. The signaled event, however, could also be generated by the application. For example, Microsoft Excel could have finished a recalculation, resulting in a need to update a displayed bar chart. In this case, Excel would send itself an "update window" message. It is also possible for Windows to generate messages, as in the case of a "close session" message. In this example, Windows must inform each application of the intent to shut down.

One last major message source could be an instrument monitoring program, such as one indicating that a critical nuclear process had reached the specified pressure. Regardless of the source of the message, your program must take the appropriate action. There are two major points to keep in mind when thinking about the role of messages in Windows.

First, it is through the message system that Windows achieves its multitasking capabilities. The message system makes it possible for Windows to share the processor among different applications. Each time Windows sends a message to the application program, it also grants processor time.

Secondly, the role of messages under Windows is to enable an application to respond to events in the environment, whether these events are generated by the application itself, by other concurrently running applications, by the user, or by Windows. Each time an event occurs, Windows makes a note of it and distributes an appropriate message to the interested applications. Thus, at the simplest level, the most important task for all versions of Windows is to process messages!

HARDWARE INDEPENDENCE

Historically, hardware devices change at a much faster rate than do operating systems. Consider, for example, the number of new printers introduced each year. Another advantage provided by Windows is hardware device independence. This section will concentrate on a discussion on how device independence is accomplished.

Windows frees the programmer from having to account for every possible variety of monitor, printer, input device, and CPU available! Currently, a non-Windows application must be written to include drivers for every possible device that it uses. This has always been one of the major inefficiencies in software development. For example, to make an application capable of printing on any printer, the developer must furnish a different driver for each printer type that may be encountered. This requires many software companies to write essentially the same device driver over and over. For instance, essentially the same Hewlett-Packard LaserJet 5 driver would be needed for WordPerfect, Microsoft Word, AutoCad, and so on. Under DOS, each software company would have to develop its own driver.

All Windows versions allow each device driver—for a video display, printer, keyboard, or mouse—to be written only once. Instead of each software company writing its own complete set, the hardware company writes one driver for the Windows environment. Microsoft includes many drivers with Windows, and others are available from the hardware or software manufacturer. One of the enhancements available with Windows is external support for font cartridges. This capability has been incorporated into the Hewlett-Packard LaserJet driver, for example. When Windows is installed, it includes one driver for each device in the current system. Whenever a command to print or draw is sent from an application, Windows feeds the output through the appropriate driver. Incorporating the necessary drivers directly into the system eliminates a great deal of redundant programming effort.

Because applications interact directly with Windows rather than with any specific device driver, from the programmer's perspective, application development has become easier. When a command is sent from the application to draw a filled rectangle, Windows will automatically carry out the task. By the same token, each device driver works with every Windows application. Developers save time, and users no longer have to worry whether each new application will support their favorite generic-brand digitizer pad. Windows achieves this device independence by specifying the capabilities the hardware must have in conjunction with the software development and/or device-driver kits.

Every routine, regardless of its complexity, is capable of breaking itself down into a minimal set of operations required for a device. For example, not every plotter is capable of drawing an ellipse. As an application developer, however, you can still use the kit routines to draw an ellipse, even if the plotter has no specific ellipse capabilities. Because every plotter connected to Windows must be minimally capable of drawing a line, Windows can break the ellipse routine down into a series of small lines.

In terms of input, Windows is also able to specify a set of minimum capabilities to ensure that your application will receive only valid, predefined input.

Windows has predefined a set of legal keystrokes. In other words, Windows predefines all the keystrokes that a Windows application can possibly receive. The valid keystroke set is very similar to that produced by the keyboard. Should a manufacturer produce a keyboard containing keys that do not exist in the Windows list of acceptable keys, the manufacturer would also have to supply additional software that would translate these "illegal" keystrokes into Windows legal keystrokes. This predefined input covers all input devices, including the mouse. Therefore, even if someone should develop a six-button mouse, you won't have to worry about compatibility issues. The manufacturer would again have to supply the software necessary to convert all mouse input to Windows predefined possibilities of mouse-button clicks.

PLUG-AND-PLAY

Windows 98 supports a feature called *Plug-and-Play*. Plug-and-Play will allow hardware devices designed for Windows 98 to be inserted into computers with no additional hardware or software adjustments. Imagine plugging in a serial port, parallel port, sound card, or modem and doing nothing else!

REUSABLE DYNAMIC LINK LIBRARIES

Just about all of Microsoft Windows' capabilities come from a set of DLLs that enhance the base operating system and provide a powerful and flexible graphics user interface (GUI). Dynamic link libraries contain predefined functions that are linked with an application program when it is loaded (dynamically) instead of when the .exe file is generated (statically). Windows did not originate the idea of linking libraries to application code, however. The C/C++ language depends heavily on libraries to implement standard functions for different systems. For example, the linker copies C/C++ run-time library functions, such as **getchar()** and **printf()**, into a program's .exe file.

This collection of routines saves a programmer from having to recreate a new procedure for a common operation, such as reading in a character or formatting output. Programmers can build their own libraries to include additional capabilities, such as changing a font and justifying text. The new function can then be made available as a general tool, eliminating redundant design. As mentioned earlier, Windows libraries are dynamically linked. With DDLs, the linker does not copy the library functions into the program's .exe file. Instead, while the program is executing, it makes calls to the functions in the library. An immediate advantage to this technique is memory conservation. No matter how many applications are running, there is only one copy of the library in the computer's RAM memory at a time.

Microsoft's new library format for Windows DLLs is more versatile. Though they have retained the same format as any other DOS .exe file (although they cannot themselves be executed), they can hold anything programs hold. In addition to functions, DLLs can also encode data and even incorporate graphics resources, such as cursor shapes and bitmaps. Windows DLLs expand the range of shared resources and save programmers even more time. Technically, when an application makes a call to a Windows function, the compiler must generate machine code for a call to the function that is located in one of the Windows DLLs. This presents a problem, because until the program is actually running under Windows, the address of the Windows function is unknown.

The solution to this problem is called *delayed binding* or *dynamic linking*. New linkers allow a program to have calls to functions that cannot be fully resolved at link time. Only when the program is loaded into memory to be run are the far function calls resolved. Windows allows your compiler to take advantage of "import libraries" that are used to properly prepare a Windows program for dynamic linking. These import libraries contain a record for each Windows function that your application can call. This record defines the Windows module that contains this function and, in many cases, an ordinal value (a numeric value) that corresponds to the function in the module.

For example, a Windows application could make a call to the Windows **PostMessage()** function. When you link the program, the linker finds the **PostMessage()** function listed in the library. The linker obtains the ordinal number for the function and embeds this information in the program's .exe file. When the program is run, Windows then links the call the program makes with the actual **PostMessage()** function.

Win16 versus Win32

Technically speaking, Windows 3.x is a sophisticated application that requires MS-DOS. It is not, although it may appear to be, a full-fledged operating system. Windows 3.x is optimized for x86 machines and uses only a small amount of system resources. For example, Windows 3.x operates very well with just 4 MB of RAM memory. By its very nature, Windows 3.x is a nonpreemptive operating environment that is very DOS-dependent. Windows operating systems are *not* based on 16-bit MS-DOS, although several DOS components have been "discovered" in Windows 98.

Both Windows 98 and NT are 32-bit operating systems. Windows 98 works well with 6–8 MB of RAM memory and Windows NT works best with 16 MB of RAM memory. Windows NT also operates on multiple hardware platforms with multiple processors. For example, you may have a server running Windows NT that uses four RISC microprocessors! Both Windows run 16-bit and 32-bit applications. This feature allows upward compatibility with older MS-DOS and Windows 3.x applications. The following discussion highlights several new components of the Windows operating systems.

PLATFORM INDEPENDENCE

One of Microsoft's major goals for Windows NT was system portability. They have succeeded. Windows NT applications are portable across several of the most popular architectures. *Hardware portability* enables code to be moved from one microprocessor to another with as little rewriting as possible. This portability allows developers and end users alike to benefit from being able to have the same operating system run on different systems. As a result, with Windows NT, a salesperson in the field can use a Windows interface on a pen-based system that matches the ones on a portable computer, on the networked microcomputer at the office, and on the minicomputer in the development lab.

For the end user, there is only one set of commands to learn. For the developer, there is only one product to design, both are happy. Financially, there is also only one initial outlay for a cross-system interface. Portability is a matter of degree. The real question is not whether software will port, but how difficult it is to port. Windows NT excels in portability. First, Windows NT is not written in a hardware-restrictive assembly language but in portable C, a programming language available on all target architectures.

Second, Windows NT minimizes the amount of code that interacts directly with the hardware. Third, because it is impossible to avoid hardware-dependent code, these routines have been localized. By not spreading hardware-dependent algorithms throughout the entire operating system, Windows NT makes porting easy. Each target environment need replace only those code sections specific to their architecture. Specifically, Windows NT encapsulates hardware-dependent code inside a DLL known as the *hardware abstraction layer* (HAL). The HAL intercepts hardware interaction, such as I/O interrupts and memory access, with a layer of software. The HAL takes care of the communication between the standard Windows NT operation and the hardware-dependent implementation. This allows the core of Windows NT to remain unchanged from architecture to architecture.

ALL PLATFORM COMPATIBILITY WITH WIN32S

With the tremendous cost of software development, designing one application that runs on multiple software platforms offers money and time savings advantages. It is extremely easy to write one Windows application that can be compiled to run under Windows 3.x, Windows 98, or Windows NT. This software portability does not exist between DOS, Windows, OS/2, and the UNIX operating systems. The success of this software portability between Windows 3.x and Windows 98 or NT lies in the Win32s and Win32 APIs. Table 1.1 lists the Win32s enhancements to Windows 3.1.

Specifically, Windows NT takes full advantage of all Win32 API features and offers access to multiple processors, distributed processing, networking, and security. Windows NT has full access to all Win32 functions and features, including **AngleLine()** and 32-bit world coordinate features. Windows 98 also

Key Elements of Windows

Table 1.1 — Improvements of Win32s over Win16.

Feature	Description
32-bit addressing	Win32 processes access a flat, 32-bit address space instead of the segmented address space of Win16.
32-bit heap	Win32 heap allocation routines, such as HeapAlloc() and HeapFree(), are supported.
Exception handling	The Win32s API also provides this Win32 capability.
Shared memory	Win32s provides some of the interprocess memory sharing support of Win32.
Virtual memory	Win 32s allows control over a program's address space. For example, some Win32 virtual memory functions and features are provided in Win32s.
File I/O	Win32s provides its own file I/O functions, replacing the MS-DOS functions used by Win16 programs but incompatible with Win32 applications.
Universal thunks	Win32s allows a Win32 application to call Win16 DLLs.

uses the 32-bit Win32 API but is currently restricted in its access to multiple processors and security features. Additionally, Windows 98 does not have access to all Win32 functions and features.

For example, Windows 98 uses a 16-bit world coordinate system and does not allow access to certain functions, such as **AngleLine()**. The official word from Microsoft is that Windows 98 will support all functions that are supported in both Win32 and Win32s—in 32-bit mode! Table 1.2 lists those features exclusive to Win32 and *not* supported by Win32s.

Windows 3.x can use a limited set of Win32 functions. However, these functions must be accessed through the 16-bit Win32s API.

Table 1.2 Win32 features not supported by Win32s.

Feature	Description
GDI improvements	The 32-bit GDI is capable of drawing paths and bezier curves, and of rotating bitmaps
Multithread support	Unlike Windows 3.1, which is a single-threaded environment, Win32 supports multithreads and processes.
Network API	Win32 provides mail slots and named pipes.
Security	Win32 provides user security to Windows NT, which is not available under Win16 or Win32s, and is not currently supported by Windows 98.
Tape backup	Win32 provides tape backup support.
Remote procedure call (RPC)	Win32 allows the control of an application from a different computer via network communication.
Console API	Character-based application development is not supported under Win32s.

MULTIPROCESSING

Very soon you are going to see a proliferation of microcomputers containing more than one microprocessor. It seems that one high-speed Pentium just isn't enough! For those high-end users, Windows NT can take advantage of multiprocessor architectures. Each additional processor added to the system delivers a linear increase in performance. A Windows NT application can allocate each thread (subtask or procedure) of the program to its own processor. Windows NT can even dedicate individual processors to system-level tasks. With this design, both the application and the operating system receive the benefits of multiprocessing. All of this is accomplished without any modifications to the application. Windows NT automatically takes full advantage of symmetric multiprocessing whenever available. Therefore, the user immediately benefits from improved performance through this transparent conversion.

SCALABILITY

Scalability is a term that refers to an operating system's ability to run on different platforms. Windows NT runs on computers ranging from notebooks to superservers, Intel-based systems, MIPS-based systems, Alpha systems, and symmetric multiprocessing machines.

DISTRIBUTED COMPUTING

One of the design goals behind Windows involved information sharing. The workplace has evolved from a company having one large mainframe computer to the proliferation of smaller and cheaper microcomputers. As a result of this hardware metamorphosis, there has come a need for these isolated microcomputer systems to communicate with one another. Windows solves this software and hardware handshaking by directly incorporating networking capabilities into the operating systems.

SECURITY

Today, more than ever, data security is an issue that more and more individuals and corporations are becoming increasingly aware of. When data storage and retrieval moved from one large mainframe to networked microcomputers, MIS managers began worrying seriously about data security. Naturally, this was not a concern of just the individual corporation, but was also an even more serious matter for our government. The government saw the need to secure one user's resources from another and to prevent any one user from garnering all of the system resources at any moment in time. Although not currently a part of Windows 98, Windows NT targets the United States Department of Defenses Class C2 security level.

This standard defines what is known as a *discretionary*, or *need-to-know*, level of protection. It also defines a set of standards that allows privilege-level audit capabilities. Basically, a C2-compliant operating system allows the owner of a system resource to decide who can access it. A system monitor keeps track of who is accessing the data and at what time. The U.S. government standard encompasses security levels from D (lowest security level) through A (highest security level). The fundamental structure of Windows NT will allow its security rating to migrate to the higher security levels.

WINDOWS OPEN SYSTEMS ARCHITECTURE

Through the use of its Windows Open Systems Architecture (WOSA), Microsoft has defined an open set of network interface standards for file sharing, print sharing, database access, electronic mail, and system configuration and administration. WOSA allows end users of Windows to access multivendor information services.

CRASH MANAGEMENT

Under Windows 98 or Windows NT, the system crashes experienced under Windows 3.x are a thing of the past. These are robust platforms with proven stability and integrity. They prevent business critical applications from experiencing any data corruption through advanced memory protection schemes. No single process—or the operating system—can bring a program down, as each is given its own unique memory space. Windows also protects from system crashes by isolating each application from direct hardware access. Windows checks each request for validity and correct privilege level. Finally, new file systems for Windows provide many file fixes, such as a full recovery system, to quickly restore file integrity. The new file systems maintain a transaction log that insures the integrity of the disk structure, even if there is a system shutdown.

VIRTUAL MEMORY

Windows takes advantage of a flat or linear programming platform, as opposed to the segmented platforms of the past. Both users and developers alike can benefit by applications that demand large amounts of RAM for peak performance. These full 32-bit operating systems, combined with a 64-bit address capability, essentially eliminate all architectural limits for your applications. One of the major goals for Windows was the operating system's ability to run MS-DOS and 16-bit Windows applications as is. This is quite an undertaking, as each environment views physical memory in a unique manner.

Microsoft's solution was to allow each of Windows environment subsystems to view memory in a manner corresponding to what each 16-bit application expects. By using a 32-bit flat address virtual memory system, an application's *virtual address space* represents a set of addresses available to a process and any of its threads. At runtime, the virtual memory manager translates or maps each virtual address into an actual physical address. Because the operating system is doing a validation between virtual addresses and physical addresses, it prevents individual processes from bumping into each other.

Many systems running Windows do not have access to large quantities of physical memory. Instead, when the virtual memory manager detects a shortage of physical memory, it automatically transfers (or pages) some of the physical memory's contents to disk. Paged data frees up the store of available physical memory. This allows needed code or data to be moved into memory. Whenever a virtual address maps to paged information, these operating systems automatically load or reload the needed data. Windows is sophisticated enough to customize itself to whatever physical RAM is available. It does this by dynamically balancing physical RAM between paged memory and a file cache.

Comparison of Windows

The list of features that each version of Windows provides is indeed confusing. Table 1.3 provides, in tabular form, a summary of features for each version of Windows.

If we are to believe the rumors that abound concerning these operating systems, the next version of Windows NT will incorporate even more Windows 98 features. This version of Windows NT, Windows 2000, is already in Beta.

Key Elements of Windows 15

Table 1.3 Features of Windows.

Feature	3.1	98	NT
features 32-bit preemptive multitasking		*	*
has auto hardware detection		*	*
has automatic recovery from a system failure			*
has C-2 security level			*
has crash protection between Win16 apps			*
has data protection			*
has desktop user profiles		*	*
fully exploits 386 to Pentium platforms		*	*
features LAN connectivity and peer-to-peer networking		*	*
has new interface		*	*
has open networking architecture		*	*
has open system management architecture		*	*
has plug-and-play technology		*	*
has remote access services		*	*
runs IBM Presentation Manager			*
runs on PowerPC, MIPS, Alpha RISC systems			*
runs Win16 device drivers	*	*	
has secure user profiles			*
supports disk compression	*	*	*
supports MS-DOS	*	*	many
supports multiple file systems + FAT		*	*
supports multiple processors			*
supports OpenGL		*	*
supports SNMP and DMI standards		*	*
supports Win16 applications	*	*	*
supports Win32 applications		*	*
uses Win32 APIs		*	*
uses Win32s APIs	*	*	*

Eventually, however, Windows 98 will merge into Windows NT as Microsoft's single operating system! Do you believe it?

Support for New Technologies

One area that may prove to be of interest to application developers is support for the Universal Serial Bus (USB). This is a new standard designed to replace the present device dependence on a limited number of hardware interrupts. Existing systems have seen ever-increasing competition by peripherals—modems, pointers, sound cards, and the like—for the limited resources represented by the 16 available hardware interrupts. The USB is designed to offer a virtually unlimited number of connections for existing and newer devices, while providing effective throughput speed orders of magnitude higher than the speed of existing channels.

Windows 98 includes support for AGP (accelerated graphics port) video cards, MMX processors, and DVD-ROM drives. In addition, you can now even connect multiple displays (using multiple display cards). Likewise, the new multilink channel aggregation (MCA) technology allows you to boost bandwidth by combining two or more communication lines.

New Wizards and Utilities

Included in Windows 98 is the Update Wizard, which allows you to connect to Microsoft's Web site to download the latest patches, drivers, and enhancements—automatically! A Tune-Up Wizard is included to defragment drives and delete unnecessary files. The System File Checker examines critical .DLL, .COM, .VXD, and other files, testing for corruption and/or modification. This utility will restore the original files if necessary. Though none of the features have any immediate impact on how you design applications for Windows, they may offer opportunities and perhaps a few suggestions for the directions of your own development projects.

Getting Started

The intent of this book is to help moderately experienced C/C++ programmers make the transition to writing applications that use the Microsoft Windows APIs. The text covers how to use all popular Windows functions, messages, and data structures to carry out useful tasks common to Windows applications. Thus, you will learn how to write common code that can be compiled and run under Windows. However, you'll also learn how to write code targeted for specific environments, such as Windows 98 or Windows NT.

The C/C++ programming language is the preferred development language for Windows applications. Many of the programming features of Windows were designed with the C/C++ programmer in mind. Windows applications can also be developed in Microsoft's Visual Basic and in Borland's Delphi and assembly language, but these languages present additional challenges and/or limitations that are typically avoided when writing applications in C/C++.

Required Software

To build all of the Windows applications in this book, you will need to have a variety of tools. For Windows application development, you will need:
- A 32-bit C/C++ Compiler. Again, we recommend either the Microsoft or Borland compilers.
- Either Windows 98 or Windows NT running on your system.
- Access to the Win32 API (usually provided by the compiler manufacturer).

System Requirements

All versions of Windows will work with 80386 or higher processors and at least 100-MB hard drives. Windows 3.x will work well with 4 MB of RAM memory. We feel that 6–8 MB of RAM memory is required for good performance under Windows 98 and 12–16 MB of RAM memory when using Windows NT.

For optimal performance for developers, we recommend the following system configuration for the best overall performance and ease of use:

- Audio board   Microsoft or Sound Blaster
- CD-ROM   4x or 6x speed CD-ROM drive
- Floppy disk type   1.44 MB 3.5"
- Hard disk   1 GB (minimum)
- Main system   Pentium running at 200 MHZ (or greater)
- Mouse   Microsoft mouse
- RAM memory   16 MB of RAM
- Video   32-bit local video bus graphics adapter

Windows 98 and NT Concepts and Terminology

Before you can begin programming a Windows application, you need to understand those concepts and terms specific to multitasking GUI applications. These new concepts and terms can be broken down into two distinct areas, visual and behind-the-scenes. Visual features include standard Windows items such as title bars, icons, radio buttons, push buttons, menus, and scroll bars. Behind-the-scenes features include invoking functions and recognizing and responding to messages.

Just like any technical area of study, for example, digital logic, knowing the correct terminology is important for correctly communicating with others. For this reason, each of the Windows features have been given a name and an associated usage. This chapter will introduce you to the basic vocabulary that will enable you to confidently discuss and develop Windows applications.

Windows versus windows

To begin, Windows, in this book, refers to the two Microsoft operating systems, Windows 98 and NT. The term *window* refers specifically to a rectangular portion of the screen representing a program, with an application-independent format. To the end user, this window is the visual interface between them and the application generating the window. To the application, this window is the rectangular area of the screen under the control of the application. How the application was written determines this window's shape, size, and screen location. In Windows, whenever the user launches an application, a new window is created. Whenever the user selects a window control or option, the program responds. One of the ways to terminate an application is simply to close this window.

As you have just seen, a window represents much more than a simple rectangle appearing on the screen. This visual interface also relates directly to specific application features, such as terminating the program. In this sense, a window represents the fundamental substructure of the Windows system and is just as important as this visual user-application information exchange. For example, though the window itself represents the graphics-oriented user interface, it is also the visible manifestation of a multitasking and hardware-independent environment. The visible overlap of applications conveys to the user the true multitasking capabilities of Windows. Because the screen is partitioned into different windows, the user can direct input to a specific application within the multitasking environment by using the keyboard or mouse to select one of the concurrently running applications. Windows then intercepts the user's input and allocates any necessary resources (such as the processor or memory) as needed.

With each window representing an individually executing application, you can easily see how this window metaphor highlights the hardware-independent substructure of Windows. From each application's viewpoint, its window is the screen. However, because Windows does not permit applications to access the physical screen directly, all interaction must be performed through the window. Because of the intervention by Windows, it doesn't matter to the application that the window may be only a portion of the entire display; to the application, the window is the entire display. It is Windows itself that sits between each application and any interaction between specific devices, such as the keyboard, monitor, printer, and so on, making all necessary translations.

Creating the "Look"

One of the main objectives to Windows was making every new application you purchase as easy as possible to learn. One way Windows accomplishes this is by requiring every Windows application to behave in a certain manner and to contain common, recognizable features. A brief list of shared characteristics might include: the Help menu and related capabilities, control boxes, About boxes, and so on. These commonalities give Windows a comforting predictability from application to application. The discussion that follows describes each of these components in detail.

The Window Border

Working from the outside in, all windows are bordered. The border consists of the lines that frame a window. To the newcomer, the border may appear only to delineate one application window from another. However, by moving the mouse pointer over a border and holding down the left mouse button, the user can alter a window's size and shape.

The Window Title Bar

In a multitasking environment, knowing which concurrently executing application you are using is important. For this reason, all application windows contain, in the top physical position, a title bar displaying the application's name. The title bar and the associated title are centered in Windows NT and placed just to the right of the applications icon under Windows 98. The title is printed left-justified in this area. Writing the code necessary to title your application is as simple as passing its title string, for example, "My Program," to the **CreateWindow()** function. **CreateWindow()**, assigns this string to the main window object's title data member (data members are functionally the same as an older high-level language's record fields).

The Control Box

The upper-left corner of all title bars contains a control box. Under Windows NT, the control box is drawn as a small square box with a flat, shadowed rectangle. Under Windows 98, the control box is usually an application-supplied and visually related icon.

The System Menu

When the user clicks on an application's control box, they see displayed a drop-down system menu. The system menu lists several standard options, such as Restore, Move, Size, Minimize, Maximize, and Close (Windows NT includes a Switch To option).

The Minimize Box

The window's minimize box appears in the upper-right hand corner of the window. Under Windows 2.1NT, this is a small, downward-pointing arrow that causes the window to shrink to a small picture, or icon. Windows 98 uses an underscore symbol to represent a collapsed window.

The Maximize Box

The upper-right hand corner of a window also houses the maximize box. Under Windows NT, this is a small, upward-pointing arrow that causes the window to expand to full size. Windows 98 uses a small rectangle with a heavy bar at the top to represent an expanded window and title bar area. When the window is maximized, this image changes to either a downward-pointing arrow or two overlapped rectangles, representing the option to return the application back to original proportions.

The Terminate Box

Windows 98 also includes one additional icon in the upper-right hand corner of the window, representing the terminate box. This is a small rectangle with a heavy "X" drawn in it, used to terminate an application whenever the user clicks the mouse over the icon.

The Vertical Scroll Bar

Scroll bars, in general, are not required window features. However, so many programs use them that they almost appear to be a standard window control. Windows demands that Vertical scroll bars be drawn vertically on the right-hand side of the client area. Vertical scroll bars have arrows at either end, pointing in opposite directions, a colored band, and a transparent window block, sometimes called the *thumb*. The thumb shows the position of the currently displayed contents in relation to the document as a whole, which is represented visually by the colored band.

A program uses the vertical scroll bar to select which page of a multiple-page file to display to the window. Clicking either arrow shifts the display one line at a time. Clicking the thumb below the upward arrow and dragging it causes screen output to move rapidly to any portion of the application's screen output. One of the best uses for the vertical scroll bar is for moving through a multiple-page word processing document.

The Horizontal Scroll Bar

Just like vertical scroll bars, horizontal scroll bars are optional window controls. If an application uses a horizontal scroll bar, it appears at the bottom of the window and runs the extent of the client area. It has arrows at its extremes that point in opposite directions, a colored band, and a transparent window block, or thumb. The thumb shows the position of the currently displayed contents in relation to the document as a whole, which is represented by the colored band.

Typically, horizontal scroll bars are used to shift the display left or right, choosing which set of multiple columns of information to be displayed. Clicking either arrow causes the screen image to shift one column at a time. Clicking the thumb to the right of the left-pointing arrow and dragging the thumb causes the screen output to shift rapidly horizontally to any portion of the application's screen output. One of the best uses for the horizontal scroll bar is to move through multiple columns of a spreadsheet application in which not all of the columns of information can't fit into one window's width.

The Menu Bar

All Windows applications have a menu bar immediately below the title bar. The menu bar is used for making menu and submenu selections (menu items are always left-justified within the menu bar). These selections can be made by pointing and clicking the menu command or, alternatively, by using a "hot-key" combination. Hot-key combinations often use the ALT key in conjunction with a letter shown in bold and underlined.

The Client or Work Area

The largest portion of a window, occupying the most screen real estate, is the client area. The client area is the application's primary location for output. It is the application's responsibility to manage the client area of the window, and only the application can output to the client area.

Object Classes to the Rescue

At this point, you are familiar with the most common components and features of a standard Windows window. From a programming perspective, the good news is that you do not have to write the bare-bones code to create each one of them. Instead you use off-the-shelf, reusable windows objects. There may even be an occasion when you will want to create two windows with a similar appearance and behavior. An excellent example of this involves the Windows Paint program. Paint allows users to clip or copy a portion of a graphics image by running two instances (or copies) of Paint. The information is copied from one instance of Paint to the other. Therefore, it is logical that each instance of Paint look and behave as its counterpart. Therefore, each instance of Paint must have its own window with an identical "look and feel."

Windows accomplishes this commonality by creating new applications based on existing window classes. Windows allows a programmer to create windows with a wide variety of characteristics. They may be of different sizes, placed on different areas of the display, have different text in the caption bars, have different display colors, or use different mouse cursors. Every window that you create in a Windows application must be based on a window class. Five of these window classes have already been registered by Windows during its initialization phase. You can also have your application register its own classes.

Windows specifies some of a window's characteristics as parameters to the **CreateWindow()** function. Other parameters are specified in a separate window class structure. To allow several windows to be created and based on the same window class, a window class needs to be registered. Once registered, the class becomes available to all programs running under Windows. Windows of similar appearance and behavior can be grouped into classes to reduce the amount of information that needs to be maintained.

Each window class has its own shareable window class structure, so there is no needless replication of the window class parameters. Also, because two windows of the same class use the same functions and any associated subroutines, classes save time and storage because there is no code duplication. The most important characteristic to shared classes, however, is that they all share the same "look and feel."

Using Object-Oriented Technology

One of the most important goals to any GUI interface deals with the common look and familiar modes of operation between different applications. If the coding for this look and user interaction were left up to the individual programmer, two things would happen. First, there would be no common look. Every programmer would have a different idea of how to draw and place an object and how it should interface with the user. Second, hardly any programs would ever get written. This later problem deals with the coding complexity involved in doing grounds-up GUI design. Fortunately, we are in the age of object-oriented programming. When you are programming for Windows, you are actually using object-oriented programming. Instead of writing the GUI code yourself, you merely use a previously written object. These objects provide the "look and feel" that end users anticipate.

By definition, in object-oriented programming, an object is an abstract data type that consists of a data structure and various functions that act on the data structure. Additionally, objects receive messages that can cause them to change. For example, a graphics object, like a vertical scroll bar, is a collection of data that can be manipulated as a single entity and is presented to the user as part of the visual interface. In particular, a graphics object represents both the data and the functions dealing with the presentation of the data. Some examples of graphics objects include menus, title bars, control boxes, and scroll bars. The next section describes several new graphics objects that affect the user's view of an application.

Icon Objects

A familiar proverb says that one picture is worth a thousand words; accordingly, icons can be very powerful. They attract the user's attention. Icons relate to program actions in the same way that assembly language mnemonics are translated into machine-code instructions. Icons and mnemonics are visual symbols associated with some sort of action. In the case of a mnemonic, this is a readable abbreviation for some action. In the case of an icon, you have a small symbol used to remind the user of a particular operation, idea, or product. For example, when a spreadsheet application is minimized, it could display a very small histogram icon to remind the user the application is still running. Clicking the histogram would cause Windows to bring the application to active status. Windows provides several stock icons, including a question mark, exclamation point, asterisk, and upturned palm. Using various Windows tools, users can create their own device-independent color icon designs. The function **DrawIcon()** allows an application to easily place an icon within the client area.

Cursor Objects

A Windows cursor is a graphic symbol, unlike the blinking underscore of DOS. The graphic symbol changes according to the placement of the pointing device; this helps to show the operations currently available. The best example of this would be the change from the standard Windows arrow cursor to the small hourglass cursor that indicates a pause while a selected command is being executed. Incorporated into Windows are several stock cursors: the original diagonal arrow, a vertical arrow, an hourglass, crosshairs, an I-beam, and several others. Using the Windows tools, your application can also create its own unique cursors.

Caret Objects

Unlike a cursor object, a caret is a graphic symbol used to show the user where input will be received. Though a typical Windows window contains many graphic markers, only the caret blinks. Most of the time, mouse input is associated with a cursor and keyboard input with a caret. However, the mouse can move or change the input emphasis of a caret. To help clarify the difference between a cursor and a caret, remember that Windows carets behave most like the standard DOS cursor. An example is the I-beam caret provided for you automatically in dialog boxes. Unlike icons and cursors, an application must create its own carets by using the **CreateCaret()** and **ShowCaret()** functions. Except for the automatic I-beam dialog box caret, there are no stock carets.

Message Box Objects

There will be many occasions on which a program will want to inform the user of a particular action. For these purposes, there are message box objects. A message box is a pop-up window that contains a title, an icon, and a message.

Programs easily generate message boxes with a simple call to the function **MessageBox()**. **MessageBox()** creates, displays, and receives the user's response from the message box. In a syntax similar to assigning data items to a structure member, your program needs only to supply the message title; the message itself; instructions on which stock icon to use (if any); and, if applicable, the stock response to use (such as OK). Other stock user responses include Yes/No, Yes/No/Cancel, OK/Cancel, Retry/Cancel. Your program can also access standard icons such as IconExclamation, IconAsterisk, IconQuestion, and IconHandand.

Dialog Box Objects

Dialog boxes are very similar to message boxes, except that they receive more complex types of user responses than do simple selections of fixed options. Dialog boxes are also pop-up window; however, dialog boxes are primarily used to receive input from the user.

A dialog box allows an application to receive information, one field or box of information at a time, rather than one character at a time. The graphic design of a dialog box is created for you automatically by Windows. Dialog boxes are considered program resources because their contents are specific to a particular application. You use your C/C++ compiler's resource editor to define dialog box objects.

Font Objects

If you understand the simple definition of an object, meaning the syntactic combination of data members (remember, a member is no different than a record field), bundled with all of the function members that make the object do something, you'll understand why even fonts are considered objects. Long gone are the days when the characters displayed on your monitor came from a single character ROM built into your system. On the contrary, today's applications seem to have unlimited font capabilities, from typefaces to point sizes to the standard bold, italics, and underline.

Your programs use font objects, or resources, to define a complete set of characters from one typeface, all with a certain size and style. Fonts can be manipulated to give text a variety of appearances. By using built-in routines, Windows allows for the dynamic modification of a typeface, including boldface or italic, underlining, or changing the font size. Windows provides all of the necessary functions for displaying text anywhere within the client area and, even better, due to Windows device independence, an application's output will have a consistent appearance from one output device to the next.

Bitmap Objects

You can think of a bitmap object as a small picture. There are two basic uses for bitmaps. First, bitmaps are used to draw pictures on the display. For example, Windows uses many small bitmaps to draw arrows in scroll bars; to display check marks when the user selects pull-down menu options; and to draw the system menu box, the size box, and many others. Bitmaps are also used for creating brushes, which will be covered shortly. These pixel pictures are stored in memory. Bitmaps are used whenever an application wants to display a graphics image quickly. Because the object is being transferred directly from memory, it can be displayed faster than the code necessary to recreate the image that can be executed.

For all of their display speed characteristics, bitmaps do have their disadvantages. First, depending on their size, bitmaps can occupy an unpredictably large portion of memory. For each pixel being displayed, there has to be an equivalent representation in memory. Displaying the same bitmap in color versus a monochrome rendering requires much more memory. In a monochrome bitmap, one bit can define a pixel as on or off. However, a color bitmap using 16 colors requires that each pixel be represented by 4 bits. In computer work, a nibble is 4 bits. Thus, as the resolution of the graphics image increases, so does the memory requirement—and what about today's 64-bit graphics devices!

A less serious disadvantage, because there are ways of coding around this, is that a bitmap is a composite picture, meaning that you cannot break apart its individual components. Take, for example, a bitmap of a personal computer. The user cannot go into this bitmap and click only on the image of the monitor to select it separately from the entire system. However, if the bitmap had been constructed from a series of routines, an application would be able to change the data supplied to these routines and modify the picture. For example, an application could modify the personal computer drawing routine to include a monitor, system unit, keyboard, and so on.

Pen Objects

You might not realize that all Windows applications use pen objects to draw lines and outline shapes. Pen objects have three basic characteristics: line width, style (dotted, dashed, solid, and so on), and color. Under Windows, a pen for drawing black lines and one for drawing white lines are always available to each application. The black pen is the default pen. Of course, you can always create your own pens. One good example of an alternate pen style is the dashed line that many spreadsheet applications use to highlight user-selected groups of cells.

Brush Objects

Many graphics applications use a small picture of a tipped paint can dribbling paint to represent a flood-fill type operation. In Windows, brushes are used to paint colors and to flood fill areas with predefined patterns. A Windows brush has a minimum size of 8 x 8 pixels and, like pens, have three basic characteristics: size, pattern, and color. With their 8 x 8 pixel minimum, brushes are said to have a pattern—not a style, as pens do. A brush's appearance may come from a compiler-supplied definition, such as a solid color to hatched to diagonal, or from an application-supplied bit-pattern.

Communication Via Messages

Because the term *multitasking* does not mean "multihardware," something has to take control of directing I/O from each concurrently running application down to the one system that all applications are sharing. Windows takes charge of the single system's keyboard, video display, mouse, parallel and serial ports, memory, and program execution. It is important to realize that Windows accomplishes all that it does because of its hardware dominance. For example, it is only by taking control of the hardware that Windows can partition the display screen into separate windows.

By managing the hardware, Windows can intercept all user input and distribute that input as messages to the appropriate applications. Finally, it is only through the total control of the hardware that Windows can ensure that an application can interface with a variety of output devices, thereby creating a "virtual machine." Under Windows, an application does not write directly to the screen, process any hardware interrupts, or output directly to the printer. Instead, the application uses the appropriate Windows functions or it waits for an appropriate message to be delivered. Applications development under Windows must now incorporate the processing of the application and the user's view of the application through Windows.

From an application's viewpoint, a message is a notification that some event of interest has occurred—an event that may or may not require a specific action. These events may have been initiated by the user by clicking, moving the mouse, changing the size of a window, or making a menu selection. However, the signaled event could have been generated by the application. The net effect of all of this is that applications must now be totally oriented toward processing messages. Applications must be capable of awakening, determining the appropriate action based on the type of message received, taking that action to completion, and returning to sleep. As a result of this new communication,

Windows applications are significantly different from their older DOS counterparts. Under Windows 3.1, over 2,300 function calls were available. Windows have access to even more.

Windows divides message processing into three general layers, called EXECUTIVE, GDI (graphics device interface), and USER. The EXECUTIVE module is responsible for memory management, loading and running an application, and scheduling. The GDI contains all of the routines to create and display graphics. The USER module takes care of all other application requirements.

Standard Message Formats

In this next section, you will take a closer look at the message system, examining the format and sources of messages, several common message types, and the ways in which both Windows and your application go about processing messages. The purpose of a message is to notify your program that an event of interest has occurred. Technically, a message is not of interest just to the application, but to a specific window within that application. Therefore, every message is addressed to a window.

There are actually two categories of message queues, the Windows system message queue and each concurrently running program's message queue. Each message in the system message queue must eventually be transferred to a program's message queue. The program's message queue stores all messages for all the windows in that program. The following four parameters are associated with all messages: a window handle (identifying which window is receiving the message), a message type, an lParam value, and a wParam value. Under Windows 3.x, handles are 16 bits, messages are 16 bits, LPARAM is 32 bits, and WPARAM is 16 bits. Under Windows 98 and NT, handles are 32 bits, messages are 32 bits, LPARAM is 32 bits and WPARAM is now 32 bits (because the parameter types are defined as symbolic constants LPARAM and WPARAM instead of standard data types, their specific meaning can be easily redefined for each target platform).

The window handle in an object-oriented programming environment is simply an identifier of an object, which for the current syntax is the identifier of the particular window to which the message is addressed. Frequently, this handle will reference an object (defined in the form of a data structure) that is located in a movable portion of memory. It is important to realize that, even though the portion of memory can be moved, the handle remains the same. This allows Windows to manage memory efficiently while leaving the relocation invisible to the application. Because multiple windows can be created based on the same window class, a single window function could process messages for more than one window within a single program. Under these circumstances, the application would use the handle to determine which window is receiving the message.

The message type obtains its meaning from one of several symbolic constants defined in the standard windows.h header file, discussed later in this chapter. Under Windows, each message type is represented by a two-character mnemonic, followed by the underscore character and, finally, a descriptor to complete the message. The most common message types include WM_CREATE, WM_PAINT, WM_CLOSE, WM_COPY, and WM_PASTE. Other message types include control window messages BM_xxxxxxxxxx, edit control messages EM_xxxxxxxxxx, and list box messages LB_xxxxxxxxxx (where xxxxxxxxxx represents different message types within the same category). If this list is not sufficient, your application can create and register its own types. Application-specific message types are not shared by other applications and are one way of generating private message types.

The contents of these last two parameters, LPARAM and WPARAM, provide any additional information necessary to interpret the message and vary, depending on the message type. Examples of the types of information that would be passed include which key was just struck, the position of the vertical or horizontal scroll bar elevators, the selected pop-up menu item, the position of the mouse, and even the status of the mouse buttons.

Who Sends Messages?

Basically, there are four sources for a message. An application can receive a message from the user, from Windows itself, from the application program itself, or from another application. It is through the underlying structure of messages that Windows is capable of multitasking. Therefore, all messages must be processed by Windows

Typical, user-input messages include keystroke information, mouse movements, point-and-click coordinates, menu selections, the location of scroll bar elevators, and so on. Your application program will devote a great deal of time to processing user messages.

When Windows itself is posting an application-specific message, Windows is usually signaling a state change—for example, when the user clicks an application's icon to make that application active. In this case, Windows tells the application that its main window is being opened, that its size and location are being modified, and so forth. Windows-originated messages can be either responded to or ignored, depending on the current state of an application.

To facilitate application-to-application message posting, Microsoft has developed the dynamic data exchange (DDE) protocol. Currently, most applications written for Windows do not take full advantage of the fourth type of message source, intertask communication. However, this category will become increasingly important as more and more applications use this integration capability.

Processing Messages

Application-specific processing of recognized message types is usually performed by functions. A Windows application will have a procedure for processing each type of message that is of interest to any of its windows. However, different windows may respond differently to messages of the same type. For example, one application may have two windows that respond in different ways to the press of the mouse button.

The first window may respond by changing the background color; the second window may respond by placing cross-hatching on a spreadsheet. Because the same message can be interpreted differently by different windows, you can understand why Windows addresses each message to a specific window within an application. Not only will the application have a different procedure to handle each message type, it will need a procedure to handle each message type for each window. The window procedure is used to group together all the message-type procedures for a Windows application.

The Standard Message Loop

All of the stand-alone functions your program uses to process messages are triggered by what is called the Windows application *message processing loop*. Each application will contain procedures to create and initialize windows, which are followed by the message processing loop and, finally, by some required closing code. The message loop is responsible for processing a message delivered by Windows to the main body of the program. Here the program acknowledges the message and requests Windows to send it to the appropriate window procedure for processing. Then the window procedure executes the desired action.

As you have already seen, messages can be sent from one of two queues, either the system queue or the application's message queue. The message queue and dispatching priority are two factors that can influence the sequence in which a message is processed. Messages are first placed in the system queue. When a message reaches the front of the queue, it is sent over to the appropriate application's message queue. This dual mode allows Windows to keep track of all messages while allowing each application to track only those messages that pertain to it. Most messages go into these queues as you would expect, in first-in–first-out order (FIFO). These are called *synchronous messages*. Most Windows applications use this type of dispatching method.

However, there are occasions when Windows will push a message to the end of the queue, thereby preventing it from being dispatched. Messages of this type are called *asynchronous messages*. Care must be taken when sending an asynchronous message that overrides the application's normal sequence of processing. There are three types of asynchronous messages; paint, timer, and quit. A timer message, for example, causes a certain action to take effect at a specified time, regardless of the messages to be processed at that moment.

Therefore, a timer message will cause all other messages in the queue to be pushed farther from the queue front.

Windows also has asynchronous messages that can be sent to other applications. This scenario is unique, in that the receiving application doesn't put the message into its queue. Instead, the message immediately calls the receiving application's appropriate window procedure, where the message then executes.

How does Windows dispatch messages that are pending for several applications at once? Windows settles this issue in one of two ways. One method of message processing is called *dispatching priority*. Each time Windows loads an application, it sets the application's priority to one of the following four levels:

- HIGH_PRIORITY_CLASS
- IDLE_PRIORITY_CLASS
- NORMAL_PRIORITY_CLASS
- REALTIME_PRIORITY_CLASS

However, an application can change its priority. All things being equal, Windows would then settle any dispatching contention by sending messages to the highest-priority application. A data communications application is an example of a program that might need to raise its priority level. If your system were connected to a distant host computer, you would want to process the information being sent long distance as soon as possible.

Normally, an application, with a properly chosen priority level won't need to change a message's priority. Because tampering with an application's priority level is very uncommon, Windows must have another method for dispatching messages to concurrent applications with the same priority level. Besides processing the messages in the queue, whenever Windows sees that a particular application has a backlog of unprocessed messages, it hangs on to any new messages for that application while continuing to dispatch other messages to other applications.

Standard Windows Resources

In general, a resource represents data that is included in a program's .exe file, although, technically speaking, it does not reside in a program's normal data segment. The graphics objects described earlier included icons, cursors, carets, message boxes, dialog boxes, fonts, bitmaps, pens, and brushes. These are all examples of Windows resources. When Windows loads a program into memory for execution, very often it will leave all of the resources on the disk. One example of this is when the user first requests to see an application's About dialog box. Before Windows can display the About box, it must first access the disk to copy this information from the program's .exe file into memory.

To make the most efficient reuse of memory possible, an application typically defines its resources as read-only and discardable. This allows Windows to discard the resource whenever more memory is required. Under Windows 3.x, resources are essentially unowned, and should the resource be requested again, Windows simply reads the disk and reloads the data into memory. Thus, multiple instances of the same application running concurrently (for instance, a word processor), will not only share the application's program code, but its resource definitions as well. Under Win32, resources are owned by the application and are not sharable.

Standard Windows Functions

The following list contains some of the most frequently used message processing functions: **RegisterWindowMessage()**, **PostMessage()**, and **DispatchMessage()**. Officially called the *API*, parameters are passed via the stack to the various modules that make up Windows. Under Windows 3.x, Windows functions returned 16-bit integer addresses. However, under Windows these addresses are now 32 bits as they are no longer the shorter 2-byte integer-offset addresses, but instead a full 4-byte integer-linear address.

Calling Convention

As just discussed, parameters to all Windows functions are passed via the stack. In a C/C++ program, for example, function parameters are first pushed onto the stack and then the function is called. Normally, the parameters are pushed starting from the right-most parameter and going to the left-most parameter. Upon return from the function, the calling procedure must adjust the stack pointer to a value equal to the number of bytes originally pushed onto the stack. In Windows, however, things look slightly different.

One of the most frequently observed function modifiers seen in Windows applications is the WINAPI modifier. The WINAPI modifier instructs the C/C++ compiler to push parameters from left to right, with the called function having the responsibility to adjust the stack before the return. It is no longer the job of the calling procedure to adjust the stack.

Windows uses this calling convention because it turns out to be more space-efficient. Therefore, the Microsoft C/C++ compiler understands that any function declared with the symbolic constant WINAPI is to use the more efficient calling convention. However, the efficiency of using the WINAPI calling convention comes with its own set of problems. This calling sequence makes coding functions with a variable number of parameters more difficult. For this reason, the Windows C/C++ compiler still uses **__cdecl** when prototyping variable argument functions.

A First Look at WINDOWS.H

Many Windows functions work with their own specified data types and variables, which your program can access. These variables and types are defined in previously mentioned header files. To use certain functions, you must include the header file in which they are defined. This is accomplished by placing an #include statement in your source program. Technically, the #define statements found in these header files associate a numeric constant with a text identifier, for example:

```
#define WM_CREATE 0x0001
```

The C/C++ compiler will use the hexadecimal constant 0x0001 as a replacement for WM_CREATE during preprocessing. Other typedef statements may appear a bit unusual, for example:

```
typedef int    INT
typedef float  FLOAT
```

In Microsoft C/C++, both int and float are reserved words. Your applications should use the uppercase INT and FLOAT for one very good reason: Should you decide to port your application over to another C/C++ compiler, it would certainly be much easier to change the typedef statements within the header file than to change all the occurrences of a particular identifier.

You may be interested to know that the original version of windows.h contained Windows-specific constants, type, and function prototypes, and occupied a mere 110 kilobytes. However, with the advent of Win32 and the introduction of Windows, this file became too unwieldy. The information contained in this header file increased from 110 kilobytes to over 567 kilobytes. Currently, windows.h simply points to more than 28 separate #include files containing this information. These files now contain over 350 constant declarations, the typedef declarations, and over 2,000 Windows function declarations. This explains just one of the reasons it takes so long to compile a Windows application.

Understanding the Style of Windows Code

Even if you already know how to code in C or C++, you may initially find Windows source code a little confusing. Not only does this new code contain never-before-seen functions, but how things are defined appears to be unique. The name for this style of coding is known as *Hungarian style*. Officially, this Hungarian style of notation can be credited to the Microsoft programmer Charles Simonyi. In Hungarian notation, variable names begin with a lowercase letter or letters that describe the data type of the variable. This variable name prefix is then followed by the name of the variable, which is represented by a

Understanding the Style of Windows Code

meaningful use of upper- and lowercase letters. This approach allows each variable to have attached a mnemonic representing the variable's data type. For example:

```
LONG LPARAM
unsigned int UINT
```

By prefacing each identifier with a reminder of its data type (L for LongPARAM and U for UnsignedINT), you can actually avoid some very common mistakes before compiling your program. The following statement looks harmless but is incorrect and may go unchecked.

```
Variable1 = Variable2;
```

However, using Hungarian notation, you would undoubtedly catch the following mistake:

```
Lvarialble1 = Uvariable2;
```

Hopefully, the following list will bring you "on board" as quickly as possible to the more frequently used Windows type prefixes:

Prefix	Data Type Represented
a	atom
b	BOOL (integer)
by	BYTE (unsigned character)
c	character (ANSI ASCII 8-bit)
dw	DWORD (unsigned long)
fn	function
h	HANDLE (unsigned integer)
hDC	HANDLE to a device context
i	integer (16 bits in Windows 3.x, 32 bits under Windows 98 and NT)
id	integral id value
l	LONG (long)
lp	long (far) pointer
lpsz	long pointer to null-terminated string
n	short integer
np	near (short) pointer
p	pointer
pfn	function pointer
pst	pointer to a structure
psz	pointer to null-terminated string
pv	pointer to void
s	string
sz	NULL (/0) terminated string
u	unsigned
v	void
w	WORD (unsigned 16-bit value)
w	character (UNICODE 16-bit)
x	short (when used as the X coordinate)
y	short (when used as the Y coordinate)

The Seven Fundamental Steps for Developing Windows Programs

All programming languages have a systematized set of steps required to build the majority of applications. Under Windows, these common steps involve:
1. A call to **WinMain()**, where program execution begins, along with any additional Widows/C/C++ functions.
2. Application-specific menu creation and menu descriptions stored in a resource script file.
3. Optional creation of the application's dialog boxes.
4. Optional creation of icons, cursors, and bitmaps.
5. Defining the project.
6. Compiling and linking all related files.
7. Debugging

As you can quickly see, creating an actual Windows application will require the use of several project development tools. The next section will take a brief look at several tools.

The Visual C/C++ Compiler

When developing a Windows application, the project file and its associated options control how the application will be built. In Chapter 4, you will learn more about project options for building Windows applications.

The Resource Editor

You use your C/C++ compiler's resource editors to create application-specific menus, dialog boxes, icons, cursors, and bitmaps. The use of these editors is almost intuitive, but on-line help is provided, should you run into a problem.

The Resource Compiler

Frequently, a Windows application will use its own resources, such as menus, icons, and dialog boxes. Each of these resources must be predefined in a file called a *resource script file*. The resource compiler does pretty much what its name suggests—it compiles the resource—and the additional information is added to the application's final .exe file by the project utility. This approach allows Windows to load and use the resources from the .exe file.

Using the Linker

All Windows applications can be linked with the C/C++ linker under the management of the project utility, which resolves all external references.

In the Next Chapter...

Because a Windows application presents the user with an incredibly rich array of features, mastering Windows application development takes some time. The first two chapters of this book have introduced you to all that Windows is capable of performing, along with a foundational foreword to Windows terminology. In these next few chapters, you will be taught the fundamentals of creating good Windows applications. Later chapters will illustrate, and teach you the programming techniques necessary to use advanced Windows capabilities.

T W O

Step by Step: Writing Simple Windows Applications

In this chapter, you will quickly learn how to use the Microsoft Visual Studio to develop a simple Windows application. This hands-on tutorial takes you through each phase of the development cycle with actual screen shots and a detailed explanation of the environment changes they produce.

The chapter also develops and explains the swt.cpp (simple windows template) file that you will use each time you begin a new project. This foundational example details the minimal code requirements needed to get a Windows application up and running, along with each statement's various options, parameters, and arguments. So, let's get started!

Ways to Develop Windows Applications

Before diving headlong into your first application, you need to know that there are various ways to generate all of the code necessary to create a Windows application. For example, Borland International uses the Object Windows Library (OWL) approach. Microsoft followed suit with the development of Microsoft Foundation Class (MFC) Library. This text does not use either approach. Why, you ask? Read on.

Historically, the typical Windows programmer was new to the following concepts: C, C++, multitasking application development, and object-oriented programming (OOP). They were, however, experienced programmers—but they needed updating to today's programming environment.

Borland International's OWL approach and Microsoft's MFC approach are attempts at streamlining the Windows application development process. Both approaches, however, are proprietary in nature. This means that they are product-specific. OWL does not work under Microsoft's environment, and, initially, MFC did not work under Borland's products. Both approaches basically added a code layer and proprietary design philosophy on top of standard Windows application development fundamentals. Problems arose from cross-platform portability issues and programmers steeped in one product's design packaging.

The approach used in this manuscript is to teach you the ins and outs of doing it yourself. The advantages to this approach are obvious. First, you are learning truly product-independent Windows programming principles that OWL and MFC automate. Second, just like driving a car with an automatic versus a standard transmission, OWL and MFC preselected options might not be exactly what you wanted. Also, the OWL/MFC approaches require a sophisticated understanding of OOP. Add to this the need for some familiarity with the demands placed on an application when it must coexist on a multitasking operating system.

At this point, you are now ready to begin developing your own Windows applications, using a procedural model, from the ground up! Throughout the text, you will learn the fundamental components of a Windows application. If you are already familiar with C/C++, you may actually be surprised to see just how straightforward the code actually is. However, pay attention to the multitasking requirements needed by a Windows application and how Microsoft Windows solves these concerns.

Starting the Visual Studio

Figure 2–1 shows an example system setup of Visual Studio (Enterprise Edition) and how you would begin your new project.

> **note**
> Figure 2–1, for variety, shows the task bar at the top of the screen—some programmers prefer this location for a drop-down look. If you like this approach, simply hold the left mouse button down to your current task bar location and drag it to the top of your screen.

The four steps are to:
1. click on the Start button
2. select the Programs group
3. select the Microsoft Visual Studio 6.0 program group
4. select the Microsoft Visual C++ 6.0 option

Starting the Visual Studio **39**

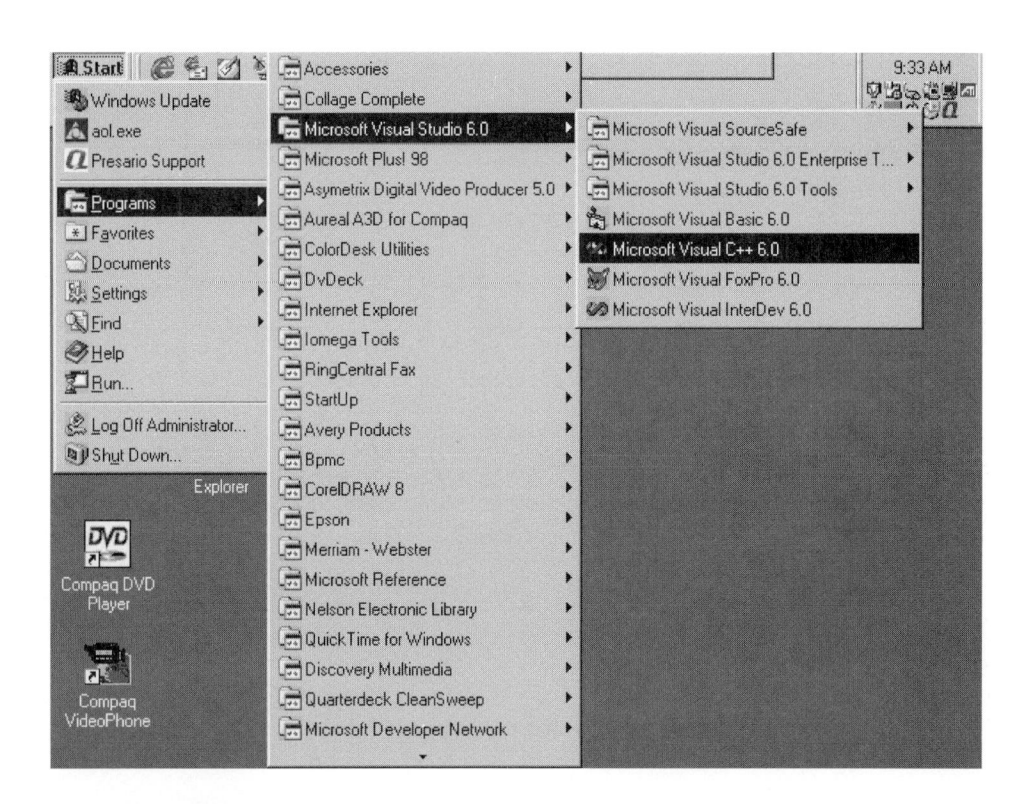

Figure 2–1   *Starting Visual C++.*

Figure 2-2 shows the initial, default windows configuration you can expect. The largest window (dark gray) is where you will enter and edit source files. The large white window at the screen's bottom displays compile/debug/link information. The medium gray window to the left provides varying information content, depending on the project's complexity. This window can easily, in a hierarchy view type, locate all of the classes, files, resources, and object properties used by the current project.

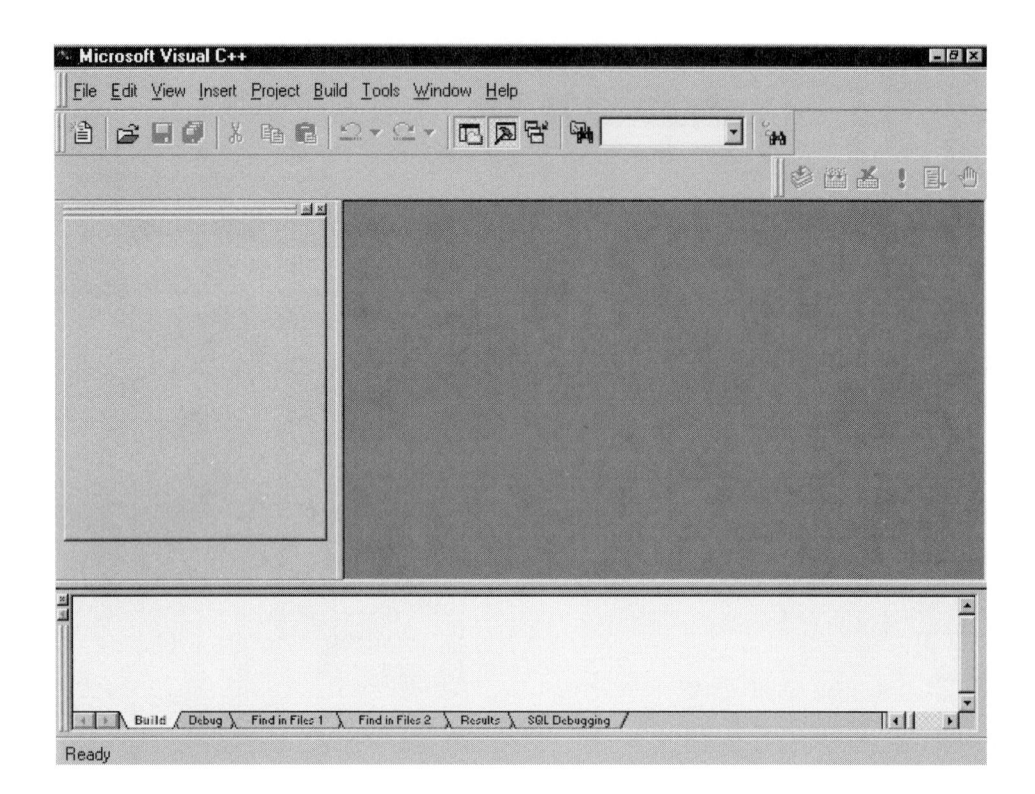

Chapter 2 • Step by Step: Writing Simple Windows Applications

Figure 2-2 *Initial Visual Studio C++ 6.0 screen.*

Starting a New Project

To begin a new project from within the Visual Studio, click on the File|New... option highlighted in Figure 2-3.

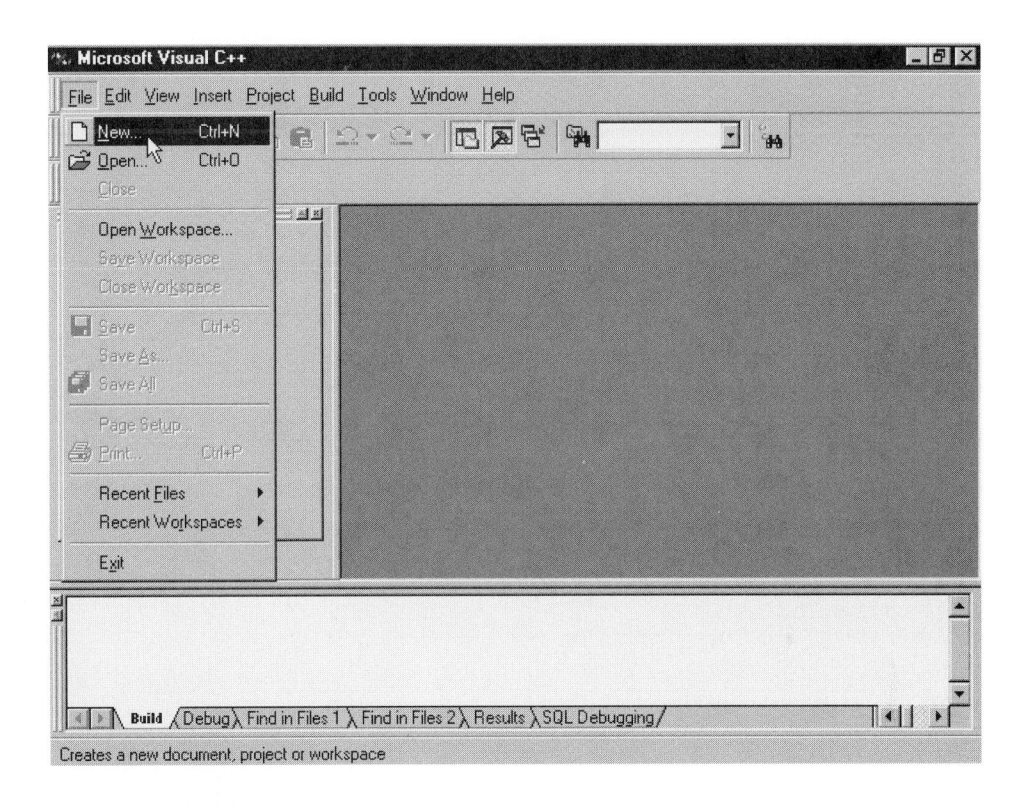

Figure 2-3 *Starting a new project.*

This opens up the New Projects window seen in Figure 2-4. At this point, you are trying to tell the Visual Studio just what type of project to create. As you can see, there are quite a few options. For this first program, choose the Win32 Application (highlighted in Figure 2-4).

The New Project window also requires you to give the project a name, for this example, *swt*. You will also need to select a location for the project's support, debug, and executable files, in this example the location *c:\swt\swt* will hold your first Simple Windows Template (swt) project. The Create new workspace radio button and Win32 Platforms check box are preselected defaults, so it's time to click on the OK button.

Chapter 2 • Step by Step: Writing Simple Windows Applications

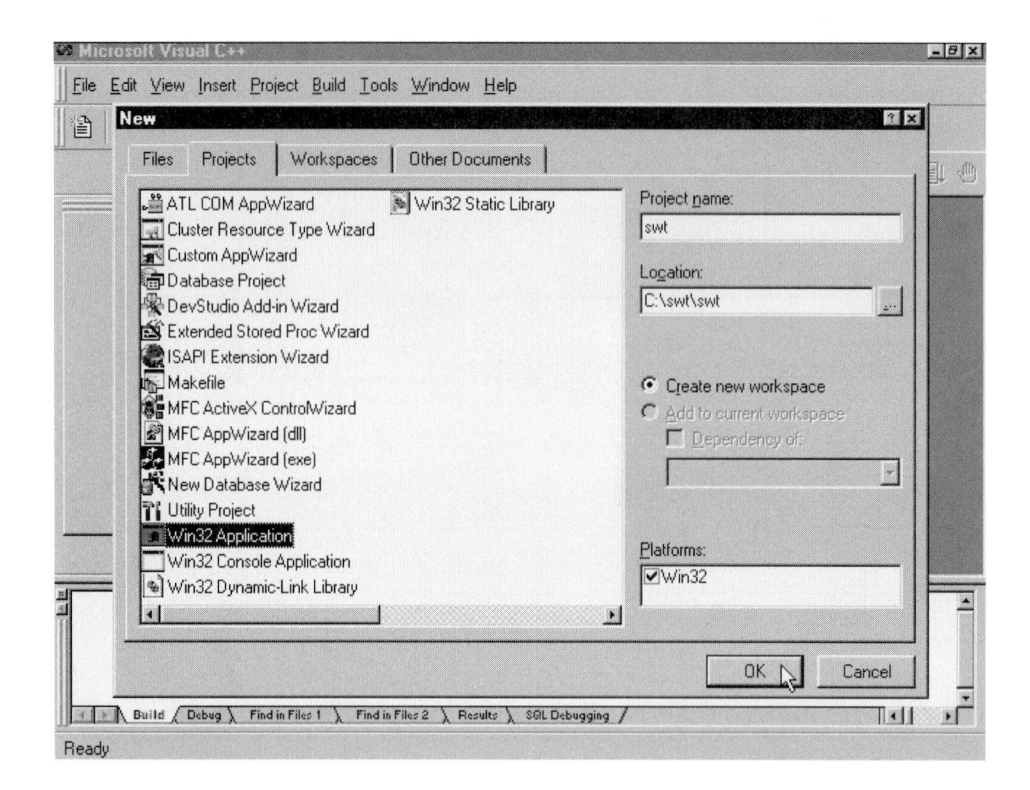

Figure 2–4 *Selecting the Win32 application and naming it* swt.

Clicking on the OK button in Figure 2-4 launches the Win32 Application—Step 1 of 1 window seen in Figure 2-5. Because this text is designed to teach the nuts and bolts of a Windows application, click on the An empty project radio button. Follow this with a quick click on the Finish button.

Starting a New Project 43

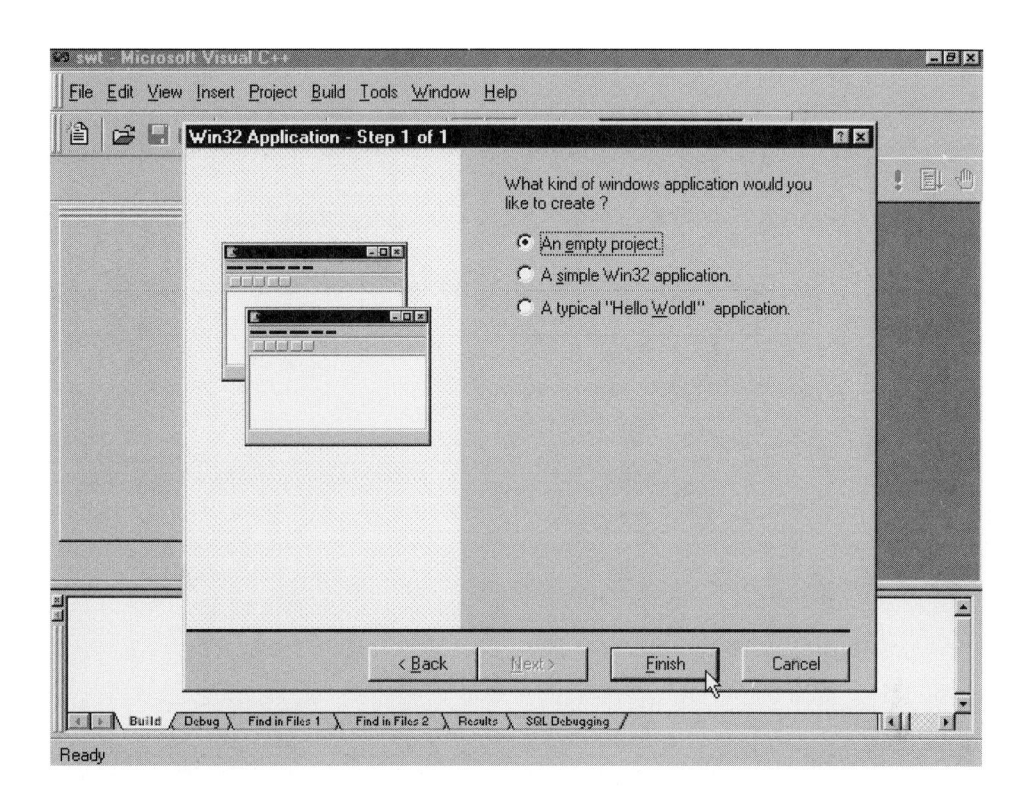

Figure 2-5 *Selecting an empty project option and clicking on Finish.*

However, you are not quite finished launching the initial phases of a project's development. Figure 2-6 displays the New Project Information window where there is a last chance to view the project's settings before actually creating any files. The "...empty application..." messages are just what we want, so one more click on OK—please.

Chapter 2 • Step by Step: Writing Simple Windows Applications

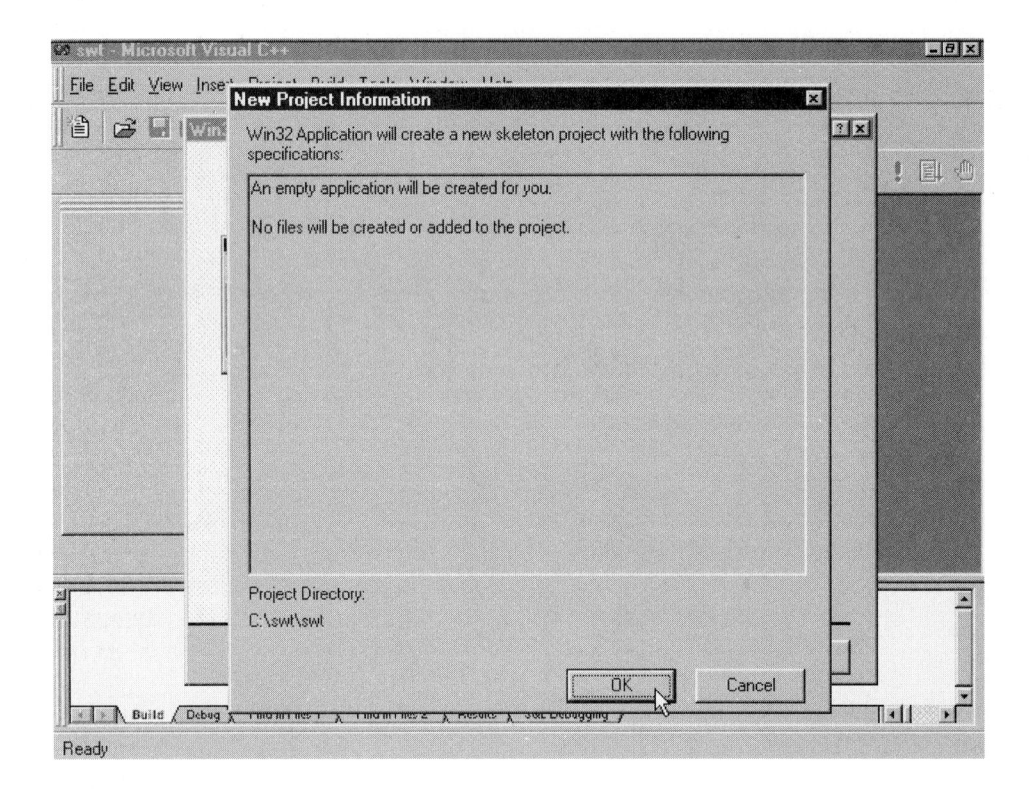

Figure 2–6 *Clicking OK to accept the New Project Information.*

At this point, the resulting screen does not look too dissimilar from the initial Visual Studio window. However, look closely at Figure 2-7. Notice the insertion of the "swt classes" entry in the left Workspace pane's ClassView.

Adding Files to a Project 45

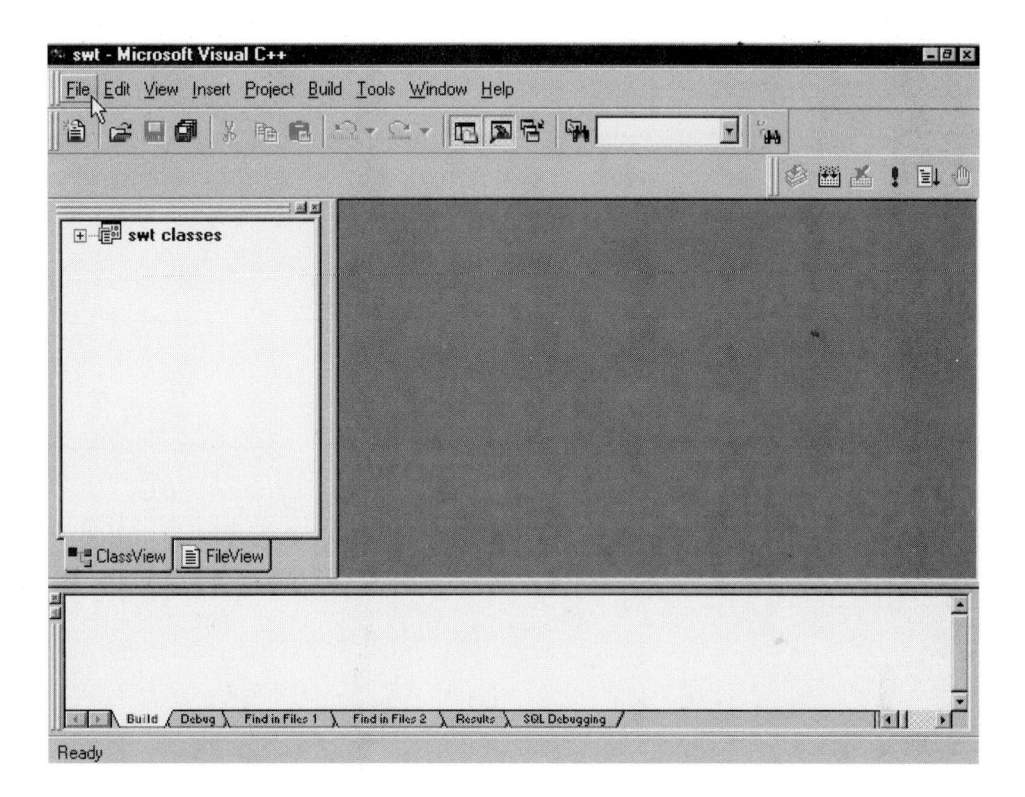

Figure 2-7 *The initial swt project view.*

Adding Files to a Project

Regardless of the type of file that is to be added to a project, the insertion process begins with clicking on the File|New... option highlighted in Figure 2-8.

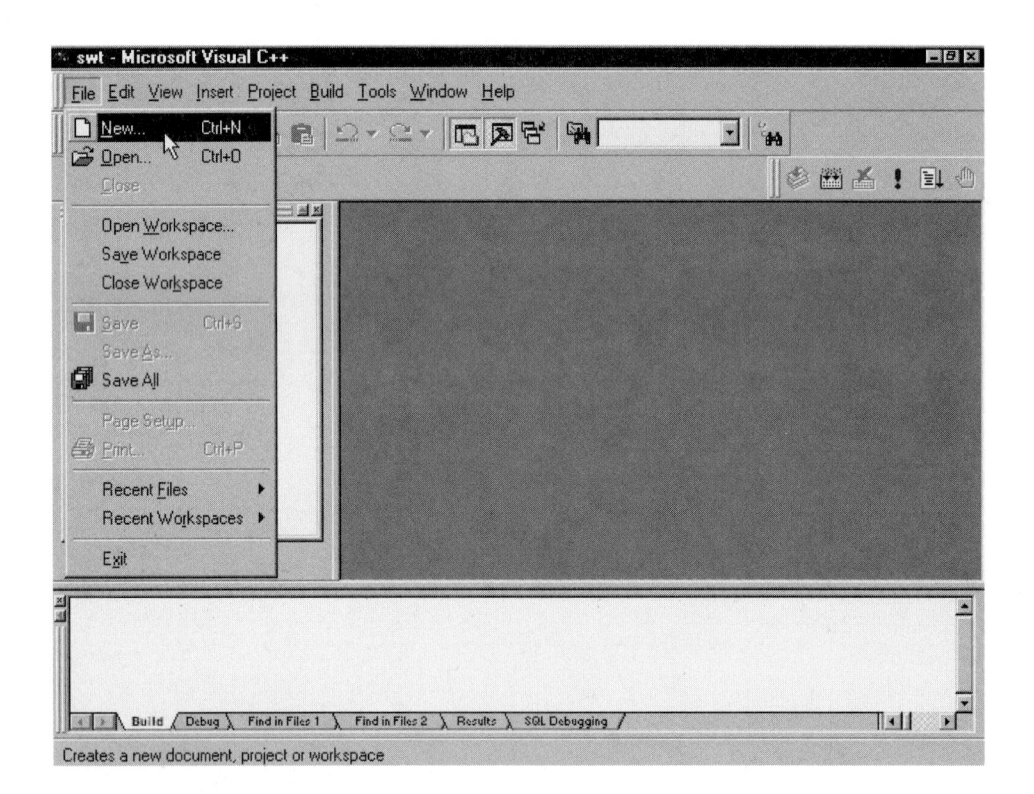

46 Chapter 2 • Step by Step: Writing Simple Windows Applications

Figure 2-8   *Adding a New...file to the swt project.*

Figure 2-9 enumerates the list of file types that can be included in a Win32 Application. For now, to enter your first Windows source file choose the C++ Source File type, give the file a name (swt in this example), then click on the OK button.

Adding Files to a Project   47

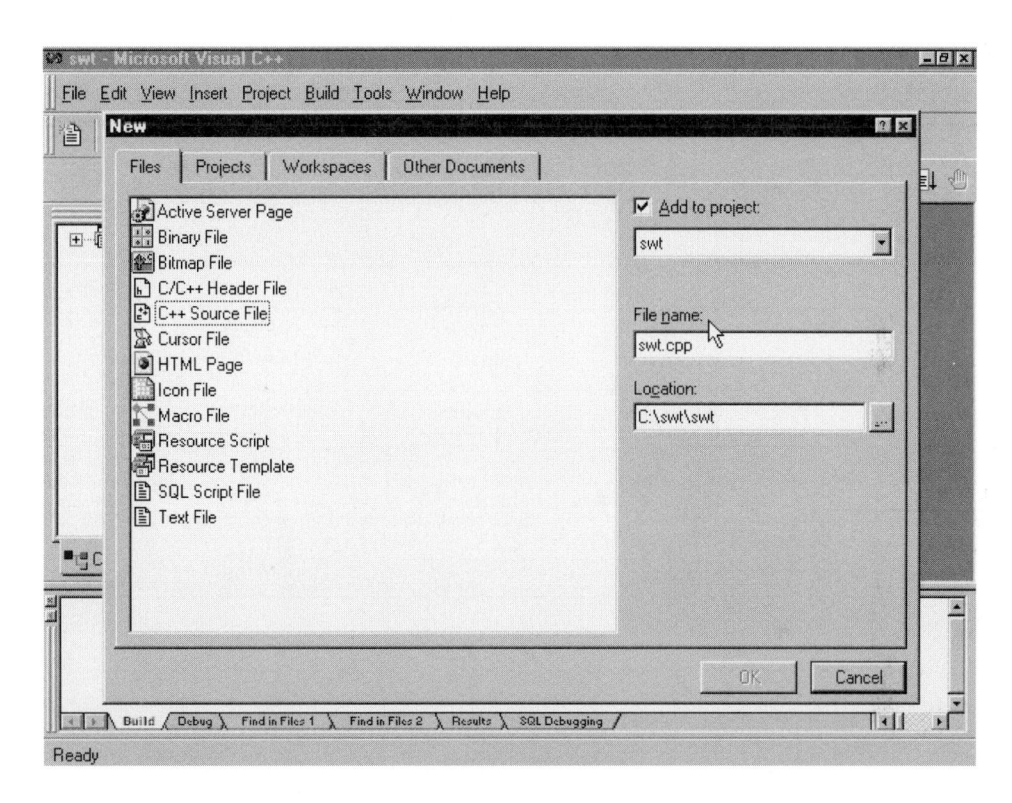

Figure 2-9   *Selecting the new file's type and giving it a name.*

The Visual Studio responds by opening up an editing window with a flashing I-beam (see Figure 2-10). It is time to begin entering your first source file.

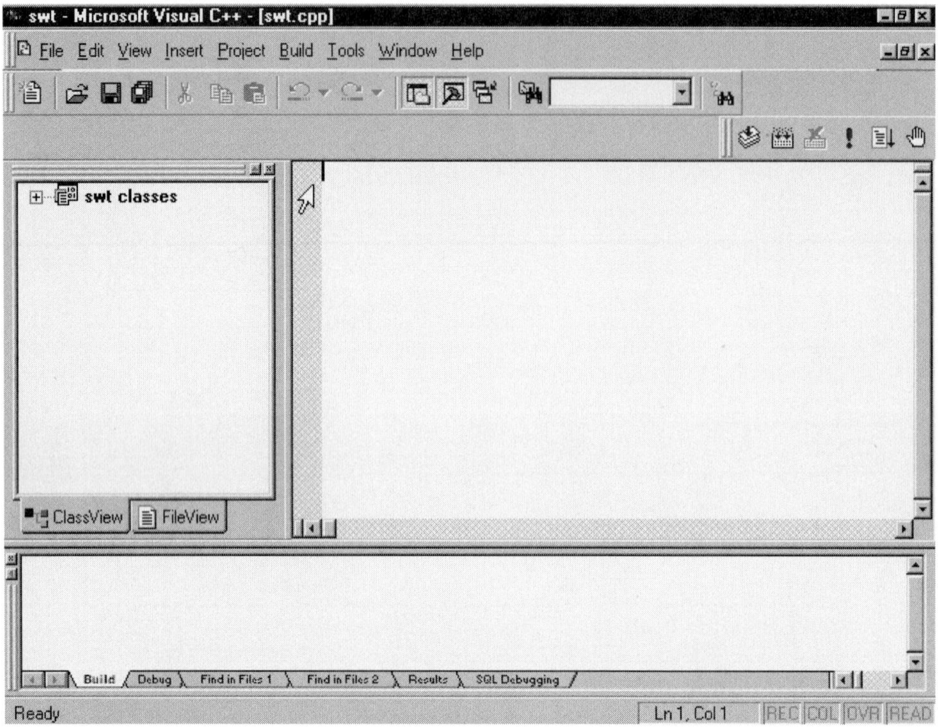

48 Chapter 2 • Step by Step: Writing Simple Windows Applications

Figure 2–10 *Arrow pointing to I-beam text insertion point for swt.cpp.*

The following listing is a complete buildable and executable example. Enter the file exactly as you see it. When you are finished entering the file, make certain to save it by clicking either on File|Save or on the diskette icon below the Edit and View main menu options.

```
//
// swt.cpp
// Simple Windows Template
// Copyright (c) William H. Murray and Chris H. Pappas, 1999
//

#include <windows.h>

LRESULT CALLBACK WndProc(HWND,UINT,WPARAM,LPARAM);
```

Adding Files to a Project

```c
char szProgName[]="ProgName";

int WINAPI WinMain(HINSTANCE hInst,HINSTANCE hPreInst,
                   LPSTR lpszCmdLine,int nCmdShow)
{
  HWND hWnd;
  MSG  lpMsg;
  WNDCLASS wcApp;

  wcApp.lpszClassName=szProgName;
  wcApp.hInstance      =hInst;
  wcApp.lpfnWndProc    =WndProc;
  wcApp.hCursor        =LoadCursor(NULL,IDC_ARROW);
  wcApp.hIcon          =0;
  wcApp.lpszMenuName   =0;
  wcApp.hbrBackground =(HBRUSH) GetStockObject(LTGRAY_BRUSH);
  wcApp.style          =CS_HREDRAW|CS_VREDRAW;
  wcApp.cbClsExtra     =0;
  wcApp.cbWndExtra     =0;
  if (!RegisterClass (&wcApp))
    return 0;

  hWnd=CreateWindow(szProgName,"Simple Windows Template",
                    WS_OVERLAPPEDWINDOW,CW_USEDEFAULT,
                    CW_USEDEFAULT,CW_USEDEFAULT,
                    CW_USEDEFAULT,(HWND)NULL,(HMENU)NULL,
                    hInst,(LPSTR)NULL);
  ShowWindow(hWnd,nCmdShow);
  UpdateWindow(hWnd);
  while (GetMessage(&lpMsg,0,0,0)) {
    TranslateMessage(&lpMsg);
    DispatchMessage(&lpMsg);
  }
  return(lpMsg.wParam);
```

}


```
LRESULT CALLBACK WndProc(HWND hWnd,UINT messg,
                         WPARAM wParam,LPARAM lParam)
{
  HDC hdc;
  PAINTSTRUCT ps;

  switch (messg)
  {
    case WM_PAINT:
      hdc=BeginPaint(hWnd,&ps);

      MoveToEx(hdc,50,60,NULL);
      LineTo(hdc,500,400);

      TextOut(hdc,200,100,"Draw a line",11);

      ValidateRect(hWnd,NULL);
      EndPaint(hWnd,&ps);
      break;
    case WM_DESTROY:
      PostQuitMessage(0);
      break;
    default:
      return(DefWindowProc(hWnd,messg,wParam,lParam));
      break;
  }
  return(0);
}
```

Your screen should now look similar to Figure 2-11 (do *not* execute a compile, build, or rebuild at this point).

Adding Files to a Project 51

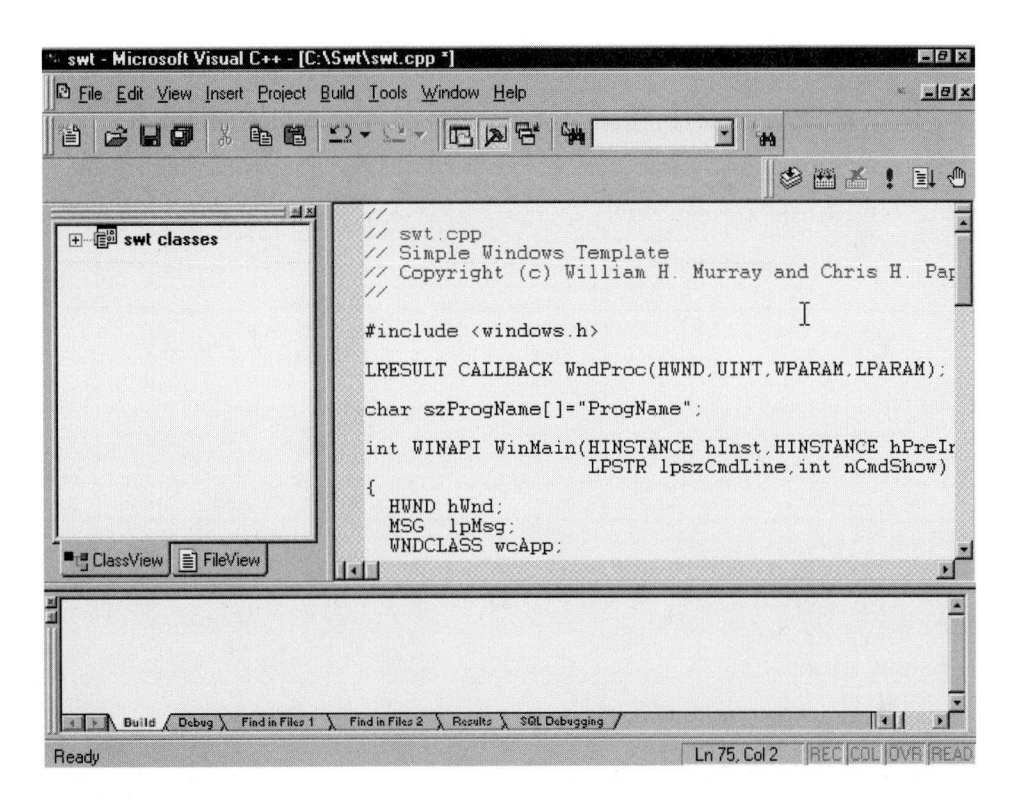

Figure 2-11 *Completed swt.cpp text file entry before any builds.*

Before explaining every aspect of the program, take a moment to fire up the Windows Explorer and route yourself over to the swt subdirectory (as seen in Figure 2-12).

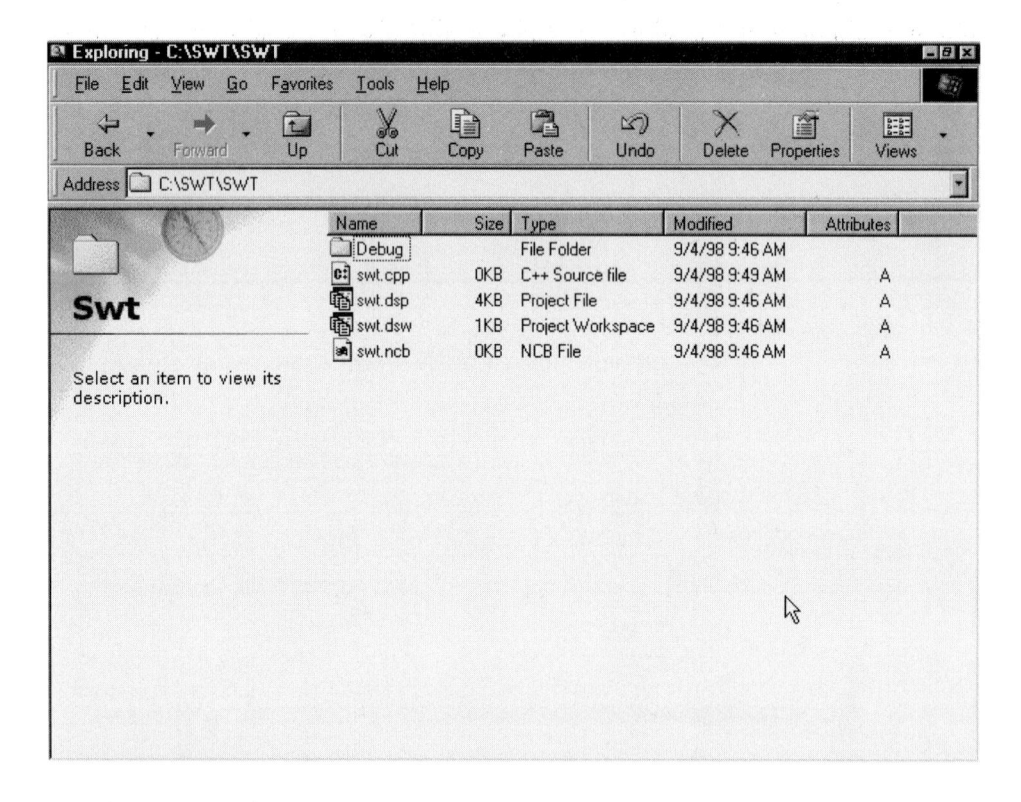

Figure 2-12 *The swt project's subdirectory prior to initial compile/build.*

You might find it interesting to see just how many and what types of files have already been created for you by the Visual Studio Win32 Application project. The following list follows the listing in Figure 2-12:

Debug—This subdirectory will eventually hold debug information and the debug .exe version of your application. You will learn later in the text how to generate a final release *.exe version, and the Visual Studio will create a special Release subdirectory to store this information.

swt.cpp—The swt C++ source file you just entered and saved.

swt.dsp—This is the project file used within the development environment. In previous versions of Visual C++, this file extension was .mak. It stores the information specific to your project. There will be a separate .dsp file for each project you create. .dsp files are not compatible with NMAKE. You must export a makefile to build with NMAKE.

swt.dsw—This is the workspace file used within the development environment. It organizes all the projects into a single workspace. To understand the terms w*orkspace* and *projects,* try and think of your boss as the workspace and each programmer under him/her as individual projects. The workspace coordinates the projects. Note, too, however, that projects can in themselves be complex in nature, with many of their own sublevels.

swt.ncb—This is the No compile Browser file. It contains information generated by the parser that is used by Visual Studio utilities such as ClassView, WizardBar, and the Component Gallery. If the file is accidentally or deliberately deleted, it is automatically regenerated.

Generating the Executable

If you have been following along with this chapter's examples step by step, you have learned how to start a project, enter a source file, and save it. At this point, it is time to create the executable version. You have several options, including a simple compile of swt.cpp, or you could choose Build or Rebuild All (see Figure 2-13).

A simple compile would *not* automatically invoke the linker, thereby generating the .exe file, but Build or Rebuild All does both. You may rightly ask what is the difference between Build and Rebuild All. The answer is time/date stamping.

Rebuild All—which this text uses exclusively, is a knock-down drag-out do-it-all approach to generating the *.exe. Rebuild All assumes you want to regenerate every intermediate and final file necessary to create the executable version of your program. For a first-time project, Build or Rebuild All behave identically.

Build, on the other hand, is very selective in what it reprocesses. Build, for anything other than a first-time Build or Rebuild All, first checks to see if an *.exe by the project's name already exists. If so, Build looks at the list of files defined by your workspace, finds each file and compares these file's time/date stamps against the time/date stamp on the existing *.exe. Build *recompiles only* support source files with newer time/date stamps. It then links only the newer updated intermediate files into the *.exe.

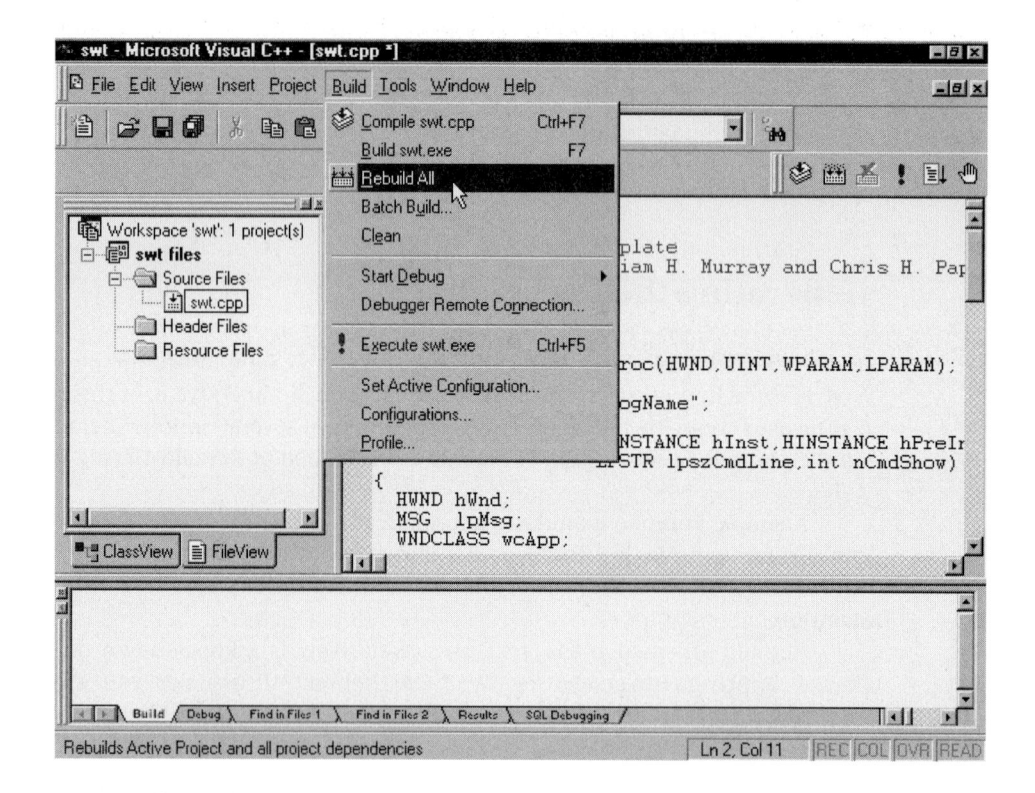

Chapter 2 • Step by Step: Writing Simple Windows Applications

Figure 2–13   Selecting the Build/Rebuild All option.

So why does this text stress the use of an apparently less efficient process? Ah, here's the rub. In a real-world workspace/project definition, support files may come from another machine in a different part of the building via network. However, these support files, in today's environment, could even be within the company's intranet. The furthest source location can even be across the Internet in another country!

Imagine this nightmare: Your team has created a semiworking Win32 Application, one of the programmers updates a workspace-defined support file on a system that proceeds to immediately crash after the file is saved. When the system is finally back up and running, something has happened to the system's internal clock. Alas, the source file is stamped with a time/date *older* than the original.

The nightmare continues as your project's manager executes a Build (which does *not* acknowledge the newer file) to incorporate the newer code, and no one has a clue as to why the application looks exactly the way it did days earlier! The lesson? If you have the time, *always* choose Rebuild All, which seeks out each file afresh.

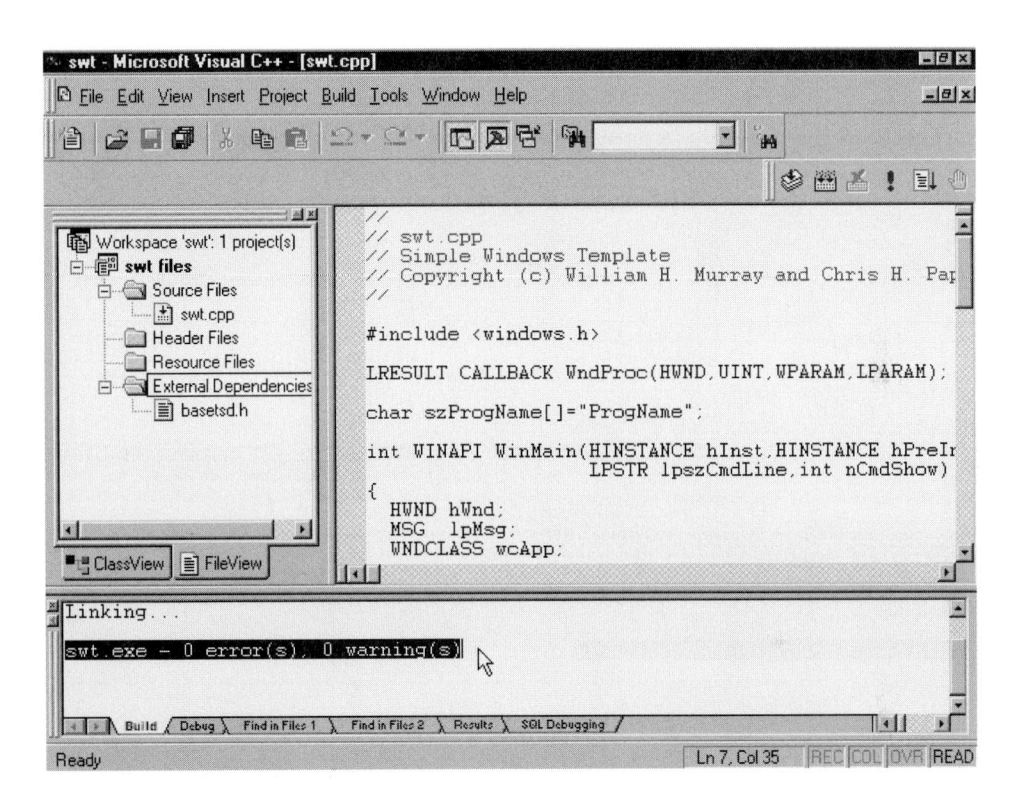

Figure 2-14 *A successful Rebuild All with 0 error(s), 0 warning(s).*

At this point you are ready to knowledgeably select the Build|Rebuild All... option. If your screen does not look like Figure 2-14, with 0 error(s) and 0 warning(s), you have simply typed something incorrectly. Cross-reference your screen copy with the listing in this chapter to find the error, save, then Rebuild All...

Executing Your First Program

Figure 2-15 illustrates the quickest ways to execute a program. Notice in the windows upper-right corner the pointed-to exclamation point. Underneath the icon is a shortcut-key reminder. You can execute your program by either clicking on the exclamation point *or* simultaneously pressing the Control key (Ctrl) and the Function 5 key (F5).

Chapter 2 • Step by Step: Writing Simple Windows Applications

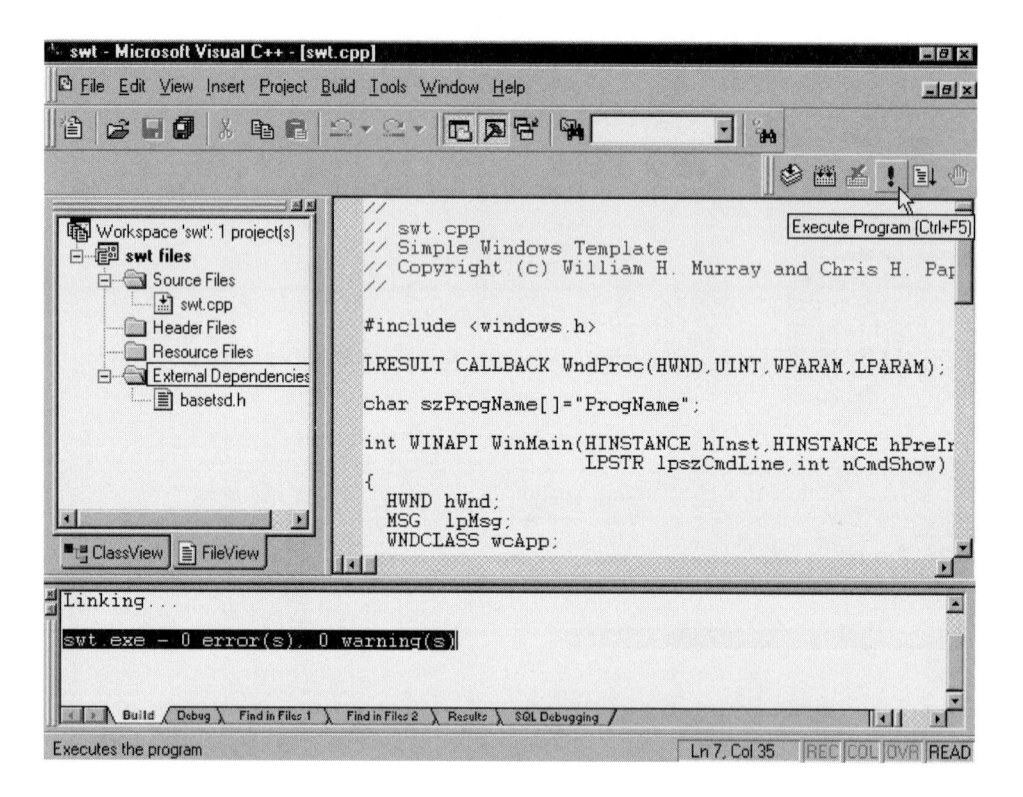

Figure 2-15 *Preparing to execute swt.exe.*

When you execute the program, you should see a new window on the screen, similar to the one shown in Figure 2-16. Your swt.cpp Win32 Application not only generated an initial window frame, program title bar, minimize, maximize, and close icons, but it drew a diagonal line with a label.

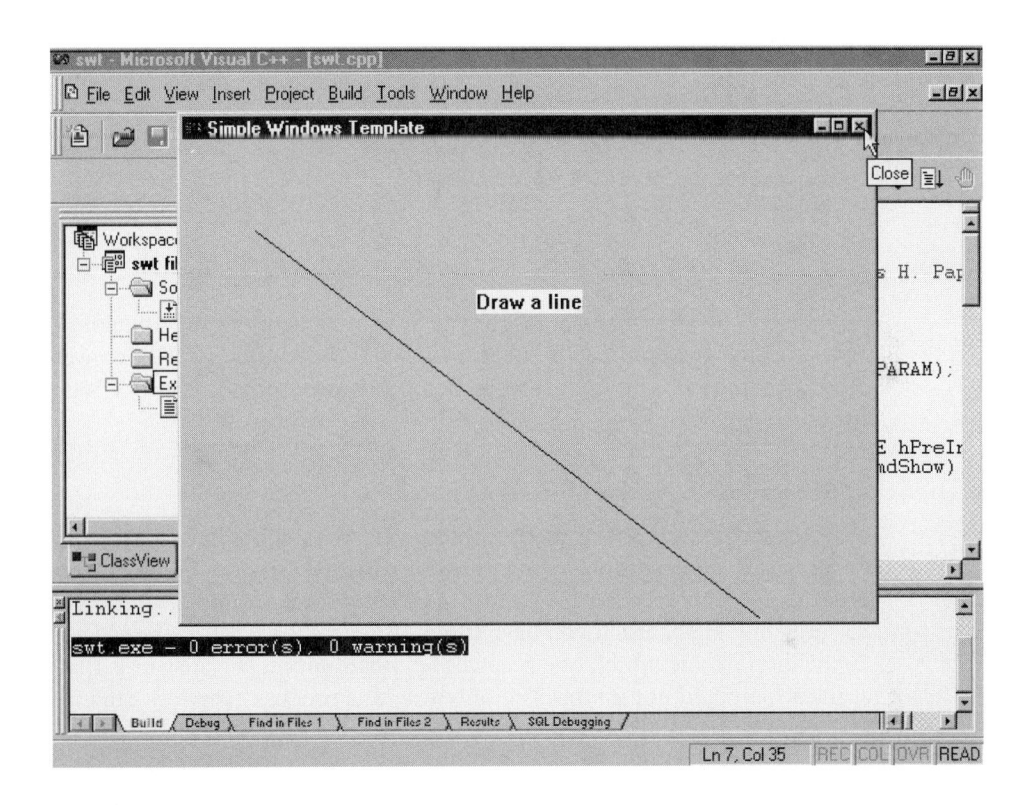

Figure 2-16 *The output from swt.exe.*

Understanding the Simple Windows Template

Now that you have practiced the steps necessary to create a simple Windows application, entered the minimal code necessary (and in this process began familiarizing yourself with its syntax and complexity), it is time to discuss each line of code in detail. Remember, this is the template you will use initially to begin the examples in this text (minus the line draw portion).

The Comment Block

Every professional programmer knows that a source file begins with a comment block identifying the file's name, title, purpose, author, and date of creation/modification:

```
//
// swt.cpp
```

```
// Simple Windows Template
// Copyright (c) William H. Murray and Chris H. Pappas, 1999
//
```

<windows.h>

The source file continues with the

```
#include <windows.h>
```

statement, which pulls in a text file named windows.h, containing Windows-specific definitions and additional #include statements. The contents of these files provide the foundational definitions necessary to build a Windows application.

The Callback Function

Unlike stand-alone MS-DOS mode applications that did not have to share system resources, Windows applications must coexist and behave themselves in relation to any previously loaded Windows programs. For example, your computer has only one keyboard. If you have three programs loaded, how would any one application decide which one receives keyboard input. The answer is that each application could not do this. The only way this process can work effectively is if the operating system oversees each application's needs. For this process to take place, every Windows application must create what is known as a *callback* function.

The purpose of the callback function is to report to Windows, via messages, what the application wants to do, while Windows informs each application, again via messages, what's out there of interest, i.e., current mouse coordinates. Let's take a detailed look at this statement in swt.cpp (the actual **WndProc()** function body is explained in detail later on in this chapter).

> **note**
> The function name WndProc() is *not* a reserved identifier. Any legal function name is allowed:
> `LRESULT CALLBACK WndProc(HWND,UINT,WPARAM,LPARAM);`

Every C/C++ function prototype begins with the function's return type, in this case LRESULT CALLBACK. LRESULT defines the type used for the return value of window procedures. It is a 32-bit value that can at times be broken down into two 16-bit values called *low* and *high*.

CALLBACK identifies the function as being an application-defined function that a system or subsystem (Windows, for example) calls. Typically, this happens when an event occurs or when windows or fonts are being enumerated. Examples of callback functions include window procedures, dialog-box procedures, and hook procedures (callback functions are also used to process dynamic data exchange [DDE] transactions).

Following CALLBACK is the function's name **WndProc()**. In a traditional program for Windows, all messages are processed in the application's "window procedure" or **WndProc()**. The **WndProc()** function is associated with a window by means of a window class registration process. The main window is registered in the **WinMain()** function, but other classes of windows can be registered anywhere in the application.

Registration depends on a structure that contains a pointer to the **WndProc()** function together with specifications for the cursor, background brush, and so forth. The structure is passed as a parameter, along with the string name of the class, in a prior call to the **RegisterClass()** function. Thus, a registration class can be shared by multiple windows. The **WndProc()** prototype in swt.cpp concludes with its formal argument list:

(HWND,UINT,WPARAM,LPARAM);

describing the number and type of arguments being passed into the function.

> **note** C/C++ code style conventions use all uppercase identifiers to define nonstandard C/C++ data types. To find the definitions for these uppercase identifiers, you need to go to their defining header files referenced via windows.h.

HWND represents a handle to a window.

UINT is a portable unsigned integer type whose size is determined by the host environment (32 bits for Windows NT and Windows 95) and is a synonym for unsigned int. It is used in place of WORD, except in the rare cases where a 16-bit unsigned quantity is desired, even on 32-bit platforms.

WPARAM is the type used for declaration of wParam, the third parameter of a windows procedure (a polymorphic data type).

LPARAM is the type used for declaration of lParam, the fourth parameter of a windows procedure.

A Brief Word about Handles

Writing a Windows application always involves the use of handles. A *handle* is a unique number that identifies many different types of objects, such as windows, controls, menus, icons, pens and brushes, memory allocation, output devices, and even window instances. In Windows terminology, each loaded copy of a program is called an *instance*.

Because Windows allows you to run more than one copy of the same application at the same time, it needs to keep track of each of these instances. It does this by attaching a unique instance handle to each running copy of the application.

Usually, the instance handle is used as an index into an internally maintained table. Having the handle reference a table element rather than an actual memory address allows Windows to rearrange all resources dynamically by simply inserting a new address into the resource's identical table position. For example, if Windows associates a particular application's resource with table look-up position 3, then no matter where Windows moves the resource in memory, table position 3 will contain the resource's current location.

Windows conserves memory resources by the way it manages multiple instances of the same application. Several multitasking environments load each duplicate instance of an application, just as if it were an entirely new application. However, Windows can conserve system resources by using the same code for all instances of an application. The only portion of each instance that is usually unique is the instance's data segment.

The first instance of an application has a very important role. It is the first instance of an application that defines all of the objects necessary for the functioning of the application. This can include controls, menus, dialog boxes, and much more, along with new window classes. A Windows application can even be instructed to allow other applications to share these new definitions.

The callback function prototype is followed by a simple program name string definition. In case you have never heard of Hungarian notation, the *sz* in front of *ProgName[]* represents an abbreviation for the variable's data type, in this case, a string (*s*) that is null-terminated (*z* = '\0').

```
char szProgName[]="ProgName";
```

The WinMain() Function

Just as a simple C or C++ MS-DOS application must have at least one function by the name **main()**, all Windows applications must have a minimum of a callback function and one by the name **WinMain()**. **WinMain()** is where normal program execution begins and ends. First, a look at WinMain()'s header:

```
int WINAPI WinMain(HINSTANCE hInst,HINSTANCE hPreInst,
          LPSTR lpszCmdLine,int nCmdShow)
```

WinMain() returns int WINAPI. The int is straightforward. WINAPI, however, is the calling convention used for the Win32 API and is used in place of FAR PASCAL in API declarations. The **WinMain()** function is called by Windows as the initial entry point for a Win32-based application. The **WinMain()** function is responsible for:

- registering the application's window class type
- performing any required initializations
- creating and initiating the application's message-processing loop (which accesses the program's message queue) terminating the program, usually upon receiving a WM_QUIT message

Understanding the Simple Windows Template

The first formal parameter to **WinMain()** is *hInst,* which contains the instance handle of the current instance of the application. This number uniquely identifies the program when it is running under Windows.

The second formal parameter, *hPreInst*, will contain a NULL value under Windows 95 and NT. This indicates that there are no previous instance of this application. Under Windows 3.x, *hPreInst* was used to indicate whether there were or were not any previous copies of the program loaded. Under Windows 98 and NT, each application runs in its own separate address space. For this reason, *hPreInst* will never return a valid previous instance, just NULL.

The third parameter, *lpszCmdLine*, is a pointer to a null-terminated string that represents the application's command line arguments. Normally, *lpszCmdLine* contains a NULL if the application was started using the Windows Run command.

The fourth and last formal parameter to **WinMain()** is *nCmdShow*. The int value stored in *nCmdShow* represents one of the many Windows predefined constants defining the possible ways a window can be displayed, such as SW_SHOWNORMAL, SW_SHOWMAXIMIZED, or SW_MINIMIZED. Table 2.1 lists the values for *nCmdShow*.

Table 2.1 Values for nCmdShow.

Symbolic Constant	Description
SW_HIDE	Hides the window and activates another window.
SW_MINIMIZE	Minimizes the window.
SW_RESTORE	The system restores it to its current size and position (same as SW_SHOWNORMAL).
SW_SHOW	Displays the window in its current size and position.
SW_SHOWMAXIMIZED	Displays the window as a maximized window.
SW_SHOWMINIMIZED	Displays the window as an icon.
SW_SHOWMINNOACTIVE	Displays a window as an icon; however, the current active window remains active.
SW_SHOWNA	Displays a window in its current state. The active window remains active.
SW_SHOWNOACTIVATE	Displays a window in its most recent size and position. The active window remains active.

Table 2.1 Values for nCmdShow. (Continued)

Symbolic Constant	Description
SW_SHOWNORMAL	Activates and displays a window. If the window is minimized or maximized, the system restores it to its original size and position (same as SW_RESTORE).

The purpose of **WinMain()** is to initialize the application, display its main window, and enter a message retrieval-and-dispatch loop that is the top-level control structure for the remainder of the application's execution. **WinMain()** should also terminate the message loop when it receives a WM_QUIT message. This terminates the application, returning the value passed in the WM_QUIT message's *wParam* parameter.

WinMain()'s swt.cpp formal definition continues with the next three declarations:

```
HWND hWnd;
MSG lpMsg;
WNDCLASS wcApp;
```

UNDERSTANDING MSG

HWND has already been defined, so it's time to discuss the MSG definition. The MSG structure defines the members that encapsulate message information from a thread's message queue. The formal definition looks like:

```
typedef struct tagMSG {
    HWND    hwnd;
    UINT    message;
    WPARAM  wParam;
    LPARAM  lParam;
    DWORD   time;
    POINT   pt;
} MSG;
```

hwnd—is the handle to the window whose window procedure receives the message.

message—defines the message number.

wParam—defines additional information about the message. The exact meaning depends on the value of the message member.

lParam—defines additional information about the message. The exact meaning depends on the value of the message member.

time—defines the time at which the message was posted.

pt—defines the cursor position, in screen coordinates, when the message was posted.

UNDERSTANDING WNDCLASS

The WNDCLASS structure contains the window class attributes used by the call to **RegisterClass()** described below. The formal definition looks like:

```
typedef struct _WNDCLASS {
    UINT     style;
    WNDPROC  lpfnWndProc;
    int      cbClsExtra;
    int      cbWndExtra;
    HANDLE   hInstance;
    HICON    hIcon;
    HCURSOR  hCursor;
    HBRUSH   hbrBackground;
    LPCTSTR  lpszMenuName;
    LPCTSTR  lpszClassName;
} WNDCLASS;
```

The individual members are described below, along with their associated parameters:

style—defines the class style(s). Any of the symbolic constants listed in Table 2.2 are legal and may be combined using the bitwise OR (|) operator.

lpfnWndProc—Contains a pointer to the window procedure.

Table 2.2 Values for *style*.

Symbolic Constant	Description
CS_BYTEALIGNCLIENT	This style affects the width of the window and its horizontal position on the display. This value aligns the window's client area on the byte boundary (in the x direction).
CS-BYTEALIGNWINDOW	This style affects the width of the window and its horizontal position on the display. It aligns a window on a byte boundary (in the x direction).
CS_CLASSDC	Creates one device context to be shared by all windows in the class.

Table 2.2 Values for *style*. (Continued)

Symbolic Constant	Description
CS_DBLCLKS	Sends double-click messages to the window procedure when the user double-clicks the mouse while the cursor is within a window belonging to the class.
CS_GLOBALCLASS	Allows an application to create a window of the class, regardless of the value of the *hInstance* parameter.
CS_HREDRAW	Redraws the entire window if a movement of size adjustment changes the width of the client area.
CS_NOCLOSE	Disables Close on the main menu.
CS_OWNDC	Creates a unique device context for each window in the class.
CS_PARENTDC	Matches the clipping region of the child window to that of the parent window so that the child can draw on the parent. A window with the CS_PARENTDC style bit receives a regular device context from the system's cache of device context or device context settings.
CS_SAVEBITS	Saves, as a bitmap, the portion of the screen image obscured by a window. The system uses the saved bitmap to re-create the screen image when the window is removed.
CS_VREDRAW	Redraws the entire window if a movement or size adjustment changes the height of the client area.

cbClsExtra— Specifies the number of extra bytes to allocate following the window-class structure. The system initializes the bytes to zero.

cbWndExtra—Specifies the number of extra bytes to allocate following the window instance. The system initializes the bytes to zero.

hInstance—A handle to the instance that the window procedure of this class is within.

hIcon—A handle to the class icon. This member must be a handle of an icon resource.

Understanding the Simple Windows Template

hCursor—A handle to the class cursor. This member must be a handle of a cursor resource.

hbrBackground—A handle to the class background brush. This member can be a handle to the physical brush to be used for painting the background or it can be a color value. A color value must be one of the following standard system colors (Note: the value 1 must be added to the chosen color):

COLOR_ACTIVEBORDER
COLOR_ACTIVECAPTION
COLOR_APPWORKSPACE
COLOR_BACKGROUND
COLOR_BTNFACE
COLOR_BTNSHADOW
COLOR_BTNTEXT
COLOR_CAPTIONTEXT
COLOR_GRAYTEXT
COLOR_HIGHLIGHT
COLOR_HIGHLIGHTTEXT
COLOR_INACTIVEBORDER
COLOR_INACTIVECAPTION
COLOR_MENU
COLOR_MENUTEXT
COLOR_SCROLLBAR
COLOR_WINDOW
COLOR_WINDOWFRAME
COLOR_WINDOWTEXT

lpszMenuName—Contains a pointer to a null-terminated character string that specifies the resource name of the class menu, as the name appears in the resource file.

lpszClassName—Contains a pointer to a null-terminated string or is an atom. If *lpszClassName* is a string, it specifies the window class name.

SWT.CPP WNDCLASS WCAPP

The listing that follows is from the swt.cpp template application and demonstrates how the WNDCLASS structure has been defined and initialized for windows applications:

```
wcApp.lpszClassName=szProgName;
wcApp.hInstance     =hInst;
wcApp.lpfnWndProc   =WndProc;
wcApp.hCursor       =LoadCursor(NULL,IDC_ARROW);
wcApp.hIcon         =0;
wcApp.lpszMenuName  =0;
```

```
wcApp.hbrBackground=(HBRUSH) GetStockObject(LTGRAY_BRUSH);
wcApp.style           =CS_HREDRAW|CS_VREDRAW;
wcApp.cbClsExtra      =0;
wcApp.cbWndExtra      =0;
```

In this example, the template assigned a generic name *szProgName* to the window's *wcApp.lpszClassName*. You should assign a unique class name for each new window class you define.

The second **WNDCLASS** field, *hInstance*, is assigned the value returned in *hInst* after **WinMain()** is invoked, indicating the current instance of the application. *lpfnWndProc* is assigned the pointer address to the window function that will carry out all of the window's tasks. For the template application, the function is called *WndProc()*.

> **note**
> *WndProc()* is a user-defined function name, not a Windows function name. The function must be prototyped before the assignment statement.

The *wcApp.hCursor* field is assigned a handle to the instance's cursor, which in this example is IDC_ARROW (representing the default tilted arrow cursor). This assignment is accomplished through a call to the **LoadCursor()** function. Because the template has no default icon, *wcApp.hIcon* is assigned a 0 value.

When *wcapp.lpszMenuName* is assigned a 0 value, Windows understands that the class has no menu. If it did, the menu would have a name and it would appear between quotation marks. The **GetStockObject()** function returns a handle to a brush used to paint the background color of the client area of windows created from this class. For the template application, the function returns a handle to one of Windows predefined brushes, WHITE_BRUSH.

The *wcApp.style* window class style has been set to CS_HREDRAW ORed (|) with CS_VREDRAW. All window class styles have identifiers in windows.h or winuser.h that begin with CS_. Each identifier represents a bit value. The bitwise OR operation | is used to combine these bit flags. The two parameters used (CS_HREDRAW or CS_VREDRAW) instruct Windows to redraw the entire client area whenever the horizontal or vertical size of the window is changed.

The last two fields, *wcApp.cbClsExtra* and *wcApp.cbWndExtra*, are frequently assigned a 0 value. These fields are used to optionally indicate the count of extra bytes that may have been reserved at the end of the window class structure and the window data structure used for each window class.

UNDERSTANDING REGISTERCLASS()

The next statement in swt.cpp's **WinMain()** function looks like:

```
if (!RegisterClass (&wcApp))
    return 0;
```

Every window you create for a Windows application must be based on a window class. **WinMain()** is responsible for registering the application's main window class. Each window class is based on a combination of user-selected styles, fonts, caption bars, icons, size, placement, and so on. The window class serves as a template that defines these attributes.

Registered window classes are available to all programs running under Windows. For this reason, the programmer should use caution when naming and registering classes to make certain that those names used do not conflict with any other applications window classes. Windows requires that every instance (loaded copy of a program), register its own window classes.

This if statement registers the new window class. It does this by sending **RegisterClass()** a pointer to the window class structure. If Windows cannot register the window class, possibly due to the lack of memory, **RegisterClass()** will return a 0, terminating the program.

Under Windows the **RegisterClassEx()** function can be used in place of the **RegisterClass()** function. RegisterClassEx() allows the inclusion of the small Windows 95/98/NT icons, via the WNDCLASSEX structure. The syntax for **RegisterClasEx()** is:

```
ATOM RegisterClassEx(CONST WNDCLASSEX FAR *lpwcx);
```

Here, *lpwcx* is a pointer to the WNDCLASSEX structure. The WNDCLASSEX structure is similar to WNDCLASS, as you can see:

```
UINT     style;
WNDPROC  lpfnWndProc;
int      cbClsExtra;
int      cbWndExtra;
HANDLE   hInstance;
HICON    hIcon;
HCURSOR  hCursor;
HBRUSH   hbrBackground;
LPCTSTR  lpszMenuName;
LPCTSTR  lpszClassName;
HICON    hIconSm;
```

The only addition of the WNDCLASSEX structure is the *hIconSm* member, which is the handle of the small icon associated with a window class.

Defining and then registering a window class has nothing to do with actually displaying a window in a Windows application. As mentioned, all windows are of some predefined and registered class type. Now that you know how to define and register a window class, you need to see the steps necessary in creating an actual window.

UNDERSTANDING CREATEWINDOW()

A window is created with a call to the Windows **CreateWindow()** function. Whereas the window class defines the general characteristics of a window, which allows the same window class to be used for many different windows, the parameters to **CreateWindow()** specify more detailed information about the window.

The **CreateWindow()** function uses the information passed to it to describe the window's class, title, style, screen position, parent handle, menu handle, and instance handle. The call to **CreateWindow()** for the template application uses the following actual parameters:

```
hWnd=CreateWindow(szProgName,"Simple Windows Template",
          WS_OVERLAPPEDWINDOW,CW_USEDEFAULT,
          CW_USEDEFAULT,CW_USEDEFAULT,
          CW_USEDEFAULT,(HWND)NULL,(HMENU)NULL,
          (HANDLE)hInst,(LPSTR)NULL);
```

The first field, *szProgName*, defines the window's class, followed by the title to be used for the window. The style of the window is the third parameter (WS_OVERLAPPEDWINDOW). This standard Windows style represents a normal overlapped window with a caption bar, a system menu box, minimize and maximize icons, and a window frame.

The next six parameters (either CW_USEDEFAULT, or NULL) represent the initial x and y positions and x and y size of the window, along with the parent window handle and window menu handle. Each of these fields has been assigned a default value. The *hInst* field contains the instance handle of the program, followed by no additional parameters (NULL).

CreateWindow() returns the handle of the newly created window if it was successful. Otherwise, the function returns NULL.

SHOWING AND UPDATING A WINDOW

At this point, you know how to define and register a window class and create its instance. However, this is still not enough to actually see your application's main window. To display a window, you need to make a call to the Windows **ShowWindow()** function. The following example is from the template application:

```
ShowWindow(hWnd,nCmdShow);
```

As described above, the *hWnd* parameter holds the handle of the window created by the call to **CreateWindow()**. The second parameter to **ShowWindow()**, *nCmdShow*, determines how the window is initially displayed, otherwise referred to as the window's *visibility state*.

The value of *nCmdShow* can specify that the window be displayed as a normal window (SW_SHOWNNORMAL) or several other possibilities. For

> **note:** In layman's terms, you can think of a *message* (usually a #define symbolic constant, found in a header file), as nothing more than a number sent to a function or object, triggering that code segment to perform a specific action.

example, substituting *nCmdShow* with the winuser.h constant SW_SHOWMINNOACTIVE causes the window to be drawn as an icon:

```
ShowWindow(hWnd,SW_SHOWMINNOACTIVE);
```

Other possibilities include, SW_SHOWMAXIMIZED, causing the window to be active and filling the entire display, along with its counterpart, SW_SHOWMINIMIZED.

The last step in displaying a window requires a call to Windows **UpdateWindow()** function:

```
UpdateWindow(hWnd);
```

Calling **ShowWindow()** with an SW_SHOWNORMAL parameter causes the function to erase the window's client area with the background brush specified in the window's class. It is the call to **UpdateWindow()** that causes the client area to be painted by generating a WM_PAINT message (WM_PAINT is explained later in the chapter).

CREATING A MESSAGE LOOP

Now that the application's window has been created and displayed, the program is ready to perform its main task, that being the processing of messages. Remember, Windows does not send input from the mouse or keyboard directly to an application. Instead, it places all input into the application's message queue. The message queue can contain messages generated by Windows or messages posted by other applications.

Once the call to **WinMain()** has taken care of creating and displaying the window, the application needs to create a message processing loop. The most common approach is to use the standard C/C++ while loop:

```
while (GetMessage(&lpMsg,NULL,0,0))
{
  TranslateMessage(&lpMsg);
  DispatchMessage(&lpMmsg);
}
```

USING GETMESSAGE()

A call to the Windows **GetMessage()** function retrieves the next message to be processed from the application's message queue. **GetMessage()** copies the message into the message structure pointed to by the long pointer, *lpMsg*, and sends it to the main body of the program.

The first NULL parameter instructs the function to retrieve any of the messages for any window that belongs to the application. The last two parameters *(0,0)*, tell **GetMessage()** not to apply any *message filters*. Message filters can restrict retrieved messages to specific categories such as keystrokes or mouse moves. These filters are referred to as *wMsgFilterMin* and *wMsgFilterMax,* and specify the numeric filter extremes to apply.

An application can normally return control to Windows any time before starting the message loop. For example, an application will normally make certain that all steps leading up to the message loop have executed properly. This can include making sure each window class is registered and has been created. However, once the message loop has been entered, only one message can terminate the loop. Whenever the message to be processed is WM_QUIT, the value returned is false. This causes the processing to proceed to the main loop's closing routine. The WM_QUIT message is the only way for an application to get out of the message loop.

USING TRANSLATEMESSAGE()

The Windows **TranslateMessage()** function translates virtual-key messages into character messages. The function call is required only by applications that need to process character input from the keyboard. For example, this can be very useful for allowing the user to make menu selections without having to use the mouse.

Technically, the **TranslateMessage()** function creates an ASCII character message (WM_CHAR) from a WM_KEYDOWN and WM_KEYUP message. As long as this function is included in the message loop, the keyboard interface will be in effect.

USING DISPATCHMESSAGE()

The Windows **DispatchMessage()** function is used to send the current message to the correct window procedure. By using this function, it is easy to add additional windows and dialog boxes to your application, allowing **DispatchMessage()** to automatically route each message to the appropriate window procedure.

WINMAIN() RETURN

WinMain() is normally responsible for terminating the message loop when it receives a WM_QUIT message. This terminates the application, returning the value passed in the WM_QUIT message's *wParam* parameter. This statement is accomplished by the last statement in **WinMain()**:

```
return(lpMsg.wParam);
```

The Required Window Function

All Windows applications must include a **WinMain()** and a Windows callback function. Because a Windows application never directly accesses any Windows functions, each application must make a request to Windows to carry out any specified operations.

> **note:** Remember that a callback function is registered with Windows and it is called back whenever Windows executes an operation on a window. The actual code size for the callback function will vary with each application. The window function itself may be very small, processing only one or two messages, or it may be large and complex.

This concept of an operating system making a call to the application can be surprising to the novice Windows programmer. The following code segment (minus application-specific statements) highlights the callback window function **WndProc()**, used in the template application:

```
LRESULT CALLBACK WndProc(HWND hWnd,UINT messg,
                   WPARAM wParam,LPARAM lParam)
{
  HDC hdc;
  PAINTSTRUCT ps;

  switch (messg)
  {
    case WM_PAINT:
      hdc=BeginPaint(hWnd,&ps);
//--------- your routines below ---------

        .
        .
        .

//--------- your routines above ---------
      ValidateRect(hWnd,NULL);
      EndPaint(hWnd,&ps);
      break;

    case WM_DESTROY:
      PostQuitMessage(0);
      break;

    default:
      return(DefWindowProc(hWnd,messg,wParam,lParam));
  }
  return(0);
}
```

One subtle detail that must not be overlooked is that Windows expects the name referenced by the *wcApp.lpfnWndProc* field of the window class structure definition to match the name used for the callback function. **WndProc()** will be the name used for the callback function for all subsequent windows created from this window class.

The following code segment reviews the placement and assignment of the callback function's name within the window class structure:

```
                .
                .
                .
wcApp.lpszClassName=szProgName;
wcApp.hInstance                                              =hInst;
wcApp.lpfnWndProc                                            =WndProc;
                .
                .
                .
```

Windows has several hundred different messages it can send to the window function. All of them are labeled with identifiers that begin with WM_. Technically, these identifiers are known as *symbolic constants*. The #define preprocessor statement is used to associate unique numeric values with each easily understood label. These symbolic constants are much easier to read and convey more information than do their numeric counterparts. Table 2.3 contains a partial list of WM_ messages found in windows.h or winuser.h.

Table 2.3   Windows messages.

Message	Value
#define WM_NULL	0x0000
#define WM_CREATE	0x0001
#define WM_DESTROY	0x0002
#define WM_MOVE	0x0003
#define WM_SIZE	0x0005
#define WM_ACTIVATE	0x0006
#define WM_SETFOCUS	0x0007
#define WM_KILLFOCUS	0x0008
#define WM_ENABLE	0x000A
#define WM_SETREDRAW	0x000B
#define WM_SETTEXT	0x000C
#define WM_GETTEXT	0x000D
#define WM_GETTEXTLENGTH	0x000E
#define WM_PAINT	0x000F

Table 2.3 — Windows messages. (Continued)

Message	Value
#define WM_CLOSE	0x0010
#define WM_QUERYENDSESSION	0x0011
#define WM_QUIT	0x0012
#define WM_QUERYOPEN	0x0013
#define WM_ERASEBKGND	0x0014
#define WM_SYSCOLORCHANGE	0x0015
#define WM_ENDSESSION	0x0016
#define WM_SHOWWINDOW	0x0018
#define WM_WININICHANGE	0x001A
#define WM_DEVMODECHANGE	0x001B
#define WM_ACTIVATEAPP	0x001C
#define WM_FONTCHANGE	0x001D
#define WM_TIMECHANGE	0x001E
#define WM_CANCELMODE	0x001F
#define WM_SETCURSOR	0x0020
#define WM_MOUSEACTIVATE	0x0021
#define WM_CHILDACTIVATE	0x0022
#define WM_QUEUESYNC	0x0023
#define WM_GETMINMAXINFO	0x0024
#define WM_PAINTICON	0x0026
#define WM_ICONERASEBKGND	0x0027
#define WM_NEXTDLGCTL	0x0028
#define WM_SPOOLERSTATUS	0x002A
#define WM_DRAWITEM	0x002B
#define WM_MEASUREITEM	0x002C
#define WM_DELETEITEM	0x002D
#define WM_VKEYTOITEM	0x002E
#define WM_CHARTOITEM	0x002F
#define WM_SETFONT	0x0030
#define WM_GETFONT	0x0031

Table 2.3 Windows messages. (Continued)

Message	Value
#define WM_SETHOTKEY	0x0032
#define WM_GETHOTKEY	0x0033
#define WM_QUERYDRAGICON	0x0037
#define WM_COMPAREITEM	0x0039
#define WM_GETOBJECT	0x003D
#define WM_COMPACTING	0x0041
#define WM_COMMNOTIFY	0x0044 /* no longer supported */
#define WM_WINDOWPOSCHANGING	0x0046
#define WM_WINDOWPOSCHANGED	0x0047
#define WM_POWER	0x0048
#define WM_COPYDATA	0x004A
#define WM_CANCELJOURNAL	0x004B
#define WM_NOTIFY	0x004E
#define WM_INPUTLANGCHANGEREQUEST	0x0050
#define WM_INPUTLANGCHANGE	0x0051
#define WM_TCARD	0x0052
#define WM_HELP	0x0053
#define WM_USERCHANGED	0x0054
#define WM_NOTIFYFORMAT	0x0055
#define WM_CONTEXTMENU	0x007B
#define WM_STYLECHANGING	0x007C
#define WM_STYLECHANGED	0x007D
#define WM_DISPLAYCHANGE	0x007E
#define WM_GETICON	0x007F
#define WM_SETICON	0x0080
#define WM_NCCREATE	0x0081
#define WM_NCDESTROY	0x0082
#define WM_NCCALCSIZE	0x0083
#define WM_NCHITTEST	0x0084

Table 2.3 Windows messages. (Continued)

Message	Value
#define WM_NCPAINT	0x0085
#define WM_NCACTIVATE	0x0086
#define WM_GETDLGCODE	0x0087
#define WM_SYNCPAINT	0x0088
#define WM_NCMOUSEMOVE	0x00A0
#define WM_NCLBUTTONDOWN	0x00A1
#define WM_NCLBUTTONUP	0x00A2
#define WM_NCLBUTTONDBLCLK	0x00A3
#define WM_NCRBUTTONDOWN	0x00A4
#define WM_NCRBUTTONUP	0x00A5
#define WM_NCRBUTTONDBLCLK	0x00A6
#define WM_NCMBUTTONDOWN	0x00A7
#define WM_NCMBUTTONUP	0x00A8
#define WM_NCMBUTTONDBLCLK	0x00A9
#define WM_KEYFIRST	0x0100
#define WM_KEYDOWN	0x0100
#define WM_KEYUP	0x0101
#define WM_CHAR	0x0102
#define WM_DEADCHAR	0x0103
#define WM_SYSKEYDOWN	0x0104
#define WM_SYSKEYUP	0x0105
#define WM_SYSCHAR	0x0106
#define WM_SYSDEADCHAR	0x0107
#define WM_KEYLAST	0x0108
#define WM_IME_STARTCOMPOSITION	0x010D
#define WM_IME_ENDCOMPOSITION	0x010E
#define WM_IME_COMPOSITION	0x010F
#define WM_IME_KEYLAST	0x010F
#define WM_INITDIALOG	0x0110
#define WM_COMMAND	0x0111

Table 2.3 — Windows messages. (Continued)

Message	Value
#define WM_SYSCOMMAND	0x0112
#define WM_TIMER	0x0113
#define WM_HSCROLL	0x0114
#define WM_VSCROLL	0x0115
#define WM_INITMENU	0x0116
#define WM_INITMENUPOPUP	0x0117
#define WM_MENUSELECT	0x011F
#define WM_MENUCHAR	0x0120
#define WM_ENTERIDLE	0x0121
#define WM_MENURBUTTONUP	0x0122
#define WM_MENUDRAG	0x0123
#define WM_MENUGETOBJECT	0x0124
#define WM_UNINITMENUPOPUP	0x0125
#define WM_MENUCOMMAND	0x0126
#define WM_CTLCOLORMSGBOX	0x0132
#define WM_CTLCOLOREDIT	0x0133
#define WM_CTLCOLORLISTBOX	0x0134
#define WM_CTLCOLORBTN	0x0135
#define WM_CTLCOLORDLG	0x0136
#define WM_CTLCOLORSCROLLBAR	0x0137
#define WM_CTLCOLORSTATIC	0x0138
#define WM_MOUSEFIRST	0x0200
#define WM_MOUSEMOVE	0x0200
#define WM_LBUTTONDOWN	0x0201
#define WM_LBUTTONUP	0x0202
#define WM_LBUTTONDBLCLK	0x0203
#define WM_RBUTTONDOWN	0x0204
#define WM_RBUTTONUP	0x0205
#define WM_RBUTTONDBLCLK	0x0206
#define WM_MBUTTONDOWN	0x0207

Table 2.3 Windows messages. (Continued)

Message	Value
#define WM_MBUTTONUP	0x0208
#define WM_MBUTTONDBLCLK	0x0209
#define WM_MOUSEWHEEL	0x020A
#define WM_MOUSELAST	0x020A
#define WM_MOUSELAST	0x0209
#define WM_PARENTNOTIFY	0x0210
#define WM_ENTERMENULOOP	0x0211
#define WM_EXITMENULOOP	0x0212
#define WM_NEXTMENU	0x0213
#define WM_SIZING	0x0214
#define WM_CAPTURECHANGED	0x0215
#define WM_MOVING	0x0216
#define WM_POWERBROADCAST	0x0218 // r_winuser pbt
#define WM_DEVICECHANGE	0x0219
#define WM_MDICREATE	0x0220
#define WM_MDIDESTROY	0x0221
#define WM_MDIACTIVATE	0x0222
#define WM_MDIRESTORE	0x0223
#define WM_MDINEXT	0x0224
#define WM_MDIMAXIMIZE	0x0225
#define WM_MDITILE	0x0226
#define WM_MDICASCADE	0x0227
#define WM_MDIICONARRANGE	0x0228
#define WM_MDIGETACTIVE	0x0229
#define WM_MDISETMENU	0x0230
#define WM_ENTERSIZEMOVE	0x0231
#define WM_EXITSIZEMOVE	0x0232
#define WM_DROPFILES	0x0233
#define WM_MDIREFRESHMENU	0x0234

Table 2.3 Windows messages. *(Continued)*

Message	Value
#define WM_IME_SETCONTEXT	0x0281
#define WM_IME_NOTIFY	0x0282
#define WM_IME_CONTROL	0x0283
#define WM_IME_COMPOSITIONFULL	0x0284
#define WM_IME_SELECT	0x0285
#define WM_IME_CHAR	0x0286
#define WM_IME_REQUEST	0x0288
#define WM_IME_KEYDOWN	0x0290
#define WM_IME_KEYUP	0x0291
#define WM_MOUSEHOVER	0x02A1
#define WM_MOUSELEAVE	0x02A3
#define WM_CUT	0x0300
#define WM_COPY	0x0301
#define WM_PASTE	0x0302
#define WM_CLEAR	0x0303
#define WM_UNDO	0x0304
#define WM_RENDERFORMAT	0x0305
#define WM_RENDERALLFORMATS	0x0306
#define WM_DESTROYCLIPBOARD	0x0307
#define WM_DRAWCLIPBOARD	0x0308
#define WM_PAINTCLIPBOARD	0x0309
#define WM_VSCROLLCLIPBOARD	0x030A
#define WM_SIZECLIPBOARD	0x030B
#define WM_ASKCBFORMATNAME	0x030C
#define WM_CHANGECBCHAIN	0x030D
#define WM_HSCROLLCLIPBOARD	0x030E
#define WM_QUERYNEWPALETTE	0x030F
#define WM_PALETTEISCHANGING	0x0310
#define WM_PALETTECHANGED	0x0311
#define WM_HOTKEY	0x0312

Table 2.3	Windows messages. (Continued)
Message	Value
#define WM_PRINT	0x0317
#define WM_PRINTCLIENT	0x0318
#define WM_HANDHELDFIRST	0x0358
#define WM_HANDHELDLAST	0x035F
#define WM_AFXFIRST	0x0360
#define WM_AFXLAST	0x037F
#define WM_PENWINFIRST	0x0380
#define WM_PENWINLAST	0x038F

Windows breaks down this impressive list of identifiers into several different categories, including window creation, resizing, moving, iconization, menu item selection, mouse manipulation of scroll bars, client area repainting, and destroying a window.

Remember the **WndProc()** callback function uses the LRESULT CALLBACK calling convention. Like many Windows functions, the first parameter to **WndProc()** is *hWnd*. *hWnd* contains the handle to the window that Windows will send the message. Because it is possible for one window function to process messages for several windows created from the same window class, this handle is used by the window function to determine which window is receiving the message.

The second parameter to the function, *messg*, specifies the actual message being processed as defined in windows.h or winuser.h. Both of the last two parameters, *wParam* and *lParam*, are involved with any additional information needed to process each specific message. Frequently, the values returned in these parameters is NULL, meaning they can be ignored; at other times, they contain a 2-byte value and a pointer, or two word values.

The **WndProc()** function continues by defining several variables; *hdc*—for the display context handle and *ps*—a PAINTSTRUCT structure needed to store client area information. The main purpose of the callback function is to examine the type of message it is about to process and select the appropriate action to be taken. This selection process usually takes the form of a standard C/C++ switch statement.

THE WM_PAINT MESSAGE

The first message **WndProc()** will process is WM_PAINT. This message calls the Windows function **BeginPaint()**, which prepares the specified window (*hWnd*), for painting, and fills a PAINTSTRUCT (*&ps*) with information about the area to be painted. The **BeginPaint()** function also returns a handle to the device context for the given window.

The device context comes equipped with a default pen, brush, and font. The default pen is black, 1 pixel wide, and draws a solid line. The default brush is white with a solid brush pattern. The default font is the system font. The device context is very important because all of the display functions used by Windows applications require a handle to the device context.

Because Windows is a multitasking environment, it becomes quite possible for one application to display its dialog box over another application's client area. This creates a problem whenever the dialog box is closed, namely, a black hole on the screen where the dialog box was displayed. Windows takes care of this problem by sending the application a WM_PAINT message. In this case, Windows is requesting that the application update its client area.

Except for the first WM_PAINT message, which is sent by a call to the **UpdateWindow()** function in **WinMain()**, additional WM_PAINT messages are sent under the following conditions:

- When a window needs resizing.
- When the application's client area needs repainting due to a recently closed menu or dialog box that has hidden a portion of a client area.
- When using scroll bar functions.
- When forcing a WM_PAINT message by calling the **InvalidateRect()** or **InvalidateRgn()** functions.

Whenever a portion of an application's client area has been corrupted by the overlay of a dialog box or menu, that part of the client area is marked as invalid. Windows manages the redrawing of the client area by keeping track of the diagonal coordinates of this invalid rectangle. The presence of an invalid rectangle prompts Windows to send a WM_PAINT message.

Windows is extremely efficient in the way it processes multiple invalidated rectangles. Should the execution of statements invalidate several portions of the client area, Windows will adjust the invalid rectangle coordinates to encapsulate all invalid regions. Therefore, it sends only one WM_PAINT, rather than one for each invalid region.

An application can force a WM_PAINT message by making a call to the **InvalidateRect()** function, which marks the application's client area as being invalid. By calling the **GetUpdateRect()** function, an application can obtain the coordinates of the invalid rectangle. A subsequent call to the **ValidateRect()** function validates any rectangular region in the client area and removes any pending WM_PAINT messages.

The **WndProc()** function ends its processing of the WM_PAINT message by calling the **EndPaint()** function. This function is called whenever the application is finished outputting information to the client area. It tells Windows that the application has finished processing all paint messages and that it is now okay to remove the display context.

THE WM_DESTROY MESSAGE

When the user selects the Close option from the application's system menu, Windows posts a WM_DESTROY message to the application's message queue. The program terminates after retrieving this message.

THE DEFWINDOWPROC() FUNCTION

The **DefWindowProc()** function call in the default section of **WndProc()**'s switch statement is needed to empty the application's message queue of any unrecognized and therefore unprocessed messages. This function ensures that all of the messages posted to the application are processed.

The basetsd.h File

Now that you have an in-depth understanding of the Simple Windows Template, swt.cpp program, it is time to turn to a few details involving your first project. For example, Figure 2-17 shows the Workspace pane set to FileView with the basetsd.h header file highlighted. If you are interested in viewing the file's contents, simply double-click on the file's name. All you need to know about basetsd.h is that it is automatically incorporated into your project and that it contains program-specific definitions for the sake of portability.

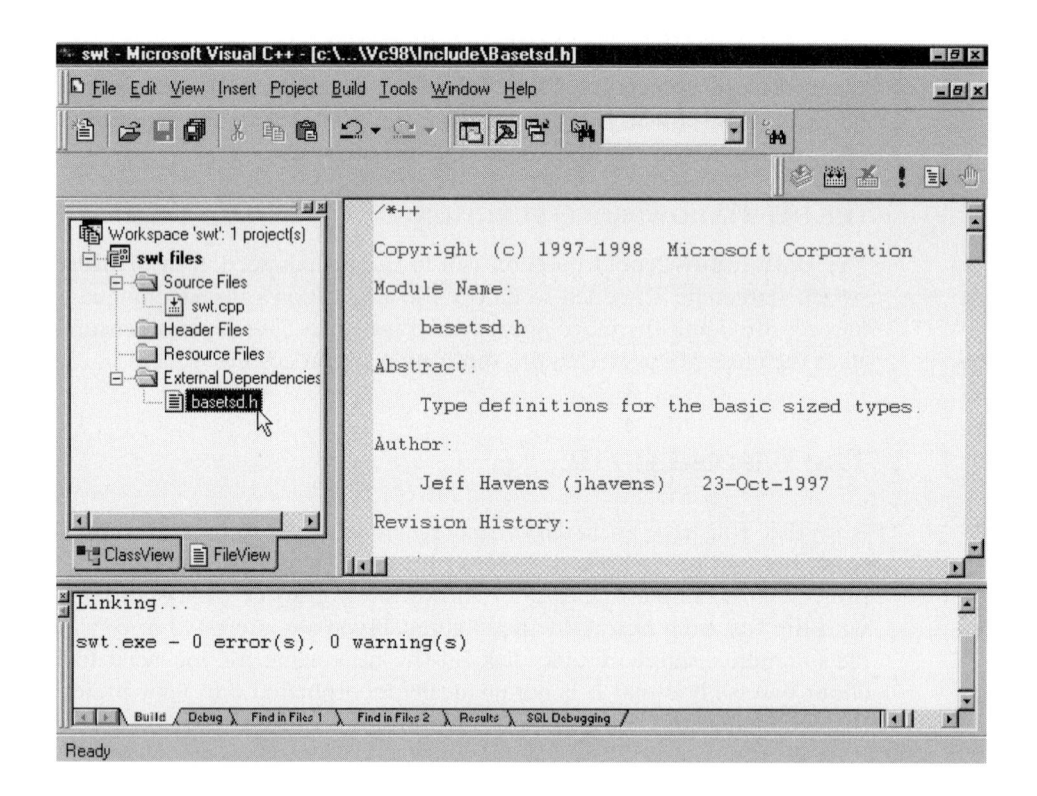

Figure 2-17 Viewing the file basetsd.h.

Using the Workspace Pane

Figure 2-18 switches the Workspace pane view from FileView (see Figure 2-17) to ClassView. ClassView can not only instantly locate any class definition within a project simply by double-clicking on the class name but, as seen in Figure 2-18, will display a class header. To do this, just leave the mouse over the class name for a few additional seconds.

Additional Rebuild All... File Entries

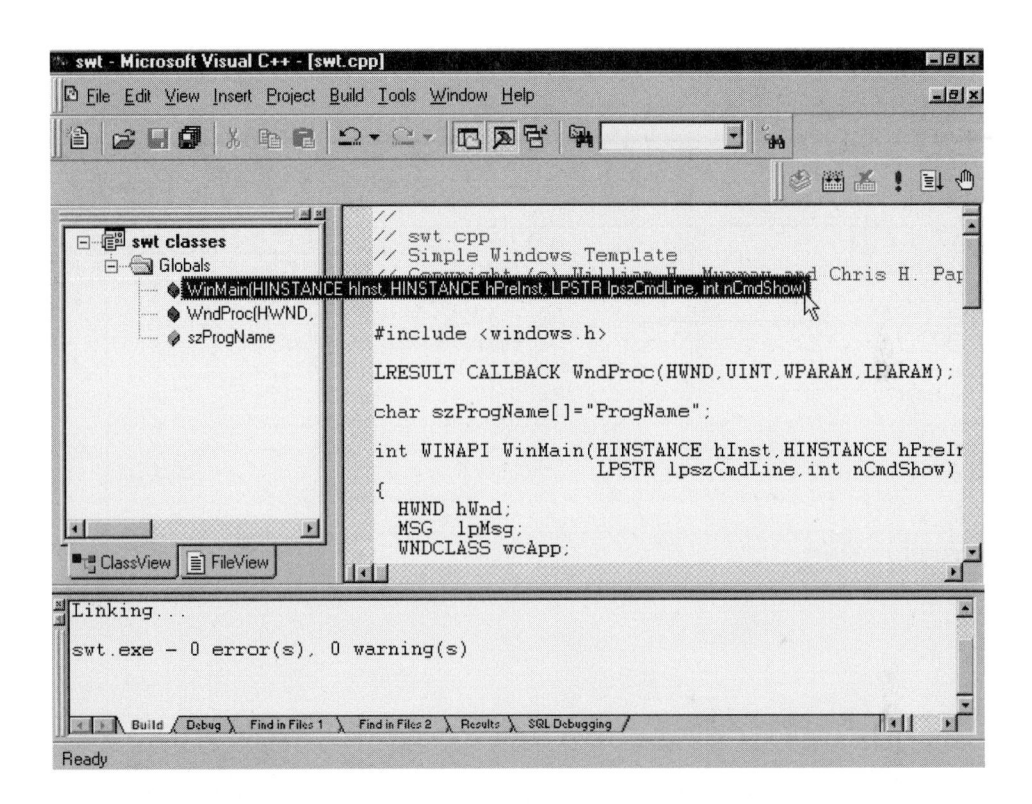

Figure 2-18 *Using the Workspace ClassView.*

Additional Rebuild All... File Entries

To round out your introduction to Microsoft Visual Studio C++ project files, take one more look at the files generated by the Rebuild All... command (see Figure 2-19).

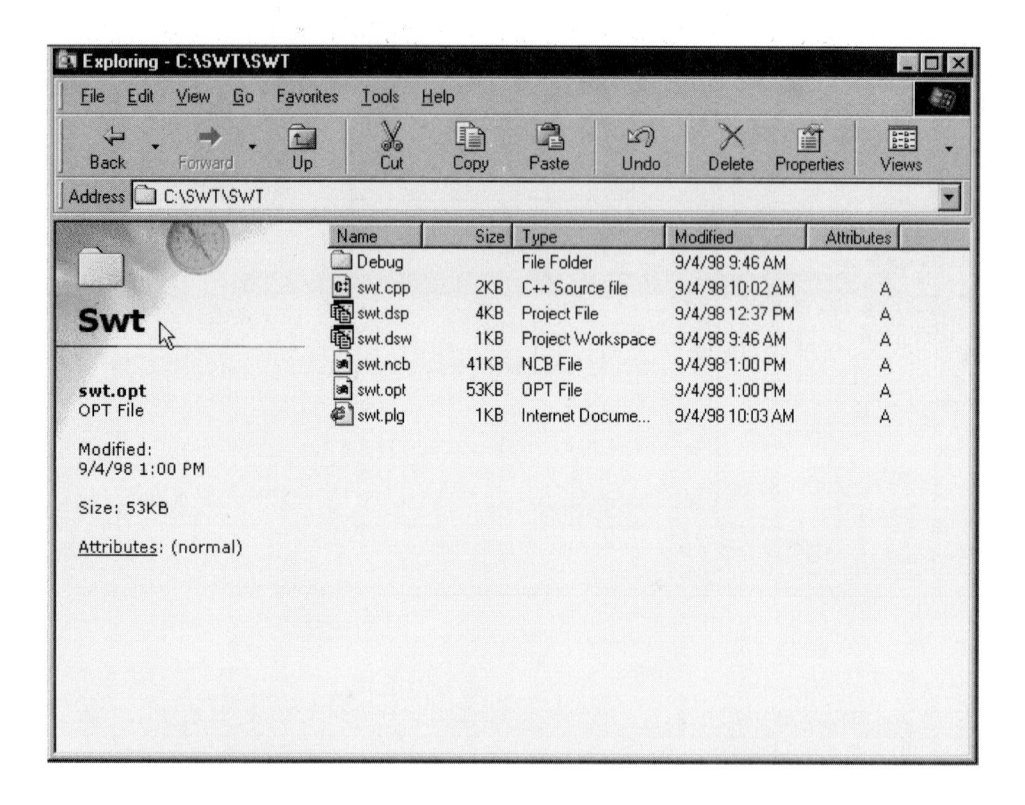

Figure 2–19 *File view of swt subdirectory.*

Many of these files have already been discussed. However, notice that there are two new ones, swt.opt and swt.plg.

swt.opt—This is the workspace options file used within the development environment. It stores all the user options you create for your workspace, so that each time you open the project workspace, it has the look and feel you want and includes any customizations you have made.

swt.plg—Optionally, you can generate a build log file (*.plg file). Any time a build occurs, the *.plg file is overwritten with the latest information. For multiple builds, save or move the *.plg file before starting the next release or debug build. The *.plg file is stored in the project directory that you build.

Additional Rebuild All... Debug File Entries

When you build the project by executing Rebuild All..., Visual Studio completes the set of files it generates, enabling you to execute and debug your Windows application. Figure 2-20 explains this list.

Additional Rebuild All... Debug File Entries

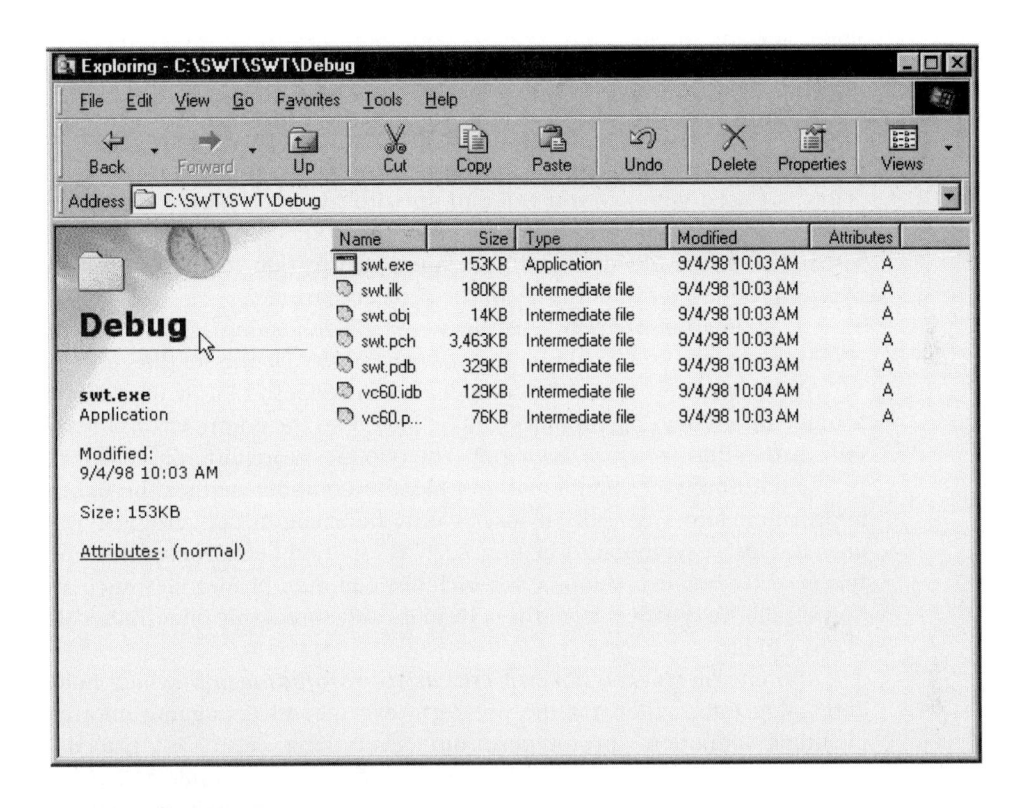

Figure 2–20 *View of Debug subdirectory.*

The first file, swt.exe, is, of course, the machine language executable version of swt.cpp However, the following files, with their unique file types are not as immediately obvious.

swt.ilk—When linking incrementally, LINK updates the *.ilk status file that it created during the first incremental link. This file has the same base name as the .exe or .dll file, and it has the extension *.ilk. During subsequent incremental links, LINK updates the *.ilk file. If the *.ilk file is missing or unusable, LINK performs a full link and creates a new file.

swt.obj—This is an intermediate file generated by the compiler and used as input to the linker.

swt.pch—These files are used to build a precompiled header file *.pch and a precompiled types file stdafx.obj. It is important that you neither #define nor #undefine any of the _afx_no_xxx macros in stdafx.h.

swt.pdb—The .pdb (program database) file holds debugging and project state information. The .pdb file provides the information needed for incremental linking of debug program versions. Although earlier, 16-bit versions of Visual C++ used .pdb files, the debugging information stored in them was appended to the end of the .exe or .dll file by the linker. Now, with 32-bit .exe's, both the linker and the integrated debugger allow .pdb files to be used directly during the debugging process. When you build projects generated by Visual C++, the compiler switch /Fd is used to rename the .pdb file to *yourprojname*.pdb. Therefore, you will have only one .pdb file for the entire project.

When you run makefiles that were not generated by Visual C++ and the /Fd is not used with /Zi, you will end up with two .pdb files:

• vc*x*0.pdb (where *x* refers to the major version of the corresponding Visual C++). This file stores all debugging information for the individual .obj files and resides in the directory of the project makefile.

• *yourprojname*.pdb. This file stores all debugging information for the resulting .exe file and resides in the *yourprojname*\Debug subdirectory.

Why two files? When the compiler is run, it doesn't know the name of the .exe file into which the .obj files will be linked, so the compiler can't insert the information into *yourprojname*.pdb. The two files store different information.

Each time you compile an .obj file, the compiler merges the debugging information into vc*x*0.pdb. It inserts only information concerning types and does not insert symbol information, such as function definitions. One benefit of this is that when every source file includes common header files, such as windows.h, all the typedefs from these headers are stored only once, rather than in every .obj file.

When you run the linker, it creates *yourprojname*.pdb, which holds the debugging information for the project's .exe file. All debugging information, including function prototypes and everything else, is placed into <project>.pdb, not just the type information found in vc*x*0.pdb. The two kinds of .pdb files share the same extension because they are architecturally similar and they both allow incremental updates. Nevertheless, they actually store different information.

The Visual C++ debugger uses the *myprojname*.pdb file created by the linker directly, and embeds the absolute path to the .pdb in the .exe or .dll file. If the debugger can't find the .pdb file at that location or if the path is invalid (for example, if the project was moved to another computer), the debugger looks for it in the current directory.

vc60.idb—The Enable Incremental Compilation option controls the incremental compiler, which compiles only those functions that have changed since the last compile. The compiler saves state information from the first compile in the projects .idb file (the default name is *myprojname*.idb or vc50.idb for files compiled without a project). The compiler uses this state information to speed subsequent compiles.

vc60.pdb—As described above.

In the Next Chapter...

In this chapter, you learned everything you need to know about creating a new project in Visual Studio C++ 6.0 along with an in-depth understanding of the minimal code necessary to get a simple Windows application up and running. Starting with Chapter 3, you will be shown the types of concerns a Windows application must take into consideration beyond what the program itself, for instance, spreadsheet, database, and so on, is trying to do.

THREE

Windows Details

Accessing the Windows Environment

Most would agree that Microsoft Windows is an easy-to-use, intuitive graphical environment that maximizes your efficiency and use of hardware resources. It is quite possible that your only prior experience with Windows has been that of an end user. Don't worry—this book does not assume that you have already programmed in Windows. If you have not written Windows code before now, you are in for quite a surprise. The difference in the learning curve for a Windows user versus a Windows programmer is quite dramatic. The good news is that learning to master Windows application development is no more difficult than mastering any new programming concept.

Think back to your first programming course and how confused you were when the instructor introduced you to the topic of functions. How long did it take you to really understand the difference between a procedure and a function?

Do you remember when your instructor boldly told you never to use the name of a function within the body of the function. If your instructor did not go into any detail explaining why this could create a problem, you likely accepted this as some sort of compiler restriction. However, sooner or later you also learned about recursion; a function that calls itself.

Probably the first time you encountered the concept of one-dimensional arrays, you were awestruck. Then came multidimensional arrays. Then there were dynamic variables!

Our educational system's approach of presenting programming concepts using an incremental scale of complexity worked to your advantage. As you solidified your understanding of programming fundamentals, you moved into deeper water. Well, it's time to put on your wet suits and scuba equipment. The ease of use provided by all Windows applications comes at the cost of programming complexity.

The software engineers who developed Windows have presented you with a large array of programming features. This chapter will begin to dive deeper into the richness of their capabilities. Many of the example programs throughout this book will make use of some or all of these important features.

> **note** Many of the topics discussed in this and following chapters include a contrasting analysis between Windows 95/98/NT and Microsoft's older Windows 3.x products. This 32-bit back to 16-bit analysis will once again reappear as Microsoft migrates its latest operating systems over to 64-bit architectures, generating a 64-bit back to 32-bit mapping.

The Coordinate System

Windows is by design a graphical environment characterized by client areas, scroll bars, visual controls, fonts, menus, and much more. All of these visual objects need positioning on the display device. The Windows environment provides the application's developer with an all-encompassing array of functions that allow you to display text and graphics in whichever coordinate system most logically or physically maps your applications needs to the display context.

The following section explains the various concepts involved in using coordinate systems. The good news is that the majority of applications can use the default coordinate system, MM_TEXT, for the most convenient placement of objects.

BASIC MAPPING MODES

Many of the Windows graphics device interface (GDI) drawing functions require coordinate values or size arguments. For example, the frequently used **TextOut()** function has X and Y values indicating where to output the beginning of a text string. The X parameter indicates the position on the horizontal axis and the Y parameter, the position on the vertical axis.

The application uses *logical units to specify* the X and Y parameters. A logical unit or *logical coordinate* represents a virtual coordinate system. Under Windows 3.x and Windows 95/98, the range of useful values for X and Y extends from −32,767 to +32,767. Under Windows NT, these values extend from −2,147,483,647 to +2,147,483,647.

> **note** Under Windows 3.x, the X and Y values are 16 bits. Under Windows 95/98, the values are 32 bits, but only the lower 16 bits are used. Under Windows NT, all 32 bits are used.

GDI output routines must map an application's logical coordinates into the correct screen coordinates for output. This mapping between logical coordinates and actual screen coordinates makes your life as a programmer much simpler. You write one application targeted for a specific display device and Windows takes care of translating all logical coordinates to realistic hardware coordinates! This translation of logical units to device units (actual screen coordinates) is governed by the current mapping mode, along with the window's viewport origin and extents.

Regardless of the mapping mode, all coordinates must fit into the signed integer range of -32,767 to +32,767 for Windows 3.x and or -2,147,483,647 to +2,147,483,647 for Windows 95/98 or Windows NT. The mapping mode also specifies an origin and orientation of the X and Y axes. Table 3.1 lists eight mapping modes defined in the windows.h header file when using Windows 3.x or in the wingdi.h header file when using Windows 95/98 and Windows NT.

Table 3.1 Mapping Modes Defined in WINGI.H.

Mapping Mode		X Axis	Y Axis	Logical Units
MM_TEXT	1	right	down	pixels
MM_LOMETRIC	2	right	up	0.1 mm
MM_HIMETRIC	3	right	up	0.01 mm
MM_LOENGLISH	4	right	up	0.01 inch
MM_HIENGLISH	5	right	up	0.001 inch
MM_TWIPS	6	right	up	1/1440 inch
MM_ISOTROPIC	7	either	either	arbitrary (x=y)
MM_ANISOTROPIC	8	either	either	arbitrary (x!=y)

Windows applications set the mapping mode with a simple call to the **SetMapMode**(*hdc,iMapMode*) function, with *iMapMode* being one of the eight mapping-mode identifiers listed in the table. While the default mapping mode is MM_TEXT, an application can obtain the current mapping mode by making a call to the **GetMapMode(hdc)** function, which would look something like this:

```
iMapMode = GetMapMode(hdc);
```

The following discussion illustrates how the different mapping modes affect the output produced by a call to the **TextOut**(*hdc,x,y,lpszString,iCount*). When the mapping mode is MM_TEXT (the default), logical units are mapped directly to physical units, or pixels. If the **TextOut()** function had been passed an *x* value of 10 and a *y* value of 20, the text output would begin 10 pixels from the left of the client area and 20 pixels from the top.

If the mapping mode had been set to MM_LOENGLISH with the **TextOut()** function being passed an *x* value of 100 and a *y* value of -200, the text output would begin 1 inch from the left of the client area and 2 inches from the top. Did you notice the -200? When using the mapping modes MM_LOENGLISH, MM_HIENGLISH, MM_LOMETRIC, MM_HIMETRIC, or MM_TWIPS, all logical coordinates are expressed in physical measurements, with the origin at the upper-left corner of the selected area. Moving down the display requires a negative value.

In order for you not to become confused, you must remember that all non-GDI functions use the device coordinate system, which returns values in device units, which are pixels. Because the mapping mode is an attribute of a device context, the only time the mapping mode will come into play is when the application is using a GDI function that requires a handle to the device context.

UNDERSTANDING DEVICE COORDINATES

All Windows device coordinate systems are expressed in terms of pixels. The X axis increases in value going from left to right. The Y axis increases in value from the top of the display to the bottom. For example, many Windows functions, such as **CreateWindow()**, **MoveWindow()**, **GetWindowRect()** (which obtains, in terms of screen coordinates, the position and size of the whole window), **WindowFromPoint()**, **GetMessagePos()**, **GetCursorPos()**, and **SetCursorPos()**, use the *screen coordinate system* described in the preceding section.

Windows uses the *whole window coordinate system* to define the application's entire window. The coordinates include access to the caption bar, main menu, any scroll bars, and the window frame itself. The **GetWindowDC()** function will map logical coordinates in GDI functions into whole window coordinates.

Of the three device coordinate systems, *client area coordinates* are the most frequently used. In this system, the upper-left corner of the client area is *(0,0)*. When using the **GetDC()** or **BeginPaint()** function, logical coordinates are translated into client area coordinates. When necessary, converting from screen coordinates to client area coordinates is as easy as making the appropriate function call to either **ScreenToClient()** or **ClientToScreen()**.

UNDERSTANDING VIEWPORTS

As you have already seen, Windows maps logical coordinates to device coordinates based on two criteria: the mapping mode selected and the particular function used to obtain the device context. Actually, there's more to the story. The mapping mode is used to define the mapping of the window's coordinates or logical units to the viewport or device coordinates.

Accessing the Windows Environment 93

A *viewport* is defined in device coordinates, or pixels, and usually refers to the client area. However, if the application has made a call to **GetWindowDC()** or **CreateDC()**, the coordinates returned will refer to the whole window or to screen coordinates, respectively. Regardless, the point *(0,0)* is at the upper-left corner of the specified area, with *X* values increasing from left to right and *Y* values increasing from top to bottom.

A w*indow,* in this context, refers to logical coordinates. These logical coordinates may be pixels, inches, millimeters, or user-defined units. Logical window coordinates are passed to GDI functions (see also Chapter 13 for more on viewport modifications).

CHANGING VIEWPORT AND WINDOW EXTENTS

To change a viewport or window extent, you must use either the MM_ISOTROPIC or MM_ANSIOTROPIC mapping modes. This allows an application-defined scaling factor for translating logical and device coordinates.

The MM_ISOTROPIC mapping mode provides a metric mapping mode where logical units on the X axis are identical to those of the Y axis. This mapping mode allows an application to display images with the correct aspect ratio, regardless of the aspect ratio of the display device itself.

Choosing the MM_ANISOTROPIC mapping mode allows an application to use arbitrary axes while providing equal logical units for both (Chapter 13 contains more examples using MM_ANSIOTROPIC).

USER-DEFINED COORDINATES

Suppose you want your application to use equal physical distances. It's simple, just use the MM_ISOTROPIC mapping mode when you call **SetMapMode()**, as seen in the listing below. With this mapping mode your program must make a call to **SetWindowExtEx()**. This function sets the *x* and *y* extents of the window associated with the device context.

For this example, the logical size of the logical window will be "hardwired" with fixed constants (500,500). The third statement makes a call to the **SetViewportExtEx()** function, passing parameters that define the actual height and width of the client area.

When Windows adjusts these extents, it has to fit the logical window within the physical viewport. Therefore, Windows makes the best use of space whenever **SetWindowExtEx()** is called before **SetViewportExtEx()**. The last statement sets the logical point *(0,0)* to the device point *(0,0)*.

```
SetMapMode(hdc,MM_ISOTROPIC);
SetWindowExtEx(hdc,500,500,NULL);
SetViewportExtEx(hdc,xClientView,yClientView,NULL);
SetViewportOrgEx(hdc,0,0,NULL);
```

Previously, you learned that if the mapping mode is set to MM_HIENGLISH with the **TextOut()** function being passed an *x* value of 100 and a *y* value of -200, the text output would begin 1 inch from the left of the client area and 2 inches from the top.

The -200 was necessary because the default window and viewport origins were *(0,0)*. This meant that the only way to display anything in the client area was to use negative values for *y*. Because this can become quite disconcerting, why not just reset the logical origin? Assuming that *yClientView* is the height of the client area in pixels, you can accomplish this with the following statement:

```
SetViewportOrgEx(hdc,0,yClientView,NULL);
```

Now that the logical origin has been set to the lower-left corner of the client area, positive values can be used to move text up the display. This approach can be used for all five of the "metric" mapping modes.

CHOOSING INITIAL WINDOW SIZES, POSITION, ICONS, CURSORS, AND STYLES

You define and create the characteristics of an overlapped, pop-up, or child window with a call to the **CreateWindow()** or **CreateWindowEx()** functions. Using these eclectic functions requires a bit of finesse. The following material is designed to explain the syntax and meaning behind the various parameters.

Here is the **CreateWindow()** function:

```
HWND CreateWindow(lpszClassName,lpszWindowName,dwStyle,
        x,y,nWidth,nHeight,hwndParent,hmenu,
        hinst,lpParam)
```

Here is the **CreateWindowEx()** function:

```
HWND CreateWindowEx(dwExStyle,lpszClassName,lpszWindowName,
        dwStyle,x,y,nWidth,nHeight,
        hwndParent,hmenu,hinst,lpvCreateParams)
```

Every Windows application must make at least one call to **CreateWindow()** or **CreateWindowEx()**. **CreateWindowEx()** offers additional capabilities over **CreateWindow()**. Either function can be used to create an overlapped, pop-up, or child window and to specify the window's class, title, and style. Either function can set the window's initial position and size. One of the arguments to **CreateWindow()**, *hWndParent*, can identify the created window's owning parent or menu, if there is one.

You can also use either function to send all necessary messages (WM_CREATE, WM_GETMINMAXINFO, and WM_NCCREATE) to the window. For example, selecting the WS_VISIBLE style option causes the function to send the window messages to activate and display the window. Listing 3.1 lists each individual parameter:

Listing 3-1   *CreateWindow() Parameters and Explanations*

Parameter *lpszClassName*(LPCSTR) points to a null-terminated character string that names the window's class.

lpszWindowName(LPCSTR) points to a null-terminated character string that identifies the window by name.

x(int) defines the initial X-coordinate position of the window.

y(int) defines the initial Y-coordinate position of the window.

nWidth(int), using device units, defines width of window.

nHeight(int), using device units, defines height of the window.

hWndParent(HWND) specifies the parent window for the window that is about to be created. Overlapped windows must *not* have a parent (*hWndParent* must be NULL). A valid parent handle must be passed when creating a child window.

hMenu(HMENU) is dependent on the window's style and specifies a menu or a child-window identifier.

hinst(HANDLE) specifies the instance of the module to be identified with the window.

dwExStyle (DWORD) specifies the extended window style (see Table 3.10).

dwStyle (DWORD) specifies the window style (see Tables 3.2 through 3.9).

lpParam specifies the address of window-creation information. *lpvCreateParams* specifies the address of window-creation information. The window being created may access this data when the CREATESTRUCT structure is passed to the window by either WM_NCCREATE or WM_CREATE.

dwStyle can be created from the various parameters in Tables 3.2 through 3.9. Table 3.2 shows possible control classes that can be applied to *dwStyle*.

Table 3.2 Possible Control Classes.

Class	Description
BUTTON	This identifies a small rectangular child window that displays a button the user can turn on or off with a press of the mouse button. Buttons usually change display appearance when selected and deselected.

BUTTON Control Styles:

BS_3STATE
BS_AUTO3STATE
BS_AUTOCHECKBOX
BS_AUTORADIOBUTTON
BS_CHECKBOX
BS_DEFPUSHBUTTON
BS_GROUPBOX
BS_LEFTTEXT
BS_OWNERDRAW
BS_PUSHBUTTON
BS_RADIOBUTTON

EDIT	This identifies a small, rectangular child window in which the user can enter text from the keyboard. Input focus can be changed by pressing the mouse button or using TAB.
	Edit control classes allow the user to select the input focus repeatedly, make entries, backspace over mistakes, and reenter information. The user inserts text whenever the control display exhibits a flashing caret.

EDIT Control Styles:

ES_AUTOHSCROLL
ES_AUTOVSCROLL
ES_CENTER
ES_LEFT
ES_LOWERCASE

Table 3.2 — Possible Control Classes. (Continued)

Class	Description
	ES_MULTILINE ES_NOHIDESEL ES_OEMCONVERT ES_PASSWORD ES_READONLY ES_RIGHT ES_UPPERCASE ES_WANTRETURN if(WINVER >= 0x030a)
LISTBOX	This identifies a list of character strings and is most frequently used when an application needs to present a list of names, such as available file names, from which the user can select. Options are selected by moving the mouse and clicking the selected item. This causes the item to be highlighted and a notification of the choice to be passed to the parent window. Whenever the list is long, LISTBOX controls can be used in conjunction with SCROLLBAR controls.
	LISTBOX Control Styles: LBS_EXTENDEDSEL LBS_HASSTRINGS LBS_MULTICOLUMN LBS_MULTIPLESEL LBS_NOINTEGRALHEIGHT LBS_NOREDRAW LBS_NOTIFY LBS_OWNERDRAWFIXED LBS_OWNERDRAWVARIABLE LBS_SORT LBS_STANDARD LBS_USETABSTOPS LBS_WANTKEYBOARDINPUT if(WINVER >= 0x030a) LBS_DISABLENOSCROLL

Table 3.2 Possible Control Classes. (Continued)

Class	Description
COMBOBOX	This designates a control consisting of a selection field similar to an EDIT control plus a list box. The list box may be displayed at all times or may be dropped down when the user selects a "pop-box" next to the selection field.
SCROLLBAR	The SCROLLBAR control displays a stretched rectangular box containing a page position reference, sometimes called a *thumb*, along with direction arrows at both ends. The user selects a position within the list by sliding the thumb up or down the bar. SCROLLBAR controls are identical in appearance to scroll bars used in ordinary windows; however, they may appear anywhere within a window.
	Automatically associated with the SCROLLBAR control is a SIZEBOX control. This small rectangle allows the user to change the size of the window.
	SCROLLBAR Control Styles:
	SBS_BOTTOMALIGN
	SBS_HORZ
	SBS_LEFTALIGN
	SBS_RIGHTALIGN
	SBS_SIZEBOX
	SBS_SIZEBOXBOTTOMRIGHTALIGN
	SBS_SIZEBOXTOPLEFTALIGN
	SBS_TOPALIGN
	SBS_VERT
STATIC	The STATIC control class—the class used most frequently to identify, box, or separate other controls—defines a simple text field, box, or rectangle. The STATIC control, therefore, outputs or inputs information.

Table 3.2 Possible Control Classes. (Continued)

Class	Description
	STATIC Control Styles: SS_BLACKFRAME SS_BLACKRECT SS_CENTER SS_GRAYFRAME SS_GRAYRECT SS_ICON SS_LEFT SS_LEFTNOWORDWRAP SS_NOPREFIX SS_RIGHT SS_SIMPLE SS_USERITEM SS_WHITEFRAME SS_WHITERECT

Table 3.3 shows possible Windows styles.

Table 3.3 Possible Window Styles.

Style	Description
WS_BORDER	Creates a bordered window.
WS_CAPTION	Adds a title bar to the bordered window.
WS_CHILD	Creates a child window. Not to be used with WS_POPUP style windows.
WS_CHILDWINDOW	Creates a child window of the WS_CHILD style.
WS_CLIPCHILDREN	Used when creating the parent window. The WS_CLIPCHILDREN window style prohibits drawing of the parent window within the area occupied by any child window.

Table 3.3 Possible Window Styles. (Continued)

Style	Description
WS_CLIPSIBLINGS	Used with the WS_CHILD style only. This style clips all other child windows whenever a particular child window receives a paint message. Without this, it would be possible to draw within the client area of another child window.
WS_DISABLED	Creates an initially disabled window.
WS_DLGFRAME	Creates a double-bordered window without a title.
WS_EX_ACCEPTFILES	Specifies that a window created with this style accepts drag-drop files.
WS_EX_CLIENTEDGE	Specifies that a window has a 3D look—that sunken edge.
WS_EX_CONTEXTHELP	Incorporates a question mark in the title bar of the window. When the user clicks the question mark, the cursor changes to a question mark with a pointer. If the user then clicks a child window, the child receives a WM_HELP message.
WS_EX_CONTROLPARENT	Allows the user to navigate among the child windows of the window by using the TAB key.
WS_EX_DLGMODALFRAME	Creates a window with a double border that can contain an optional title bar. This style can be used only in the *dwExStyle*.
WS_EX_LEFT	Gives the window a generic left-aligned property (default mode).
WS_EX_LEFTSCROLLBAR	Adds a vertical scroll bar to the left of the client area.
WS_EX_LTRREADING	Outputs window text using left-to-right reading order (default mode).
WS_EX_MDICHILD	Creates an MDI child window.
WS_EX_NOPARENTNOTIFY	Specifies that a child window created in this style will not send the WM_PARENTNOTIFY message to its parent window when the child window is created or destroyed.

Table 3.3 Possible Window Styles. (Continued)

Style	Description
WS_EX_OVERLAPPEDWINDOW	Combines WS_EX_CLIENTEDGE and WS_EX_WINDOWEDGE
WS_EX_PALETTEWINDOW	Combines WS_EX_WINDOWEDGE and WS_EX_TOPMOST.
WS_EX_RIGHT	Gives the window right-aligned properties (depends on window class).
WS_EX_RIGHTSCROLLBAR	Inserts a vertical scroll bar on right edge of client area (default).
WS_EX_RTLREADING	Displays the window's text using right-to-left reading order.
WS_EX_STATICEDGE	Specifies a window with a 3D border style for items not accepting user input.
WS_EX_TOOLWINDOW	Creates a tool window intended to be used as a floating toolbar. The title bar is shorter and in a smaller font than a normal title bar. Tool windows do not appear in the task bar or in the window that appears when the user presses Alt+Tab.
WS_EX_TOPMOST	Specified that a window created with this style should be placed above all nontopmost windows and stay above them, even when the window is deactivated.
WS_EX_TRANSPARENT	Specifies that a window created of this style is to be transparent. Any windows that are beneath the window are not obscured by the window.
WS_EX_WINDOWEDGE	Defines a window that has a border with a raised edge.
WS_GROUP	Used only by dialog boxes. This window style defines the first control of a group of controls. The user can move from one control to another by using the direction keys.
WS_HSCROLL	Creates a window with a horizontal scroll bar.
WS_MAXIMIZE	Creates a window of maximum size.
WS_MAXIMIZEBOX	Creates a window that includes a maximize box.
WS_MINIMIZE	Creates a window of minimum size.

Chapter 3 • Windows Details

Table 3.3	Possible Window Styles. (Continued)
Style	**Description**
WS_MINIMIZEBOX	Creates a window that includes a minimize box.
WS_OVERLAPPED	Creates an overlapped window.
WS_OVERLAPPEDWINDOW	Uses the WS_CAPTION, WS_OVERLAPPED, WS_THICKFRAME, and WS_SYSMENU styles to create an overlapped window.
WS_POPUP	Creates a pop-up window. Not to be used with the WS_CHILD style.
WS_POPUPWINDOW	Uses the WS_BORDER, WS_POPUP, and WS_SYSMENU styles to create a pop-up window.
WS_SYSMENU	Creates a window with a system-menu box displayed in its title bar. When used with a child window, this style creates a close box instead of the standard system-menu box. WS_SYSMENU is used only with windows that include title bars.
WS_TABSTOP	Used only by dialog boxes. Indicates any number of controls the user can move by using TAB. Successive presses of TAB move through the controls specified by the WS_TABSTOP style.
WS_THICKFRAME	Creates a thick-framed window that can be used to size the window.
WS_VISIBLE	Creates a window that is automatically displayed. Can be used with overlapped and pop-up windows.
WS_VSCROLL	Creates a window with a vertical scroll bar.

Table 3.4 shows the various BUTTON class control styles that can be used with dwStyle.

Table 3.4	BUTTON Class Control Styles.
Style	**Description**
BS_AUTOCHECKBOX	Identical in usage to BS_CHECKBOX, except that the button automatically toggles its state when the user selects it by pressing the mouse button.

Table 3.4 BUTTON Class Control Styles. (Continued)

Style	Description
BS_AUTORADIOBUTTON	Identical in usage to BS_RADIOBUTTON, except that when the button is selected, a BN_CLICKED message is sent to the application, removing check marks from any other radio buttons in the group.
BS_AUTO3STATE	Identical to BX_3STATE, except that the button automatically toggles its state when the user selects it by pressing the mouse button.
BS_CHECKBOX	Defines a small rectangular button that can be checked. The check box is shown in bold when it is selected. Any associated text is printed to the right of the button.
BS_DEFPUSHBUTTON	Defines a small elliptical bold-bordered button. Usually used to identify a user's default response. Any associated text is displayed within the button.
BS_GROUPBOX	Defines a rectangular region bounding a button group. Text is displayed within the rectangle's upper-left corner.
BS_LEFTTEXT	Forces text to be displayed on the left side of the radio button or checkbox button. Can be used with the control styles, BX_3STATE.
BS_OWNERDRAW	Designates an "owner-draw" button. The parent window is notified whenever a button is clicked. This notification includes a request to paint, invert, and then disable the button.
BS_PUSHBUTTON	Defines a small elliptical button containing the specified text. This control sends a message to the parent window whenever the user clicks the button.
BS_RADIOBUTTON	Defines a small circular button with a border that is shown in bold when it has been selected with a click. The parent window is also notified via a message. A subsequent click produces a normal border, and another message is sent to the parent window to indicate the change.

Table 3.4	BUTTON Class Control Styles. (Continued)
Style	**Description**
BS_3STATE	Identical to BS_CHECKBOX, but the button can be grayed as well as checked. The grayed state is a visual reminder that the current check box has been disabled.

Table 3.5 shows the various EDIT Class Control styles that can be combined with *dwStyle*.

Table 3.5	EDIT Class Control Style.
Style	**Description**
ES_AUTOHSCROLL	Automatically scrolls text to the right 10 characters whenever the user enters data at the end of a line. When the user presses ENTER<, the text scrolls back to the left-edge border.
ES_AUTOVSCROLL	Automatically scrolls text up one page when the user presses ENTER at the last line.
ES_CENTER	Centers text.
ES_LEFT	Uses flush-left text alignment.
ES_LOWERCASE	Converts all characters to lowercase as they are typed.
ES_MULTILINE	Provides a multiple-line editing control. When used in conjunction with the ES_AUTOVSCROLL style, scrolls text vertically when the user presses ENTER. If ES_AUTOVSROLL style is not specified, the system beeps when the user presses ENTER; no more lines can be displayed. A similar condition exists when used with the ES_AUTOHSCROLL style. If selected, the style will allow the user to remain on the same line, shifting text to the left. When deactivated, text not fitting on the same line within the window causes a new line to be created. ES_MULTILINE styles can include scroll bars.

Table 3.5 EDIT Class Control Style. (Continued)

Style	Description
ES_NOHIDESEL	Overrides the default action, preventing the EDIT control from hiding the selection whenever the control loses the input focus. ES_NOHIDESEL does not invert the selection when the control receives the input focus.
ES_OEMCONVERT	Converts text entered in the EDIT control from the Windows character set to the OEM character set and back again.
ES_PASSWORD	Displays each character as an asterisk (*) as the character is typed.
ES_READONLY	Prevents the user from typing or editing text.
ES_UPPERCASE	Converts all characters to uppercase as they are typed.
ES_RIGHT	Uses a flush-right text alignment.
ES_WANTRETURN	Inserts a carriage return when the user presses the ENTER key.

Table 3.6 shows LISTBOX Class Control styles that can be combined with *dwStyle*.

Table 3.6 LISTBOX Class Control Styles.

Style	Description
LBS_DISABLENOSCROLL	Disables vertical scroll bar display for a list box when the box does not contain enough items to scroll.
LBS_EXTENDEDSEL	Allows multiple items to be selected by using the SHIFT key and the mouse or by using special keys.
LBS_HASSTRINGS	Maintains the memory and pointers for strings that appear in "owner-draw" list boxes. LBS_HASSTRINGS allows the application to use the LB_GETTEXT message to retrieve the text for a particular string.

Table 3.6   LISTBOX Class Control Styles. (Continued)

Style	Description
LBS_MULTICOLUMN	Specifies a multicolumn list box that is scrolled horizontally.
LBS_MULTIPLESEL	Allows selection of any number of strings, with the string selection toggling each time the user clicks or double-clicks the string.
LBS_NOINTEGRALHEIGHT	Defines the size of the list box as being exactly the size specified by the application when the list box was created.
LBS_NOREDRAW	Ensures that the LISTBOX display is not updated when changes are made.
LBS_NOTIFY	Ensures that, whenever the user clicks or double-clicks a string, the parent window receives an input message.
LBS_OWNERDRAWFIXED	Indicates that the owner of the list box is responsible for drawing its contents; the items in the list box are the same height.
LBS_OWNERDRAWVARIABLE	Indicates that the owner of the list box is responsible for drawing its contents; however, unlike LBS_OWNERDRAWFIXED, the strings are of variable height.
LBS_SORT	Sorts the strings in the LISTBOX alphabetically.
LBS_STANDARD	Sorts the strings within the LISTBOX alphabetically, sending a message to the parent window whenever the user clicks or double-clicks a string. The LISTBOX contains a vertical scroll bar and borders on all sides.
LBS_USETABSTOPS	Permits a list box to recognize and expand all tab characters when drawing strings. The default tab positions are 32 dialog units. Using the **GetDialogBaseUnits()** function, an application can obtain the current dialog base units in pixels. One horizontal dialog unit is equal to one-fourth of the current dialog base width unit. Dialog base units are calculated on the height and width of the current system font.

Accessing the Windows Environment 107

Table 3.6 LISTBOX Class Control Styles. (Continued)

Style	Description
LBS_WANTKEYBOARDINPUT	Ensures that, whenever the user presses a key and the list box has the input focus, the owner of the list box receives WM_VKEYTOITEM or WM_CHARTOITEM messages.

Table 3.7 shows the various COMBOBOX class control styles that can be combined with *dwStyle*.

Table 3.7 COMBOBOX Class Control Styles.

Style	Description
CBS_AUTOHSCROLL	Automatically scrolls the text in the EDIT control to the right whenever the user types a character at the end of the line.
CBS_DISABLENOSCROLL	Disables vertical scroll bar display for a list box when the box does not contain enough items to scroll.
CBS_DROPDOWN	Causes the list box not to be displayed unless the user selects an icon next to the selection field.
CBS_DROPDOWNLIST	Replaces the EDIT control with a static text item that displays the current selection in the list box.
CBS_HASSTRINGS	Allows GETTEXT to return the text for a particular item.
CBS_NOINTEGRALHEIGHT	Identifies the text as having no integral height.
CBS_OEMCONVERT	Identifies an OEM convert.
CBS_OWNERDRAWFIXED	Indicates that the owner of the list box is responsible for drawing its contents; the items in the list box are the same height.
CBS_OWNERDRAWVARIABLE	Indicates that the owner of the list box is responsible for drawing its contents; however, unlike LBS_OWNERDRAWFIXED, the strings are of variable height.

Table 3.7 COMBOBOX Class Control Styles. (Continued)

Style	Description
CBS_SIMPLE	Displays the list box at all times. The current selection in the list box is displayed in the EDIT control.
CBS_SORT	Automatically sorts strings that are entered into the list box. This style does not apply to "owner-draw" combo boxes.

Table 3.8 shows the various SCROLLBAR class control styles that can be combined with *dwStyle*.

Table 3.8 SCROLLBAR Class Control Styles.

Style	Description
SBS_BOTTOMALIGN	Used in conjunction with SBS_HORZ style. Using the system-default scroll bar height, SBS_BOTTOMALIGN aligns the scroll bar with the bottom edge of the rectangle defined by *x, y, nWidth,* and *nHeight*.
SBS_HORZ	Defines a horizontal scroll bar. The height, width, and position of the scroll bar are determined by the **CreateWindow()** function if neither SBS_BOTTOMALIGN nor SBS_TOPALIGN style is requested.
SBS_LEFTALIGN	Used in conjunction with SBS_VERT style. Using the system-default scroll bar height, SBS_LEFTALIGN aligns the left edge of the scroll bar with the left edge of a rectangle defined by *x, y, nWidth,* and *nHeight*.
SBS_RIGHTALIGN	Used in conjunction with SBS_VERT style. Using the system-default scroll bar height, SBS_RIGHTALIGN aligns the lower-right corner of the scroll bar with the right edge of the rectangle defined by *x, y, nWidth,* and *nHeight*.

Accessing the Windows Environment

Table 3.8 SCROLLBAR Class Control Styles. (Continued)

Style	Description
SBS_SIZEBOX	Defines a size box. The height, width, and position of the size box are determined by the **CreateWindow()** function if neither the SBS_SIZEBOXBOTTOMRIGHTALIGN nor the SBS_SIZEBOXTOPLEFTALIGN style is selected.
SBS_SIZEBOXBOTTOMRIGHT-ALIGN	Used in conjunction with the SBS_SIZEBOX style. Using the system-default scroll bar height, SBS_SIZEBOXBOTTOMRIGHTALIGN aligns the scroll bar with the lower-right corner of the rectangle defined by *x, y, nWidth*, and *nHeight*.
SBS_SIZEBOXTOPLEFTALIGN	Used in conjunction with the SBS_SIZEBOX style. Using the system-default scroll bar height, SBS_SIZEBOXTOPLEFTALIGN aligns the upper-left corner of the scroll bar with the upper-left corner of the rectangle defined by *x, y, nWidth*, and *nHeight*.
SBS_TOPALIGN	Using the system-default scroll bar height, SBS_TOPALIGN aligns the scroll bar along the top edge of the rectangle defined by *x, y, nWidth*, and *nHeight*.
SBS_VERT	Defines a vertical scroll bar. The height, width, and position of the scroll bar are determined by the **CreateWindow()** function if neither the SBS_RIGHTALIGN nor the SBS_LEFTALIGN style is requested.

Table 3.9 shows the various STATIC class control styles that can be combined with *dwStyle*.

Table 3.9 STATIC Class Control Styles.

Style	Description
SS_BLACKFRAME	Defines a box with a black frame.
SS_BLACKRECT	Defines a black-filled rectangle.

Table 3.9 STATIC Class Control Styles. (Continued)

Style	Description
SS_CENTER	Takes the given text and centers it within a simple rectangle. All text is formatted. Any text not fitting on one line is automatically wrapped to the next line and centered.
SS_GRAYFRAME	Defines a gray-framed box.
SS_GRAYRECT	Defines a gray-filled rectangle.
SS_ICON	Automatically sizes and displays an icon within the dialog box.
SS_LEFT	Works similarly to SS_CENTER, except that the text displayed within the rectangle is aligned flush left. This includes automatic word wrap and flush-left alignment of the next line.
SS_LEFTNOWORDWRAP	Turns word wrapping off.
SS_NOPREFIX	Overrides usual interpretation of the ampersand (&). Normally, Windows interprets an ampersand in the control's text as an accelerator prefix character; this causes the next character to be underlined. If a static control is to contain no underlined text, SS_NOPREFIX (when used with with the bit-wise logical operator OR) can be used with other styles.
SS_RIGHT	Works similarly to SS_CENTER, except that the text displayed within the rectangle is aligned flush right. This includes automatic word wrap and flush-right alignment of the next line.
SS_SIMPLE	Defines a rectangle that will display a single line of flush-left text.
SS_USERITEM	Defines a user-defined item.
SS_WHITEFRAME	Defines a white-framed box.
SS_WHITERECT	Defines a white-filled rectangle.

Table 3.10 shows the various extended styles that can be applied to *dwExStyle*.

Table 3.10 Extended Styles.

Style	Meaning
WS_EX_ACCEPTFILES	A window created with this style will accept drag-drop files.
WS_EX_CLIENTEDGE	A window created with 3D look (sunken edge).
WS_EX_CONTEXTHELP	A window that includes a question mark. Clicking on the question mark causes the image to change to a pointer message.
WS_EX_DLGMODALFRAME	A window with a double border. It may also be created with a title bar if the WS_CAPTION style flag is used in the dwStyle parameter.
WS_EX_CONTROLPARENT	A window that allows the user to navigate among the child windows using the Tab key.
WS_EX_DLGMODALFRAME	A window with a double border (optionally a title bar using WS_CAPTION dwStyle.
WS_EX_LEFT	Assigns a generic left-edge-align property (default mode).
WS_EX_LEFTSCROLLBAR	Inserts a left-aligned vertical scroll bar in client area.
WS_EX_LTRREADING	Assigns left-or-right reading order (default mode).
WS_EX_MIDICHILD	Defines a MDI child window.
WS_EX_NOPARENTNOTIFY	A child window is created and no WM_PARENTNOTIFY message is sent to its parent window when the child window is created or destroyed.
WS_EX_OVERLAPPEDWINDOW	Combines WS_EX_CLIENTEDGE and WS_EX_WINDOWEDGE styles.
WS_EX_PALETTEWINDOW	Combines WS_EX_WINDOWEDGE and WS_EX_TOPMOST styles.
WS_EX_RIGHT	Assigns a right-aligned property, depending on window class.
WS_EX_RIGHTSCROLLBAR	Inserts a vertical scroll bar on right edge of client window.
WS_EX_RTLREADING	Outputs text using right-to-left reading order.
WS_EX_STATICEDGE	Defines a window with a 3D border style used for nonuser input items.

Table 3.10 Extended Styles. (Continued)

Style	Meaning
WS_EX_TOOLWINDOW	Creates a tool window intended to be used as a floating toolbar. The title bar is shorter and in a smaller font than a normal title bar. Tool windows do not appear in the task bar or in the window that appears when the user presses Alt+Tab.
WS_EX_TOPMOST	A window is created with this style and placed above all nontopmost windows. It will stay above them even when deactivated. **SetWindowPos()** can add or remove this attribute.
WS_EX_TRANSPARENT	A window created with this style is transparent. Any windows that are beneath the window are not obscured by the window. WM_PAINT messages are received after all sibling windows have been updated.
ws_EX_WINDOWEDGE	Defines a window with a raised edge border.

It is easy to understand why all windows are created with the use of one of these functions! The functions give the programmer the flexibility through their style and extended style options to create just about any type of window.

Displaying the Window with ShowWindow()

Windows is instructed to show a window with a call to the **ShowWindow()** function. However, each application must make a call to the **ShowWindow()** function using the *nCmdShow* parameter from the **WinMain()** function.

```
ShowWindow(hWnd,nCmdShow)
```

Subsequent calls to **ShowWindow()** must come from the window states defined in Table 3.11.

Table 3.11 Window States.

State	Description
SW_FORCEMINIMIZE	(Windows NT 5.0 or later) Minimizes a window, even if the threat that owns the window is hung.
SW_HIDE	Hides the window and passes activation to another window.
SW_MAXIMIZE	Maximizes the specified window.

Table 3.11	Window States. (Continued)
State	**Description**
SW_MINIMIZE	Minimizes the window and activates the top-level window in the window manager's list.
SW_RESTORE	Does the same work as SW_SHOWNORMAL.
SW_SHOW	Activates the window and displays it in its current position and at its current size.
SW_SHOWDEFAULT	Activates the window and displays it using default settings.
SW_SHOWMAXIMIZED	Activates the window and displays it fully maximized.
SW_SHOWMINIMIZED	Activates the window and displays it as an icon.
SW_SHOWMINNOACTIVATE	Displays the window as an icon; the window that is currently active remains active.
SW_SHOWNA	Displays the window in its current state; whichever window is currently active remains active.
SW_SHOWNOACTIVATE	Displays the window in its most recent position and at its most recent size; whichever window is currently active remains active.
SW_SHOWNORMAL	Activates and displays the window. If the window had been an icon or was zoomed, Windows will restore the window to its original position and size.
SW_SHOWSMOOTH	Activates the window with a smoothed appearance.

note

The primary difference between SW_MINNOACTIVATE and SW_SHOWMINIMIZED is that the former does not make the window the active window, but the latter does.

Changing the Window with SetClassWord() or SetClassLong()

You can make a call to **SetClassWord()** under Windows 3.x or to **SetClassLong()** under Windows 95/98 and NT. As an example, the syntax for the **SetClassLong()** function looks like this:

```
SetClassLong(hWnd,nIndex,wNewWord)
```

hWnd identifies the handle to the window. *nIndex* designates which long value in the WNDCLASSA data structure is to be changed; the *wNewWord* parameter specifies the replacement value (LONG). **SetClassWord()** simply uses wordsized values.

The following code sequence shows how a call to **SetClassLong()** can be made to change the background color of a window by using the LTGRAY_BRUSH value:

```
switch (messg)
  case WM_CREATE:
    GetClassLong(hWnd,GCL_HBRBACKGROUND);
    DeleteObject(hWnd);
    SetClassLong(hWnd,GCL_HBRBACKGROUND,LTGRAY_BRUSH);
    InvalidateRect(hWnd,NULL,TRUE);
    UpdateWindow(hWnd);
    break;
```

Commonly Used Controls and Dialog Boxes

Most Windows applications use controls and dialog boxes. These predefined child windows have features and capabilities that other window styles do not. Their purpose is to provide an easy method by which the user can interact with the application.

Windows provides several ready-made control classes. Controls have their characteristics and functions defined by their window class, just as any other window would. The window function determines how the window will appear to the user. It also determines what actions are to be taken based on the user's responses. Even better is the fact that control window functions are predefined by Windows, thereby sidestepping any need to create additional code.

WHAT IS A STATIC CONTROL?

Generally, a *static control* is used in conjunction with other controls. A static control typically produces a small window containing text or graphics elements, such as icons, and can be used to separate a group of controls. Static controls do not accept user input.

WHAT IS A PUSH-BUTTON CONTROL?

A *push-button control* style defines a small rectangle with rounded corners and containing text. Examples of push buttons are the OK and CANCEL choices provided by many Windows applications. Clicking the push button causes the application to take some form of immediate action.

WHAT IS A RADIO-BUTTON CONTROL?

You use a *radio-button control* to create an open circle with text to its right. The user can select this circle to turn the associated control on or off. When the control is on, the circle will be filled in. Radiobuttons work like the buttons on your car radio. You can select only one at a time. (Ever tried to play two stations at once?) Radio buttons list mutually exclusive application options.

Most applications group radio buttons into logical groups, with the user able to select only one of the choices. When the user selects a second radio-button control, the previously selected item is deselected.

For example, you could use radio-button controls to give the user a list of disk drives to select from. Naturally, you can read from only one drive at a time. Selecting both Drive C and Drive A has no meaning. If used properly, radio buttons can prevent the user from making a mistake.

WHAT IS A CHECK-BOX CONTROL?

You can visually distinguish a *check-box control* from a radio button by the small square with text to the right. Unlike radio buttons, this control can be used in multiples that are not mutually exclusive. In other words, the check-box control permits concurrent selections.

For example, a desktop publishing application could present the user with several text-format options—bold, underlining, italic, subscripts, and so on—that could be combined in numerous ways. The user could specify bold italic, for instance, or an underlined subscript.

WHAT IS A LIST BOX?

A *list box control* responds to both keyboard and mouse input. They list character strings—for example, file names. The user can select one or several items. Control styles include list boxes that have their contents automatically sorted (LBS_SORT), which automatically notify the parent window of a selection (LBS_NOTIFY), and that can include scroll bar styles (WS_VSCROLL). When an LBS_STANDARD style is chosen, all three of these styles are selected.

Users select list box items by pressing the spacebar or by double-clicking with the mouse. Either response will cause Windows to highlight the text in the selected character string. Messages returned include LBN_SELCHANGE and LBN_DBLCLK (if the mouse button was pressed).

Retrieving the index of the selected character string is as easy as making a call to **SendDlgItemMessage()**, using LB_GETCURSEL (the selected item's index) and LB_GETTEXT (which contains a copy of the selected text).

WHAT IS AN EDIT BOX?

A Windows *edit box control* functions like a mini word processor. It is a window in which the user can enter and edit text. The application can define an EDIT control with multiple-line editing and scrolling by selecting the appropriate control style (ES_MULTILINE, ES_AUTOHSCROLL, or ES_AUTOVSCROLL). The last two options shift the window horizontally or vertically whenever the user enters text extending beyond the box's borders.

WHAT IS A SCROLL BAR CONTROL?

Scroll bars are a very common feature of Windows applications. *Scroll bar controls* permit the user to move through lists, text, columns of information, or graphics displays that do not fit on a single screen.

The vertical and horizontal scroll bars allow the user to see the part of the surface that, because of the size constraints of the active window or screen, are temporarily out of view. With the two scroll bars, the user can shift the displayed image up and down, left or right.

Actually, there are two types of scroll bars used by Windows: window scroll bars and scroll bar controls. As you've already seen, the **CreateWindow()** function wears many hats. As it turns out, the function is also responsible for adding horizontal window scroll bars (WS_HSCROLL) or vertical window scroll bars (WS_VSCROLL).

Vertical scroll bars are always displayed along the right side of the window and extend the full height of the client area. Horizontal scroll bars are always positioned at the bottom of the window and extend the full width of the client area. The following highlights show how to add scroll bars to a window. (Notice the syntax and placement for using WS_VSCROLL and WS_HSCROLL. Also, Chapter 5 continues the discussion of scroll bars.)

```
CreateWindow(lpszClassName,      // Registered Class Name
        "Adding Scroll Bars",// Window text
        WS_VSCROLL |
        WS_HSCROLL,          // Adding the scroll bars
        CW_USEDEFAULT,       // Use x default position
        0,                   // Use y default position
        CW_USEDEFAULT,       // cx - default width
        0,                   // cy - default height
        NULL,                // Window has no parent
        NULL,                // Use the class menu
        hInstance,           // Who created window
        NULL                 // No window creation data
        );
```

In contrast, scroll bar controls are, technically, child windows. They can be any size and dimension, and can be placed anywhere within the client area of the window. They are created by making a call to (you guessed it) **CreateWindow()**. This call requests the creation of a child window that contains a scroll bar.

What Is a Virtual Key?

Windows applications often need to deal with multiple-language keyboard input. This means that the key marked "J" may be used to enter a kanji glyph. To help developers with this situation, Windows has defined a set of virtual key codes.

This set of virtual keys defines the set of all possible keystrokes that can occur in the Windows environment. This set of keystrokes is defined in winuser.h and constitutes the only keystrokes a Windows application can receive.

The virtual key code identifies the key that was either pressed or released. Because the developers of Windows defined virtual keys for many different hardware configurations, some virtual key codes cannot be generated on an IBM system. Table 3.12 lists the more common identifiers, along with the numeric key codes and the keyboard key that corresponds to the virtual key (see Chapter 11 for more on virtual keys).

Table 3.12 Virtual Key Codes.

Required Windows Virtual Key	WINUSER.H Identifier	PC Key	Hex value
	VK_LBUTTON		01
	VK_RBUTTON		02
Yes	VK_CANCEL	Ctrl-Break	03
	VK_MBUTTON		04
Yes	VK_BACK	Backspace	08
Yes	VK_TAB	Tab	09
	VK_CLEAR	Keypad #5	0C
Yes	VK_RETURN	Enter	0D
Yes	VK_SHIFT	Shift	10
Yes	VK_CONTROL	Ctrl	11

Chapter 3 • Windows Details

Table 3.12 Virtual Key Codes.(Continued)

Yes	VK_MENU	Alt	12
	VK_PAUSE		13
Yes	VK_CAPITAL	Caps Lock	14
Yes	VK_ESCAPE	Esc	1B
Yes	VK_SPACE	Spacebar	20
Yes	VK_PRIOR	PgUp	21
Yes	VK_NEXT	PgDn	22
	VK_END	End	23
Yes	VK_HOME	Home	24
Yes	VK_LEFT	Left arrow	25
Yes	VK_UP	Up arrow	26
Yes	VK_RIGHT	Right arrow	27
Yes	VK_DOWN	Down arrow	28
	VK_SELECT		29
	VK_PRINT		2A
	VK_EXECUTE		2B
	VK_SNAPSHOT		2C
Yes	VK_INSERT	Ins	2D
Yes	VK_DELETE	Del	2E
	VK_HELP		2F
		Keyboard	
	VK_[0-9]	0–9	30-39
	VK_[A-Z]	A–Z	41-5A
	VK_NUMPAD0	Keypad 0	60
	VK-NUMPAD1	Keypad 1	61
	VK_NUMPAD2	Keypad 2	62
	VK_NUMPAD3	Keypad 3	63
	VK_NUMPAD4	Keypad 4	64
	VK_NUMPAD5	Keypad 5	65
	VK_NUMPAD6	Keypad 6	66
	VK_NUMPAD7	Keypad 7	67

Table 3.12 Virtual Key Codes.(Continued)

	VK_NUMPAD8	Keypad 8	68
	VK_NUMPAD9	Keypad 9	69
	VK_MULTIPLY	Keypad *	6A
	VK_ADD	Keypad +	6B
	VK_SEPARATOR		6C
	VK_SUBTRACT	Keypad -	6D
	VK_DECIMAL	Keypad.	6E
	VK_DIVIDE	Keypad /	6F
Yes	VK_F1	F1	70
Yes	VK_F2	F2	71
Yes	VK_F3	F3	72
Yes	VK_F4	F4	73
Yes	VK_F5	F5	74
Yes	VK_F6	F6	75
Yes	VK_F7	F7	76
Yes	VK_F8	F8	77
Yes	VK_F9	F9	78
Yes	VK_F10	F10	79
	VK_F11	F11	7A
	VK_F12	F12	7B
	VK_F13		7C
	VK_F14		7D
	VK_F15		7E
	VK_F16		7F
	VK_F17		80
	VF_F18		81
	VF_F19		82
	VF_F20		83
	VF_F21		84
	VF_F22		85
	VF_F23		86

Table 3.12	Virtual Key Codes.(Continued)		
	VK_F24		87
	VK_NUMLOCK	Num Lock	90
	VK_SCROLL	Scroll Lock	91
	VK_LSHIFT		
	VK_RSHIFT		
	VK_ALT		
	VK_LCONTROL		
	VK_RCONTROL		
	VK_LMENU		
	VK_RMENU		
	VK_ATTN		
	VK_CRSEL		
	VK_EXCEL		
	VK_EREOF		
	VK_PLAY		
	VK_ZOOM		
	VK_NONAME		
	VK_PA1		
	VK_OEM_CLEAR		
	VK_ACCEPT		
	VK_BACK_QUOTE		
	VK_BACK_SLASH		
	VK_BACK_SPACE		
	VK_CAPS_LOCK		
	VK_CLOSE_BRACKER		
	VK_CONVERT		
	VK_MODECHANGE		

What Is a System Timer?

Windows provides every application with access to a system timer. The system timer is an input device that instructs Windows how often to give the application a "buzz." This causes Windows to send the application recurrent WM_TIMER messages at the specified interval.

Windows 3.x is a nonpreemptive multitasking environment. The main purpose of a timer is to provide a method whereby a large, time-consuming process can be subdivided into smaller, interruptible tasks. In Windows 3.x, each subtask is activated whenever it receives a WM_TIMER message. This prevents any one application from monopolizing the CPU.

Windows 95/98 and NT are fully preemptive multitasking environments. Timers are still needed so that, with the correct priority, Windows can take control of the processor as needed. Additionally, Windows timers can be used to activate a preset alarm used in a scheduling program, to generate an auto save for a word processor at predefined intervals, to control the speed of a graphics display, to control the update for a clock display, and to do many other meaningful tasks (additional examples in Chapter 14).

WHAT MAKES THE TIMER TICK?

The *uElapseMs* parameter to the **SetTimer()** function defines the elapsed time (in milliseconds) between timer events. The interval can range from 1 to 65,535 milliseconds, or up to 65.5 seconds. For example, if *uElapseMs* were 4,000 milliseconds, Windows would send the application program a WM_TIMER message about every 4 seconds. The *pfnTimerFunc* parameter to **SetTimer()** points to the procedure-instance address of the callback function.

The Windows WM_TIMER message is accomplished through a virtualized MS-DOS call implemented in Win32. The message instructs it to decrement each of the system timer counters set by Windows. Whenever the count reaches 0, a WM_TIMER message is sent to the application's message queue. After this, the counter is set back to its original starting value.

Because all Windows applications receive the WM_TIMER messages from the normal message queue, the application won't suddenly be interrupted in the middle of an important process. When writing an application that uses system timers, however, the developer must be careful to enable the application to continue proper execution if there are no timers available. There are approximately 16 timers available at any one time. Therefore, applications should stop any timer messages no longer needed by making a call to the **KillTimer()** function.

EFFECTIVE USE OF TIMERS

Most Windows applications use timers in one of two ways. The first and the easiest approach to use includes error checking. This method involves a call to the **SetTimer()** function from the **WinMain()** function or during the processing of a WM_CREATE message.

This approach gives the application the earliest means of dealing with an unavailable timer. It is ended by terminating the timer with a call to **KillTimer()** in response to a WM_DESTROY message. With this method, all WM_TIMER messages are sent directly to the normal window function.

The second approach to using the timer causes Windows to send the WM_TIMER message to a function within the application program (a callback function) instead of to the **WinMain()** function.

MEMORY

Allocating and accessing memory from within a Windows application has changed dramatically over the evolution of Windows. For example, under Windows NT, an application can access up to 2 gigabytes of virtual address space. This virtually unlimited domain, however, has the typical size-versus-speed trade-off associated with all virtual storage. For this reason, it is still imperative that all Windows applications manage this resource.

Windows 95/98 uses a page-based memory management scheme. With paging, Windows 95/98 and the CPU fool applications into believing there is more system memory than is actually available. When memory requirements exceed actual memory, Windows 95/98 will swap information to the hard drive.

The most significant factor influencing the speed of your Windows applications is the amount of available memory. When you want to execute multiple programs, Windows will attempt to place as many of these programs into system memory as possible. However, it seems that no matter how much memory you purchase, you never have enough just when you want it!

If you attempt to load several large programs under Windows, the majority of your system memory may be allocated. At this point, any additional programs you invoke will cause Windows to make space for the program in memory by temporarily taking a current application out of memory and placing it on the fixed disk. One can quickly see that, as the number of programs executing becomes very large, the amount of memory and disk swapping that Windows must perform increases proportionately.

Regardless of the access time on your fixed disk, it is still a snail's pace compared with the speed of the electronic circuits making up the RAM memory. Because of this access-time limitation, disk input and output operations are one of the major causes of computer processing delays. Performance is also degraded by the additional overhead required by all disk I/O operations generated by the frequent swapping.

All Windows applications work on information when it is in RAM memory. This means that everything must eventually get into memory. For example, before Windows can draw a menu or an icon, the description of the menu and the contents of the icon must be loaded into memory. The picture becomes even more complex, as Windows also requires the display context, code segments, data segments, the window itself, and on and on, to reside in memory before they can be executed.

Considering the tremendous amount of memory required by the Windows graphics-oriented environment, as well as the fact that Windows accomplishes its multitasking in a finite amount of memory, you begin to appreciate why memory management is such an important issue in Windows programming.

MEMORY ALLOCATION VIA THE OPERATING SYSTEM

To give you an idea of just how quickly a typical Windows application can use up memory look at the following example. As soon as the user selects a program by double-clicking the application's name in the Program Manager, the first instance of the application begins to execute. For a minimal application, this would require Windows to load at least one code segment and data segment, for a total of two objects loaded into memory. On top of this, each Windows application must register a window class and create a window of that class. Most Windows applications use at least one menu and an icon. Total objects in memory: six.

Now consider what Windows must do to manage this finite memory resource. Suppose the user chooses to start a second instance of the application. The second instance shares the same code segment as its predecessor, along with the application's icon. However, the second instance has its own data segment. Though the second instance has a window of the same class as the first instance, it is still a new window object. Because of the modifications (selection, activation, and deactivation of options) each instance can make, the menu of the first instance cannot be shared with the second instance. This brings the memory-object total to nine. Finally, most Windows applications create their own font, pen, and brush. Total objects: twelve.

A poorly written Windows application (one not sharing objects) would cause the second instance to create its own font, pen, and brush, bringing the memory object tally to 15, and the application hasn't even done anything yet!

As you can see, memory gets consumed at a startling rate in the Windows environment, as graphics objects are an integral part of an application's basic functioning, and multiple instances can be invoked at any moment. You can, however, minimize the amount of space an application requires by using special memory management techniques.

MANAGING YOUR MEMORY

Under Windows there is no way of knowing ahead of time just how much memory an application will need at any particular moment. For this reason, it is up to each application to manage this limited resource. Though Windows does provide several memory management routines for your application to use, memory itself is a different type of resource, as Windows is unable to abstract or separate it from the application.

Though Windows is quite capable of mediating the use of a display or printer, it cannot arbitrate an application's need for memory. Each Windows application controls how much memory it requires, while at the same time specifying how much memory is unavailable for other applications to use. This last point highlights the need for each Windows application to manage memory efficiently.

You can enhance the overall performance of Windows applications by remembering four basic memory management principles:

- Limit the number of objects used.
- Minimize the size of each object.
- Share objects whenever possible.
- Define objects as relocatable.

REDUCING THE NUMBER OF OBJECTS • Your application can use one of two approaches when limiting the number of objects in memory. The first approach shares objects as much as possible, rather than forcing each task to create its own copy of the object. The second is to make certain that unused objects are not accidentally left in memory.

All objects can be considered shareable whenever the object is not likely to be modified during program execution. Under these conditions, the object can be shared not only by multiple instances of an application, but also between different applications. Icons; standard cursors; and user-created brushes, pens, and objects are all examples of shareable objects.

REDUCING OBJECT SIZE • The size of an application's objects can be reduced using one of three common approaches. The first method involves making sure you segment your code. Follow Microsoft's recommendation of limiting the size of your code segments to 4 kilobytes; this will also minimize the amount of code you have lying around in memory at one time.

You can also reduce the final size of an object by allocating the minimum amount of memory required to represent the object. One example of this approach would involve a disk file containing both graphics and text information. At one point in the application, only the text information is required. Rather than dynamically allocating a portion of memory large enough to contain the entire text, a better approach would be to allocate enough memory for a small number of records, read more records, reallocate memory, and so on. With this last approach, the amount of memory used most closely represents the actual size of the object.

You've probably heard it said that one picture is worth a thousand words; when it comes to the use of memory, however, it might be better to use the thousand words. The last method in reducing the size of memory objects involves the conservative use of bitmaps. The problem with bitmaps is the tremendous amounts of memory they can require. Additionally, due to varying display resolutions, the size of a bitmap is somewhat unpredictable. On a monochrome monitor, a bitmap may occupy 100 x 100 / 8 (1 bit per pixel) bytes; on another device, 200 x 200 / 2 (4 bits per pixel for 16 colors) bytes. A high-resolution graphics full-screen bitmap would require 1024 x 1024 x 3 (24-bit color resolution), or a whopping 3072 kilobytes of memory!

USING RELOCATABLE OBJECTS • Each time an application is started, new memory objects are created. Each time Windows loads an object into memory, it uses tangential pieces of memory. When the application terminates, the memory objects are removed. This dynamic memory allocation-deallocation process is most efficient whenever Windows is told that it can move or relocate an object.

A poorly written Windows application will create and then subsequently destroy fixed memory objects, thereby fragmenting memory. Because Windows will allocate only contiguous memory for each subsequent object, it is quite possible that a memory fragment will not be large enough for the new object. If the fragmentation is severe enough, an out-of-memory error can be generated—even though sufficient total memory is actually available. The solution is to allow Windows to move objects within memory dynamically.

If you are unfamiliar with OOP, you are probably flinching at the thought of movable memory objects. Frequently, memory objects are kept track of with pointers. Moving memory objects would then require acquiring new pointers—a dynamic variable nightmare!

In an OOP environment, handles keep track of objects. Technically, a handle is a pointer—but not to the memory object. Instead, handles are pointers to pointers. A program needs only to know where to look (the handle) for the object; Windows supplies the address of the object (the pointer pointed to by the handle).

A properly written Windows application creates two types of objects, nonrelocatable and relocatable. By choosing the last type—relocatable, you allow Windows to move memory objects to maximize memory "real estate." About the only time an application will need to lock or mark a memory object as nonrelocatable is when it needs to write or read data in an object or when it is subscript-indexing through the object.

Any Windows application that creates a relocatable object can subsequently lock the object and eventually return it to the original relocatable state as needed. It is best to keep locked objects to an absolute minimum between messages. Leaving a memory object locked while waiting for new messages can create additional problems if the new message is not addressed to the nonrelocatable memory object.

Changing a Windows Background Color

The first example application, named *backgnd.cpp*, will show you how to change a Windows background color with the **GetClassLong()** function. To create this application with Visual C++, you'll need to create Win32 application workspace and name it *backgnd*. Then add a C++ source code file named *backgnd.cpp*. The following listing shows the contents that should appear in your source code file.

```cpp
//
// Backgnd.cpp
// An application that shows how to
// manipulate features, such as background color with
// the GetClassLong() and SetClassLong() functions.
// Copyright (c) William H. Murray and Chris H. Pappas, 1999
//

#include <windows.h>

LRESULT CALLBACK WndProc(HWND,UINT,WPARAM,LPARAM);

char szProgName[]="ProgName";

int WINAPI WinMain(HINSTANCE hInst,HINSTANCE hPreInst,
                   LPSTR lpszCmdLine,int nCmdShow)
{
  HWND hWnd;
  MSG  lpMsg;
  WNDCLASS wcApp;

  wcApp.lpszClassName=szProgName;
  wcApp.hInstance     =hInst;
  wcApp.lpfnWndProc   =WndProc;
  wcApp.hCursor       =LoadCursor(NULL,IDC_ARROW);
  wcApp.hIcon         =0;
  wcApp.lpszMenuName  =0;
  wcApp.hbrBackground=(HBRUSH) GetStockObject(WHITE_BRUSH);
  wcApp.style         =CS_HREDRAW|CS_VREDRAW;
  wcApp.cbClsExtra    =0;
  wcApp.cbWndExtra    =0;
  if (!RegisterClass (&wcApp))
    return 0;
```

Changing a Windows Background Color

```
    hWnd=CreateWindow(szProgName,"Changing the Background Color",
                WS_OVERLAPPEDWINDOW,
                CW_USEDEFAULT,CW_USEDEFAULT,
                CW_USEDEFAULT,CW_USEDEFAULT,
                (HWND)NULL,(HMENU)NULL,
                hInst,(LPSTR)NULL);
  ShowWindow(hWnd,nCmdShow);
  UpdateWindow(hWnd);
  while (GetMessage(&lpMsg,0,0,0)) {
    TranslateMessage(&lpMsg);
    DispatchMessage(&lpMsg);
  }
  return(lpMsg.wParam);
}

LRESULT CALLBACK WndProc(HWND hWnd,UINT messg,
                WPARAM wParam,LPARAM lParam)
{
  HDC hdc;
  PAINTSTRUCT ps;

  switch (messg) {
    case WM_CREATE:  // initial settings for window.
    GetClassLong(hWnd,GCL_HBRBACKGROUND);
                DeleteObject(hWnd);
                SetClassLong(hWnd,GCL_HBRBACKGROUND,LTGRAY_BRUSH);
                InvalidateRect(hWnd,NULL,TRUE);
                UpdateWindow(hWnd);
        return 0;

    case WM_PAINT:
      hdc=BeginPaint(hWnd,&ps);

        Ellipse(hdc,50,50,100,100);
```

```
        Ellipse(hdc,200,200,400,400);
        Ellipse(hdc,400,50,300,200);

        ValidateRect(hWnd,NULL);
        EndPaint(hWnd,&ps);
        return 0;

     case WM_DESTROY:
        PostQuitMessage(0);
        return 0;

     default:
        return(DefWindowProc(hWnd,messg,wParam,lParam));
        return 0;
   }
   return 0;
}
```

Examining the Application File (backgnd.cpp)

The first change to the change to Chapter 2's swt.cpp template is:

`wcApp.hbrBackground=(HBRUSH) GetStockObject(WHITE_BRUSH);`

which is an alternate way to change a brush's color. This statement sets the color when the window is created, instead of afterward. This parameter can be any one of the following values (see Table 3.13):

Table 3.13 Predefined stock pens, brushes, fonts, or palettes.

Value	Meaning
BLACK_BRUSH	Black brush.
DKGRAY_BRUSH	Dark gray brush.
DC_BRUSH	Used in Windows 98, Windows NT 5.0, and later: Solid color brush. The default color is white. The color can be changed by using the **SetDCBrushColor()** function.
GRAY_BRUSH	Gray brush.

Changing a Windows Background Color

Table 3.13	Predefined stock pens, brushes, fonts, or palettes. (Continued)
Value	**Meaning**
HOLLOW_BRUSH	Hollow brush (same as NULL_BRUSH).
LTGRAY_BRUSH	Light gray brush.
NULL_BRUSH	Null brush (same as HOLLOW_BRUSH).
WHITE_BRUSH	White brush.
BLACK_PEN	Black pen.
DEFAULT_PALETTE	Default palette. This palette consists of the static colors in the system palette.

The swt.cpp template continues unchanged until entering the **WndProc()** callback function, as seen below:

```
        case WM_CREATE:    // initial settings for window .
GetClassLong(hWnd,GCL_HBRBACKGROUND);
            DeleteObject(hWnd);
            SetClassLong(hWnd,GCL_HBRBACKGROUND,LTGRAY_BRUSH);
            InvalidateRect(hWnd,NULL,TRUE);
            UpdateWindow(hWnd);
```

The WM_CREATE case is new. The WM_CREATE message is sent when an application requests that a window be created by calling the **CreateWindowEx()** or **CreateWindow()** function. The window procedure of the new window receives this message after the window is created, but before the window becomes visible. The message is sent before the **CreateWindowEx()** or **CreateWindow()** function returns. This code segment allows you to modify the background color whenever the WM_CREATE message is issued. Figure 3-1 shows the brush color results with the three ellipses painted in WHITE_BRUSH while the background is LTGRAY_BRUSH.

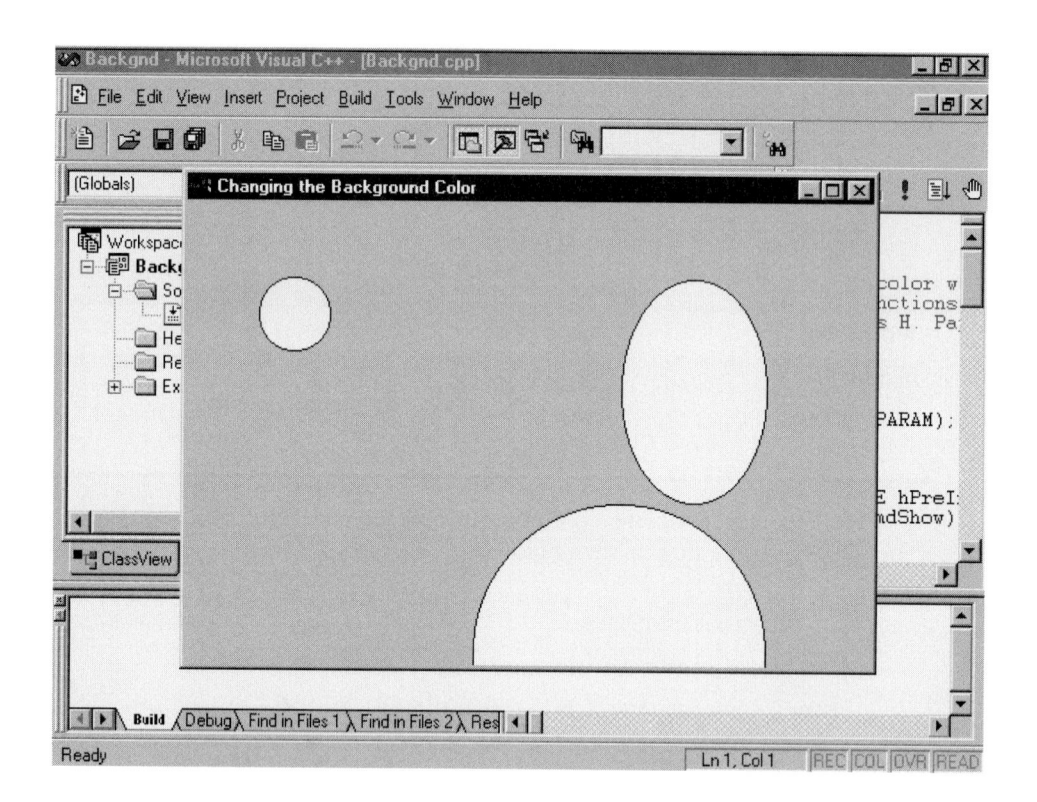

Figure 3-1 *Using WHITE_BRUSH and LTGRAY_BRUSH.*

Changing a Windows Mapping Mode

The second example application, named *mapper.cpp*, will show you how to change a windows mapping mode. To create this application with Visual C++, you'll need to create Win32 application workspace and name it *mapper*. Then add a C++ source code file named *mapper.cpp*. The following listing shows the contents that should appear in your source code file.

```
//
// Mapper.cpp
// An application that shows how to
// manipulate the mapping mode, viewport, etc.
// Copyright (c) William H. Murray and Chris H. Pappas, 1999
//
```

```c
#include <windows.h>

LRESULT CALLBACK WndProc(HWND,UINT,WPARAM,LPARAM);
char szProgName[]="ProgName";

int WINAPI WinMain(HINSTANCE hInst,HINSTANCE hPreInst,
                   LPSTR lpszCmdLine,int nCmdShow)
{
  HWND hWnd;
  MSG  lpMsg;
  WNDCLASS wcApp;

  wcApp.lpszClassName=szProgName;
  wcApp.hInstance     =hInst;
  wcApp.lpfnWndProc   =WndProc;
  wcApp.hCursor       =LoadCursor(NULL,IDC_ARROW);
  wcApp.hIcon         =0;
  wcApp.lpszMenuName =0;
  wcApp.hbrBackground=(HBRUSH) GetStockObject(WHITE_BRUSH);
  wcApp.style         =CS_HREDRAW|CS_VREDRAW;
  wcApp.cbClsExtra    =0;
  wcApp.cbWndExtra    =0;
  if (!RegisterClass (&wcApp))
    return 0;

  hWnd=CreateWindow(szProgName,"Mapping Modes, Etc.",
                    WS_OVERLAPPEDWINDOW,
                    CW_USEDEFAULT,CW_USEDEFAULT,
                    CW_USEDEFAULT,CW_USEDEFAULT,
                    (HWND)NULL,(HMENU)NULL,
                    hInst,(LPSTR)NULL);
  ShowWindow(hWnd,nCmdShow);
  UpdateWindow(hWnd);
  while (GetMessage(&lpMsg,0,0,0)) {
```

132 Chapter 3 • Windows Details

```
      TranslateMessage(&lpMsg);
      DispatchMessage(&lpMsg);
   }
   return(lpMsg.wParam);
}

LRESULT CALLBACK WndProc(HWND hWnd,UINT messg,
                        WPARAM wParam,LPARAM lParam)
{
   HDC hdc;
   PAINTSTRUCT ps;

   static int xClientView,yClientView; //dim of client area

   switch (messg) {
      case WM_SIZE:   // get the dimensions of the client
                                        area.
         yClientView=HIWORD (lParam);
         xClientView=LOWORD (lParam);
         return 0;

      case WM_PAINT:
         hdc=BeginPaint(hWnd,&ps);

//       SetMapMode(hdc,MM_ISOTROPIC);
//       SetWindowExtEx(hdc,500,500,NULL);
//       SetViewportExtEx(hdc,600,-600,NULL);
//       SetViewportOrgEx(hdc,250,250,NULL);

         Rectangle(hdc,50,50,100,200);
         Ellipse(hdc,200,200,300,400);


         ValidateRect(hWnd,NULL);
         EndPaint(hWnd,&ps);
```

```
    return 0;

  case WM_DESTROY:
    PostQuitMessage(0);
    return 0;

  default:
    return(DefWindowProc(hWnd,messg,wParam,lParam));
    return 0;
  }
  return 0;
}
```

Examining the Application File (mapper.cpp)

In this application, the first line of code to vary from the Simple Windows Template is:

```
static int xClientView,yClientView; //dim of client area
```

which declares two integer variables to hold the dimensions of the client area. The following WM_SIZE message case:

```
  case WM_SIZE:  // get the dimensions of the client area.
    yClientView=HIWORD (lParam);
    xClientView=LOWORD (lParam);
```

is responsible for initializing the variables to their current extents. Notice how the **WndProc()** *lParam* argument is being broken down into its high and low word components using the HIWORD and LOWORD Windows macros. The WM_SIZE message is sent to a window after its size has changed. The related information looks like:

```
WM_SIZE
fwSizeType = wParam;          // resizing flag
nWidth = LOWORD(lParam);      // width of client area
nHeight = HIWORD(lParam);     // height of client area
```

While mapper.cpp never actually changes these values, this example demonstrates how your application can find out the current settings before any specific manipulations. Figure 3-2 draws the rectangle and ellipse using the maximum width and height.

134 Chapter 3 • Windows Details

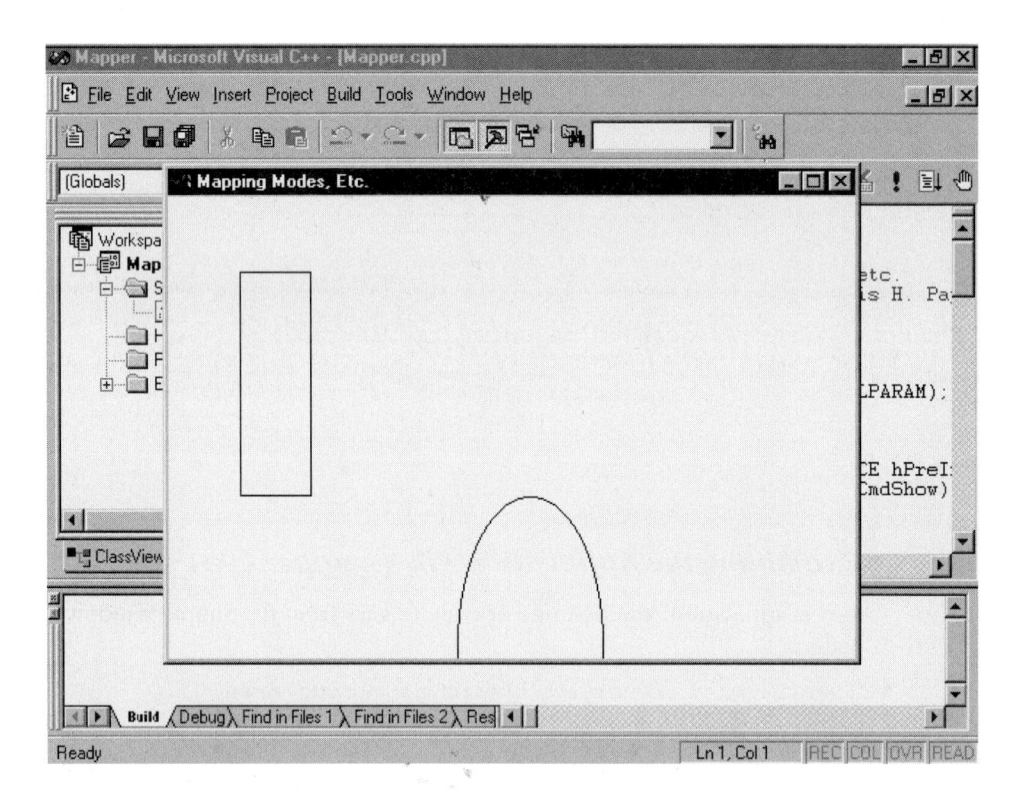

Figure 3-2 *Drawing the rectangle and ellipse without changing the window viewport.*

The following commented-out statements:

```
//SetMapMode(hdc,MM_ISOTROPIC);
//SetWindowExtEx(hdc,500,500,NULL);
//SetViewportExtEx(hdc,600,-600,NULL);
//SetViewportOrgEx(hdc,250,250,NULL);
```

set the mapping mode to MM_ISOTROPIC, where logical units are converted to arbitrary units with equally scaled axes; that is, 1 unit along the x-axis is equal to 1 unit along the y-axis. The **SetWindowExt()** and **SetViewportExt()** member functions specify the desired units and the orientation of the axes. GDI makes adjustments as necessary to ensure that the *x* and *y* units remain the same size.

The **SetWindowExtEx()** function sets the horizontal and vertical extents of the window for a device context by using the specified values. In this example, both *x* and *y* extents will be 500 logical units.

Changing a Windows Mapping Mode   135

```
BOOL SetWindowExtEx(
   HDC hdc,          // handle of device context
   int nXExtent,     // new horizontal window extent
   int nYExtent,     // new vertical window extent
   LPSIZE lpSize     // original window extent
);
```

The **SetViewportExtEx()** function sets the horizontal and vertical extents of the viewport for a device context by using the specified values—in this example, 600, -600. Notice the negative y value. This provides more positive values at the top of the window and more negative values at the bottom.

```
BOOL SetViewportExtEx(
   HDC hdc,          // handle of device context
   int nXExtent,     // new horizontal viewport extent
   int nYExtent,     // new vertical viewport extent
   LPSIZE lpSize     // original viewport extent
);
```

The **SetViewportOrgEx()** function sets the viewport origin of a device context by using the specified coordinates. Here, the origin is set to 250, 250, or the center of the 500 x 500 viewport extent (Figure 3-3).

```
BOOL SetViewportOrgEx(
   HDC hdc,           // handle of device context
   int X,             // new x-coordinate of viewport origin
   int Y,             // new y-coordinate of viewport origin
   LPPOINT lpPoint    // address of structure receiving original origin
);
```

If you remove the comment symbols // and rebuild the application, you will see that the positions of the rectangle and ellipses have moved, even though their specific dimensions remain unchanged. The apparent shifting to the right and up of these images is a result of changing the viewport and origins.

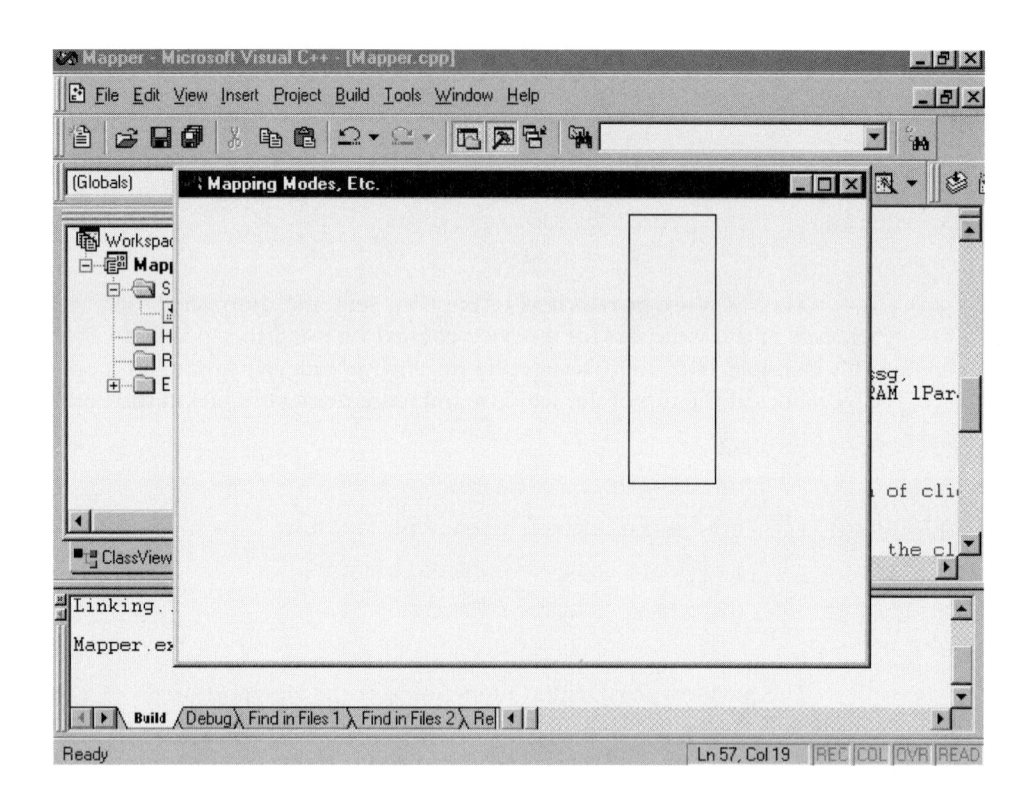

Figure 3-3 *Using specific mapping modes, viewport, and origins.*

Using the System Timer to Control Messages

The first example application, named *systimer.cpp*, will show you how to use the system timer to control messages. To create this application with Visual C++, you'll need to create Win32 application workspace and name it *systimer*. Then add a C++ source code file named *systimer.cpp*. The following listing shows the contents that should appear in your source code file.

```
//
// Systimer.cpp
// An application that shows how to
// use the System Timer to control messages.
// Copyright (c) William H. Murray and Chris H. Pappas, 1999
//
#include <windows.h>
```

```
#include <stdlib.h>
#define TIMERDELAY 1000
//Timer delay set to 1 second
LRESULT CALLBACK WndProc(HWND,UINT,WPARAM,LPARAM);

char szProgName[]="ProgName";

int WINAPI WinMain(HINSTANCE hInst,HINSTANCE hPreInst,
                   LPSTR lpszCmdLine,int nCmdShow)
{
  HWND hWnd;
  MSG   lpMsg;
  WNDCLASS wcApp;

  wcApp.lpszClassName=szProgName;
  wcApp.hInstance     =hInst;
  wcApp.lpfnWndProc   =WndProc;
  wcApp.hCursor       =LoadCursor(NULL,IDC_ARROW);
  wcApp.hIcon         =0;
  wcApp.lpszMenuName =0;
  wcApp.hbrBackground=(HBRUSH) GetStockObject(WHITE_BRUSH);
  wcApp.style         =CS_HREDRAW|CS_VREDRAW;
  wcApp.cbClsExtra    =0;
  wcApp.cbWndExtra    =0;
  if (!RegisterClass (&wcApp))
     return 0;

  hWnd=CreateWindow(szProgName,"Changing A System Timer",
                    WS_OVERLAPPEDWINDOW,
                    CW_USEDEFAULT,CW_USEDEFAULT,
                    CW_USEDEFAULT,CW_USEDEFAULT,
                   (HWND)NULL,(HMENU)NULL,
                    hInst,(LPSTR)NULL);
```

Chapter 3 • Windows Details

```
    if (!SetTimer(hWnd,1,TIMERDELAY,NULL))
    {
       MessageBox(hWnd,"Too many timers started!",
                  szProgName,MB_OK);
       return FALSE;
    }

    ShowWindow(hWnd,nCmdShow);
    UpdateWindow(hWnd);
    while (GetMessage(&lpMsg,0,0,0)) {
      TranslateMessage(&lpMsg);
      DispatchMessage(&lpMsg);
    }
    return(lpMsg.wParam);
}


LRESULT CALLBACK WndProc(HWND hWnd,UINT messg,
                         WPARAM wParam,LPARAM lParam)
{
   HDC hdc;
   PAINTSTRUCT ps;
   static int i=1;
   char sbuffer[1],*strptr;

   switch (messg)
   {
     case WM_TIMER:
        i++;
        InvalidateRect(hWnd,NULL,TRUE);
        return 0;

     case WM_PAINT:
        hdc=BeginPaint(hWnd,&ps);
        TextOut(hdc,160,180,"A Simple Counter",16);
```

```
        strptr=_itoa(i,sbuffer,10);
        TextOut(hdc,200,200,strptr,1);
        if (i>=10)
           i=1;

        ValidateRect(hWnd,NULL);
        EndPaint(hWnd,&ps);
        return 0;

      case WM_DESTROY:
        PostQuitMessage(0);
        return 0;

      default:
        return(DefWindowProc(hWnd,messg,wParam,lParam));
        return 0;
    }
    return 0;
}
```

Examining the Application File (systimer.cpp)

The systimer.cpp file uniqueness begins with the inclusion of <stdlib.h>, providing access to the **_itoa()** or integer-to-alpha function and followed by the symbolic constant definition of TIMERDELAY:

```
#define TIMERDELAY 1000      //Timer delay set to 1 second
```

Next, systimer.cpp's **WinMain** is modified to include the following statements:

```
if (!SetTimer(hWnd,1,TIMERDELAY,NULL))
   {
      MessageBox(hWnd,"Too many timers started!",
             szProgName,MB_OK);
      return FALSE;
   }
```

140 Chapter 3 • Windows Details

This code section takes care of outputting a warning message if the application is unable to capture one of the available system timers. The **WndProc()** function also has several code changes, including:

```
static int i=1;
char sbuffer[1], *strptr;
```

The variable *i* maintains the current timer count and is inialized to 1, while *sbuffer* and its related pointer, *strptr*, are declared for the purposes of holding the string representation of the current integer value stored in *i*. The WM_TIMER case:

```
case WM_TIMER:
  i++;
  InvalidateRect(hWnd,NULL,TRUE);
  return 0;
```

increments the timer count (*i*), makes a call to **InvalidateRect()** to inform Windows that it needs to repaint the window with updated information. The last code change involves the WM_PAINT case, which now includes the statements:

```
strptr=_itoa(i,sbuffer,10);
TextOut(hdc,200,200,strptr,1);
```

The first statement converts the numeric count in *i* to a string equivalent. The second statement actually outputs the updated string count. Figure 3-4 displays a snapshot of the generated counting sequence.

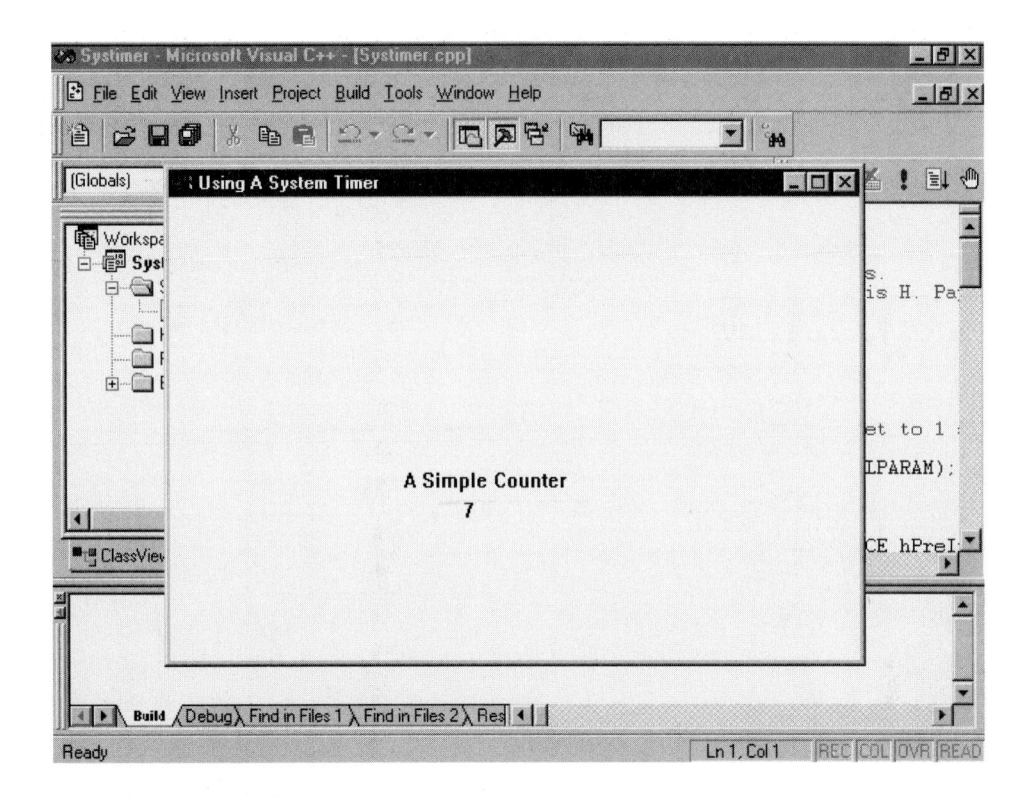

Figure 3-4 *Using System Timers to generate a counter.*

What's Next?

Now that you have had a thorough introduction to the Windows philosophy, its underlying structure, and basic introductory programming fundamentals, it is time to build your first cross-platform Windows applications. In Chapter 4, you will learn how to manage the various project options available with your compiler. Also in Chapter 4, you will learn the fundamental code requirements for writing and understanding the minimal code necessary to get a cross-platform Windows applications up and running.

F O U R

Using Graphics Device Interface Drawing Primitives

This chapter contains important information on how to effectively use the Windows drawing environment. Here you will learn how to use simple graphics primitives for drawing basic shapes such as lines, circles, and arcs. You will also learn how to control the graphics environment by changing pen, brush, and text colors. A major portion of the chapter will teach you interesting bitmap tricks using the **BitBlt()** function.

The Graphics Device Interface

The graphics device interface (GDI) is the Windows code module that manages graphics instructions. The GDI contains a large number of graphics functions that are capable of drawing dots, lines, rectangles, arcs, ellipses, circles, and so on. We call these basic drawing functions *graphics primitives*. The GDI is also responsible for translating these graphics commands for all output device drivers, including monitors, printers, and plotters. As such, the GDI is a device-independent interface. Thus, graphics programs that adhere to the Windows standards will draw on any installed printer, plotter, or graphics display.

This chapter will introduce you to the basic concepts of using the GDI. You will learn much of the basic terminology used in association with the GDI environment. The most frequently used graphics primitives will be introduced, along with many pieces of sample code to teach you about drawing basic shapes. As the chapter progresses, you will learn more and more techniques for building advanced graphics windows.

The GDI Environment

The GDI uses the list of installed drivers on a system to determine how to interface with the various hardware items that are part of the computer system. For example, raster devices, such as monochrome and color monitors, must be handled differently than vector devices, such as plotters. Even among display monitors, further differentiation must be considered because resolution, color, and aspect ratios differ. The device-independent environment of the GDI gives Windows the portability that many operating systems cannot offer, along with the ability to perform powerful bitmap manipulations.

The GDI environment is limited in some areas, however. For example, the GDI lacks the built-in ability to directly produce three-dimensional images and to animate screens. If these effects are desired, they must be programmed manually. Simple animation is still possible, and a simple technique that involves erasing and redrawing the figure will be shown in Chapter 14.

The Default Pixel Mapping Mode

The GDI operates, by default, in a pixel coordinate mode. It obtains information about the device driver and adjusts its graphics output to produce a figure in the correct aspect ratio and in the correct resolution for the hardware device. Seven other *mapping modes* are available for mapping in metric, English, and user-defined units. These will be discussed in Chapter 5. The default MM_TEXT mapping mode will use 0 to 639 pixels horizontally and 0 to 479 pixels vertically when drawing on a VGA screen. If the application is moved to an SVGA or XGA system, the GDI will adjust the screen accordingly.

Information on Installed Devices

Information regarding the installed hardware that the GDI must contend with can be obtained by using the **GetDeviceCaps()** function. This function returns information on numerous hardware device attributes. These attributes include horizontal and vertical resolutions, aspect ratios, color planes, and so forth.

```
GetDeviceCaps(hdc,nIndex);
```

The index value, *nIndex*, is an integer that specifies the item to return. **GetDeviceCaps()** returns a type **int**. Table 4.1 gives a description of these attributes.

Table 4.1 Device-Specific Information returned by GetDeviceCaps.

Index	Meaning
DRIVER VERSION	Version number

Table 4.1 Device-Specific Information returned by GetDeviceCaps. (Continued)

Index	Meaning
TECHNOLOGY	DT_PLOTTER DT_RASDISPLAY DT_RASPRINTER DT_RASCAMERA DT_CHARSTREAM DT_METAFILE DT_DISPFILE
HORZSIZE	Width of display in millimeters
VERTSIZE	Height of display in millimeters
HORZRES	Width of the display, in pixels
VERTRES	Height of the display, in raster lines
LOGPIXELSX	Number of pixels in logical inch along display width
LOGPIXELSY	Number of pixels in logical inch along display height
BITSPIXEL	Number of adjacent color bits per pixel
PLANES	Number of color planes
NUMBRUSHES	Number of device-specific brushes
NUMPENS	Number of device-specific pens
NUMMARKERS	Number of device-specific markers
NUMFONTS	Number of device-specific fonts
NUMCOLORS	Number of entries in the device's color table
ASPECTX	Relative width of device pixel
ASPECTY	Relative height of device pixel
ASPECTXY	Diagonal width of device pixel
PDEVICESIZE	Size of the PDEVICE internal structure, in bytes
CLIPCAPS	Clipping capabilities supported: CP_NONE CP_RECTANGLE CP_REGION
SIZEPALETTE	Number of entries in the system palette

Table 4.1 Device-Specific Information returned by GetDeviceCaps. (Continued)

Index	Meaning
NUMRESERVED	Number of reserved entries in the system palette
COLORRES	Color resolution of the device, in bits per pixel
RASTERCAPS	Raster capabilities the device supports: RC_BANDING Banding RC_BIGFONT Fonts larger than 64K RC_BITBLT Transfers bitmaps RC_BITMAP64 Bitmaps larger than 64K RC_DEVBITS Device bitmaps RC_DI_BITMAP Supports SetDIBits and GetDIBits RC_DIBTODEV Supports SetDIBitsToDevice RC_FLOODFILL Performs flood fills RC_GDI20_OUTPUT For Windows version 2.0 features RC_GDI20_STATE Puts a state block in device context RC_NONE No raster operations supported RC_OP_DX_OUTPUT Supports dev opaque and DX array
RC_PALETTE	Specifies a palette-based device
RC_SAVEBITMAP	Saves bitmaps locally
RC_SCALING	Scaling
RC_STRETCHBLT	Supports StretchBlt
RC_STRETCHDIB	Supports StretchDIBits
CURVECAPS	Curve capabilities the device supports:
CC_NONE	Curves
CC_CIRCLES	Circles
CC_PIE	Pie wedges
CC_CHORD	Chords
CC_ELLIPSES	Ellipses
CC_WIDE	Wide borders
CC_STYLED	Styled borders
CC_WIDESTYLED	Wide styled borders

Table 4.1 Device-Specific Information returned by GetDeviceCaps. (Continued)

Index	Meaning
CC_INTERIORS	Interiors
CC_ROUNDRECT	Rectangles with rounded corners
LINECAPS	Line capabilities the device supports:
LC_NONE	No lines
LC_POLYLINE	Polylines
LC_MARKER	Markers
LC_POLYMARKER	Polymarkers
LC_WIDE	Wide lines
LC_STYLED	Styled lines
LC_WIDESTYLED	Wide styled lines
LC_INTERIORS	Interiors
POLYGONALCAPS	Polygonal capabilities the device supports:
PC_NONE	No polygons
PC_POLYGON	Alternate fill polygonsF
PC_RECTANGLE	Rectangles
PC_WINDPOLYGON	Winding number fill polygons
PC_SCANLINE	Scan lines
PC_WIDE	Wide borders
PC_STYLED	Styled borders
PC_WIDESTYLED	Wide styled borders
PC_INTERIORS	Interiors
TEXTCAPS	Text capabilities the device supports:
TC_OP_CHARACTER	Device can place fonts at any pixel
TC_OP_STROKE	Device can omit any stroke of a font
TC_CP_STROKE	Device can clip fonts to a pixel
TC_CR_90	90-degree character rotation
TC_CR_ANY	Any degree character rotation
TC_SF_X_YINDEP	Independent scaling x and y direction
TC_SA_DOUBLE	Doubled character scaling
TC_SA_INTEGER	Integer multiples for scaling

Table 4.1 Device-Specific Information returned by GetDeviceCaps. (Continued)

Index	Meaning
TC_SA_CONTIN	Any multiples for exact scaling
TC_EA_DOUBLE	Double-weight characters
TC_IA_ABLE	Italics
TC_UA_ABLE	Underlining
TC_SO_ABLE	Strikeouts
TC_RA_ABLE	Raster fonts
TC_VA_ABLE	Vector fonts
TC_RESERVED	Reserved; must be zero
LOGPIXELSX	Pixels/inch in X direction
LOGPIXELSY	Pixels/inch in Y direction

Also included in this arsenal of information are details on built-in hardware capabilities, such as a device's ability to draw ellipses, pie wedges, circles, and so on, without directly using the GDI routines. If the hardware device does not have these abilities built in, Windows will provide an equivalent software routine through the GDI.

Many VGA displays, for example, have a horizontal size of 240 mm and a vertical size of 180 mm. These dimensions produce a horizontal and vertical aspect ratio for the default mapping mode that allows 20 dots, for example, drawn in either the X or Y direction to produce lines of the same length in the window.

In the default mapping mode, the GDI has its origin in the upper left part of the window. The X axis increases positively to the right and the Y axis positively downward, as shown in Figure 4-1.

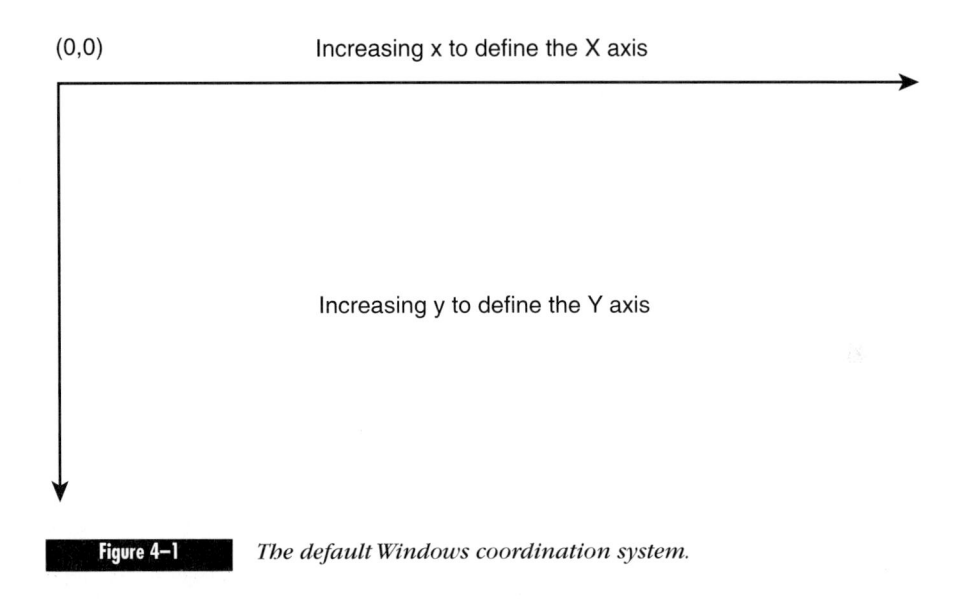

Figure 4-1 *The default Windows coordination system.*

USING THE DEVICE CONTEXT HANDLE

All GDI graphics functions require a handle to a device context. The technique used most frequently to obtain the handle is with a call to the **BeginPaint()** function.

```
hdc=BeginPaint(hWnd,&ps);
```

In this case, *hWnd* is the handle of the current window and *ps* is a pointer to a structure of type **PAINTSTRUCT**, as described in the windows.h or wingdi.h header file.

```
typedef struct tagPAINTSTRUCT {
  HDC   hdc;
  BOOL  fErase;
  RECT  rcPaint;
  BOOL  fRestore;
  BOOL  fIncUpdate;
  BYTE  rgbReserved[32];
} PAINTSTRUCT;
```

The device context handle, *hdc*, is actually returned from the **PAINTSTRUCT** structure. **PAINTSTRUCT** allows drawing only on a valid region of the screen. The invalid region is described by the **rcPaint** structure, which is of type **RECT**.

```
typedef struct tagRECT {
  long left;
  long top;
  long right;
```

```
    long bottom;
} RECT;
```

A call to the **EndPaint()** function completes all drawing in a window.

```
EndPaint(hWnd,&ps);
```

For every **BeginPaint()** function call, there should be a corresponding call to the **EndPaint()** function.

An Introduction to GDI Drawing Primitives

Starting with earlier Windows versions, Microsoft has provided an environment rich in graphic functions. The world outside this operating environment is not always so friendly. Assembly language programmers, for example, have only two basic graphics primitives: draw dot and read dot. From there they must write their own line, box, and circle functions. Programmers specializing in high-level languages have had it a little easier. BASIC, C/C++, and Pascal, for example, contain many powerful graphics functions. Unfortunately, these functions do not necessarily extend from language to language. Thus, BASIC's rectangle function syntax is not necessarily the same as that of Pascal's.

Windows provides a consistent and complete graphics environment. Program developers, however, must adhere to the programming constraints and guidelines of this environment. As a result of this consistent environment, once you learn how to use the various GDI functions, they will always work the same way for you and for all other programmers.

The graphics primitives are the building blocks of all other graphics drawing functions. They are not the "cake mixes" of graphics, but the raw materials: flour, sugar, and eggs. Graphics primitives are the components of all graphics applications, small and large.

Frequently Used Graphics Primitives

There are numerous categories of drawing primitives. Most of these categories are composed of a single function. The most often used categories include functions for drawing arcs, chords, circles, ellipses, lines, pie wedges, polygons, polylines, rectangles, rectangles with rounded corners, and single pixels, as well as techniques for setting cursor positions.

All drawing primitives draw with the current pen style and color and, where applicable, fill the shape with the current brush style and color. Details about pen and brush selections are included later in this chapter.

THE ARC() AND ARCTO() FUNCTIONS

The **Arc()** function is used to draw an elliptical arc. The center of the arc is also the center of a bounding rectangle described by the points *x1,y1* and *x2,y2*, as shown in Figure 4-2.

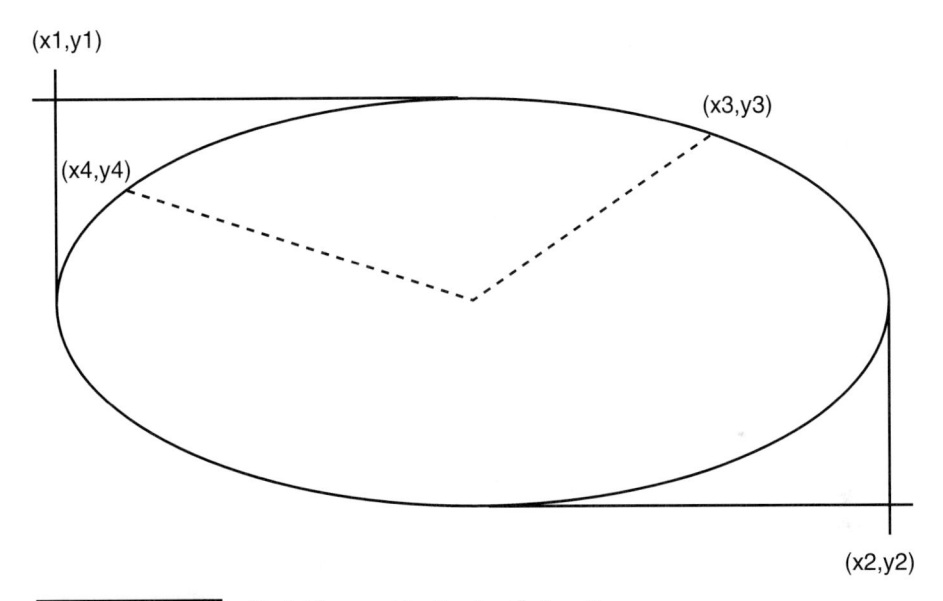

Figure 4–2 *Variables used by the Arc() function.*

The actual length of the arc is described as lying between points *x3,y3* and *x4,y4*, with the drawing performed in a counterclockwise direction. An arc cannot be filled as it is not a closed figure. The **Arc()** function will not update the coordinates of the current point. The handle for the device context is given by *hdc*. All other parameters are of type **int**. This function returns a type **BOOL**.

The function can be called by supplying parameters in the following manner:

```
Arc(hdc,x1,y1,x2,y2,x3,y3,x4,y4)
```

For example, the following line of code draws a small arc in the user's window:

```
Arc(hdc,25,125,175,225,175,225,100,125);
```

The **ArcTo()** function, new for Windows, is similar to **the Arc()** function, except that it does update the current point once it is called.

THE CHORD() FUNCTION

The **Chord()** function is identical to the **Arc()** function, with the added feature that the figure is closed by a line between the two arc points *x3,y3* and *x4,y4*. Figure 4-3 shows these points.

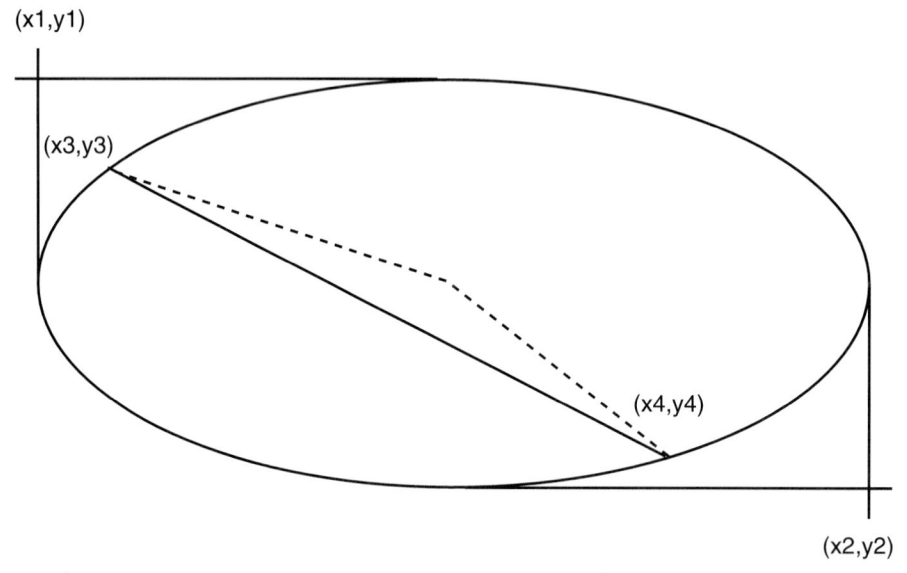

Figure 4-3 *Variables used by the **Chord()** function.*

A chord is filled with the current brush because it is a closed figure. The handle for the device context is given by *hdc*. All other parameters are of type *int*. This function returns a type **BOOL**.

The function can be called in the following manner:

```
Chord(hdc,x1,y1,x2,y2,x3,y3,x4,y4)
```

For example, the following line of code draws a small chord in the user's window:

```
Chord(hdc,125,125,275,225,275,225,200,125);
```

THE ELLIPSE() (AND CIRCLE) FUNCTIONS

The **Ellipse()** function is used to draw an ellipse or a circle. The center of the ellipse is also the center of an imaginary rectangle described by the points *x1,y1* and *x2,y2*, as shown in Figure 4-4.

(x1,y1)

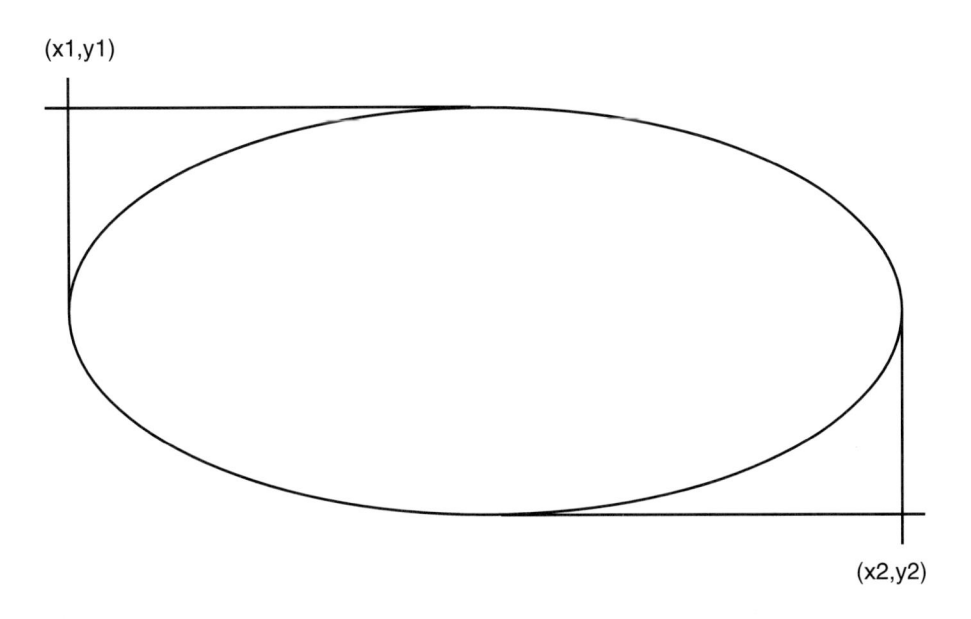

(x2,y2)

Figure 4-4 *Variables used by the **Ellipse()** (circle) function.*

An ellipse is filled because it is a closed figure. The handle for the device context is given by *hdc*. All other parameters are of type **int**. This function returns a type **BOOL**.

The function is called with the following parameters:

```
Ellipse(hdc,x1,y1,x2,y2)
```

For example, the following line of code draws a small ellipse in the user's window:

```
Ellipse(hdc,275,300,200,250);
```

A special case of the **Ellipse()** function specifies a circle when the boundary rectangle is a square. The following code draws a circle:

```
Ellipse(hdc,375,75,525,225);
```

THE LINETO() FUNCTION

The **LineTo()** function draws a line from the current point up to, but not including, the specified point. The current point can be set with the **MoveToEx()** function. The current point will be *x,y* when the function is successful. The handle for the device context is given by *hdc*. All other parameters are of type **int**. This function returns a type **BOOL**.

The function can be called with the following parameters:

```
LineTo(hdc,x,y)
```

Here are some values for drawing a diagonal line in the user's window:

```
MoveToEx(hdc,20,20,NULL);
LineTo(hdc,100,100);
```

THE MOVETOEX() FUNCTION

The **MoveToEx()** function moves the current point to the specified point and returns the original point to a data structure. The handle for the device context is given by *hdc*. The *x* and *y* values are of type **int**. This function returns a type **BOOL**. The *x* and *y* coordinates of the original point are returned in an **lpPoint** structure.

This function can be called with the following parameters:

```
MoveToEx(hdc,x,y,lpPt)
```

If the original point's values are not desired, a **NULL** value may be inserted in the function.

```
MoveToEx(hdc,x,y,NULL)
```

In this manner, the function behaves like the earlier, but outdated, **MoveTo()** Windows function. The following line of code illustrates a typical call to this function:

```
MoveToEx(hdc,20,20,NULL);
```

THE PIE() FUNCTION

The **Pie()** function is used to draw pie-shaped wedges. The center of the elliptical arc is also the center of an imaginary rectangle described by the points *x1,y1* and *x2,y2*, as shown in Figure 4-5.

The starting and ending points of the arc are points *x3,y3* and *x4,y4*. Two lines are drawn from each end point to the center of the rectangle in a counterclockwise direction. The pie wedge is filled because it is a closed figure. The handle for the device context is given by *hdc*. All other parameters are of type **int**. This function returns a type **BOOL**.

This function can be called in the following manner:

```
Pie(hdc,x1,y1,x2,y2,x3,y3,x4,y4)
```

For example, the following line of code draws a small pie-shaped wedge in the user's window:

```
Pie(hdc,200,0,300,100,200,50,250,100);
```

An Introduction to GDI Drawing Primitives   **155**

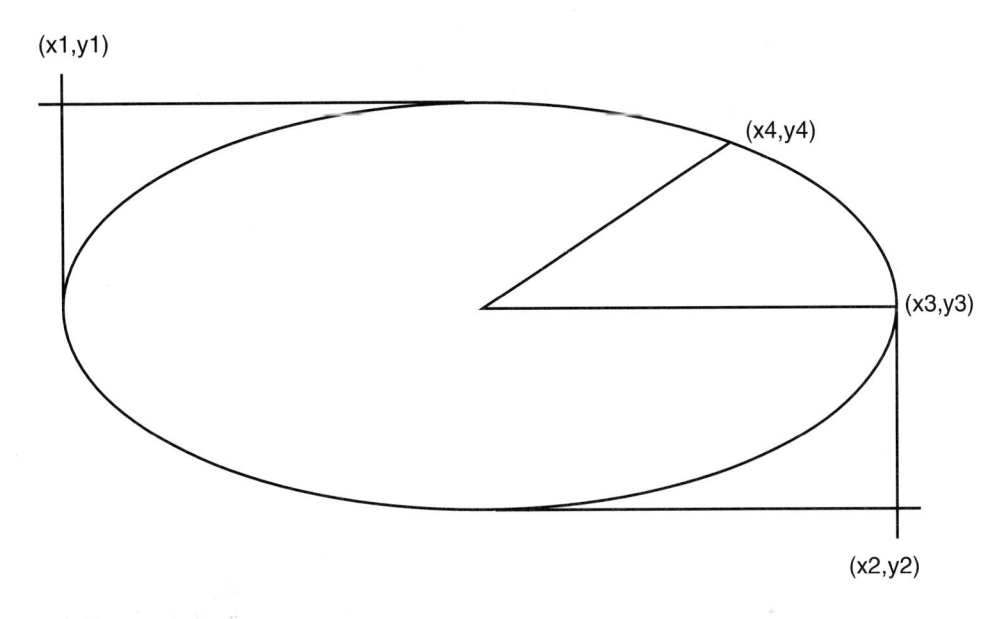

Figure 4–5   *Variables used by the **Pie()** function.*

THE POLYGON() FUNCTION

The **Polygon()** function draws a polygon that consists of points connected by lines. How the lines are drawn is dependent on the filling mode. In *alternate mode,* lines are drawn from the first point to the last. In *winding mode,* the points are used to calculate a border; then the border is drawn. Both modes use the current pen for drawing and the current brush for filling. The polygon is filled, since it is a closed figure. Figure 4-6 shows an example of a polygon.

The handle for the device context is given by *hdc.* The location of the data points is held in an array of type **POINT** in the example that follows. The number of points in the array is an integer. This function returns a type **BOOL**.

This function can be called in the following manner:

```
Polygon(hdc,pointarray,nCount)
```

The following lines of code draw a polygon in the user's window:

```
polygpts[0].x=40;
polygpts[0].y=200;
polygpts[1].x=100;
polygpts[1].y=270;
polygpts[2].x=80;
polygpts[2].y=290;
polygpts[3].x=20;
polygpts[3].y=220;
```

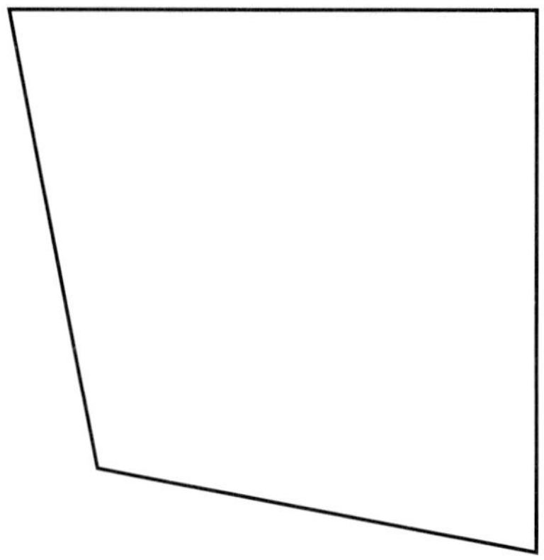

Figure 4-6 *An example of a closed polygon.*

```
polygpts[4].x=40;
polygpts[4].y=200;
Polygon(hdc,polygpts,5);
```

THE POLYLINE() AND POLYLINETO() FUNCTIONS

The **Polyline()** function draws a group of connected line segments given in a type **POINT** array. This function behaves like multiple **MoveToEx()** and **LineTo()** function calls, except that the position of the starting point is not changed. **PolylineTo()** is a Win32 function that also returns the starting point. A shape drawn by **Polyline()** is not filled. The handle for the device context is given by *hdc*. In the example that follows, the location of the data points is held in an array of type **POINT**. The number of points in the array is an integer. This function returns a type **BOOL**.

This function can be called in the following manner:

```
Polyline(hdc,pointarray,nCount)
```

The following lines of code draw a polyline figure in the user's window:

```
polylpts[0].x=10;
polylpts[0].y=30;
polylpts[1].x=10;
polylpts[1].y=100;
polylpts[2].x=50;
polylpts[2].y=100;
polylpts[3].x=10;
polylpts[3].y=30;
Polyline(hdc,polylpts,4);
```

The **PolylineTo()** function is similar to the **Polyline()** function, except that it updates the current point once it is called.

THE RECTANGLE() FUNCTION

The **Rectangle()** function draws a rectangle, or box, described by *x1,y1* and *x2,y2*. The rectangle is filled because it is a closed shape. The handle for the device context is given by *hdc*. All other parameters are of type **int**. This function returns a type **BOOL**.

This function can be called in the following manner:

```
Rectangle(hdc,x1,y1,x2,y2)
```

The following line of code draws a rectangular figure in the user's window:

```
Rectangle(hdc,25,300,150,375);
```

THE ROUNDRECT() FUNCTION

The **RoundRect()** function draws a round-cornered rectangle, or box, described by *x1,y1* and *x2,y2*. The values *x3* and *y3* specify the width and height of the ellipse used to round the corners. The rounded rectangle is filled because it is a closed figure. The handle for the device context is given by *hdc*. All other parameters are of type **int**. This function returns a type **BOOL**.

This function can be called in the following manner:

```
RoundRect(hdc,x1,y1,x2,y2,x3,y3)
```

The following line of code draws a rectangular figure in the user's window:

```
RoundRect(hdc,350,250,400,290,20,20);
```

THE SETPIXEL() AND GETPIXEL() FUNCTIONS

The **SetPixel()** function is used to light a pixel at the location specified by *x* and *y*. It will select the RGB color closest to that requested. The handle for the device context is given by *hdc*. The *x* and *y* parameters are of type **int**. *crColor* is of type **COLORREF**. This function returns a type **COLORREF**.

This function can be called in the following manner:

```
SetPixel(hdc,x,y,crColor)
```

The following line of code lights one pixel in the user's window:

```
SetPixel(hdc,40,150,240L);
```

The **GetPixel()** Function retrieves the RGB color value at the specified point and returns it as a type **COLORREF**.

This function can be called in the following manner:

```
GetPixel(hdc,x,y)
```

GDI Tools and Techniques

Windows provides an environment rich in graphical tools and drawing techniques. For example, stock tools can be chosen, or special tools can be designed for a particular application. Stock brushes and pens are described in the wingdi.h header file. If you have not printed a copy of this file for your own use, you should do so now. Stock brushes and pens include:

WHITE_BRUSH
LTGRAY_BRUSH
GRAY_BRUSH
DKGRAY_BRUSH
BLACK_BRUSH
HOLLOW_BRUSH (or NULL_BRUSH)
WHITE_PEN
BLACK_PEN
NULL_PEN

You will learn shortly how to select stock pens and brushes and how to create custom pens and brushes that allow you to use dazzling colors for drawing and filling shapes.

PENS

Pens are used to draw the outlines for all GDI graphics functions. Pens can be specified with three attributes: color, style, and width. The default pen is a black pen (BLACK_PEN), which draws a solid line (PS_SOLID) one device pixel wide. Other stock pen color choices include a white pen (WHITE_PEN) and a pen that does not draw (NULL_PEN), which is useful for drawing figures without an outline.

PS_INSIDEFRAME creates a pen that draws inside the frame of closed shapes. The basic stock line styles are still:

PS_SOLID_____
PS_DASH- - - - - - - -
PS_DOT............
PS_DASHDOT_._._._._
PS_DASHDOTDOT_.._.._..
PS_NULL
PS_INSIDEFRAME Draws a solid rule inside a frame

Line widths are specified in logical units as integer numbers. Thus, a width of 10 in the default mode, MM_TEXT, will draw a line 10 pixels wide. All pens greater than one logical unit default to either a null or a solid line style.

Pens are referenced with the use of a handle of type **HPEN**. Stock pens can be obtained with the **GetStockObject()** function. To change the pen just selected to the current pen use the **SelectObject()** function.

```
HPEN       hPen;
hPen=SelectObject(hdc,GetStockObject(WHITE_PEN));
```

Creating a customized pen is a little different from creating a stock pen. A custom pen is created and selected with the **CreatePen()** function, in conjunction with the **SelectObject()** function. The **CreatePen()** function creates a logical pen with the syntax:

```
CreatePen(nPenStyle,nWidth,rgbColor);
```

The parameter, *nPenStyle*, is a type **int** and can be specified by any of the values given earlier—for example, PS_SOLID. The value *nWidth* is also of type **int** and is described in logical units. The value *rgbColor* is a type **COLORREF**, given in terms of an RGB color value. For example:

```
hPenRed=SelectObject(CreatePen(PS_SOLID,
           2,RGB(255,0,0)));
```

In this case, a pen is created and selected for drawing solid lines two pixels wide in red. By carefully combining RGB values, a wide variety of colors can be obtained. RGB is a macro defined as a type **COLORREF**. For example:

RGB(0,0,0)= a black pen
RGB(255,255,255)= a white pen
RGB(255,0,0)= a red pen
RGB(0,255,0)= a green pen
RGB(0,0,255)= a blue pen
RGB(255,0,255)= a magenta pen
RGB(255,255,0)= a yellow pen
RGB(0,255,255)= a cyan pen

The RGB value, if specified as a single hexadecimal value, ranges from 0x00000000 to 0x00FFFFFF. For monochrome screens, hexadecimal values less than 800000H default to a black pen; larger values default to a white pen.

Once a pen is selected, only that pen can be used to draw within the device context. To use another pen, the first pen must be deselected. This is done by calling the **DeleteObject()** function.

```
DeleteObject(hPenRed);
```

You should not attempt to delete stock pens. If multiple pens are desired in a program, they can all be created at the same time and selected individually. When the drawing is complete, the entire group can be deleted.

BRUSHES

Brushes are used to fill the closed figures created with GDI graphics functions. Brushes can be specified with several attributes. These attributes include colors, brush styles, and hatch styles. The default brush is a white brush (WHITE_BRUSH) that fills the object with a solid pattern (BS_SOLID). *Solid*, in this context, refers to the fill pattern used by the brush, not the "purity" of the color. Other stock brush color choices include LTGRAY_BRUSH, GRAY_BRUSH, DKGRAY_BRUSH, BLACK_BRUSH, and HOLLOW_BRUSH or NULL_BRUSH.

The colors of the stock brushes are achieved by dithering. Dithering produces shades of colors. On a monochrome screen, gray shades are obtained by using a block of pixels in which the number of black and white pixels is varied. Varying the number of black and white dots creates the illusion of different shades. A large palette of colors can be obtained in a similar manner. The most frequently used stock fill patterns include:

BS_SOLID The fill is the color of the brush.
BS_HOLLOW (BS_NULL) The color of the brush is ignored.
BS_HATCHED The hatching is the color of the brush.
BS_PATTERN The color of the brush is ignored.
BS_INDEXED The color is selected from a color table.
BS_DIBPATTERN The color is defined by a device-independent bitmap.

Cross-hatching can be selected from the following group of hatch patterns:

HS_HORIZONTAL- - - - -
HS_VERTICAL| | | |
HS_FDIAGONAL/////
HS_BDIAGONAL\\\
HS_CROSS+++++
HS_DIAGCROSSxxxxx

Other patterns described in wingdi.h include HS_BDIAGONAL1, HS_NOSHADE, HS_HALFTONE, HS_FDIAGONAL1 and HS_DENSE1 to HS_DENSE8. Brushes are referenced with the use of a handle of type **HBRUSH**. Stock brushes can be obtained with the **GetStockObject()** function. The **SelectObject()** function changes the brush just selected to the current brush.

```
HBRUSH      hBrush;
hBrush=SelectObject(hdc,GetStockObject(LTGRAY_BRUSH));
```

To create and select a customized brush, you must use one of the create brush functions: **CreateSolidBrush()**, **CreateHatchBrush()**, **CreatePatternBrush()**, **CreateDIBPatternBrush()**, etc. Once created, the brush is selected with the **SelectObject()** function. Here are two examples:

```
//(a green solid brush)
hGBrush=SelectObject(hdc,CreateSolidBrush(RGB(0,225,0)));

//(a red hatched (+++) brush)
hRHBrush=SelectObject(hdc,CreateHatchBrush(HS_CROSS,
           RGB(225,0,0)));
```

RGB brush colors can be made of several color combinations. Here are just a few:

RGB(0,0,0)= a black brush
RGB(255,255,255)= a white brush
RGB(255,0,0)= a red brush
RGB(0,255,0)= a green brush
RGB(0,0,255)= a blue brush
RGB(255,0,255)= a magenta brush
RGB(255,255,0)= a yellow brush
RGB(0,255,255)= a cyan brush

Recall that the RGB value is of type **COLORREF.** If the color value is specified as a single hexadecimal number, ranges from 0x00000000 to 0x00FFFFFF are acceptable. For monochrome screens, hexadecimal values less than 800000H default to a black brush; larger values default to white.

Once a brush is selected, only that brush can be used to fill objects within the device context. To use a brush of another color or pattern, the previous brush must be deselected. This is done by calling the **DeleteObject()** function. For example:

```
DeleteObject(hGBrush);
```

The **DeleteObject()** function should not be used to delete stock brushes. If multiple brushes are desired in a program, they can all be created at the same time and selected individually. When the drawing is complete, the entire group of brushes can be deleted.

CHANGING TEXT COLORS

The foreground and background colors of text sent to the graphics screen are very easy to alter. The foreground color of text can be changed with the **SetTextColor()** function. For example:

```
SetTextColor(hdc,RGB(255,0,255));
```

This RGB value sets the text color to magenta. The background of each text color, by default, is based on the setting of the background mode and color. The background mode is either *opaque* or *transparent*. In the opaque mode (the default), the background color fills the space between the letters. This space is white unless the background color is changed. In transparent mode, the background color is ignored, and the space between characters is not filled. If you plan to have labels within solidly filled objects, you will probably choose the transparent mode. If you plan to have labels within a hatch-filled object, the opaque mode is the better selection. The background mode can be set with a call to the **SetBkMode()** function.

```
SetBkMode(hdc,TRANSPARENT);
```

The background text color can be altered with a call to the **SetBkColor()** function.

```
SetBkColor(hdc,RGB(0,255,255));
```

In this case, the background text color is set to cyan.

DRAWING MODE SELECTION

The drawing mode selected determines how pens and brushes will be combined with objects already on the display screen. The **SetROP2()** function selects the drawing mode. The syntax of the function is

`SetROP2(hdc,nDrawMode);`

SetROP2() returns a type **int**. *nDrawMode* is a type **int**. The value for *nDrawMode* can be any of the values shown in Table 4.2. The default value is R2_COPYPEN.

Table 4.2 Available drawing modes.

Value	Meaning
R2_BLACK	pixel is black
R2_NOTMERGEPEN	pixel inverse of R2_MERGEOPEN color
R2_MASKNOTPEN	pixel combination of display and inverse of pen
R2_NOTCOPYPEN	pixel is inverse of pen color
R2_MASKPENNOT	pixel combination of pen color and inverse of screen
R2_NOT	pixel inverse of display color
R2_XORPEN	pixel of colors in pen and display but not in both
R2_NOTMASKPEN	pixel inverse of R2_MASKPEN
R2_MASKPEN	pixel colors common to pen and display
R2_NOTXORPEN	pixel inverse of R2_XORPEN
R2_NOP	pixel unchanged
R2_MERGENOTPEN	pixel display color and inverse pen color
R2_COPYPEN	pixel is pen color
R2_MERGEPENNOT	pixel pen color and inverse display color merged
R2_MERGEPEN	pixel pen color and display color merged
R2_WHITE	pixel is white

Drawing modes are actually binary raster operation codes, or masks. The various options shown earlier in Table 4.2 are made from Boolean operations such as AND, OR, XOR, and NOT.

Simple Applications Using GDI Tools and Techniques

The next five applications will illustrate many of the techniques just discussed. The first application, graph1.cpp, will teach you how to draw many graphics primitives with default pen and brush styles. The second application, graph2.c, uses a wide array of pen, brush, text, and background styles and colors. This application creates a simple bar chart in the window. The next application, graph3.cpp, will show you how to use bitmaps. Graph4.cpp and graph5.cpp demonstrate how to use external bitmaps.

All five applications illustrate the various graphics primitives just discussed. Study each application listing and identify the values used for creating each figure.

In this chapter, we will break with the tradition of discussing the contents of each file for each application. Instead, we will concentrate only on the new features introduced with each application. If there are questions concerning application overhead, etc., we encourage you to return to a previous chapter for more detail.

DRAWING A VARIETY OF SHAPES

Graph1.c, is not modest when it comes to drawing shapes. This application makes specific use of the **MoveToEx()**, **LineTo()**, **Arc()**, **Chord()**, **Ellipse()**, **Pie()**, **Rectangle()**, **RoundRect()**, **SetPixel()**, **Polyline()**, and **Polygon()** functions.

Don't give up, however. Each function is called in the simplest manner possible. Parameter values, where possible, are supplied as immediate values, making it easy to understand the placement and size of the figure within the window.

The following listing is the source code needed to build the graph1.cpp application. You'll need to also create a project file from within your C/C++ compiler.

```
//
// Graph1.cpp
// Experimenting with various GDI graphics drawing
// primitives.
// Copyright (c) William H. Murray and Chris H. Pappas, 1999
//

#include <windows.h>

LRESULT CALLBACK WndProc(HWND,UINT,WPARAM,LPARAM);
```

```
char szProgName[]="ProgName";

int WINAPI WinMain(HINSTANCE hInst,HINSTANCE hPreInst,
                   LPSTR lpszCmdLine,int nCmdShow)
{
  HWND hWnd;
  MSG  lpMsg;
  WNDCLASS wcApp;

  wcApp.lpszClassName=szProgName;
  wcApp.hInstance    =hInst;
  wcApp.lpfnWndProc  =WndProc;
  wcApp.hCursor      =LoadCursor(NULL,IDC_ARROW);
  wcApp.hIcon        =0;
  wcApp.lpszMenuName =0;
  wcApp.hbrBackground=(HBRUSH) GetStockObject(WHITE_BRUSH);
  wcApp.style        =CS_HREDRAW|CS_VREDRAW;
  wcApp.cbClsExtra   =0;
  wcApp.cbWndExtra   =0;
  if (!RegisterClass (&wcApp))
     return 0;

  hWnd=CreateWindow(szProgName,
                    "Experimenting with Drawing Primitives",
                    WS_OVERLAPPEDWINDOW,CW_USEDEFAULT,
                    CW_USEDEFAULT,CW_USEDEFAULT,
                    CW_USEDEFAULT,(HWND)NULL,(HMENU)NULL,
                    hInst,(LPSTR)NULL);
  ShowWindow(hWnd,nCmdShow);
  UpdateWindow(hWnd);
  while (GetMessage(&lpMsg,0,0,0)) {
     TranslateMessage(&lpMsg);
     DispatchMessage(&lpMsg);
  }
```

An Introduction to GDI Drawing Primitives   165

```c
    return(lpMsg.wParam);
}

LRESULT CALLBACK WndProc(HWND hWnd,UINT messg,
                        WPARAM wParam,LPARAM lParam)
{
  HDC hdc;
  PAINTSTRUCT ps;
  POINT polylpts[4],polygpts[5];

  int xcoord;

  switch (messg) {
    case WM_PAINT:
      hdc=BeginPaint(hWnd,&ps);
      // draw an arc with Arc()
      Arc(hdc,25,125,175,225,175,225,100,125);
      TextOut(hdc,100,150,"Arc ->",6);

      // draw a chord with Chord()
      Chord(hdc,125,125,275,225,275,225,200,125);
      TextOut(hdc,280,150,"<- Chord",8);

      // draw a circle with Ellipse()
      Ellipse(hdc,375,75,525,225);
      TextOut(hdc,435,150,"Ellipse",7);

      // draw a line with MoveToEx() and LineTo()
      MoveToEx(hdc,20,20,NULL);
      LineTo(hdc,100,100);
      TextOut(hdc,60,20,"<- LineTo",9);

      // draw an ellipse with Ellipse()
      Ellipse(hdc,275,300,200,250);
```

```
TextOut(hdc,220,265,"Ellipse",7);

// set several pixels with SetPixel()
for(xcoord=400;xcoord<450;xcoord+=5)
  SetPixel(hdc,xcoord,350,0L);
TextOut(hdc,460,345,"<- SetPixel",11);

// draw a pie wedge with Pie()
Pie(hdc,200,0,300,100,200,50,250,100);
TextOut(hdc,260,80,"<- Pie",6);

// draw a rectangle with Rectangle()
Rectangle(hdc,25,300,150,375);
TextOut(hdc,50,325,"Rectangle",9);

// draw a rounded rectangle with RoundRect()
RoundRect(hdc,350,250,400,290,20,20);
TextOut (hdc,410,270,"<--RoundRect",12);

// drawing lines with Polyline()
polylpts[0].x=10;
polylpts[0].y=30;
polylpts[1].x=10;
polylpts[1].y=100;
polylpts[2].x=50;
polylpts[2].y=100;
polylpts[3].x=10;
polylpts[3].y=30;
Polyline(hdc,polylpts,4);
TextOut(hdc,10,110,"Polyline",8);

// draw a polygon with Polygon()
polygpts[0].x=40;
polygpts[0].y=200;
```

```
      polygpts[1].x=100;
      polygpts[1].y=270;
      polygpts[2].x=80;
      polygpts[2].y=290;
      polygpts[3].x=20;
      polygpts[3].y=220;
      polygpts[4].x=40;
      polygpts[4].y=200;
      Polygon(hdc,polygpts,5);
      TextOut(hdc,80,230,"<- Polygon",10);

      ValidateRect(hWnd,NULL);
      EndPaint(hWnd,&ps);
      break;

    case WM_DESTROY:
      PostQuitMessage(0);
      break;
    default:
      return(DefWindowProc(hWnd,messg,wParam,lParam));
      break;
  }
  return(0);
}
```

All drawing is done with Windows default settings. The default pen draws a black line. The default brush is white. The default mapping mode is MM_TEXT. The values supplied for the various GDI function parameters are pixel values that will plot on a VGA screen.

The various shapes are shown and labeled in Figure 4-7. You should determine from the application listing which function calls produce each shape in the window.

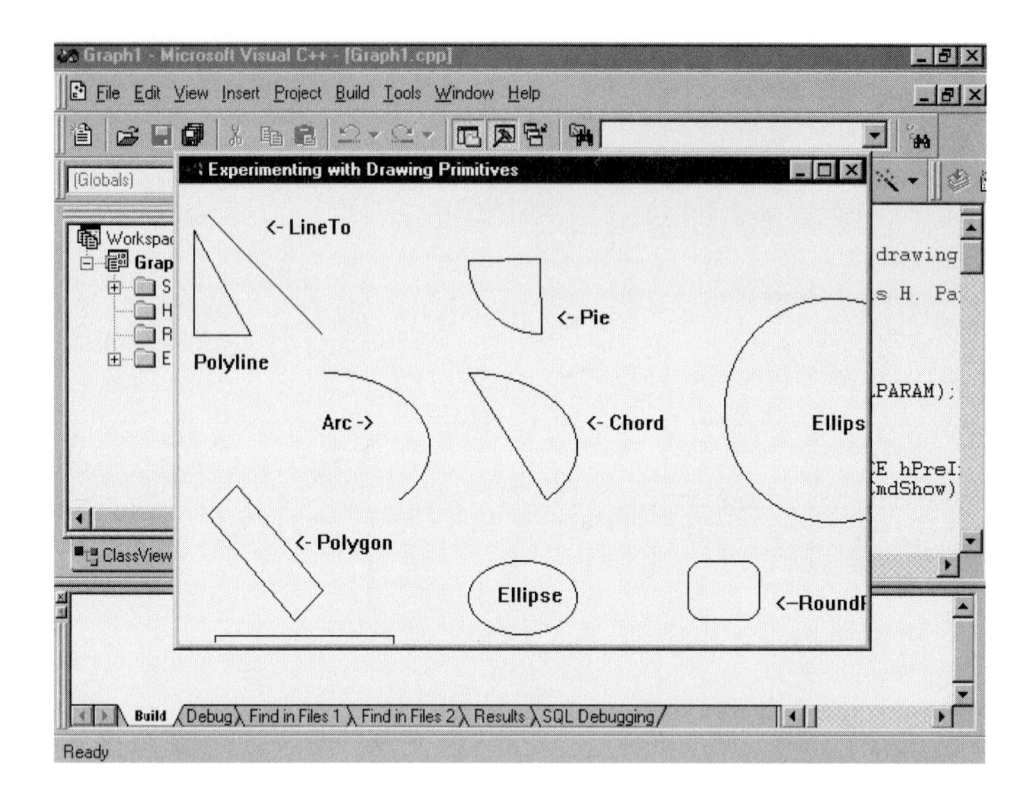

Figure 4-7 *Drawing numerous shapes with Windows graphics primitives.*

Next, try a little cut-and-paste operation with this application. For example, why not try drawing a simple house using just lines and rectangles? If you're successful, try doing it again with a single call to the **Polyline()** function.

CREATING A SIMPLE BAR CHART

Business and scientific graphs put graphics primitives to practical use. In this section, a very simple bar chart graph will be drawn with the **MoveToEx()**, **LineTo()**, and **Rectangle()** functions.

You have learned the theory behind changing pen, brush, text, and background colors. This application will show you how to change all four and make your application come alive with color.

Recall that the background color is set to white when the drawing window is created. To change the background color, this stock white brush value must be replaced. Also, the default text color is black. The **SetTextColor()** function will be used to change text colors.

An Introduction to GDI Drawing Primitives

The following listing is the source code needed to build the graph2.c application. You'll also need to create a project file from within your C/C++ compiler. Additionally, if you are building a 16-bit version of this application, you will need a module definition file. For this example, the default module definition file, offered by the C/C++ compiler, is acceptable. Here is the graph2.cpp source code file:

```
//
// Graph2.cpp
// Use the Rectangle() function to create a simple
// Bar Chart. Pen, Brush and Text colors are changed.
// Copyright (c) William H. Murray and Chris H. Pappas, 1999
//

#include <windows.h>

LRESULT CALLBACK WndProc(HWND,UINT,WPARAM,LPARAM);

char szProgName[]="ProgName";

int WINAPI WinMain(HINSTANCE hInst,HINSTANCE hPreInst,
                   LPSTR lpszCmdLine,int nCmdShow)
{
  HWND hWnd;
  MSG  lpMsg;
  WNDCLASS wcApp;

  wcApp.lpszClassName=szProgName;
  wcApp.hInstance     =hInst;
  wcApp.lpfnWndProc   =WndProc;
  wcApp.hCursor       =LoadCursor(NULL,IDC_ARROW);
  wcApp.hIcon         =0;
  wcApp.lpszMenuName  =0;
  wcApp.hbrBackground=(HBRUSH) GetStockObject(WHITE_BRUSH);
  wcApp.style         =CS_HREDRAW|CS_VREDRAW;
  wcApp.cbClsExtra    =0;
```

```c
   wcApp.cbWndExtra    =0;
   if (!RegisterClass (&wcApp))
      return 0;

   hWnd=CreateWindow(szProgName,
                     "Creating a simple Bar Chart",
                     WS_OVERLAPPEDWINDOW,CW_USEDEFAULT,
                     CW_USEDEFAULT,CW_USEDEFAULT,
                     CW_USEDEFAULT,(HWND)NULL,(HMENU)NULL,
                     hInst,(LPSTR)NULL);
   ShowWindow(hWnd,nCmdShow);
   UpdateWindow(hWnd);
   while (GetMessage(&lpMsg,0,0,0)) {
      TranslateMessage(&lpMsg);
      DispatchMessage(&lpMsg);
   }
   return(lpMsg.wParam);
}

LRESULT CALLBACK WndProc(HWND hWnd,UINT messg,
                         WPARAM wParam,LPARAM lParam)
{
   HDC hdc;
   PAINTSTRUCT ps;
   static HPEN hNPen;
   static HBRUSH hNBrush;

   switch (messg) {
      case WM_PAINT:
         hdc=BeginPaint(hWnd,&ps);

         // draw x & y coordinate axes
         MoveToEx(hdc,99,49,NULL);
         LineTo(hdc,99,350);
```

An Introduction to GDI Drawing Primitives

```
LineTo(hdc,500,350);

// blue brush & pen color for first bar
hNBrush=CreateHatchBrush(HS_HORIZONTAL,RGB(0,255,255));
SelectObject(hdc,hNBrush);
hNPen=CreatePen(PS_SOLID,2,RGB(0,255,255));
SelectObject(hdc,hNPen);
Rectangle(hdc,100,350,200,150);

// yellow brush & pen color for second bar
hNBrush=CreateHatchBrush(HS_FDIAGONAL,RGB(255,255,0));
SelectObject(hdc,hNBrush);
hNPen=CreatePen(PS_SOLID,2,RGB(255,255,0));
SelectObject(hdc,hNPen);
Rectangle(hdc,200,350,300,75);

// red brush & pen color for third rectangle
hNBrush=CreateHatchBrush(HS_CROSS,RGB(255,0,0));
SelectObject(hdc,hNBrush);
hNPen=CreatePen(PS_SOLID,1,RGB(255,0,0));
SelectObject(hdc,hNPen);
Rectangle(hdc,300,350,400,100);

// green brush & pen color for fourth rectangle
hNBrush=CreateHatchBrush(HS_VERTICAL,RGB(0,255,0));
SelectObject(hdc,hNBrush);
hNPen=CreatePen(PS_SOLID,1,RGB(0,255,0));
SelectObject(hdc,hNPen);
Rectangle(hdc,400,350,500,250);

// chart title
TextOut(hdc,240,30,"Car Color Selector",18);

// vertical scale values
```

```
      TextOut(hdc,65,70,"100",3);
      TextOut(hdc,75,160,"75",2);
      TextOut(hdc,75,250,"50",2);
      TextOut(hdc,85,340,"0",1);

      // horizontal colored labels
      SetTextColor(hdc,RGB(0,0,255));
      TextOut(hdc,130,370,"BLUE",4);
      SetTextColor(hdc,RGB(255,255,0));
      TextOut(hdc,220,370,"YELLOW",6);
      SetTextColor(hdc,RGB(255,0,0));
      TextOut(hdc,340,370,"RED",3);
      SetTextColor(hdc,RGB(0,255,0));
      TextOut(hdc,425,370,"GREEN",5);

      ValidateRect(hWnd,NULL);
      EndPaint(hWnd,&ps);
      break;

    case WM_DESTROY:
      DeleteObject(hNPen);
      DeleteObject(hNBrush);
      PostQuitMessage(0);
      break;
    default:
      return(DefWindowProc(hWnd,messg,wParam,lParam));
      break;
  }
  return(0);
}
```

Notice that in this application, the initial window is set to start at coordinates CW_USEDEFAULT. This was done because the font used for the labels is not scaled in this simple application. Scaling would have added a layer of complexity to the application and masked the important new points. You will learn better ways of drawing scaled figures and text when you study the charting examples in Chapter 14.

DRAWING BARS • The viewport for this figure is changed as the size of the window is altered. When this is done under the MM_ISOTROPIC mapping mode, figures can be scaled to the window's size.

The X and Y coordinate axes for this figure are drawn with three familiar function calls.

```
// draw x & y coordinate axes
MoveToEx(hdc,99,49,NULL);
LineTo(hdc,99,350);
LineTo(hdc,500,350);
```

The first of four bars is drawn with a call to the **Rectangle()** function.

```
Rectangle(hdc,100,350,200,150);
```

The remaining three bars are specified in a similar manner. There is nothing magic about this process, nor is there any flexibility. The heights and widths of the four bars are *hard wired* into the application's code. A good bar chart application will allow user interaction in specifying bar heights, etc. A more complete bar chart application can be found in Chapter 13.

CHANGING PEN AND BRUSH COLORS • Earlier in the chapter, the various functions for creating brushes and pens were discussed. Here is an example of how the **CreateHatchBrush()** function can be used to create a yellow brush with a horizontal hatch pattern.

```
hNBrush=CreateHatchBrush(HS_HORIZONTAL,RGB(255,255,0));
SelectObject(hdc,hNBrush);
```

Once the brush is created, it must be selected as a current drawing brush with the use of the **SelectObject()** function. Likewise, you will find creating new pen colors with the **CreatePen()** function just as easy. In the following code, a solid yellow pen is created.

```
hNPen=CreatePen(PS_SOLID,1,RGB(255,255,0));
SelectObject(hdc,hNPen);
```

Like the brush, the pen must be selected as the current drawing device with a call to the **SelectObject()** function.

CHANGING TEXT COLORS • In this application, four labels are printed within each bar chart bar. The labels are printed in the same color with which the bar was drawn and filled. This is possible because the labels are drawn using the default opaque mode. Here the characters are printed in the specified color, but the block containing each character is, by default, white.

```
SetTextColor(hdc,RGB(0,0,255));
TextOut(hdc,130,370,"BLUE",4);
```

While in the opaque mode, you have the ability to change the color that surrounds each color with a call to the **SetBkColor()** function. If you prefer a gray character block surrounding each character, try this:

```
SetBkColor(hdc,RGB(127,127,127));
SetTextColor(hdc,RGB(0,0,255));
TextOut(hdc,130,370,"BLUE",4);
```

It is also possible that you would like the screen color (the background color of the screen) surrounding each color. If that is the case, you will need to switch from the default opaque mode to the transparent mode. This is a simple operation:

```
SetBkMode(hdc,TRANSPARENT);
SetTextColor(hdc,RGB(0,0,255));
TextOut(hdc,120,370,"BLUE",4);
```

Now you'll see yellow text surrounded by the current background color, even within each character cell!

Figure 4-8 is the figure produced by the original listing. You have to admit, it is colorful and appealing, even for such a simple application.

Why not make some of the programming changes suggested in the previous paragraphs and see the results of your experimentation?

An Introduction to GDI Drawing Primitives   **175**

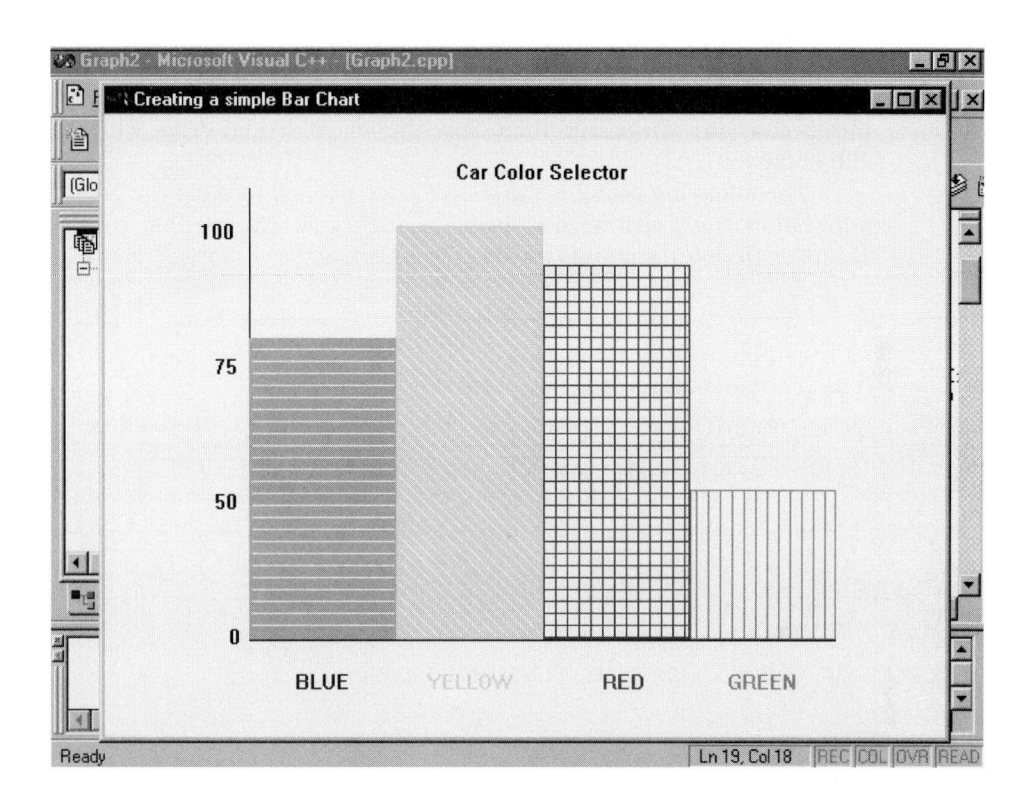

Figure 4-8 *A simple bar chart drawn with different brush, pen, and text styles and colors.*

Manipulating Bitmapped Images

Bitmaps give the programmer the ability to copy, save, and replicate portions of a window. On a monochrome screen, for example, the information about which pixels are turned on and off is saved in memory as a simple bitmap pattern. That bitmap can be played back at a later date to duplicate the original screen quickly.

Windows has several important functions created for drawing, moving, masking, and manipulating bitmapped images. In the following section, two applications are used to help you learn how to use the **BitBlt()** function. In this chapter, you will learn how to create, load, and store bitmapped images. Additional uses for bitmaps will be examined in Chapter 14.

176 Chapter 4 • Using Graphics Device Interface Drawing Primitives

THE BITBLT() BITMAP FUNCTION

In the graph3.c application, you will learn how to create a simple bitmapped image, copy the image, and then draw the image several times with the **BitBlt()** function.

The following listing is the source code needed to build the graph3.cpp application. You'll also need to create a project file from within your C/C++ compiler. Here is the graph3.cpp source code file:

```cpp
//
// Graph3.cpp
// Use the BitBlt() functions to replicate
// a small bitmap image.
// Copyright (c) William H. Murray and Chris H. Pappas, 1999
//

#include <windows.h>

LRESULT CALLBACK WndProc(HWND,UINT,WPARAM,LPARAM);

char szProgName[]="ProgName";

int WINAPI WinMain(HINSTANCE hInst,HINSTANCE hPreInst,
                   LPSTR lpszCmdLine,int nCmdShow)
{
  HWND hWnd;
  MSG  lpMsg;
  WNDCLASS wcApp;

  wcApp.lpszClassName=szProgName;
  wcApp.hInstance     =hInst;
  wcApp.lpfnWndProc   =WndProc;
  wcApp.hCursor       =LoadCursor(NULL,IDC_ARROW);
  wcApp.hIcon         =0;
  wcApp.lpszMenuName  =0;
  wcApp.hbrBackground=(HBRUSH) GetStockObject(WHITE_BRUSH);
  wcApp.style         =CS_HREDRAW|CS_VREDRAW;
```

An Introduction to GDI Drawing Primitives

```
  wcApp.cbClsExtra    =0;
  wcApp.cbWndExtra    =0;
  if (!RegisterClass (&wcApp))
    return 0;

  hWnd=CreateWindow(szProgName,
                    "Playing with Bitmaps",
                    WS_OVERLAPPEDWINDOW,CW_USEDEFAULT,
                    CW_USEDEFAULT,CW_USEDEFAULT,
                    CW_USEDEFAULT,(HWND)NULL,(HMENU)NULL,
                    hInst,(LPSTR)NULL);
  ShowWindow(hWnd,nCmdShow);
  UpdateWindow(hWnd);
  while (GetMessage(&lpMsg,0,0,0)) {
    TranslateMessage(&lpMsg);
    DispatchMessage(&lpMsg);
  }
  return(lpMsg.wParam);
}

LRESULT CALLBACK WndProc(HWND hWnd,UINT messg,
                         WPARAM wParam,LPARAM lParam)
{
  HDC hdc;
  PAINTSTRUCT ps;
  static HBRUSH hBlueBrush;
  int newx,newy;

  switch (messg) {
    case WM_PAINT:
      hdc=BeginPaint(hWnd,&ps);

      // Using the Rectangle() function.
      // draw a small blue rectangle on left
```

```
        hBlueBrush=CreateSolidBrush(RGB(0,0,255));
        SelectObject(hdc,hBlueBrush);
        Rectangle(hdc,20,10,70,60);
        TextOut(hdc,25,30,"BitBlt",6);

        // Using the BitBlt() function to copy
        // the rectangle just drawn and
        // then drawing it diagonally in the window.
        newy=10;
        for(newx=80;newx<600;newx+=60) {
          BitBlt(hdc,newx,newy,50,50,hdc,20,10,SRCCOPY);
                   newy+=50;
        }

        ValidateRect(hWnd,NULL);
        EndPaint(hWnd,&ps);
        break;

      case WM_DESTROY:
        DeleteObject(hBlueBrush);
        PostQuitMessage(0);
        break;
      default:
        return(DefWindowProc(hWnd,messg,wParam,lParam));
        break;
    }
    return(0);
}
```

USING BITBLT() • The **BitBlt()** function was designed to move a bitmap from the source device context to the destination context. If the source and destination context are the same, the function can be used to replicate a pattern anywhere on the screen.

The function can be called in the following manner:

```
BitBlt(hDestDC,x,y,nWidth,nHeight,
     hSrcDC,xSrc,ySrc,dwRop);
```

In the **BitBlt()** function, *hDestDC* is the handle of the receiving device context; *hSrcDC* is the handle of the device context that the bitmap will be copied from. The *x* and *y* values are of type **int** and specify the logical coordinates of the upper left corner of the destination rectangle. The *nWidth* and *nHeight* values are of type **int** and specify the width and height of the destination rectangle and source bitmap. The *xSrc* and *ySrc* values are of type **int** and specify the logical X and Y coordinates of the upper left corner of the source bitmap. The *dwRop* value is of type **DWORD**. Table 4.3 shows possible values for *dwRop*.

Table 4.3 Raster Operation Codes for Bitblt Function.

Value	Description
SRCPAINT	OR together destination and source bitmaps
SRCCOPY	copies source to destination bitmap
SRCAND	AND together destination and source bitmaps
SRCINVERT	XORs destination and source bitmaps
SRCERASE	ANDs an inverted destination bitmap with source bitmap
NOTSRCCOPY	copies inverted source bitmap to destination
NOTSRCERASE	source and destination are ANDed together and then inverted
MERGECOPY	ANDs the pattern and source bitmap
MERGEPAINT	OR inverted source and destination bitmap
PATCOPY	copies pattern to destination bitmap
PATPAINT	OR inverted source with pattern bitmap
PATINVERT	OR destination with pattern bitmap
DSTINVERT	inverts destination bitmap
BLACKNESS	output all black
WHITENESS	output all white

Bitmaps can be created in a variety of ways. This application will draw a small rectangle in the upper left portion of the window with GDI graphics primitives. The rectangle will be filled with a yellow brush. The function name **BitBlt()** will be drawn inside the rectangle.

```
// draw a small blue rectangle on left
    hBlueBrush=CreateSolidBrush(RGB(0,0,255));
```

```
SelectObject(hdc,hBlueBrush);
Rectangle(hdc,20,10,70,60);
TextOut(hdc,25,30,"BitBlt",6);
```

This small rectangular bitmapped image can then be copied and drawn in a different location using the **BitBlt()** function.

```
// Using the BitBlt() function to copy
// the rectangle just drawn and
// then drawing it diagonally in the window.
newy=10;
for(newx=80;newx<600;newx+=60) {
  BitBlt(hdc,newx,newy,50,50,hdc,20,10,SRCCOPY);
      newy+=50;
}
```

Can you determine how the various parameters were derived? First, the original image was drawn to the upper left corner of the rectangle at 20,10. You can see those numbers in both the **Rectangle()** and **BitBlt()** functions. The horizontal dimension of the rectangle is derived by taking 70 --20 = 50. The vertical dimension of the rectangle is derived by taking 60 --10 = 50. Both the horizontal and vertical dimensions are used by **BitBlt()**. The variables *newx* and *newy* point to window locations for the placement of the new bitmapped image. In this case, **BitBlt()** is in a loop that will replicate the image 10 times. The device context is the same for the original and replicated images. Figure 4-9 shows the finished screen containing the results of **BitBlt()**.

Can you think of additional uses for these functions? In the next application, you will learn how to use an external bitmapped image.

An Introduction to GDI Drawing Primitives **181**

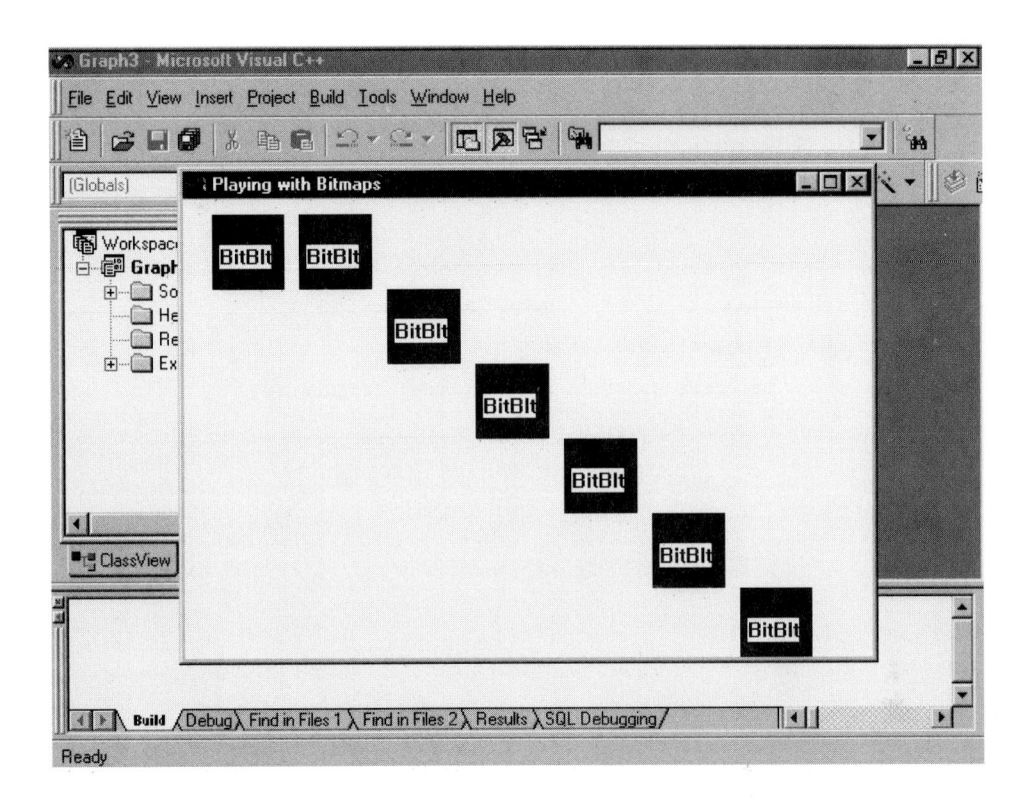

Figure 4-9 *BitBlt() can be used to replicate bitmapped images.*

LOADING AND DRAWING BITMAPPED IMAGES

In the application graph4.c you will learn how recreate a bitmapped image in the current window. This image can be a scanned image or a bitmap file you obtained from an external bulletin board, etc. The image for this example was saved in the root directory as *Graph4.bmp*.

> **note** By using a scanner, all types of images can be scanned and saved, including color and black and white pictures. Just be prepared to allocate ample disk storage for these objects. If you have access to a scanner, perhaps there is a favorite picture you might like to scan and experiment with.

The following listing is the resource script file and the source code needed to build the graph4.cpp application. You'll also need to create a project file from within your C/C++ compiler and have access to a previously saved bitmap image named *graph4.bmp*. Here is the graph4.rc resource script file:

```
#include "windows.h"

BMImage BITMAP graph4.bmp
```

This application, again, makes use of the **BitBlt()** function. Here is the source code file, graph4.cpp:

```
//
// Graph4.cpp
// Reading in an external bitmap image and drawing it
// with the BitBlt() function.
// Note: Create a resource script file named Graph4.rc
//    This file contains: #include "window.h"
//                        BMImage BITMAP c:\Graph4.bmp
// Copyright (c) William H. Murray and Chris H. Pappas, 1999
//

#include <windows.h>

LRESULT CALLBACK WndProc(HWND,UINT,WPARAM,LPARAM);

char szProgName[]="ProgName";
char szBMName[]="BMImage";
HBITMAP hBitmap;

int WINAPI WinMain(HINSTANCE hInst,HINSTANCE hPreInst,
                   LPSTR lpszCmdLine,int nCmdShow)
{
  HWND hWnd;
  MSG   lpMsg;
  WNDCLASS wcApp;

  hBitmap=LoadBitmap(hInst,szBMName);

  wcApp.lpszClassName=szProgName;
  wcApp.hInstance     =hInst;
  wcApp.lpfnWndProc   =WndProc;
```

```
    wcApp.hCursor       =LoadCursor(NULL,IDC_ARROW);
    wcApp.hIcon         =0;
    wcApp.lpszMenuName  =0;
    wcApp.hbrBackground=(HBRUSH) GetStockObject(WHITE_BRUSH);
    wcApp.style         =CS_HREDRAW|CS_VREDRAW;
    wcApp.cbClsExtra    =0;
    wcApp.cbWndExtra    =0;
    if (!RegisterClass (&wcApp))
       return 0;

    hWnd=CreateWindow(szProgName,
                    "Drawing an External Bitmap Image",
                    WS_OVERLAPPEDWINDOW,CW_USEDEFAULT,
                    CW_USEDEFAULT,CW_USEDEFAULT,
                    CW_USEDEFAULT,(HWND)NULL,(HMENU)NULL,
                    hInst,(LPSTR)NULL);
    ShowWindow(hWnd,nCmdShow);
    UpdateWindow(hWnd);
    while (GetMessage(&lpMsg,0,0,0)) {
       TranslateMessage(&lpMsg);
       DispatchMessage(&lpMsg);
    }
    return(lpMsg.wParam);
}

LRESULT CALLBACK WndProc(HWND hWnd,UINT messg,
                         WPARAM wParam,LPARAM lParam)
{
    HDC hdc;
    PAINTSTRUCT ps;
    HDC hmdc;
    static BITMAP bm;

    switch (messg) {
```

Chapter 4 • Using Graphics Device Interface Drawing Primitives

```
    case WM_PAINT:
      hdc=BeginPaint(hWnd,&ps);

      // Create a compatible memory device context
      hmdc=CreateCompatibleDC(hdc);
      // Select the image into the memory device context
      SelectObject(hmdc,hBitmap);
      // Get the object and obtain the size of the image
      GetObject(hBitmap,sizeof(bm),(LPSTR) &bm);
      // Draw the bitmap image from memory to hdc
      BitBlt(hdc,0,0,bm.bmWidth,bm.bmHeight,hmdc,0,0,
             SRCCOPY);
      // Remove the memory device context
      DeleteDC(hmdc);

      ValidateRect(hWnd,NULL);
      EndPaint(hWnd,&ps);
      break;

    case WM_DESTROY:
      PostQuitMessage(0);
      break;
    default:
      return(DefWindowProc(hWnd,messg,wParam,lParam));
      break;
  }
  return(0);
}
```

RETRIEVING THE IMAGE • The bitmapped image was saved in a file with a .bmp file extension. The name of the bitmapped file, graph4.bmp, is identified as a resource in the application's resource script file. The resource script file shows the file as a BITMAP resource. This bitmapped image is named *BMImage*.

```
#include "windows.h"
```

An Introduction to GDI Drawing Primitives

```
BMImage BITMAP graph4.bmp
```

The bitmapped image is loaded with a call to the **LoadBitmap()** function and a handle, *hBitmap*, is returned.

```
char szBMName[]="BMImage";
HBITMAP hBitmap;

int WINAPI WinMain(HINSTANCE hInst,HINSTANCE hPreInst,
            LPSTR lpszCmdLine,int nCmdShow)
{
  HWND hWnd;
  MSG    lpMsg;
  WNDCLASS wcApp;

  hBitmap=LoadBitmap(hInst,szBMName);
```

The **LoadBitmap()** function anticipates an instance handle and a bitmap identified by a null terminated string. Once the bitmap is loaded, it can be accessed with the **BitBlt()** function.

USING BITBLT() • The code for drawing the bitmapped image is relatively easy but involves several new functions. First, information regarding the bitmap will be needed.

```
static BITMAP bm;
```

The variable *bm* is associated with a **BITMAP** structure. This structure contains the following members:

typedef struct tagBITMAP {
   LONG   bmType;
   LONG   bmWidth;
   LONG   bmHeight;
   LONG   bmWidthBytes;
   WORD   bmPlanes;
   WORD   bmBitsPixel;
   LPVOID bmBits;
} BITMAP;

This structure defines the type, width, height, color format, and bit values of a bitmap. The bmType must be zero. The bmWidth and bmHeight members specify the width and height of the bitmap in pixels. The bmWidthBytes member gives the number of bytes in each scan line. This value must be divisible by four. The number of color planes is given in bmPlanes. The number of bits used to indicate the color of a pixel is given in bmBitsPixel. Finally, bmBits points to the location of the bit values for the bitmap. In this application, only bmWidth and bmHeight are needed.

In this application, it is necessary to create a compatible memory device context compatible with the device specified by *hdc*. This can be done with a call to the **CreateCompatibleDC()** function.

```
hmdc=CreateCompatibleDC(hdc);
```

The handle to the memory device context is returned to *hmdc*. The bit-mapped image is now selected to the memory device context using the **SelectObject()** function. The **SelectObject()** function has been used in earlier applications primarily to select fonts, brushes, and pens.

```
SelectObject(hmdc,hBitmap);
```

The **GetObject()** function will get the previously selected object. **GetObject()** requires the handle of the bitmapped image, the size of the bitmap structure, in bytes, and the location of the structure.

```
GetObject(hBitmap,sizeof(bm),(LPSTR) &bm);
```

All that is needed now is a call to **BitBlt()** to draw the image in the window.

```
BitBlt(hdc,0,0,bm.bmWidth,bm.bmHeight,hmdc,0,0,SRCCOPY);
```

Unlike the previous application, the device context for the drawing and image are not the same. Here, *hdc* identifies the device context where the image will be drawn, and *hmdc* is the compatible memory device context for the image.

The image will be drawn to the upper left corner of the window (0,0). The width and height of the image are retrieved from the **BITMAP** structure.

Before leaving the application, the memory device context should be deleted with a call to the **DeleteDC()** function.

```
DeleteDC(hmdc);
```

After all of this work, what does our example image look like? Examine Figure 4-10 for a view of the scanned image.

Why not put your knowledge to work and see if you can copy and draw another image of your own bitmap to the window with **BitBlt()**?

Writing GDI Applications   **187**

Figure 4-10   *Working with a small scanned bitmap image.*

Writing GDI Applications

Now that you have studied this chapter, it might be a good spot to do a little experimentation. Why not see what you can do with the various graphics primitives in terms of pen and brush colors? Or you might substitute the **Ellipse()** function in place of the **Rectangle()** function for the previous application and see what happens.

F I V E

Taking Control of the Window

In Chapter 3, you learned that there are many options for changing the appearance of the display of the window you create. For example, under Windows 98 and NT, you have a choice of mapping modes, origins, viewports, pen colors, brush colors, and so on. In Chapter 4, you learned about the various graphical device interface (GDI) graphics primitives for drawing lines, circles, rectangles and so on. In this chapter we'll continue to investigate several important control features provided under Windows. The main emphasis of this chapter is to investigate the use of scroll bars and the system timer. Using four applications, you'll learn how to use scroll bars to aid in viewing a large text document, create a simple ticker tape application, generate a loan amortization table, and develop an application that will allow you to scroll large graphics screens.

There is a variety of ways for a programmer to position a program's screen output. One common approach is to write the application to recognize PgUp and PgDn, or cursor keystrokes. However, in the Windows graphical environment, this is not always the best approach.

For most users, the mouse has become the easiest interface between them and an application. For this reason, Windows allows the use of horizontal and vertical scroll bars. These optional graphical objects allow a user to shift screen output by visually selecting where they want to go and clicking the mouse. Scroll bars always appear at the bottom and right edges of a window. Scroll bars are fundamentally different, in terms of programming, from scroll bar controls. For example, scroll bar controls can be placed at any location within a user's window. Scroll bar controls are discussed in Chapter 12.

In this chapter, you will learn how to add scroll bars to a text-based application and how to interconnect a scroll bar with a system timer. You'll also learn how to control the output sent to a window in a simple loan amortization program.

Understanding Scroll Bars

You have seen many examples of Windows applications that must display more information than can fit inside the program's client area. You probably use these applications all the time. For example, word processors, spreadsheets, and graphics programs are all capable of generating files too large to fit inside one window.

In the early days of programming, when only the DOS environment was available, shifting screen output was confusing with just a keyboard interface. Many applications used unique key combinations to perform identical screen actions. As you moved from one application to another, you would often find that the same key combination would perform quite different actions. Windows has helped solve this problem. Adding scroll bars to a Windows application immediately provides the user with a visual control that looks and functions the same way across all Windows programs.

The scroll bar is one of the best graphical features provided by the Windows mouse interface. Scroll bars come in two varieties. A vertical scroll bar moves the display contents up and down. A horizontal scroll bar shifts the display contents left and right. You can use either a vertical scroll bar, horizontal scroll bar, or both scroll bars in an application. All Windows scroll bars have the same visual characteristics. At the extreme ends of a scroll bar, you will find an arrow displayed. Clicking one of them causes the display to shift in the direction of the arrow.

Visually, scroll bars also incorporate a thumb. A thumb is a lightly shaded rectangle visible inside a scroll bar. A thumb represents the relative position of the image being displayed in relation to the size of the entire file. Clicking the mouse in the space between the thumb and one of the arrows causes the displayed image to shift in a manner similar to pressing the PgUp or PgDn keys. The user can also left click on the thumb and drag it along the scroll bar. This usually changes the area displayed in the window in increments of more than a page.

Speaking of Scroll Bars

Scroll bars have a unique language that is used to define their type and behavior. This section introduces you to this terminology and will make it much easier for you to understand applications that use scroll bars.

SCROLL BAR CONSTANTS

Imagine that a user is running a word processing application and has loaded a 20-page document. After viewing the first screen of the document, the user wants to scroll down a few lines. Though the user wants to move *down* the document, in reality, the application must move the displayed text *up!* The developers of Windows have approached the declarations for certain scroll bar symbolic constants from the user's perspective. These *constants* are found in the winuser.h header file. The header file contains many self-documenting identifiers such as SB_LINEDOWN and SB_PAGEDOWN, which correspond to the user's desire to move down the document. Table 5.1 shows various constants and commands from this header file.

Table 5.1 Scroll bar constants.

Name	Value
SB_HORZ	0
SB_VERT	1
SB_CTL	2
SB_BOTH	3
SB_LINEUP	0
SB_LINELEFT	0
SB_LINEDOWN	1
SB_LINERIGHT	1
SB_PAGEUP	2
SB_PAGELEFT	2
SB_PAGEDOWN	3
SB_PAGERIGHT	3
SB_THUMBPOSITION	4
SB_THUMBTRACK	5
SB_TOP	6
SB_LEFT	6
SB_BOTTOM	7
SB_RIGHT	7
SB_ENDSCROLL	8

Using these unique constants provides two advantages. First, it makes the application easier to design because you do not have to understand the intricacies of scroll bars. All you have to do is pick an easily read and understood constant, such as SB_RIGHT. The second advantage to using these constants is that it makes your code more readable and, therefore, more easily debugged and modified.

> **note**: Notice that many constants share a similar value. That means, for example, that SB_BOTTOM could be used successfully where a programmer should have used SB_RIGHT for scrolling to the right.

SCROLL BAR RANGE

Scroll bars are used in all types of applications, from word processors to CAD programs. With such a wide diversity of applications, something must tell the scroll bar control its valid minimum and maximum positions. You do this by defining the range.

The scroll bar's *range* is defined using integer values. These values define the scroll bar's minimum and maximum extents. The minimum value for a vertical scroll bar occurs when the thumb is at the top of the scroll bar; when the thumb is positioned at the bottom, the scroll bar is in its maximum position. For horizontal scroll bars, the minimum is to the extreme left, and the maximum is to the scroll bar's extreme right. The default scroll bar range is from 0 (top or left) to 100 (bottom or right).

SCROLL BAR POSITION

The scroll bar thumb is used to remind the user visually of the relative position of the displayed data in relation to the overall file. The scroll bar's *position* is determined by the location of the thumb and is represented by an integer value. For example, if the range for a scroll bar is from 0 to 10, there would be 11 actual thumb positions.

TWO TYPES OF SCROLL BARS

As we mentioned earlier, there are two basic types of scroll bars. The first type can be used by all windows and has a predefined size and screen location. This is the type of scroll bar discussed in this chapter. The second type of scroll bar is called a *scroll bar control*. This type of scroll bar behaves like a child window. Scroll bar controls will be discussed in Chapter 12.

In the examples in this chapter, you'll see that vertical-window scroll bars are automatically positioned along the right side of the client area. Horizontal-window scroll bars are always placed along the bottom of the client area. Note that the client area does not include the space occupied by the scroll bar. The height and width of window scroll bars are dependent on the particular display driver.

In contrast to the type of scroll bar discussed in this chapter, a scroll bar control is actually a child window that can be drawn in any size, height, and width. They are created by making a call to the **CreateWindow()** function and requesting a child window with a scroll bar style. Again, more on this type of control in Chapter 12.

Adding Scroll Bars to an Application

The first example application, named *scroll.cpp*, will show you how to create and use both vertical and horizontal scroll bars. To create this application with Visual C++, you'll need to create Win32 application workspace and name it *scroll*. Then add a C++ source code file named *scroll*. The following listing shows the contents that should appear in your source code file.

```
//
// scroll.cpp
// A simple scroll bar application
// Copyright (c) William H. Murray and Chris H. Pappas, 1999
//

#include <windows.h>
#include <stdio.h>
#include <string.h>

#define LINES 600    // number of lines in document

LRESULT CALLBACK WndProc(HWND,UINT,WPARAM,LPARAM);

char szProgName[]="ProgName";

int WINAPI WinMain(HINSTANCE hInst,HINSTANCE hPreInst,
                   LPSTR lpszCmdLine,int nCmdShow)
{
  HWND hWnd;
  MSG  lpMsg;
  WNDCLASS wcApp;

  wcApp.lpszClassName=szProgName;
  wcApp.hInstance     =hInst;
  wcApp.lpfnWndProc   =WndProc;
  wcApp.hCursor       =LoadCursor(NULL,IDC_ARROW);
  wcApp.hIcon         =0;
  wcApp.lpszMenuName  =0;
  wcApp.hbrBackground=(HBRUSH) GetStockObject(WHITE_BRUSH);
  wcApp.style         =CS_HREDRAW|CS_VREDRAW;
```

```
  wcApp.cbClsExtra    =0;
  wcApp.cbWndExtra    =0;
  if (!RegisterClass (&wcApp))
    return 0;

  hWnd=CreateWindow(szProgName,"Working with Scroll Bars",
                    WS_OVERLAPPEDWINDOW,
                    20,20,240,240,
                     (HWND)NULL,(HMENU)NULL,
                    hInst,(LPSTR)NULL);
  ShowWindow(hWnd,nCmdShow);
  UpdateWindow(hWnd);
  while (GetMessage(&lpMsg,0,0,0)) {
    TranslateMessage(&lpMsg);
    DispatchMessage(&lpMsg);
  }
  return(lpMsg.wParam);
}


LRESULT CALLBACK WndProc(HWND hWnd,UINT messg,
                        WPARAM wParam,LPARAM lParam)
{
  HDC hdc;
  PAINTSTRUCT ps;
  SCROLLINFO si;
  TEXTMETRIC tm;
  FILE *fp;

  char szBuffer[500];        // set buffer size

  static int xClientView,yClientView; //dim of client area
  static int xClientViewMax; // maximum width of client area
  static int xChWidth;       // horizontal scrolling unit
  static int yChHeight;      // vertical scrolling unit
  static int xUpper;         // avg width of uppercase letters
  static int xPos,yPos;      // current scrolling positions
  static int xMax,yMax;      // maximum scrolling positions
  int xInc,yInc;             // scrolling increments
  int i,t,ch;                // a few needed variables

  switch (messg) {
    case WM_CREATE:
      // handle to client area device context
      hdc=GetDC (hWnd);
      // font dimensions from the text metrics structure
      GetTextMetrics(hdc,&tm);
      xChWidth=tm.tmAveCharWidth;
      xUpper=(tm.tmPitchAndFamily & 1 ? 3 : 2)*xChWidth/2;
      yChHeight=tm.tmHeight+tm.tmExternalLeading;
```

```
      // release device context.
      ReleaseDC(hWnd,hdc);
      // set maximum width for client area
      // make xClientViewMax the sum of the widths of 48
      // lowercase letters and 12 uppercase letters.)
      xClientViewMax=48*xChWidth+12*xUpper;
      return 0;

   case WM_SIZE:    // get the dimensions of the client area.
      yClientView=HIWORD (lParam);
      xClientView=LOWORD (lParam);
      // get the maximum vertical scrolling position
      // add some white space
      yMax=max (0,LINES+2-yClientView/yChHeight);
      // check that the current vertical scrolling position
      // does not exceed the maximum
      yPos=min (yPos, yMax);
      // adjust vertical scrolling range and scroll box
      // position for the new yMax and yPos
      si.cbSize=sizeof(si);
      si.fMask=SIF_ALL;
      si.nMin=0;
      si.nMax=yMax;
      si.nPage=yClientView/yChHeight;
      si.nPos=yPos;
      SetScrollInfo(hWnd,SB_VERT,&si,TRUE);
      // get the maximum horizontal scrolling position.
      // add some white space
      xMax=max (0,2+(xClientViewMax-xClientView)/xChWidth);
      // check that the horizontal scrolling position
      // does not exceed the maximum
      xPos=min (xPos,xMax);
      // adjust the horizontal scrolling range and scroll box
      // position for the new xMax and xPos
      si.cbSize=sizeof(si);
      si.fMask=SIF_ALL;
      si.nMin=0;
      si.nMax=xMax;
      si.nPage=xClientView/xChWidth;
      si.nPos=xPos;
      SetScrollInfo(hWnd,SB_HORZ,&si,TRUE);
      return 0;

   case WM_HSCROLL:
      switch(LOWORD (wParam))
      {
         // clicked space left of thumb
         case SB_PAGELEFT:
            xInc=-28;
            break;
```

Chapter 5 • Taking Control of the Window

```
      // clicked space right of thumb
      case SB_PAGERIGHT:
        xInc=28;
        break;
      // clicked left arrow
      case SB_LINELEFT:
        xInc=-1;
        break;
      // clicked right arrow
      case SB_LINERIGHT:
        xInc=1;
        break;
      // dragged the thumb
      case SB_THUMBTRACK:
        xInc=HIWORD(wParam)-xPos;
        break;
      default:
        xInc=0;
    }
    // check to see if scrolling increment takes
    // scrolling position out of scrolling range
    if (xInc=max (-xPos,min (xInc, xMax-xPos)))
    {
      xPos+=xInc;
      ScrollWindowEx(hWnd,-xChWidth * xInc,0,
            (CONST RECT *) NULL,(CONST RECT *) NULL,
            (HRGN) NULL,(LPRECT) NULL,SW_INVALIDATE);
      si.cbSize=sizeof(si);
      si.fMask=SIF_POS;
      si.nPos=xPos;
      SetScrollInfo(hWnd,SB_HORZ,&si,TRUE);
      UpdateWindow(hWnd);
      InvalidateRect(hWnd,NULL,TRUE);
    }
    return 0;

case WM_VSCROLL:
    switch(LOWORD (wParam))
    {
      // clicked the space above the thumb
      case SB_PAGEUP:
        yInc=min(-1,-yClientView/yChHeight);
        break;
      // clicked the space below the thumb
      case SB_PAGEDOWN:
        yInc=max(1,yClientView/yChHeight);
        break;
      // clicked top arrow
      case SB_LINEUP:
        yInc=-1;
```

```
      break;
    // clicked bottom arrow
    case SB_LINEDOWN:
      yInc=1;
      break;
    // dragged the thumb
    case SB_THUMBTRACK:
      yInc=HIWORD(wParam)-yPos;
      break;
    default:
      yInc=0;
  }
  // check to see if scrolling increment takes
  // scrolling position out of scrolling range
  if (yInc=max(-yPos,min(yInc,yMax - yPos)))
  {
    yPos+=yInc;
    ScrollWindowEx(hWnd,0,-yChHeight * yInc,
            (CONST RECT *) NULL,(CONST RECT *) NULL,
            (HRGN) NULL,(LPRECT) NULL,SW_INVALIDATE);
    si.cbSize=sizeof(si);
    si.fMask=SIF_POS;
    si.nPos=yPos;
    SetScrollInfo(hWnd,SB_VERT,&si,TRUE);
    UpdateWindow(hWnd);
    InvalidateRect(hWnd,NULL,TRUE);
  }
  return 0;

case WM_PAINT:
  hdc=BeginPaint(hWnd,&ps);


  // open a document and draw text to the window
  t=0;
  if ((fp=fopen("c:\\scroll\\test.txt","r"))!=NULL)
  {
    while(!feof(fp))
    {
      ch=fgetc(fp);
      i=0;
      while((ch!='\n') && (ch!=EOF))
      {
        szBuffer[i]=(char)ch;
        ch=fgetc(fp);
        i++;
      }
      TextOut(hdc,-xChWidth*(xPos),
              yChHeight*(t-yPos),szBuffer,i);
      t++;
```

```
            }
        }
        fclose(fp);

        ValidateRect(hWnd,NULL);
        EndPaint(hWnd,&ps);
        return 0;

    case WM_DESTROY:
        PostQuitMessage(0);
        return 0;

    default:
        return(DefWindowProc(hWnd,messg,wParam,lParam));
        return 0;
    }
    return 0;
}
```

There is one more file, test.txt, that you'll need to run the program. This is the text file used by the application that will let you scroll up, down, left, and right, demonstrating how scroll bars work. You can use any text file you choose. However, to take full advantage of the horizontal scroll bar's ability to shift text left and right, your original document should be wider than 80 characters. Text that is significantly narrower than this will not emphasize horizontal displacement. Also note that Windows will not draw the scroll bar when it is not needed. So, you may ask for a horizontal scroll bar, but if one is not needed to view the entire document, it will not be drawn.

Figure 5-1 is a sample document used in our application. Notice the placement of both scroll bars and the thumb position in each.

Adding Scroll Bars to an Application **199**

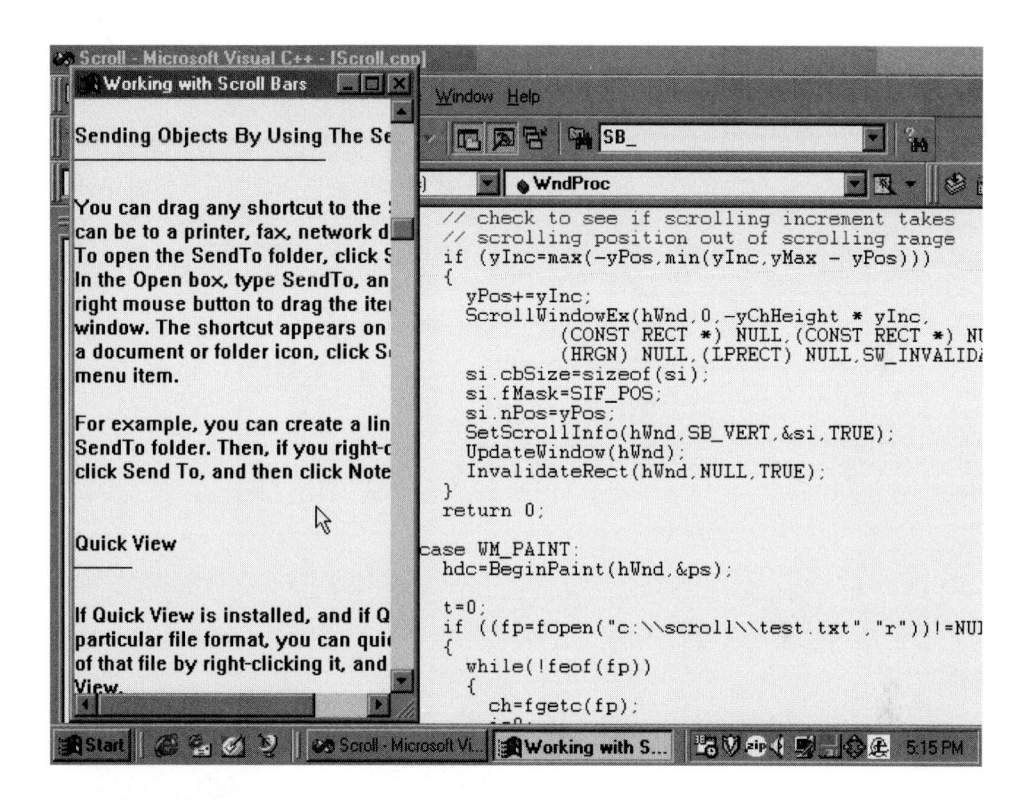

Figure 5-1 *A document being scrolled in the scroll application.*

Examining the Application File (scroll.cpp)

There is a wide variety of scroll bar functions available to the Windows programmer. For Win32 applications, it is best to use the **GetScrollInfo()** and **SetScrollInfo()** functions to ensure accurate scrolling results across all sizes of documents. Before we examine the use of these functions, let's see how this program differs from the programs in the previous chapters.

One important change over earlier applications is that the program's window is set to a specific size. This is done with the **CreateWindow()** function.

```
hWnd=CreateWindow(szProgName,"Working with Scroll Bars",
                  WS_OVERLAPPEDWINDOW,
                  20,20,240,240,
                  (HWND)NULL,(HMENU)NULL,
                  hInst,(LPSTR)NULL);
```

In this case, the window is drawn starting at a point (20,20) that specifies the upper left corner of a rectangular viewing area. The window extends to a point (240,240) that specifies the lower-right corner of a rectangular viewing area. This will ensure that a relatively small window is created so that most documents will require both vertical and horizontal scroll bars.

> **note:** With some scroll bar functions, it is necessary to specify WS_VSCROLL and WS_HSCROLL in the **CreateWindow()** function to make the scroll bars visible. This requirement is not necessary for the **GetScrollInfo()** and **SetScrollInfo()** functions. Their use ensures that the scroll bars are automatically drawn.

Both the **GetScrollInfo()** and **SetScrollInfo()** functions use information stored in a **SCROLLINFO** structure.

```
typedef struct tagSCROLLINFO {  // si
    UINT cbSize;
    UINT fMask;
    int  nMin;
    int  nMax;
    UINT nPage;
    int  nPos;
    int  nTrackPos;
}           ;
typedef     FAR *LPSCROLLINFO;
```

The structure uses seven members: cbSize gives the size, in bytes, of this structure; fMask gives the scroll bar parameters to set or retrieve; fmask is a combination of the values shown in Table 5.2.

Table 5.2 SCROLLINFO fmask values.

Constant	Definition
SIF_ALL	A combination of SIF_PAGE, SIF_POS, SIF_RANGE, and SIF_TRACKPOS.
SIF_DISABLENOSCROLL	Use only when setting a scroll bar's parameters. If the scroll bar parameters make the scroll bar unnecessary, the scroll bar should be disabled but not removed.
SIF_POS	Use when the nPos member contains the scroll thumb position that is not updated while the user drags the thumb.
SIF_RANGE	Use when the nMin and nMax members contain the minimum and maximum values for the scrolling range.
SIF_TRACKPOS	Use when the nTrackPos member contains the current position of the thumb while it is being dragged

The nMin and nMax values specify the minimum and maximum scrolling positions. nPage gives the page size. This value is used to determine the appropriate size of the proportional thumb. nPos gives the position of the thumb. nTrackPos gives the current position of a scroll bar thumb being moved by the user. This information is obtained by processing the SB_THUMBTRACK message.

Examine the **WndProc()** function in the scroll.cpp file listing shown earlier. You'll see the SCROLLINFO structure used there. Here is a portion of that code:

```
HDC hdc;
PAINTSTRUCT ps;
SCROLLINFO si;
TEXTMETRIC tm;
FILE *fp;
```

Immediately below the SCROLLINFO structure is another structure named TEXTMETRIC. Unfortunately, this is one of those cases where we must use something before adequately explaining its use. The TEXTMETRIC structure is used to return information on text fonts. It will be explained in detail in Chapter 6. For now, resign yourself to the fact that this will aid us in calculating scrolling distances for a given font. The FILE structure is a standard structure for use in opening, reading, writing, and closing standard C++ files.

Windows applications process messages as you have already learned. In the message processing section of this application, notice that the WM_CREATE, WM_SIZE, WM_HSCROLL, and WM_VSCROLL message sections are new to this application.

WM_CREATE

A WM_CREATE message is received and processed when the window is first created. It is at this time that the information is collected for the TEXTMETRIC structure by calling the **GetTextMetrics()** function. If you examine this code you'll see a variety of calculations being made that will help determine the vertical and horizontal scrolling parameters. Remember that the TEXTMETRIC structure and various font functions will be explained in Chapter 6. This information only needs to be gathered at the creation of the window.

WM_SIZE

WM_SIZE messages are used by the programmer to determine the current size of the window. In this example the information is returned to the variables *yClientView* and *xClientView*.

If you examine the WM_SIZE portion of code in the scroll.cpp listing you will notice two almost identical code sections. Actually, one portion of code sets the horizontal scroll bar information and the other portion of code the vertical scroll bar information. Here is a portion of that listing:

```
yMax=max (0,LINES+2-yClientView/yChHeight);
// check that the current vertical scrolling position
// does not exceed the maximum
yPos=min (yPos, yMax);
// adjust vertical scrolling range and scroll box
// position for the new yMax and yPos
si.cbSize=sizeof(si);
si.fMask=SIF_ALL;
si.nMin=0;
si.nMax=yMax;
si.nPage=yClientView/yChHeight;
si.nPos=yPos;
SetScrollInfo(hWnd,SB_VERT,&si,TRUE);
```

The *yMax* variable holds the maximum vertical scrolling range for the scroll bar. It should be no surprise that it is based upon a preset number of lines, LINES, and the vertical dimensions of the window divided by the character heights.

The *yPos* variable is used for setting the current scroll bar position. You saw the **SCROLLINFO** structure in the previous section. Examine the portion of code just shown to see how each parameter is set. When the **SetScrollInfo()** function is called, the vertical scroll bar is adjusted, and the window is redrawn to reflect the new data. The **SetScrollInfo()** function sets the parameters of a scroll bar, including the minimum and maximum scrolling positions, the page size, and the position of the thumb (scroll box). The function also redraws the scroll bar, if requested.

The **SetScrollInfo()** function accepts four parameters. The hwnd parameter is a handle to the window using the scroll bar. The fnBar parameter is the scroll bar flag. Flag values for this parameter are shown in Table 5.3.

Table 5.3   Flag values for the fnBar parameter.

Value	Definition
SB_CTL	Specifies the parameters of a scroll bar control. Where *hwnd* is a handle to the scroll bar control.
SB_HORZ	Specifies the parameters of the window's horizontal scroll bar.
SB_VERT	Specifies the parameters of the window's vertical scroll bar.

The third parameter points to a **SCROLLINFO** structure. The values used in this structure were discussed earlier in this chapter. The fourth parameter, Redraw, specifies whether the scroll bar is to be redrawn to reflect the changes to the scroll bar values. When this value is set to TRUE, the scroll bar will be redrawn. If set to FALSE, it will not be redrawn.

Values for the horizontal scroll bar are calculated in a similar manner.

WM_HSCROLL

WM_SCROLL messages contain information on the type of scrolling action initiated. For example, the user could click in the space between the thumb and the scroll bar arrow to initiate a page left advance. This corresponds to the SB_PAGELEFT constant. In a similar manner, a SB_PAGERIGHT, SB_LINELEFT, SB_LINERIGHT, or SB_THUMBTRACK value could be returned. Each possibility is processed with a case statement to determine the movement of the scroll bar. Increment information is set in the *xInc* variable for use by the **ScrollWindowEx()** function.

Here is the portion of code used to control the horizontal scrolling action.

```
// check to see if scrolling increment takes
// scrolling position out of scrolling range
if (xInc=max (-xPos,min (xInc, xMax-xPos)))
{
  xPos+=xInc;
  ScrollWindowEx(hWnd,-xChWidth * xInc,0,
       (CONST RECT *) NULL,(CONST RECT *) NULL,
       (HRGN) NULL,(LPRECT) NULL,SW_INVALIDATE);
  si.cbSize=sizeof(si);
  si.fMask=SIF_POS;
  si.nPos=xPos;
  SetScrollInfo(hWnd,SB_HORZ,&si,TRUE);
  UpdateWindow(hWnd);
  InvalidateRect(hWnd,NULL,TRUE);
}
return 0;
```

Here the window is scrolled based on the information supplied to the **ScrollWindowEx()** function. The scroll bar itself is adjusted with a call to the **SetScrollInfo()** function. At this point, you might want to use your Visual C++ help screen to investigate each of the **ScrollWindowEx()** parameters.

A call to the **UpdateWindow()** and **InvalidateRect()** functions force a screen update and redraw.

WM_VSCROLL

If you study the code listed under WM_VSCROLL in the scroll.cpp file, you'll see that it is very similar to the code used to process WM_HSCROLL messages. Here, however, the constants returned consist of SB_PAGEUP, SB_PAGEDOWN, SB_LINEUP, SB_LINEDOWN, and SB_THUMBTRACK.

A WORD ABOUT WM_PAINT

When either a WM_HSCROLL or WM_VSCROLL message is processed, the screen is updated and redrawn by calling the **UpdateWindow()** and **InvalidateRect()** functions. Essentially, this causes Windows to generate a WM_PAINT message. All the code under WM_PAINT is executed again. In this application, the text will be redrawn, but with possibly different parameters for the horizontal or vertical values passed to the **TextOut()** function. Recall that the variables *xPos* and *yPos* contain current scroll bar information based on the position of the scroll bar thumb. To actually scroll the screen, the horizontal and vertical values used in the **TextOut()** function must reflect the position of the scroll bar thumb. These positions are based on the scroll bar thumb and the font's character height or width.

The code used to open, read, and close the text file is standard C++ code that we'll assume you are already familiar with.

Now here is the good news! Once you master how to create and control a scroll bar, you'll find that the code doesn't change much from one application to another. We'll illustrate this fact as we investigate the remaining three applications in this chapter.

Using Scroll Bars and the System Timer

The second example application, named *ticker.cpp*, will show you how to use a horizontal scroll bar and system timer to create a simple ticker tape program. To create this application with Visual C++, you'll need to create Win32 application workspace and name it *ticker*. Then add a C++ source code file named *ticker*. The following listing shows the contents that should appear in your source code file.

```
//
// ticker.cpp
// A System Timer and Scroll bar application
// Copyright (c) William H. Murray and Chris H. Pappas, 1999
//

// This application uses a text file which you need to create
// and name text.txt.  This file must be located in the ticker
// subdirectory.
// To make the application appear like a ticker tape, use
// approx 30 character message followed by approx 200 periods.

#include <windows.h>
#include <stdio.h>
#include <string.h>

#define TIMEDELAY 200    // delay in milliseconds
```

Using Scroll Bars and the System Timer   205

```
LRESULT CALLBACK WndProc(HWND,UINT,WPARAM,LPARAM);

char szProgName[]="ProgName";

int WINAPI WinMain(HINSTANCE hInst,HINSTANCE hPreInst,
                   LPSTR lpszCmdLine,int nCmdShow)
{
  HWND hWnd;
  MSG  lpMsg;
  WNDCLASS wcApp;

  wcApp.lpszClassName=szProgName;
  wcApp.hInstance    =hInst;
  wcApp.lpfnWndProc  =WndProc;
  wcApp.hCursor      =LoadCursor(NULL,IDC_ARROW);
  wcApp.hIcon        =0;
  wcApp.lpszMenuName =0;
  wcApp.hbrBackground=(HBRUSH) GetStockObject(WHITE_BRUSH);
  wcApp.style        =CS_HREDRAW|CS_VREDRAW;
  wcApp.cbClsExtra   =0;
  wcApp.cbWndExtra   =0;
  if (!RegisterClass (&wcApp))
    return 0;

  hWnd=CreateWindow(szProgName,"Ticker Tape",
                    WS_OVERLAPPEDWINDOW,
                    0,390,639,69,           // VGA screen pos.
                    (HWND)NULL,(HMENU)NULL,
                    hInst,(LPSTR)NULL);
  if (!SetTimer(hWnd,1,TIMEDELAY,NULL))
  {
    MessageBox(hWnd,"Too many timers started!",
               szProgName,MB_OK);
    return FALSE;
  }

  ShowWindow(hWnd,nCmdShow);
  UpdateWindow(hWnd);
  while (GetMessage(&lpMsg,0,0,0)) {
    TranslateMessage(&lpMsg);
    DispatchMessage(&lpMsg);
  }
  return(lpMsg.wParam);
}


LRESULT CALLBACK WndProc(HWND hWnd,UINT messg,
                         WPARAM wParam,LPARAM lParam)
{
  HDC hdc;
```

Chapter 5 • Taking Control of the Window

```
        PAINTSTRUCT ps;
        SCROLLINFO si;
        TEXTMETRIC tm;
        FILE *fp;

        char szBuffer[300];        // set buffer size

        static int xClientView;    // dim of client area
        static int xChWidth;       // horizontal scrolling unit
        static int xPos;           // current scrolling positions
        int xInc;                  // scrolling increments
        int i,ch;                  // a few needed variables

        switch (messg) {
          case WM_CREATE:
            // handle to client area device context
            hdc=GetDC (hWnd);
            // font dimensions from the text metrics structure
            GetTextMetrics(hdc,&tm);
            xChWidth=tm.tmAveCharWidth;
            // release device context.
            ReleaseDC (hWnd,hdc);
            // adjust the horizontal scrolling range and scroll box
            // position for the new xMax and xPos
            si.cbSize=sizeof(si);
            si.fMask=SIF_ALL;
            si.nPage=xClientView/xChWidth;
            si.nPos=xPos;
            SetScrollInfo(hWnd,SB_HORZ,&si,TRUE);
            return 0;

          case WM_SIZE:  // dimension of the horz client area.
            xClientView=LOWORD (lParam);
            return 0;

          case WM_TIMER:
            xInc=1;
            if (xPos >=120)
               xPos=0;
            if (xPos <0)
               xPos=0;
            xPos+=xInc;
            ScrollWindowEx (hWnd,-xChWidth * xInc,0,
                    (CONST RECT *) NULL,(CONST RECT *) NULL,
                    (HRGN) NULL,(LPRECT) NULL,SW_INVALIDATE);
            si.cbSize=sizeof(si);
            si.fMask=SIF_POS;
            si.nPos=xPos;
            SetScrollInfo(hWnd,SB_HORZ,&si,TRUE);
            UpdateWindow(hWnd);
```

```
      InvalidateRect(hWnd,NULL,TRUE);
      return 0;

    case WM_PAINT:
      hdc=BeginPaint(hWnd,&ps);

      if ((fp=fopen("c:\\ticker\\test.txt","r"))!=NULL)
      {
        while(!feof(fp))
        {
          ch=fgetc(fp);
          i=0;
          while((ch!='\n') && (ch!=EOF))
          {
            szBuffer[i]=(char)ch;
            ch=fgetc(fp);
            i++;
          }
          TextOut(hdc,xClientView-(xPos*xChWidth),
                  12,szBuffer,i);
        }
      }
      fclose(fp);

      ValidateRect(hWnd,NULL);
      EndPaint(hWnd,&ps);
      return 0;

    case WM_DESTROY:
      PostQuitMessage(0);
      return 0;

    default:
      return(DefWindowProc(hWnd,messg,wParam,lParam));
      return 0;
  }
  return 0;
}
```

Under Windows a system timer is an input device that can generate Windows messages at preset intervals. An application can use a timer to instruct Windows on how often to give it a "buzz." Whenever the specified interval elapses, Windows sends the application a WM_TIMER message. The ticker application uses this message to update the ticker-tape message, one character per timer interval.

As you study the previous listing, you'll notice several familiar components. Most of the scroll bar action is similar to the scroll.cpp application, with the exception that only a horizontal scroll bar is employed by the ticker application.

Examining the Application File (ticker.cpp)

Examine the source code of the application file, ticker.cpp, and notice the definition of a new type of constant named TIMEDELAY.

```
#define TIMEDELAY 200        // delay in milliseconds
```

TIMEDELAY is used to set the timing interval (in milliseconds) that Windows will use when generating WM_TIMER messages.

To create a window that takes on the appearance of an actual ticker tape, the **CreateWindow()** function forces the window to a rectangular size that fits a VGA screen. If you are working in super VGA (SVGA), you'll need to adjust these coordinates. The upper left corner of the rectangle is set to (0,639) and the lower right corner to (390,69).

```
hWnd=CreateWindow(szProgName,"Ticker Tape",
          WS_OVERLAPPEDWINDOW,
          0,390,639,69,           // VGA screen pos.
          (HWND)NULL,(HMENU)NULL,
          hInst,(LPSTR)NULL);
```

At this point, the application is ready to try to set the system timer. The timer is set with a call to the **SetTimer()** function. This function uses the following syntax:

```
SetTimer(HWND hWnd, UINT nIDEvent, UINT uElapse,
        TIMERPROC lpTimerFunc);
```

The hWnd parameter is a handle to the window to be associated with the timer. If this parameter is set to NULL, no window will be associated with the timer, and the nIDEvent parameter is ignored. The nIDEvent parameter is an identifier for the new timer. The uElapse parameter specifies the timer's time-out value, in milliseconds. The lpTimerFunc parameter is a pointer to the function to be notified when the time-out value elapses. When lpTimerFunc is set to NULL, the system posts a WM_TIMER message to the application queue.

In this case, the **SetTimer()** function is set with the following values:

```
if (!SetTimer(hWnd,1,TIMEDELAY,NULL))
{
  MessageBox(hWnd,"Too many timers started!",
            szProgName,MB_OK);
  return FALSE;
}
```

This timer is identified as timer #1 and set with a time delay specified in the TIMEDELAY constant. The NULL value given for the fourth parameter specifies that we want WM_TIMER messages generated at each timer interval.

If the timer can't be created, it is usually the result of too many timers being created. If that is the case, a Windows message box is created with the **MessageBox()** function to warn the user.

If you examine the ticker.cpp source code, shown earlier, you'll see that the call back function, **WndProc()**, is designed to process WM_CREATE, WM_SIZE, WM_TIMER, and WM_PAINT messages.

The WM_CREATE and WM_SIZE case statements are very similar to the ones used in the scroll.cpp application discussed earlier in this chapter. Their brevity is a result of using just a horizontal scroll bar in the program.

The new action in this program takes place in the WM_TIMER and WM_PAINT sections.

WM_TIMER

In the scroll.cpp application, discussed earlier in this chapter, the user could move a horizontal or vertical bar and scroll a document left-right or up-down. In this application, the system timer will do all of the work. Each time a system timer message is intercepted the WM_TIMER message handler will increment the horizontal scroll bar by one character. Depending on the message and the defined timer interval, the output from this program will appear as a ticker-tape message scrolling across the screen from right to left.

The following portion of code shows how WM_TIMER messages are processed in this application:

```
case WM_TIMER:
  xInc=1;
  if (xPos >=120)
     xPos=0;
  if (xPos <0)
     xPos=0;
  xPos+=xInc;
  ScrollWindowEx (hWnd,-xChWidth * xInc,0,
        (CONST RECT *) NULL,(CONST RECT *) NULL,
        (HRGN) NULL,(LPRECT) NULL,SW_INVALIDATE);
  si.cbSize=sizeof(si);
  si.fMask=SIF_POS;
  si.nPos=xPos;
  SetScrollInfo(hWnd,SB_HORZ,&si,TRUE);
  UpdateWindow(hWnd);
  InvalidateRect(hWnd,NULL,TRUE);
  return 0;
```

If you examine this code, you might recall seeing it before. This code is almost identical to the code used in the WM_HSCROLL and WM_VSCROLL message handlers of the scroll.cpp application. However, in this section we're not interested in user-generated scroll bar messages but in system timer-generated messages.

Each time a WM_TIMER message is received, the *xInc* variable will increase the value in the *xPos* variable by one. The new scroll bar position is then processed by the **ScrollWindowEx()** and **SetScrollInfo()** functions, as in the scroll.cpp application.

WHAT'S HAPPENING IN WM_PAINT

Examine the following portion of code from the ticker.cpp application. Here you'll see what transpires when a WM_PAINT message is received.

```
case WM_PAINT:
  hdc=BeginPaint(hWnd,&ps);

  if ((fp=fopen("c:\\ticker\\test.txt","r"))!=NULL)
  {
    while(!feof(fp))
    {
      ch=fgetc(fp);
      i=0;
      while((ch!='\n') && (ch!=EOF))
      {
        szBuffer[i]=(char)ch;
        ch=fgetc(fp);
        i++;
      }
      TextOut(hdc,xClientView-(xPos*xChWidth),
              12,szBuffer,i);
    }
  }
  fclose(fp);

  ValidateRect(hWnd,NULL);
  EndPaint(hWnd,&ps);
  return 0;
```

Remember that WM_PAINT messages are issued every time a WM_TIMER message is processed. This occurs because the WM_TIMER message handler contains a call to the **UpdateWindow()** and **InvalidateRect()** functions.

When a WM_PAINT message is received, the window is redrawn, moving the text one character to the left. No vertical movement is necessary in this application. The code for opening, reading, and closing the external text file is identical to the previous example.

Figure 5-2 shows a typical screen with the ticker-tape message appearing in the lower portion of the screen.

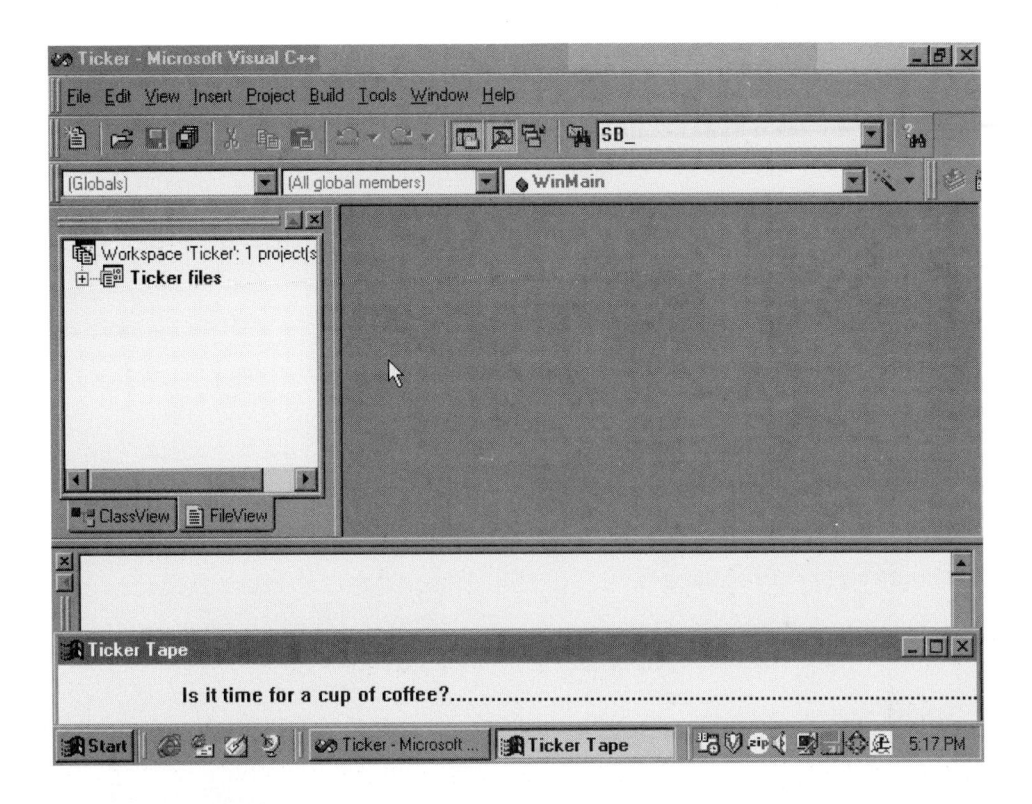

Figure 5-2 *A ticker tape message is sent by the ticker.cpp application.*

Is it time for a cup of coffee yet? By this time, you are probably ready for a caffeine hit.

In the next example, we'll return to the use of a horizontal and vertical scroll bar and investigate how to scroll through a table of numeric values.

Scroll Bars Used to Scroll a Table of Information

The third example application, named *loan.cpp*, will show you how use a vertical and horizontal scroll bar to scroll through a large table of numeric values. The numeric values represent a loan amortization table showing payments, interest, and so on. To create this application with Visual C++, you'll need to create Win32 application workspace and name it *loan*. Then add a C++ source code file named *loan*. The following listing shows the contents that should appear in your source code file.

```cpp
//
// loan.cpp
// A scroll bar application that
// prints a loan amortization table.
// Copyright (c) William H. Murray and Chris H. Pappas, 1999
//

#include <windows.h>
#include <stdio.h>
#include <strstrea.h>
#include <string.h>
#include <math.h>


#define LINES 100         // lines in document
#define HORIZONTAL 120    // width of data

LRESULT CALLBACK WndProc(HWND,UINT,WPARAM,LPARAM);

char szProgName[]="ProgName";

int WINAPI WinMain(HINSTANCE hInst,HINSTANCE hPreInst,
                   LPSTR lpszCmdLine,int nCmdShow)
{
  HWND hWnd;
  MSG  lpMsg;
  WNDCLASS wcApp;

  wcApp.lpszClassName=szProgName;
  wcApp.hInstance       =hInst;
  wcApp.lpfnWndProc     =WndProc;
  wcApp.hCursor         =LoadCursor(NULL,IDC_ARROW);
  wcApp.hIcon           =0;
  wcApp.lpszMenuName    =0;
  wcApp.hbrBackground=(HBRUSH) GetStockObject(WHITE_BRUSH);
  wcApp.style           =CS_HREDRAW|CS_VREDRAW;
  wcApp.cbClsExtra      =0;
  wcApp.cbWndExtra      =0;
  if (!RegisterClass (&wcApp))
    return 0;

  hWnd=CreateWindow(szProgName,"Loan Amortization",
                    WS_OVERLAPPEDWINDOW,
                    0,0,639,479,
                     (HWND)NULL,(HMENU)NULL,
                    hInst,(LPSTR)NULL);
  ShowWindow(hWnd,nCmdShow);
  UpdateWindow(hWnd);
  while (GetMessage(&lpMsg,0,0,0)) {
    TranslateMessage(&lpMsg);
```

```
      DispatchMessage(&lpMsg);
   }
   return(lpMsg.wParam);
}

LRESULT CALLBACK WndProc(HWND hWnd,UINT messg,
                         WPARAM wParam,LPARAM lParam)
{
   HDC hdc;
   PAINTSTRUCT ps;
   SCROLLINFO si;
   TEXTMETRIC tm;
   RECT rc;

   char szBuffer[200];        // set buffer size

   static int xClientView,yClientView; //dim of client area
   static int xChWidth;       // horizontal scrolling unit
   static int yChHeight;      // vertical scrolling unit
   static int xPos,yPos;      // current scrolling positions
   static int xMax,yMax;      // maximum scrolling positions
   int xInc,yInc;             // scrolling increments
   int i,t;                   // a few needed variables

   // Variables for mortgage calculations
   double Balance,Payment,Interest,Amortized;
   double TInterest,Temp1,NewRate;
   double FPayment,FInterest,FAmortized;
   double FBalance,FTInterest;

   // set your mortgage amounts below
   double Principal=8000.0;   // amount of loan
   double Rate=10.5;          // yearly interest
   int Term=5;                // terms in years
   int PayYear=12;            // payments per year
   // set your mortgage amounts above

   switch (messg) {
     case WM_CREATE:
       // handle to client area device context
       hdc=GetDC (hWnd);
       // font dimensions from the text metrics structure
       GetTextMetrics (hdc, &tm);
       xChWidth=tm.tmAveCharWidth;
       yChHeight=tm.tmHeight+tm.tmExternalLeading;
       // release device context.
       ReleaseDC (hWnd,hdc);
       return 0;

     case WM_SIZE:   // get the dimensions of the client area.
```

```
        yClientView=HIWORD (lParam);
        xClientView=LOWORD (lParam);
        // set the maximum vertical scrolling position
        yMax=LINES;
        // check that the current vertical scrolling position
        // does not exceed the maximum
        yPos=min (yPos, yMax);
        // adjust vertical scrolling range and scroll box
        // position for the new yMax and yPos
        si.cbSize=sizeof(si);
        si.fMask=SIF_ALL;
        si.nMin=0;
        si.nMax=yMax;
        si.nPage=yClientView/yChHeight;
        si.nPos=yPos;
        SetScrollInfo(hWnd,SB_VERT,&si,TRUE);
        // set the maximum horizontal scrolling position.
        xMax=HORIZONTAL;
        // check that the horizontal scrolling position
        // does not exceed the maximum
        xPos=min (xPos,xMax);
        // adjust the horizontal scrolling range and scroll box
        // position for the new xMax and xPos
        si.cbSize=sizeof(si);
        si.fMask=SIF_ALL;
        si.nMin=0;
        si.nMax=xMax;
        si.nPage=xClientView/xChWidth;
        si.nPos=xPos;
        SetScrollInfo(hWnd,SB_HORZ,&si,TRUE);
        return 0;

        case WM_HSCROLL:
        switch(LOWORD (wParam))
        {
          // clicked space left of thumb
          case SB_PAGELEFT:
            xInc=-28;
            break;
          // clicked space right of thumb
          case SB_PAGERIGHT:
            xInc=28;
            break;
          // clicked left arrow
          case SB_LINELEFT:
            xInc=-1;
            break;
          // clicked right arrow
          case SB_LINERIGHT:
            xInc=1;
```

```
      break;
    // dragged the thumb
    case SB_THUMBTRACK:
      xInc=HIWORD(wParam)-xPos;
      break;
    default:
      xInc=0;
  }
  // check to see if scrolling increment takes
  // scrolling position out of scrolling range
  if (xInc=max (-xPos,min (xInc, xMax-xPos)))
  {
    xPos+=xInc;
    ScrollWindowEx (hWnd,-xChWidth * xInc,0,
        (CONST RECT *) NULL,(CONST RECT *) NULL,
        (HRGN) NULL,(LPRECT) NULL,SW_INVALIDATE);
    si.cbSize=sizeof(si);
    si.fMask=SIF_POS;
    si.nPos=xPos;
    SetScrollInfo(hWnd,SB_HORZ,&si,TRUE);
    UpdateWindow(hWnd);
    InvalidateRect(hWnd,NULL,TRUE);
  }
  return 0;

case WM_VSCROLL:
  switch(LOWORD (wParam))
  {
    // clicked the space above the thumb
    case SB_PAGEUP:
      yInc=min(-1,-yClientView/yChHeight);
      break;
    // clicked the space below the thumb
    case SB_PAGEDOWN:
      yInc=max(1,yClientView/yChHeight);
      break;
    // clicked top arrow
    case SB_LINEUP:
      yInc=-1;
      break;
    // clicked bottom arrow
    case SB_LINEDOWN:
      yInc=1;
      break;
    // dragged the thumb
    case SB_THUMBTRACK:
      yInc=HIWORD(wParam)-yPos;
      break;
    default:
      yInc=0;
```

```
      }
      // check to see if scrolling increment takes
      // scrolling position out of scrolling range
      if (yInc=max(-yPos,min(yInc,yMax - yPos)))
      {
        yPos+=yInc;
        ScrollWindowEx(hWnd,0,-yChHeight * yInc,
              (CONST RECT *) NULL,(CONST RECT *) NULL,
              (HRGN) NULL,(LPRECT) NULL,SW_INVALIDATE);
        si.cbSize=sizeof(si);
        si.fMask=SIF_POS;
        si.nPos=yPos;
        SetScrollInfo(hWnd,SB_VERT,&si,TRUE);
        UpdateWindow(hWnd);
        InvalidateRect(hWnd,NULL,TRUE);
      }
      return 0;

    case WM_PAINT:
      hdc=BeginPaint(hWnd,&ps);

      t=0;
      TInterest=0.0;
      NewRate=Rate/100.00;
      Temp1=pow(NewRate/PayYear+1,PayYear*Term);
      Payment=NewRate*Principal/PayYear/(1-1/Temp1);
      Balance=Principal;

      // prepare to print table headers
      ostrstream(szBuffer,200) << "PERIOD" << '\t'
                               << "PAYMENT" << '\t'
                               << "INTEREST" << '\t'
                               << "AMORTIZED" << '\t'
                               << "BALANCE" << '\t' << '\t'
                               << "TOTAL INT"
                               << endl;
      rc.left=-xChWidth*(xPos);
      rc.top=yChHeight*(t-yPos);
      rc.right=rc.left+1024;
      rc.bottom=rc.top + yChHeight;
      DrawText(hdc,szBuffer,strlen(szBuffer),
             &rc,DT_EXPANDTABS);

      // prepare to print table data
      for(i=1;i<=Term*PayYear;i++) {
        t++;
        Interest=Balance*NewRate/12;
        FPayment=((long) (Payment*100.005))/100.0;
        FInterest=((long) (Interest*100.005))/100.0;
        Amortized=Payment-Interest;
```

```
        FAmortized=((long) (Amortized*100.005))/100.0;
        Balance-=Amortized;
        FBalance=((long) (Balance*100.005))/100.0;
        TInterest+=Interest;
        FTInterest=((long) (TInterest*100.005))/100.0;
        ostrstream(szBuffer,200) << i << '\t'
                                 << FPayment << '\t' << '\t'
                                 << FInterest << '\t' << '\t'
                                 << FAmortized << '\t' << '\t'
                                 << FBalance << '\t' << '\t'
                                 << FTInterest << endl;
        rc.left=-xChWidth*(xPos);
        rc.top=yChHeight*(t-yPos);
        rc.right=rc.left+1024;
        rc.bottom=rc.top + yChHeight;
        DrawText(hdc,szBuffer,strlen(szBuffer),
                 &rc,DT_EXPANDTABS);
      }

      ValidateRect(hWnd,NULL);
      EndPaint(hWnd,&ps);
      return 0;

    case WM_DESTROY:
      PostQuitMessage(0);
      return 0;

    default:
      return(DefWindowProc(hWnd,messg,wParam,lParam));
      return 0;
  }
  return 0;
}
```

This application generates a mortgage amortization table and prints it to the window. Because of the size of such tables, horizontal and vertical scroll bars are often necessary. In this application, the initial loan values are part of the application. These include the principal, interest rate, term, and number of payments per year. In Chapter 11, you will learn how to use dialog boxes to allow users to enter data interactively.

For this example, a loan of $8,000 is taken for a 5-year period. The interest rate is 10.5%, and 12 payments are made each year. The program will list the payment period, the payment amount, the interest charge for each payment, the amortized amount, the loan balance, and the total interest paid to date. All of these values are calculated using standard mathematical equations. The treatment of such equations is a topic covered in many business math and other financial books. (Remember, under certain circumstances, mortgage interest is still deductible on your income-tax statement!)

> **note**
>
> As you may have noticed, this program uses some heavy-duty C++ formatting. At the top of the application, *strstrea.h* header file is included. If you need to study C++ formatting, we recommend reading *Visual C++ Complete Reference*, by Pappas and Murray, published by Osborne/McGraw-Hill. This book discusses C++ formatting in detail.

The purpose of this program is to give you an additional application that is built around the framework of a practical example. Once you master the Windows concepts in later chapters, you may want to return to this application and study the code more thoroughly. However, let us take a look at the code you are familiar with.

Examining the Application File (loan.cpp)

Study the code in the loan.cpp listing and satisfy yourself that you understand how scroll bar action is controlled in this example. You will notice that this particular section of code is very similar to the scroll.cpp scroll bar example discussed at the beginning of this chapter.

The loan amortization calculations make up the heart of this application's code. Let's start by looking at the data that will be used for this particular loan calculation. You can easily change these initial values to fit your particular needs.

For example, you may wish to take out a loan for $20,000 to buy that new Pentium 600 MHz computer. How much would your payments be each month if you could obtain a loan at 12.5% over a 4-year period? To do this you'll have to change the initial values specified in this program.

```
// set your mortgage amounts below
double Principal=8000.0;   // amount of loan
double Rate=10.5;          // yearly interest
int Term=5;                // terms in years
int PayYear=12;            // payments per year
// set your mortgage amounts above
```

As you examine the loan.cpp listing, you'll see that the callback function, **WndProc()**, processes WM_CREATE, WM_SIZE, WM_HSCROLL, WM_VSCROLL, and WM_PAINT messages. From earlier examples, you should be comfortable with the actions that are taking place in the WM_CREATE, WM_SIZE, WM_HSCROLL, and WM_VSCROLL sections. These sections contain the code for what has become a rather standard way of controlling scroll bar actions. It is the WM_PAINT message handler that is adding a unique flavor to this application.

THE WM_PAINT MESSAGE HANDLER

The code contained in the WM_PAINT message handler makes all of the loan calculations for the application. Initial amortization values, including the monthly payment, are calculated first.

```
t=0;
TInterest=0.0;
NewRate=Rate/100.00;
Temp1=pow(NewRate/PayYear+1,PayYear*Term);
Payment=NewRate*Principal/PayYear/(1-1/Temp1);
Balance=Principal;
```

Next, C++ ostrstream is used to store the amortization chart title in the buffer, *szBuffer*.

```
// prepare to print table headers
ostrstream(szBuffer,200) << "PERIOD" << '\t'
                        << "PAYMENT" << '\t'
                        << "INTEREST" << '\t'
                        << "AMORTIZED" << '\t'
                        << "BALANCE" << '\t' << '\t'
                        << "TOTAL INT"
                        << endl;
```

This table header information is sent to the screen by determining the characteristics of the rectangle (rc) into which the text is to be drawn. Notice that the rectangle's dimensions are determined by the positions of the scroll bars.

```
rc.left=-xChWidth*(xPos);
rc.top=yChHeight*(t-yPos);
rc.right=rc.left+1024;
rc.bottom=rc.top + yChHeight;
```

The **DrawText()** function is used to draw each line of information to the window. This function is very useful for producing formatted columns, and it warrants additional study.

```
DrawText(hdc,szBuffer,strlen(szBuffer),
         &rc,DT_EXPANDTABS);
```

The **DrawText()** function has five parameters. The handle, hdc, is the handle of the device context. The second parameter, *szBuffer*, is the address of the string to draw. The third parameter is simply the string length. The fourth parameter is the address of the rectangular structure, with formatting dimensions. The final parameter is used for a variety of text-drawing flags. The values for this flag are listed in Table 5.4.

The **DrawText()** function, in this application, draws formatted text into the specified rectangle. For this example the scroll bar positions help determine the rectangle's dimensions. Most importantly, for applications that require tabular data columns, the **DrawText()** function formats text by expanding tabs

Table 5.4 DrawText() formatting characteristics.

Value	Use
DT_BOTTOM	Used to justify the text to the bottom of the rectangle. This value must be combined with DT_SINGLELINE.
DT_CALCRECT	Finds the width and height of the rectangle. If there are multiple lines of text, it uses the width of the rectangle pointed to by the *lpRect* parameter. The base of the rectangle is extended to bound the last line of text. If there is only one line of text, it changes the right side of the rectangle so that it bounds the last character in the line.
DT_CENTER	Used to center text horizontally in the rectangle.
DT_EDITCONTROL	Duplicates the text-displaying characteristics of a multiline edit control. Here the average character width is calculated in the same manner as for an edit control. The function does not display a partially visible last line.
DT_END_ELLIPSIS or DT_PATH_ELLIPSIS	Used to replace part of the given string with ellipses, in order that the result fit into the given rectangle. The DT_MODIFYSTRING flag must be used for modification to take place. DT_END_ELLIPSIS can be used to replace characters at the end of the string. DT_PATH_ELLIPSIS can be used to replace characters in the middle of the string.
DT_EXPANDTABS	Used to expand tab characters. Eight is the number of default characters per tab.
DT_EXTERNALLEADING	Includes the font external leading in line height.
DT_INTERNAL	The system font is used to calculate text metrics.
DT_LEFT	Used to align text to the left.
DT_MODIFYSTRING	Changes the string to match the displayed text. To be effective the DT_END_ELLIPSIS or DT_PATH_ELLIPSIS flag must also be used.
DT_NOCLIP	Used to draw without clipping.
DT_NOPREFIX	Used to prevent the processing of prefix characters.
DT_RIGHT	Used to align text to the right.

Table 5.4 DrawText() formatting characteristics. (Continued)

Value	Use
DT_RTLREADING	Used for layout in right to left reading order for bi-directional text when the font selected into the *hdc* is a Hebrew or Arabic font. The default is for reading from left to right.
DT_SINGLELINE	Used to draw text on a single line. Carriage returns and linefeeds do not break the line.
DT_TABSTOP	Used to set tab stops. Bits 15.8 (high-or-word) of the *uFormat* parameter give the number of characters for each tab stop. By default the number of characters per tab is eight.
DT_TOP	Used to top-justify text. For single lines only.
DT_VCENTER	Used to center text vertically. For single lines only.
DT_WORDBREAK	Used to break words. Lines are broken between words when a word would extend past the edge of the given rectangle. A carriage return-linefeed sequence can also break a line.
DT_WORD_ELLIPSIS	Used to truncate text that does not fit in the rectangle and adds ellipses.

into appropriate spaces, aligning text (to the left or right or centering it), and breaking text into lines that fit in the specified rectangle. This is why the **DrawText()** function is used in this example instead of the popular **TextOut()** function.

The text-drawing flags permit tight control over the text drawn to the rectangle. In this example, DT_EXPANDTABS is used to expand tab characters. The default number of characters per tab is eight.

Once the table headers are drawn to the screen, numeric values must be calculated. A **for** loop is used to calculate and draw each line of amortization data to the screen. Numerous values must be calculated during each trip around the loop.

```
// prepare to print table data
for(i=1;i<=Term*PayYear;i++) {
  t++;
  Interest=Balance*NewRate/12;
  FPayment=((long) (Payment*100.005))/100.0;
  FInterest=((long) (Interest*100.005))/100.0;
  Amortized=Payment-Interest;
  FAmortized=((long) (Amortized*100.005))/100.0;
```

```
Balance-=Amortized;
FBalance=((long) (Balance*100.005))/100.0;
TInterest+=Interest;
FTInterest=((long) (TInterest*100.005))/100.0;
ostrstream(szBuffer,200) << i << '\t'
                        << FPayment << '\t' << '\t'
                        << FInterest << '\t' << '\t'
                        << FAmortized << '\t' << '\t'
                        << FBalance << '\t' << '\t'
                        << FTInterest << endl;
rc.left=-xChWidth*(xPos);
rc.top=yChHeight*(t-yPos);
rc.right=rc.left+1024;
rc.bottom=rc.top + yChHeight;
DrawText(hdc,szBuffer,strlen(szBuffer),
         &rc,DT_EXPANDTABS);
}
```

Notice the repeated use of the **DrawText()** function while in the **for** loop. Each time the horizontal or vertical tab is set, the screen's text will be redrawn reflecting the new tabular position.

Figure 5-3 shows a typical window displaying this tabular data for a given set of loan values.

All numeric values for a given payment period are packed into the *szBuffer*. **DrawText()** uses this information to maintain column alignment in the table as it is scrolled.

At this point, you're probably acknowledging that tables and text are okay but wondering about graphics. Well, graphics are handled in an almost identical manner. The example in the next chapter will illustrate scrolling techniques on screens with GDI graphics.

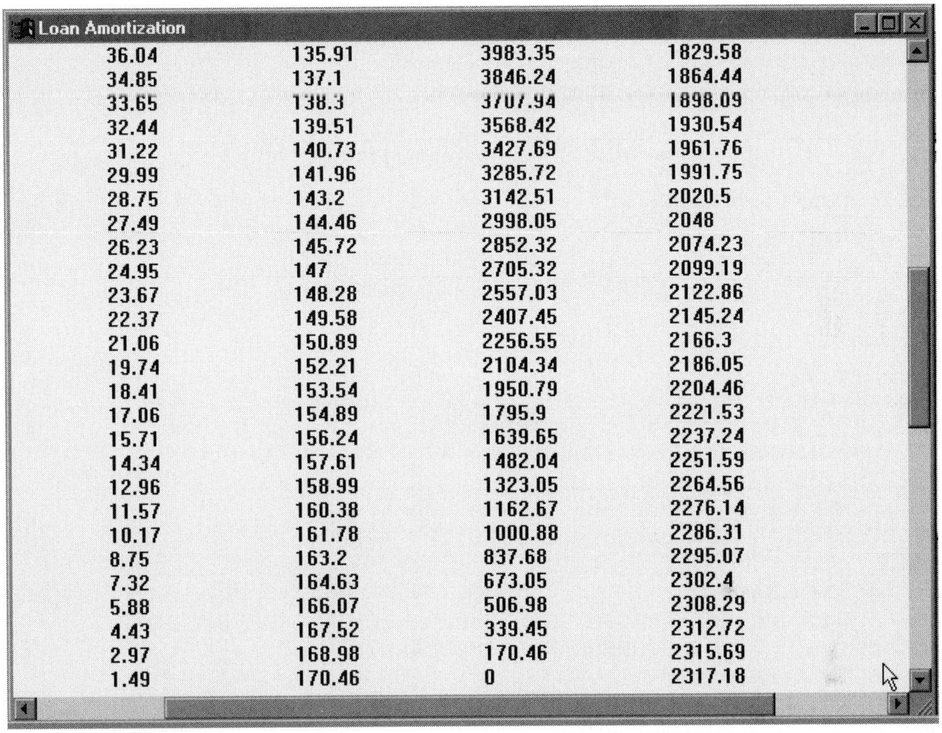

36.04	135.91	3983.35	1829.58
34.85	137.1	3846.24	1864.44
33.65	138.3	3707.94	1898.09
32.44	139.51	3568.42	1930.54
31.22	140.73	3427.69	1961.76
29.99	141.96	3285.72	1991.75
28.75	143.2	3142.51	2020.5
27.49	144.46	2998.05	2048
26.23	145.72	2852.32	2074.23
24.95	147	2705.32	2099.19
23.67	148.28	2557.03	2122.86
22.37	149.58	2407.45	2145.24
21.06	150.89	2256.55	2166.3
19.74	152.21	2104.34	2186.05
18.41	153.54	1950.79	2204.46
17.06	154.89	1795.9	2221.53
15.71	156.24	1639.65	2237.24
14.34	157.61	1482.04	2251.59
12.96	158.99	1323.05	2264.56
11.57	160.38	1162.67	2276.14
10.17	161.78	1000.88	2286.31
8.75	163.2	837.68	2295.07
7.32	164.63	673.05	2302.4
5.88	166.07	506.98	2308.29
4.43	167.52	339.45	2312.72
2.97	168.98	170.46	2315.69
1.49	170.46	0	2317.18

Figure 5-3 *The output from the default values in the loan.cpp application.*

Scroll Bars and Graphics

The final example for this chapter is a graphics application named *graphics.cpp*. The graphics application will show you how to scroll vertically and horizontally in a window with several GDI graphics shapes. To create this application with Visual C++, you'll need to create Win32 application workspace and name it *graphics*. Then add a C++ source code file named *graphics*. The following listing shows the contents that should appear in your source code file.

```
//
// Graphics.cpp
// A scroll bar application that shows how
// to scroll through a simple graphics program.
// Copyright (c) William H. Murray and Chris H. Pappas, 1999
//
#include <windows.h>
```

Chapter 5 • Taking Control of the Window

```c
#define LINES 500         // height of graphics
#define HORIZONTAL 240    // width of graphics
#define XSTEP 60          // graphics step
#define YSTEP 60          // graphics step

LRESULT CALLBACK WndProc(HWND,UINT,WPARAM,LPARAM);

char szProgName[]="ProgName";

int WINAPI WinMain(HINSTANCE hInst,HINSTANCE hPreInst,
                   LPSTR lpszCmdLine,int nCmdShow)
{
  HWND hWnd;
  MSG  lpMsg;
  WNDCLASS wcApp;

  wcApp.lpszClassName=szProgName;
  wcApp.hInstance     =hInst;
  wcApp.lpfnWndProc   =WndProc;
  wcApp.hCursor       =LoadCursor(NULL,IDC_ARROW);
  wcApp.hIcon         =0;
  wcApp.lpszMenuName =0;
  wcApp.hbrBackground=(HBRUSH) GetStockObject(LTGRAY_BRUSH);
  wcApp.style         =CS_HREDRAW|CS_VREDRAW;
  wcApp.cbClsExtra    =0;
  wcApp.cbWndExtra    =0;
  if (!RegisterClass (&wcApp))
     return 0;

  hWnd=CreateWindow(szProgName,"Graphics Scrolling",
                    WS_OVERLAPPEDWINDOW,
                    0,0,639,479,
                     (HWND)NULL,(HMENU)NULL,
                     hInst,(LPSTR)NULL);
  ShowWindow(hWnd,nCmdShow);
  UpdateWindow(hWnd);
  while (GetMessage(&lpMsg,0,0,0)) {
    TranslateMessage(&lpMsg);
    DispatchMessage(&lpMsg);
  }
  return(lpMsg.wParam);
}

LRESULT CALLBACK WndProc(HWND hWnd,UINT messg,
                          WPARAM wParam,LPARAM lParam)
{
  HDC hdc;
  PAINTSTRUCT ps;
  SCROLLINFO si;
```

```
      static int xClientView,yClientView; //dim of client area
      static int xPos,yPos;        // current scrolling positions
      static int xMax,yMax;        // maximum scrolling positions
      int xInc,yInc;               // scrolling increments

    switch (messg) {
      case WM_CREATE:
        // handle to client area device context
        hdc=GetDC (hWnd);
        // release device context.
        ReleaseDC (hWnd,hdc);
        return 0;

      case WM_SIZE:   // get the dimensions of the client area.
        yClientView=HIWORD (lParam);
        xClientView=LOWORD (lParam);
        // set the maximum vertical scrolling position
        yMax=LINES;
        // check that the current vertical scrolling position
        // does not exceed the maximum
        yPos=min (yPos, yMax);
        // adjust vertical scrolling range and scroll box
        // position for the new yMax and yPos
        si.cbSize=sizeof(si);
        si.fMask=SIF_ALL;
        si.nMin=0;
        si.nMax=yMax;
        si.nPage=yClientView/YSTEP;
        si.nPos=yPos;
        SetScrollInfo(hWnd,SB_VERT,&si,TRUE);
        // set the maximum horizontal scrolling position.
        xMax=HORIZONTAL;
        // check that the horizontal scrolling position
        // does not exceed the maximum
        xPos=min (xPos,xMax);
        // adjust the horizontal scrolling range and scroll box
        // position for the new xMax and xPos
        si.cbSize=sizeof(si);
        si.fMask=SIF_ALL;
        si.nMin=0;
        si.nMax=xMax;
        si.nPage=xClientView/XSTEP;
        si.nPos=xPos;
        SetScrollInfo(hWnd,SB_HORZ,&si,TRUE);
        return 0;

        case WM_HSCROLL:
        switch(LOWORD (wParam))
        {
          // clicked space left of thumb
```

```
      case SB_PAGELEFT:
        xInc=-28;
        break;
     // clicked space right of thumb
      case SB_PAGERIGHT:
        xInc=28;
        break;
     // clicked left arrow
      case SB_LINELEFT:
        xInc=-1;
        break;
     // clicked right arrow
      case SB_LINERIGHT:
        xInc=1;
        break;
     // dragged the thumb
      case SB_THUMBTRACK:
        xInc=HIWORD(wParam)-xPos;
        break;
      default:
        xInc=0;
   }
   // check to see if scrolling increment takes
   // scrolling position out of scrolling range
   if (xInc=max (-xPos,min (xInc, xMax-xPos)))
   {
     xPos+=xInc;
     ScrollWindowEx (hWnd,-XSTEP * xInc,0,
            (CONST RECT *) NULL,(CONST RECT *) NULL,
            (HRGN) NULL,(LPRECT) NULL,SW_INVALIDATE);
     si.cbSize=sizeof(si);
     si.fMask=SIF_POS;
     si.nPos=xPos;
     SetScrollInfo(hWnd,SB_HORZ,&si,TRUE);
     UpdateWindow(hWnd);
     InvalidateRect(hWnd,NULL,TRUE);
   }
   return 0;

case WM_VSCROLL:
   switch(LOWORD (wParam))
   {
     // clicked the space above the thumb
     case SB_PAGEUP:
        yInc=min(-1,-yClientView/YSTEP);
        break;
     // clicked the space below the thumb
     case SB_PAGEDOWN:
        yInc=max(1,yClientView/YSTEP);
        break;
```

```
      // clicked top arrow
      case SB_LINEUP:
        yInc=-1;
        break;
      // clicked bottom arrow
      case SB_LINEDOWN:
        yInc=1;
        break;
      // dragged the thumb
      case SB_THUMBTRACK:
        yInc=HIWORD(wParam)-yPos;
        break;
      default:
        yInc=0;
    }
    // check to see if scrolling increment takes
    // scrolling position out of scrolling range
    if (yInc=max(-yPos,min(yInc,yMax - yPos)))
    {
      yPos+=yInc;
      ScrollWindowEx(hWnd,0,-YSTEP * yInc,
              (CONST RECT *) NULL,(CONST RECT *) NULL,
              (HRGN) NULL,(LPRECT) NULL,SW_INVALIDATE);
      si.cbSize=sizeof(si);
      si.fMask=SIF_POS;
      si.nPos=yPos;
      SetScrollInfo(hWnd,SB_VERT,&si,TRUE);
      UpdateWindow(hWnd);
      InvalidateRect(hWnd,NULL,TRUE);
    }
    return 0;

  case WM_PAINT:
    hdc=BeginPaint(hWnd,&ps);

    Rectangle(hdc,50-xPos,100-yPos,200-xPos,300-yPos);
    Ellipse(hdc,350-xPos,300-yPos,800-xPos,600-yPos);

    ValidateRect(hWnd,NULL);
    EndPaint(hWnd,&ps);
    return 0;

  case WM_DESTROY:
    PostQuitMessage(0);
    return 0;

  default:
    return(DefWindowProc(hWnd,messg,wParam,lParam));
    return 0;
  }
  return 0;
}
```

If you have been studying the previous examples in this chapter, you'll probably notice a large amount of familiar code. The **WndProc()** function, for example, still uses message handlers for create, size, vertical scroll, horizontal scroll, and paint messages. The WM_CREATE, WM_SIZE, WM_HSCROLL, and WM_VSCROLL message handlers process scroll bar information just like they did for all of the previous examples—with one exception. When working with graphics, you are not usually concerned with text characteristics. That is why there is no need for the **TEXTMETRICS** structure or for obtaining information on character heights and widths. As a programmer, you can decide the scrolling increments that best suit your application's needs.

Examining the Application File (graphics.cpp)

For this application, the following constants were declared at the start of the code:

```
#define LINES 500          // height of graphics
#define HORIZONTAL 240     // width of graphics
#define XSTEP 60           // graphics step
#define YSTEP 60           // graphics step
```

These constants are used to define the width and height of the scroll area and the step size when the scroll bars are activated. You might want to do a little experimenting with different values to observe how the application's window is affected.

You'll see that most of the code is redundant to the code in earlier examples. The real difference takes place when WM_PAINT messages are received.

SCROLLING IMAGES UNDER WM_PAINT

You have probably already guessed that scrolling graphics images is achieved in the same manner as the text we have been *drawing* to the window. The emphasis is on the word drawing. Under windows text, GDI graphics and bitmap images are drawn to the window. If that is true (and it is), there should be no difference in the way text and graphics are handled.

Our message handlers have basically sent a request to WM_PAINT to repaint the screen each time a scroll bar message is received. The WM_PAINT message handler has simply updated the starting position of the text it is to draw and repaints the screen. With a GDI graphics primitive, applications proceed in the same fashion. Examine these two GDI graphics primitives:

```
Rectangle(hdc,50-xPos,100-yPos,200-xPos,300-yPos);
Ellipse(hdc,350-xPos,300-yPos,800-xPos,600-yPos);
```

They simply draw the rectangle and ellipse at a fixed screen position, adjusted by the current values in the *xPos* and *yPos* variables. The values in the *xPos* and *yPos* variables are passed to this message handler by the WM_HSCROLL and WM_VSCROLL message handlers.

Scroll Bars and Graphics 229

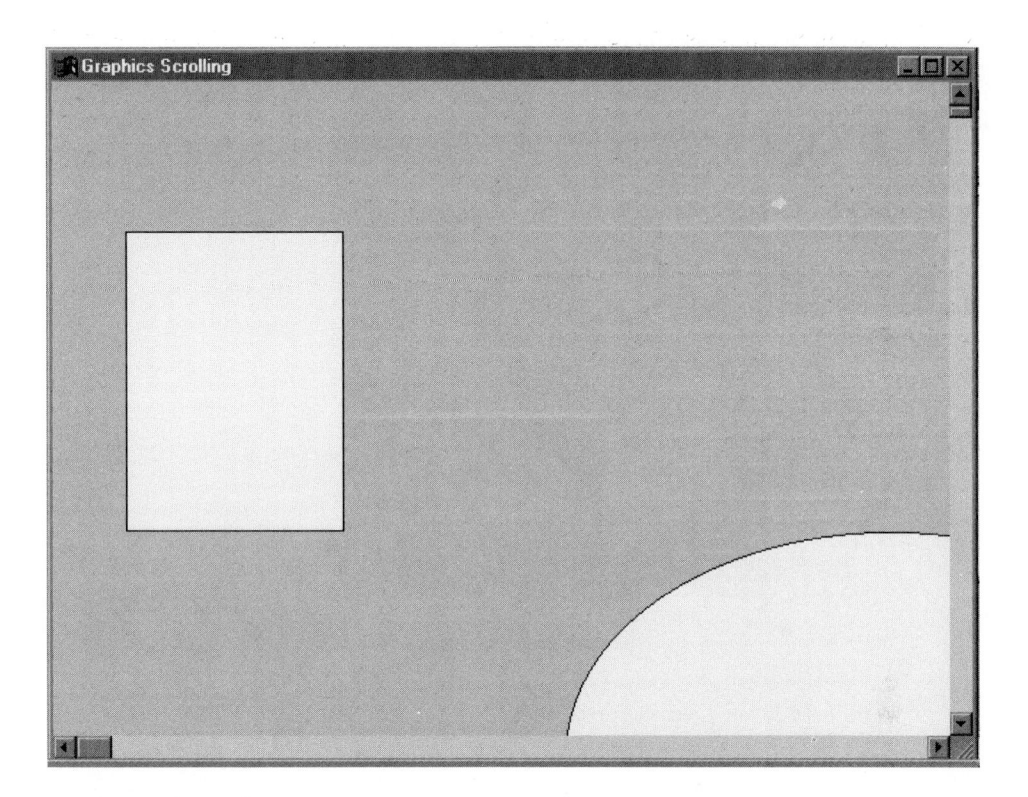

Figure 5-4 *A graphics example before scrolling.*

That's all that is needed! If you develop a graphics application that might need to be scrolled, simply include the scroll bar information as you have seen in the previous example.

Figure 5-4 shows the initial graphics window with a rectangle and partial ellipse on the screen.

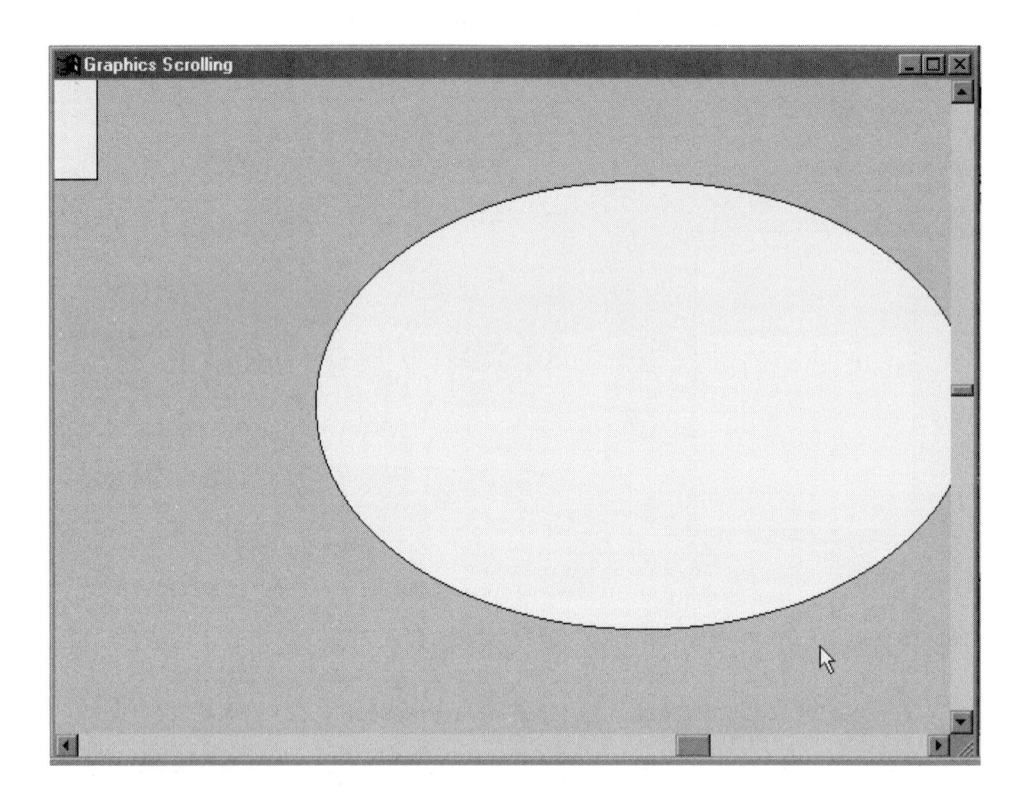

Figure 5-5 *The position of the graphics image is adjusted with the vertical and horizontal scroll bars.*

Figure 5-5 shows the same example after the scroll bar thumbs have been moved to a different location.

Once you learn how to include bitmap resources in an application, you'll find that they can be scrolled just as easily as graphics created with GDI drawing primitives.

What's Next?

In this chapter, you learned how to implement several important features of Windows that control how documents are viewed in a window. With the programming knowledge you gained from Chapters 3 and 4 combined with this chapter, you are truly on your way to a complete understanding of the Windows environment.

In the next section of this book, you'll investigate many important resources that are available to the Windows programmer. These resources include fonts, icons, cursors, bitmaps, sound, and so on. As you work with these resources, you'll always find yourself returning the programming fundamentals that you learned in the first five chapters of this book.

S I X

Using Fonts

Appearances count as much for text displays in a window as they do for graphics images. Printer or videotext displays that look as if they have the "zaggies" leave you wondering why you paid so much for a particular software package.

This chapter will teach you about Windows font capabilities that will work across Windows platforms. You'll learn how to incorporate the latest font technology in your applications. Font terminology, definitions, and how to utilize new font features available with TrueType fonts and Windows will be fully explained. With this new knowledge, your text appearance will improve dramatically.

Windows Font Definitions

Before looking at the various Windows font functions that can be used in your applications, let's examine some basic font terminology. First, a typeface is a basic character design. As such, it is defined by stroke width and serifs (serifs are the small lines used to finish off main strokes, such as at the top and bottom of the uppercase letters *M* or *T*). Some typefaces are sans serif—in other words, they have no serifs.

A font is defined as a complete set of characters of the same typeface and size, including letters, punctuation marks, and other symbols. The size of a font is measured in points. For example, a 12-point TrueType Times New Roman font is different from a 12-point TrueType Times New Roman italic font. Likewise, a 14-point TrueType Times New Roman font is different from a 14-point TrueType Arial font. A point is the smallest unit of measure used in typography.

There are 72 points in an inch and 12 points in a pica. A pica is a unit of measure in typography; a pica equals approximately 1/6 inch.

Mastering all the font capabilities that Windows offers could take a very long time. To make life easier, many of these capabilities are defined in several frequently referenced structures; **TEXTMETRIC**, **NEWTEXTMETRIC**, and **LOGFONT**. These structures can be found in the Windows wingdi.h header file shipped with your Visual C++ compiler. Take a minute to examine this file and look at these declarations. This will give you a feeling for the richness of character-display possibilities.

Font Constants

The following font constants are also included in the wingdi.h header file. Here is a portion of that file listing for your convenience. It might be handy to print a complete hard copy of wingdi.h for future reference.

```
/* Font Weights */
#define FW_DONTCARE         0
#define FW_THIN             100
#define FW_EXTRALIGHT       200
#define FW_LIGHT            300
#define FW_NORMAL           400
#define FW_MEDIUM           500
#define FW_SEMIBOLD         600
#define FW_BOLD             700
#define FW_EXTRABOLD        800
#define FW_HEAVY            900
#define FW_ULTRALIGHT       FW_EXTRALIGHT
#define FW_REGULAR          FW_NORMAL
#define FW_DEMIBOLD         FW_SEMIBOLD
#define FW_ULTRABOLD        FW_EXTRABOLD
#define FW_BLACK            FW_HEAVY

/* CharSet values */
#define ANSI_CHARSET        0
#define DEFAULT_CHARSET     1
#define SYMBOL_CHARSET      2
#define SHIFTJIS_CHARSET    128
#define HANGEUL_CHARSET     129
#define HANGUL_CHARSET      129
#define GB2312_CHARSET      134
#define CHINESEBIG5_CHARSET 136
#define OEM_CHARSET         255
#if(WINVER >= 0x0400)
#define JOHAB_CHARSET       130
#define HEBREW_CHARSET      177
#define ARABIC_CHARSET      178
#define GREEK_CHARSET       161
#define TURKISH_CHARSET     162
```

```
#define VIETNAMESE_CHARSET       163
#define THAI_CHARSET             222
#define EASTEUROPE_CHARSET       238
#define RUSSIAN_CHARSET          204
#define MAC_CHARSET              77
#define BALTIC_CHARSET           186

/* OutPrecision values */
#define OUT_DEFAULT_PRECIS           0
#define OUT_STRING_PRECIS            1
#define OUT_CHARACTER_PRECIS         2
#define OUT_STROKE_PRECIS            3
#define OUT_TT_PRECIS                4
#define OUT_DEVICE_PRECIS            5
#define OUT_RASTER_PRECIS            6
#define OUT_TT_ONLY_PRECIS           7
#define OUT_OUTLINE_PRECIS           8
#define OUT_SCREEN_OUTLINE_PRECIS    9

/* ClipPrecision values */
#define CLIP_DEFAULT_PRECIS      0
#define CLIP_CHARACTER_PRECIS    1
#define CLIP_STROKE_PRECIS       2
#define CLIP_MASK                0xf
#define CLIP_LH_ANGLES           (1<<4)
#define CLIP_TT_ALWAYS           (2<<4)
#define CLIP_EMBEDDED            (8<<4)

/* Quality values */
#define DEFAULT_QUALITY          0
#define DRAFT_QUALITY            1
#define PROOF_QUALITY            2
#if(WINVER >= 0x0400)
#define NONANTIALIASED_QUALITY   3
#define ANTIALIASED_QUALITY      4

/* PitchAndFamily pitch values (low 4 bits) */
#define DEFAULT_PITCH            0
#define FIXED_PITCH              1
#define VARIABLE_PITCH           2
#if(WINVER >= 0x0400)
#define MONO_FONT                8

/* PitchAndFamily values (high 4 bits */
#define FF_DONTCARE      (0<<4)
#define FF_ROMAN         (1<<4)
#define FF_SWISS         (2<<4)
#define FF_MODERN        (3<<4)
#define FF_SCRIPT        (4<<4)
#define FF_DECORATIVE    (5<<4)
```

Chapter 6 • Using Fonts

```
/* Stock fonts for use with GetStockObject() */
#define OEM_FIXED_FONT      10
#define ANSI_FIXED_FONT     11
#define ANSI_VAR_FONT       12
#define SYSTEM_FONT         13
#define DEVICE_DEFAULT_FONT 14
#define DEFAULT_PALETTE     15
#define SYSTEM_FIXED_FONT   16

/* tmPitchAndFamily flags */
#define TMPF_FIXED_PITCH    0x01
#define TMPF_VECTOR         0x02
#define TMPF_DEVICE         0x08
#define TMPF_TRUETYPE       0x04
```

These constants are used as parameter values for various font functions and structures. For example, in the applications that follow, you will learn how to set the weight, character set, quality, etc., of fonts with these values.

The TEXTMETRIC Structure

The **TEXTMETRIC** structure, used in earlier Windows versions, has been redefined to include new data types. **TEXTMETRIC** is now associated with either **TEXTMETRICA** or **TEXTMETRICW**. These two structures are necessary in order to accommodate both ANSI ASCII and UNICODE programming. **TEXTMETRICA** is for ANSI ASCII, and **TEXTMETRICW** is used in UNICODE applications. Likewise, the **NEWTEXTMETRIC** structure is associated with **NEWTEXTMETRICA** or **NEWTEXTMETRICW**. **NEWTEXTMETRICA** is for ANSI ASCII and **NEWTEXTMETRICW** is used in UNICODE applications. These data structures are also listed in wingdi.h. As an example, examine the **NEWTEXTMETRICA** structure.

```
typedef struct tagNEWTEXTMETRICA
{
    LONG    tmHeight;
    LONG    tmAscent;
    LONG    tmDescent;
    LONG    tmInternalLeading;
    LONG    tmExternalLeading;
    LONG    tmAveCharWidth;
    LONG    tmMaxCharWidth;
    LONG    tmWeight;
    LONG    tmOverhang;
    LONG    tmDigitizedAspectX;
    LONG    tmDigitizedAspectY;
    BYTE    tmFirstChar;
    BYTE    tmLastChar;
    BYTE    tmDefaultChar;
    BYTE    tmBreakChar;
```

```
    BYTE    tmItalic;
    BYTE    tmUnderlined;
    BYTE    tmStruckOut;
    BYTE    tmPitchAndFamily;
    BYTE    tmCharSet;
    DWORD   ntmFlags;
    UINT    ntmSizeEM;
    UINT    ntmCellHeight;
    UINT    ntmAvgWidth;
} NEWTEXTMETRICA, *PNEWTEXTMETRICA, NEAR *NPNEWTEXTMETRICA, FAR
*LPNEWTEXTMETRICA;
```

This structure and its cousins form the foundation for most font manipulation work in Windows. The last four structure members are used specifically by TrueType fonts. Other than this, **TEXTMETRICA** and **NEWTEXTMETRICA** are identical.

The most frequently used values for specifying a font are identified with the following structure parameters: *tmHeight, tmAscent, tmDescent, tmInternalLeading, tmExternalLeading,* and *tmAveCharWidth*. Figure 6-1 shows how these fields are used to define a basic font.

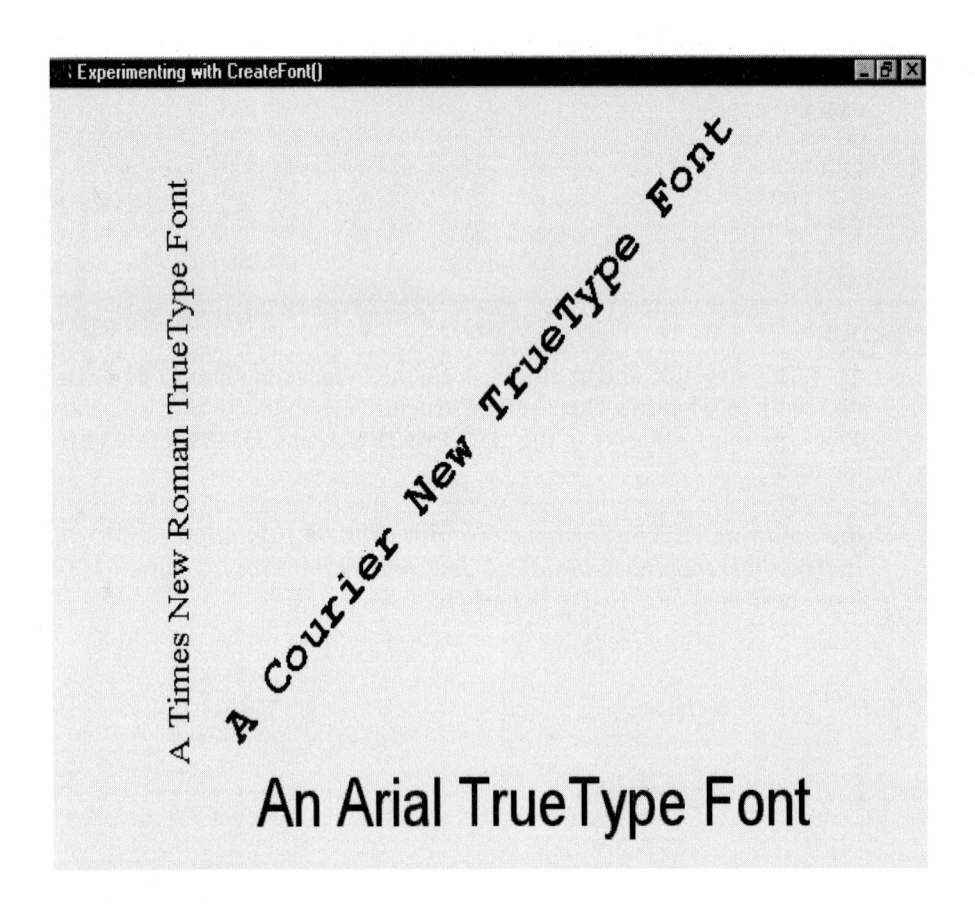

Figure 6-1 *Fonts are defined using various fields.*

The LOGFONTA *Structure*

In addition to the various **TEXTMETRIC** structures, the **LOGFONTA** data structure is also frequently used in applications. This structure makes creating logical fonts a very easy process. Here is a copy of the **LOGFONTA** structure:

```
typedef struct tagLOGFONTA
{
    LONG     lfHeight;
    LONG     lfWidth;
    LONG     lfEscapement;
    LONG     lfOrientation;
    LONG     lfWeight;
    BYTE     lfItalic;
    BYTE     lfUnderline;
    BYTE     lfStrikeOut;
```

```
    BYTE        lfCharSet;
    BYTE        lfOutPrecision;
    BYTE        lfClipPrecision;
    BYTE        lfQuality;
    BYTE        lfPitchAndFamily;
    CHAR        lfFaceName[LF_FACESIZE];
} LOGFONTA, *PLOGFONTA, NEAR *NPLOGFONTA, FAR *LPLOGFONTA;
```

The members in this structure allow the manipulation of certain unique font characteristics. For example, it is possible to specify the rotation of a character or the rotation of an entire string by changing the *lfOrientation* or *lfEscapement* parameters. This ability is important for charts and graphs, where both vertical and horizontal labels are needed. The **LOGFONTW** data structure is used for UNICODE applications and can also be found in wingdi.h.

The Font Character Cell

Table 6.1 describes the basic elements of a font character.

Table 6.1 Basic Elements of a Font.

Point of Measurement	Description
Ascent	The distance in character cell rows from the character cell baseline to the top of the character cell.
Baseline	The base on which characters stand. Lowercase letters such as *p* and *q* have descenders that extend below the baseline.
Descent	The distance in character cell rows from the character cell baseline to the bottom of the character cell.
Height	The height of a character cell row.
Origin	The upper left corner of the character cell. It is used as a point of reference when a character is output to a particular device or display.
Width	The width of a character cell column.

Font characters are much more complex than what the symbols themselves imply when viewed on an output device. The Windows graphics device interface (GDI) places each symbol within a rectangular region called a *character cell*. Each cell consists of a predefined number of rows and columns and is described by six specific measurement points: ascent, baseline, descent, height, origin, and width. The meanings of some of these terms are obvious, although others are not quite as clear. A little knowledge about the field of typography will help your understanding.

Within the **NEWTEXTMETRICA** and **LOGFONTA** data structures, there are some obvious parameters, such as *lfItalic* and *lfUnderline*. However, what does *tmInternalLeading* do? The *tmInternalLeading* parameter defines how much space is to be inserted within the character cell for characters such as accents, umlauts, and tildes in foreign language character sets. Similarly, *tmExternalLeading* defines how much white space is to be inserted between the top and bottom of a character cell in adjacent rows.

The *lfPitchAndFamily* parameter is used to set the number of characters from a particular font that will fit in a single inch. In Windows, this is either fixed pitch or variable pitch. (See the description of "Font Widths," later in this chapter for more detail.)

Together, *tmDigitizedAspectX* and *tmDigitizedAspectY* are used whenever a raster font is created (raster fonts are also discussed later in this chapter). A font's aspect ratio is based on the relationship between the width and height of a device's pixel. Together, *tmDigitizedAspectX* and *tmDigitizedAspectY* represent the ideal X and Y aspect ratio for each individual font, as supplied by the GDI. (The X and Y aspect ratio will be explained later.)

The *tmOverhang* parameter is very important. This parameter tells the GDI to synthesize a font. Whenever an application requests a font that is unavailable on a device, such as the monitor or printer, the GDI creates one. The difference in width (the amount of extra character cell columns) between a string created with the normal font and a string created with the synthesized font is called the overhang.

Font Basics

Remember that a font represents a complete set of characters from one specific typeface, all with the same specific size and style. (The style could be italics or boldface.) Usually, the system owns all the font resources and shares them with the application. Fonts are not usually compiled into the final executable version of a program. An exception to this is TrueType's ability to be embed fonts within a document. Embedded TrueType fonts come in two varieties, read-only and read/write. In the first case, documents can contain the font but users cannot edit the document. The second case allows full editing options. Microsoft's TrueType Font Packs are read/write. Certainly, embedded fonts offer a greater degree of flexibility to the programmer and end user alike.

Applications treat fonts as other drawing objects, such as circles and rectangles; therefore, they are manipulated through the use of handles. An application will create a font and can repeatedly associate the font with different contexts before deleting the font.

> **note:** The **AnsiToOem()** and **OemToAnsi()** functions are obsolete. For compatibility with 16-bit versions of Windows, this function is implemented as a macro that calls the **OemToChar()** function, which should be used for new Win32-based applications.

Font Widths

Fonts in which all characters are the same width are called *fixed fonts*. Fixed fonts make alignment easier, as narrow characters such as *i*, occupy the same space as do wide characters, such as *W*. They also make it easier to center strings in graphs and charts.

On the other hand, variable-width fonts, also called *proportionally spaced fonts* and *variable-pitch fonts*, allocate differing amounts of space to each character. This occurs in the window or printer just as it would if you were writing them by hand. In a proportionally spaced font, the *i* occupies much less space than does the *W*.

One of the easiest ways to spot a fixed font is to locate the letters *i* and *W* or *M*. In a fixed font, the uppercase *W* or *M* is just as wide as the lowercase *i*. Windows uses variable-width fonts by default.

Automatic Leading and Kerning

Leading refers to the amount of vertical space, measured in points between the baselines of two lines of text. Remember that the baseline is the invisible line on which letters set. A descender is the part of a lowercase letter that extends below this invisible line. Descenders appear in the lowercase letters *g* and *y*, for example.

Kerning means to subtract space between certain letter combinations. For example, when an uppercase *T* and lowercase *o* are adjacent characters in words such as *To* and *Toward*, kerning moves the pair closer together. Kerning creates a visually consistent image. Windows is capable of querying a font's metrics or characteristics and adjusting the output accordingly.

OEM Versus ANSI Character Sets

Manufacturers sometimes include their own definitions for character sets. These definitions are called original equipment manufacturer (OEM) definitions. OEM definitions are different from the American National Standards Institute (ANSI) character set definitions, which in turn differ from IBM's extended character set definitions. This jumble of definitions can create a problem when mapping certain graphics symbols, mathematic symbols, and foreign letters. Although it is beyond the scope of this chapter, Windows does provide for character set redefinition by means of the **AnsiToOem()** and **OemToAnsi()** functions.

Logical Versus Physical Fonts

In one respect, you could think of a logical font as a means of satisfying your wildest dream of font manipulation. A logical font, for example, can allow you to specify a character font that consists of widely spaced bold italics characters, even if that font is not actually available. A physical font is the actual device context translation of that specification. It is the Windows-supplied match that comes closest to your request. Many of the GDI character functions have been written to provide as close a match as possible between the two.

Vector, Raster, and TrueType Fonts

In addition to determining whether a font is supplied by Windows or by the device, whether it is in ANSI format, and so on, you will need to know whether it is a vector, raster, or a TrueType font.

A vector font, frequently called a *stroke font* (most frequently used by plotters), defines each character as a set of points connected by lines. Vector fonts can be easily scaled. The drawback to vector fonts occurs with very small fonts and very large fonts. Small fonts tend to cramp the lines together, and large fonts suffer from large characters with thin lines.

A raster font is created in much the same way that a dot matrix printer prints, as a miniature bitmapped image. Scaling, though limited, can be achieved by producing multiples of the *bitmap's* lines and columns. Raster fonts suffer from the fact that the images can be scaled only in integer multiples of the original font. This means that what you see in the window may or may not be closely related to what you asked for in the application.

TrueType font technology combines many of the characteristics of vector and raster fonts. TrueType fonts are easily scalable, like vector fonts, but differ in the way their specifications for lines and curves are stored. When creating a TrueType font of a particular scale, information embedded within the font's specification is used to draw the lines and curves. This image is then converted to a miniature bitmapped image, like that used for a raster font. The embedded TrueType information is responsible for adjusting character information to overcome the previously defined weaknesses of vector and raster fonts.

A Scheme for Mapping Fonts

Windows has a very powerful scheme, for non-TrueType font requests that it uses to decide which fonts "match" a user's request. Remember that it is quite possible for an application to select a raster display font that isn't available for a particular printer. The process of selecting the physical font that bears the closest resemblance to the specified logical font is known as *font mapping*.

Basically, the font mapper assigns certain penalty values to physical fonts with characteristics that do not match the characteristics of the specified logical font. The physical font with the lowest penalty total is the one Windows selects. Table 6.2 lists the penalty values from the most to the least severe. The **SelectObject()** function is used to select the physical font (applicant font) that most closely matches the logical font

Table 6.2 Font Mapping Penalty Weights.

Selector	Penalty Weight	Description
CharSets	4	Whenever the character sets do not match, the applicant font is penalized severely.
Pitch	3	Whenever a proportionally pitched font is requested, the applicant font with fixed-pitch is penalized very severely, or vice versa.
Family	3	Whenever the font families do not match, the applicant font is severely penalized.
FaceName	3	Whenever the typeface names do not match, the applicant font is severely penalized.
Height	2	Whenever the applicant font height is less than the requested font, Windows will multiply (up to a factor of 8) the applicant font height to produce a match. A penalty is assessed for any modifications made and for any additional height changes.
Width	2	The same approach is used here as is applied to differences in height.
Weight	1	Whenever the applicant font weight is not what was requested, Windows assigns a penalty.
Slant	1	Whenever the applicant font is not italicized, the applicant font is penalized, or vice versa.
Underline	1	Whenever the applicant font is not underlined, the applicant font is penalized, or vice versa.
StrikeOut	1	Whenever the applicant font is not struck out, the applicant font is penalized, or vice versa.

Font Families

There are several types of fonts available for your Windows applications. From the simplest fonts (default fonts) to the more difficult and complex (custom-designed fonts), Windows provides a very rich type foundry.

System Default Fonts

Windows supplies several standard fonts: System, Terminal, Courier, Helvetica, Modern, Roman, Script, Times Roman. Additionally, TrueType fonts, such as Arial, Courier New, and Times New Roman are also available. These provide a much better WYSIWYG (what-you-see-is-what-you-get) mapping between screen and output device. These resources are installed automatically with Windows and become part of a common environment shared between systems.

Using Printer Fonts

A printer font can be a device font supplied by the printer manufacturer. Printer device fonts are never display fonts. This can create some confusion in regard to certain types of applications. For example, a desktop publishing application might provide a WYSIWYG screen display. The user could then select a raster script font for writing an informal letter. However, to the user's surprise, when the application attempts to print the letter, there is no matching script font available for the printer. The letter might be printed in Courier! Windows always tries to make the best match possible.

If, on the other hand, the user was working with a TrueType font, the letter would be printed as it appears on the screen. This is, of course, the advantage of TrueType font technology.

Font Change Example Programs

In the following section, three applications are developed to illustrate various font, TrueType, and Windows capabilities. The first applications will work directly with the **CreateFont()** function; the remaining applications will use the **CreateFontIndirect()** function. The first application will show you how to print text horizontally and vertically on the screen with two TrueType fonts.

The second application changes the font's point size as it prints a string several times with a TrueType font. The third application will combine information from Chapter 3 (timer information) with the font information you have learned to produce a large digit counter. Before studying these individual applications, let us examine in detail the **CreateFont()** and **CreatFontIndirect()** functions.

The CreateFont() Function

The **CreateFont()** function is of type **HFONT**, as defined in the wingdi.h header file. The syntax for **CreateFont()** is:

```
HFONT CreateFont(Height,Width,Escapement,
         Orientation,Weight,
```

Font Change Example Programs

```
Italic,Underline,StrikeOut,
CharSet,OutputPrecision,
ClipPrecision,Quality,
PitchAndFamily,Facename)
```

With 14 parameters, **CreateFont()** carries quite a bit of baggage. Naturally, each time you make a call to **CreateFont()**, you must provide the specifications for each piece of this baggage (Table 6.3).

Table 6.3 Fourteen parameters of **CreateFont()**.

Parameter	Description
(int) nHeight	Desired font height in logical units
(int) nWidth	Average font width in logical units
(int) nEscapement	Angle (tenths of a degree) for each line written in the font
(int) nOrientation	Angle (tenths of a degree) for each character's baseline
(int) fnWeight	Weight of font (0 to 1000); 400 is normal, 700 is bold
(DWORD) fdwItalic	Italic font
(DWORD) fdwUnderline	Underline font
(DWORD) fdwStrikeOut	Strike-through font (Such a font is sometimes called a redline font.)
(DWORD) fdwCharSet	Character set (ANSI_CHARSET, DEFAULT_CHARSET, OEM_CHARSET, SYMBOL_CHARSET)
(DWORD) fdwOutputPrecision	match the requested specifications (OUT_CHARACTER_PRECIS, OUT_DEFAULT_PRECIS, OUT_DEVICE_PRECIS)

Chapter 6 • Using Fonts

Table 6.3 Fourteen parameters of **CreateFont()**. (Continued)

Parameter	Description
(DWORD) fdwClipPrecision	How to clip characters outside of clipping range (CLIP_CHARACTER_PRECIS, CLIP_DEFAULT_PRECIS, CLIP_ENCAPSULATE, CLIP_LH_ANGLES, CLIP_STROKE_PRECIS, CLIP_MASK, CLIP_TT_ALWAYS)
(DWORD) fdwQuality	How carefully the logical attributes are mapped to the physical font (DEFAULT_QUALITY, DRAFT_QUALITY, PROOF_QUALITY)
(DWORD) fdwPitchAndFamily	Pitch and family of font (DEFAULT_PITCH, FIXED_PITCH, PROOF_QUALITY, FF_DECORATIVE, FF_DONTCARE, FF_MODERN, FF_ROMAN, FF_SCRIPT, FF_SWISS)
(LPCTSTR) lpszFacename	A string pointing to the name of the desired font's typeface

This function selects the logical font from the GDI's pool of physical fonts—that is, **CreateFont()** selects the font whose characteristics most closely match those the developer specified in the function call. Once created, this logical font can be used by any device.

The CreateFontIndirect Function

The **CreateFontIndirect()** function frees the programmer from the baggage of **CreateFont()**. This function creates or modifies a logical font with the characteristics given in the data structure specified by *lpLogFont*. Only those characteristics that are to be changed need be specified.

The syntax is:

```
HFONT CreateFontIndirect(lpLogFont)
```

where *lpLogFont* points to a **LOGFONTA** data structure specified in wingdi.h. The **LOGFONTA** data structure was discussed and shown earlier in this chapter.

The CF Application

The application that follows will illustrate how to use the **CreateFont()** function to print two strings to the screen. One string will be printed horizontally; the other will be printed vertically. One string will be displayed in the TrueType Arial font and the other in the TrueType Times New Roman font.

The cf.cpp application consists of just the source code file. There is no header or resource information for this simple application. Here is the code:

```
//
// cf.cpp
// This application illustrates the use of the
// CreateFont() function.  With this function you
// can incorporate a wide variety of fonts into
// an application and also manipulate various
// font properties.
// Copyright (c) William H. Murray and Chris H. Pappas, 1999
//

#include <windows.h>
#include <string.h>

LRESULT CALLBACK WndProc(HWND,UINT,WPARAM,LPARAM);

char szProgName[]="ProgName";

int WINAPI WinMain(HINSTANCE hInst,HINSTANCE hPreInst,
                   LPSTR lpszCmdLine,int nCmdShow)
{
  HWND hWnd;
  MSG  lpMsg;
  WNDCLASS wcApp;
  wcApp.lpszClassName=szProgName;
  wcApp.hInstance     =hInst;
  wcApp.lpfnWndProc   =WndProc;
  wcApp.hCursor       =LoadCursor(NULL,IDC_ARROW);
  wcApp.hIcon         =0;
  wcApp.lpszMenuName  =0;
  wcApp.hbrBackground=(HBRUSH) GetStockObject(WHITE_BRUSH);
  wcApp.style         =CS_HREDRAW|CS_VREDRAW;
  wcApp.cbClsExtra    =0;
  wcApp.cbWndExtra    =0;
  if (!RegisterClass (&wcApp))
    return 0;
```

```
    hWnd=CreateWindow(szProgName,
                    "Experimenting with CreateFont()",
                    WS_OVERLAPPEDWINDOW,CW_USEDEFAULT,
                    CW_USEDEFAULT,CW_USEDEFAULT,
                    CW_USEDEFAULT,(HWND)NULL,(HMENU)NULL,
                    hInst,(LPSTR)NULL);
    ShowWindow(hWnd,nCmdShow);
    UpdateWindow(hWnd);
    while (GetMessage(&lpMsg,0,0,0)) {
      TranslateMessage(&lpMsg);
      DispatchMessage(&lpMsg);
    }
    return(lpMsg.wParam);
}

LRESULT CALLBACK WndProc(HWND hWnd,UINT messg,
                        WPARAM wParam,LPARAM lParam)
{
    HDC hdc;
    PAINTSTRUCT ps;
    char szXString[]="An Arial TrueType Font";
    char szXYString[]="A Courier New TrueType Font";
    char szYString[]="A Times New Roman TrueType Font";
    HGDIOBJ hNFont,hOFont;

    switch (messg)
    {
      case WM_PAINT:
        hdc=BeginPaint(hWnd,&ps);

        // Print TrueType Horizontal Text to Screen
        // in Arial Font
        hNFont=CreateFont(45,0,0,0,FW_NORMAL,
                        FALSE,FALSE,FALSE,ANSI_CHARSET,
                        OUT_DEFAULT_PRECIS,
                        CLIP_DEFAULT_PRECIS,
                        DEFAULT_QUALITY,
                        34,
                        "Arial");
        hOFont=SelectObject(hdc,hNFont);
        TextOut(hdc,150,400,szXString,strlen(szXString));
        DeleteObject(hOFont);


        // Print TrueType Text 45 degrees to Screen
        // in Times New Roman Font
        hNFont=CreateFont(35,0,450,450,FW_BOLD,
                        FALSE,FALSE,FALSE,
                        ANSI_CHARSET,
                        OUT_DEFAULT_PRECIS,
```

```
                       CLIP_DEFAULT_PRECIS,
                       DEFAULT_QUALITY,
                       18,
                       "Courier New"),
   hOFont=SelectObject(hdc,hNFont);
   TextOut(hdc,120,370,szXYString,strlen(szXYString));
   DeleteObject(hOFont);


   // Print TrueType Vertical Text to Screen
   // in Times New Roman Font
   hNFont=CreateFont(25,0,900,900,FW_NORMAL,
                     FALSE,FALSE,FALSE,
                     ANSI_CHARSET,
                     OUT_DEFAULT_PRECIS,
                     CLIP_DEFAULT_PRECIS,
                     DEFAULT_QUALITY,
                     18,
                     "Times New Roman");
   hOFont=SelectObject(hdc,hNFont);
   TextOut(hdc,80,400,szYString,strlen(szYString));
   DeleteObject(hOFont);

   ValidateRect(hWnd,NULL);
   EndPaint(hWnd,&ps);
   break;

 case WM_DESTROY:
   PostQuitMessage(0);
   break;
 default:
   return(DefWindowProc(hWnd,messg,wParam,lParam));
   break;
 }
 return(0);
}
```

When you build this application your project file will need to include this source code file.

THE CF.CPP APPLICATION FILE

If you examine the application file, you will notice that—except for the declaration of *hOFont, hNFont,* and several strings—the structure of the applications code is identical to the simple platform developed in Chapter 2. All font action takes place when WM_PAINT messages are processed.

The first time **CreateFont()** is called, the parameters are set to the following values:

```
Height = 45
```

```
Width = 0
Escapement = 0
Orientation = 0
Weight = FW_NORMAL
Italic = FALSE
Underline = FALSE
StrikeOut = FALSE
CharSet = ANSI_CHARSET
OutputPrecision = OUT_DEFAULT_PRECIS
ClipPrecision = CLIP_DEFAULT_PRECIS
Quality = DEFAULT_QUALITY
PitchAndFamily = 34
Facename = "Arial"
```

The function will attempt to find a font to match these specifications. This font is used to print the horizontal string of text to the window.

The second time **CreateFont()** is called, the parameters are set to these values:

```
Height = 35
Width = 0
Escapement = 450
Orientation = 450
Weight = FW_BOLD
Italic = FALSE
Underline = FALSE
StrikeOut = FALSE
CharSet = ANSI_CHARSET
OutputPrecision=OUT_DEFAULT_PRECIS
ClipPrecision = CLIP_DEFAULT_PRECIS
Quality = DEFAULT_QUALITY
PitchAndFamily = 18
Facename = "Courier New"
```

Notice that both the Escapement and Orientation values have changed. These parameters have angles specified in tenths of a degree. In this case, the value 450 is understood to be 45.0 degrees. Thus, the Escapement parameter rotates the line of text from horizontal to a 45.0-degree angle. Orientation

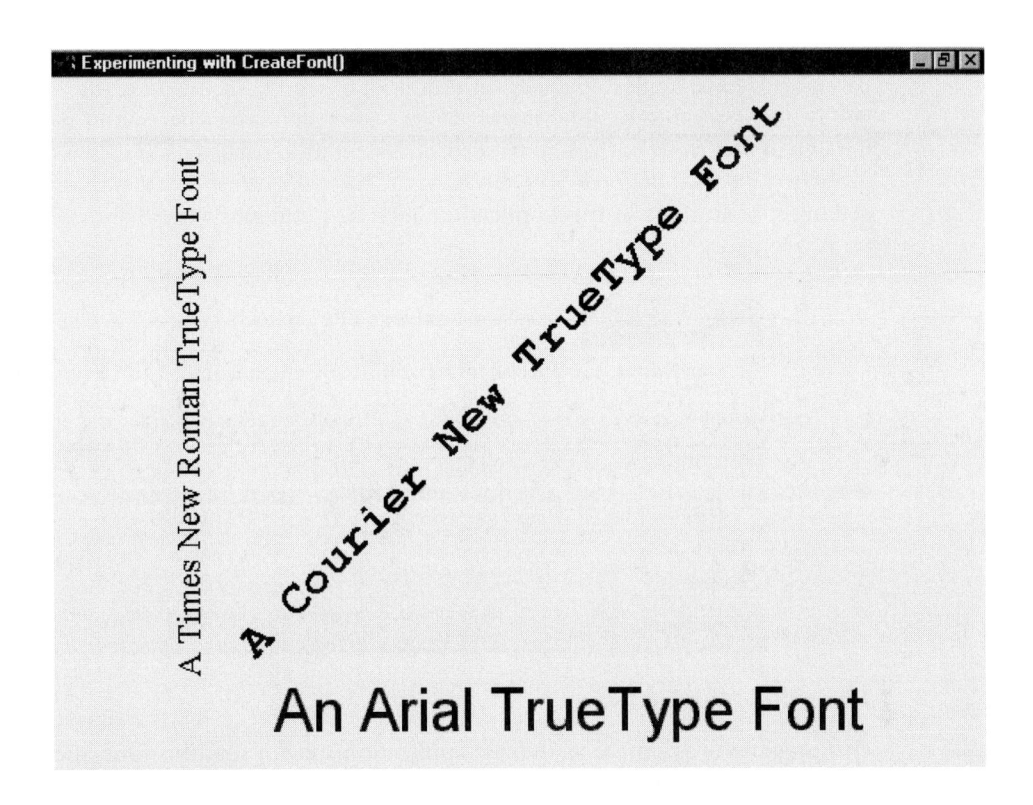

Font Change Example Programs

Figure 6-2 *Window output from the CF application.*

rotates each character in the string by 45.0 degrees. Both rotations are necessary to obtain the results shown in Figure 6-2.

The third time **CreateFont()** is called, the parameters are set to these values:

```
Height = 25
Width = 0
Escapement = 900
Orientation = 900
Weight = FW_NORMAL
Italic = FALSE
Underline = FALSE
StrikeOut = FALSE
CharSet = ANSI_CHARSET
OutputPrecision=OUT_DEFAULT_PRECIS
ClipPrecision = CLIP_DEFAULT_PRECIS
Quality = DEFAULT_QUALITY
PitchAndFamily = 18
Facename = "Times New Roman"
```

250 Chapter 6 • Using Fonts

Again, both the Escapement and Orientation values have changed. These parameters have angles specified in tenths of a degree. In this case, the value 900 is understood to be 90.0 degrees. Thus, the Escapement parameter rotates the line of text from horizontal to vertical. Orientation rotates each character in the string by 90.0 degrees. You can experiment with other TrueType fonts by making substitutions in this application. Table 6.4 contains some handy values for you to use.

Table 6.4 TrueType Names and Parameters.

FaceName	PitchAndFamily	CharSet
Arial	34	0 (ANSI_Charset)
Courier New	49	0
Symbol	18	2 (Symbol_Charset)
Times New Roman	18	0
Wingdings	2	2

The CFI Application

This program is as simple as the last application, except that this time, the size of the font will be changed. Changing just the height or width of a font is a simple task when using the **CreateFontIndirect()** function. Here is a listing of the cfi.cpp source code file.

```
//
// cfi.cpp
// This application illustrates the use of the
// CreateFontIndirect() function. With this function you
// can incorporate a wide variety of fonts into
// an application and also manipulate various
// font properties often with more ease than with
// the CreateFont() function.
// Copyright (c) William H. Murray and Chris H. Pappas, 1999
//

#include <windows.h>
#include <memory.h>
#include <string.h>

LRESULT CALLBACK WndProc(HWND,UINT,WPARAM,LPARAM);

char szProgName[]="ProgName";

int WINAPI WinMain(HINSTANCE hInst,HINSTANCE hPreInst,
```

```
                      LPSTR lpszCmdLine,int nCmdShow)
{
  HWND hWnd;
  MSG   lpMsg;
  WNDCLASS wcApp;

  wcApp.lpszClassName=szProgName;
  wcApp.hInstance    =hInst;
  wcApp.lpfnWndProc  =WndProc;
  wcApp.hCursor      =LoadCursor(NULL,IDC_ARROW);
  wcApp.hIcon        =0;
  wcApp.lpszMenuName =0;
  wcApp.hbrBackground=(HBRUSH) GetStockObject(WHITE_BRUSH);
  wcApp.style        =CS_HREDRAW|CS_VREDRAW;
  wcApp.cbClsExtra   =0;
  wcApp.cbWndExtra   =0;
  if (!RegisterClass (&wcApp))
    return 0;

  hWnd=CreateWindow(szProgName,
                    "Experimenting with CreateFontIndirect()",
                    WS_OVERLAPPEDWINDOW,CW_USEDEFAULT,
                    CW_USEDEFAULT,CW_USEDEFAULT,
                    CW_USEDEFAULT,(HWND)NULL,(HMENU)NULL,
                    hInst,(LPSTR)NULL);
  ShowWindow(hWnd,nCmdShow);
  UpdateWindow(hWnd);
  while (GetMessage(&lpMsg,0,0,0)) {
    TranslateMessage(&lpMsg);
    DispatchMessage(&lpMsg);
  }
  return(lpMsg.wParam);
}

LRESULT CALLBACK WndProc(HWND hWnd,UINT messg,
                         WPARAM wParam,LPARAM lParam)
{
  HDC hdc;
  PAINTSTRUCT ps;
  char szXString[]="An Arial TrueType Font";
  HGDIOBJ hNFont,hOFont;
  LOGFONT lf;
  int i,ypos;

  switch (messg)
  {
    case WM_PAINT:
      hdc=BeginPaint(hWnd,&ps);

      ypos=0;
```

```
      for (i=1;i<10;i+=2) {
        // allocate memory for LOGFONT
        memset(&lf,0,sizeof(LOGFONT));
        // Arial TrueType Font Characteristics
        lf.lfWeight=FW_HEAVY;
        lf.lfCharSet=ANSI_CHARSET;
        lf.lfPitchAndFamily=34;
        lf.lfHeight=8+(8*i);
        // create and select the new font
        hNFont=CreateFontIndirect(&lf);
        hOFont=SelectObject(hdc,hNFont);
        // draw the string with the new font and position
        TextOut(hdc,0,ypos,szXString,strlen(szXString));
        ypos+=20*i;
        // delete the font object
        DeleteObject(hOFont);
      }

      ValidateRect(hWnd,NULL);
      EndPaint(hWnd,&ps);
      break;

    case WM_DESTROY:
      PostQuitMessage(0);
      break;
    default:
      return(DefWindowProc(hWnd,messg,wParam,lParam));
      break;
  }
  return(0);
}
```

When you build this application, your project file will need to include only the source code file, cfi.cpp.

THE CFI.CPP APPLICATION FILE

In this application, a simple loop is used within WM_PAINT to repeatedly increase the height of the TrueType Arial font and draw it to the window. Notice in the application code that the weight, character set, and font family are specified by setting members of the logical font structure to specified values. The logical font structure member that alters the height, *lf.lfHeight*, is placed within the loop.

Can you determine the font heights for each pass through the loop? Figure 6-3 shows the output sent to the window.

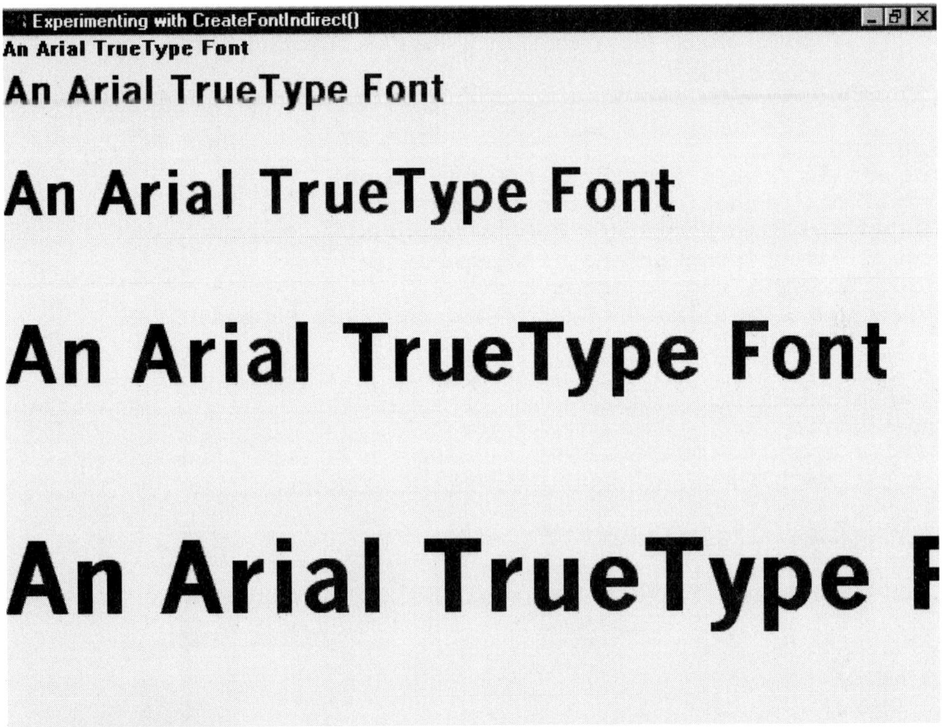

[Figure 6-3 screenshot showing "An Arial TrueType Font" rendered at progressively larger sizes in a window titled "Experimenting with CreateFontIndirect()"]

Figure 6-3 *A Font's character heights are changed with the CreateFontIndirect() function.*

Now, having studied the last two examples, what would you say was the greatest shortcoming of the **CreateFont()** function? You would probably agree that it is the function's parameter list, as the list must be repeated for each font change. The **CreateFontIndirect()** function allows the font height to be changed without the need for repeating all other parameters.

The Count Application

The count.cpp application is a practical program that you might want to put to use. It is a count-up timer that displays very large digits on a VGA screen. Just the thing for parties, etc. This program makes use of the information you just learned about fonts and incorporates a system timer. System timers were discussed in Chapter 3. When you study the listing for the count.cpp source code, note that the **CreateFont()** function is used to produce the large Arial TrueType fonts for the program.

254 Chapter 6 • Using Fonts

The count application consists of just a source code file, along with the typical project files created by Visual C++. Here is the listing for the count.cpp source code.

```
//
// count.cpp
// This application illustrates the use of the
// CreateFont() function and the system timer.
// This application shows you how to build a
// large digit up counter that increments in
// approximately 1 second intervals.
// Copyright (c) William H. Murray and Chris H. Pappas, 1999
//

#include <windows.h>
#include <string.h>

LRESULT CALLBACK WndProc(HWND,UINT,WPARAM,LPARAM);

char szProgName[]="ProgName";

int WINAPI WinMain(HINSTANCE hInst,HINSTANCE hPreInst,
                   LPSTR lpszCmdLine,int nCmdShow)
{
  HWND hWnd;
  MSG  lpMsg;
  WNDCLASS wcApp;

  wcApp.lpszClassName=szProgName;
  wcApp.hInstance     =hInst;
  wcApp.lpfnWndProc   =WndProc;
  wcApp.hCursor       =LoadCursor(NULL,IDC_ARROW);
  wcApp.hIcon         =0;
  wcApp.lpszMenuName  =0;
  wcApp.hbrBackground=(HBRUSH) GetStockObject(WHITE_BRUSH);
  wcApp.style         =CS_HREDRAW|CS_VREDRAW;
  wcApp.cbClsExtra    =0;
  wcApp.cbWndExtra    =0;
  if (!RegisterClass (&wcApp))
     return 0;

  hWnd=CreateWindow(szProgName,
                    "CreateFont() and the System Timer",
                    WS_OVERLAPPEDWINDOW,CW_USEDEFAULT,
                    CW_USEDEFAULT,CW_USEDEFAULT,
                    CW_USEDEFAULT,(HWND)NULL,(HMENU)NULL,
                    hInst,(LPSTR)NULL);
  ShowWindow(hWnd,nCmdShow);
  UpdateWindow(hWnd);
  while (GetMessage(&lpMsg,0,0,0)) {
```

```
      TranslateMessage(&lpMsg);
      DispatchMessage(&lpMsg);
   }
   return(lpMsg.wParam);
}

LRESULT CALLBACK WndProc(HWND hWnd,UINT messg,
                         WPARAM wParam,LPARAM lParam)
{
   HDC hdc;
   PAINTSTRUCT ps;
   char szString[]="";
   static HGDIOBJ hNFont,hOFont;
   static int iCount;

   switch (messg)
   {
     case WM_CREATE:
        // create a system timer with an
        // approximate 1000 millisecond
        // timer interval.
        SetTimer(hWnd,0,1000,NULL);
        break;

     case WM_TIMER:
        // increment count when a timer message is
        // received
        iCount++;
        // keep the count between 0 and 99
        if(iCount>=100) iCount=0;
        // refresh the screen to display the new time
        InvalidateRect(hWnd,NULL,TRUE);
        UpdateWindow(hWnd);
        break;

     case WM_PAINT:
        hdc=BeginPaint(hWnd,&ps);

        // Print TrueType Digits to Screen
        // in Arial Font
        hNFont=CreateFont(500,0,0,0,FW_NORMAL,
                         FALSE,FALSE,FALSE,ANSI_CHARSET,
                         OUT_DEFAULT_PRECIS,
                         CLIP_DEFAULT_PRECIS,
                         DEFAULT_QUALITY,
                         34,"Arial");
        hOFont=SelectObject(hdc,hNFont);

        itoa(iCount,szString,10);

        TextOut(hdc,50,0,szString,strlen(szString));
```

Chapter 6 • Using Fonts

```
        DeleteObject(hOFont);

        ValidateRect(hWnd,NULL);
        EndPaint(hWnd,&ps);
        break;

    case WM_DESTROY:
      PostQuitMessage(0);
      break;
    default:
      return(DefWindowProc(hWnd,messg,wParam,lParam));
      break;
  }
  return(0);
}
```

Build the application and give it a try. Neat!

THE COUNT.CPP APPLICATION FILE

When you examine the complete source code listing for the count.cpp application, you will observe that this application is built of the standard building blocks of all previous applications. The interesting and unique features start with the WM_TIMER block.

```
case WM_TIMER:
  // increment count when a timer message is
  // received
  iCount++;
  // keep the count between 0 and 99
  if(iCount>=100) iCount=0;
  // refresh the screen to display the new time
  InvalidateRect(hWnd,NULL,TRUE);
  UpdateWindow(hWnd);
  break;
```

When timer messages are generated by the system timer, WM_TIMER responds by incrementing *iCount*. The variable, *iCount*, holds the number that will eventually be displayed to the screen. As long as the *iCount* is not smaller than 0 or greater than 99, the **InvalidateRect()** and **UpdateWindow()** functions are called to update the windows display by issuing a WM_PAINT message.

Under WM_PAINT, when *iCount* is changed, the Arial font will be created. The point size requested is 500 point. In the next portion of code you'll see how the digits are actually drawn to the screen.

```
        itoa(iCount,szString,10);

        TextOut(hdc,50,0,szString,strlen(szString));
        DeleteObject(hOFont);
```

![CreateFont() and the System Timer window showing large "11"]

Figure 6-4 *The count.cpp draws large digits to the window.*

The numeric value contained in *iCount* is converted to a string with a call to the **itoa()** function. Single- or double-digit values are drawn to the screen with the call to **TextOut()**. Figure 6-4 shows the Count.cpp countdown timer in action.

Looking Ahead

The applications in this chapter are only a preview of what can be done with custom fonts under Windows. To gain experience with font characteristics, start with simple programs, such as the previous examples, and change one or two characteristics at a time. You'll be surprised just how easy it is to create professional-looking fonts in no time at all. Many of the techniques developed in this chapter will be used for printing labels on graphs and charts in future chapters.

If you are really getting into fonts, just wait until you get to Chapter 11 and see how easy it is to use Microsoft's Common Font Dialog Box resource.

SEVEN

Working with Icons and Cursors

Windows makes it very easy for you to visually enhance your application with custom icons and cursors. The Visual C++ Resource Editor is used to create custom icons and cursors. In this chapter, you will learn how to use the Resource Editor and how to incorporate the icon and cursor resource into your Windows application. Under Windows 98, it is possible to use a standard icon, a small icon, or both. We'll show you how Windows 98 can make the proper decision.

The Resource Editor is just one of the useful application development tools provided in your Visual C++ compiler's toolkit. With the Resource Editor you can design device-independent color icons and cursors. These custom icons and cursors are functionally device-independent with respect to their resolutions.

Windows provides a file format that allows you to tailor each resource so that it looks good in any display resolution. For example, one icon might consist of four definitions (called *device independent bitmaps* [DIBs]): one designed for monochrome displays, one for CGAs, one for EGAs, and one for VGAs. Whenever the application displays the icon, it simply refers to it by name; then Windows automatically selects the icon image best suited to the current display!

Icons and the Resource Editor

The Visual C++ Resource editor is very easy to use. The Resource Editor can be started from within the compiler's integrated environment by selecting the

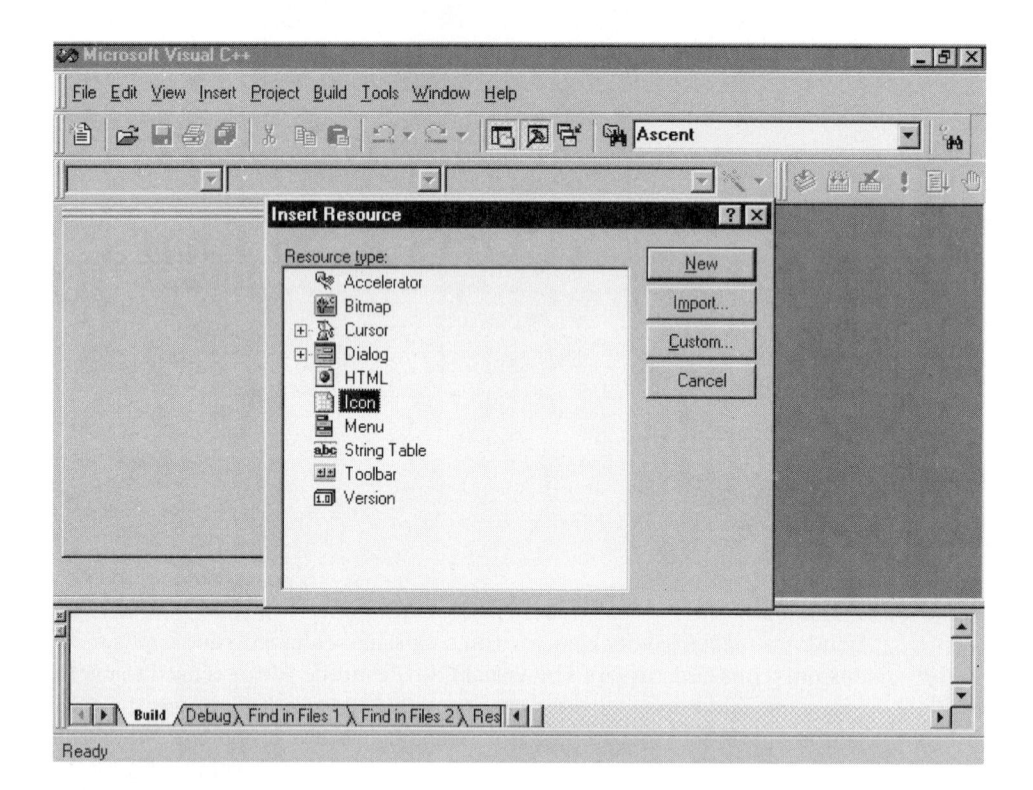

Figure 7-1 *The Resource Editor's list box allows the developer to select the proper resource.*

Insert menu and picking the Resource menu item. A list box will then allow you to choose the appropriate resource which, in this case, will be an icon. Figure 7-1 shows the list box provided for selecting the proper resource.

Within the Resource Editor are a selection of tools and palettes for creating the perfect icon. The use of the resource editor is self-explanatory, but patience is needed as you develop complicated icon designs. Let's examine a few properties associated with icons before designing our first custom icon.

Icon Sizes

Windows can use four sizes of icons; shell large, shell small, system large, and system small. The system large and system small are frequently called class icons.

The shell large icon is used on the desktop. The shell small icon is used in Windows Explorer and in the various common dialogs. The shell small icon defaults to the system small size. The system large icon is used mainly by applications. The system large icon is frequently manipulated with calls to the **Cre-**

ateIconFromResource(), **DrawIcon()**, **ExtractIcon()**, and **LoadIcon()** functions. The actual size of the system large icon is associated with the video driver and cannot be changed. The system small icon is displayed in the window caption.

To manipulate icons other than the system large icon, use function calls to the **CreateIcon()**, **CreateIconFromResourceEx()**, and **CreateIconIndirect()** functions.

The Start menu and Explorer can use either the shell small icon or the shell large icon. The selection is based on which view (large icon or small icon) is selected in the check box. Microsoft recommends that icons be supplied in groups with the sizes and color shown in Table 7.1.

Table 7.1 Recommended icon sizes and colors.

Pixel Sizes	Number of Colors
48 x 48	256 color
32 x 32	16 color
16 x 16	16 color

If you are developing an application that uses a small system icon, you will need to use the **WNDCLASSEX** structure and associated **RegisterClassEx()** function to register the window class. In these cases, it is possible to specify a large system icon (32 x 32) and a small system icon (16 x 16). In these cases, the hIcon member is set to the large system icon, and the hIconSm member is set to the small system icon.

If the hIcon or hIconSm structure members are set to a NULL value, Windows uses the default application icon (the icon appears as a small window) as the large and small system icons for the window class. If a large system icon is specified and a small one is not, Windows creates a small system icon based on the large one. This is achieved by using alternate pixels. However, if a small system icon is specified and a large one is not, Windows uses the default application icon as the large system icon and the specified icon as the small system icon. The second application in this chapter will allow you to experiment with these properties.

Custom or Standard Icons?

It is possible to design custom icons in the Visual C++ Resource Editor or to use standard icons provided by the Visual C++ compiler. You can find the standard system icons in the winuser.h header file. Table 7.2 is a list of these icons and a brief description.

Table 7.2 — Standard Windows 98 Icons and descriptions.

Icon ID	Description
IDI_APPLICATION	small window icon
IDI_HAND	red circle with white X
IDI_QUESTION	question mark symbol
IDI_EXCLAMATION	exclamation mark symbol
IDI_ASTERISK	asterisk symbol
IDI_WINLOGO	small Windows 98 logo
IDI_WARNING	same as IDI_EXCLAMATION
IDI_ERROR	same as IDI_HAND
IDI_INFORMATION	same as IDI_ASTERISK

The second application in this chapter illustrates the use of standard Windows icons.

Working with a Large Custom Icon

In this section, you will learn how to incorporate a large custom icon into your Windows application.

note: Large icons normally measure 32 x 32 pixels. When small icons aren't specified in an application, Windows 98 will shrink the large icon down to 16 x 16 pixel icons.

To build this application from your Visual C++ compiler, you will need a project file, a C++ source code file (Icon.cpp), a resource script file (Icon.rc), and a new icon (Icon.ico). Remember that the icon is designed in the Resource Editor and is saved, along with the resource script file. It will be up to you to design your own unique icon for this example. Figure 7-2 shows the icon we designed for this example.

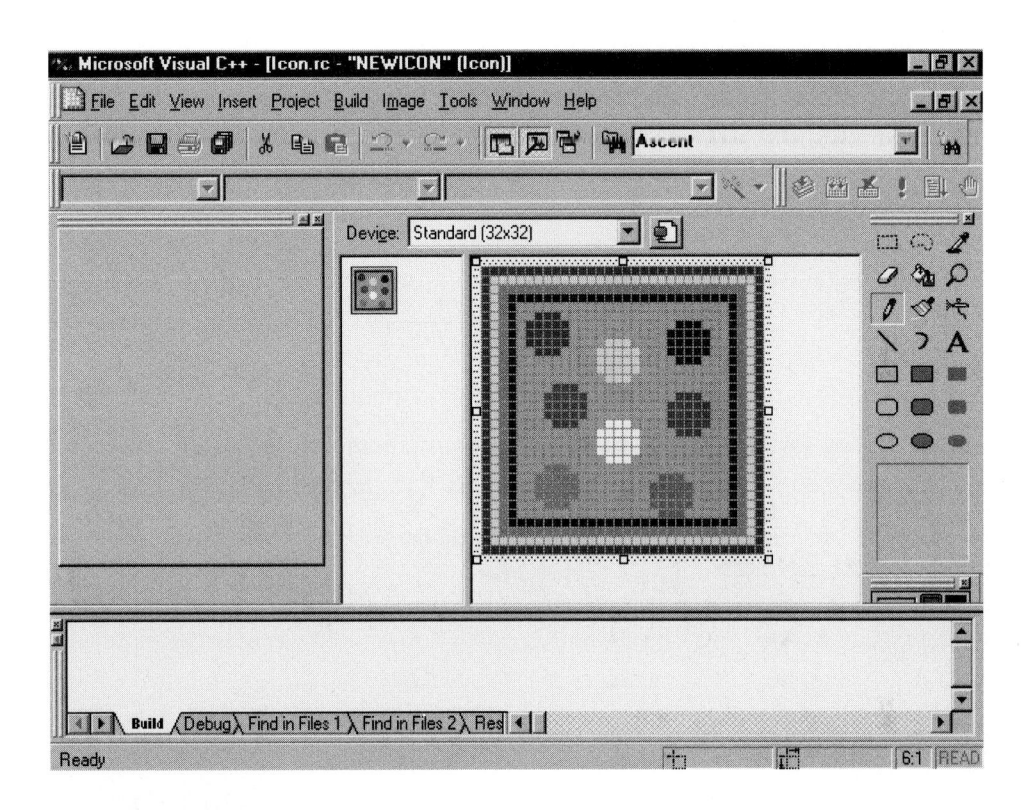

Icons and the Resource Editor 263

Figure 7-2 *A custom icon (Icon.ico) is created in the Resource Editor for the first application.*

If you have designed and saved a new icon in the Resource Editor, a resource script file has already been generated for your project. The resource script file is a text description of project resources such as menus, dialog boxes, toolbars, icon and cursor identifications, and so on. Here is the Icon.rc resource script file for this project:

```
//Microsoft Developer Studio generated resource script.
//
#include "resource.h"

#define APSTUDIO_READONLY_SYMBOLS
/////////////////////////////////////////////////////////////
//
// Generated from the TEXTINCLUDE 2 resource.
//
#include "afxres.h"


/////////////////////////////////////////////////////////////
#undef APSTUDIO_READONLY_SYMBOLS
```

```
/////////////////////////////////////////////////////////
// English (U.S.) resources

#if !defined(AFX_RESOURCE_DLL) || defined(AFX_TARG_ENU)
#ifdef _WIN32
LANGUAGE LANG_ENGLISH, SUBLANG_ENGLISH_US
#pragma code_page(1252)
#endif //_WIN32


/////////////////////////////////////////////////////////
//
// Icon
//

// Icon with lowest ID value placed first to ensure
// application icon remains consistent on all systems.
NewIcon      ICON     DISCARDABLE       "Icon.ico"

#ifdef APSTUDIO_INVOKED
/////////////////////////////////////////////////////////
//
// TEXTINCLUDE
//

1 TEXTINCLUDE DISCARDABLE
BEGIN
    "resource.h\0"
END

2 TEXTINCLUDE DISCARDABLE
BEGIN
    "#include""afxres.h""afxres.h""\r\n"
    "\0"
END

3 TEXTINCLUDE DISCARDABLE
BEGIN
    "\r\n"
    "\0"
END

#endif    // APSTUDIO_INVOKED

#endif    // English (U.S.) resources
/////////////////////////////////////////////////////////

#ifndef APSTUDIO_INVOKED
/////////////////////////////////////////////////////////
//
// Generated from the TEXTINCLUDE 3 resource.
```

```
//
///////////////////////////////////////////////////////
#endif    // not APSTUDIO INVOKED
```

This listing shows the unedited resource script file for the project. Normally, you will not have to pay any attention to the contents of this file. The bolded text, in this listing, is the portion of code inserted by the Resource Editor to identify the icon resource for the project. In this listing, the name of the iconic resource (Icon.ico) is associated with the name *NewIcon*. NewIcon will be used in the C++ source code file to reference this resource.

Here is the Icon.cpp source code file for this project:

```
//
// Icon.cpp
// A simple windows application that teaches you how to
// incorporate a custom icon into your application.
// Copyright (c) William H. Murray and Chris H. Pappas, 1999
//

#include <windows.h>

LRESULT CALLBACK WndProc(HWND,UINT,WPARAM,LPARAM);

char szProgName[]="ProgName";
char szIconName[]="NewIcon";    // name of icon resource

int WINAPI WinMain(HINSTANCE hInst,HINSTANCE hPreInst,
                   LPSTR lpszCmdLine,int nCmdShow)
{
  HWND hWnd;
  MSG  lpMsg;
  WNDCLASS wcApp;

  wcApp.lpszClassName=szProgName;
  wcApp.hInstance     =hInst;
  wcApp.lpfnWndProc   =WndProc;
  wcApp.hCursor       =LoadCursor(NULL,IDC_ARROW);
  // include the icon resource here
  wcApp.hIcon         =LoadIcon(hInst,szIconName);
  wcApp.lpszMenuName  =0;
  wcApp.hbrBackground=(HBRUSH) GetStockObject(WHITE_BRUSH);
  wcApp.style         =CS_HREDRAW|CS_VREDRAW;
  wcApp.cbClsExtra    =0;
  wcApp.cbWndExtra    =0;
  if (!RegisterClass (&wcApp))
     return 0;

  hWnd=CreateWindow(szProgName,"Displaying A Custom Icon",
```

```
                     WS_OVERLAPPEDWINDOW,CW_USEDEFAULT,
                     CW_USEDEFAULT,CW_USEDEFAULT,
                     CW_USEDEFAULT,(HWND)NULL,(HMENU)NULL,
                     hInst,(LPSTR)NULL);
  ShowWindow(hWnd,nCmdShow);
  UpdateWindow(hWnd);
  while (GetMessage(&lpMsg,0,0,0)) {
    TranslateMessage(&lpMsg);
    DispatchMessage(&lpMsg);
  }
  return(lpMsg.wParam);
}


LRESULT CALLBACK WndProc(HWND hWnd,UINT messg,
                         WPARAM wParam,LPARAM lParam)
{
  HDC hdc;
  PAINTSTRUCT ps;
  static char szString1[]= "View the icon in the";
  static char szString2[]= "upper-left corner";

  switch (messg)
  {
    case WM_PAINT:
      hdc=BeginPaint(hWnd,&ps);

      TextOut(hdc,50,100,szString1,sizeof(szString1)-1);
      TextOut(hdc,50,120,szString2,sizeof(szString2)-1);

      ValidateRect(hWnd,NULL);
      EndPaint(hWnd,&ps);
      break;

    case WM_DESTROY:
      PostQuitMessage(0);
      break;

    default:
      return(DefWindowProc(hWnd,messg,wParam,lParam));
      break;
  }
  return(0);
}
```

Pulling a custom icon into an application takes only two steps. First, *szIconName* is assigned the name of the icon defined in the Icon.rc resource script file:

```
szIconName[]="NewIcon";
```

The large icon is assigned to the **WNDCLASS** structure with the following assignment to the hIcon structure member.

```
wcApp.hIcon=LoadIcon(hInst,szIconName);
```

When the window is created, it automatically contains the large custom icon.

When you build this project, make sure the source code file (Icon.cpp) and the resource script file (Icon.rc) are specified in the project's build list. Use the Project|Add To Project|Files menu selections to open the files selection dialog box. The project utility will automatically include, compile, and link these resources to your executable file, Icon.exe.

Figure 7-3 shows the new icon in the upper left portion of the window when the application is run.

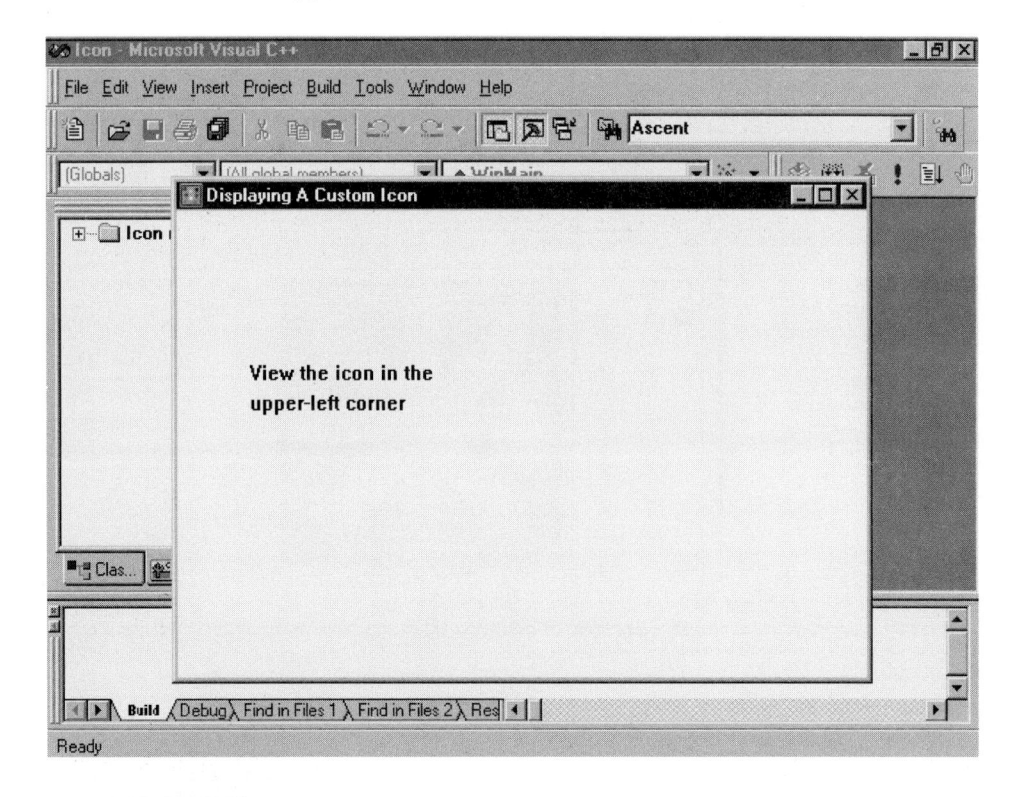

Figure 7-3 *The new icon is displayed in the upper left portion of the window.*

Remember that the large system icon is converted to a small system icon when a small system icon is not specified in the project. The icon you are viewing in Figure 7-3 is actually 16 x 16 pixels.

Working with Large and Small Icons

In this section, you will learn how to use both a large custom icon and a small standard icon for a Windows 98 application. Remember that large icons measure 32 x 32 pixels, but Windows 98 can also user a smaller 16 x 16 icon. If a unique 16 x 16 pixel icon isn't supplied to Windows 98, it will shrink a 32 x 32 pixel icon to 16 x 16. Sometimes, the results are less than satisfactory with custom-designed icons.

To build this application, you will need a project file, a C++ source code file, a resource script file, and a large custom icon. The large system icon is created in the Resource Editor. A standard system icon will be used for the small icon resource and thus will not have to be designed. The large icon is designed and saved as Icon98.ico. Figure 7-4 shows the large icon we designed for this application.

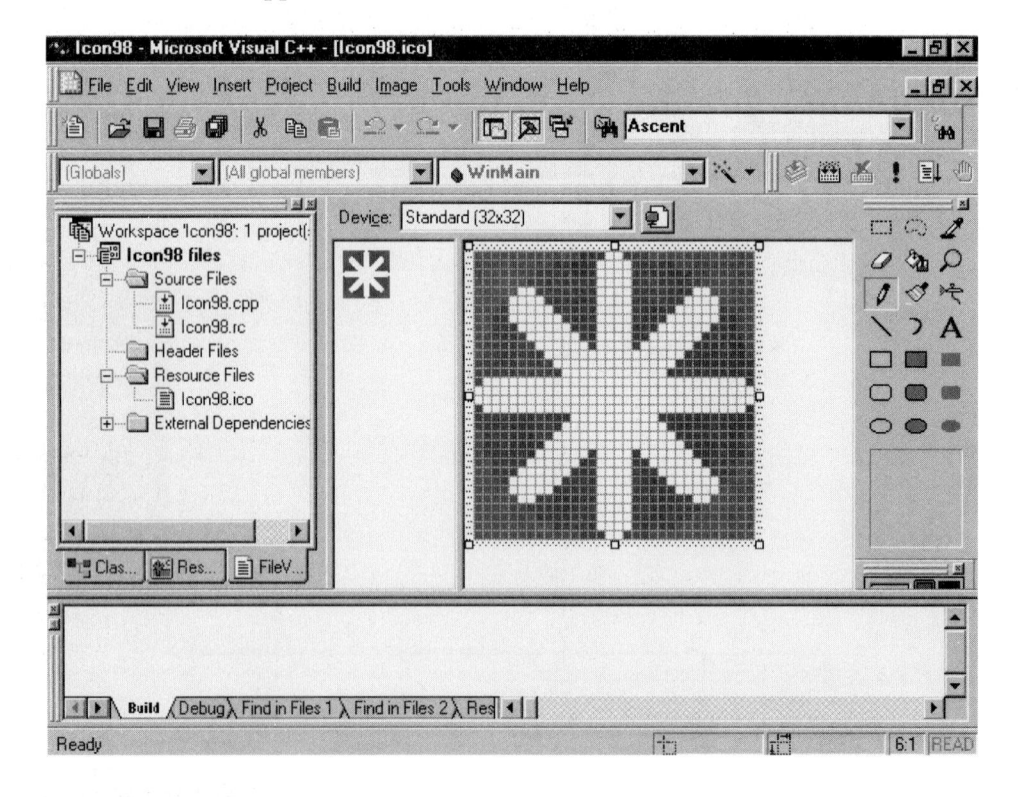

Figure 7-4 *A large icon is created in the Resource Editor for the Icon98 application.*

The small 16 x 16 icon is selected from the list of icons shown in Table 7.2. For this example, we'll use the icon identified by IDI_ERROR for the project.

This project will have a resource script file similar to the resource script file of the first project. Here is an edited version of the ICON98.rc resource script file showing how the large iconic resource is identified. Remember, this resource script file is automatically generated by the Resource Editor when you design the new icon and save it with the appropriate project name.

```
//Microsoft Developer Studio generated resource script.
//
#include "resource.h"
    .
    .
    .
/////////////////////////////////////////////////////////////
//
// Icon
//
// Icon with lowest ID value placed first to ensure
// application icon remains consistent on all systems.
LargeIcon       ICON    DISCARDABLE     "c:Icon98.ico"

#ifdef APSTUDIO_INVOKED
    .
    .
    .
```

In the resource script file, the name of the large iconic resource (Icon98.ico) is associated with the name *LargeIcon*. LargeIcon will be referenced by the C++ source code file.

Here is the Icon98.cpp source code file for this project:

```
//
// Icon98.cpp
// A windows application that allows you to
// experiment with large and small icons.
// Copyright (c) William H. Murray and Chris H. Pappas, 1999
//

#include <windows.h>

LRESULT CALLBACK WndProc(HWND,UINT,WPARAM,LPARAM);

char szProgName[]="ProgName";
char szIconName[]="LargeIcon";

int WINAPI WinMain(HINSTANCE hInst,HINSTANCE hPreInst,
                   LPSTR lpszCmdLine,int nCmdShow)
{
```

Chapter 7 • Working with Icons and Cursors

```c
  HWND hWnd;
  MSG  lpMsg;
  WNDCLASSEX wcApp;

  wcApp.lpszClassName=szProgName;
  wcApp.hInstance    =hInst;
  wcApp.lpfnWndProc  =WndProc;
  wcApp.hCursor      =LoadCursor(NULL,IDC_ARROW);
  // include the large icon resource here
  wcApp.hIcon        =LoadIcon(hInst,szIconName);
  wcApp.lpszMenuName =0;
  wcApp.hbrBackground=(HBRUSH) GetStockObject(WHITE_BRUSH);
  wcApp.style        =CS_HREDRAW|CS_VREDRAW;
  wcApp.cbClsExtra   =0;
  wcApp.cbWndExtra   =0;
  wcApp.cbSize       =sizeof(WNDCLASSEX);
  // include the small icon resource here
  wcApp.hIconSm      =LoadIcon(NULL,IDI_ERROR);
  if (!RegisterClassEx (&wcApp))
    return 0;

  hWnd=CreateWindow(szProgName,"Large and Small Icons",
                    WS_OVERLAPPEDWINDOW,CW_USEDEFAULT,
                    CW_USEDEFAULT,CW_USEDEFAULT,
                    CW_USEDEFAULT,(HWND)NULL,(HMENU)NULL,
                    hInst,(LPSTR)NULL);
  ShowWindow(hWnd,nCmdShow);
  UpdateWindow(hWnd);
  while (GetMessage(&lpMsg,0,0,0)) {
    TranslateMessage(&lpMsg);
    DispatchMessage(&lpMsg);
  }
  return(lpMsg.wParam);
}


LRESULT CALLBACK WndProc(HWND hWnd,UINT messg,
                         WPARAM wParam,LPARAM lParam)
{
  HDC hdc;
  PAINTSTRUCT ps;
  static char szString1[]= "View the small icon in the";
  static char szString2[]= "upper-left corner";
  static char szString3[]= "View the large icon in the";
  static char szString4[]= "Explorer Window";

  switch (messg)
  {
    case WM_PAINT:
      hdc=BeginPaint(hWnd,&ps);
```

```
            TextOut(hdc,50,100,szString1,sizeof(szString1)-1);
            TextOut(hdc,50,120,szString2,sizeof(szString2)-1);
            TextOut(hdc,50,160,szString3,sizeof(szString3)-1);
            TextOut(hdc,50,180,szString4,sizeof(szString4) 1);

            ValidateRect(hWnd,NULL);
            EndPaint(hWnd,&ps);
            break;

        case WM_DESTROY:
            PostQuitMessage(0);
            break;

        default:
            return(DefWindowProc(hWnd,messg,wParam,lParam));
            break;
    }
    return(0);
}
```

You should be able to compare the source code file for the first project with this source code file and see where the differences occur. Actually, all of the action takes place with the use of the **WNDCLASSEX** structure and **RegisterClassEx()** function call. Both the new structure and the new function call are required to take advantage of the small icon resource. Here is a portion of the previous listing:

.
.
.

```
WNDCLASSEX wcApp;

wcApp.lpszClassName=szProgName;
wcApp.hInstance     =hInst;
wcApp.lpfnWndProc   =WndProc;
wcApp.hCursor       =LoadCursor(NULL,IDC_ARROW);
// include the large icon resource here
wcApp.hIcon         =LoadIcon(hInst,szIconName);
wcApp.lpszMenuName  =0;
wcApp.hbrBackground=(HBRUSH) GetStockObject(WHITE_BRUSH);
wcApp.style         =CS_HREDRAW|CS_VREDRAW;
wcApp.cbClsExtra    =0;
wcApp.cbWndExtra    =0;
wcApp.cbSize        =sizeof(WNDCLASSEX);
// include the small icon resource here
wcApp.hIconSm       =LoadIcon(NULL,IDI_ERROR);
if (!RegisterClassEx (&wcApp))
    return 0;
```
.
.
.

A **WNDCLASSEX** structure is required to specify a small icon. This structure is similar to the familiar **WNDCLASS** structure used in all previous examples but includes two additional structure members; cbSize and hIconSm. The size of the structure is returned to the cbSize structure member with a call to the **sizeof()** function. The hIconSm structure member is handled in the same manner as structure member, hIcon, for the large icon. Notice that in this example, a custom icon is not used for the small system icon. Rather, the standard icon identified with IDI_ERROR and found in the winuser.h header file is used.

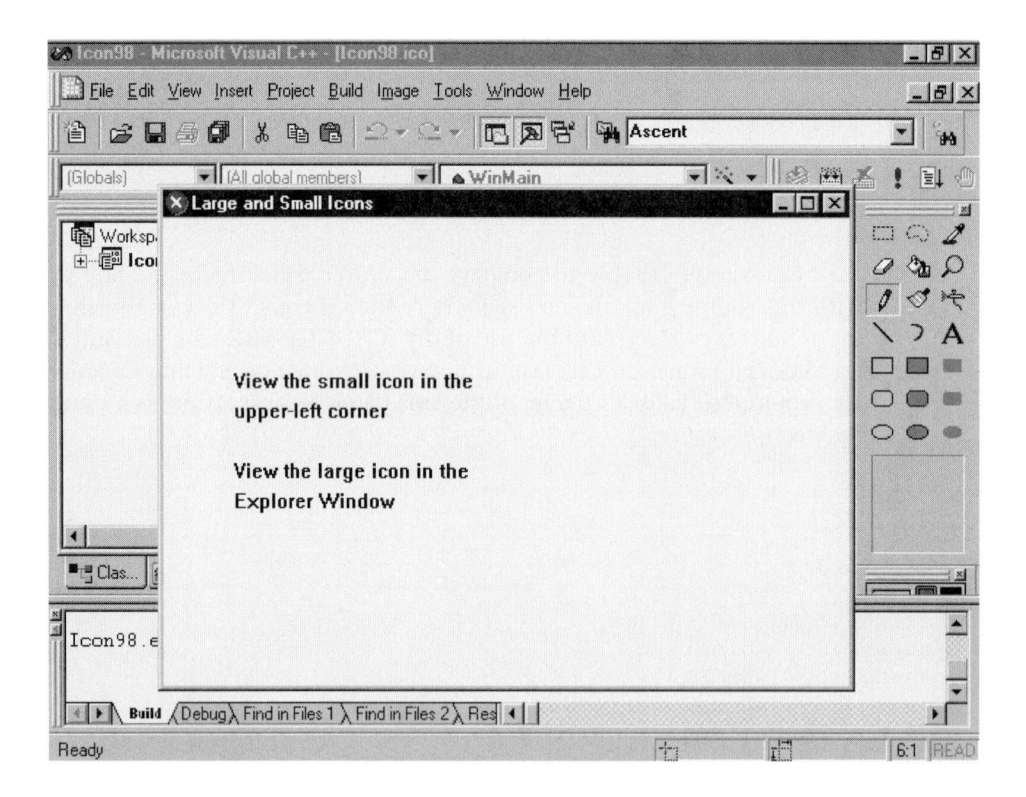

Figure 7-5 *The small standard icon is visible in this application.*

Figure 7-5 shows the application during execution. The small standard icon is visible in the upper-left corner of the window.

Now open Windows Explorer and move to the subdirectory that contains the executable file for this project. Make sure you set your view options to use a large icon. You should see the large icon used here. Figure 7-6 shows the large icon we designed for the project.

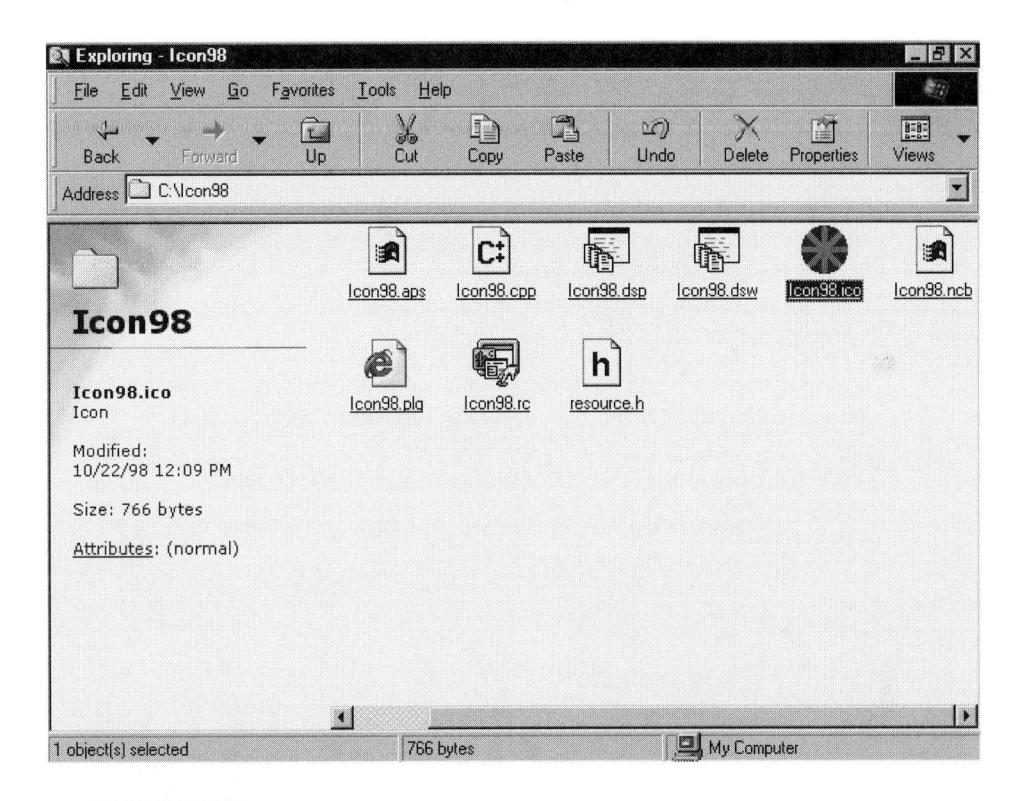

Icons and the Resource Editor 273

Figure 7-6 *The large custom icon is visible for this application under the Windows Explorer.*

Custom icons can add a professional touch to any project. Now that you see how easy they are to add, we're sure you'll want to include them with every project you create. But wait, you'll find that cursors are just as easy to use. In the next section, we'll show you how to add custom cursor resources to your projects.

Special Icon Functions

There is a number of functions designed to manipulate icons once an application is started. In this section, we'll discuss the syntax of a few of the popular functions. With this knowledge, you can experiment with iconic resources. For example, you might want to replace an icon once an application is started.

THE LOADICON() FUNCTION

The **LoadIcon()** function loads the specified icon resource from the executable (.exe) file associated with an application instance.

```
HICON LoadIcon(
  HINSTANCE hInstance,
  LPCTSTR lpIconName
);
```

hInstance is a handle to an instance of the module whose executable file contains the icon to be loaded. This parameter must be NULL when a standard icon is being loaded.

lpIconName is a pointer to a null-terminated string that contains the name of the icon resource to be loaded.

RETURN VALUES • If the function succeeds, the return value is a handle to the newly loaded icon. If the function fails, the return value is NULL.

THE DRAWICON() AND DRAWICONEX() FUNCTIONS

The **DrawIcon()** function draws an icon in the client area of the window of the specified device context.

```
BOOL DrawIcon(
  HDC hDC,
  int X,
  int Y,
  HICON hIcon
);
```

hDC is a handle to the device context for a window.

X defines the logical *x*-coordinate of the upper left corner of the icon.

Y defines the logical *y*-coordinate of the upper left corner of the icon.

hIcon is a handle to the icon to be drawn. The icon resource must have been previously loaded using the **LoadIcon()** or **LoadImage()** functions.

RETURN VALUES • On success, the return value is nonzero. If the function fails, the return value is zero.

THE CREATEICONINDIRECT() FUNCTION

The **CreateIconIndirect()** function creates an icon or cursor from an **ICONINFO** structure.

```
HICON CreateIconIndirect(
  PICONINFO piconinfo
);
```

piconinfo is a pointer to an ICONINFO structure the function uses to create the icon or cursor.

RETURN VALUES • On success, the return value is a handle to the icon or cursor that is created. If the function fails, the return value is NULL.

THE DESTROYICON() FUNCTION

The **DestroyIcon()** function destroys an icon and frees any memory the icon occupied.

```
BOOL DestroyIcon(
  HICON hIcon
);
```

hIcon is a handle to the icon to be destroyed. The icon must not be in use.

RETURN VALUES • On success, the return value is nonzero. If the function fails, the return value is zero.

Cursors and the Resource Editor

The Visual C++ Resource Editor makes cursor design just as easy as icon design. The Resource Editor is started from within the compiler's integrated environment by selecting the Insert menu and picking the Resource menu item. From the list box provided, select the cursor resource.

The Resource Editor will provide a selection of tools and palettes for creating the perfect cursor. Figure 7-7 shows the initial cursor design screen.

Again, the use of the Resource Editor is self-explanatory, but patience is needed as you develop complicated cursor designs. In the next section, we'll examine some unique cursor properties.

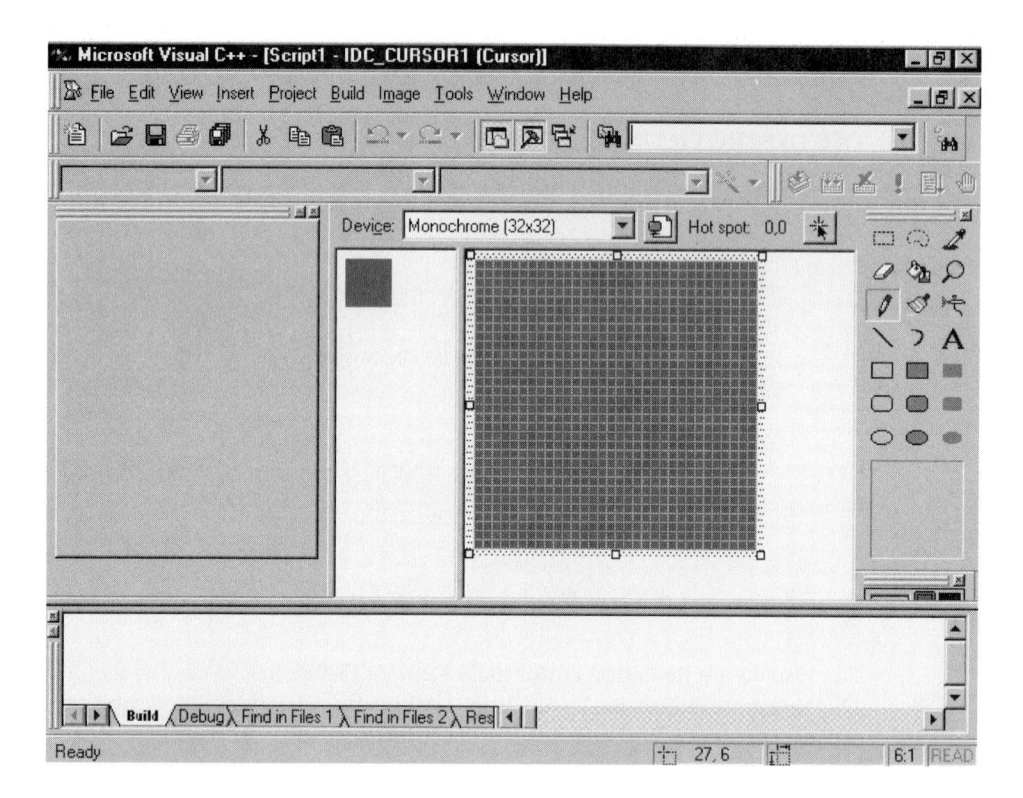

Figure 7-7 *The initial design window for a new cursor in the Resource Editor.*

Custom or Standard Cursors

Figure 7-8 shows the design of a unique cursor that an application could use to highlight important selections.

When looking at the completed designs, notice that there are actually two renditions of the design. The larger rendition allows your eyes to create an exploded image easily. The smaller rendition represents the actual size of the design as it would appear in the application.

Remember that it takes a great deal of patience and experience coupled with good design talent to create a meaningful cursor. The process usually involves a little trial and error coupled with your creative abilities. Whenever you come up with a design that has possibilities, stop and save a copy of it.

A cursor can include an optional hot spot. A hot spot is identified by selecting the hot spot tool from the toolbar. The hot spot tool selects which

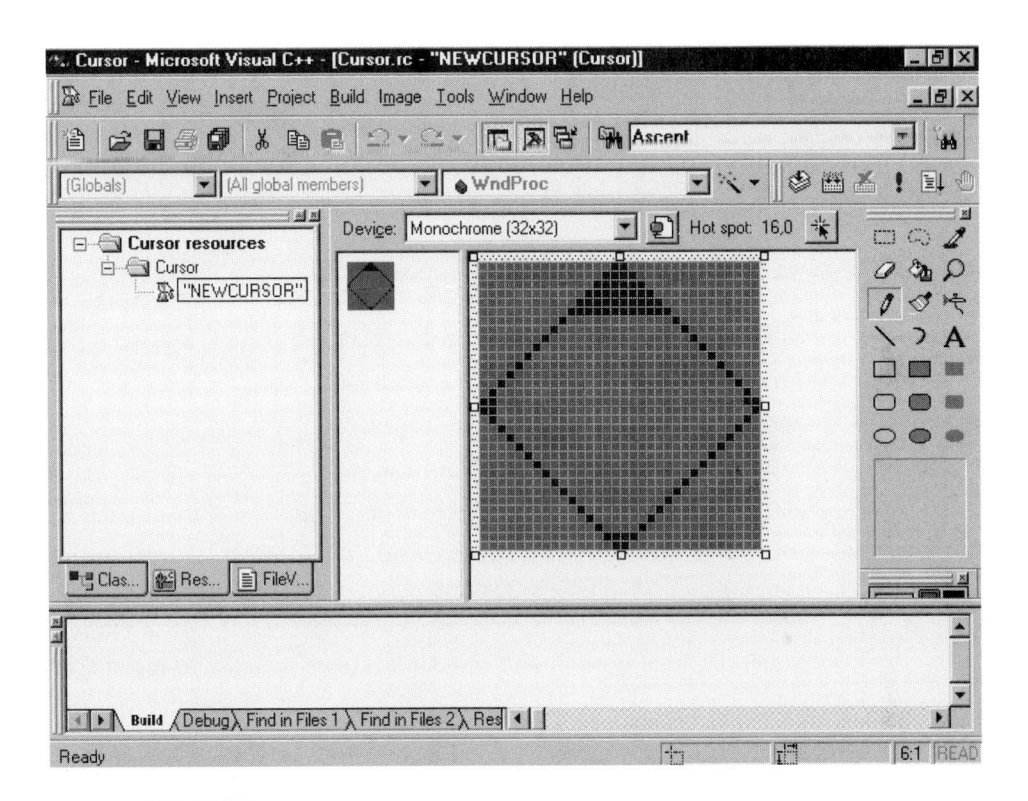

Cursors and the Resource Editor **277**

Figure 7-8 *A unique cursor design (Cursor.cur) shown in the Visual C++ Resource Editor.*

portion of the cursor (pixel) will be used to return the current screen coordinates when the cursor is positioned on a portion of the screen.

Once the hot spot tool is selected, notice that a very small mark appears in the drawing window. Simply place the mark on whichever pixel you want to select as the hot spot and press the mouse button. The coordinates of the selected hot spot are added to the display windows list of statistics. Only one hot spot per cursor is allowed.

Applications can also select a cursor resource from a list of available resources provided in the winuser.h header file. Standard cursor ID values start with IDC_. Table 7.3 shows the current group of available cursors.

Table 7.3 Standard Windows 98 cursors.

Cursor ID	Description
IDC_ARROW	standard cursor arrow
IDC_CROSS	cross cursor

Table 7.3 Standard Windows 98 cursors. (Continued)

Cursor ID	Description
IDC_IBEAM	I-beam cursor
IDC_ICON	obsolete, use IDC_ARROW
IDC_NO	no cursor
IDC_SIZE	obsolete, use IDC_SIZEALL
IDC_SIZEALL	size all cursor
IDC_SIZENESW	NESW cursor arrows
IDC_SIZENS	NS cursor arrows
IDC_SIZENWSE	NWSE cursor arrows
IDC_SIZEWE	WE cursor arrows
IDC_UPARROW	up arrow cursor
IDC_WAIT	hourglass cursor

You'll find that custom and standard cursors are easy to include in your projects.

Working with a Custom Cursor

To build this application from your Visual C++ compiler, you will need a project file, the C++ source code file (Cursor.cpp), a resource script file (Cursor.rc), and a new cursor (Curosr.cur). In the last section, we illustrated the design for the custom cursor used in this section. You may want to design your own unique cursor for this example.

When the custom cursor is designed and saved from the Resource Editor, a new resource script file is also created for the project. Here is an edited portion of the Cursor.rc resource script file created for this project.

```
//Microsoft Developer Studio generated resource script.
//
#include "resource.h"
    .
    .
    .
/////////////////////////////////////////////////////////
//
// Cursor
//
NewCursor       CURSOR  DISCARDABLE     "Cursor.cur"
```

Notice in the resource script file that the name of the cursor resource (Cursor.cur) is associated with the name NewCursor. The C++ source code file will reference the NewCursor resource.

Here is the Cursor.cpp source code file:

```cpp
//
// Cursor.cpp
// A simple windows application that teaches you how to
// incorporate a custom cursor into your application.
// Copyright (c) William H. Murray and Chris H. Pappas, 1999
//

#include <windows.h>

LRESULT CALLBACK WndProc(HWND,UINT,WPARAM,LPARAM);

char szProgName[]="ProgName";
char szCursorName[]="NewCursor";    // name of cursor resource

int WINAPI WinMain(HINSTANCE hInst,HINSTANCE hPreInst,
                   LPSTR lpszCmdLine,int nCmdShow)
{
  HWND hWnd;
  MSG  lpMsg;
  WNDCLASS wcApp;

  wcApp.lpszClassName=szProgName;
  wcApp.hInstance     =hInst;
  wcApp.lpfnWndProc   =WndProc;
  // include the new cursor resource here
  wcApp.hCursor       =LoadCursor(hInst,szCursorName);
  wcApp.hIcon         =0;
  wcApp.lpszMenuName  =0;
  wcApp.hbrBackground=(HBRUSH) GetStockObject(WHITE_BRUSH);
  wcApp.style         =CS_HREDRAW|CS_VREDRAW;
  wcApp.cbClsExtra    =0;
  wcApp.cbWndExtra    =0;
  if (!RegisterClass (&wcApp))
    return 0;

  hWnd=CreateWindow(szProgName,"Displaying A Custom Cursor",
                    WS_OVERLAPPEDWINDOW,CW_USEDEFAULT,
                    CW_USEDEFAULT,CW_USEDEFAULT,
                    CW_USEDEFAULT,(HWND)NULL,(HMENU)NULL,
                    hInst,(LPSTR)NULL);
  ShowWindow(hWnd,nCmdShow);
  UpdateWindow(hWnd);
  while (GetMessage(&lpMsg,0,0,0)) {
    TranslateMessage(&lpMsg);
    DispatchMessage(&lpMsg);
```

Chapter 7 • Working with Icons and Cursors

```
  }
  return(lpMsg.wParam);
}


LRESULT CALLBACK WndProc(HWND hWnd,UINT messg,
                        WPARAM wParam,LPARAM lParam)
{
  HDC hdc;
  PAINTSTRUCT ps;
  static char szString1[]= "Move the mouse around and";
  static char szString2[]= "watch the new cursor move";

  switch (messg)
  {
    case WM_PAINT:
      hdc=BeginPaint(hWnd,&ps);

      TextOut(hdc,50,100,szString1,sizeof(szString1)-1);
      TextOut(hdc,50,120,szString2,sizeof(szString2)-1);

      ValidateRect(hWnd,NULL);
      EndPaint(hWnd,&ps);
      break;

    case WM_DESTROY:
      PostQuitMessage(0);
      break;

    default:
      return(DefWindowProc(hWnd,messg,wParam,lParam));
      break;
  }
  return(0);
}
```

Adding a custom cursor to an application is easy. First, *szCursorName* is assigned the name of the cursor defined in the Cursor.rc resource script file:

```
szCursorName[]="NewCursor";
```

Next, the WNDCLASS hCursor structure member is set to the new resource with the following portion of code.

```
wcApp.hCursor=LoadCursor(hInst,szCursorName);
```

When the window is created, the custom cursor is automatically associated with the current mouse position.

Again, when you create this project, make sure the Cursor.cpp source code file and the Cursor.rc resource script file are included in the project's

Cursors and the Resource Editor

build list. The project utility will automatically include, compile and link these resources to your executable file, Cursor.exe.

Figure 7-9 shows the application running with the new custom cursor clearly visible.

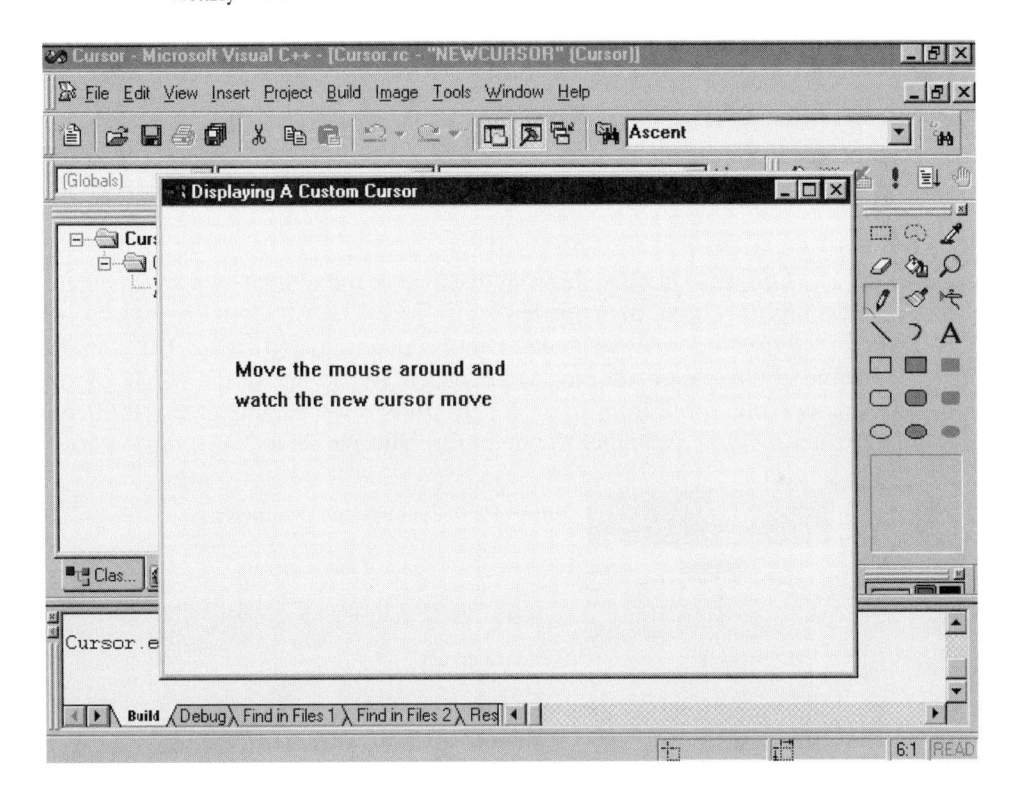

Figure 7-9 *A new custom cursor is added to an application.*

If you desire to use a standard cursor instead of a custom cursor, the code change is elementary. For example, to add an hourglass icon to a project, use this code to change the hCursor structure member:

```
wcApp.hCursor=LoadCursor(NULL,IDC_WAIT);
```

That's all there is to it. Couple your knowledge of custom icons to your knowledge of custom cursors and you are really ready to add professional touches to your applications.

Special Cursor Functions

There is a number of functions designed to manipulate cursors once an application is started. These functions are very similar in structure to the special icon functions discussed earlier in this chapter. In this section, we'll examine a few of the popular functions used to manipulate cursors.

THE LOADCURSOR() FUNCTION

The **LoadCursor()** function loads the specified cursor resource from the .exe file associated with an application instance.

```
HCURSOR LoadCursor(
  HINSTANCE hInstance,
  LPCTSTR lpCursorName
);
```

hInstance is a handle to an instance of the module whose executable file contains the cursor to be loaded.

lpCursorName is a pointer to a null-terminated string that contains the name of the cursor resource to be loaded. To use one of the Win32 predefined cursors, the application must set the *hInstance* parameter to NULL and the *lpCursorName* parameter to one of the values in Table 7.4.

Table 7.4 Values for lpCursorName parameter.

Value	Description
IDC_APPSTARTING	Standard arrow and small hourglass
IDC_ARROW	Standard arrow
IDC_CROSS	Crosshair
IDC_HAND	Windows NT 5.0 and later: Hand
IDC_HELP	Arrow with question mark
IDC_IBEAM	I-beam
IDC_ICON	No longer valid for applications marked version 4.0 or later
IDC_NO	The standard slashed circle
IDC_SIZE	No longer valid for applications marked version 4.0 or later. Use IDC_SIZEALL
IDC_SIZEALL	Four-pointed arrow
IDC_SIZENESW	Double-pointed arrow pointing northeast and southwest
IDC_SIZENS	Double-pointed arrow pointing north and south
IDC_SIZENWSE	Double-pointed arrow pointing northwest and southeast

Table 7.4 Values for lpCursorName parameter. (Continued)

Value	Description
IDC_SIZEWE	Double-pointed arrow pointing west and east
IDC_UPARROW	Vertical arrow
IDC_WAIT	Hourglass

RETURN VALUES • On success, the return value is the handle to the newly loaded cursor. If the function fails, the return value is NULL.

THE LOADCURSORFROMFILE() FUNCTION

The **LoadCursorFromFile()** function creates a cursor based on data contained in a file. The file is specified by its name or by a system cursor identifier. The function returns a handle to the newly created cursor. Files containing cursor data may be in either cursor (.cur) or animated cursor (.ani) format.

```
HCURSOR LoadCursorFromFile(
  LPCTSTR lpFileName
);
```

lpFileName specifies the source of the file data to be used to create the cursor. The data in the file must be in either .cur or .ani format. When the high-order word of *lpszFileName* is nonzero, it is a pointer to a string that is a fully qualified name of a file containing cursor data. When the high-order word of *lpszFileName* is zero, the low-order word is a system cursor identifier. The function then searches the [Cursors] entry in the WIN.INI file for the file associated with the name of that system cursor. Here is a list of system cursor names and identifiers:

Table 7.5 System cursor names and identifiers.

System Cursor Name	System Cursor Identifier
AppStarting	OCR_APPSTARTING
Arrow	OCR_NORMAL
Crosshair	OCR_CROSS
Hand	Windows NT 5.0 and later: OCR_HAND
Help	OCR_HELP
IBeam	OCR_IBEAM
Icon	OCR_ICON

Table 7.5 — System cursor names and identifiers. (Continued)

System Cursor Name	System Cursor Identifier
No	OCR_NO
Size	OCR_SIZE
SizeAll	OCR_SIZEALL
SizeNESW	OCR_SIZENESW
SizeNS	OCR_SIZENS
SizeNWSE	OCR_SIZENWSE
SizeWE	OCR_SIZEWE
UpArrow	OCR_UP
Wait	OCR_WAIT

RETURN VALUES • On success, the return value is a handle to the new cursor. If the function fails, the return value is NULL.

THE SETCURSOR() FUNCTION

The **SetCursor()** function establishes the cursor shape.

```
HCURSOR SetCursor(
  HCURSOR hCursor
);
```

hCursor is a handle to the cursor. The cursor must have been created by the **Createcursor()** or loaded by the **LoadCursor()** function. If this parameter is NULL, the cursor is removed from the screen.

RETURN VALUES • The handle to the previous cursor, if there was one. If there was no previous cursor, the return value is NULL.

THE SETCURSORPOS() FUNCTION

The **SetCursorPos()** function moves the cursor to the specified screen coordinates. If the new coordinates are not within the screen rectangle set by the most recent **ClipCursor()** function, the system automatically adjusts the coordinates so that the cursor stays within the rectangle.

```
BOOL SetCursorPos(
  int X,
  int Y
```

```
);
```

X defines the new *x*-coordinate of the cursor in screen coordinates.

Y defines the new *y*-coordinate of the curso in screen coordinates,

RETURN VALUES • On success, the return value is nonzero. If the function fails, the return value is zero.

THE SHOWCURSOR() FUNCTION

The **ShowCursor()** function displays or hides the cursor.

```
int ShowCursor(
  BOOL bShow
);
```

bShow defines whether the internal display counter is to be incremented or decremented. If *bShow* is TRUE, the display count is incremented by one. If *bShow* is FALSE, the display count is decremented by one.

RETURN VALUES • The return value specifies the new display counter.

What's Next?

At this point, you should be thoroughly comfortable with creating and incorporating custom Windows icons and cursors. In the next chapter, we'll look at a close relative to the icon and cursor—the bitmap. You'll learn how to incorporate bitmaps into applications and manipulate their properties. Bitmaps can be anything from a drawing you make to photographs of loved ones.

E I G H T

Adding Multimedia Sound Resources

You learned in Chapter 7 that Windows makes it very easy for you to visually enhance your application with custom icons and cursors. It is just as easy to add multimedia sound resources that will make your programs even more dynamic by giving your applications full digital sound capabilities.

In Chapter 7, you learned how to use Visual C++ compiler's Resource Editor to create custom icons and cursors. In this chapter, you'll discover that multimedia sound resources can be found in a number of unique locations, such as files already installed in a subdirectory or found on the Internet. If you want to create your own multimedia sound files, you'll learn how to use the Windows sound recorder. The Windows sound recorder is provided with Windows 98 and is not part of the Visual C++ compiler package. The multimedia sound files used in this chapter and those created by the Windows sound recorder are wave files. You'll always know a wave file by the .wav file extension attached to it.

Finding and Making Sound Resources

As you work your way through the remainder of this chapter, you'll discover that sound resources can be added to an application with just a single function call. As such, the application code is simple and straightforward. In the following sections, we'll concentrate on a discussion of the where, how, and why of finding or creating unique sound resources. Later, you'll learn how to write a simple application capable of playing any sound resource you desire.

Finding Resources Already on Your Computer

One of the ways to locate your system's sound and wave files is to use the Sound Properties dialog box by opening the Control Panel, then the Sounds folder, and looking in the list box. Figure 8-1 launches this process for Windows 98.

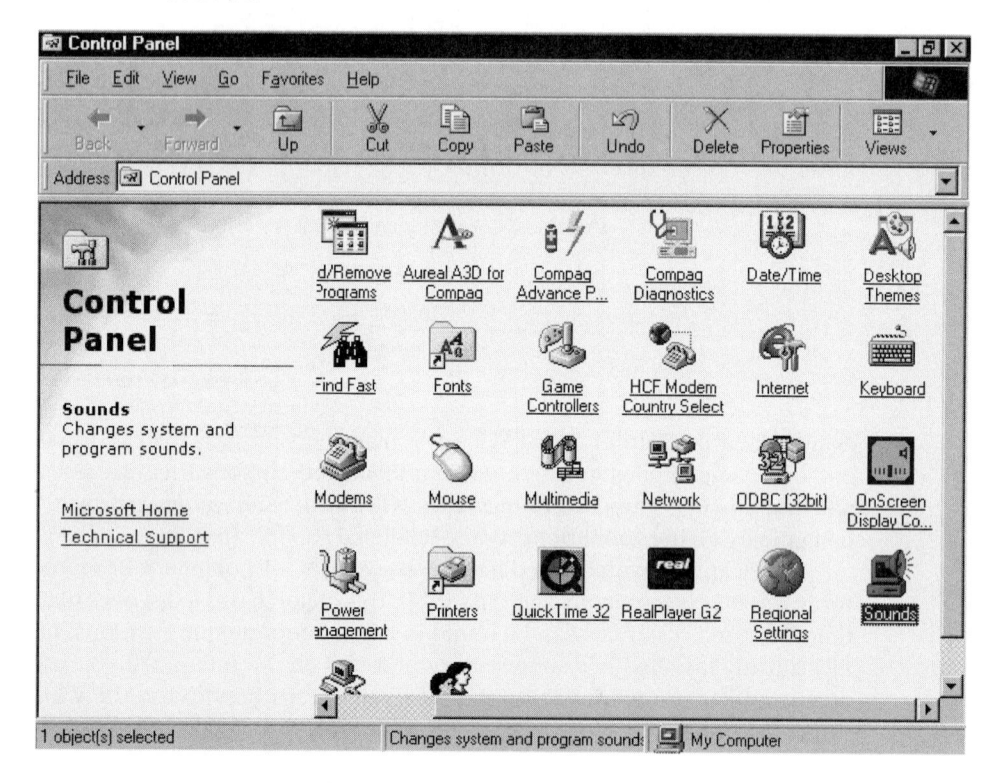

Figure 8-1 *Launching the Windows 98 Control Panel Sound Utility.*

Finding and Making Sound Resources **289**

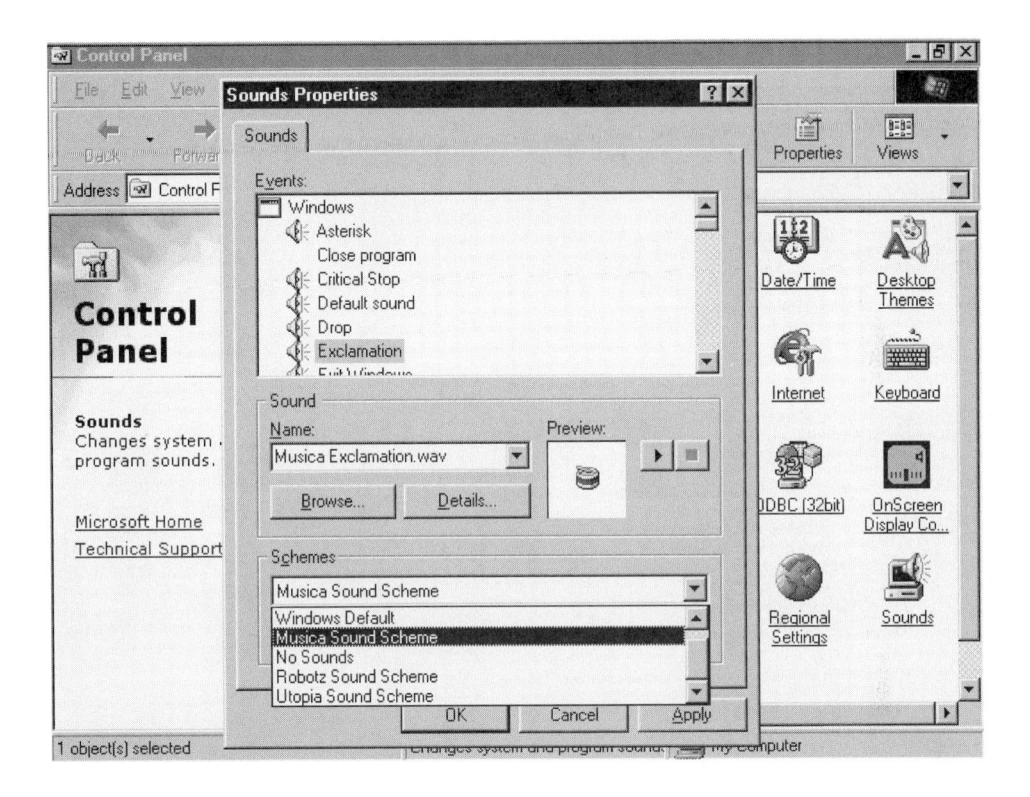

Figure 8-2 *Viewing Sound Scheme details.*

Figure 8-2 may look different here than on your screen, depending on installed options. However, you will have a list of default Schemes. Selecting one of these schemes updates the Events list. To test one of these sounds, simply click on the item in the Events list, then click on the right arrow button to the right of the Preview icon.

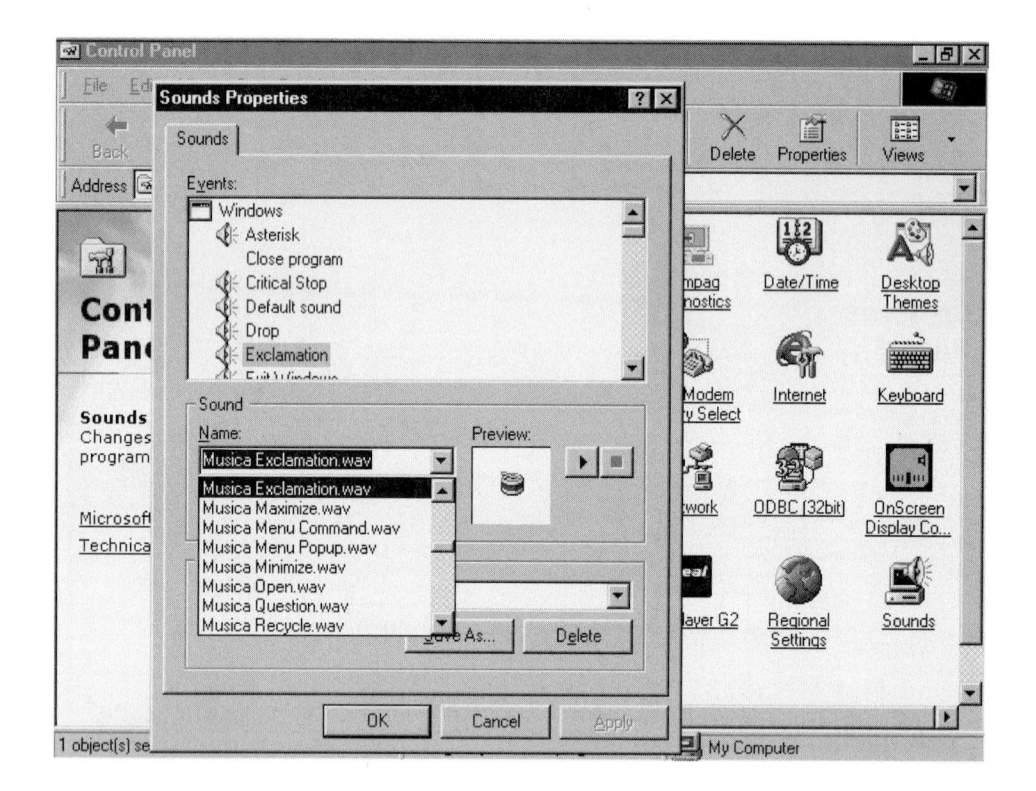

290 Chapter 8 • Adding Multimedia Sound Resources

Figure 8-3 *Expanded drop-down list of sound file names.*

Another option provided by the Windows Sounds utility is to reassociate a Windows event with a different sound file. For example, Figure 8-3 shows the file name associated with the Exclamation event. Should you wish to associate this action with a different sound file, this is where you would search for an alternate wave file and link its physical location with each event.

Finding and Making Sound Resources 291

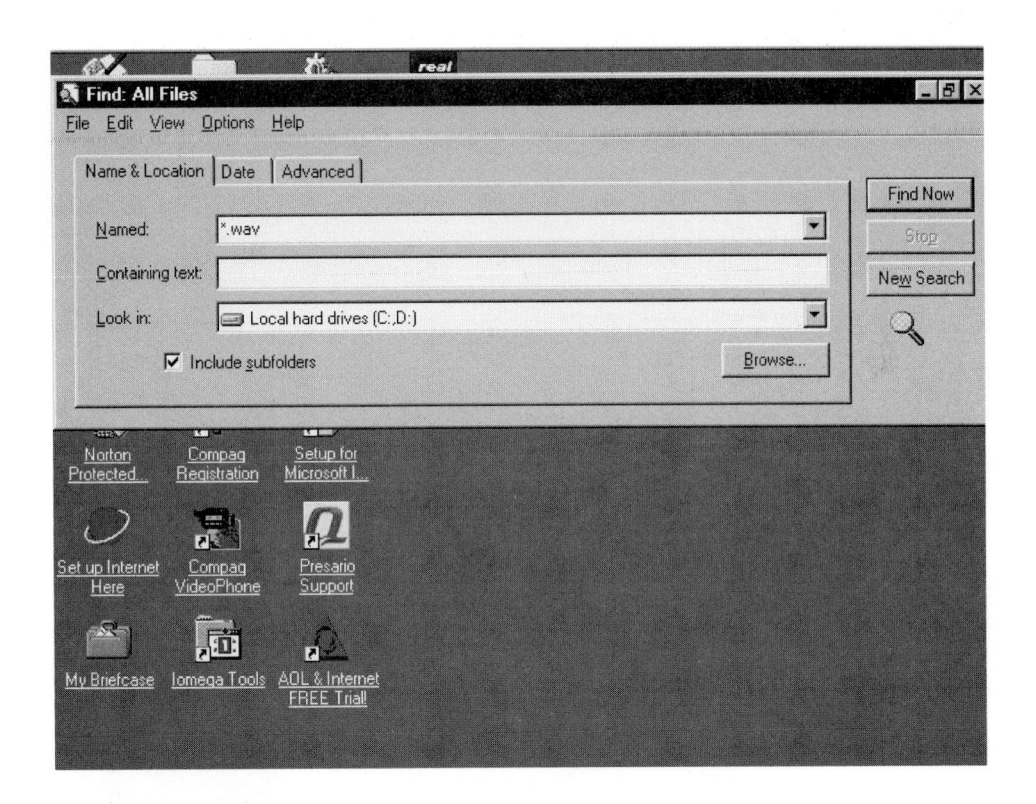

Figure 8–4 *Finding other system wave files with File | Find.*

By selecting the Start | Find | Files option, you can locate all of the sound files on your system. Figure 8-4 shows the Find: All Files window set to locate all files with a .wav file extension on drives C and D.

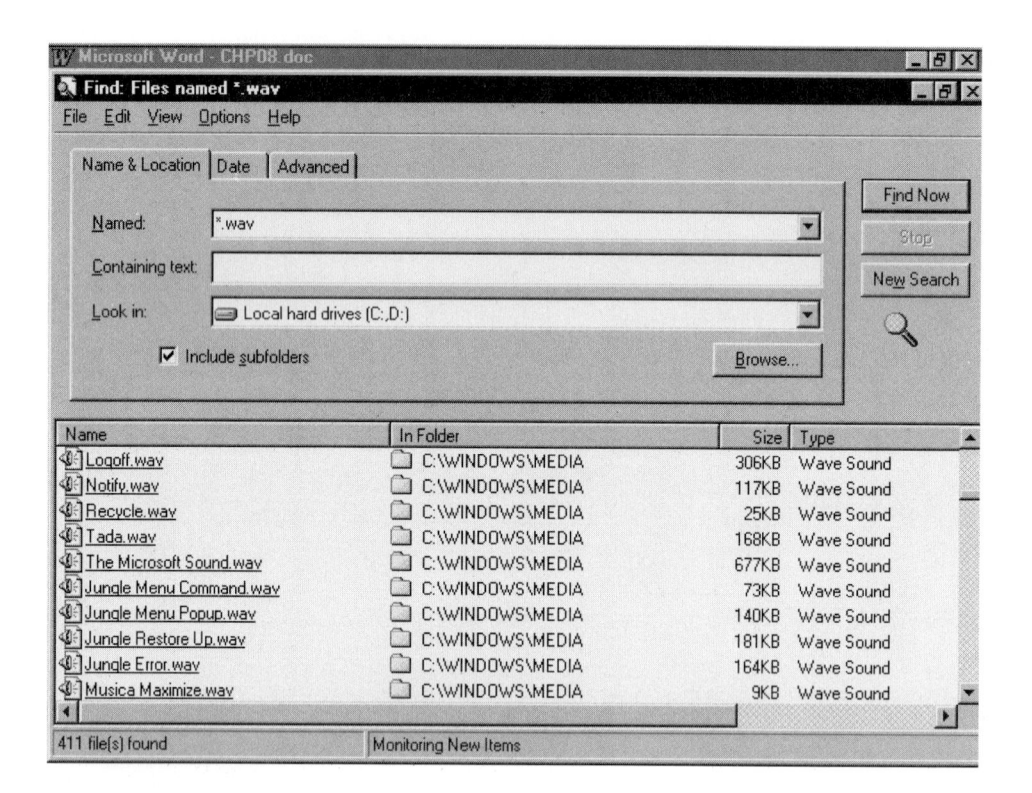

Figure 8-5 Sample results from Find:All Files *.wav (on C and D drives).

Figure 8-5 displays a sample Find:All Files *.wav results window. The window's contents were scrolled down to display one of the more popular file subdirectories used by Windows to locate .wav files. This list was created by installing Windows 98 Plus! along with its additional screen savers and associated sounds.

Finding Resources on the Internet

Of course, in today's computer environment, just about everyone is on the Internet. From product-specific upgrades to musical groups, everyone involved in this multimedia explosion posts sound files.

Accessing these files is as easy as starting your Internet Connection Service. Figure 8-6 shows AOL (America Online) 4.0 accessing the Lycos (www.lycos.com) search engine.

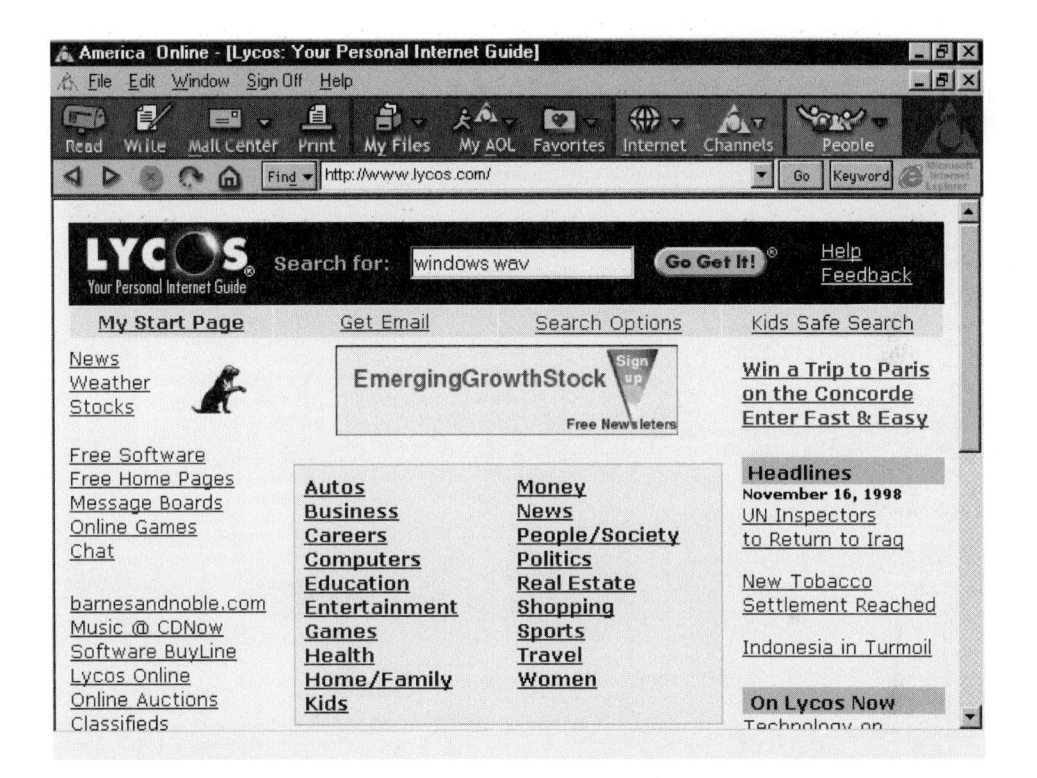

Figure 8-6 *Using AOL 4.0 and www.lycos.com to search for windows .wav files.*

Notice that the Lycos search engine is set to "Search for: windows .wav" files. Figure 8-7 displays one of the results pages referencing Windows-related updates.

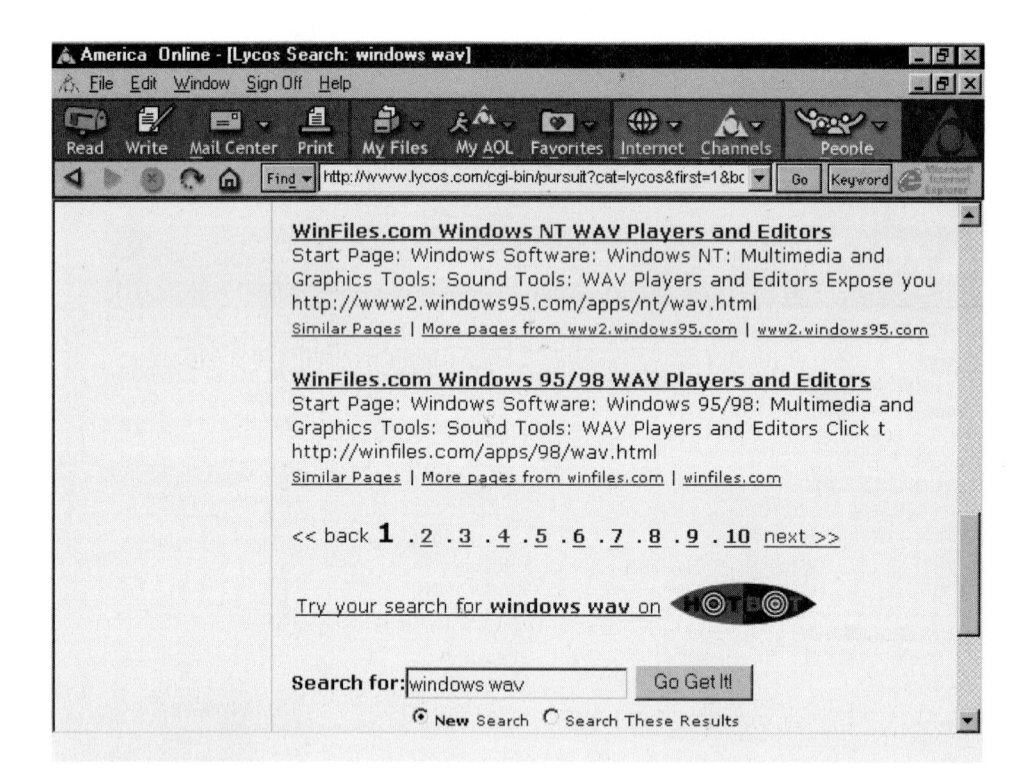

Figure 8-7 *Sample Lycos search results locating Windows WAV updates.*

Making Your Own Sound Resources with the Sound Recorder

Unquestionably, the most exciting option provided by Windows is the ability to create your *own* sound files. This simple process begins by opening the Start | Programs | Accessories | Entertainment | Sound Recorder (well, it is simple to use, if not simple to find!). Figure 8-8 illustrates this nested selection process.

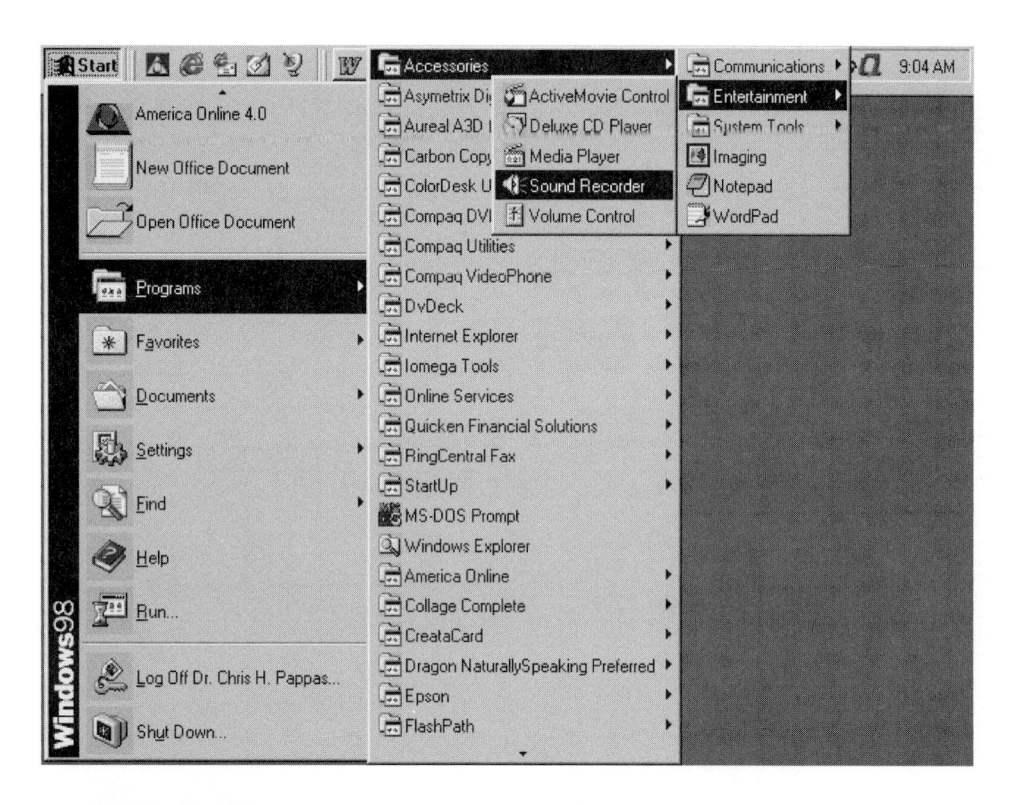

Finding and Making Sound Resources

Figure 8–8 *Launching the Start | Programs | Accessories | Entertainment | Sound Recorder.*

Make certain your system has a microphone connected and is active before clicking on the *red* begin-recording button seen in Figure 8-9.

Chapter 8 • Adding Multimedia Sound Resources

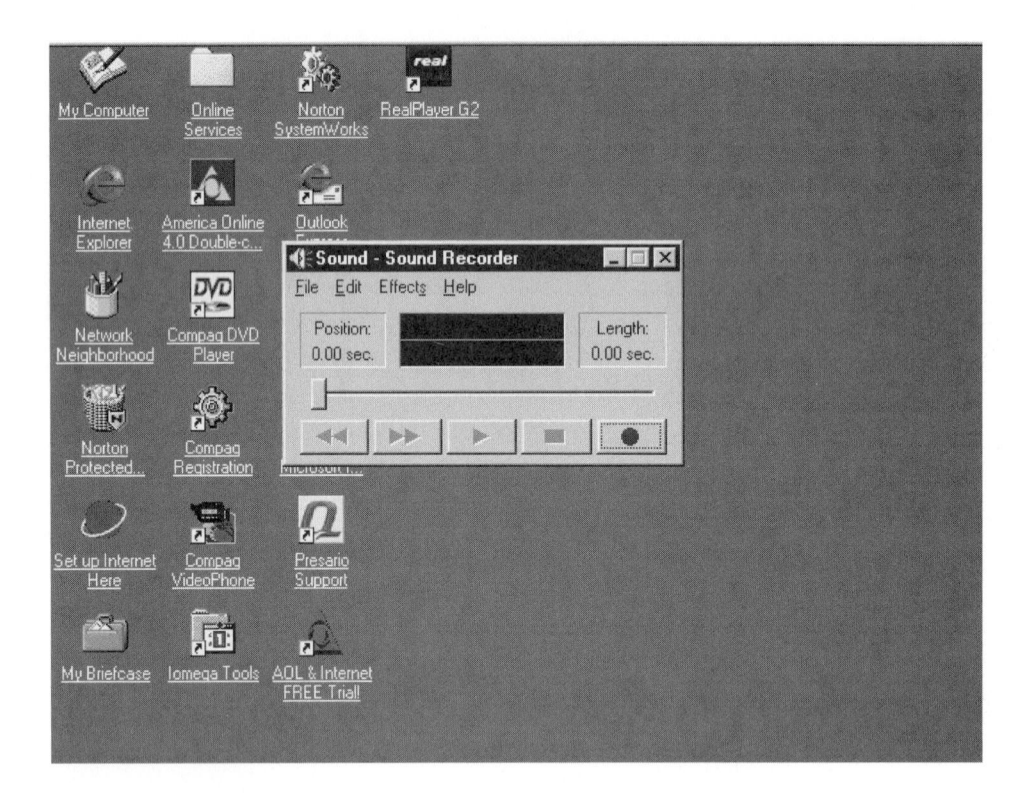

Figure 8-9 *Initial Sound Recorder window set to record.*

Clicking on the red dot (black in Figure 8-9) starts the recording process. As you speak, you will see the frequency bar fluctuate as it visually displays your spoken phonemes. To stop the recording process, simply click on the stop button (which was the round red button before you clicked on it). Now all that is left is for you to select File | Save, give your file a name with a .wav file extension. *Voila*.

Remember, you can associate these new files with any Windows Event by restarting the Control Panel Sound Utility, selecting an event, then browsing into the subdirectory where you just stored your "Declaration of Independence." Have fun personalizing your Windows environment for friends, family, and business associates. Wave files are easily copied to a floppy for system transfer. Take them to work and surprise everyone.

The sndPlaySound() Function

Windows programs can call the **sndPlaySound()** function to play a waveform sound. The function allows you to select the file by file name or by an entry in the registry or the WIN.INI file. This function offers a subset of the functionality of the **PlaySound()** function; **sndPlaySound()** is being maintained for backward compatibility. The function is defined in the following listing:

```
BOOL sndPlaySound(
  LPCSTR lpszSound,
  UINT fuSound
);
```

The first parameter, *lpszSound*, contains a string that specifies the sound to play. This parameter can be either an entry in the registry or in WIN.INI that identifies a system sound; or it can be the name of a waveform-audio file. (If the function does not find the entry, the parameter is treated as a file name.) If this parameter is NULL, any currently playing sound is stopped.

The second parameter, *fuSound*, uses specific predefined flags for playing the sound. These flags include SND_ASYNC, which plays the sound asynchronously, and the function returns immediately after beginning the sound. To terminate an asynchronously played sound, you must call **sndPlaySound()** with *lpszSoundName* set to NULL.

If *fuSound* is set to SND_LOOP, Windows plays the sound repeatedly until **sndPlaySound()** is called again with the *lpszSoundName* parameter set to NULL. You must also specify the SND_ASYNC flag to loop sounds.

If set to SND_MEMORY, *lpszSoundName* must define an image of a waveform sound in memory. SND_NODEFAULT can be ORed with any other SND_ parameter telling Windows not to play any sound— even the default sound— when the specified file name does not exist.

For your **sndPlaySound()** request not to interrupt a currently playing sound, select the SND_NOSTOP flag. If a sound is currently playing, the function immediately returns FALSE, without playing the requested sound.

The last flag option is SND_SYNC, which instructs Windows to play the sound synchronously, and the function does not return until the sound ends.

sndPlaySound() returns TRUE if successful or FALSE otherwise. When **sndPlaySound()** cannot find the specified file, **sndPlaySound()** by default plays the system default sound. If there is no system default entry in the registry or WIN.INI file or if the default sound cannot be found, the function makes no sound and returns FALSE.

Also, the selected sound file must fit in available physical memory and be playable by an installed waveform-audio device driver. When **sndPlaySound()** does not find the sound in the current directory, the function searches for it, using the standard directory-search order.

Adding Multimedia Sound Resources to an Application

One of the easiest resources you can add to a Windows application is sound. Once you have found or created a wave file, your application accesses the digitized file with a call to the **sndPlaySound()** function discussed in the previous section.

To build this application from your Visual C++ compiler you will need to create a project file named *Wave*. The C++ source code file is named *Wave.cpp*. You'll also need to find or create a sound file named *Test.wav* and save it in the project's subdirectory.

Here is the Wave.cpp source code:

```
//
// Wave.cpp
// Simple Windows Application for playing multimedia
// sound files (wave files).
// Copyright (c) William H. Murray and Chris H. Pappas, 1999
//

#include <windows.h>
#include <mmsystem.h>

LRESULT CALLBACK WndProc(HWND,UINT,WPARAM,LPARAM);

char szProgName[]="ProgName";

int WINAPI WinMain(HINSTANCE hInst,HINSTANCE hPreInst,
                   LPSTR lpszCmdLine,int nCmdShow)
{
  HWND hWnd;
  MSG  lpMsg;
  WNDCLASS wcApp;

  wcApp.lpszClassName=szProgName;
  wcApp.hInstance      =hInst;
  wcApp.lpfnWndProc    =WndProc;
  wcApp.hCursor        =LoadCursor(NULL,IDC_ARROW);
  wcApp.hIcon          =0;
  wcApp.lpszMenuName   =0;
  wcApp.hbrBackground=(HBRUSH) GetStockObject(WHITE_BRUSH);
  wcApp.style          =CS_HREDRAW|CS_VREDRAW;
  wcApp.cbClsExtra     =0;
  wcApp.cbWndExtra     =0;
  if (!RegisterClass (&wcApp))
    return 0;

  hWnd=CreateWindow(szProgName,"Playing A Sound File",
                    WS_OVERLAPPEDWINDOW,CW_USEDEFAULT,
```

```
               CW_USEDEFAULT,CW_USEDEFAULT,
               CW_USEDEFAULT,(HWND)NULL,(HMENU)NULL,
               hInst,(LPSTR)NULL);
  ShowWindow(hWnd,nCmdShow);
  UpdateWindow(hWnd);
  while (GetMessage(&lpMsg,0,0,0)) {
    TranslateMessage(&lpMsg);
    DispatchMessage(&lpMsg);
  }
  return(lpMsg.wParam);
}


LRESULT CALLBACK WndProc(HWND hWnd,UINT messg,
                         WPARAM wParam,LPARAM lParam)
{
  HDC hdc;
  PAINTSTRUCT ps;

  switch (messg)
  {
    case WM_PAINT:
      hdc=BeginPaint(hWnd,&ps);

      TextOut(hdc,30,20,"This simple application plays",29);
      TextOut(hdc,30,60,"a single sound file each time",29);
      TextOut(hdc,30,100,"this window is resized.",23);

      // play the sound file named Test.wav
      // found in the project's subdirectory
      sndPlaySound("c:Test.wav",SND_ASYNC);

      ValidateRect(hWnd,NULL);
      EndPaint(hWnd,&ps);
      break;

    case WM_DESTROY:
      PostQuitMessage(0);
      break;

    default:
      return(DefWindowProc(hWnd,messg,wParam,lParam));
      break;
  }
  return(0);
}
```

This application demonstrates the simplest approach to adding audible output to a Windows application. If you examine the code, you see it is very similar to the template code we've been using for several chapters. When you look closely at the source code, however, you probably noticed a new

#include file. The mmsystem.h header file contains many of the constants, macros, and function prototypes needed to control wave files. This header file should be included immediately after the windows.h header file.

When this application is executed, it will display a message to the user, telling them that they will hear the sound file each time the window is resized. The application then calls the **sndPlaySound()** function, sending it the name of the file to play and its mode.

When you build this application, it is **very** important that you specify that the Visual C++ linker will also include the winmm.lib during the linking phase of the build process. If you don't, you'll get several error messages and no executable file! Examine your project utility's link statements and add this library if it does not already exist.

More Resources?

By this time, we're sure you are thoroughly comfortable with adding icons, cursors, and sound resources. In the next chapter, you will learn how to enhance your application's user interface with bitmap resources. Bitmaps can be made of GDI graphics primitives or even photographs. As such, they are an important resource for many professional applications.

N I N E

Creating and Displaying Bitmaps

In recent chapters, you have learned how to add important resources to your Windows applications. Icons, cursors, fonts, and sound resources are all important means of making applications appear with a professional touch.

You will learn how to create, store, load, and manipulate bitmapped images in this chapter.

Images in the Window

There are basically two methods of creating images in a window. The first method involves the use of graphics device interface (GDI) drawing primitives and the second involves the use of bitmaps.

In Chapter 4, you learned how to dynamically draw objects in the client area of a window with the use of GDI drawing primitives. GDI drawing primitives are one of the chief means of creating graphical images. They are dynamic because the images are not stored but drawn each time the function is encountered. If you resize a window, for example, each function is called again with each issue of a WM_PAINT message. When the drawing cycle becomes long enough, the user must wait for the full rendering of the screen. This is seen as one of the disadvantages of using complicated GDI images. Of course, there is the other disadvantage! Have you ever tried to create a photographic-quality image with GDI graphics? It's almost impossible and must proceed at almost a pixel at a time.

The alternate means of placing images on the screen is with a bitmap. Think of a bitmap image as a digital photograph of a screen. Once created, it can be stored and quickly retrieved. Bitmaps can be composed of simple graphics objects such as lines, circles, or rectangles, or complicated images such as photographs. Bitmaps must be created, before they can be stored, so some means of drawing or photographing an image must be available. Bitmaps can be easily stored, but the storage requirements can be very large for photographic-quality bitmaps. If you have become involved with digital photography, you already know that 32-bit 1024 x 1024 images can easily exceed several megabytes. As long as you have a large amount of hard disk storage, this will not be a major problem. The other downside of bitmapped images is the fact that they are not easily scalable. You learned, in Chapter 5 that GDI graphics images could easily be scaled to fit the screen. Bitmaps are a little harder as the manipulation of each of the image's pixels is at stake. There are several ways bitmaps can be resized, and we will look at a very popular technique in this chapter.

Important Windows Bitmap Functions

There are several key functions that are used when working with bitmaps. Perhaps the most famous is the **BitBlt()** function. Another popular function is the **StretchBlt()** function and its associated support function **SetStretchBltMode()**. The **StretchBlt()** function can scale a bitmapped image based upon the parameters supplied with the function. If you venture into the world of Windows NT programming, you'll find additional bitmap functions, such as **PlgBlt()** and **MaskBlt()**. These special NT functions will not be discussed here, but full details on each of them is available with the Visual C++ Help facility.

In the following sections we'll examine the details for using the **BitBlt()** and **StretchBlt()** functions because these functions operate across all Windows platforms.

The BitBlt() Function

The **BitBlt()** function was designed to move a bitmap from the source device context to the destination context. If the source and destination contexts are the same, the function can be used to replicate a pattern anywhere on the screen.

The function can be called in the following manner:

```
BitBlt(hDestDC,x,y,nWidth,nHeight,
       hSrcDC,xSrc,ySrc,dwRop);
```

In the **BitBlt()** function, the *hDestDC* parameter is the handle of the receiving device context. The *hSrcDC* parameter is the handle of the device context that the bitmap will be copied from. The *x* and *y* parameters are of type **int** and specify the logical coordinates of the upper left corner of the des-

Important Windows Bitmap Functions **303**

tination rectangle. The *nWidth* and *nHeight* parameters are of type **int** and specify the width and height of the destination rectangle and source bitmap. The *xSrc* and *ySrc* parameters are of type **int** and specify the logical X and Y coordinates of the upper left corner of the source bitmap. The *dwRop* parameter is of type **DWORD**. Table 9.1 shows possible values for the *dwRop* parameter.

Table 9.1 Raster operation codes for **BitBit()** Function.

Value	Description
BLACKNESS	output all black
DSTINVERT	inverts destination bitmap
MERGECOPY	ANDs the pattern and source bitmap
MERGEPAINT	ORs inverted source and destination bitmap
NOTSRCCOPY	copies inverted source bitmap to destination
NOTSRCERASE	source and destination are ANDed together
PATCOPY	copies pattern to destination bitmap
PATINVERT	ORs destination with pattern bitmap
PATPAINT	ORs inverted source with pattern bitmap and source bitmap
SRCAND	ANDs together destination and source bitmaps
SRCCOPY	copies source to destination bitmap
SRCERASE	ANDs an inverted destination bitmap with source bitmap
SRCINVERT	XORs destination and source bitmaps
SRCPAINT	ORs together destination and source bitmaps
WHITENESS	output all white

Bitmaps can be created in a variety of ways—after all, they are merely digital photographs of a full or partial window.

WORKING WITH GDI IMAGES

The following portion of code will draw a small rectangle in the upper left portion of the window with GDI graphics primitives. The rectangle will be filled with a yellow brush. The string *BitBlt* will be drawn inside the rectangle.

```
// draw a small yellow rectangle on left
hYellowBrush=CreateSolidBrush(RGB(255,255,0));
hOrgBrush=SelectObject(hdc,hYellowBrush);
Rectangle(hdc,20,10,70,60);
```

```
TextOut(hdc,25,30,"BitBlt",6);
```

A digital photograph can be taken of this small rectangular bitmapped image using the **BitBlt()** function. Here is a portion of code that can do this.

```
// copy the single image drawn above and
// print across the window, in a rectangle, with
// the BitBlt function.
newy=10;
for(newx=80;newx<600;newx+=60)
BitBlt(hdc,newx,newy,50,50,hdc,20,10,SRCCOPY);
```

Once the image is copied, it can be replicated any number of times on the screen. Hey, this would be a neat way to create digital wallpaper!

When you examine the **BitBlt()** function, can you determine how the various parameters were derived? First, the original image was drawn with the upper left corner of the rectangle at 20,10. You can see those numbers used in the calls to the **Rectangle()** and **BitBlt()** functions. The horizontal dimension of the rectangle is derived by taking 70 - 20 = 50. The vertical dimension of the rectangle is derived by taking 60 - 10 = 50. Both the horizontal and vertical dimensions are used by **BitBlt()**. The variables *newx* and *newy* point to window locations for the placement of the new bitmapped image. In this case, **BitBlt()** is in a loop that will replicate the image ten times. The device context is the same for the original and replicated images.

It is also possible to use a *memory device context*. The handle for a memory device context is often *hmdc*. When a memory device context is used to store a bitmapped image, the image is saved in memory rather than displaying it in the window.

> **note** In truth, the image is ALWAYS in memory, whether it is displayed on the screen or not.

WORKING WITH PHOTOGRAPHS AND SCANNED IMAGES

The bitmapped image used in this example was scanned by a scanner and saved in a file with a .bmp file extension. We'll load the bitmap resource and use the **BitBlt()** function to display the image.

The bitmap resource is identified as a BITMAP resource.

```
BMImage BITMAP scan.bmp
```

The bitmap resource is loaded with a call to the **LoadBitmap()** function. A handle to the bitmap is then returned. In the following example, the handle is *hBitmap*.

```
char szBMName[]="BMImage";
```

```
HBITMAP hBitmap;
   .
   .
   .
hBitmap-LoadBitmap(hInst,szBMName);
```

The **LoadBitmap()** function returns the handle, which can then be used by the **BitBlt()** function.

The code for drawing the bitmapped image is relatively easy but involves the use of the **BITMAP** structure. The BITMAP structure holds information regarding the bitmap.

```
  static BITMAP bm;
```

The variable *bm* is associated with the **BITMAP** structure. This structure contains the following members:

```
typedef struct tagBITMAP {
   LONG    bmType;
   LONG    bmWidth;
   LONG    bmHeight;
   LONG    bmWidthBytes;
   WORD    bmPlanes;
   WORD    bmBitsPixel;
   LPVOID  bmBits;
} BITMAP;
```

This structure holds information on this bitmap's type, width, height, color format, and bit values. The *bmType* member must be zero. The *bmWidth* and *bmHeight* members specify the width and height of the bitmap in pixels. The *bmWidthBytes* member gives the number of bytes in each scan line. This value must be divisible by four. The number of color planes is given by the *bmPlanes* member. The number of bits used to indicate the color of a pixel is given by the *bmBitsPixel* member. Finally, the *bmBits* member points to the location of the bit values for the bitmap. For this example, only *bmWidth* and *bmHeight* are needed.

First, a memory device context (identified with the *hmdc* handle) that is compatible with the device context (identified with the *hdc* handle) is created. This is achieved with a call to the **CreateCompatibleDC()** function.

```
hmdc=CreateCompatibleDC(hdc);
```

The bitmapped image is now selected to the memory device context using the **SelectObject()** function. You've seen the **SelectObject()** function in earlier chapters used to select fonts, brushes, and pens.

```
SelectObject(hmdc,hBitmap);
```

The **GetObject()** function will get the previously selected object. The **GetObject()** function requires the handle of the bitmapped image, the size of the bitmap structure, in bytes, and the location of the structure.

```
GetObject(hBitmap,sizeof(bm),(LPSTR) &bm);
```

All that is needed now is a call to **BitBlt()** to draw the image in the window.

```
BitBlt(hdc,0,0,bm.bmWidth,bm.bmHeight,hmdc,0,0,SRCCOPY);
```

Unlike the GDI bitmap example, the device context for the drawing and image are not the same. Here, *hdc* is the handle that identifies the device context where the image will be drawn, and *hmdc* is the handle to the compatible memory device context for the image.

The image will be drawn to the upper left corner of the window (0,0). The width and height information for the image is retrieved from the **BITMAP** structure.

Before leaving the example, remember to delete the memory device context with a call to the **DeleteDC()** function.

```
DeleteDC(hmdc);
```

Most bitmapped work can be handled by one of these two techniques. In the next section, we'll examine a function that is very similar to the **BitBlt()** function. **StretchBlt()** performs many of the same operations at **BitBlt()**, with the added feature of allowing us to shrink or stretch a bitmapped image.

The StretchBlt() Function

In the previous section, you learned various methods for employing the **BitBlt()** function. You'll find that the **StretchBlt()** function operates in a similar manner but with the added capability of shrinking or stretching a bitmapped image. In many cases, the two functions can be swapped in program code, with just the necessary function parameters being supplied. Let's examine the syntax of using the **StretchBlt()** function.

The **StretchBlt()** function is used to copy a bitmap from a source rectangle into a destination rectangle, stretching or compressing the bitmap to fit the dimensions of the destination rectangle. The system stretches or compresses the bitmap according to the stretching mode currently set in the destination device context.

```
BOOL StretchBlt(HDC hdcDest,int nXOriginDest,int nYOriginDest,
          int nWidthDest,int nHeightDest,HDC hdcSrc,
          int nXOriginSrc,int nYOriginSrc,int nWidthSrc,
          int nHeightSrc,DWORD dwRop);
```

Here, the *hdcDest* parameter serves as the handle to the destination device context. The *nXOriginDest* parameter is the *x*-coordinate, in logical units, of the upper left corner of the destination rectangle. The *nYOriginDest* parameter is the *y*-coordinate, in logical units, of the upper left corner of the destination rectangle. The *nWidthDest* parameter is the width, in logical units, of the destination rectangle. The *nHeightDest* parameter is the height, in logical units, of the destination rectangle. The *hdcSrc* parameter serves as the handle to the source device context. The *nXOriginSrc* parameter is the *x*-coordinate, in logical units, of the upper left corner of the source rectangle. The *nYOriginSrc* parameter is the *y*-coordinate, in logical units, of the upper left corner of the source rectangle. The *nWidthSrc* parameter is the width, in logical units, of the source rectangle. The *nHeightSrc* parameter is the height, in logical units, of the source rectangle. Finally, the *dwRop* parameter is the raster operation that is to be performed. The raster operation codes are similar to those used for **BitBlt()**.

The function, **StretchBlt()**, shrinks or stretches the source bitmap in memory and copies the result to the destination rectangle. The color data for pattern or destination pixels is merged after the shrinking or stretching takes place. The system will use the currently selected brush when a brush is required and select it into the destination device context.

In cases where the source and pattern bitmaps do not have the same color format, the function will attempt to convert them to match the destination bitmap.

The destination coordinates for the bitmap are transformed using the transformation given for the destination device context. The source coordinates for the bitmap are transformed using the transformation given for the source device context. The source transformation cannot have a rotation or shear.

The **StretchBlt()** function can be used to convert monochrome bitmaps to color bitmaps. In these cases the function will set white pixels to the background color and black pixels to the foreground color. If the reverse process is required, the function sets pixels matching the background color to white and all other pixels to black. The results of these conversions are often not what was anticipated!

Here is an actual portion of code that uses the **StretchBlt()** function to stretch a bitmap to twice its original size.

```
hmdc=CreateCompatibleDC(hdc);
SelectObject(hmdc,hBitmap);
GetObject(hBitmap,sizeof(bm),(LPSTR) &bm);

StretchBlt(hdc,100,100,2*bm.bmWidth,
           2*bm.bmHeight,hmdc,0,0,bm.bmWidth,
           bm.bmHeight,SRCCOPY);

DeleteDC(hmdc);
```

The stretched image is started at coordinate positions 100,100. The bitmap then extends a width of 2*bm.bmWidth and a height of 2*bm.bmHeight. The width and height parameters from the **BITMAP** structure represent the dimensions of the original bitmapped image.

The Photo project, discussed later in this chapter, makes use of the **StretchBlt()** function to stretch a photographic image.

The SetStretchBltMode() Function

The **SetStretchBltMode()** function is used to set the bitmap stretching mode in the given device context. It is often used in conjunction with the **StretchBlt()** function. The syntax for this function is:

```
int SetStretchBltMode(HDC hdc, int iStretchMode);
```

Here, the *hdc* parameter represents the handle to the device context. The *iStretchMode* parameter gives the stretching mode. Table 9.2 shows valid values for the stretching mode.

Table 9.2 *iStretchMode* parameter values.

Value	Description
BLACKONWHITE	Uses a Boolean AND operation with the color values for the existing and deleted pixels. When a monochrome bitmap is used, this mode saves black pixels at the expense of white pixels. Used to preserve foreground pixels.
COLORONCOLOR	Deletes the eliminated lines of pixels. Typically used to preserve color in color bitmaps.
HALFTONE	Pixels are mapped from the source rectangle into blocks of pixels at the destination rectangle. The color over the destination block of pixels is an average that approximates the color of the source pixels. This mode requires extended source image processing compared to the other modes, but renders higher quality images
STRETCH_ANDSCANS	See BLACKONWHITE.
STRETCH_DELETESCANS	See COLORONCOLOR.
STRETCH_HALFTONE	See HALFTONE.
STRETCH_ORSCANS	Uses a Boolean OR operation with the color values for the existing and deleted pixels. When a monochrome bitmap is used, this mode saves white pixels at the expense of black pixels. Used to preserve foreground pixels.
WHITEONBLACK	See STRETCH_ORSCANS.

This function determines how the system combines rows or columns of a bitmap with existing pixels on a display device. The function can be used in conjunction with the **StretchBlt()** function to achieve desired results.

Complete Bitmap Examples

In the previous sections of this chapter, we examined portions of code for creating, storing, and retrieving bitmapped images. The following examples are complete applications that illustrate how to work with bitmapped images created by a variety of sources.

A GDI Graphics Example

The following project, named *GDI*, draws a small rectangular figure on the screen then copies that portion of the screen as a bitmap. Once in memory, the image can be replicated several times in the window without the need for calling the GDI drawing functions.

Create this project in the normal manner and use the swt.cpp template code for the initial source code. You can then simply add the code unique to this application. The complete source code listing, named *GDI.cpp*, is shown next.

```
//
// GDI.cpp
// This application will illustrate how to draw an image
// with simple GDI graphics primitives, capture it as a
// bitmapped image and replicate it several times in the
// window.
// Copyright (c) William H. Murray and Chris H. Pappas, 1999
//

#include <windows.h>

LRESULT CALLBACK WndProc(HWND,UINT,WPARAM,LPARAM);

char szProgName[]="ProgName";

int WINAPI WinMain(HINSTANCE hInst,HINSTANCE hPreInst,
                   LPSTR lpszCmdLine,int nCmdShow)
{
  HWND hWnd;
  MSG  lpMsg;
  WNDCLASS wcApp;

  wcApp.lpszClassName=szProgName;
  wcApp.hInstance     =hInst;
  wcApp.lpfnWndProc   =WndProc;
```

310 Chapter 9 • Creating and Displaying Bitmaps

```
  wcApp.hCursor       =LoadCursor(NULL,IDC_ARROW);
  wcApp.hIcon         =0;
  wcApp.lpszMenuName  =0;
  wcApp.hbrBackground=(HBRUSH) GetStockObject(WHITE_BRUSH);
  wcApp.style         =CS_HREDRAW|CS_VREDRAW;
  wcApp.cbClsExtra    =0;
  wcApp.cbWndExtra    =0;
  if (!RegisterClass (&wcApp))
    return 0;

  hWnd=CreateWindow(szProgName,
                    "A Bitmap created from GDI Graphics",
                    WS_OVERLAPPEDWINDOW,CW_USEDEFAULT,
                    CW_USEDEFAULT,CW_USEDEFAULT,
                    CW_USEDEFAULT,(HWND)NULL,(HMENU)NULL,
                    hInst,(LPSTR)NULL);
  ShowWindow(hWnd,nCmdShow);
  UpdateWindow(hWnd);
  while (GetMessage(&lpMsg,0,0,0)) {
    TranslateMessage(&lpMsg);
    DispatchMessage(&lpMsg);
  }
  return(lpMsg.wParam);
}


LRESULT CALLBACK WndProc(HWND hWnd,UINT messg,
                         WPARAM wParam,LPARAM lParam)
{
  HDC hdc;
  PAINTSTRUCT ps;
  static HBRUSH hOrgBrush;
  static HBRUSH hYellowBrush;
  int newx,newy;

  switch (messg)
  {
    case WM_PAINT:
      hdc=BeginPaint(hWnd,&ps);

      // draw a small yellow rectangle on left
      hYellowBrush=CreateSolidBrush(RGB(255,255,0));
      hOrgBrush=(HBRUSH) SelectObject(hdc,hYellowBrush);
      Rectangle(hdc,20,10,70,60);
      TextOut(hdc,25,30,"BitBlt",6);

      // copy the single image drawn above and
      // print across the window, in a rectangle, with
      // the BitBlt function.
      newy=10;
```

```
        for(newx=80;newx<600;newx+=60)
           BitBlt(hdc,newx,newy,50,50,hdc,20,10,SRCCOPY);

        ValidateRect(hWnd,NULL);
        EndPaint(hWnd,&ps);
        break;

     case WM_DESTROY:
        DeleteObject(hYellowBrush);
        PostQuitMessage(0);
        break;

     default:
        return(DefWindowProc(hWnd,messg,wParam,lParam));
        break;
   }
   return(0);
}
```

As you can see, the core programming code looks very similar to the partial programming example discussed earlier in this chapter.

```
// draw a small yellow rectangle on left
hYellowBrush=CreateSolidBrush(RGB(255,255,0));
hOrgBrush=(HBRUSH) SelectObject(hdc,hYellowBrush);
Rectangle(hdc,20,10,70,60);
TextOut(hdc,25,30,"BitBlt",6);

// copy the single image drawn above and
// print across the window, in a rectangle, with
// the BitBlt function.
newy=10;
for(newx=80;newx<600;newx+=60)
   BitBlt(hdc,newx,newy,50,50,hdc,20,10,SRCCOPY);
```

The key here is to first draw the rectangular object and text with normal GDI graphics functions. The **BitBlt()** function is then employed in a **for** loop to copy the portion of the window with the figure and replicate it several more times by incrementing the drawing position.

Return to the section devoted to the discussion of the **BitBlt()** function and make sure you understand where and why each parameter for the function is obtained as you study this program code.

Figure 9-1 shows the window when this application is executed.

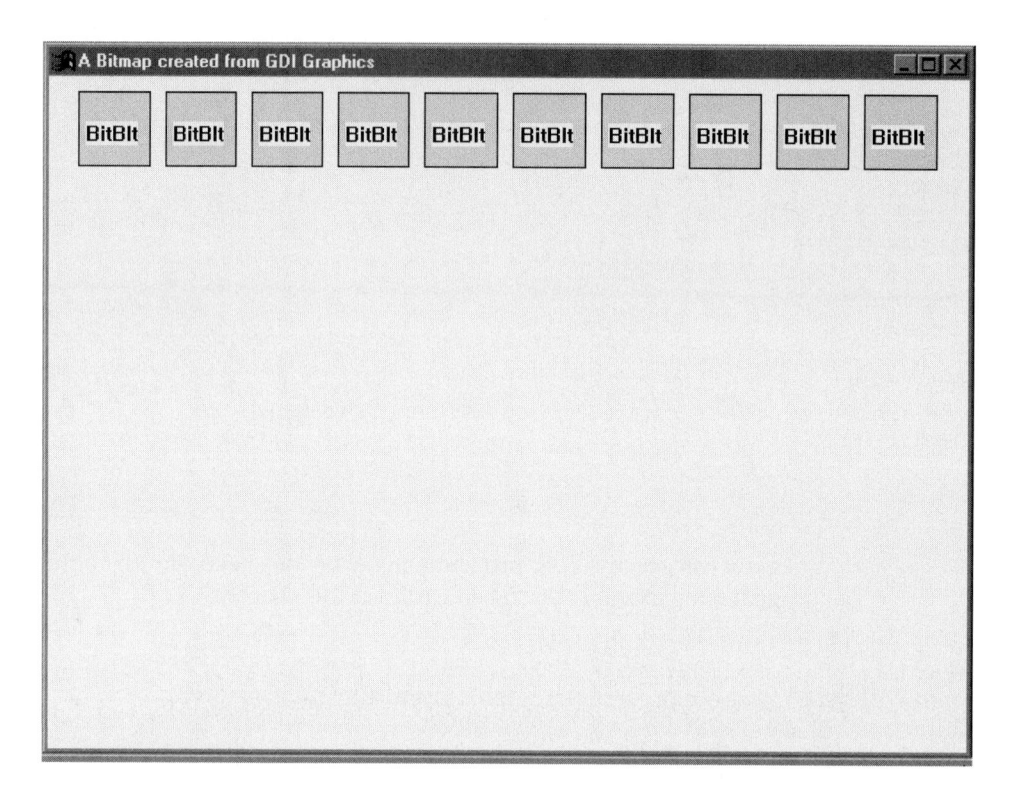

Figure 9-1 *A small portion of the window is replicated several times.*

The bitmapped image doesn't have to be obtained from figures already drawn in the window. Bitmaps can be drawn with any properly stored image. In the next example, we'll use an image obtained from a scanner.

Using a Scanned Bitmap Image

Scanners are another popular means of obtaining a bitmapped image. Select a document or piece of art work to scan and save the final image in a bitmap format. This is one of the first places where you'll see how the document size, resolution, and number of colors affects the overall file size. Don't be surprised to see file sizes well over one megabyte for large documents.

This project is named *Image*. You can create the project in the normal manner with your Visual C++ compiler. Use the swt.cpp template code, developed in Chapter 2, as the base code for the source code file. Then add the unique code, shown in this project's source code listing, to complete your application.

Because this project will use an external bitmapped file obtained with a scanner, it will have to be brought into the project with the Resource Editor.

Complete Bitmap Examples **313**

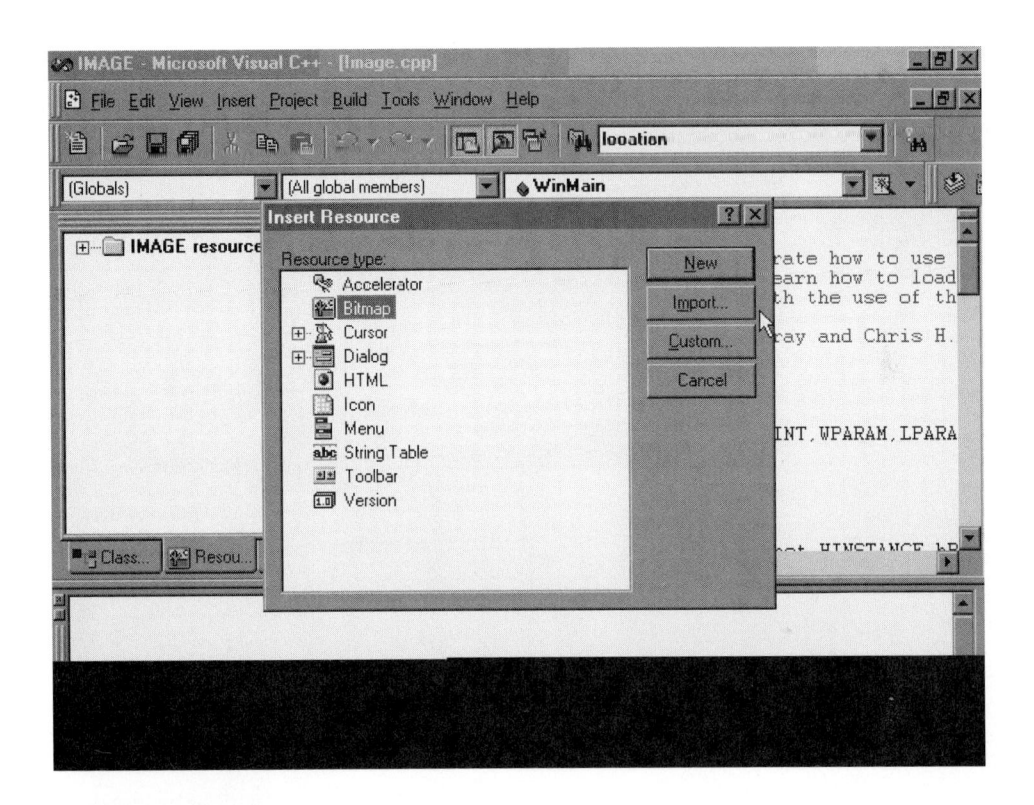

Figure 9-2 *Adding a previously defined bitmap image to the IMAGE project.*

Use the Visual C++ Insert|Resource menu option to add a predefined bitmap resource, as shown in Figure 9-2.

Once the resource is added, change the default ID value for the resource to BMImage, as shown in Figure 9-3.

314 Chapter 9 • Creating and Displaying Bitmaps

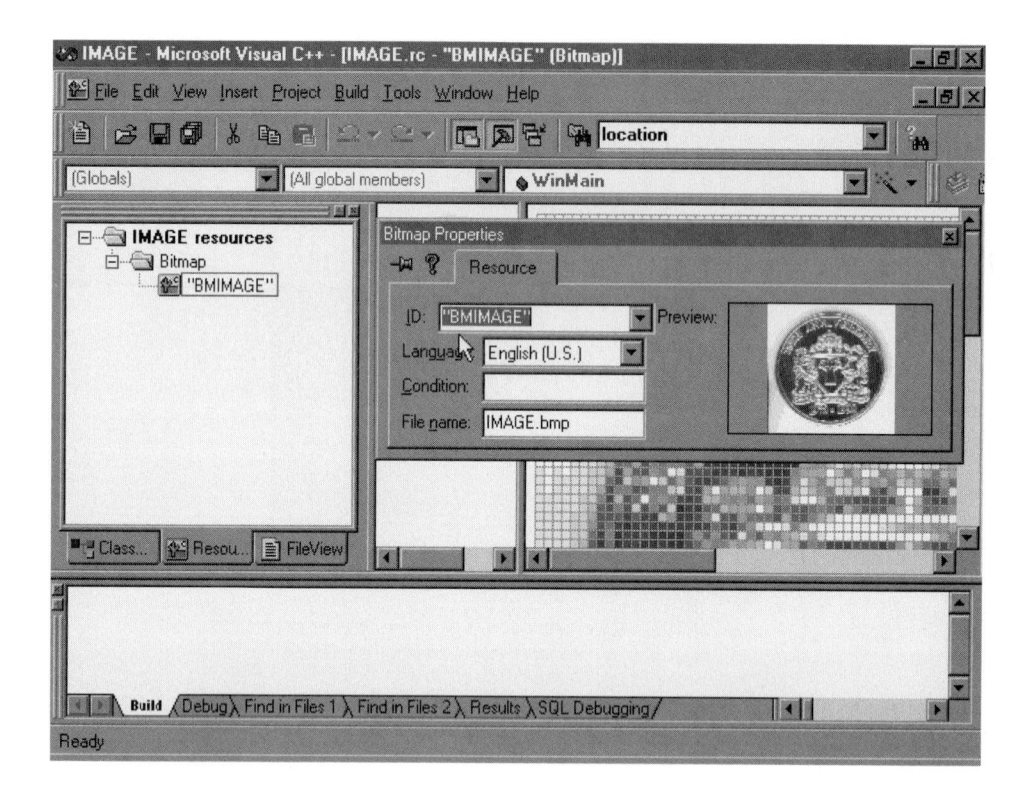

Figure 9-3   *The default ID value for the image is changed to BMImage.*

At this point, it is possible to load the bitmapped image into the Resource Editor for any final editing, as you can see in Figure 9-4.

Complete Bitmap Examples **315**

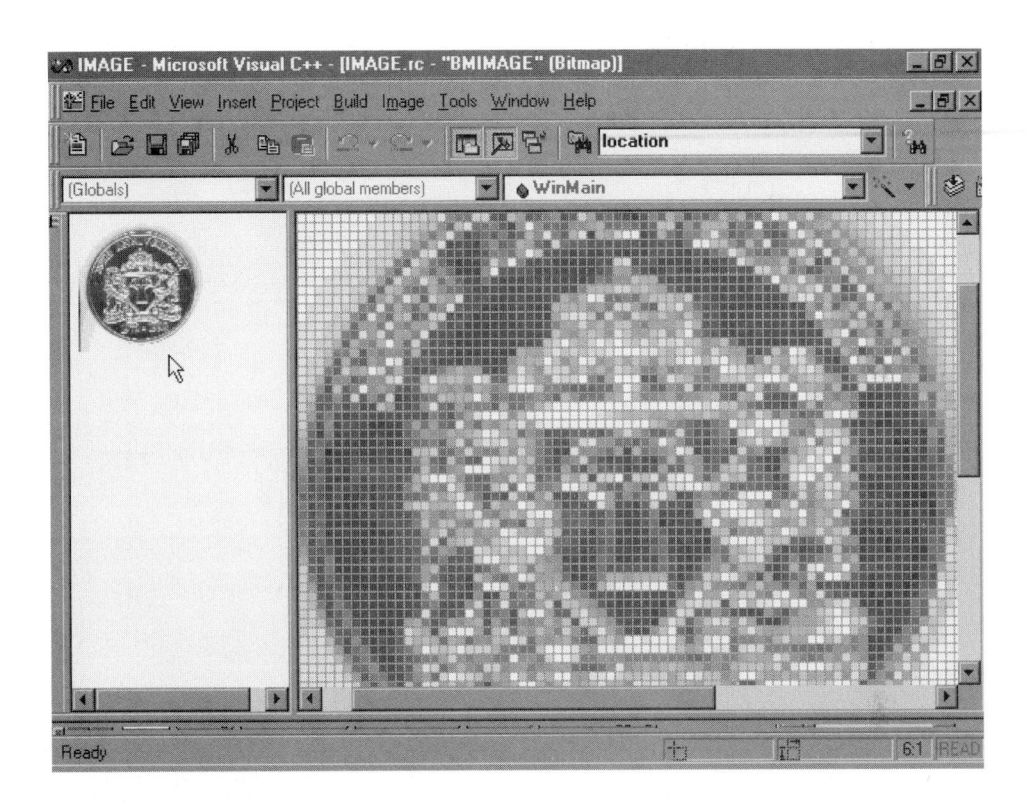

Figure 9-4 *The scanned image can be edited in the Resource Editor.*

Use the Visual C++ Project|Add To Project|Files... menu selection to add the image resource to the project, as shown in Figure 9-5.

316 Chapter 9 • Creating and Displaying Bitmaps

Figure 9–5 *The image resource file is added to the Image project.*

The Resource Editor automatically generates a resource script file for the project. Resource script files hold resource information for a project. In this example, we're interested in just the portion of the resource script file dealing with the bitmapped image. Here is an edited portion of the IMAGE.rc resource script file for this project.

```
//Microsoft Developer Studio generated resource script.
//
#include "resource.h"
    .
    .
    .
/////////////////////////////////////////////////////////////
//
// Bitmap
//

BMImage     BITMAP  DISCARDABLE     "IMAGE.bmp"
    .
    .
    .
```

Remember that the Resource Editor generates the IMAGE.rc resource script file. Resource script files are not entered by the programmer.

The next listing is the source code listing for the project. If you study this listing carefully, you'll see the components of the swt.cpp file, as well as code similar to that used in the GDI project, discussed in the previous section.

```cpp
//
// IMAGE.cpp
// This application will illustrate how to use a scanned
// image as a bitmap. You'll learn how to load the image,
// and draw it in the window with the use of the
// BitBlt() function.
// Copyright (c) William H. Murray and Chris H. Pappas, 1999
//

#include <windows.h>

LRESULT CALLBACK WndProc(HWND,UINT,WPARAM,LPARAM);

char szProgName[]="ProgName";
char szBMName[]="BMImage";
HBITMAP hBitmap;

int WINAPI WinMain(HINSTANCE hInst,HINSTANCE hPreInst,
                   LPSTR lpszCmdLine,int nCmdShow)
{
  HWND hWnd;
  MSG  lpMsg;
  WNDCLASS wcApp;

  hBitmap=LoadBitmap(hInst,szBMName);

  wcApp.lpszClassName=szProgName;
  wcApp.hInstance     =hInst;
  wcApp.lpfnWndProc   =WndProc;
  wcApp.hCursor       =LoadCursor(NULL,IDC_ARROW);
  wcApp.hIcon         =0;
  wcApp.lpszMenuName  =0;
  wcApp.hbrBackground=(HBRUSH) GetStockObject(WHITE_BRUSH);
  wcApp.style         =CS_HREDRAW|CS_VREDRAW;
  wcApp.cbClsExtra    =0;
  wcApp.cbWndExtra    =0;
  if (!RegisterClass (&wcApp))
    return 0;
    hWnd=CreateWindow(szProgName,
                      "A Scanned Image and BitBlt()",
                      WS_OVERLAPPEDWINDOW,CW_USEDEFAULT,
                      CW_USEDEFAULT,CW_USEDEFAULT,
                      CW_USEDEFAULT, (HWND)NULL, (HMENU)NULL,
                      hInst,(LPSTR)NULL);
```

318   Chapter 9 • Creating and Displaying Bitmaps

```
  ShowWindow(hWnd,nCmdShow);
  UpdateWindow(hWnd);
  while (GetMessage(&lpMsg,0,0,0)) {
    TranslateMessage(&lpMsg);
    DispatchMessage(&lpMsg);
  }
  return(lpMsg.wParam);
}


LRESULT CALLBACK WndProc(HWND hWnd,UINT messg,
                         WPARAM wParam,LPARAM lParam)
{
  HDC hdc;
  HDC hmdc;
  PAINTSTRUCT ps;
  static BITMAP bm;

  switch (messg)
  {
    case WM_PAINT:
      hdc=BeginPaint(hWnd,&ps);

      hmdc=CreateCompatibleDC(hdc);
      SelectObject(hmdc,hBitmap);
      GetObject(hBitmap,sizeof(bm),(LPSTR) &bm);
      BitBlt(hdc,0,0,bm.bmWidth,bm.bmHeight,hmdc,0,0,
             SRCCOPY);

      DeleteDC(hmdc);

      ValidateRect(hWnd,NULL);
      EndPaint(hWnd,&ps);
      break;

    case WM_DESTROY:
      DeleteObject(hBitmap);
      PostQuitMessage(0);
      break;

    default:
      return(DefWindowProc(hWnd,messg,wParam,lParam));
      break;
  }
  return(0);
}
```

As you study this source code, see if you can find each of the following key lines of programming code in this listing.

```
char szBMName[]="BMImage";
```

```
HBITMAP hBitmap;
   .
   .
   .
hBitmap=LoadBitmap(hInst,szDMName);
   .
   .
   .
HDC hdc;
HDC hmdc;
PAINTSTRUCT ps;
static BITMAP bm;
   .
   .
   .
hmdc=CreateCompatibleDC(hdc);
SelectObject(hmdc,hBitmap);
GetObject(hBitmap,sizeof(bm),(LPSTR) &bm);
BitBlt(hdc,0,0,bm.bmWidth,bm.bmHeight,hmdc,0,0,
       SRCCOPY);

DeleteDC(hmdc);
   .
   .
   .
DeleteObject(hBitmap);
```

Have you seen these lines of code before? Of course you have—they were discussed in the section dealing with the **BitBlt()** function. They represent the second method of bringing in a bitmapped image.

Figure 9-6 shows the execution of the project.

Now you know that this image could be drawn multiple times in the window with the **BitBlt()** function from the techniques you learned in the GDI project. However, wouldn't it be great to be able to change the size of the image? In the next section, you'll learn how to use the **StretchBlt()** function to do just that!

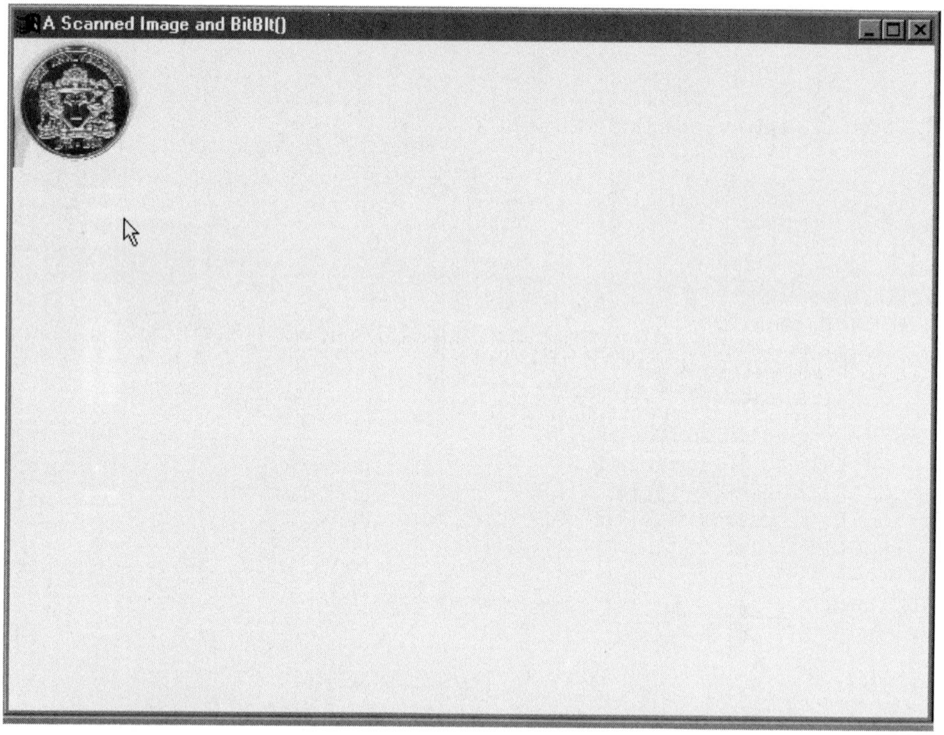

Figure 9–6 *The external bitmapped image is rendered in the Image project's window.*

Working with a Bitmapped Photograph

In this section, we'll investigate the use of the **StretchBlt()** function. Recall that this function is capable of shrinking or stretching a bitmapped image.

There are probably applications that you can think of where a smaller or larger image would work best. Perhaps you want to create a slide-viewer project. On one screen would be small images of all of the slides in the slide tray. These images would, of course, be images that were shrunk by the **StretchBlt()** function. The user could then click on a particular image to view it in normal size.

This project is named **Photo**. You can create the project in the normal manner with your Visual C++ compiler. Use the swt.cpp template code as the base code for the source code file. Then add the unique Photo source code to complete your application.

Because this project will use an external bitmapped photograph file obtained from a camera, it will have to be brought into the project with the

Complete Bitmap Examples **321**

Resource Editor, just like the scanned image of the Image project. The process is similar, but we'll repeat the steps here to avoid confusion.

Use the Visual C++ Insert|Resource menu option to add a predefined bitmap resource, as shown in Figure 9-7.

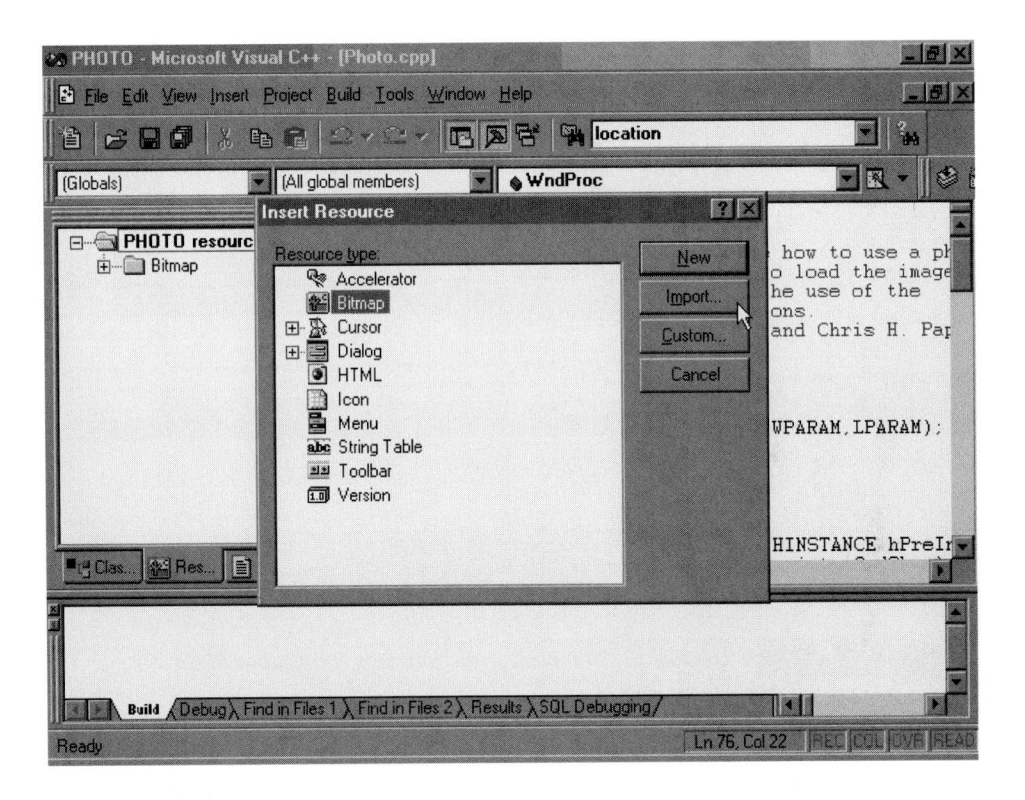

Figure 9-7 *Adding a previously defined bitmap photograph to the Photo project.*

322 Chapter 9 • Creating and Displaying Bitmaps

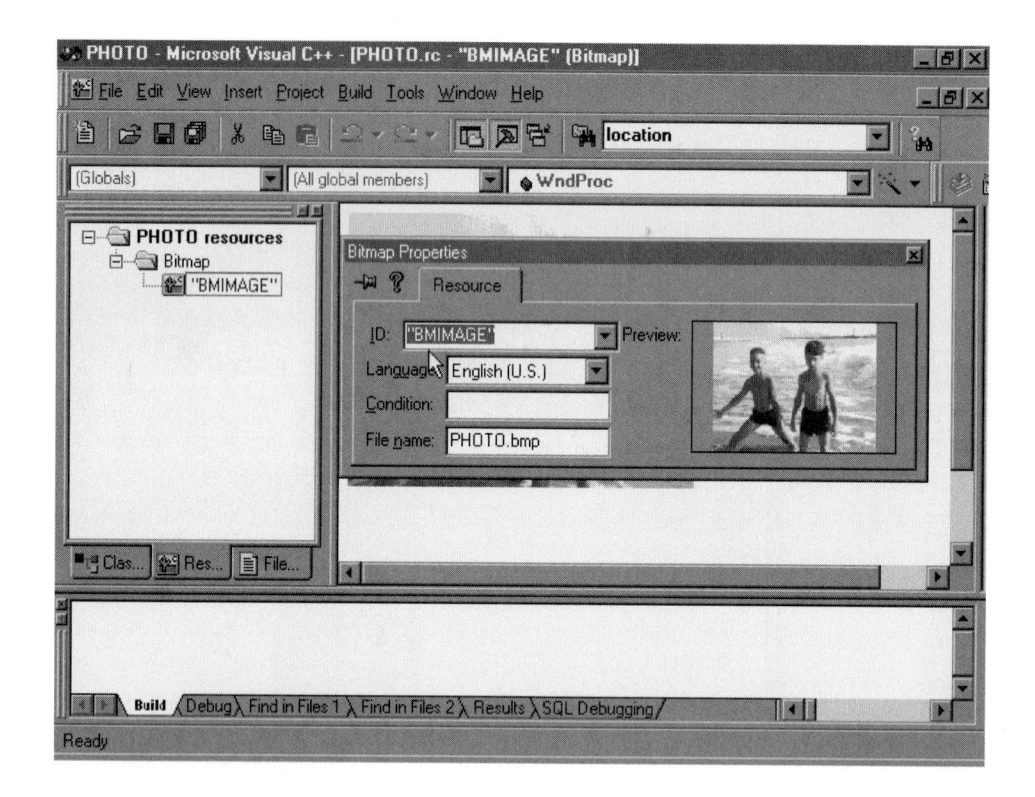

Figure 9-8 *The default ID value for the image is changed to BMImage.*

Once the resource is added, change the default ID value for the resource to BMImage, as shown in Figure 9-8.

At this point, it is possible to load the bitmapped photograph into the Resource Editor, as you can see in Figure 9-9.

Complete Bitmap Examples **323**

Figure 9-9 *The photograph can be edited in the Resource Editor.*

Use the Visual C++ Project|Add To Project|Files... menu selection to add the image resource to the project, as shown in Figure 9-10.

324 Chapter 9 • Creating and Displaying Bitmaps

Figure 9-10 *The image resource file is added to the Photo project.*

Remember that the Resource Editor automatically generates a resource script file for the project. Here is an edited portion of the PHOTO.rc resource script file for this project.

```
//Microsoft Developer Studio generated resource script.
//
#include "resource.h"
    .
    .
    .
/////////////////////////////////////////////////////////
//
// Bitmap
//

BMImage     BITMAP   DISCARDABLE      "PHOTO.bmp"
    .
    .
    .
```

Complete Bitmap Examples 325

The next listing is the source code listing for the project. If you study this listing carefully, you'll see that the basis code of the Photo project has not changed significantly from the code used in the Image project. There is one key change, however. See if you can find it.

```cpp
//
// PHOTO.cpp
// This application will illustrate how to use a photograph
// as a bitmap.  You'll learn how to load the image,
// and draw it in the window with the use of the
// BitBlt() and StretchBlt() functions.
// Copyright (c) William H. Murray and Chris H. Pappas, 1999
//

#include <windows.h>

LRESULT CALLBACK WndProc(HWND,UINT,WPARAM,LPARAM);

char szProgName[]= "ProgName";
char szBMName[]="BMImage";
HBITMAP hBitmap;

int WINAPI WinMain(HINSTANCE hInst,HINSTANCE hPreInst,
                   LPSTR lpszCmdLine,int nCmdShow)
{
  HWND hWnd;
  MSG  lpMsg;
  WNDCLASS wcApp;

  hBitmap=LoadBitmap(hInst,szBMName);

  wcApp.lpszClassName=szProgName;
  wcApp.hInstance     =hInst;
  wcApp.lpfnWndProc   =WndProc;
  wcApp.hCursor       =LoadCursor(NULL,IDC_ARROW);
  wcApp.hIcon         =0;
  wcApp.lpszMenuName  =0;
  wcApp.hbrBackground=(HBRUSH) GetStockObject(WHITE_BRUSH);
  wcApp.style         =CS_HREDRAW|CS_VREDRAW;
  wcApp.cbClsExtra    =0;
  wcApp.cbWndExtra    =0;
  if (!RegisterClass (&wcApp))
    return 0;

  hWnd=CreateWindow(szProgName,
                    "The BitBlt() and StretchBlt() Functions",
                    WS_OVERLAPPEDWINDOW,CW_USEDEFAULT,
                    CW_USEDEFAULT,CW_USEDEFAULT,
                    CW_USEDEFAULT,(HWND)NULL,(HMENU)NULL,
                    hInst,(LPSTR)NULL);
```

Chapter 9 • Creating and Displaying Bitmaps

```
  ShowWindow(hWnd,nCmdShow);
  UpdateWindow(hWnd);
  while (GetMessage(&lpMsg,0,0,0)) {
    TranslateMessage(&lpMsg);
    DispatchMessage(&lpMsg);
  }
  return(lpMsg.wParam);
}

LRESULT CALLBACK WndProc(HWND hWnd,UINT messg,
                         WPARAM wParam,LPARAM lParam)
{
  HDC hdc;
  HDC hmdc;
  PAINTSTRUCT ps;
  static BITMAP bm;

  switch (messg)
  {
    case WM_PAINT:
      hdc=BeginPaint(hWnd,&ps);

      hmdc=CreateCompatibleDC(hdc);
      SelectObject(hmdc,hBitmap);
      GetObject(hBitmap,sizeof(bm),(LPSTR) &bm);
      BitBlt(hdc,0,0,bm.bmWidth,bm.bmHeight,hmdc,0,0,
             SRCCOPY);

      TextOut(hdc, 400,50,"Paul and Mark at the beach",26);
      TextOut(hdc, 460,80,"1980",4);

      StretchBlt(hdc,bm.bmWidth,bm.bmHeight,2*bm.bmWidth,
                 2*bm.bmHeight,hmdc,0,0,bm.bmWidth,
                 bm.bmHeight,SRCCOPY);

      DeleteDC(hmdc);

      ValidateRect(hWnd,NULL);
      EndPaint(hWnd,&ps);
      break;

    case WM_DESTROY:
      DeleteObject(hBitmap);
      PostQuitMessage(0);
      break;

    default:
      return(DefWindowProc(hWnd,messg,wParam,lParam));
      break;
```

```
  }
  return(0);
}
```

If you scanned this code, we're sure you detected the first use of the **StretchBlt()** function. Here is a portion of the key code used in this project.

```
hmdc=CreateCompatibleDC(hdc);
SelectObject(hmdc,hBitmap);
GetObject(hBitmap,sizeof(bm),(LPSTR) &bm);
BitBlt(hdc,0,0,bm.bmWidth,bm.bmHeight,hmdc,0,0,
        SRCCOPY);
      .
      .
      .
StretchBlt(hdc,bm.bmWidth,bm.bmHeight,2*bm.bmWidth,
           2*bm.bmHeight,hmdc,0,0,bm.bmWidth,
           bm.bmHeight,SRCCOPY);

DeleteDC(hmdc);
```

The original photograph (bitmap) is loaded *and* placed on the screen with a call to the **BitBlt()** function. This code is similar to that used by the Image project of the previous section. However, this project uses code to draw the image again. This time, the **StretchBlt()** function renders, the photograph to twice the size of the original bitmapped image.

Figure 9-11 shows the project's window when it is executed.

Figure 9-11 *The **Stretch Blt()** function can stretch original bitmapped images.*

More detail on the **StretchBlt()** function can be found earlier in this chapter. Take the time to understand where each parameter value for this function was obtained and why. It will go a long way toward your complete understanding of the **BitBlt()** and **StretchBlt()** functions.

This would be a great place to do a little experimenting. Why not go back into the project and try to shrink the original bitmap? You could also do an experiment on size versus resolution by making the image even larger.

We intentionally kept the bitmap file sizes small in this chapter. However, as you experiment with your own scanned images and photographs, you'll soon discover the downside to bitmaps—large file sizes.

More Resources?

Icons, cursors, and bitmaps are just the tip of the iceberg when it comes to Windows resources. In the next two chapters, you'll be introduced to menu and dialog box resources. Menus and dialog boxes are major components to any Windows project.

T E N

Adding Menu and Keyboard Accelerators

In the last four chapters, you have learned how to add a variety of resources to basic Windows applications. You know that resources such as icons, cursors, bitmaps, and sound resources greatly enhance the overall appeal of an application to the user.

Menus are yet another important Windows resource. They are considered by many programmers to be the gateway for easy, consistent interfacing across applications. Because of their ability to produce a consistent interface many developers consider them the most important Windows resource.

Menus allow the user to point and click on menu items that have been predefined by the programmer in a resource file. Menu item selections can be screen color choices, sizing options, directory listings, etc. Menus also perform an additional important role. Menus, acting as a gateway, allow the user to select dialog boxes from the menu list. Dialog boxes are important because they permit direct data entry from the keyboard. Dialog boxes are used to gather strings of characters, integers, and real numbers from the user. Because dialog boxes are such a large and important topic, they are discussed separately in Chapter 11. Menus serve not only as a path to dialog boxes, but also as the first line of active interfacing with the user. This chapter is, therefore, devoted to exploring the use of menus.

This chapter will use four separate menu applications to illustrate the most important aspects of creating menus. These applications will show you how to use menus to change the size of objects, alter the background color, retrieve information about your computer system, and even produce directory listings for various hard and disk drives.

Menu Concepts

What is a menu? What do menus look like? How are menus created as a resource? What menu options are available to the programmer? What are keyboard accelerators? These are all important questions regarding menus. In the following sections, we'll answer each of these questions as we explore the menu resource. You'll find that menus are easy to create and easy to include in all Windows applications.

What Is a Menu?

A menu is defined simply as a list of items of names that represent options that a user can interactively select when running an application. Menu items usually include a list of simple choices but can also include bitmaps and lead to dialog boxes. Users can select a menu option by using either the mouse or the keyboard and by moving to the desired item. Then the left mouse button or a combination of keystrokes actually selects the item. Windows will then respond to the selection by sending a message to the application, stating which item was selected. These messages are generated automatically.

Designing a Menu

The Visual C++ Resource Editor will allow you to graphically design a menu for your application. To illustrate this process, the menu for the second application in this chapter will be discussed.

To add a new menu resource to an application, open the Visual C++ Insert menu and select the Resource...menu item, as shown in Figure 10–1.

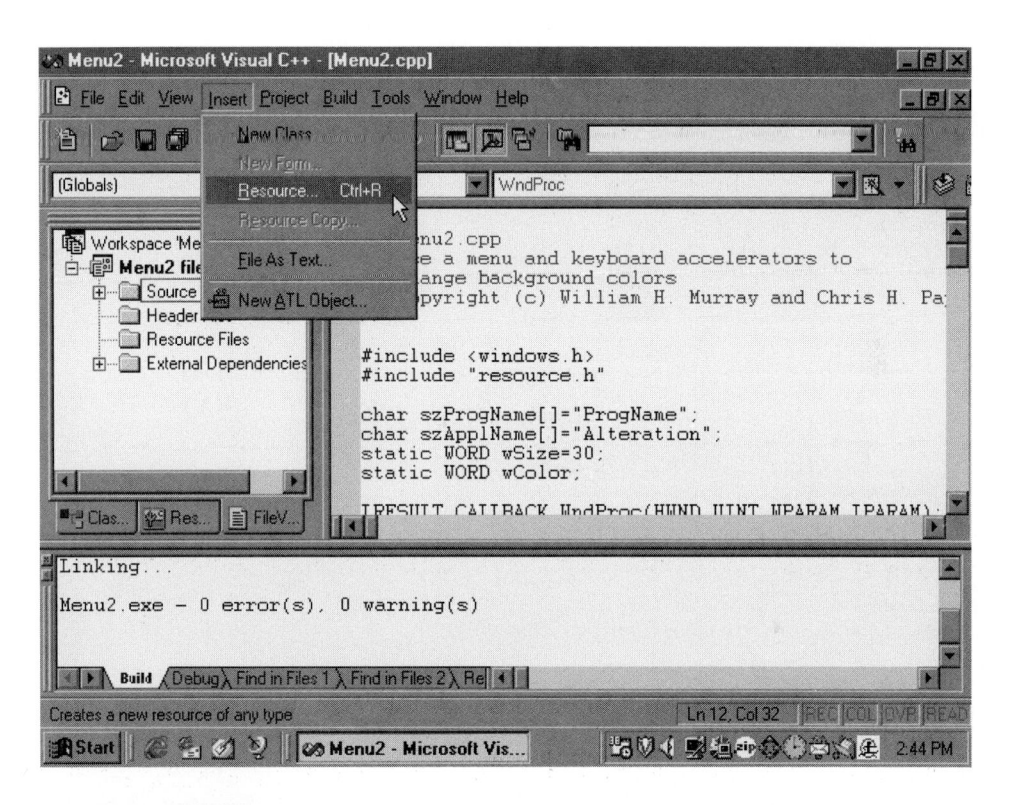

Menu Concepts **331**

Figure 10-1 Use the Visual C++ Insert menu and select the Resource...menu item.

When the Resource...menu item is selected, an Insert Resource dialog box will open with various resource options. Select the Menu item, as illustrated in Figure 10-2.

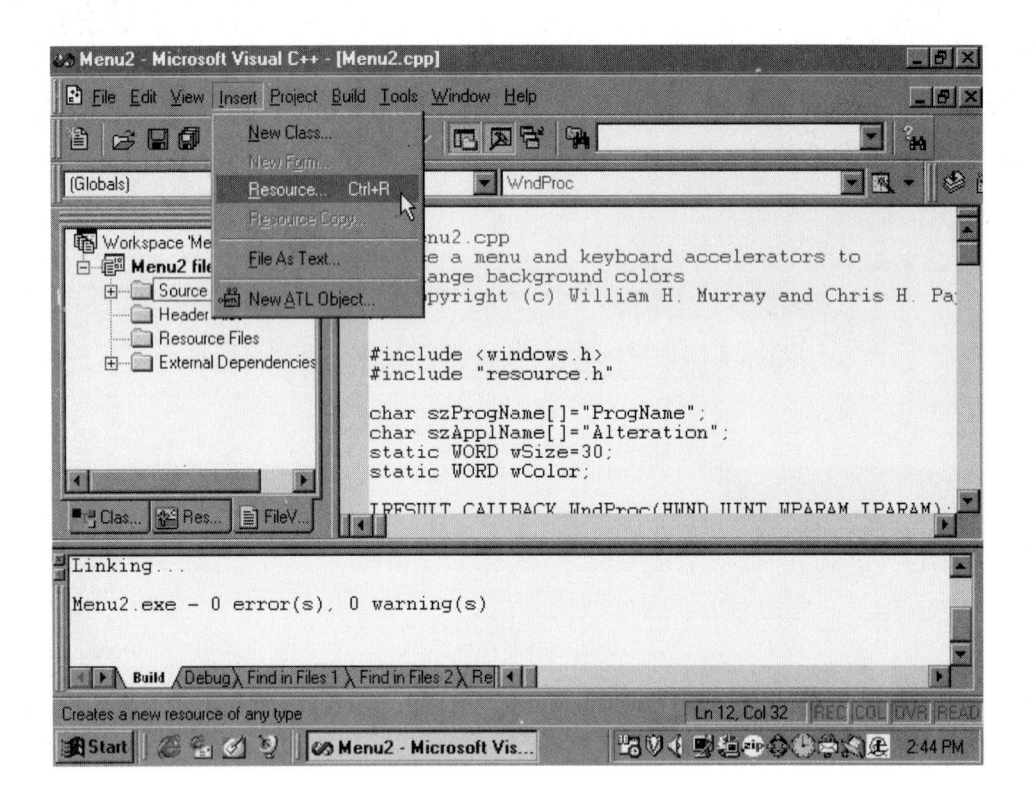

332 Chapter 10 • Adding Menu and Keyboard Accelerators

Figure 10-2 *Select the Menu item in the Insert Resource dialog box.*

If the menu resource is a new resource, use the New button to start the resource editor. If you want to view existing menu resources, you can simply double-click on the Menu item.

The Resource Editor frequently assigns an ID value to a new menu, such as IDR_MENU1 for this example. Figure 10-3 shows that we have changed the default menu name to *ALTERATION* for this example.

Menu Concepts **333**

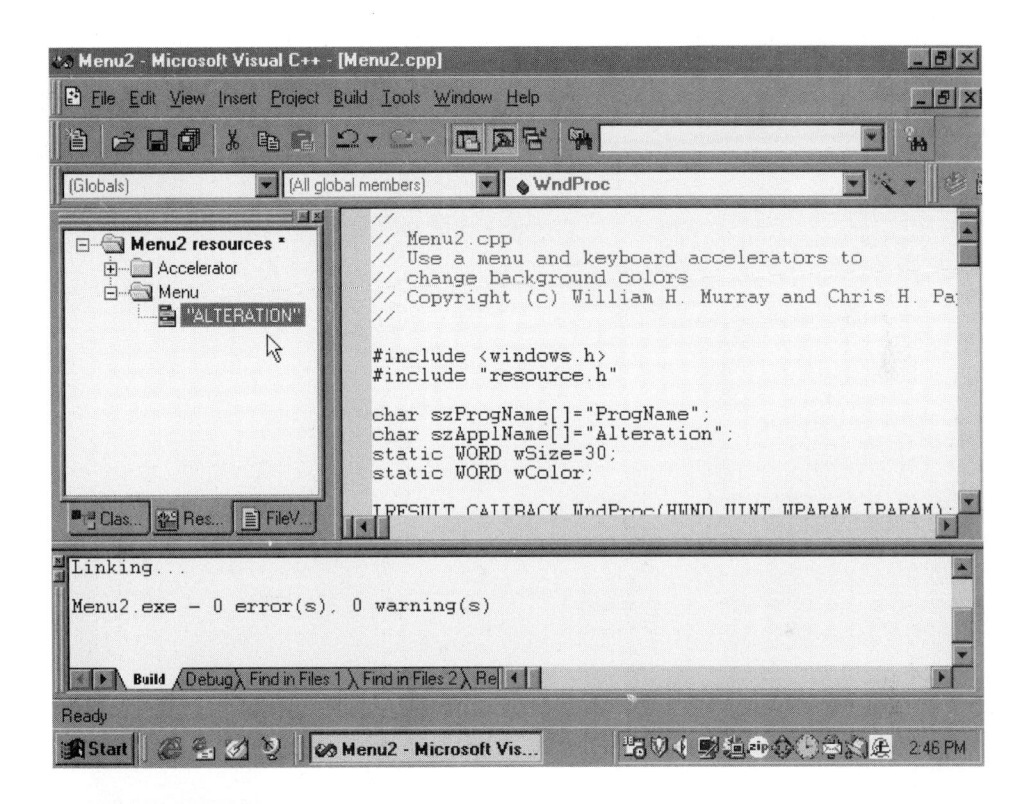

Figure 10-3 *Change the default menu name to a meaningful name for your application.*

Notice, in Figure 10–3, that the *szApplName[]* variable has been changed in the source code listing to *Alteration* in order to reflect the new menu name.

Menu titles and menu items can be added to a menu by clicking on the dotted rectangular area in the design area and typing in the appropriate name. Figure 10–4 shows two menu titles, Ellipse_Size and Background_Colors.

334 Chapter 10 • Adding Menu and Keyboard Accelerators

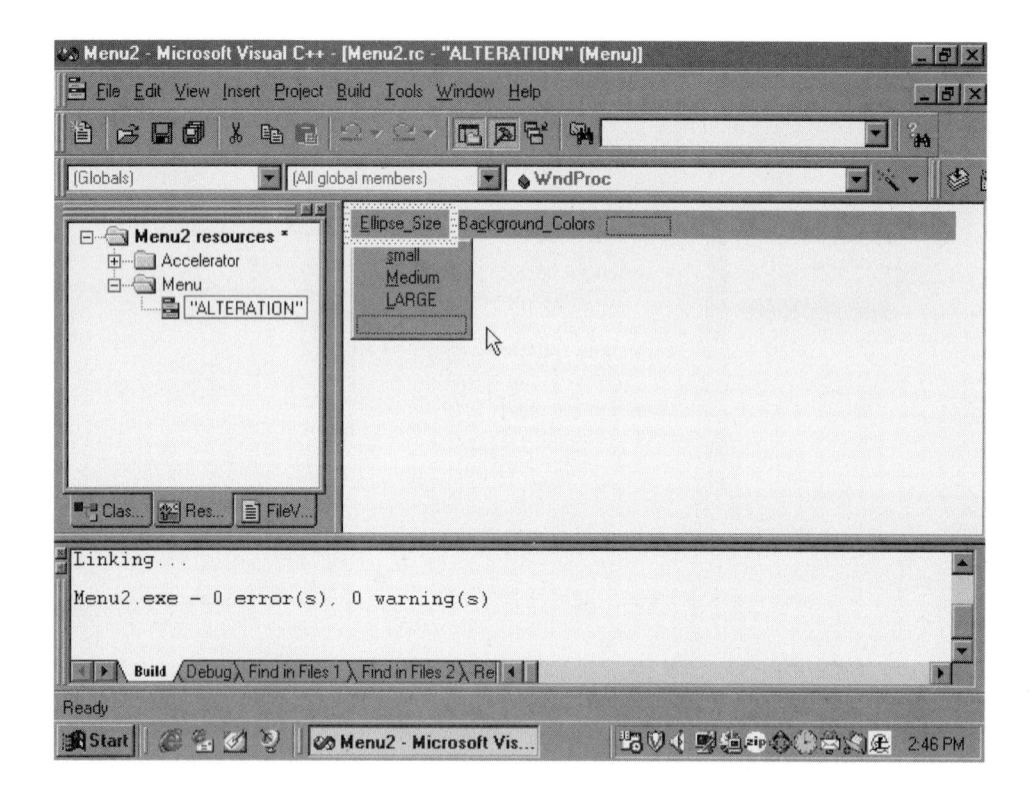

Figure 10-4 *Menu titles and items are added at the dotted-rectangle prompt.*

In Figure 10-4, also notice that the three size choices have been added to the Ellipse_Size menu. These are small, Medium, and LARGE.

Click the mouse on the Background_Colors menu name to add menu item to this menu. Figure 10-5 shows that 12 menu items and a separator bar have been added to this menu.

Menu Concepts **335**

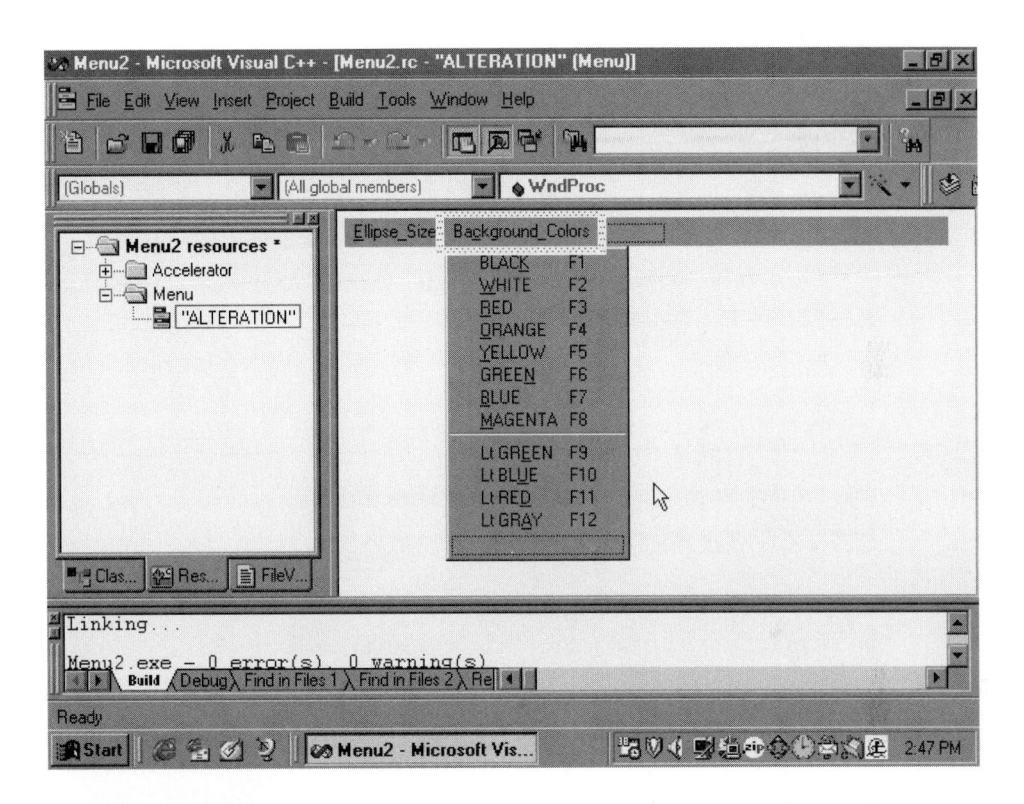

Figure 10-5 *Menu items and a separator bar are added to the Background_Colors menu.*

The function keys that you see at each menu item are going to be used as keyboard accelerators. These will be discussed shortly.

The properties of any menu title or item can be examined, set, or changed by double-clicking the mouse on the item in question. Figure 10-6 shows the Menu Item Property dialog box obtained by double-clicking the mouse on the Ellipse_Size menu title.

336 Chapter 10 • Adding Menu and Keyboard Accelerators

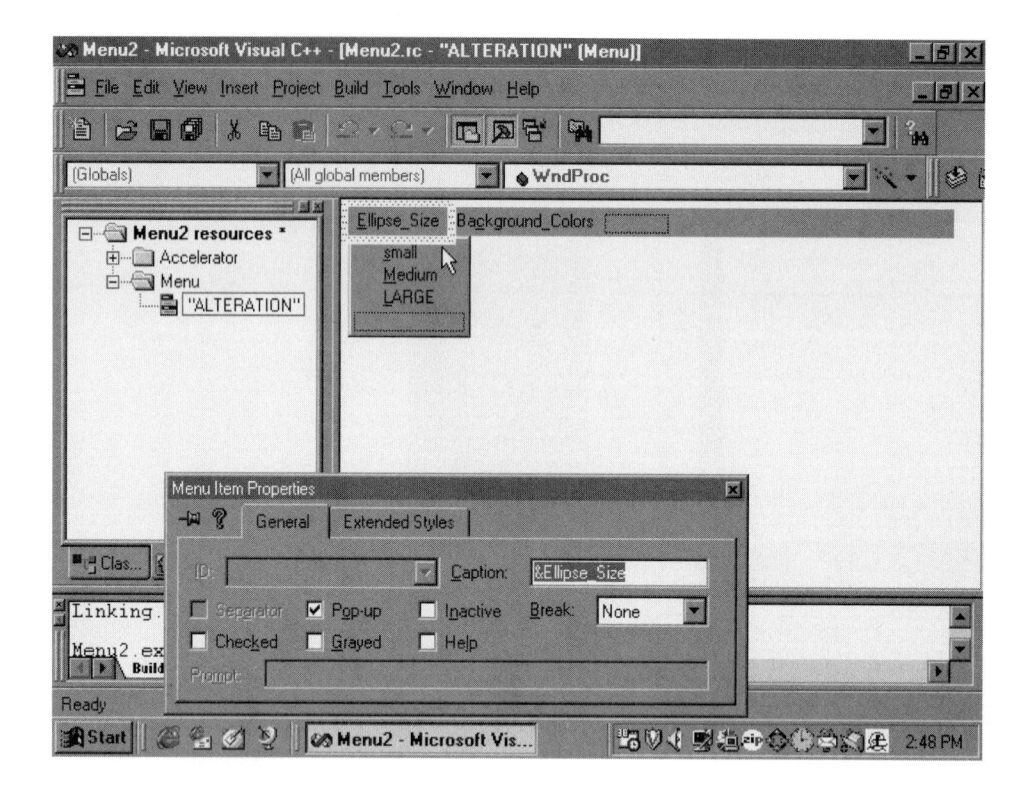

Figure 10–6 *The Menu Item Properties dialog box for a menu.*

By default, menus are designated as pop-up menus as you can see in Figure 10–6. By placing the ampersand character in front of a letter, you insure that letter is underscored in the final menu. Underscored characters allow menus and menu items to be selected without the mouse by using the Alt key and the underscored character. The only restriction is that the underscored character can be used only once in a given pop-up menu. This has led to some interesting key combinations in Windows applications, as we're sure you have noticed. Menu names do not have ID values attached.

Figure 10–7 shows a Menu Item Properties dialog box for the Medium menu choice of the Ellipse_Size menu.

Menu Concepts **337**

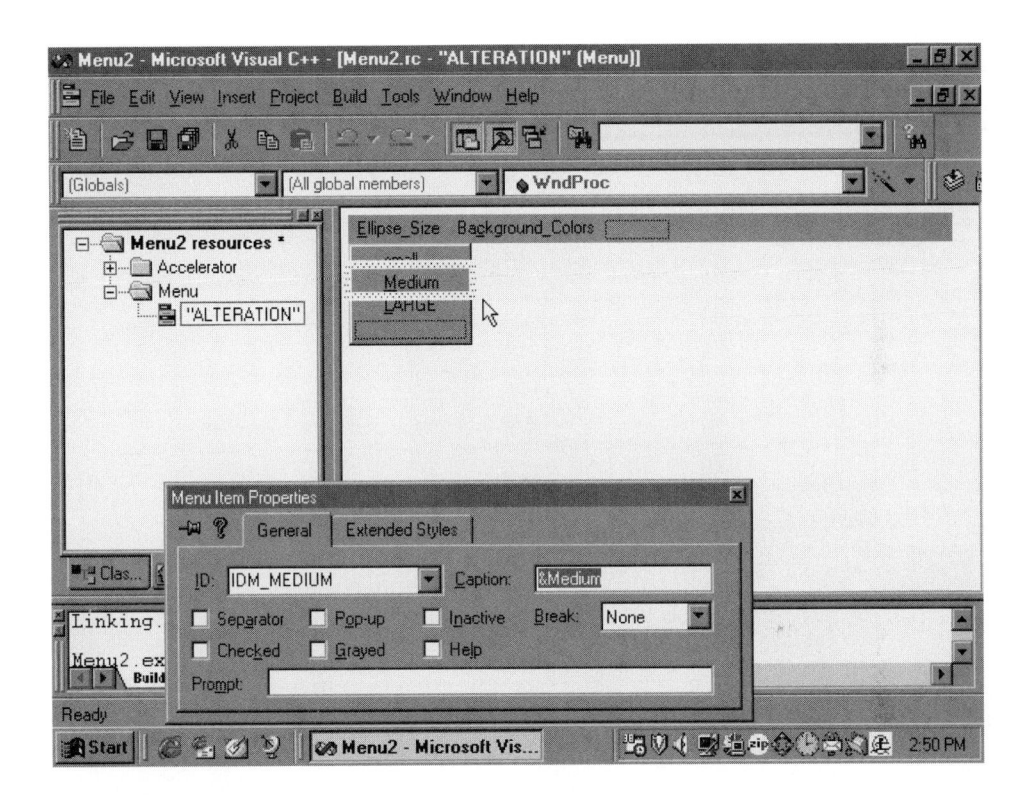

Figure 10–7 *The Menu Item Properties dialog box for a menu item.*

In Figure 10–7, notice that the ampersand character appears before the *M* in the word *Medium*. Then observe that the Medium menu item does have the letter *M* underscored. Notice, too, that menu items do use ID values. Menu ID values should be unique identifiers. It is common practice to start the name of each identifier with *IDM_*. For this case, then, the name is *IDM_MEDIUM*. In this menu, we would also use IDM_SMALL and IDM_LARGE.

Figure 10–8 shows a similar Menu Item Properties dialog box for the ORANGE menu item of the Background_Colors menu.

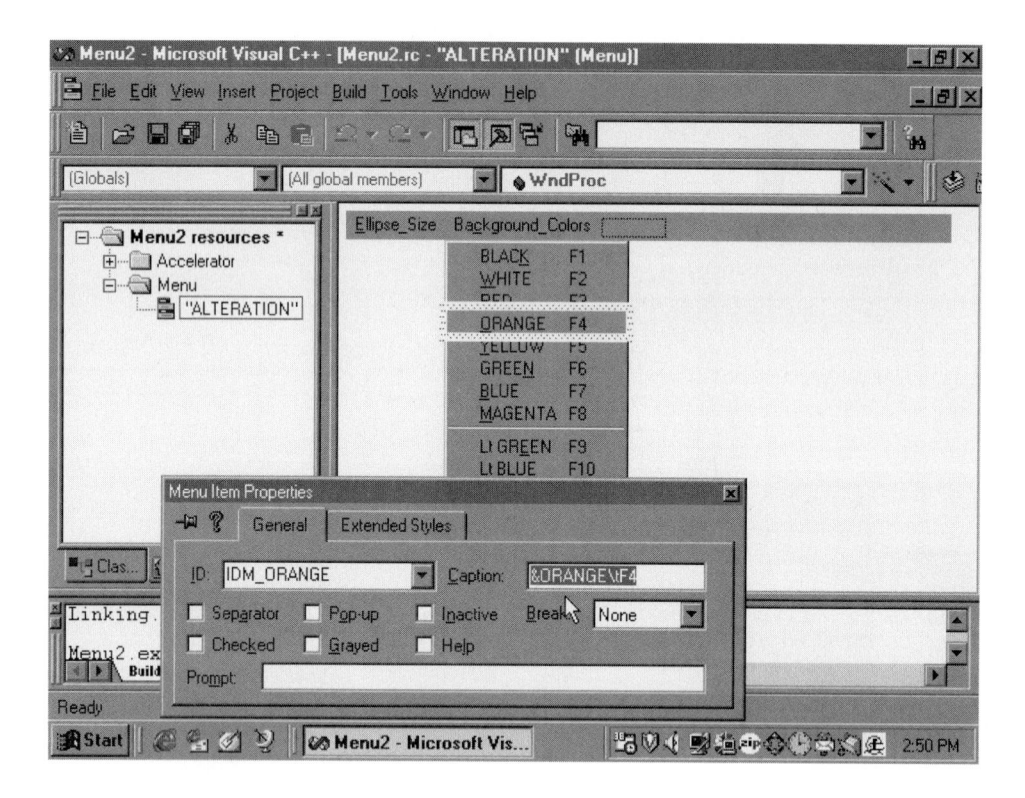

Chapter 10 • Adding Menu and Keyboard Accelerators

Figure 10–8 *Properties are set for the ORANGE menu item.*

Notice in Figure 10–8 that the caption for the ORANGE menu item contains the characters \tF4. The \t combination is simply a tab stop that will place F4 to the right of the menu item. The characters F4 have no function other than to remind the user that this program will allow the use of accelerator keys when making color selections.

The Resource Editor will also create a header file for this resource. The header file will hold the ID values for the menu items just created. By default the header file is named *resource.h*. Header file information is required by both the resource script file and the C++ source code file. When you actually build this project, it is important to include the C++ source code file, the resource script file, and the resource header file during the build process.

Several additional menu options will be discussed later. For now, save the menu resource for use in the application.

Designing Keyboard Accelerators

Windows provides several methods for making menu selections. We have already discussed mouse and keyboard selections based on the Alt key and underscored character in a menu item's name. However, there is an even faster way to make selections that appear in a menu item list. Keyboard accelerators are used by menu designers as a sort of "hot key." For example, the menu being created in this example lists 12 colors that the user can choose from to set the background color of a window. In the normal selection process, the user can point and click the mouse for a specific color. This means that the menu and the menu item must first be selected. Keyboard accelerators can be used to speed up this process. The function keys (F1 to F12) can be designated for this purpose and used without having to select the menu or menu item at all!

Return to Figure 10–2 and notice that an Accelerator resource option appears at the top to the Insert Resource dialog box. To add a group of keyboard accelerators, select and add an Accelerator resource to your project.

When keyboard accelerators are added to reflect menu item selections, you'll need to know the menu item ID value. This is why menus are usually designed before adding accelerator resources. Figure 10–9 shows the list of accelerator keys that should be added to this project in order to reflect each possible menu item selection.

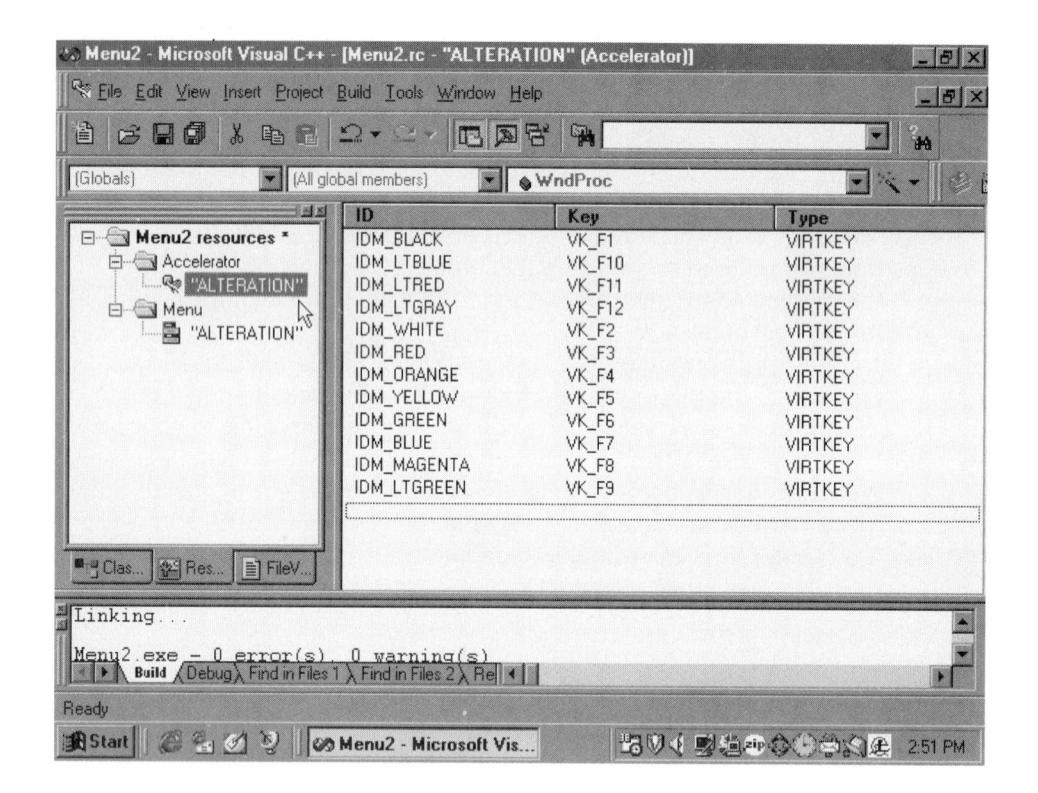

340 Chapter 10 • Adding Menu and Keyboard Accelerators

Figure 10-9 A group of keyboard accelerators is used to reflect menu item color selections.

The Key designator *VK_* stands for "virtual key" and is used to incorporate the function keys F1 to F12 into the project.

The properties for each accelerator key are set by double-clicking the mouse on a given key and opening the Accel Properties dialog box, as shown in Figure 10–10.

ID value and Key names can be selected from drop-down list boxes. In Figure 10–10, the ID and Key values that will reflect the IDM_BLACK menu item selection are set. When you have added all of the keyboard accelerators, simply save the resource file.

Menu Concepts **341**

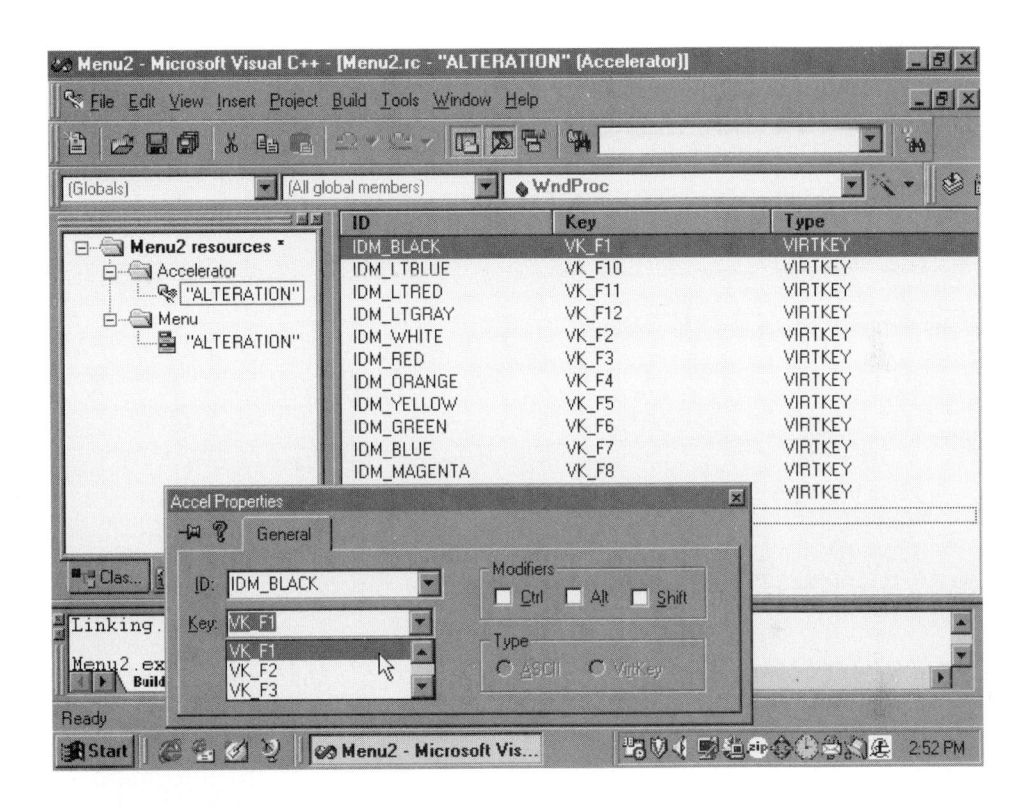

[Screenshot of Microsoft Visual C++ showing the Menu2.rc ALTERATION Accelerator editor with a list of IDM_ identifiers mapped to VK_F1 through VK_F12 as VIRTKEY entries, and an Accel Properties dialog box open on the General tab with ID set to IDM_BLACK and Key set to VK_F1.]

Figure 10-10 *Accelerator key properties are set with the Accel Properties dialog box.*

The Resource File

When resources are added to a project, they are eventually saved in a resource script file. This is a file with an .rc file extension. If you want to see how the Resource Editor translated the graphical menu design and keyboard accelerator information to a text file, simply open the resource script file with Microsoft Word or any text editor. Note: If you open the resource script file with Visual C++, you will be returned to the graphical design environment.

The following listing is the resource script file generated for the example we have developed in this section. As you examine the listing, notice that the menu and keyboard accelerator information has been set in a bold font for easy identification.

```
//Microsoft Developer Studio generated resource script.
//
#include "resource.h"
```

```
#define APSTUDIO_READONLY_SYMBOLS
/////////////////////////////////////////////////////////////////////
//////
//
// Generated from the TEXTINCLUDE 2 resource.
//
#include "afxres.h"

/////////////////////////////////////////////////////////////////////
//////
#undef APSTUDIO_READONLY_SYMBOLS

/////////////////////////////////////////////////////////////////////
//////
// English (U.S.) resources

#if!defined(AFX_RESOURCE_DLL) || defined(AFX_TARG_ENU)
#ifdef _WIN32
LANGUAGE LANG_ENGLISH, SUBLANG_ENGLISH_US
#pragma code_page(1252)
#endif //_WIN32

/////////////////////////////////////////////////////////////////////
//////
//
// Menu
//

Alteration MENU DISCARDABLE
BEGIN
    POPUP "&Ellipse_Size"
    BEGIN
        MENUITEM "&small",                    IDM_SMALL
        MENUITEM "&Medium",                   IDM_MEDIUM
        MENUITEM "&LARGE",                    IDM_LARGE
    END
    POPUP "Ba&ckground_Colors"
    BEGIN
        MENUITEM "BLAC&K\tF1",                IDM_BLACK
        MENUITEM "&WHITE\tF2",                IDM_WHITE
        MENUITEM "&RED\tF3",                  IDM_RED
        MENUITEM "&ORANGE\tF4",               IDM_ORANGE
        MENUITEM "&YELLOW\tF5",               IDM_YELLOW
        MENUITEM "GREE&N\tF6",                IDM_GREEN
        MENUITEM "&BLUE\tF7",                 IDM_BLUE
        MENUITEM "&MAGENTA\tF8",              IDM_MAGENTA
        MENUITEM SEPARATOR
        MENUITEM "Lt GR&EEN\tF9",             IDM_LTGREEN
        MENUITEM "Lt BL&UE\tF10",             IDM_LTBLUE
        MENUITEM "Lt RE&D\tF11",              IDM_LTRED
```

```
            MENUITEM "Lt GR&AY\tF12",              IDM_LTGRAY
        END
END


#ifdef APSTUDIO_INVOKED
///////////////////////////////////////////////////////////////////
//////
//
// TEXTINCLUDE
//

1 TEXTINCLUDE DISCARDABLE
BEGIN
    "resource.h\0"
END

2 TEXTINCLUDE DISCARDABLE
BEGIN
    "#include ""afxres.h""afxres.h""\r\n"
    "\0"
END

3 TEXTINCLUDE DISCARDABLE
BEGIN
    "\r\n"
    "\0"
END

#endif    // APSTUDIO_INVOKED


///////////////////////////////////////////////////////////////////
//////
//
// Accelerator
//

Alteration ACCELERATORS DISCARDABLE
BEGIN
    VK_F1,          IDM_BLACK,          VIRTKEY, NOINVERT
    VK_F10,         IDM_LTBLUE,         VIRTKEY, NOINVERT
    VK_F11,         IDM_LTRED,          VIRTKEY, NOINVERT
    VK_F12,         IDM_LTGRAY,         VIRTKEY, NOINVERT
    VK_F2,          IDM_WHITE,          VIRTKEY, NOINVERT
    VK_F3,          IDM_RED,            VIRTKEY, NOINVERT
    VK_F4,          IDM_ORANGE,         VIRTKEY, NOINVERT
    VK_F5,          IDM_YELLOW,         VIRTKEY, NOINVERT
    VK_F6,          IDM_GREEN,          VIRTKEY, NOINVERT
    VK_F7,          IDM_BLUE,           VIRTKEY, NOINVERT
```

344 Chapter 10 • Adding Menu and Keyboard Accelerators

```
    VK_F8,         IDM_MAGENTA,          VIRTKEY, NOINVERT
    VK_F9,         IDM_LTGREEN,          VIRTKEY, NOINVERT
END

#endif    // English (U.S.) resources
/////////////////////////////////////////////////////////////////////////////



#ifndef APSTUDIO_INVOKED
/////////////////////////////////////////////////////////////////////////////
//
// Generated from the TEXTINCLUDE 3 resource.
//


/////////////////////////////////////////////////////////////////////////////
#endif    // not APSTUDIO_INVOKED
```

Menus can use a variety of menu keywords. Study the listing and identify keywords such as **MENU, POPUP, MENUITEM,** and **SEPARATOR**. Brackets ({}) can be interchanged with the menu keywords **BEGIN** and **END**, if desired. It should also be easy to identify the menu items, in this example, for each of the two pop-up menus. The most frequently used menu keywords are shown in Table 10.1.

Table 10.1 Menu keywords.

Option	Use
CHECKED	Menu item has a check mark next to it.
END	Menu item is the last item in a pop-up or static menu.
GRAYED	Menu item is set inactive and appears as a faded option on the menu list.
HELP	Menu item is a right-justified static menu, selected with the keyboard.
INACTIVE	Menu item is displayed but cannot be selected under the current set of circumstances.
MENUBREAK	Menu item is placed in a new column.
SEPARATOR	Menu item is placed in a new row/column. Items are separated by a bar.

Table 10.1 Menu keywords. (Continued)

Option	Use
OWNERDRAW	The owner of the menu is responsible for drawing all visual aspects of the menu item, including highlighted, inactive, and checked states.
POPUP	A sublist of items is displayed when this option is selected.

At one time, the programmer created menus using text files. At that time, no graphical design tools were available. Paramount to menu design were the knowledge and use of menu keywords. With the graphical design tools available in the Visual C++ compiler, the memorization and hand-coding of keywords is obsolete.

However, you may find it interesting in the future to compare various menu options during the design process with menu keywords used in the resource script file.

Menus—A Variety of Options

Menus are the critical path for most user interaction under Windows. The remainder of this chapter is devoted to guiding you through the creation of the four menu applications. Each project will be created with a unique source code and resource script file. For example, the first project is named *Menu1*. This application includes the Menu1.cpp source code file and the Menu1.rc resource script file.

Each of these applications can be built in a manner similar to those of earlier chapters. Just remember to include both the source code file and the resource script file in the list of files to put with the project.

If you are creating your own applications or entering those in the chapter, be extremely careful as you enter the code. As listing size increases, so does the likelihood of data entry mistakes.

Using a Menu to Change the Size of Graphics Shapes

The first example application, named *Menu1*, will produce a single menu with three menu items that allow the user to size a graphics figure. By selecting one of these menu items from the menu, an ellipse will be drawn on the screen in the predetermined size.

To create this application with Visual C++, you'll need to create Win32 application workspace and name it *Menu1*. Then add a resource file containing menu information in a file named *Menu1.rc* and the C++ source code file named *Menu1.cpp*. Remember that the resource editor will create a header file name Resource.h that holds the resource script file ID values.

The first listing is a portion of the Menu1.rc resource script file needed for this project. From the section that is shown in this listing, you should be able to determine how the menu was designed and the various ID values selected.

Do not use this file to directly create your menu. Use the Resource Editor supplied with your Visual C++ compiler to create your own menu visually.

```
/////////////////////////////////////////////////////
//
// Menu
//

ShapeMenu MENU DISCARDABLE
BEGIN
    POPUP "&Ellipse_Size"
    BEGIN
        MENUITEM "&small",              IDM_SMALL
        MENUITEM "&Medium",             IDM_MEDIUM
        MENUITEM "&LARGE",              IDM_LARGE
    END
END
```

Figure 10-11 shows the menu, in the Resource Editor, during design.

The next listing is the C++ source code needed for the project. This file is named *Menu1.cpp*.

Menus—A Variety of Options 347

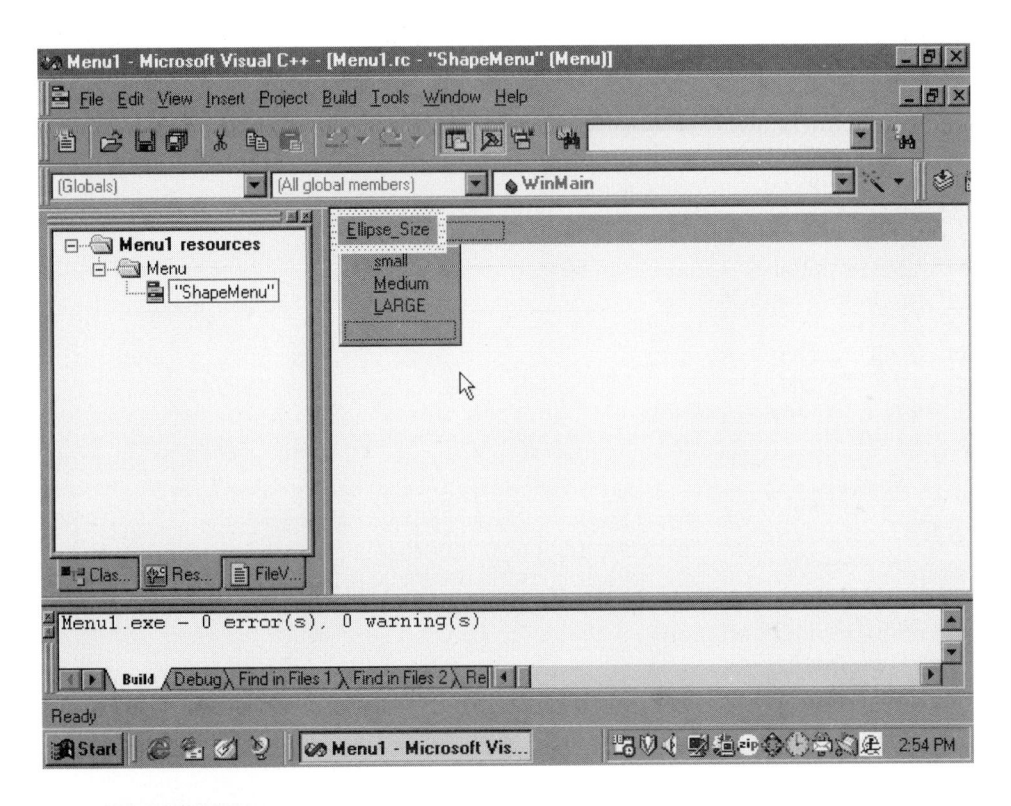

Figure 10-11 *The menu for the Menu1 project is designed in the Resource Editor.*

```
//
// Menu1.cpp
// Using a menu to size a shape.
// Copyright (c) William H. Murray and Chris H. Pappas, 1999
//

#include <windows.h>
#include "resource.h"

char szProgName[]="ProgName";
char szApplName[]="ShapeMenu";
static WORD wSize=30;

LRESULT CALLBACK WndProc(HWND,UINT,WPARAM,LPARAM);

int WINAPI WinMain(HINSTANCE hInst,HINSTANCE hPreInst,
                   LPSTR lpszCmdLine,int nCmdShow)
{
  HWND hWnd;
```

Chapter 10 • Adding Menu and Keyboard Accelerators

```
  MSG     lpMsg;
  WNDCLASS wcApp;

  wcApp.lpszClassName=szProgName;
  wcApp.hInstance    =hInst;
  wcApp.lpfnWndProc  =WndProc;
  wcApp.hCursor      =LoadCursor(NULL,IDC_ARROW);
  wcApp.hIcon        =0;
  wcApp.lpszMenuName =szApplName;
  wcApp.hbrBackground=(HBRUSH) GetStockObject(LTGRAY_BRUSH);
  wcApp.style        =CS_HREDRAW|CS_VREDRAW;
  wcApp.cbClsExtra   =0;
  wcApp.cbWndExtra   =0;
  if (!RegisterClass (&wcApp))
     return 0;

  hWnd=CreateWindow(szProgName,"Selecting Size with a Menu",
                    WS_OVERLAPPEDWINDOW,CW_USEDEFAULT,
                    CW_USEDEFAULT,CW_USEDEFAULT,
                    CW_USEDEFAULT,(HWND)NULL,(HMENU)NULL,
                    hInst,(LPSTR)NULL);
  ShowWindow(hWnd,nCmdShow);
  UpdateWindow(hWnd);
  while (GetMessage(&lpMsg,0,0,0)) {
     TranslateMessage(&lpMsg);
     DispatchMessage(&lpMsg);
  }
  return(lpMsg.wParam);
}


LRESULT CALLBACK WndProc(HWND hWnd,UINT messg,
                         WPARAM wParam,LPARAM lParam)
{

  HDC hdc;
  PAINTSTRUCT ps;
  static int xClientView,yClientView;

  switch (messg) {
    case WM_COMMAND:
      switch (LOWORD(wParam)) {
        case IDM_SMALL:
          wSize=30;
          break;
        case IDM_MEDIUM:
          wSize=60;
          break;
        case IDM_LARGE:
          wSize=90;
```

```
            break;
         default:
            break;
      }
      InvalidateRect(hWnd,NULL,TRUE);
      break;

   case WM_SIZE:
      xClientView=LOWORD(lParam);
      yClientView=HIWORD(lParam);
      break;

   case WM_PAINT:
      hdc=BeginPaint(hWnd,&ps);

      // Change mapping mode, window extents and viewport
      SetMapMode(hdc,MM_ISOTROPIC);
      SetWindowExtEx(hdc,500,500,NULL);
      SetViewportExtEx(hdc,xClientView,-yClientView,NULL);
      SetViewportOrgEx(hdc,xClientView/2,yClientView/2,NULL);

      // Draw a simple shape to size and some text
      Ellipse(hdc,-(wSize*2),-wSize,
              (wSize*2),wSize);
      TextOut(hdc,-100,230,
              "Changing the size of an Ellipse",31);

      ValidateRect(hWnd,NULL);
      EndPaint(hWnd,&ps);
      break;

   case WM_DESTROY:
      PostQuitMessage(0);
      break;
   default:
      return(DefWindowProc(hWnd,messg,wParam,lParam));
      break;
   }
   return(0);
}
```

Once the menu design is completed and the C++ source code is entered, build the project. When the Menu1 application is executed, a simple menu will appear on the menu bar, as shown in Figure 10.12.

A LARGE shape is selected from the menu and drawn to the screen. Let's investigate how all of this works.

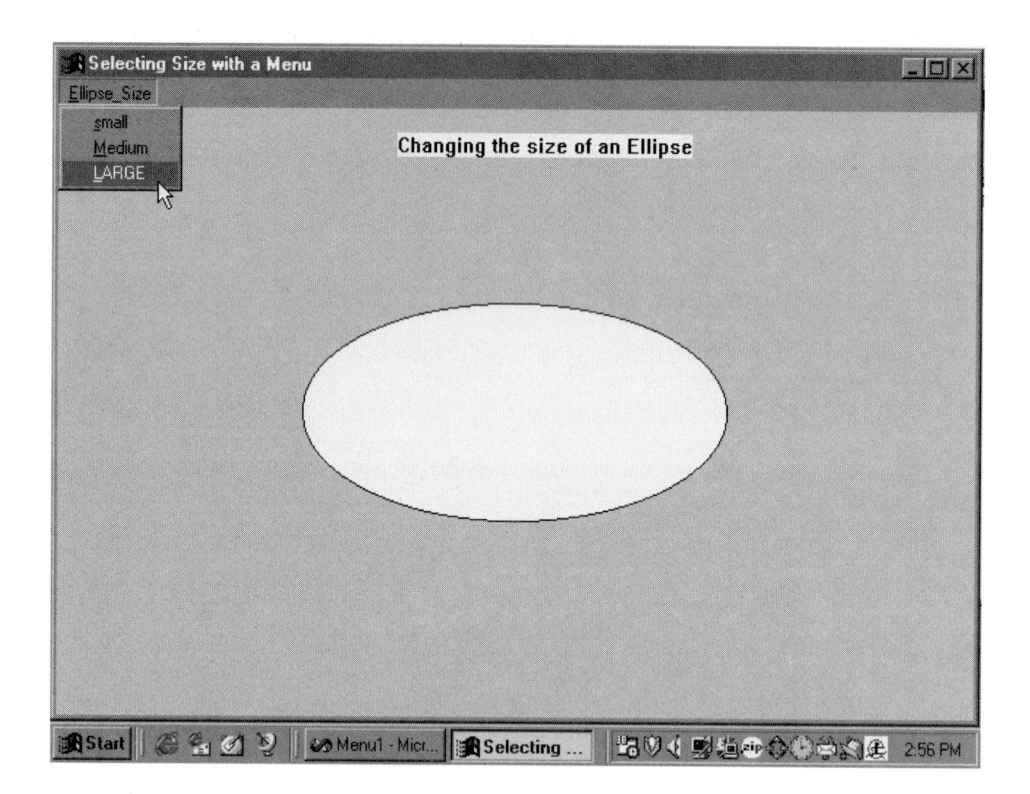

Figure 10-12 *The Menu1 project is run.*

THE HEADER FILE (RESOURCE.H)

A small header file, named *resource.h*, is created for this project. This header file is used to hold the ID values associated with the menu shapes.

```
//{{NO_DEPENDENCIES}}
// Microsoft Developer Studio generated include file.
// Used by Menu1.rc
//
#define IDR_MENU1                       104
#define IDM_SMALL                       40001
#define IDM_MEDIUM                      40002
#define IDM_LARGE                       40003

// Next default values for new objects
//
#ifdef APSTUDIO_INVOKED
#ifndef APSTUDIO_READONLY_SYMBOLS
#define _APS_NEXT_RESOURCE_VALUE        105
```

```
#define _APS_NEXT_COMMAND_VALUE      40004
#define _APS_NEXT_CONTROL_VALUE      1000
#define _APS_NEXT_SYMED_VALUE        101
#endif
#endif
```

Both the resource file and the application file use this header file information.

THE C++ SOURCE CODE FILE (MENU1.CPP)

Examine the complete listing for Menu1.cpp, shown earlier, and notice the inclusion of three lines of code near the top of the application.

```
char szProgName[]="ProgName";
char szApplName[]="ShapeMenu";
static WORD wSize=30;
```

The null terminated string, held in *szApplName*, identifies the name of the menu—*ShapeMenu*. Remember that the name of the menu was changed from an ID value of IDR_MENU1 to *ShapeMenu* during the menu design process. This name is passed to the *lpszMenuName* **WNDCLASS** structure member.

```
wcApp.lpszMenuName =szApplName;
```

The variable, *wSize*, is global and is declared as a static WORD initialized to 30. This value will form the default value for the ellipse's size.

When the menu is selected, WndProc receives a WM_COMMAND message to act upon.

```
case WM_COMMAND:
  switch (LOWORD(wParam)) {
    case IDM_SMALL:
      wSize=30;
      break;
    case IDM_MEDIUM:
      wSize=60;
      break;
    case IDM_LARGE:
      wSize=90;
      break;
    default:
      break;
  }
  InvalidateRect(hWnd,NULL,TRUE);
  break;
```

The LOWORD value of *wParam* is checked with three case statements. If "Small" is selected from the menu, *wSize* is set to 30. "Medium" returns a 60 and "Large" returns 90. Regardless of which value is selected, the **InvalidateRect()** function will send a message to WM_PAINT to update the entire window and draw the ellipse to the size specified by *wSize*. The global variable, *wSize*, is used to size the ellipse under WM_PAINT.

```
// Draw a simple shape to size and some text
Ellipse(hdc,-(wSize*2),-wSize,
        (wSize*2),wSize);
TextOut(hdc,-100,230,
        "Changing the size of an Ellipse",31);
```

The **InvalidateRect()**, **Ellipse()** and **TextOut()** functions used in WM_PAINT were discussed in detail in Chapter 4.

Notice that the combination of functions **SetMapMode()**, **SetWindowExtEx()**, **SetViewportExtEx()**, and **SetViewportOrgEx()** are used to change the default mapping mode, set the extents of the window and viewport, and reposition the window's origin.

```
// Change mapping mode, window extents and viewport
SetMapMode(hdc,MM_ISOTROPIC);
SetWindowExtEx(hdc,500,500,NULL);
SetViewportExtEx(hdc,xClientView,-yClientView,NULL);
SetViewportOrgEx(hdc,xClientView/2,yClientView/2,NULL);
```

The ellipse figure is scaled to fit the size of the window drawn to the screen using the MM_ISOTROPIC mapping mode, in combination with the viewport extents and origin determined by *xClientView* and *yClientView*. The use of these four functions was discussed in Chapter 3.

Changing a Background Color with a Menu

In the Menu2 project, two menus are used. The first menu is similar to the menu used in the first project, Menu1. The second menu allows the user to select a new background color from a list of 12 predefined colors. This menu incorporates keyboard accelerators that will allow the use of the function keys in making color selections.

To create this application with Visual C++, you'll need to create Win32 application workspace and name it *Menu2*. Then add a resource file containing menu information in a file named *Menu2.rc* and the C++ source code file named *Menu2.cpp*. Remember that a header file named *resource.h* is created, along with the resource script file.

The first file shown is a partial listing of the *Menu2.rc* resource script file needed for this project. Use this listing to determine how the menu and keyboard accelerators were designed and to find the various ID values used for menu items.

Remember, don't type in this file. Use the Resource Editor supplied with your Visual C++ compiler to graphically design the menu.

```
//////////////////////////////////////////////////////
//
// Menu
```

```
//

Alteration MENU DISCARDABLE
BEGIN
    POPUP "&Ellipse_Size"
    BEGIN
        MENUITEM "&small",                  IDM_SMALL
        MENUITEM "&Medium",                 IDM_MEDIUM
        MENUITEM "&LARGE",                  IDM_LARGE
    END
    POPUP "Ba&ckground_Colors"
    BEGIN
        MENUITEM "BLAC&K\tF1",              IDM_BLACK
        MENUITEM "&WHITE\tF2",              IDM_WHITE
        MENUITEM "&RED\tF3",                IDM_RED
        MENUITEM "&ORANGE\tF4",             IDM_ORANGE
        MENUITEM "&YELLOW\tF5",             IDM_YELLOW
        MENUITEM "GREE&N\tF6",              IDM_GREEN
        MENUITEM "&BLUE\tF7",               IDM_BLUE
        MENUITEM "&MAGENTA\tF8",            IDM_MAGENTA
        MENUITEM SEPARATOR
        MENUITEM "Lt GR&EEN\tF9",           IDM_LTGREEN
        MENUITEM "Lt BL&UE\tF10",           IDM_LTBLUE
        MENUITEM "Lt RE&D\tF11",            IDM_LTRED
        MENUITEM "Lt GR&AY\tF12",           IDM_LTGRAY
    END
END
    .
    .
    .
    .

////////////////////////////////////////////////////////
//
// Accelerator
//

Alteration ACCELERATORS DISCARDABLE
BEGIN
    VK_F1,          IDM_BLACK,      VIRTKEY, NOINVERT
    VK_F10,         IDM_LTBLUE,     VIRTKEY, NOINVERT
    VK_F11,         IDM_LTRED,      VIRTKEY, NOINVERT
    VK_F12,         IDM_LTGRAY,     VIRTKEY, NOINVERT
    VK_F2,          IDM_WHITE,      VIRTKEY, NOINVERT
    VK_F3,          IDM_RED,        VIRTKEY, NOINVERT
    VK_F4,          IDM_ORANGE,     VIRTKEY, NOINVERT
    VK_F5,          IDM_YELLOW,     VIRTKEY, NOINVERT
    VK_F6,          IDM_GREEN,      VIRTKEY, NOINVERT
    VK_F7,          IDM_BLUE,       VIRTKEY, NOINVERT
    VK_F8,          IDM_MAGENTA,    VIRTKEY, NOINVERT
```

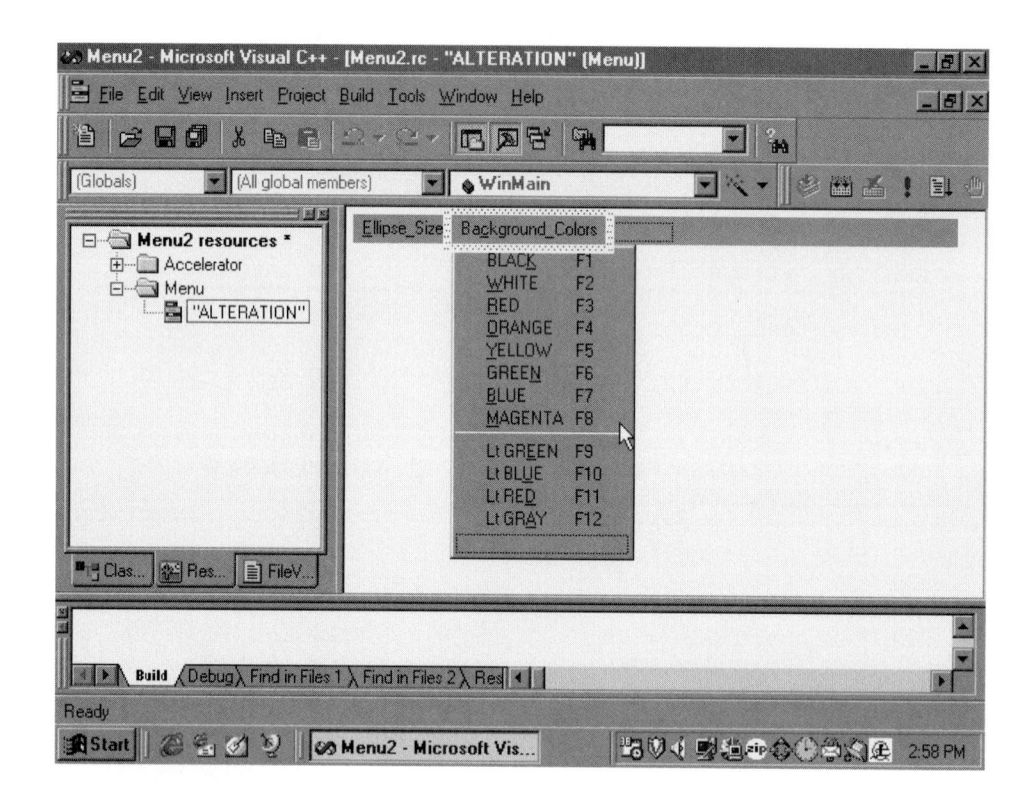

354 Chapter 10 • Adding Menu and Keyboard Accelerators

Figure 10–13 *The second menu for the Menu2 project is designed in the Resource Editor.*

```
VK_F9,          IDM_LTGREEN,         VIRTKEY, NOINVERT
END
```

Figure 10–3 shows the second menu, in the Resource Editor, during design.

The next listing is the C++ source code needed for the project. This file is named *Menu2.cpp*.

```
//
// Menu2.cpp
// Use a menu and keyboard accelerators to
// change background colors
// Copyright (c) William H. Murray and Chris H. Pappas, 1999
//

#include <windows.h>
#include "resource.h"
char szProgName[]="ProgName";
char szApplName[]="Alteration";
static WORD wSize=30;
```

```
static WORD wColor;

LRESULT CALLBACK WndProc(HWND,UINT,WPARAM,LPARAM);

int WINAPI WinMain(HINSTANCE hInst,HINSTANCE hPreInst,
                   LPSTR lpszCmdLine,int nCmdShow)
{
  HWND hWnd;
  HACCEL hAccel;
  MSG lpMsg;
  WNDCLASS wcApp;

  wcApp.lpszClassName=szProgName;
  wcApp.hInstance    =hInst;
  wcApp.lpfnWndProc  =WndProc;
  wcApp.hCursor      =LoadCursor(NULL,IDC_ARROW);
  wcApp.hIcon        =0;
  wcApp.lpszMenuName =szApplName;
  wcApp.hbrBackground=(HBRUSH) GetStockObject(WHITE_BRUSH);
  wcApp.style        =CS_HREDRAW|CS_VREDRAW;
  wcApp.cbClsExtra   =0;
  wcApp.cbWndExtra   =0;
  if (!RegisterClass (&wcApp))
    return 0;

  hWnd=CreateWindow(szProgName,
                    "Select Background Colors with a Menu",
                    WS_OVERLAPPEDWINDOW,CW_USEDEFAULT,
                    CW_USEDEFAULT,CW_USEDEFAULT,
                    CW_USEDEFAULT,(HWND)NULL,(HMENU)NULL,
                    hInst,(LPSTR)NULL);
  // Load Accelerators
  hAccel=LoadAccelerators(hInst,szApplName);

  ShowWindow(hWnd,nCmdShow);
  UpdateWindow(hWnd);
  while (GetMessage(&lpMsg,0,0,0)) {
    if (!TranslateAccelerator(hWnd,hAccel,&lpMsg)) {
      TranslateMessage(&lpMsg);
      DispatchMessage(&lpMsg);
    }
  }
  return(lpMsg.wParam);
}


LRESULT CALLBACK WndProc(HWND hWnd,UINT messg,
                         WPARAM wParam,LPARAM lParam)
{
```

```
HDC hdc;
PAINTSTRUCT ps;
HMENU hmenu;
static int xClientView,yClientView;
static int wColorValue[12][3]={0,0,0,         //BLACK
                               255,255,255,   //WHITE
                               255,0,0,       //RED
                               255,96,0,      //ORANGE
                               255,255,0,     //YELLOW
                               0,255,0,       //GREEN
                               0,0,255,       //BLUE
                               255,0,255,     //MAGENTA
                               128,255,0,     //LT GREEN
                               0,255,255,     //LT BLUE
                               255,0,159,     //LT RED
                               180,180,180};  //LT GRAY
switch (messg) {
  case WM_COMMAND:
    switch (LOWORD(wParam)) {
      case IDM_SMALL:
        wSize=30;
        break;
      case IDM_MEDIUM:
        wSize=60;
        break;
      case IDM_LARGE:
        wSize=90;
        break;
      case IDM_BLACK:
      case IDM_WHITE:
      case IDM_RED:
      case IDM_ORANGE:
      case IDM_YELLOW:
      case IDM_GREEN:
      case IDM_BLUE:
      case IDM_MAGENTA:
      case IDM_LTGREEN:
      case IDM_LTBLUE:
      case IDM_LTRED:
      case IDM_LTGRAY:
        hmenu=GetMenu(hWnd);
        CheckMenuItem(hmenu,wColor,MF_UNCHECKED);
        wColor=LOWORD(wParam);
        CheckMenuItem(hmenu,wColor,MF_CHECKED);
        SetClassLong(hWnd,GCL_HBRBACKGROUND,
                (LONG) CreateSolidBrush(RGB
                (wColorValue[wColor-IDM_BLACK][0],
                wColorValue[wColor-IDM_BLACK][1],
                wColorValue[wColor-IDM_BLACK][2])));
```

```
            break;
         default:
            break;
      }
      InvalidateRect(hWnd,NULL,TRUE);
      break;

   case WM_SIZE:
      xClientView=LOWORD(lParam);
      yClientView=HIWORD(lParam);
      break;

   case WM_PAINT:
      hdc=BeginPaint(hWnd,&ps);

      // Change mapping mode, window extents and viewport
      SetMapMode(hdc,MM_ISOTROPIC);
      SetWindowExtEx(hdc,500,500,NULL);
      SetViewportExtEx(hdc,xClientView,-yClientView,NULL);
      SetViewportOrgEx(hdc,xClientView/2,yClientView/2,NULL);

      // Draw a simple shape to size and some text
      Ellipse(hdc,-(wSize*2),-wSize,
              wSize*2,wSize);
      TextOut(hdc,-80,230,
              "Changing Sizes and Colors",25);

      ValidateRect(hWnd,NULL);
      EndPaint(hWnd,&ps);
      break;

   case WM_DESTROY:
      PostQuitMessage(0);
      break;
   default:
      return(DefWindowProc(hWnd,messg,wParam,lParam));
      break;
   }
   return(0);
}
```

In the following sections, we'll examine the additions and differences in this project, as compared with the Menu1 project.

THE HEADER FILE (RESOURCE.H)

The Resource Editor creates a header file when the menus are designed graphically. Here is a header file that has been edited slightly.

```
//{{NO_DEPENDENCIES}}
```

```
// Microsoft Developer Studio generated include file.
// Used by Menu2.rc
//
#define IDM_SMALL                       40001
#define IDM_MEDIUM                      40002
#define IDM_LARGE                       40003
#define IDM_BLACK                       40004
#define IDM_WHITE                       40005
#define IDM_RED                         40006
#define IDM_ORANGE                      40007
#define IDM_YELLOW                      40008
#define IDM_GREEN                       40009
#define IDM_BLUE                        40010
#define IDM_MAGENTA                     40011
#define IDM_LTGREEN                     40012
#define IDM_LTBLUE                      40013
#define IDM_LTRED                       40014
#define IDM_LTGRAY                      40015

// Next default values for new objects
//
#ifdef APSTUDIO_INVOKED
#ifndef APSTUDIO_READONLY_SYMBOLS
#define _APS_NEXT_RESOURCE_VALUE        103
#define _APS_NEXT_COMMAND_VALUE         40016
#define _APS_NEXT_CONTROL_VALUE         1000
#define _APS_NEXT_SYMED_VALUE           101
#endif
#endif
```

It contains all of the ID values necessary for the resource script and source code files. The ID values are really divided into two groups. One group holds menu IDs for sizing and one the IDs for the color options. You can see from examining the listing that three ellipse sizes and 12 background colors have been identified and assigned unique numeric values. Remember that the numeric values associated with the ID values can vary, as long as each of them is a unique value.

THE RESOURCE FILE (MENU2.RC)

The resource file contains menu and accelerator key information. The structure of both menus is very similar. For this application, the system's 12 function keys (F1–F12) are used as accelerator keys for color selection. When the application is run, background colors can be selected from the menu in the normal fashion or by simply pushing a function key. For example, the *F4* function key will change the background color to orange.

THE C++ SOURCE CODE FILE (MENU2.CPP)

When you study the Menu2.cpp source code listing you will notice initially that it is very similar to the source code used in the Menu1 project. One difference you'll observe is the addition of a new global variable named *wColor* at the start of the listing. This variable will hold the color selection value for the background color, but in an indirect manner, that will be explained shortly.

The first real change in this project over the Menu1 project is necessary to include the accelerator keys. A handle for the accelerator keys is obtained with a call to the **LoadAccelerators()** function. The *szApplName* name represents both the menu and the accelerator resources.

```
// Load Accelerators
  hAccel=LoadAccelerators(hInst,szApplName);
```

Next, access to the accelerators is included within the message loop of the application by a call to the **TranslateAccelerator()** function.

```
while (GetMessage(&lpMsg,0,0,0)) {
  if (!TranslateAccelerator(hWnd,hAccel,&lpMsg)) {
    TranslateMessage(&lpMsg);
    DispatchMessage(&lpMsg);
  }
}
```

WndProc() contains the bulk of the program code that is unique to this application. The handle for the menu, *hmenu,* is of type **HMENU**. A look-up table of RGB color values is used to create a custom brush. This custom brush is then used to paint the window's background. Notice that the look-up table, *wColorValue,* is a two-dimensional array. This array defines 12 colors by specifying three integer values for each. The integer values give the amount of each of the primary colors (red, green, blue) that are to be mixed for the brush. These range from 0 to 255 for each primary color.

When a WM_COMMAND message is received, sizing and color values must be processed. Notice that the case statements for the color selection take on a unique appearance.

```
case IDM_BLACK:
case IDM_WHITE:
case IDM_RED:
case IDM_ORANGE:
case IDM_YELLOW:
case IDM_GREEN:
case IDM_BLUE:
case IDM_MAGENTA:
case IDM_LTGREEN:
case IDM_LTBLUE:
case IDM_LTRED:
case IDM_LTGRAY:
hmenu=GetMenu(hWnd);
```

In this portion of code, the **GetMenu()** function will be called to return the menu handle. It doesn't matter which color has been selected, from IDM_BLACK to IDM_LTGRAY. The structure of this code is typical for menu items that are related. The only catch is that the menu items must have sequential identification numbers. We'll discuss this in more detail when we look at the **SetClassLong()** function.

Menus permit listed items to be checked or unchecked. If you desire to build an application that checks menu items when they are selected, you must use the **CheckMenuItem()** function.

```
CheckMenuItem(hmenu,wColor,MF_UNCHECKED);
wColor=LOWORD(wParam);
CheckMenuItem(hmenu,wColor,MF_CHECKED);
```

The **CheckMenuItem()** function has the ability to place or remove a check mark next to the specified menu item. It is customary to remove a previously placed check (*MF_UNCHECKED*) before placing a new check mark (*MF_CHECKED*). Therefore, the process is to remove the old value, retrieve the new *wColor* value, and place the new check mark at the appropriate location on the menu.

The **SetClassLong()** function is used to change the background color.

```
SetClassLong(hWnd,GCL_HBRBACKGROUND,
             (LONG) CreateSolidBrush(RGB
             (wColorValue[wColor-IDM_BLACK][0],
             wColorValue[wColor-IDM_BLACK][1],
             wColorValue[wColor-IDM_BLACK][2])));
```

The **SetClassLong()** function uses three parameters. The first parameter holds the handle *hWnd*. The second parameter, called the *index*, is selected from seven possible options: GCL_CBCLSEXTRA, GCL_CBWNDEXTRA, GCL_HBRBACKGROUND, GCL_HCURSOR, GCL_HICON, GCL_HMODULE, AND GCL_STYLE. These options permit the replacement of the given parameter in the **WNDCLASS** structure at the beginning of each application. GCL_HBRBACKGROUND sets a new handle to a background brush. The third parameter specifies the replacement value. For this example, the replacement value is derived from the color value, *wColor*. Here is an explanation of why the color values had to be sequential. Suppose the user selected an orange background. In that case, *wColor* will be passed the ID value of 40007. Also notice that the color black has an ID value of 40004. The black ID number is subtracted from the orange ID number, giving a result of 3. The value of 3 is used as an index into the *wColorValue* array. The orange values in the array correspond to [3][0], [3][1], and [3][2]. Now you know why the values must be sequential.

The remainder of the Menu2 project is very similar to the Menu1 project. Figure 10–14 shows a medium-sized elliptical shape against a light gray background.

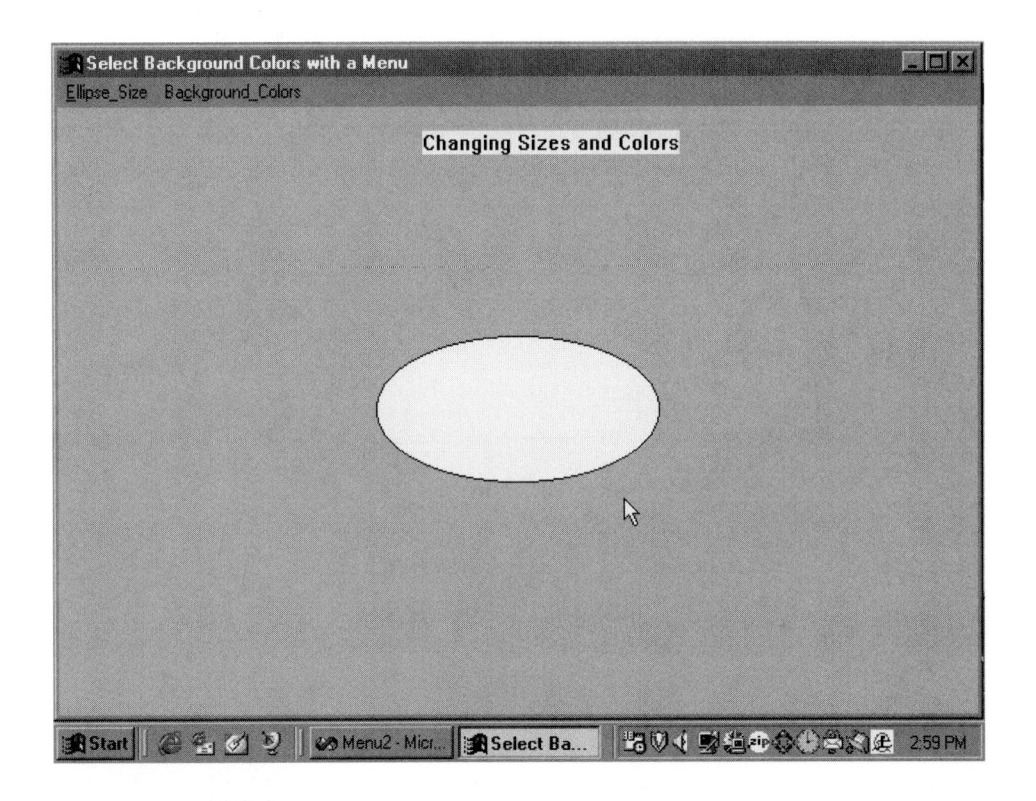

Figure 10-14 A graphics shape set against a light gray background.

For all other color selections, you'll have to try the application yourself. Hey, this is kind of neat!

Determining System Information with a Menu

Many times you'll need to determine information about the computer system you are using. In the third project, Menu3, we'll retrieve some vital information about the computer system on which the application is running. For example, before saving a file you might want to determine the amount of disk space available. It's possible that you may have a need for the Windows version number or even the current time and date. All of this information and more is available through Windows function calls. If you are a former DOS programmer, don't even think of using interrupts to obtain this information! DOS interrupts are not allowed under Windows 98 or NT. If interrupt calls were possible, they could compromise the integrity of the entire operating environment.

To create this application with Visual C++, you'll need to create Win32 application workspace and name it *Menu3*. Then add a resource file containing menu information in a file named *Menu3.rc* and the C++ source code file named *Menu3.cpp*.

The first file listed is a portion of the *Menu3.rc* resource script file needed for this project. Use the section to determine how the menus were designed and to find the various ID values used for menu items. The menu resource is assigned an ID value of IDR_MENU3. This was changed to *SystemInfo* before saving the resource script file.

Remember, don't type in this file. Use the Resource Editor supplied with your Visual C++ compiler to graphically design the menu.

```
/////////////////////////////////////////////////////////////////////
//
// Menu
//

SystemInfo MENUEX DISCARDABLE
BEGIN
    POPUP "&Disk_Information",              65535
    BEGIN
        MENUITEM "&Total Disk Space",       40001
        MENUITEM "&Free Disk Space",        40002
        MENUITEM SEPARATOR
        MENUITEM "&Current Drive and Path", 40003
        MENUITEM "&Windows Version",        40004
    END
    POPUP "&Time / Date",                   65535
    BEGIN
        MENUITEM "&Date",                   40005
        MENUITEM "&Time",                   40006
    END
END
```

As you can see from this listing, two menus are used. The first menu includes four menu items that allow the user to select total disk space, free disk space, the current disk drive and path, and the Windows version number. The second menu permits the selection of either the current time or the current date, as held by the system.

The next listing is the C++ source code listing for the project. This file is named *Menu3.cpp*.

```
//
// Menu3.cpp
// Menu selection of System Information
// Copyright (c) William H. Murray and Chris H. Pappas, 1999
//

#include <windows.h>
#include <stdio.h>
```

```
#include "resource.h"

char szProgName[]="ProgName";
char szApplName[]="SystemInfo";
char szMessage[50];
long int iLength;

LRESULT CALLBACK WndProc(HWND,UINT,WPARAM,LPARAM);

int WINAPI WinMain(HINSTANCE hInst,HINSTANCE hPreInst,
                   LPSTR lpszCmdLine,int nCmdShow)
{
  HWND hWnd;
  MSG   lpMsg;
  WNDCLASS wcApp;

  wcApp.lpszClassName=szProgName;
  wcApp.hInstance     =hInst;
  wcApp.lpfnWndProc   =WndProc;
  wcApp.hCursor       =LoadCursor(NULL,IDC_ARROW);
  wcApp.hIcon         =0;
  wcApp.lpszMenuName  =szApplName;
  wcApp.hbrBackground=(HBRUSH) GetStockObject(LTGRAY_BRUSH);
  wcApp.style         =CS_HREDRAW|CS_VREDRAW;
  wcApp.cbClsExtra    =0;
  wcApp.cbWndExtra    =0;
  if (!RegisterClass (&wcApp))
    return 0;

  hWnd=CreateWindow(szProgName,
                    "System Information with a Menu",
                    WS_OVERLAPPEDWINDOW,CW_USEDEFAULT,
                    CW_USEDEFAULT,CW_USEDEFAULT,
                    CW_USEDEFAULT,(HWND)NULL,(HMENU)NULL,
                    hInst,(LPSTR)NULL);
  ShowWindow(hWnd,nCmdShow);
  UpdateWindow(hWnd);
  while (GetMessage(&lpMsg,0,0,0)) {
    TranslateMessage(&lpMsg);
    DispatchMessage(&lpMsg);
  }
  return(lpMsg.wParam);
}


LRESULT CALLBACK WndProc(HWND hWnd,UINT messg,
                         WPARAM wParam,LPARAM lParam)
{
  HDC hdc;
  PAINTSTRUCT ps;
```

```c
         SYSTEMTIME st;
         WORD month,day,year,hrs,mins,secs,msec;
         DWORD dVer;
         WORD  wMainver,wFracver;
         ULARGE_INTEGER lpFreeBytesAvailableToCaller,
                        lpTotalNumberOfBytes,
                        lpTotalNumberOfFreeBytes;
         char lpszCurDir[MAX_PATH];

         switch (messg) {
           case WM_COMMAND:
             switch (LOWORD(wParam)) {
               case IDM_TDS:
                 // Use new function for disk space information
                 GetDiskFreeSpaceEx("c:\\",
                                   &lpFreeBytesAvailableToCaller,
                                   &lpTotalNumberOfBytes,
                                   &lpTotalNumberOfFreeBytes);
                 iLength=sprintf(szMessage,
                               "Total C Drive Disk Space (MB) \
                               -> %f",
                               DWORD(lpTotalNumberOfBytes. \
                               QuadPart/1000)/1000.0);
                 break;
               case IDM_FDS:
                 // Use new function for disk space information
                 GetDiskFreeSpaceEx("c:\\",
                                   &lpFreeBytesAvailableToCaller,
                                   &lpTotalNumberOfBytes,
                                   &lpTotalNumberOfFreeBytes);
                 iLength=sprintf(szMessage,
                               "Total C Drive Free Space (MB) \
                               -> %f",
                               DWORD(lpTotalNumberOfFreeBytes. \
                               QuadPart/1000)/1000.0);
                 break;
               case IDM_DD:
                 // form current directory and path
                 GetCurrentDirectory(MAX_PATH,lpszCurDir);
                 iLength=sprintf(szMessage,lpszCurDir);
                 break;
               case IDM_WV:
                 // form version number
                 // Windows 98 is reported as version 4.1
                 dVer=GetVersion();
                 wFracver=(WORD) dVer >> 8;
                 wMainver=(WORD) dVer & 255;
                 iLength=sprintf(szMessage,
                               "Windows Version Number ->  %d.%d",
                               wMainver,wFracver);
```

```
          break;
        case IDM_DATE:
          // get date information
          GetLocalTime(&st);
          year=st.wYear;
          month=st.wMonth;
          day=st.wDay;
          iLength=sprintf(szMessage,
                          "Current Date ->   %d/%d/%d",
                          month,day,year);
          break;
        case IDM_TIME:
          // get time information
          GetLocalTime(&st);
          hrs=st.wHour;
          mins=st.wMinute;
          secs=st.wSecond;
          msec=st.wMilliseconds;
          iLength=sprintf(szMessage,
                          "Current Time ->   %d:%d:%d:%d",
                          hrs,mins,secs,msec);
          break;
        default:
          break;
      }
      InvalidateRect(hWnd,NULL,TRUE);
      break;

    case WM_PAINT:
      hdc=BeginPaint(hWnd,&ps);

      TextOut(hdc,10,50,szMessage,iLength);

      ValidateRect(hWnd,NULL);
      EndPaint(hWnd,&ps);
      break;

    case WM_DESTROY:
      PostQuitMessage(0);
      break;
    default:
      return(DefWindowProc(hWnd,messg,wParam,lParam));
      break;
  }
  return(0);
}
```

We'll examine the important parts of this application in the following sections.

THE HEADER FILE (RESOURCE.H)

A unique header file, named *resource.h*, contains ID information for the menu items in this project. The ID values are assigned in the following manner:

```
//{{NO_DEPENDENCIES}}
// Microsoft Developer Studio generated include file.
// Used by Menu3.rc
//
#define IDR_MENU1                       101
#define IDM_TDS                         40001
#define IDM_FDS                         40002
#define IDM_DD                          40003
#define IDM_WV                          40004
#define IDM_DATE                        40005
#define IDM_TIME                        40006

// Next default values for new objects
//
#ifdef APSTUDIO_INVOKED
#ifndef APSTUDIO_READONLY_SYMBOLS
#define _APS_NEXT_RESOURCE_VALUE        102
#define _APS_NEXT_COMMAND_VALUE         40007
#define _APS_NEXT_CONTROL_VALUE         1000
#define _APS_NEXT_SYMED_VALUE           101
#endif
#endif
```

These ID values are used by both the resource script and source code files for the Menu3 project.

THE RESOURCE FILE (MENU3.RC)

The resource file for this application will produce two menus. The first menu, Disk Information, allows the user to select information pertaining to disk and version numbers. The second menu, Time / Date, will display time or date options. Notice in the resource file listing that the first pop-up menu contains a MENUITEM SEPARATOR after IDM_DD. The results of using the MENUITEM SEPARATOR option are shown in Figure 10–15.

Menus—A Variety of Options   **367**

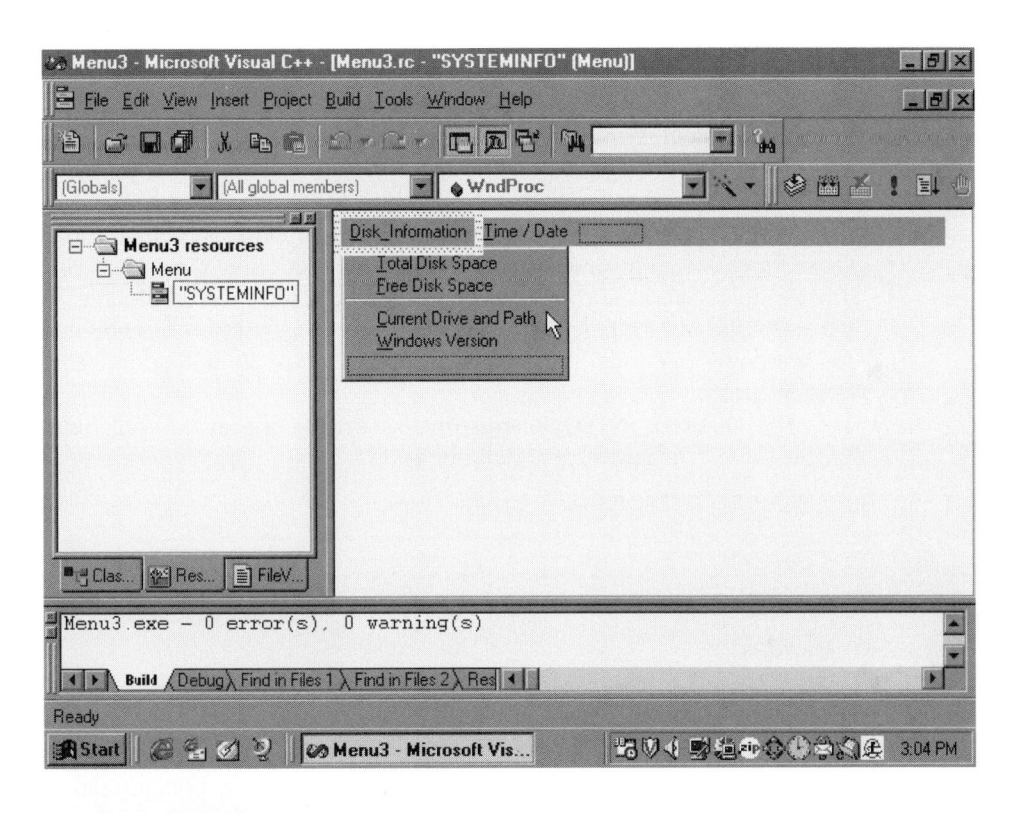

Figure 10-15 *The MENUITEM SEPARATOR divides the first menu into two sections.*

Breaking a menu into parts is often desirable when more than one group of items is contained in a menu.

THE C++ SOURCE CODE FILE (MENU3.CPP)

Study the source code listing for this project. Notice that in this application all screen information, regardless of the menu item selected, will be returned to the *szMessage* array. The array is initialized to hold 50 characters. The actual length of the string is an integer and is held in the variable *iLength*. Both of these global variables are declared at the start of the *Menu3.cpp* source code.

There are some unique features to be found in the variable declaration section of **WndProc()**.

```
HDC hdc;
PAINTSTRUCT ps;
SYSTEMTIME st;
WORD month,day,year,hrs,mins,secs,msec;
```

```
DWORD dVer;
WORD   wMainver,wFracver;
ULARGE_INTEGER lpFreeBytesAvailableToCaller,
               lpTotalNumberOfBytes,
               lpTotalNumberOfFreeBytes;
char lpszCurDir[MAX_PATH];
```

Windows provides many functions for retrieving system information. These functions, in turn, return information in a variety of data sizes. The variables in this section are an assortment of characters, words, double words, and unsigned large integers. These hold the information returned by the various Windows functions. Time and date information will be held in a **SYSTEMTIME** structure.

The **ULARGE_INTEGER** structure is used to specify a 64-bit unsigned integer value. The structure is defined as:

```
typedef union _ULARGE_INTEGER {
    struct {
        DWORD LowPart;
        DWORD HighPart;
    };
    ULONGLONG QuadPart;
} ULARGE_INTEGER;
```

A 64-bit integer value is ideal for storing the size of large disk drives. Applications developed for Windows 98 and Windows NT can make use of this large size and use the **GetDiskFreeSpaceEx()** function instead of the older **GetDiskFreeSpace()** function used by earlier Windows versions.

WM_COMMAND messages are used to process selected menu items with case statements. Notice the six case values, previously assigned to the menu items: IDM_TDS, IDM_FDS, IDM_DD, IDM_WV, IDM_DATE, and IDM_TIME.

As an example, consider how the total disk space is determined. When the request is made for total disk space (IDM_TDS) from the menu, a WM_COMMAND message is sent and processed by the appropriate **case** statement. The total disk space is determined by making a call to the **GetDiskFreeSpaceEx()** function.

```
case IDM_TDS:
  // Use new function for disk space information
  GetDiskFreeSpaceEx("c:\\",
                     &lpFreeBytesAvailableToCaller,
                     &lpTotalNumberOfBytes,
                     &lpTotalNumberOfFreeBytes);
```

The **GetDiskFreeSpaceEx()** function accepts four parameters. The first parameter, *lpDirectoryName*, is a pointer to a null-terminated string that gives a directory on the disk. The string can be a UNC name. If it is a UNC name it should be followed with an additional backslash. In this example, we're asking for the total disk space on the C drive. The value can also be set to NULL. When the parameter is set to NULL, the function finds information about the disk that contains the current directory. The second parameter, *lpFreeBytesAvailableToCaller*, is a pointer to a variable that receives the total number of free bytes on the disk. Actually, the value returned represents the total number of free bytes that are available to the user with regard to the calling thread. The third parameter, *lpTotalNumberOfBytes*, is a pointer to a variable that receives the total number of bytes on the disk. Again, this is measured with respect to the calling thread. The fourth parameter, *lpTotalNumberOfFreeBytes*, is a pointer to a variable that receives the total number of free bytes on the disk.

The total disk space is returned via the *lpTotalNumberOfBytes* parameter. Use **sprintf()** to format a string of information returned by this function.

```
iLength=sprintf(szMessage,
           "Total C Drive Disk Space (MB) \
           ->   %f",
           DWORD(lpTotalNumberOfBytes. \
           QuadPart/1000)/1000.0);
```

The number returned to the **ULARGE_INTEGER** structure is a 64-bit value. A little fancy arithmetic reduces that large number to a managable number that can be reported to the window. This arithmetic allows the application to report drive sizes in megabytes instead of bytes.

In another example, the current time can be requested by selecting the appropriate menu item. The **GetLocalTime()** function is used for this purpose. Time and date information is returned to *st*, which is a **SYSTEMTIME** structure.

```
case IDM_TIME:
  // get time information
  GetLocalTime(&st);
  hrs=st.wHour;
  mins=st.wMinute;
  secs=st.wSecond;
  msec=st.wMilliseconds;
  iLength=sprintf(szMessage,
              "Current Time ->   %d:%d:%d:%d",
              hrs,mins,secs,msec);
  break;
```

The **SYSTEMTIME** structure is defined in the winbase.h header file.

```
typedef struct _SYSTEMTIME {
    WORD wYear;
    WORD wMonth;
    WORD wDayOfWeek;
    WORD wDay;
    WORD wHour;
```

```
    WORD wMinute;
    WORD wSecond;
  WORD wMilliseconds;
} SYSTEMTIME;
```

To assemble a composite time value, structure members *st.wHour*, *st.wMinute*, *st.wSecond,* and *st.wMilliseconds* are returned to the variables *hrs*, *mins*, *secs,* and *msec,* respectively. These values are assembled and saved in *szMessage* with the help of the **sprintf()** function. The length of the string is returned to *iLength*. The time and date information returned represents the system's current time and date.

All other menu choices for this project are processed in a manner similar to these two examples. If you desire additional information on the **GetDiskFreeSpaceEx()**, **GetCurrentDirectory()**, and **GetVersion()** functions, help is immediately available from the Windows on-line Help facility. One special note—Windows 98 correctly reports a version number of 4.1 with this application.

Regardless of which menu item is selected, information is saved in *szMessage* and drawn to the window by sending a WM_PAINT message. The window information is updated each time a new menu selection is processed because of the call to the **InvalidateRect()** function at the end of WM_COMMAND. Figures 10–16 and 10–17 show the information returned by two different menu selections.

Test the other menu items and learn more about your disk drive and Windows.

Obtaining Directory Listings with a Menu

The fourth application will use a single menu that will allow the user to select a disk drive (A, B, C, or D) from which to obtain a directory listing. The directory listing will then be displayed in the window. Because directory listings can be quite long, a vertical scroll bar will be used with this window. Menus do not allow the user to input data directly from the keyboard, so the application will be restricted to the root directories of the four drives just mentioned. One major drawback of this application is that only the directory for the current drive and path can be listed. No provision is made for switching directory paths. This problem could be overcome, and the application greatly enhanced, with the use of a dialog box. Dialog boxes, explained in the next chapter, allow the user to enter information interactively from the keyboard.

To create this application with Visual C++, you'll need to create Win32 application workspace and name it *Menu4*. Then add a resource file containing menu information in a file named *Menu4.rc* and the C++ source code file named *Menu4.cpp*.

The first file listed is a portion of the *Menu4.rc* resource script file needed for this project. Use the section to determine how the menus were designed and to find the various ID values used for menu items. The menu resource is assigned an ID value of IDR_MENU4. This was changed to *Directory* before saving the resource script file.

Remember, don't type in this file. Use the Resource Editor supplied with your Visual C++ compiler to graphically design the menu.

```
//////////////////////////////////////////////////
//
// Menu
//

Directory MENU DISCARDABLE
BEGIN
    POPUP "&Directory_Information"
    BEGIN
        MENUITEM "Directory &A:",           IDM_AFILES
        MENUITEM "Directory &B:",           IDM_BFILES
        MENUITEM "Directory &C:",           IDM_CFILES
        MENUITEM "Directory &D:",           IDM_DFILES
    END
END
```

As you can see from this listing, one menu is used. The menu includes four menu items that allow the user to select a disk drive from which to obtain a directory listing.

The next listing is the C++ source code listing for the project. This file is named *Menu4.cpp*.

```
//
// Menu4.cpp

// Reading root directories with a menu
// Copyright (c) William H. Murray and Chris H. Pappas, 1999
//

#include <windows.h>
#include <string.h>
#include <stdio.h>
#include "resource.h"

#define LINES 500   // number of lines to scroll
LRESULT CALLBACK WndProc(HWND,UINT,WPARAM,LPARAM);

char szProgName[]="ProgName";
char szApplName[]="Directory";
char szMessage[100];
```

Chapter 10 • Adding Menu and Keyboard Accelerators

```c
char szMyfile[20] = "c:\\windows";   // initial directory
int   iLength;
int WINAPI WinMain(HINSTANCE hInst,HINSTANCE hPreInst,
                   LPSTR lpszCmdLine,int nCmdShow)
{
  HWND hWnd;
  MSG  lPMsg;
  WNDCLASS wcApp;

  wcApp.lpszClassName=szProgName;
  wcApp.hInstance    =hInst;
  wcApp.lpfnWndProc  =WndProc;
  wcApp.hCursor      =LoadCursor(NULL,IDC_ARROW);
  wcApp.hIcon        =0;
  wcApp.lpszMenuName =szApplName;
  wcApp.hbrBackground=(HBRUSH)GetStockObject(LTGRAY_BRUSH);
  wcApp.style        =CS_HREDRAW|CS_VREDRAW;
  wcApp.cbClsExtra   =0;
  wcApp.cbWndExtra   =0;
  if (!RegisterClass (&wcApp))
    return 0;

  hWnd=CreateWindow(szProgName,"Reading a Root Directory",
                    WS_OVERLAPPEDWINDOW,CW_USEDEFAULT,
                    CW_USEDEFAULT,CW_USEDEFAULT,
                    CW_USEDEFAULT,(HWND)NULL,(HMENU)NULL,
                    hInst,(LPSTR)NULL);
  ShowWindow(hWnd,nCmdShow);
  UpdateWindow(hWnd);
  while (GetMessage(&lPMsg,0,0,0)) {
    TranslateMessage(&lPMsg);
    DispatchMessage(&lPMsg);
  }
  return(lPMsg.wParam);
}


LRESULT CALLBACK WndProc(HWND hWnd,UINT messg,
                         WPARAM wParam,LPARAM lParam)
{
 HDC hdc;
  PAINTSTRUCT ps;
  HANDLE hFindFile;
  WIN32_FIND_DATA ffd;
  TEXTMETRIC tm;
  SCROLLINFO si;
```

Menus—A Variety of Options

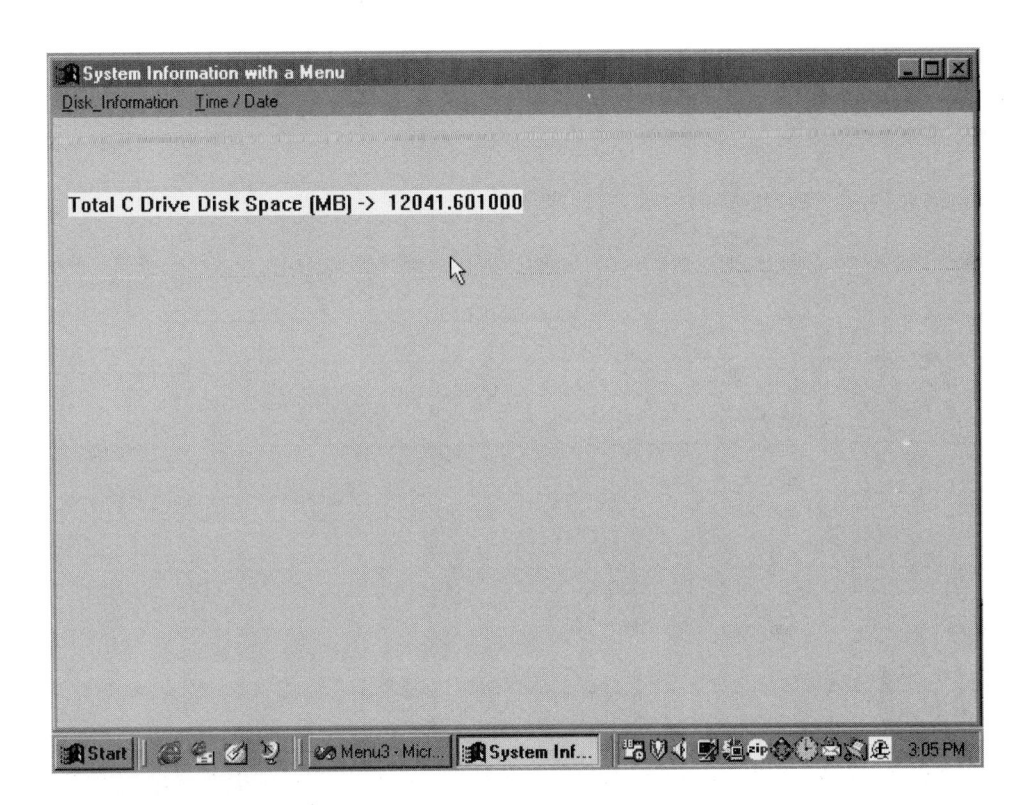

Figure 10-16   Disk size is reported for 12-gigabyte hard disk.

```
BOOL fRC;
LPTSTR lpszSearchFile="*.*";
int i, yInc;
static yChHeight;
static int yPos, yMax;
static int yClientView;

switch (messg) {
  case WM_CREATE:
    // handle to client area device context
    hdc=GetDC (hWnd);
    // font dimensions from the text metrics structure
    GetTextMetrics (hdc, &tm);
    yChHeight=tm.tmHeight+tm.tmExternalLeading;
    // release device context.
```

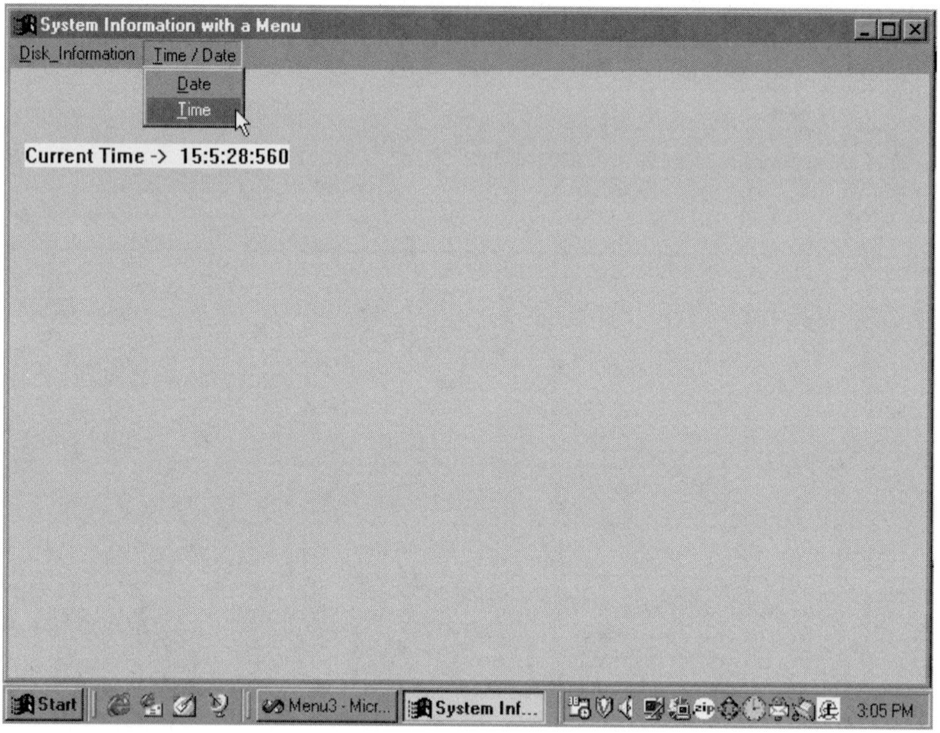

374 Chapter 10 • Adding Menu and Keyboard Accelerators

Figure 10-17 *The current system time is returned.*

```
      ReleaseDC (hWnd,hdc);
      return 0;

case WM_SIZE:   // get the dimensions of the client area.
   yClientView=HIWORD (lParam);
   // set the maximum vertical scrolling position
   yMax=LINES;
   // check that the current vertical scrolling position
   // does not exceed the maximum
   yPos=min (yPos, yMax);
   // adjust vertical scrolling range and scroll box
   // position for the new yMax and yPos
   si.cbSize=sizeof(si);
   si.fMask=SIF_ALL;
   si.nMin=0;
   si.nMax=yMax;
   si.nPage=yClientView/yChHeight;
   si.nPos=yPos;
   SetScrollInfo(hWnd,SB_VERT,&si,TRUE);
```

```c
      return 0;

case WM_VSCROLL:
  switch(LOWORD (wParam))
  {
    // clicked the space above the thumb
    case SB_PAGEUP:
      yInc=min(-1,-yClientView/yChHeight);
      break;
    // clicked the space below the thumb
    case SB_PAGEDOWN:
      yInc=max(1,yClientView/yChHeight);
      break;
    // clicked top arrow
    case SB_LINEUP:
      yInc=-1;
      break;
    // clicked bottom arrow
    case SB_LINEDOWN:
      yInc=1;
      break;
    // dragged the thumb
    case SB_THUMBTRACK:
      yInc=HIWORD(wParam)-yPos;
      break;
    default:
      yInc=0;
  }
  // check to see if scrolling increment takes
  // scrolling position out of scrolling range
  if (yInc=max(-yPos,min(yInc,yMax - yPos)))
  {
    yPos+=yInc;
    ScrollWindowEx(hWnd,0,-yChHeight * yInc,
            (CONST RECT *) NULL,(CONST RECT *) NULL,
            (HRGN) NULL,(LPRECT) NULL,SW_INVALIDATE);
    si.cbSize=sizeof(si);
    si.fMask=SIF_POS;
    si.nPos=yPos;
    SetScrollInfo(hWnd,SB_VERT,&si,TRUE);
    UpdateWindow(hWnd);
    InvalidateRect(hWnd,NULL,TRUE);
  }
  return 0;

case WM_COMMAND:
  switch (LOWORD(wParam)) {
    // select root directory to scan
    case IDM_AFILES:
      strcpy(szMyfile,"a:\\");
```

```
        break;
      case IDM_BFILES:
        strcpy(szMyfile,"b:\\");
        break;
      case IDM_CFILES:
        strcpy(szMyfile,"c:\\");
        break;
      case IDM_DFILES:
        strcpy(szMyfile,"d:\\");
        break;
      default:
        break;
    }
    InvalidateRect(hWnd,NULL,TRUE);
break;

case WM_PAINT:
  hdc=BeginPaint(hWnd,&ps);

  i=0;
  // set directory to scan
  SetCurrentDirectory(szMyfile);
  // use FindFirstFile() to get handle
  hFindFile=FindFirstFile(lpszSearchFile,&ffd);
  // create and print a string with the file name
  iLength=sprintf(szMessage,ffd.cFileName);
  TextOut(hdc,0,yChHeight*(i-yPos),
          szMessage,iLength);
  i++;
  for(;;) {
    // get subsequent file names and print
    fRC=FindNextFile(hFindFile,&ffd);
    if (fRC==FALSE) {
      // use FindClose() to close the file
      FindClose(hFindFile);
      break;
    }
    else
      // continue to print file names
      // until there are none remaining
      FindNextFile(hFindFile,&ffd);
      iLength=sprintf(szMessage,ffd.cFileName);
      TextOut(hdc,0,yChHeight*(i-yPos),
              szMessage,iLength);
      i++;
  }

  ValidateRect(hWnd,NULL);
  EndPaint(hWnd,&ps);
  break;
```

```
    case WM_DESTROY:
      PostQuitMessage(0);
      break;
    default:
      return(DefWindowProc(hWnd,messg,wParam,lParam));
      break;
  }
  return(0);
}
```

In the following sections, we'll investigate the new features of this program.

THE HEADER FILE (RESOURCE.H)

The header file uses four unique IDs and associated numbers for each drive's directory: IDM_AFILES, IDM_BFILES, IDM_CFILES, and IDM_DFILES.

```
//{{NO_DEPENDENCIES}}
// Microsoft Developer Studio generated include file.
// Used by Menu4.rc
//
#define IDR_MENU1                       101
#define IDM_AFILES                      40001
#define IDM_BFILES                      40002
#define IDM_CFILES                      40003
#define IDM_DFILES                      40004

// Next default values for new objects
//
#ifdef APSTUDIO_INVOKED
#ifndef APSTUDIO_READONLY_SYMBOLS
#define _APS_NEXT_RESOURCE_VALUE        102
#define _APS_NEXT_COMMAND_VALUE         40005
#define _APS_NEXT_CONTROL_VALUE         1000
#define _APS_NEXT_SYMED_VALUE           101
#endif
#endif
```

THE RESOURCE FILE (MENU4.RC)

The application uses a single menu named *Directory_Information*. Four menu items allow the user to select a directory listing for either the A, B, C, or D disk drives, using the current path.

THE C++ SOURCE CODE FILE (MENU4.CPP)

This is quite a long file because of the inclusion of a vertical scroll bar. You may want to review the information on scroll bars contained in Chapter 5 before proceeding with this project.

This application handles the establishment of the application's menu in the normal fashion. Five important messages are processed by this application: WM_CREATE, WM_SIZE, WM_VSCROLL, WM_COMMAND, and WM_PAINT. You should be familiar with many of these messages by this time.

WM_CREATE, for example, processes preliminary information about the current text height using the **GetTextMetrics()** function. This information is returned in the **tm** structure. The **tm** structure is of type **TEXTMETRIC**. This structure was discussed in Chapter 6. Recall that information regarding character height is necessary when scrolling a page of information up and down on the screen. The *tm* structure holds important information concerning current and available fonts.

WM_SIZE returns information on the current window size. This application is interested only in the vertical component of the window's size. This information is needed when scrolling a window a page at a time. Information on the initial scroll bar position and range is also obtained when the window is sized.

WM_COMMAND processes the drive option selected from the menu. As mentioned, this application limits the choice to root directories of drives A, B, C, and D. Regardless of the user's choice, the selection is saved in *szMyfile*. When processing a WM_PAINT message, this string information will be used in conjunction with several Windows function calls. WM_COMMAND ends with a call to **InvalidateRect()**. Remember from previous examples that this function posts a message to WM_PAINT for a screen update.

WM_PAINT uses three Windows function calls to obtain a complete directory listing: **SetCurrentDirectory()**, **FindFirstFile()** and **FindNextFile()**. The current directory is set from information returned to *szMyfile*.

```
SetCurrentDirectory(szMyfile);
```

Once the user selects a drive, the **FindFirstFile()** function is used to locate the first file in the directory that meets the *lpszSearchFile* criterion.

```
// set directory to scan
SetCurrentDirectory(szMyfile);
// use FindFirstFile() to get handle
hFindFile=FindFirstFile(lpszSearchFile,&ffd);
// create and print a string with the file name
iLength=sprintf(szMessage,ffd.cFileName);
TextOut(hdc,0,yChHeight*(i-yPos),
        szMessage,iLength);
```

In this case, the search criterion uses "*.*" to search for all files and file extensions. The address for the transferred information is contained in *ffd*. *ffd* is associated with the **WIN32_FIND_DATA** Windows structure.

```
typedef struct _WIN32_FIND_DATA {
    DWORD dwFileAttributes;
    FILETIME ftCreationTime;
    FILETIME ftLastAccessTime;
    FILETIME ftLastWriteTime;
    DWORD nFileSizeHigh;
    DWORD nFileSizeLow;
    DWORD dwReserved0;
    DWORD dwReserved1;
    CHAR cFileName[ MAX_PATH ];
    CHAR cAlternateFileName[ 14 ];
} WIN32_FIND_DATA;
```

The information returned to the structure is processed by the **sprintf()** function, stored in *szMessage*, and eventually printed to the window with a call to the **TextOut()** function.

The next function call occurs within a **for** loop. The **FindNextFile()** function is repeatedly checked for an end-of-directory match.

```
for(;;) {
  // get subsequent file names and print
  fRC=FindNextFile(hFindFile,&ffd);
  if (fRC==FALSE) {
    // use FindClose() to close the file
    FindClose(hFindFile);
    break;
  }
  else
    // continue to print file names
    // until there are none remaining
    FindNextFile(hFindFile,&ffd);
    iLength=sprintf(szMessage,ffd.cFileName);
    TextOut(hdc,0,yChHeight*(i-yPos),
            szMessage,iLength);
    i++;
}
```

If the directory is complete, a call is made to **FindClose()**, otherwise, the next file name is returned and drawn to the screen.

File names are drawn in the current window font, against the left border of the window. Notice that the second parameter in **TextOut()** is set to 0. The vertical position is determined by the character height (*yChHeight*) times the combination of the file number (*i*) minus the position of the vertical scrolls (*yPos*).

```
vertical position = yChHeight * (i - yPos)
```

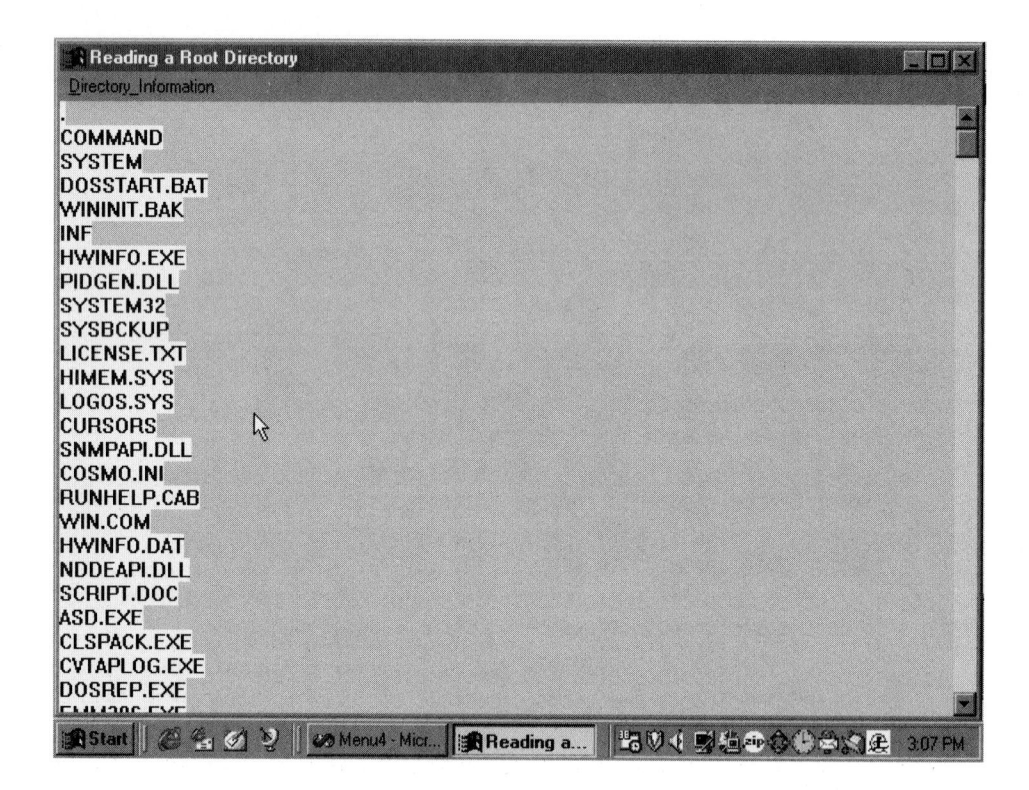

Figure 10-18 *A sample file listing for the Windows root directory.*

Figure 10–18 shows a sample listing for the default drive. This might be a surprise as the default was set to list the files in the Windows root directory.

What's Next?

Menus give us the ability to perform simple interactions with applications. Menus are, therefore, important in their own right. Menus, however, serve another important role. They are the gateway for a more important form of data entry—the dialog box. The next chapter will show you how to add dialog box options to menus.

ELEVEN

Adding Dialog Boxes

In the previous chapter, you learned that menus and keyboard accelerators are simple ways to interact with a Windows application. This chapter will take program interaction one step further. This chapter will present a more significant means of data entry—the dialog box. You'll learn that dialog boxes are the preferable data entry technique for maintaining consistency among all Windows platforms.

Dialog boxes, with associated controls, can be used to check items in a list, set radio buttons for various choices, enter strings and integer numbers, and indirectly enter real numbers (*floats*). It is even possible to combine controls. Windows combo box controls, for example, are a form of dialog box that allows a combination of a single-line edit field control and a list box control. Dialog boxes give the user true interactive communications with an application. Dialog boxes are also easy to implement as Windows handles all the necessary overhead.

The pathway to a dialog box is usually through a menu item in a standard Windows menu. When a menu item is selected that leads to a dialog box, the dialog box will appear as a pop-up window to the user. To set dialog box menu items apart from normal menu items, dialog box menu items are followed by three dots, or ellipses (...). Therefore, as you view various Windows menus and see three dots following a menu item, you know that a dialog box will pop up if that menu item is selected. Figure 11–1 shows a menu with a dialog box menu item (the screen is part of an example developed later in this chapter).

Chapter 11 • Adding Dialog Boxes

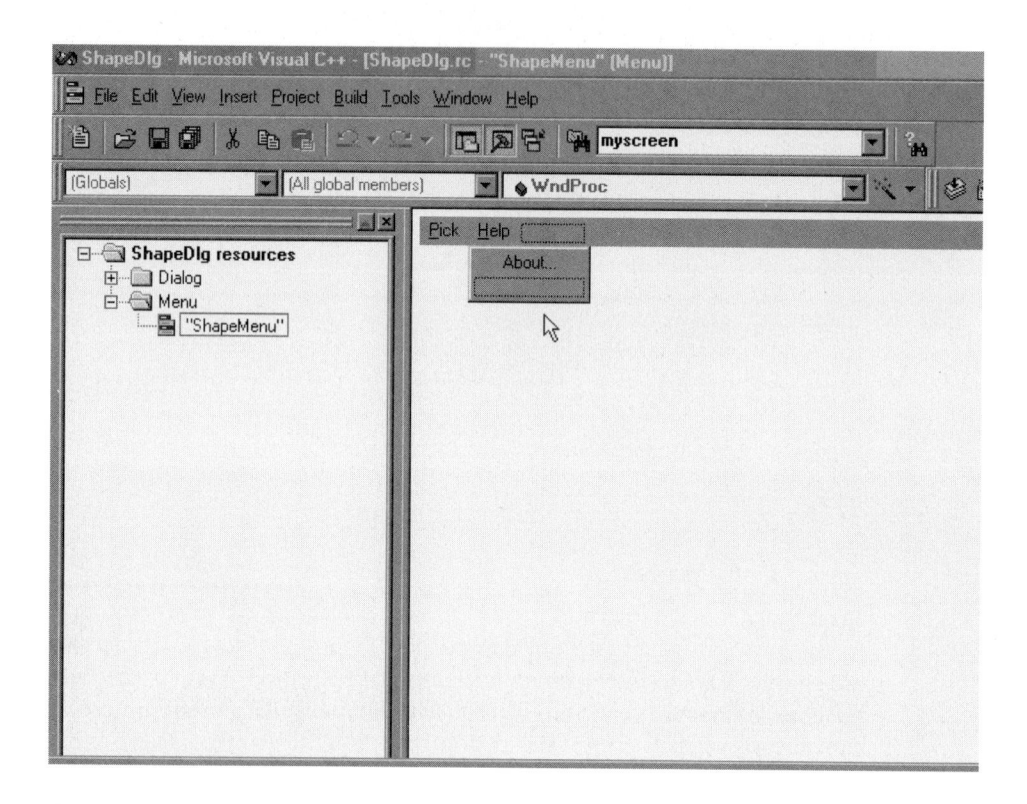

Figure 11-1 *A menu containing an About dialog box menu item.*

The specifications for the dialog box are designed by you, then generated by the Resource Editor supplied with the Microsoft Visual C++ compiler. The information provided by the Resource Editor when creating a dialog box resource eventually becomes part of the resource script file (a file with an .rc file extension) for the application. Figure 11.2 shows a simple About box dialog box. About dialog boxes can relay information to the user about the application's name, copyright date, designer, and so on.

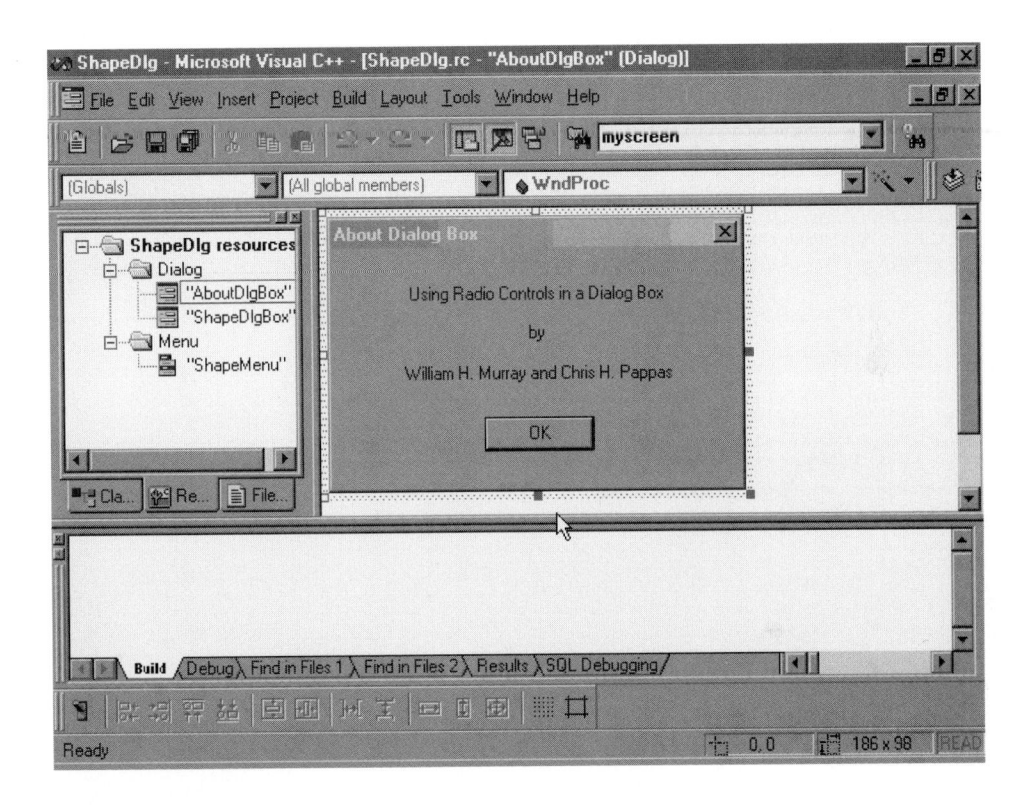

Figure 11-2 *A simple About dialog box.*

Figure 11-3 shows a dialog box that contains radio button controls. Like radio buttons on a car radio, only one radio button in a group can be selected at a time.

Chapter 11 • Adding Dialog Boxes

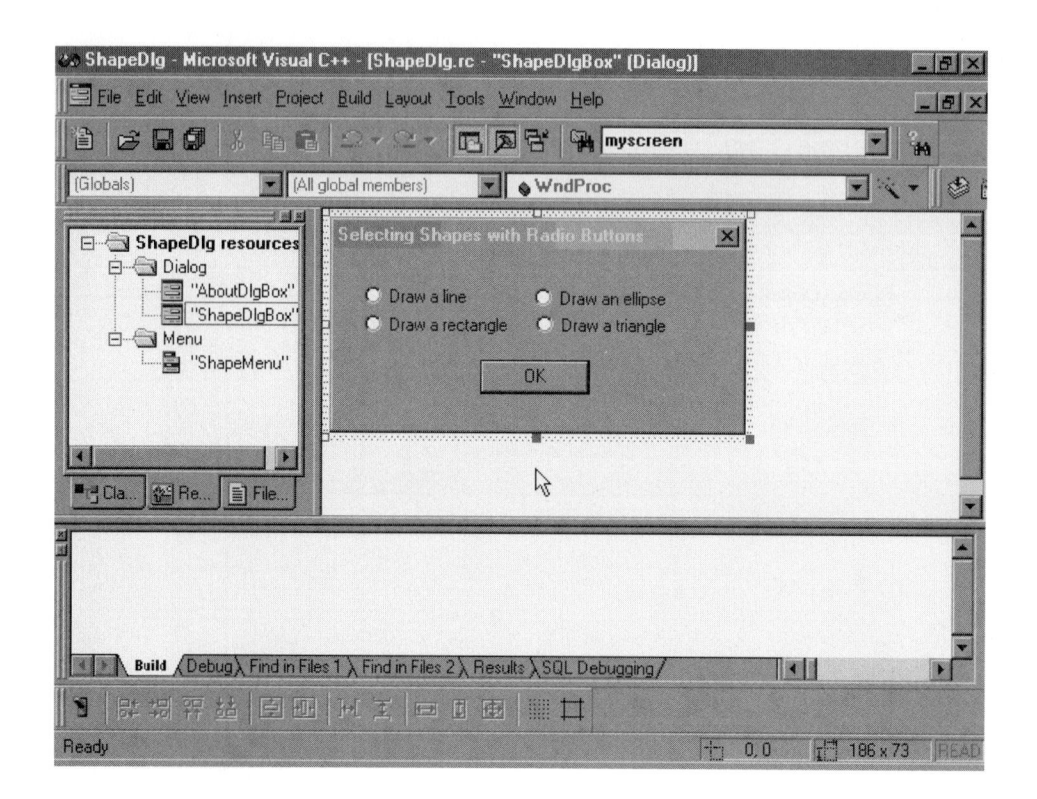

Figure 11-3 *Radio button controls can be used to make simple selections.*

Figure 11–4 shows a dialog box with an edit control. Edit controls allow the user to enter text that can be incorporated into the application. Dialog boxes can make programs truly interactive.

[Figure 11-4 screenshot of Microsoft Visual C++ showing a Text Entry Dialog Box]

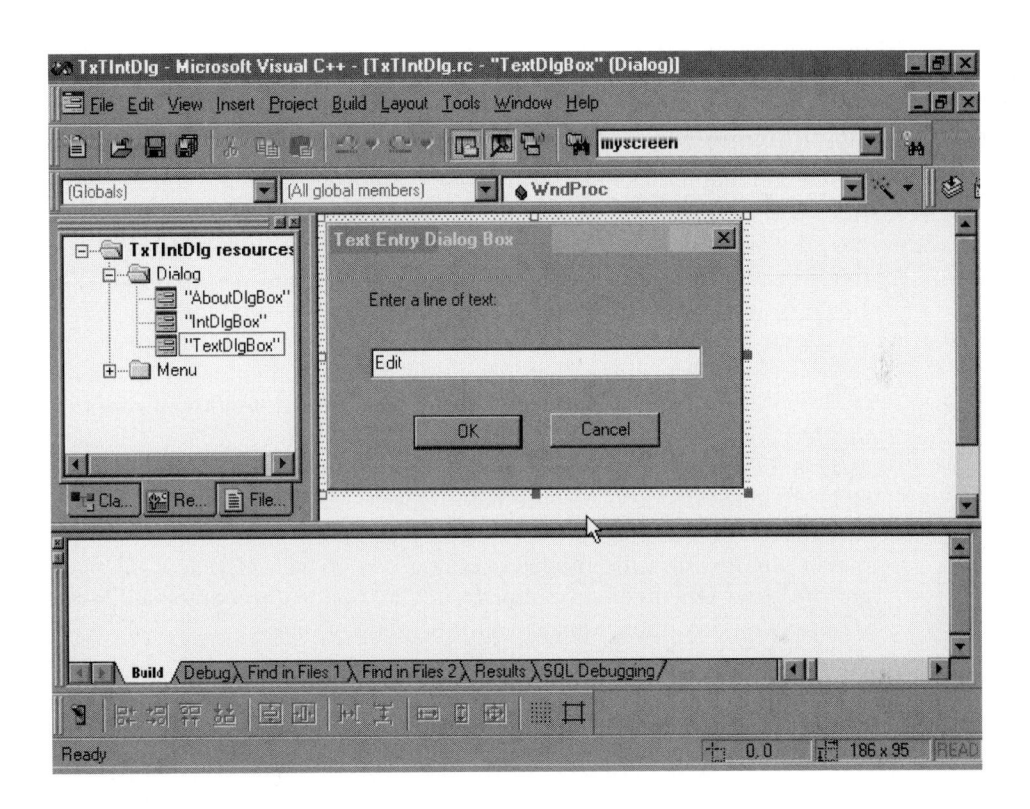

Figure 11-4 *Dialog boxes can allow the user to enter text in an edit control.*

Static text controls, edit controls, buttons, and radio buttons are very popular controls and frequently appear in dialog box designs. However, there are many additional controls that can be added to dialog boxes. These will be discussed in the following sections.

What Is a Dialog Box?

Dialog boxes are a special case of a child window. They are made to "pop up" when a dialog box menu item is selected. If the user selects a control contained in a dialog box, Windows provides the necessary means to process the message information. In the applications in this chapter, dialog box messages will be passed to a function in the application. We use a naming technique that uses an identifier name followed by *DlgProc*. For example, AboutDlgProc, ShapeDlgProc, or TextDlgProc identify unique dialog box functions. These functions have the primary responsibility of initializing various dialog box controls when the dialog box is created, evaluating the dialog box messages, and ending the dialog box.

The coded descriptions of the dialog boxes reside in resource script files. We replace the default names provided by the resource editor with more meaningful names such as *AboutDlgBox*, *ShapeDlgBox,* and *TextDlgBox*.

Dialog boxes can be created in two different styles: *modal* and *modeless*. Modal dialog boxes are the most frequently used dialog boxes. They are used for all of the applications in this chapter. When a modal dialog box is created, no other options within the current application are available to the user until a click of the Okay or Cancel buttons ends the current dialog box session. The Okay button will allow any new information to be processed, and the Cancel button returns the user to the original window without changing any of the previous information. The Resource Editor automatically assigns ID values to the Okay and Cancel button controls, IDOK and IDCANCEL. Modeless dialog boxes are more closely related to ordinary windows. A modeless dialog box can be created so that the user can switch between the parent window and the modeless dialog box at will. Modeless dialog boxes are preferred when certain options, such as options in a color-select or font-select dialog box, must remain on the screen.

The Resource Editor

Dialog boxes are resources, just like menus. The Resource Editor, provided with the Microsoft Visual C++ compiler, can be used to graphically design and compile dialog box resources. Because dialog box resources are usually used in conjunction with menus, you'll find that the Resource Editor can combine all related resources into a resource script file (a file with an .rc file extension).

The resource script file is a text file that is eventually compiled by the resource compiler and combined with the project's source code. As a text file, it is possible to enter, edit, and delete dialog box information in a text editor.

Why Use Resource Editor?

It is always best to design and edit dialog boxes within the graphical environment of the Resource Editor. Here is a portion of the code generated by the Resource Editor and placed in a resource script file. One look at this code should convince you of the need for a resource editor.

```
REALDLGBOX DIALOG DISCARDABLE 0, 0, 186, 95
STYLE DS_MODALFRAME | WS_POPUP | WS_CAPTION | WS_SYSMENU
CAPTION "Real Number Dialog Box"
FONT 8, "MS Sans Serif"
BEGIN
```

```
    DEFPUSHBUTTON "OK",IDOK,31,71,50,14
    PUSHBUTTON "Cancel",IDCANCEL,112,71,50,14
    LTEXT "Enter the radius of a circle as a real number:",
          IDC_STATIC,9,9,165,12
    EDITTEXT IDC_REAL,9,29,107,13,ES_AUTOHSCROLL
END
```

Where do all those terms come from? What is a DEFPUSHBUTTON? Without the Resource Editor, you would have to learn the terms used with all of the controls, then learn how to code them correctly. But that's not the worst of it. Those groups of four numbers, such as 0, 0, 186, 95 are used to size and locate the dialog box and/or control. Without a Resource Editor, you have to visualize the size and placement of controls. The Resource Editor, on the other hand, will do all this for you automatically.

Using the Resource Editor

During an application's creation, the dialog box development process will usually involve the creation of a menu resource and a dialog box resource. Both of these resources can reside in the same resource script file (.rc).

The Resource Editor can be started by using the Insert | Resource menu selection from the Visual C++ compiler. To create a dialog box, for example, you would then select Dialog from the Insert Resource dialog box, as shown in Figure 11-5.

Chapter 11 • Adding Dialog Boxes

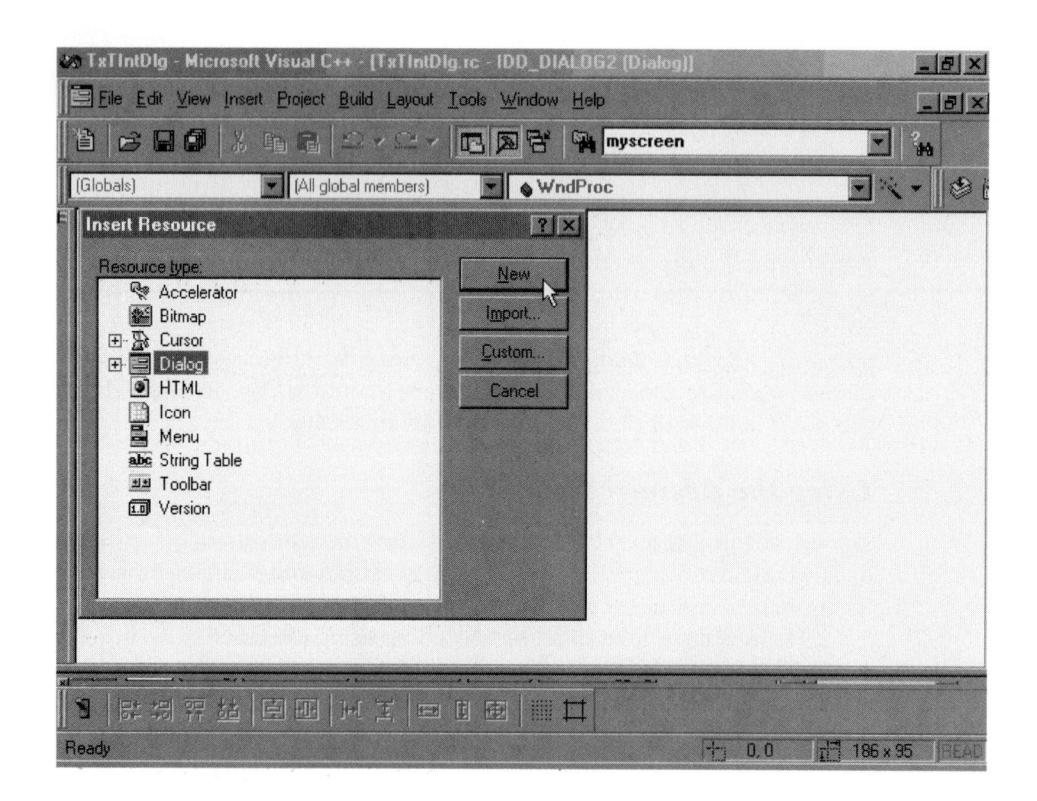

Figure 11-5 *Preparing to create a Dialog box resource in the Resource Editor.*

When the dialog box option is selected from the previous list, the Resource Editor will open with an initial outline of a new dialog box resource. This outline can be moved around the screen and sized to fit your needs. An example, of a dialog box resource under development is shown in Figure 11–6.

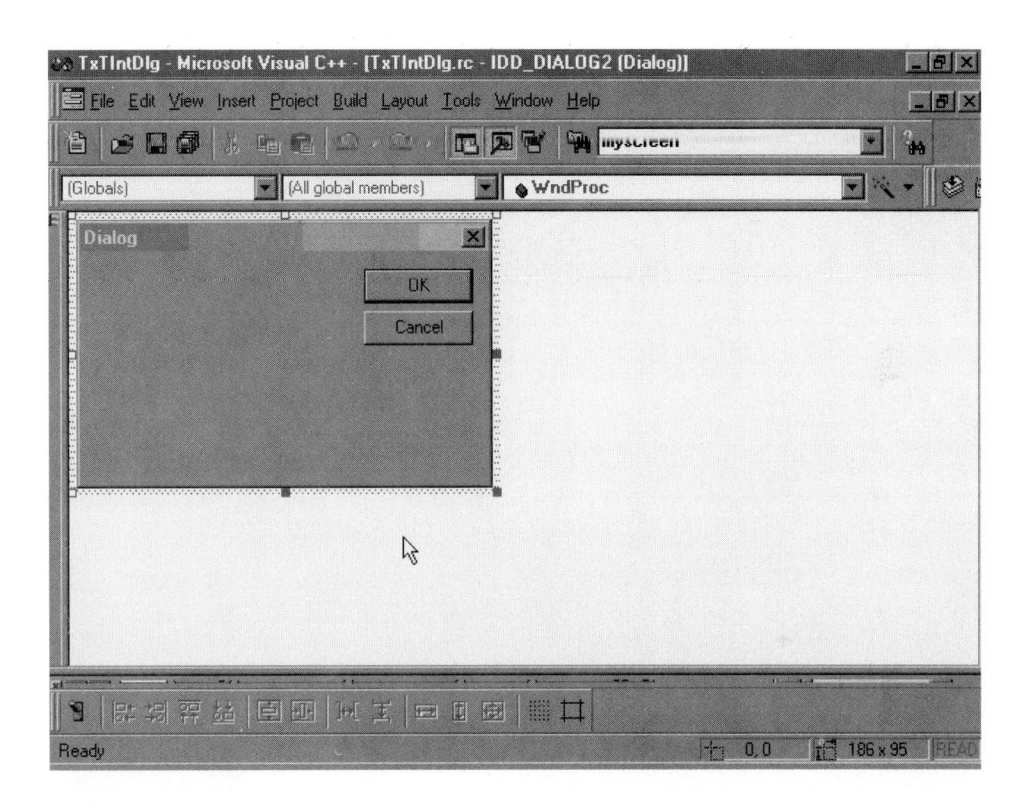

Figure 11-6 *A new dialog box being created in the Resource Editor.*

Using Controls in a Dialog Box

Controls give dialog boxes their real power. The proper placement of controls is the most important reason for using the Resource Editor. Controls are selected from the toolbox with a click of the mouse and dragged to the desired location within the dialog box prototype. When a control is positioned, a click of the mouse button will "fix" the selected control at the desired spot. If the position of the control needs to be changed, just click the mouse over the control and drag the control to the new position within the dialog box.

Chapter 11 • Adding Dialog Boxes

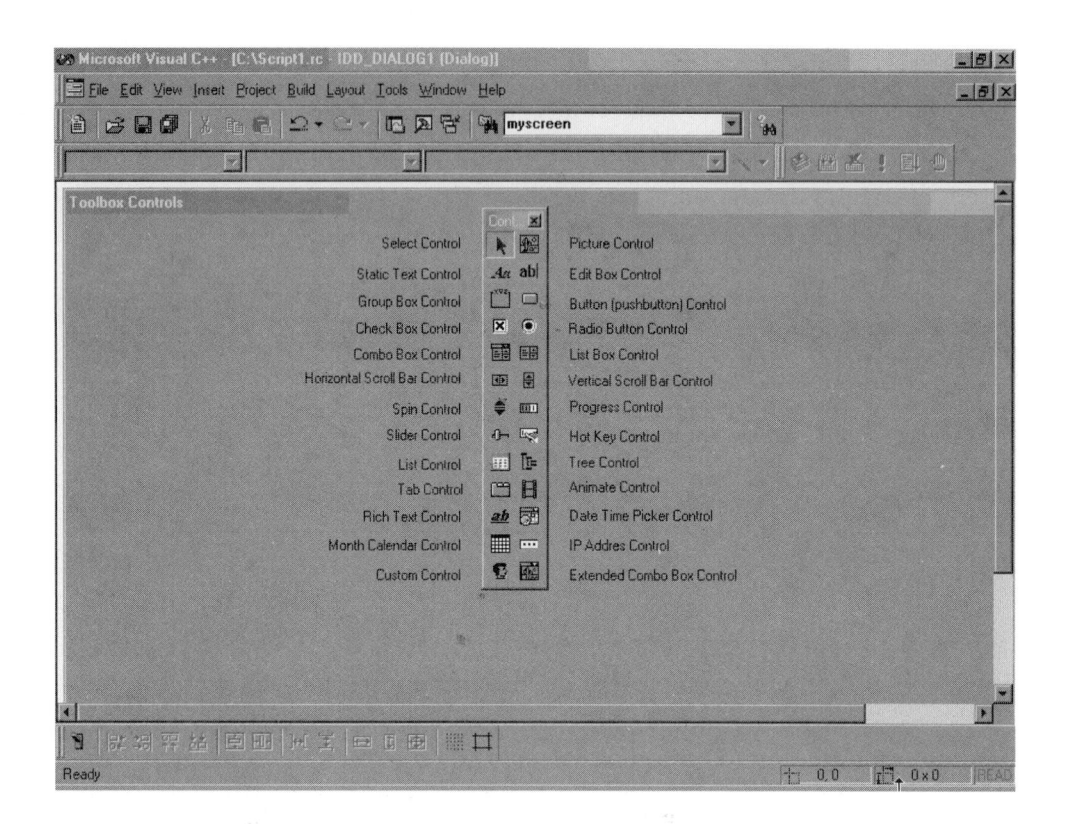

Figure 11-7 *Controls are contained in the Editor's Toolbox.*

A brief explanation of the most frequently used Toolbox controls is given in the following section. Refer to Figure 11-7 for the location of individual controls in the Toolbox.

Additional information for any Toolbox control can be found by using the on-line Help facilities provided with your Visual C++ compiler.

THE BUTTON (PUSH BUTTON) CONTROL • The button control is a small, rounded rectangle that can also be sized. The button control contains a label. Buttons are used for making an immediate choice, such as accepting or canceling the dialog box selections made by the user. The dialog boxes in this chapter usually contain one or two buttons: Okay and/or Cancel.

THE CHECK BOX CONTROL • The check box control draws a small square box (a check box) with a label to its right. Check boxes are marked, or checked, by clicking the left mouse button while positioned over the check box. Check boxes can also be selected by using the keyboard. Check boxes usually appear in groups and allow the user to check one or more features at the same time.

THE COMBO BOX CONTROL • The combo box control is made up of two elements. It is a combination of a single-line edit field (a static text control) and a list box. The combo box gives the user the ability to enter text into the edit box or to scroll through the list box, looking for an appropriate selection. Windows provides several styles of combo boxes.

THE CUSTOM CONTROL • The custom control option allows the creation of customized controls. Many such controls can be created and saved in a catalog recognized by the Resource Editor. Custom controls are made up of dynamic link libraries that also contain the window procedure for the control. The catalog is contained in the win.ini file.

THE DATE TIME PICKER CONTROL • The date time picker control is a control that can provide the current date or time to the user. This is useful when an application prompts the user for such information, as in the case of a product registration questionnaire.

THE EDIT BOX CONTROL • The edit box control draws a small interactive rectangle on the screen. The user can enter string information, within the rectangle from the keyboard. The edit box control can be sized to accept short or long strings. The string information can be processed directly (as character or numeric integer data) and indirectly (as real number data). The edit box is the most important control for data entry. Several applications in this chapter use edit box controls.

THE GROUP BOX CONTROL • The group box control draws a rectangular outline within a dialog box. The outline encloses a group of controls that are to be used together. These controls often share a common feature. For example, a group box might contain check boxes and radio buttons for setting foreground and background colors, and so on. The group box has a user-defined label on its upper left edge.

THE LIST CONTROL • The list control allows the user to make a selection from a list of presented options.

THE LIST BOX CONTROL • The List Box control draws a rectangular outline with a vertical scroll bar. List boxes are useful when scrolling is needed for long lists.

THE MONTH CALENDAR CONTROL • This month calendar control draws the current month's calendar to the screen when selected. The control provides a variety of properties that allows dates to be selected and changed and so on. This control is very easy to implement and provides outstanding visual effects.

THE PROGRESS CONTROL • The progress control is used to show the progress of an operation, such as a file transfer.

THE RADIO BUTTON CONTROL • The radio button control draws a small circle (a radio button) with a label to its right. Radio button controls, like check box controls, typically appear in groups. However, unlike check box controls, only one radio button control at a time can be selected in any given group. Radio button controls can be selected with the mouse or keyboard.

THE SCROLL BAR CONTROLS • The horizontal and vertical scroll bar controls draw the horizontal or vertical scroll bars for the dialog box. These are usually used in conjunction with another window or control that contains text or graphics information. Scroll bar controls can be placed anywhere within the dialog box and are not restricted to the bottom or right edges of the dialog box.

THE SLIDER CONTROL • The slider control behaves like a sliding volume control on a stereo. They can be moved from left to right or designed to move from top to bottom.

THE SPIN CONTROL • The spin control provides two arrows (up and down). By clicking on either arrow, the user can move up or down in a selection. Spin controls behave like the up and down arrows in a scroll bar control.

THE STATIC TEXT CONTROL • The static text control allows the insertion of labels and strings within the dialog box. These can be used, for example, to place labels before edit box controls.

THE TAB CONTROL • The tab control is frequently used to divide a large dialog box into related folders. The individual folders are then selected via the tab control.

Creating an About Dialog Box

An About dialog box is the simplest dialog box to design and implement. About dialog boxes are used to identify the application and the programmer, to give a copyright date if desired, and so on. They typically contain a single button control—Okay. Figure 11–8 shows a completed About box in the Resource Editor.

Using Controls in a Dialog Box 393

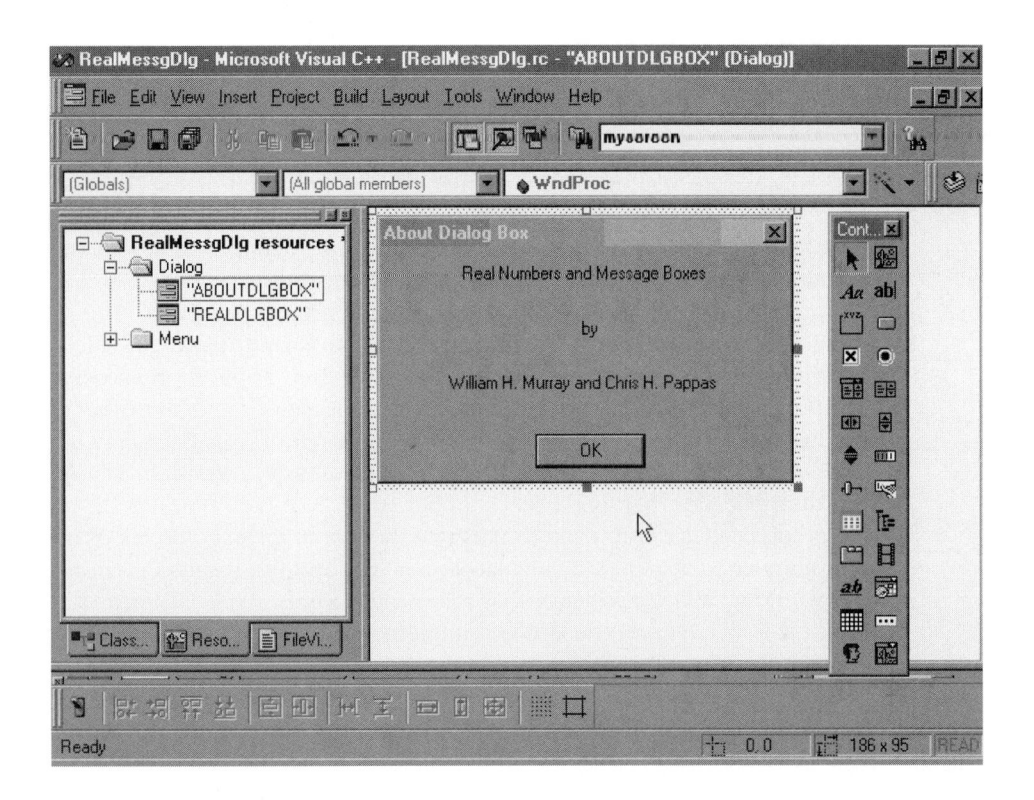

Figure 11-8 *A completed About dialog box in the Resource Editor.*

In this example, only two types of controls are used—static text control and a button control. To place a static text control, just click the static text control icon in the Toolbox and drag the icon to the dialog box being constructed. The mouse can be used to position and size the static text control in the dialog box. Pressing the mouse button after positioning the static text control will allow you to edit the text string that appears in the control. Text can be aligned left, centered, or to the right. ID values are automatically supplied for static text controls.

Using the Resource Editor efficiently is a skill learned over a period of time. Large dialog boxes with many controls will take hours to design. Again, we urge you to read the detailed information contained in the on-line Help. Start with simple dialog boxes and work toward more complicated types. Be sure to save your work at several stages during the design.

Dialog Boxes Solve a Variety of Input Needs

Four applications are illustrated in this section to show a variety of dialog box options. The applications represent a good cross-section of data entry types and will expose you to the use of many frequently used dialog box controls. For example, you will learn how to enter text, integers, and real numbers into your application. Future chapters continue to use dialog boxes, so you'll see additional examples as you progress through this book.

The first application incorporates a single About dialog box. The second application allows the user to select a graphics shape based on selecting a radio button control within the dialog box. The third application uses two dialog boxes. One dialog box gathers string information, and the other dialog box gathers four integer numbers from the user. The text is then drawn to the screen, and the four integer values are used to size a graphics shape. The fourth application permits a real number (C++ float data type) to be entered in an edit box. It is also used to illustrate the use of message boxes. When the real number is obtained, a calculation is made and the results drawn back to the window. You'll also learn that a message box is a special form of dialog box that is very easy to design and implement.

Each example in this chapter is designed to be as straightforward as possible. Each example carefully introduces only a few new concepts and builds on the material discussed in the previous example.

To build the applications in this chapter, you will need to enter the C++ source code shown in the listing. In addition, you will have to design the menu and dialog box resources in the Resource Editor. Your project file will use both the source code file (.cpp file extension) and resource script file (.rc file extension) to build the application. Remember to change the names of the menu resource and dialog box resources to match those that we use. The Resource Editor's default values were changed to meaningful names throughout this chapter.

One word of caution as you prepare to build these applications. The listings for each application are quite long. You must be very careful if you are typing the code so that it is entered correctly.

Windows is a dynamic product. From time to time, Microsoft changes the names of tools or components. If you can't find a particular tool or component mentioned in this chapter, search around for a similar tool. As always, make use of your compiler's on-line Help facilities.

An About Dialog Box Application

This About dialog box application, AboutDlg.cpp, is as simple as it can be in terms of implementing a dialog box resource. Your project file should be named *AboutDlg*. When you complete the menu and dialog box design, your

Dialog Boxes Solve a Variety of Input Needs

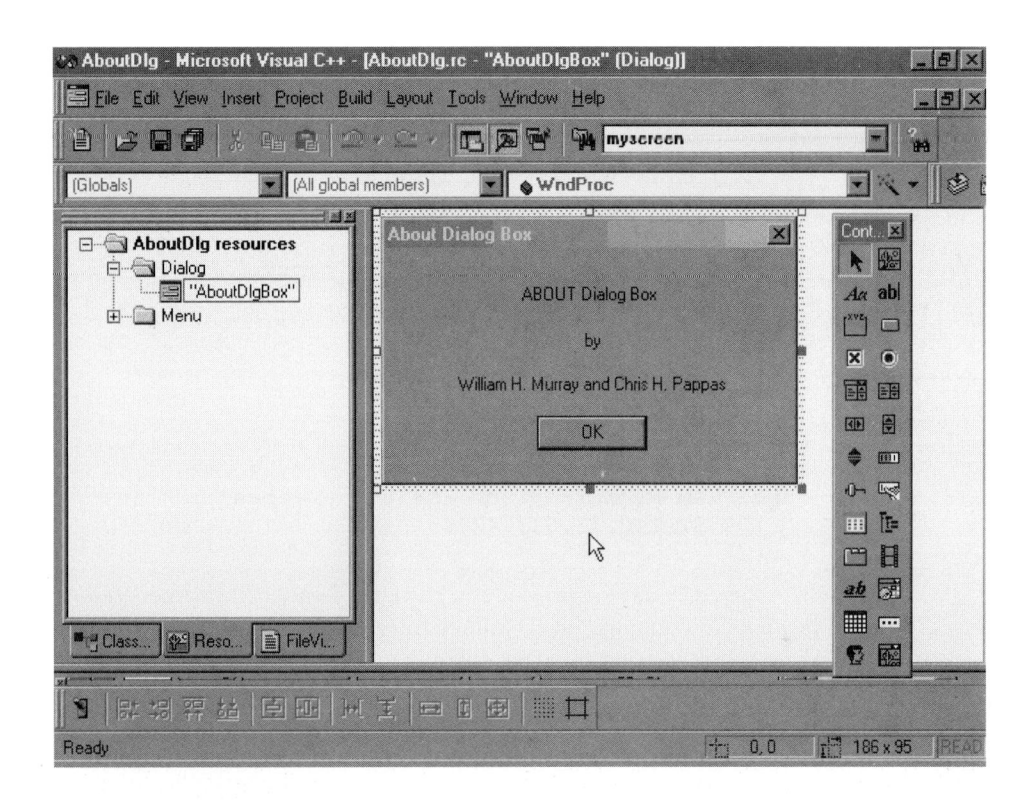

Figure 11-9 *The About Dialog Box used for the AboutDlg project.*

resource script file will contain the following code, describing both resources. Figure 11-9 shows the About dialog box in the Resource Editor.

Note that the resource script file, AboutDlg.rc, has been edited. This listing shows just the portion of the listing used to describe the menu and dialog box.

```
/////////////////////////////////////////////////////////
//
// Menu
//

ABOUTMENU MENU DISCARDABLE
BEGIN
  POPUP "&Help"
  BEGIN
    MENUITEM "&About...",        ID_HELP_ABOUT
    MENUITEM "&Exit",            ID_HELP_EXIT
  END
END
```

```
//////////////////////////////////////////////////////////
//
// Dialog
//

AboutDlgBox DIALOG DISCARDABLE  0, 0, 186, 95
STYLE DS_MODALFRAME | WS_POPUP | WS_CAPTION | WS_SYSMENU
CAPTION "About Dialog Box"
FONT 8, "MS Sans Serif"
BEGIN
    DEFPUSHBUTTON     "OK",IDOK,69,68,50,14
    CTEXT             "ABOUT Dialog Box",IDC_STATIC,
                       17,14,152,11
    CTEXT             "by",IDC_STATIC,76,33,37,12
    CTEXT             "William H. Murray and Chris H. Pappas",
                       IDC_STATIC,23,51,142,13
END
```

The Resource Editor produces a resource header file named *resource.h*. This header file contains the ID values for various controls used in the menu and dialog box resources. The following listing shows a portion of the resource.h header file.

```
//{{NO_DEPENDENCIES}}
// Microsoft Developer Studio generated include file.
// Used by AboutDlg.rc
//
#define IDR_MENU1                       101
#define ID_HELP_ABOUT                   40001
#define ID_HELP_EXIT                    40002
    .
    .
    .
```

The source code file for the AboutDlg.cpp application includes an additional procedure for handling the About dialog box. Locate the new file prototype and function as you study the following listing.

```
//
// AboutDlg.cpp
// Application demonstrates how to create and access
// a simple About dialog box.
// Copyright (c) William H. Murray and Chris H. Pappas, 1999
//

#include <windows.h>
#include "resource.h"

HINSTANCE hInst;
```

```
LRESULT CALLBACK WndProc(HWND,UINT,WPARAM,LPARAM);
BOOL CALLBACK AboutDlgProc(HWND,UINT,WPARAM,LPARAM);

char szProgName[]="ProgName";
char szApplName[]="AboutMenu";

int WINAPI WinMain(HINSTANCE hInst,HINSTANCE hPreInst,
                   LPSTR lpszCmdLine,int nCmdShow)
{
  HWND hWnd;
  MSG  lpMsg;
  WNDCLASS wcApp;

  wcApp.lpszClassName=szProgName;
  wcApp.hInstance    =hInst;
  wcApp.lpfnWndProc  =WndProc;
  wcApp.hCursor      =LoadCursor(NULL,IDC_ARROW);
  wcApp.hIcon        =0;
  wcApp.lpszMenuName =szApplName;
  wcApp.hbrBackground=(HBRUSH) GetStockObject(WHITE_BRUSH);
  wcApp.style        =CS_HREDRAW|CS_VREDRAW;
  wcApp.cbClsExtra   =0;
  wcApp.cbWndExtra   =0;
  if (!RegisterClass (&wcApp))
    return 0;

  hWnd=CreateWindow(szProgName,"About Dialog Box",
                    WS_OVERLAPPEDWINDOW,CW_USEDEFAULT,
                    CW_USEDEFAULT,CW_USEDEFAULT,
                    CW_USEDEFAULT,(HWND)NULL,(HMENU)NULL,
                    hInst,(LPSTR)NULL);
  ShowWindow(hWnd,nCmdShow);
  UpdateWindow(hWnd);
  while (GetMessage(&lpMsg,0,0,0)) {
    TranslateMessage(&lpMsg);
    DispatchMessage(&lpMsg);
  }
  return(lpMsg.wParam);
}


// Process the About dialog box control selection
BOOL CALLBACK AboutDlgProc(HWND hDlg,UINT messg,
                    WPARAM wParam,LPARAM lParam)
{
  switch (messg) {
    case WM_INITDIALOG:
    break;
    case WM_COMMAND:
      switch (LOWORD(wParam)) {
```

```
          case IDOK:
            EndDialog(hDlg,0);
            break;
          default:
            return FALSE;
        }
        break;
    default:
      return FALSE;
  }
  return TRUE;
}

LRESULT CALLBACK WndProc(HWND hWnd,UINT messg,
                         WPARAM wParam,LPARAM lParam)
{
  HDC hdc;
  PAINTSTRUCT ps;
  static HPEN hPen;

  switch (messg)
  {
    // Process the menu item selection
    case WM_COMMAND:
      switch (LOWORD(wParam)) {
        // Draw the About dialog box
        case ID_HELP_ABOUT:
          DialogBox(hInst,"AboutDlgBox",hWnd,
                (DLGPROC)AboutDlgProc);
          break;
        // Exit the application
        case ID_HELP_EXIT:
          SendMessage(hWnd,WM_CLOSE,0,0L);
          break;
        default:
          break;
      }
    break;

    case WM_PAINT:
      hdc=BeginPaint(hWnd,&ps);

      // Create a red pen, 12 pixels wide
      hPen=CreatePen(PS_SOLID,12,RGB(255,0,0));
      SelectObject(hdc,hPen);

      // Draw a little information on the screen
      MoveToEx(hdc,50,60,NULL);
      LineTo(hdc,500,400);
```

```
        TextOut(hdc,200,100,"Draw a thick red line",21);
        ValidateRect(hWnd,NULL);
        EndPaint(hWnd,&ps);
        break;

    case WM_DESTROY:
        DeleteObject(hPen);
        PostQuitMessage(0);
        break;
    default:
        return(DefWindowProc(hWnd,messg,wParam,lParam));
        break;
    }
    return(0);
}
```

Remember that the header file and the resource script file for this project are generated by the Resource Editor and should not be typed in by hand. They are provided as a reference to help you identify ID values and so on. The C++ source code listing must be entered. The source code file and the resource script file must be included in the project before you build the application.

THE APPLICATION FILE (ABOUTDLG.CPP)

Did you find the additional AboutDlgProc in the AboutDlg.cpp source code file? Here is the AboutDlgProc portion of code. This code is responsible for processing the About dialog box message.

```
// Process the About dialog box control selection
BOOL CALLBACK AboutDlgProc(HWND hDlg,UINT messg,
                           WPARAM wParam,LPARAM lParam)
{
  switch (messg) {
    case WM_INITDIALOG:
    break;
  case WM_COMMAND:
    switch (LOWORD(wParam)) {
    case IDOK:
      EndDialog(hDlg,0);
      break;
    default:
      return FALSE;
    }
    break;
    default:
      return FALSE;
  }
  return TRUE;
```

The procedure uses a handle, *hDlg*, as the handle for the dialog box window. You will also notice that the dialog procedure is of type **BOOL**, which sets it apart from regular Windows procedures. As such, the dialog box procedure returns either a TRUE or FALSE. A TRUE is returned if the dialog box processes a message and FALSE if it does not.

The first of the two messages that the procedure processes is sent to WM_INITDIALOG. If a TRUE is returned, the input will be channeled to the first control in the dialog box. This is the focus. The second message is WM_COMMAND. This message will be sent to the application program if the Okay button is selected with the mouse or Return key. In order to remove the dialog box from the application's main window, the user must select the button option. In the case where IDOK is TRUE, a call will be made to the **End-Dialog()** function, and the dialog box session ends. All other messages return FALSE. The switch and case statements used in this procedure follow normal C++ programming style.

The dialog box is called from the AboutMenu menu. This option is added during the processing of **WndProc()**. If you study this section of code, you will notice the addition of a new case statement—WM_COMMAND.

```
// Process the menu item selection
case WM_COMMAND:
  switch (LOWORD(wParam)) {
    // Draw the About dialog box
    case ID_HELP_ABOUT:
      DialogBox(hInst,"AboutDlgBo", hWnd,
            (DLGPROC)AboutDlgProc);
      break;
    // Exit the application
    case ID_HELP_EXIT:
      SendMessage(hWnd,WM_CLOSE,0,0L);
      break;
    default:
      break;
  }
break;
```

The AboutMenu menu for this application allows one of two selections: a view of the About dialog box or an exit from the program.

Both of these options are handled by WM_COMMAND. For the case of ID_HELP_ABOUT, the **DialogBox()** function establishes the predefined dialog box on the screen. This dialog box will not be erased until the **EndDialog()** function, discussed earlier, receives the message formed by selecting the IDOK button. An exit from the entire program can be achieved by selecting the ID_HELP_EXIT case and utilizing the **SendMessage()** function.

Many of the programs in this chapter draw simple graphics shapes to the screen, in addition to processing the dialog box information. Chapter 4 was devoted to explaining the various Windows graphics primitives and func-

Dialog Boxes Solve a Variety of Input Needs   401

tions completely. For this particular program, a thick red diagonal line is drawn to the screen when a WM_PAINT message is processed. This requires creating a drawing pen of the specified color, moving the pen to a particular spot on the screen, and using the **LineTo()** function to actually draw the line. The **TextOut()** function is used to print a text label to the screen.

Figure 11–10 shows the application with the About Dialog Box visible.

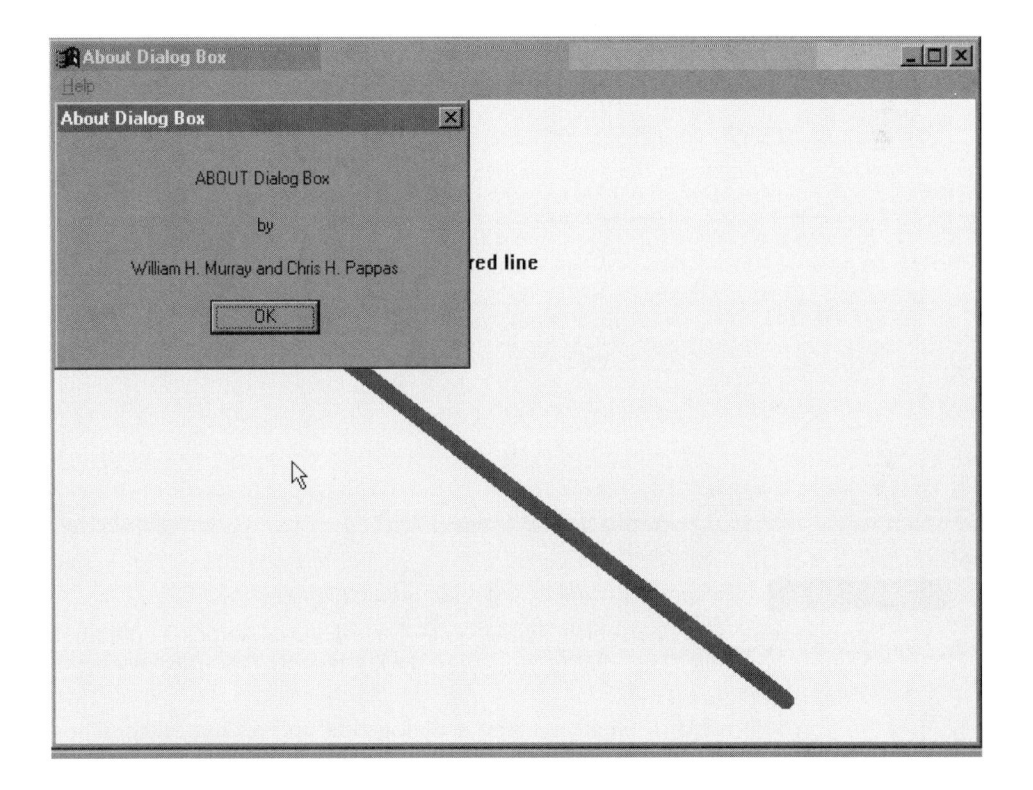

Figure 11-10 *The About Dialog Box is opened during program execution.*

About Dialog Boxes are simple by their very design. In the next section, we'll add some radio buttons to make the dialog box more interactive.

Using Radio Buttons in a Dialog Box

In this application, we'll use radio button controls within a dialog box to allow user interaction. Specifically, the user will be permitted to select a predefined graphics shape from a dialog box. The selected shape will be drawn to the screen when the dialog box information is processed. This application uses two dialog boxes: an About dialog box and a data entry dialog box. The About dialog box description is similar to the dialog box from the previous

Chapter 11 • Adding Dialog Boxes

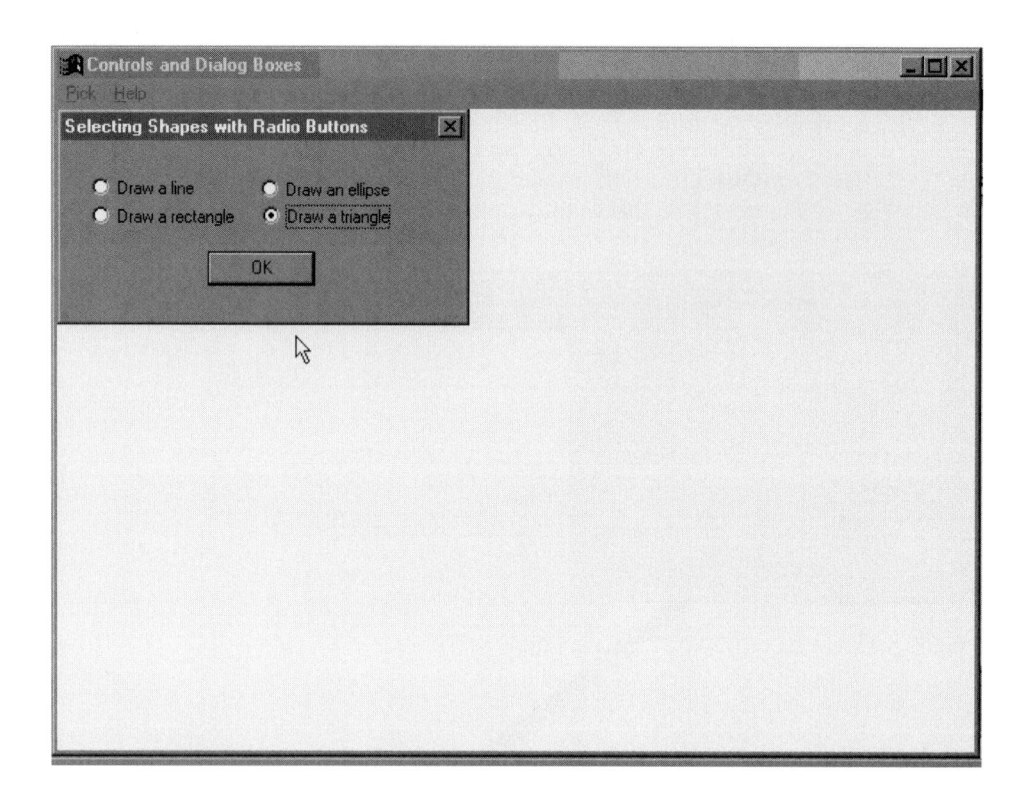

Figure 11-11 *The data entry dialog box with radio button controls.*

application. The data entry dialog box—for selecting shapes—contains radio button controls. The dialog box with radio buttons for this application is shown in Figure 11-11.

You'll need to create an About dialog box and a data entry dialog box similar to the one shown in Figure 11-11.

Here is the resource.h header file that contains ID information for the application's menu and two dialog boxes. It has been edited to show just the relative information.

```
//{{NO_DEPENDENCIES}}
// Microsoft Developer Studio generated include file.
// Used by ShapeDlg.rc
//
#define IDC_RADIO1                      1001
#define IDC_RADIO2                      1002
#define IDC_RADIO3                      1003
#define IDC_RADIO4                      1004
#define ID_PICK_SHAPE                   40001
#define ID_PICK_EXIT                    40002
```

```
#define ID_HELP_ABOUT                    40003
```

The resource script file, named *ShapeDlg.rc*, contains the menu description and the descriptions of both dialog boxes returned by the Resource Editor. Again, the listing has been edited to show just this information.

```
//////////////////////////////////////////////////////
//
// Menu
//

ShapeMenu MENU DISCARDABLE
BEGIN
  POPUP "&Pick"
  BEGIN
    MENUITEM "&Select a shape..."  ID_PICK_SHAPE
    MENUITEM "&Exit",              ID_PICK_EXIT
  END
  POPUP "&Help"
  BEGIN
    MENUITEM "About...",           ID_HELP_ABOUT
  END
END
     .
     .
     .

//////////////////////////////////////////////////////
//
// Dialog
//

AboutDlgBox DIALOG DISCARDABLE  0, 0, 186, 98
STYLE DS_MODALFRAME | DS_3DLOOK | WS_POPUP |
    WS_CAPTION | WS_SYSMENU
CAPTION "About Dialog Box"
FONT 8, "MS Sans Serif"
BEGIN
    DEFPUSHBUTTON   "OK",IDOK,69,69,50,14
    CTEXT "Using Radio Controls in a Dialog Box",
          IDC_STATIC,17,14,152,11
    CTEXT "William H. Murray and Chris H. Pappas",
          IDC_STATIC,17,47,153,15
    CTEXT "by",IDC_STATIC,85,30,16,12
END

ShapeDlgBox DIALOG DISCARDABLE  0, 0, 186, 73
STYLE DS_MODALFRAME | WS_POPUP | WS_CAPTION | WS_SYSMENU
CAPTION "Selecting Shapes with Radio Buttons"
FONT 8, "MS Sans Serif"
BEGIN
```

```
        DEFPUSHBUTTON    "OK",IDOK,67,45,50,14
        CONTROL "Draw a line",IDC_RADIO1,"Button",
                BS_AUTORADIOBUTTON |
                WS_GROUP,13,14,71,10
        CONTROL "Draw a rectangle",IDC_RADIO2,"Button",
                BS_AUTORADIOBUTTON,13,26,70,10
        CONTROL "Draw an ellipse",IDC_RADIO3,"Button",
                BS_AUTORADIOBUTTON,91,15,64,10
        CONTROL "Draw a triangle",IDC_RADIO4,"Button",
                BS_AUTORADIOBUTTON,92,26,63,10
END
```

In the ShapeDlg.cpp source file, shown in the following listing, see if you can find the function prototypes for each dialog box procedure. Once you have located the AboutDlgProc and ShapeDlgProc prototypes, locate the procedures themselves.

```
//
// ShapeDlg.cpp
// Application demonstrates how to use a dialog box
// with radio button controls to make selections.
// Copyright (c) William H. Murray and Chris H. Pappas, 1999
//

#include <windows.h>
#include "resource.h"

HINSTANCE hInst;

LRESULT CALLBACK WndProc(HWND,UINT,WPARAM,LPARAM);
BOOL CALLBACK AboutDlgProc(HWND,UINT,WPARAM,LPARAM);
BOOL CALLBACK ShapeDlgProc(HWND,UINT,WPARAM,LPARAM);

char szProgName[]="ProgName";
char szApplName[]="ShapeMenu";
int myshape;

int WINAPI WinMain(HINSTANCE hInst,HINSTANCE hPreInst,
                   LPSTR lpszCmdLine,int nCmdShow)
{
  HWND hWnd;
  MSG  lpMsg;
  WNDCLASS wcApp;

  wcApp.lpszClassName=szProgName;
  wcApp.hInstance     =hInst;
  wcApp.lpfnWndProc   =WndProc;
  wcApp.hCursor       =LoadCursor(NULL,IDC_ARROW);
  wcApp.hIcon         =0;
  wcApp.lpszMenuName  =szApplName;
  wcApp.hbrBackground=(HBRUSH) GetStockObject(WHITE_BRUSH);
```

```
  wcApp.style            =CS_HREDRAW|CS_VREDRAW;
  wcApp.cbClsExtra       =0;
  wcApp.cbWndExtra       =0;
  if (!RegisterClass (&wcApp))
    return 0;

  hWnd=CreateWindow(szProgName,"Controls and Dialog Boxes",
                    WS_OVERLAPPEDWINDOW,CW_USEDEFAULT,
                    CW_USEDEFAULT,CW_USEDEFAULT,
                    CW_USEDEFAULT,(HWND)NULL,(HMENU)NULL,
                    hInst,(LPSTR)NULL);
  ShowWindow(hWnd,nCmdShow);
  UpdateWindow(hWnd);
  while (GetMessage(&lpMsg,0,0,0)) {
    TranslateMessage(&lpMsg);
    DispatchMessage(&lpMsg);
  }
  return(lpMsg.wParam);
}

// Process the Shape dialog box control selection
BOOL CALLBACK ShapeDlgProc(HWND hDlg,UINT messg,
                           WPARAM wParam,LPARAM lParam)
{
  switch (messg) {
    case WM_INITDIALOG:
      break;
    case WM_COMMAND:
      switch (LOWORD(wParam)) {
        case IDOK:
          EndDialog(hDlg,0);
          break;
        case IDC_RADIO1:
          myshape=1;
          CheckRadioButton(hDlg,IDC_RADIO1,
                    IDC_RADIO4,wParam);
          break;
        case IDC_RADIO2:
          myshape=2;
          CheckRadioButton(hDlg,IDC_RADIO1,
                    IDC_RADIO4,wParam);
          break;
        case IDC_RADIO3:
          myshape=3;
          CheckRadioButton(hDlg,IDC_RADIO1,
                    IDC_RADIO4,wParam);
          break;
        case IDC_RADIO4:
          myshape=4;
          CheckRadioButton(hDlg,IDC_RADIO1,
```

Chapter 11 • Adding Dialog Boxes

```
                           IDC_RADIO4,wParam);
            break;
          default:
             return FALSE;
        }
        break;
      default:
        return FALSE;
    }
  return TRUE;
}

// Process the About dialog box control selection
BOOL CALLBACK AboutDlgProc(HWND hDlg,UINT messg,
                           WPARAM wParam,LPARAM lParam)
{
  switch (messg) {
     case WM_INITDIALOG:
        break;
     case WM_COMMAND:
        switch (LOWORD(wParam)) {
           case IDOK:
             EndDialog(hDlg,0);
              break;
           default:
              return FALSE;
        }
        break;
      default:
        return FALSE;
    }
  return TRUE;
}

LRESULT CALLBACK WndProc(HWND hWnd,UINT messg,
                         WPARAM wParam,LPARAM lParam)
{
  HDC hdc;
  PAINTSTRUCT ps;
  static HPEN hPen;
     switch (messg)
    {
    // Process the menu item selection
    case WM_COMMAND:
       switch (LOWORD(wParam)) {
          // Draw the Shape dialog box
          case ID_PICK_SHAPE:
            DialogBox(hInst,"ShapeDlgBox",hWnd,
                   (DLGPROC)ShapeDlgProc);
             InvalidateRect(hWnd,NULL,TRUE);
```

```
            UpdateWindow(hWnd);
          break;
        // End the application
        case ID_PICK_EXIT:
          SendMessage(hWnd,WM_CLOSE,0,0L);
          break;
        // Draw the About dialog box
        case ID_HELP_ABOUT:
          DialogBox(hInst,"AboutDlgBox",hWnd,
                 (DLGPROC)AboutDlgProc);
        break;
      default:
        break;
          }
    break;

  case WM_PAINT:
    hdc=BeginPaint(hWnd,&ps);

    // Create a blue pen, 8 pixels wide
    hPen=CreatePen(PS_SOLID,8,RGB(0,0,255));
    SelectObject(hdc,hPen);

    // Draw the appropriate shape
    if (myshape==1) {
      MoveToEx(hdc,50,60,NULL);
      LineTo(hdc,100,300);
    }
    else
      if (myshape==2) {
        Rectangle(hdc,20,30,200,300);
      }
      else
        if (myshape==3) {
          Ellipse(hdc,10,30,300,200);
        }
        else
          if (myshape==4) {
            MoveToEx(hdc,200,120,NULL);
            LineTo(hdc,320,300);
            LineTo(hdc,200,300);
            LineTo(hdc,200,120);
          }
    ValidateRect(hWnd,NULL);
    EndPaint(hWnd,&ps);
    break;
  case WM_DESTROY:
    DeleteObject(hPen);
    PostQuitMessage(0);
    break;
```

```
      default:
        return(DefWindowProc(hWnd,messg,wParam,lParam));
        break;
    }
    return(0);
}
```

Have you noticed how long these listing are getting? If you are entering the applications from the keyboard, take your time and enter the code carefully.

To build this application, create a project named *ShapeDlg*. You will then need to design the menu and dialog boxes to obtain the resource.h and ShapeDlg.rc files. Make sure you name the menu and dialog resources using the names we selected instead of the default names provided by the Resource Editor. Next, enter the ShapeDlg.cpp source code. When you are ready to build the applications, include the ShapeDlg.cpp and ShapeDlg.rc in the build list of files.

The Application File (ShapeDlg.cpp)

When you study the ShapeDlg.cpp listing, notice that AboutDlgProc is processed in exactly the same way as it was in the previous example. Once you have designed a good About box, you may want to copy it from application to application.

The ShapeDlgProc is used to process information from the shape dialog box. Examine the following portion of code.

```
// Process the Shape dialog box control selection
BOOL CALLBACK ShapeDlgProc(HWND hDlg,UINT messg,
                           WPARAM wParam,LPARAM lParam)
{
  switch (messg) {
    case WM_INITDIALOG:
      break;
    case WM_COMMAND:
      switch (LOWORD(wParam)) {
        case IDOK:
          EndDialog(hDlg,0);
          break;
        case IDC_RADIO1:
          myshape=1;
          CheckRadioButton(hDlg,IDC_RADIO1,
                           IDC_RADIO4,wParam);
          break;
        case IDC_RADIO2:
          myshape=2;
          CheckRadioButton(hDlg,IDC_RADIO1,
                           IDC_RADIO4,wParam);
          break;
```

```
        case IDC_RADIO3:
          myshape=3;
          CheckRadioButton(hDlg,IDC_RADIO1,
                      IDC_RADIO4,wParam);
          break;
        case IDC_RADIO4:
          myshape=4;
          CheckRadioButton(hDlg,IDC_RADIO1,
                      IDC_RADIO4,wParam);
          break;
        default:
          return FALSE;
      }
      break;
    default:
      return FALSE;
  }
  return TRUE;
}
```

The WM_COMMAND message handler is responsible for processing five case statements. IDOK represents the dialog box button for accepting input and removing the dialog box. The other four case statements represent the radio buttons corresponding to the specified shapes. Each case statement is then examined. If a case is TRUE, the global variable, *myshape,* is set to a pre-defined integer value. The integer value will be used in WM_PAINT by **WndProc()** to determine which shape is actually drawn in the window. The **CheckRadioButton()** function is used to "check" the button circle on the dialog box (i.e., darken the radio button). This function is also responsible for sending the *wParam* part of the message to WM_COMMAND. The range of radio button IDs must be sequential when using **CheckRadioButton()**. The first ID is IDC_RADIO1, and the last is IDC_RADIO4, as you can observe from the resource.h header file.

The ShapeDlgProc does not provide a Cancel button. Once the user opens the dialog box, they must make a selection in order to close the dialog box with the Okay button. Typically, dialog boxes include the Cancel button to return the user to the application window without making changes. You'll see the use of a Cancel button with the remaining applications in this chapter.

Shapes are drawn when WM_PAINT messages are received. To select and draw the correct figure when a WM_PAINT message is received, an **if-else** ladder is used.

```
// Draw the appropriate shape
if (myshape==1) {
  MoveToEx(hdc,50,60,NULL);
  LineTo(hdc,100,300);
}
else
```

Chapter 11 • Adding Dialog Boxes

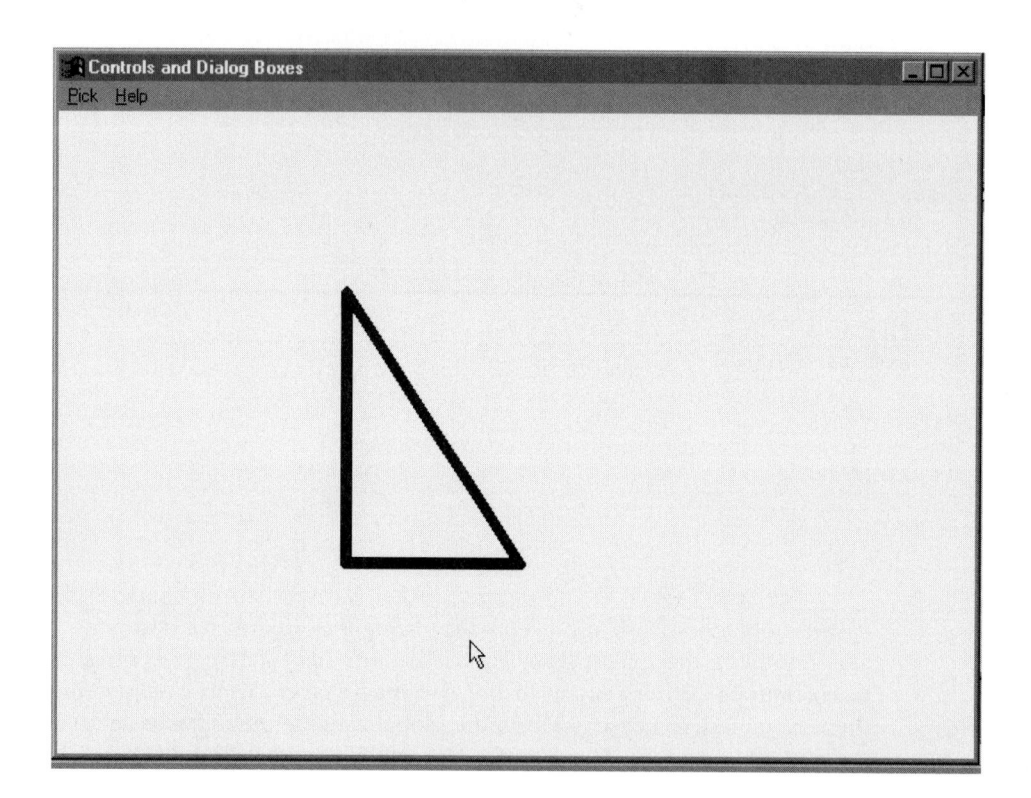

Figure 11-12 *A triangle is selected from the dialog box and drawn to the screen.*

```
if (myshape==2) {
  Rectangle(hdc,20,30,200,300);
}
else
  if (myshape==3) {
    Ellipse(hdc,10,30,300,200);
  }
  else
    if (myshape==4) {
      MoveToEx(hdc,200,120,NULL);
      LineTo(hdc,320,300);
      LineTo(hdc,200,300);
      LineTo(hdc,200,120);
    }
```

The variable *myshape* is global and is checked to determine which shape is drawn. Figure 11–12 shows one figure, a triangle, that can be drawn with this application.

Dialog Boxes Solve a Variety of Input Needs   **411**

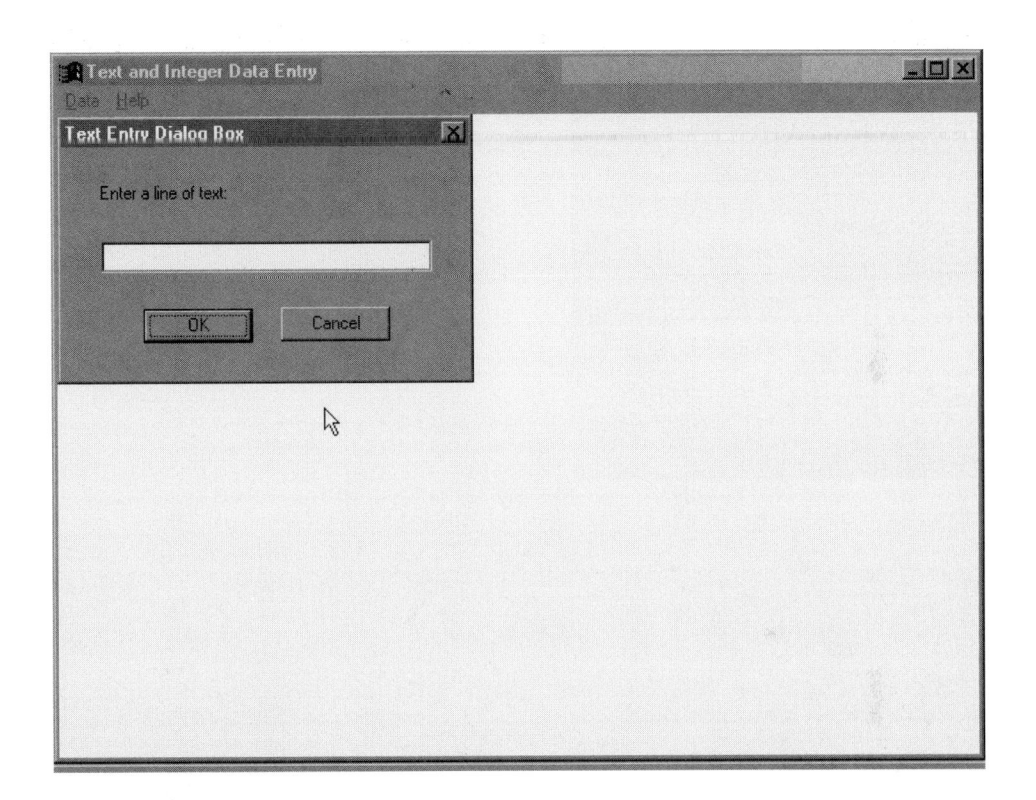

Figure 11-13   *A dialog box that allows a user to enter text into an application.*

The various shapes are drawn with several different graphics functions: **MoveToEx()**, **LineTo()**, **Rectangle()**, and **Ellipse()**. Details on these and other graphics functions are contained in Chapter 4.

Entering Text and Integers in a Dialog Box

Using radio button controls gives the user a limited interaction, but giving the user the ability to enter text and numbers gives them real power! Text and integer information is entered through the dialog box's edit box control. Text information is processed with the **GetDlgItemText()** function while integer information uses a call to the **GetDlgItemInt()** function.

This project, named *TxtIntDlg*, uses three dialog boxes. One dialog box is a standard About dialog box. The second dialog box is for text, and the third for entering integer data. The text entry dialog box is shown in Figure 11-13.

412 Chapter 11 • Adding Dialog Boxes

Figure 11-14 *A dialog box that allows the user to enter integer numbers into an application.*

This dialog box contains two buttons. Okay will accept the new text and print it to the screen. The Cancel button will cancel the dialog box without changing the current message on the screen.

The integer entry dialog box is shown in Figure 11-14.

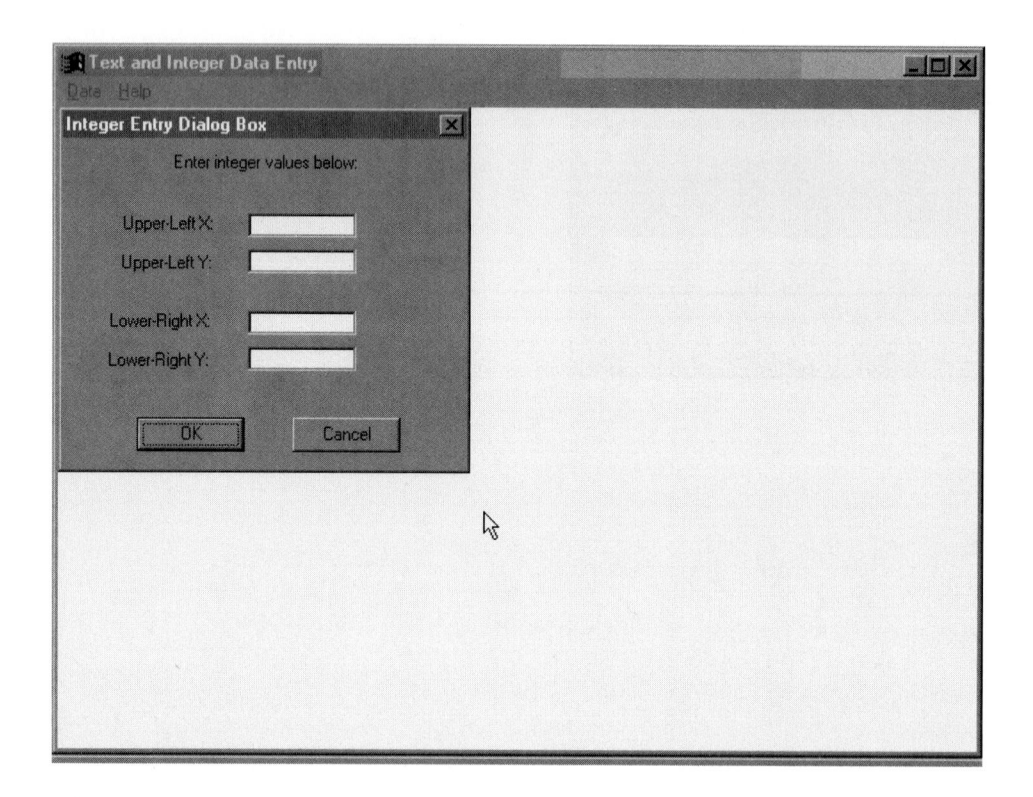

In this dialog box, the coordinates for diagonally adjacent corners of a defining rectangle will be entered by the user in four separate edit box controls. The information, if it is in the form of numeric digits, will be converted to integer values and used by the **Rectangle()** function when a WM_PAINT message is processed.

Here is the resource.h header file for the TxtIntDlg project. Remember that the header file contains the ID information for the menu, the About dialog box, and the two data entry dialog boxes. This information is generated after the menu and dialog boxes are designed in the Resource Editor. This listing has been abbreviated to show just these components.

```
// Microsoft Developer Studio generated include file.
// Used by TxtIntDlg.rc
//
```

```
#define IDD_DIALOG1              101
#define IDC_UPPERX               1000
#define IDC_UPPERY               1001
#define IDC_LOWERX               1002
#define IDC_LOWERY               1003
#define IDC_TEXT                 1004
#define ID_DATA_TEXT             40001
#define ID_DATA_INT              40002
#define ID_HELP_ABOUT            40003
#define ID_HELP_EXIT             40004
```

The TxtIntDlg.rc file is generated by the Resource Editor after you have graphically designed the menu and three dialog boxes. Here is an abbreviated listing of that file.

```
//////////////////////////////////////////////////////////
//
// Dialog
//

AboutDlgBox DIALOG DISCARDABLE  0, 0, 186, 90
STYLE DS_MODALFRAME | WS_POPUP | WS_CAPTION | WS_SYSMENU
CAPTION "About Dialog Box"
FONT 8, "MS Sans Serif"
BEGIN
   DEFPUSHBUTTON   "OK",IDOK,71,68,50,14
   CTEXT  "Text and Integer Data Entry Dialog Box",
          IDC_STATIC,15,10,151,10
   CTEXT  "by",IDC_STATIC,80,25,30,10
   CTEXT  "William H. Murray and Chris H. Pappas",
          IDC_STATIC,12,43,160,10
END

TextDlgBox DIALOG DISCARDABLE  0, 0, 186, 95
STYLE DS_MODALFRAME | WS_POPUP | WS_CAPTION | WS_SYSMENU
CAPTION "Text Entry Dialog Box"
FONT 8, "MS Sans Serif"
BEGIN
   DEFPUSHBUTTON   "OK",IDOK,37,66,50,14
   PUSHBUTTON      "Cancel",IDCANCEL,100,65,50,14
   LTEXT           "Enter a line of text:",
                   IDC_STATIC,17,14,150,13
   EDITTEXT        IDC_TEXT,18,38,151,13,ES_AUTOHSCROLL
END

IntDlgBox DIALOG DISCARDABLE  0, 0, 186, 135
STYLE DS_MODALFRAME | WS_POPUP | WS_CAPTION | WS_SYSMENU
CAPTION "Integer Entry Dialog Box"
FONT 8, "MS Sans Serif"
BEGIN
   DEFPUSHBUTTON   "OK",IDOK,34,114,50,14
```

```
    PUSHBUTTON         "Cancel",IDCANCEL,106,114,50,14
    CTEXT              "Enter integer values below:",
                       IDC_STATIC,15,5,156,12
    RTEXT              "Upper-Left X:",IDC_STATIC,25,30,44,11
    RTEXT              "Upper-Left Y:",IDC_STATIC,23,46,45,15
    RTEXT              "Lower-Right X:",IDC_STATIC,20,70,48,12
    RTEXT              "Lower-Right Y:",IDC_STATIC,17,86,50,10
    EDITTEXT           IDC_UPPERX,85,30,50,10,ES_AUTOHSCROLL
    EDITTEXT           IDC_UPPERY,85,45,50,10,ES_AUTOHSCROLL
    EDITTEXT           IDC_LOWERX,85,70,50,10,ES_AUTOHSCROLL
    EDITTEXT           IDC_LOWERY,85,85,50,10,ES_AUTOHSCROLL
END

////////////////////////////////////////////////////////////
//
// Menu
//

DataMenu MENU DISCARDABLE
BEGIN
  POPUP "&Data"
  BEGIN
    MENUITEM "&Text...",            ID_DATA_TEXT
    MENUITEM "&Integer...",         ID_DATA_INT
  END
  POPUP "&Help"
  BEGIN
    MENUITEM "&About...",           ID_HELP_ABOUT
    MENUITEM "&Exit",               ID_HELP_EXIT
  END
END
```

By this time, we're sure that several menu keywords are beginning to look familiar to you.

The source code for TxtIntDlg.cpp application immediately identifies the functions used in this application with the function prototype list. Each of the previously described dialog boxes uses a separate function prototype: AboutDlgProc, TextDlgProc, and IntDlgProc. Can you locate them in the source code listing?

```
//
// TxTIntDlg.cpp
// Application demonstrates how to use a dialog box
// to enter text and integer numbers.
// Copyright (c) William H. Murray and Chris H. Pappas, 1999
//

#include <windows.h>
#include "resource.h"
```

```
HINSTANCE hInst;

LRESULT CALLBACK WndProc(HWND,UINT,WPARAM,LPARAM);
BOOL CALLDACK AboutDlgProc(HWND,UINT,WPARAM,LPARAM);
BOOL CALLBACK TextDlgProc(HWND,UINT,WPARAM,LPARAM);
BOOL CALLBACK IntDlgProc(HWND,UINT,WPARAM,LPARAM);

char szProgName[]="ProgName";
char szApplName[]="DataMenu";
char screentext[80]="An initial line of text.";
int iupperx,iuppery,ilowerx,ilowery;

int WINAPI WinMain(HINSTANCE hInst,HINSTANCE hPreInst,
                   LPSTR lpszCmdLine,int nCmdShow)
{
  HWND hWnd;
  MSG   lpMsg;
  WNDCLASS wcApp;

  wcApp.lpszClassName=szProgName;
  wcApp.hInstance    =hInst;
  wcApp.lpfnWndProc  =WndProc;
  wcApp.hCursor      =LoadCursor(NULL,IDC_ARROW);
  wcApp.hIcon        =0;
  wcApp.lpszMenuName =szApplName;
  wcApp.hbrBackground=(HBRUSH) GetStockObject(WHITE_BRUSH);
  wcApp.style        =CS_HREDRAW|CS_VREDRAW;
  wcApp.cbClsExtra   =0;
  wcApp.cbWndExtra   =0;
  if (!RegisterClass (&wcApp))
    return 0;

  hWnd=CreateWindow(szProgName,"Text and Integer Data Entry",
                    WS_OVERLAPPEDWINDOW,CW_USEDEFAULT,
                    CW_USEDEFAULT,CW_USEDEFAULT,
                    CW_USEDEFAULT,(HWND)NULL,(HMENU)NULL,
                    hInst,(LPSTR)NULL);
  ShowWindow(hWnd,nCmdShow);
  UpdateWindow(hWnd);
  while (GetMessage(&lpMsg,0,0,0)) {
    TranslateMessage(&lpMsg);
    DispatchMessage(&lpMsg);
  }
  return(lpMsg.wParam);
}

// Process the Text dialog box control selection
BOOL CALLBACK TextDlgProc(HWND hDlg,UINT messg,
                          WPARAM wParam,LPARAM lParam)
{
```

Chapter 11 • Adding Dialog Boxes

```c
  switch (messg) {
    case WM_INITDIALOG:
      break;
    case WM_COMMAND:
      switch (LOWORD(wParam)) {
        case IDOK:
          GetDlgItemText(hDlg,IDC_TEXT,screentext,80);
          EndDialog(hDlg,TRUE);
          break;
        case IDCANCEL:
          EndDialog(hDlg,FALSE);
          break;
        default:
          return FALSE;
      }
      break;
    default:
      return FALSE;
  }
  return TRUE;
}

// Process the Integer dialog box control selection
BOOL CALLBACK IntDlgProc(HWND hDlg,UINT messg,
                         WPARAM wParam,LPARAM lParam)
{
  switch (messg) {
    case WM_INITDIALOG:
      break;
    case WM_COMMAND:
      switch (LOWORD(wParam)) {
        case IDOK:
          iupperx=GetDlgItemInt(hDlg,IDC_UPPERX,NULL,0);
          iuppery=GetDlgItemInt(hDlg,IDC_UPPERY,NULL,0);
          ilowerx=GetDlgItemInt(hDlg,IDC_LOWERX,NULL,0);
          ilowery=GetDlgItemInt(hDlg,IDC_LOWERY,NULL,0);
          EndDialog(hDlg,TRUE);
          break;
        case IDCANCEL:
          EndDialog(hDlg,FALSE);
          break;
        default:
          return FALSE;
      }
      break;
    default:
      return FALSE;
  }
  return TRUE;
}
```

```c
// Process the About dialog box control selection
BOOL CALLBACK AboutDlgProc(HWND hDlg,UINT messg,
                           WPARAM wParam,LPARAM lParam)
{
  switch (messg) {
    case WM_INITDIALOG:
      break;
    case WM_COMMAND:
      switch (LOWORD(wParam)) {
        case IDOK:
          EndDialog(hDlg,0);
          break;
        default:
          return FALSE;
      }
      break;
    default:
      return FALSE;
  }
  return TRUE;
}

LRESULT CALLBACK WndProc(HWND hWnd,UINT messg,
                         WPARAM wParam,LPARAM lParam)
{
  HDC hdc;
  PAINTSTRUCT ps;
  static HPEN hPen;
  static int xClientView,yClientView;

  switch (messg)
  {
    // Process the menu item selection
    case WM_COMMAND:
      switch (LOWORD(wParam)) {
        // Draw the Text dialog box
        case ID_DATA_TEXT:
          DialogBox(hInst,"TextDlgBox",hWnd,
                    (DLGPROC)TextDlgProc);
          InvalidateRect(hWnd,NULL,TRUE);
          UpdateWindow(hWnd);
          break;
        // Draw the Integer dialog box
        case ID_DATA_INT:
          DialogBox(hInst,"IntDlgBox",hWnd,
                    (DLGPROC)IntDlgProc);
          InvalidateRect(hWnd,NULL,TRUE);
          UpdateWindow(hWnd);
          break;
        // Draw the About dialog box
```

Chapter 11 • Adding Dialog Boxes

```
      case ID_HELP_ABOUT:
        DialogBox(hInst,"AboutDlgBox",hWnd,
                  (DLGPROC)AboutDlgProc);
        break;
      // End the application
      case ID_HELP_EXIT:
        SendMessage(hWnd,WM_CLOSE,0,0L);
        break;
      default:
        break;
    }
    break;

  case WM_PAINT:
    hdc=BeginPaint(hWnd,&ps);

    // Create a green pen, 10 pixels wide
    hPen=CreatePen(PS_SOLID,10,RGB(0,255,0));
    SelectObject(hdc,hPen);

    Rectangle(hdc,iupperx,iuppery,ilowerx,ilowery);
    TextOut(hdc,100,100,screentext,strlen(screentext));

    ValidateRect(hWnd,NULL);
    EndPaint(hWnd,&ps);
    break;

  case WM_DESTROY:
    DeleteObject(hPen);
    PostQuitMessage(0);
    break;
  default:
    return(DefWindowProc(hWnd,messg,wParam,lParam));
    break;
  }
  return(0);
}
```

This is a fairly long file. We'll investigate its unique features in the next section.

THE APPLICATION FILE (TXTINTDLG.CPP)

The length of the application file TxtIntDlg.cpp may be a little overwhelming. However, recall that much of this code hasn't changed dramatically from the basic code first described in Chapter 2.

For this application, the first new feature appears in the TextDlgProc procedure.

```
// Process the Text dialog box control selection
```

```
BOOL CALLBACK TextDlgProc(HWND hDlg,UINT messg,
                          WPARAM wParam,LPARAM lParam)
{
  switch (messg) {
    case WM_INITDIALOG:
      break;
    case WM_COMMAND:
      switch (LOWORD(wParam)) {
        case IDOK:
          GetDlgItemText(hDlg,IDC_TEXT,screentext,80);
          EndDialog(hDlg,TRUE);
          break;
        case IDCANCEL:
          EndDialog(hDlg,FALSE);
          break;
        default:
          return FALSE;
      }
      break;
    default:
      return FALSE;
  }
  return TRUE;
}
```

When the TxtDlgBox dialog box is selected from the menu and the user enters a string of text, that information will be processed by the **GetDlgItemText()** function. This function will return the text string to the global variable, *myscreen*, when the IDOK button is selected by the user. In this case, the handle, the ID value, the location for the string (*myscreen*), and the maximum length of the string are passed to the function. If the user selects the Cancel button, the dialog box is erased without further window updating.

The text string is finally printed to the screen when a WM_PAINT message is received. This program also draws a little graphics figure in the window. The **TextOut()** function is used to print the information returned by TextDiaProc to the global character array, *myscreen*.

The structure of the IntDlgProc is similar to the TextDlgProc.

```
// Process the Integer dialog box control selection
BOOL CALLBACK IntDlgProc(HWND hDlg,UINT messg,
                         WPARAM wParam,LPARAM lParam)
{
  switch (messg) {
    case WM_INITDIALOG:
      break;
    case WM_COMMAND:
      switch (LOWORD(wParam)) {
        case IDOK:
          iupperx=GetDlgItemInt(hDlg,IDC_UPPERX,NULL,0);
          iuppery=GetDlgItemInt(hDlg,IDC_UPPERY,NULL,0);
```

420 Chapter 11 • Adding Dialog Boxes

```
            ilowerx=GetDlgItemInt(hDlg,IDC_LOWERX,NULL,0);
            ilowery=GetDlgItemInt(hDlg,IDC_LOWERY,NULL,0);
            EndDialog(hDlg,TRUE);
            break;
          case IDCANCEL:
            EndDialog(hDlg,FALSE);
            break;
          default:
            return FALSE;
        }
        break;
     default:
       return FALSE;
  }
  return TRUE;
}
```

The four variables are named *iupperx*, *iuppery*, *ilowerx*, and *ilowery*. The **GetDlgItemInt()** function returns an integer value to each of these variables. The function is passed a handle, an ID value, a NULL, and a 0 if the translation is to be an unsigned integer; 1 would replace the 0 for signed integer numbers. Unsigned integer numbers can range up to UINT_MAX and signed numbers to INT_MAX. The *lpTranslated* parameter, which in this case receives a NULL, can be used to warn of errors in data entry. Only the numeric digits 0–9 are considered valid (hexadecimal integers cannot be entered with this technique). As in the previous examples, this information is processed with the selection of the IDOK button.

The four variables containing the coordinate information are used directly by the **Rectangle()** function under WM_PAINT to draw a green rectangle in the window. These parameters are for the defining rectangle that specifies the range of the ellipse.

```
// Create a green pen, 10 pixels wide
hPen=CreatePen(PS_SOLID,10,RGB(0,255,0));
SelectObject(hdc,hPen);

Rectangle(hdc,iupperx,iuppery,ilowerx,ilowery);
TextOut(hdc,100,100,screentext,strlen(screentext));
```

Figure 11–15 shows the rectangle and text previously described with the use of the two data entry dialog boxes.

Dialog Boxes Solve a Variety of Input Needs **421**

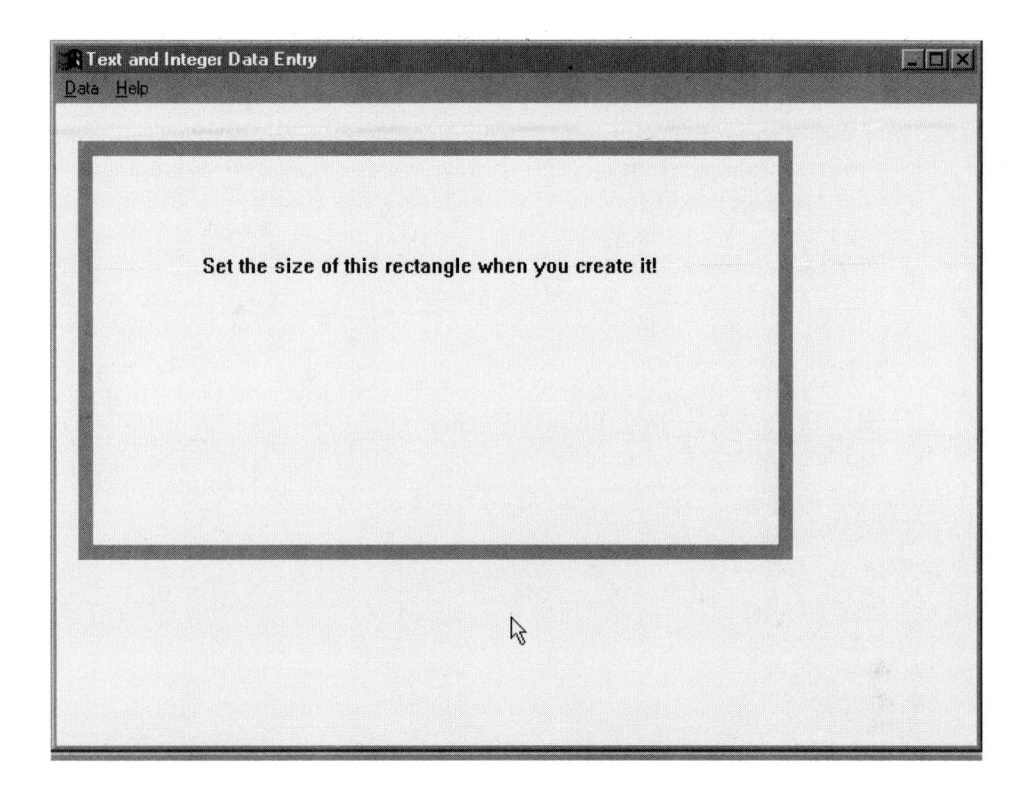

Figure 11-15 *Text and integer data were used to create this window.*

If this is the first time you have been able to create an application that allows text and numeric information to be entered by the user, we're sure you are impressed with the results. However, integers are not the only type of number you're likely to encounter. What about real numbers? The solution to this form of data entry rests with the next application.

Entering Real Numbers in a Dialog Box

Real numbers are just as easy to process as integer numbers in Windows. One quick way to obtain real number information across many Windows functions is to store the real number in a global variable. The global variable will be immediately available to all functions. In this application, a real number will be entered, using an edit box control in a dialog box. The application will then treat that number as the radius of a circle and calculate the circle's area. Recall that the area of a circle is given by the equation:

```
Area of a circle = pi * r²
```

This application, RealMessgDlg, will accept a real number by the user, then calculate and return a real number for the circle's area. In addition, this application will illustrate the use of message boxes. Message boxes are an express form of dialog box. Message boxes are often used to report system status, warnings, cautions, and stop messages to the user. Windows provides the **MessageBox()** function for processing this easy-to-use dialog box. This application will allow you to look at several message boxes and learn how to use the message box function.

Message boxes do not require a formal design (i.e., the use of the Resource Editor). They are predefined dialog boxes and are automatically handled by Windows.

Here is the resource.h header file for the menu and dialog box information designed with the Resource Editor. Remember that this file is generated automatically.

```
// Microsoft Developer Studio generated include file.
// Used by RealMessgDlg.rc
//
#define IDC_REAL                        1000
#define ID_DATA_REAL                    40001
#define ID_HELP_ABOUT                   40002
#define ID_HELP_EXIT                    40003
#define ID_DATA_STATUS                  40004
#define ID_DATA_WARNING                 40005
#define ID_DATA_INFORMATION             40006
#define ID_DATA_STOP                    40007
```

The first four ID values in the resource.h header file pertain to the menu and dialog boxes used in this application. The final four ID values are used by four separate Message Boxes.

The RealMessgDlg.rc resource script file returned by the Resource Editor is listed next. This is a partial listing showing the menu and dialog box information.

```
/////////////////////////////////////////////////////////
//
// Menu
//

DataMenu MENU DISCARDABLE
BEGIN
  POPUP "&Data"
  BEGIN
    MENUITEM "&Real Numbers...",    ID_DATA_REAL
    MENUITEM "&Status Box...",      ID_DATA_STATUS
    MENUITEM "&Warning Box...",     ID_DATA_WARNING
    MENUITEM "&Information...",     ID_DATA_INFORMATION
    MENUITEM "S&top...",            ID_DATA_STOP
  END
```

```
    POPUP "&Help"
    BEGIN
      MENUITEM "&About...",          ID_HELP_ABOUT
      MENUITEM "&Exit",              ID_HELP_EXIT
    END
END

/////////////////////////////////////////////////////////
//
// Dialog
//

ABOUTDLGBOX DIALOG DISCARDABLE  0, 0, 186, 95
STYLE DS_MODALFRAME | WS_POPUP | WS_CAPTION | WS_SYSMENU
CAPTION "About Dialog Box"
FONT 8, "MS Sans Serif"
BEGIN
  DEFPUSHBUTTON    "OK",IDOK,70,76,50,14
  CTEXT    "Real Numbers and Message Boxes",
              IDC_STATIC,7,6,170,11
  CTEXT    "by",IDC_STATIC,79,29,30,14
  CTEXT    "William H. Murray and Chris H. Pappas",
              IDC_STATIC,7,51,168,13

  END

  REALDLGBOX DIALOG DISCARDABLE  0, 0, 186, 95
  STYLE DS_MODALFRAME | WS_POPUP | WS_CAPTION | WS_SYSMENU
  CAPTION "Real Number Dialog Box"
  FONT 8, "MS Sans Serif"
  BEGI
    DEFPUSHBUTTON    "OK",IDOK,31,71,50,14
    PUSHBUTTON "Cancel",IDCANCEL,112,71,50,14
    LTEXT    "Enter the radius of a circle as a real number:",
          IDC_STATIC,9,9,165,12
    EDITTEXT IDC_REAL,9,29,107,13,ES_AUTOHSCROLL
  END
```

In this listing, you can easily identify two menus. The first menu uses five menu items. The first menu item opens a data entry dialog box. The remaining four menu items open appropriate message boxes. The second menu allows the user to view an About dialog box or exit the application.

The About dialog box description is similar to the earlier applications. The data entry dialog box, REALDLGBOX, is also a more-or-less standard dialog box with two buttons, a line of static text, and an edit box control. Figure 11–16 shows the data entry dialog box.

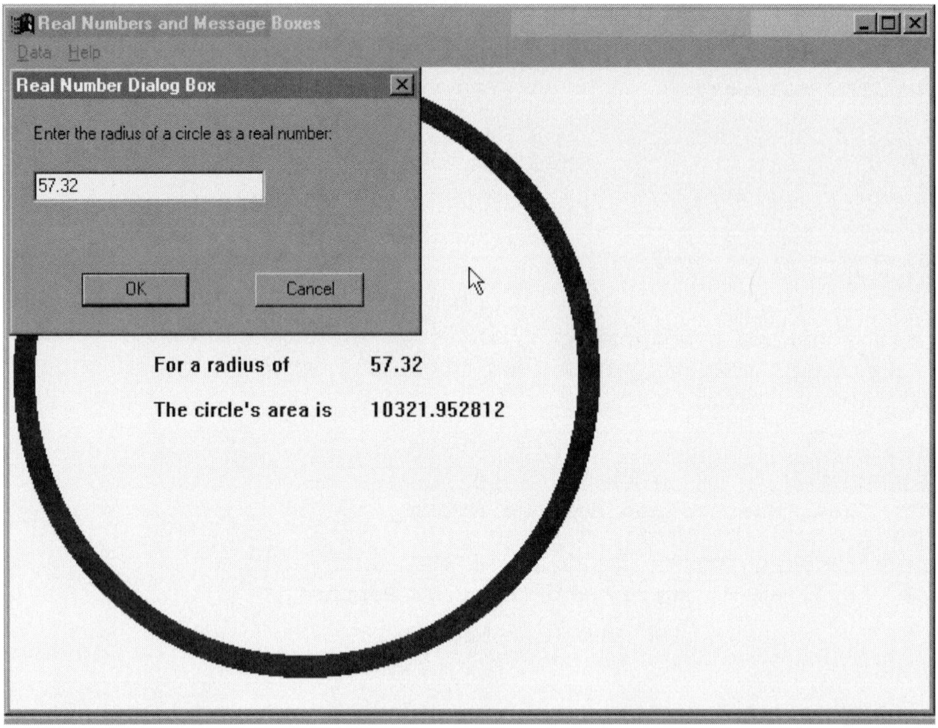

424 Chapter 11 • Adding Dialog Boxes

Figure 11-16 *The data entry dialog box for the RealMessgDlg project.*

The following listing is the source code for this application, named *RealMessgDlg.cpp*.

```
//
// RealMessgDlg.cpp
// Application demonstrates how to use a dialog box
// to enter real numbers.
// Message Boxes are also illustrated.
// Copyright (c) William H. Murray and Chris H. Pappas, 1999
//

#include <windows.h>
#include <stdlib.h>
#include <string.h>
#include <math.h>
#include "resource.h"
HINSTANCE hInst;

LRESULT CALLBACK WndProc(HWND,UINT,WPARAM,LPARAM);
BOOL CALLBACK AboutDlgProc(HWND,UINT,WPARAM,LPARAM);
```

```
BOOL CALLBACK RealDlgProc(HWND,UINT,WPARAM,LPARAM);

char szProgName[]="ProgName";
char szApplName[]="DataMenu";
char numberstring[30]="57.32";
double circleradius;

int WINAPI WinMain(HINSTANCE hInst,HINSTANCE hPreInst,
                   LPSTR lpszCmdLine,int nCmdShow)
{
  HWND hWnd;
  MSG  lpMsg;
  WNDCLASS wcApp;

  wcApp.lpszClassName=szProgName;
  wcApp.hInstance    =hInst;
  wcApp.lpfnWndProc  =WndProc;
  wcApp.hCursor      =LoadCursor(NULL,IDC_ARROW);
  wcApp.hIcon        =0;
  wcApp.lpszMenuName =szApplName;
  wcApp.hbrBackground=(HBRUSH) GetStockObject(WHITE_BRUSH);
  wcApp.style        =CS_HREDRAW|CS_VREDRAW;
  wcApp.cbClsExtra   =0;
  wcApp.cbWndExtra   =0;
  if (!RegisterClass (&wcApp))
    return 0;

  hWnd=CreateWindow(szProgName,"Real Numbers and Message Boxes",
                    WS_OVERLAPPEDWINDOW,CW_USEDEFAULT,
                    CW_USEDEFAULT,CW_USEDEFAULT,
                    CW_USEDEFAULT,(HWND)NULL,(HMENU)NULL,
                    hInst,(LPSTR)NULL);
  ShowWindow(hWnd,nCmdShow);
  UpdateWindow(hWnd);
  while (GetMessage(&lpMsg,0,0,0)) {
    TranslateMessage(&lpMsg);
    DispatchMessage(&lpMsg);
  }
  return(lpMsg.wParam);
}

// Process the Real dialog box control selection
BOOL CALLBACK RealDlgProc(HWND hDlg,UINT messg,
                          WPARAM wParam,LPARAM lParam)
{
  switch (messg) {
    case WM_INITDIALOG:
      break;
    case WM_COMMAND:
      switch (LOWORD(wParam)) {
```

```
        case IDOK:
          GetDlgItemText(hDlg,IDC_REAL,numberstring,30);
                    EndDialog(hDlg,TRUE);
          break;
        case IDCANCEL:
          EndDialog(hDlg,FALSE);
          break;
        default:
          return FALSE;
      }
      break;
    default:
      return FALSE;
  }
  return TRUE;
}

// Process the About dialog box control selection
BOOL CALLBACK AboutDlgProc(HWND hDlg,UINT messg,
                           WPARAM wParam,LPARAM lParam)
{
  switch (messg) {
    case WM_INITDIALOG:
      break;
    case WM_COMMAND:
      switch (LOWORD(wParam)) {
        case IDOK:
          EndDialog(hDlg,0);
          break;
        default:
          return FALSE;
      }
      break;
    default:
      return FALSE;
  }
  return TRUE;
}

LRESULT CALLBACK WndProc(HWND hWnd,UINT messg,
                         WPARAM wParam,LPARAM lParam)
{
  HDC hdc;
  PAINTSTRUCT ps;
  static HPEN hPen;
  double circlearea;
  char numberstring2[30];

  switch (messg)
  {
```

```
// Process the menu item selection
case WM_COMMAND:
  switch (LOWORD(wParam)) {
    // Draw the Real dialog box
    case ID_DATA_REAL:
      DialogBox(hInst,"RealDlgBox",hWnd,
             (DLGPROC)RealDlgProc);
      InvalidateRect(hWnd,NULL,TRUE);
      UpdateWindow(hWnd);
      break;
    // Draw four message boxes
    case ID_DATA_STATUS:
      MessageBox(hWnd,"A Status Message Box",
             "Status",MB_ICONEXCLAMATION|MB_OK);
      break;
    case ID_DATA_WARNING:
      MessageBox(hWnd,"A Warning Message Box",
             "Warning",MB_ICONQUESTION|MB_OK);
      break;
    case ID_DATA_INFORMATION:
      MessageBox(hWnd,"An Information Message Box",
              "Information",
              MB_ICONINFORMATION|MB_OK);
      break;
    case ID_DATA_STOP:
      MessageBox(hWnd,"A Stop Message Box",
             "Stop",MB_ICONSTOP|MB_OK);
      break;
    // Draw the About dialog box
    case ID_HELP_ABOUT:
      DialogBox(hInst,"AboutDlgBox",hWnd,
             (DLGPROC)AboutDlgProc);
      break;
    // End the application
    case ID_HELP_EXIT:
      SendMessage(hWnd,WM_CLOSE,0,0L);
      break;
    default:
       break;
  }
  break;

case WM_PAINT:
  hdc=BeginPaint(hWnd,&ps);

  circleradius=atof(numberstring);
  circlearea=(3.14159*circleradius*circleradius);

  // Create a blue pen, 15 pixels wide
  hPen=CreatePen(PS_SOLID,15,RGB(0,0,255));
```

428 Chapter 11 • Adding Dialog Boxes

```
      SelectObject(hdc,hPen);

      Ellipse(hdc,10,10,400,400);

      _gcvt(circlearea,12,numberstring2);
      TextOut(hdc, 100,190,"For a radius of ",16);
      TextOut(hdc,250,190,numberstring,strlen(numberstring));
      TextOut(hdc,100,220,"The circle's area is ",21);
      TextOut(hdc,250,220,numberstring2,strlen(numberstring2));

      ValidateRect(hWnd,NULL);
      EndPaint(hWnd,&ps);
      break;

    case WM_DESTROY:
      DeleteObject(hPen);
      PostQuitMessage(0);
      break;
    default:
      return(DefWindowProc(hWnd,messg,wParam,lParam));
      break;
  }
  return(0);
}
```

In the next section, we'll investigate the unique features of this application.

THE APPLICATION FILE (REALMESSGDLG.CPP)

This application uses the FloatDlgProc function to return the text string (containing characters that will be converted to real number information) to a global string array named *numberstring[30]*. This string holds an initial group of characters representing the real number 57.32.

```
char szProgName[]="ProgName";
char szApplName[]="DataMenu";
char numberstring[30]="57.32";
double circleradius;
```

You might recall that this same technique was used when text information was being entered for the screen in earlier examples. The **GetDlgItemText()** function returns a "numeric-appearing" character string of up to 20 characters to *numberstring*. The Microsoft C++ language contains functions and macros that allow the conversion of strings containing numeric digits into actual numbers and back. Can you find two of them in the following partial listing?

```
circleradius=atof(numberstring);
circlearea=(3.14159*circleradius*circleradius);
```

```
// Create a blue pen, 15 pixels wide
hPen=CreatePen(PS_SOLID,15,RGB(0,0,255));
SelectObject(hdc,hPen);

Ellipse(hdc,10,10,400,400);

_gcvt(circlearea,12,numberstring2);
TextOut(hdc, 100,190,"For a radius of ",16);
TextOut(hdc,250,190,numberstring,strlen(numberstring));
TextOut(hdc,100,220,"The circle's area is ",21);
TextOut(hdc,250,220,numberstring2,strlen(numberstring2));
```

The variable *circleradius* is a *double* that will hold the numeric data returned by the **atof()** function. To use this function, either the math.h or stdlib.h must be included in your application program. The **atof()** function expects a string containing numeric digits. It will stop the conversion process upon receiving the first nonnumeric character. For correctly entered string data, this will be the null character that terminates the string. Once converted, *circleradius* is immediately used to calculate the area of the circle, *circlearea*. Can you think of any other C++ functions that would allow you to convert string information to numeric data? (Hint: Use your compiler's on-line Help to examine the **atof()** function.)

We'd like to print the circle's area to the screen, but here is the catch. Only string information can be printed with the **TextOut()** function. Because *circlearea* holds numeric data, that data will have to be converted back to a string! The Microsoft C++ language has a macro, _gcvt, or a function, **gcvt()**, that will help make this conversion. The macro will convert a double into a string of the specified length and return it to the given character array.

The four remaining **TextOut()** function calls draw the required information to the screen, as shown in Figure 11–17.

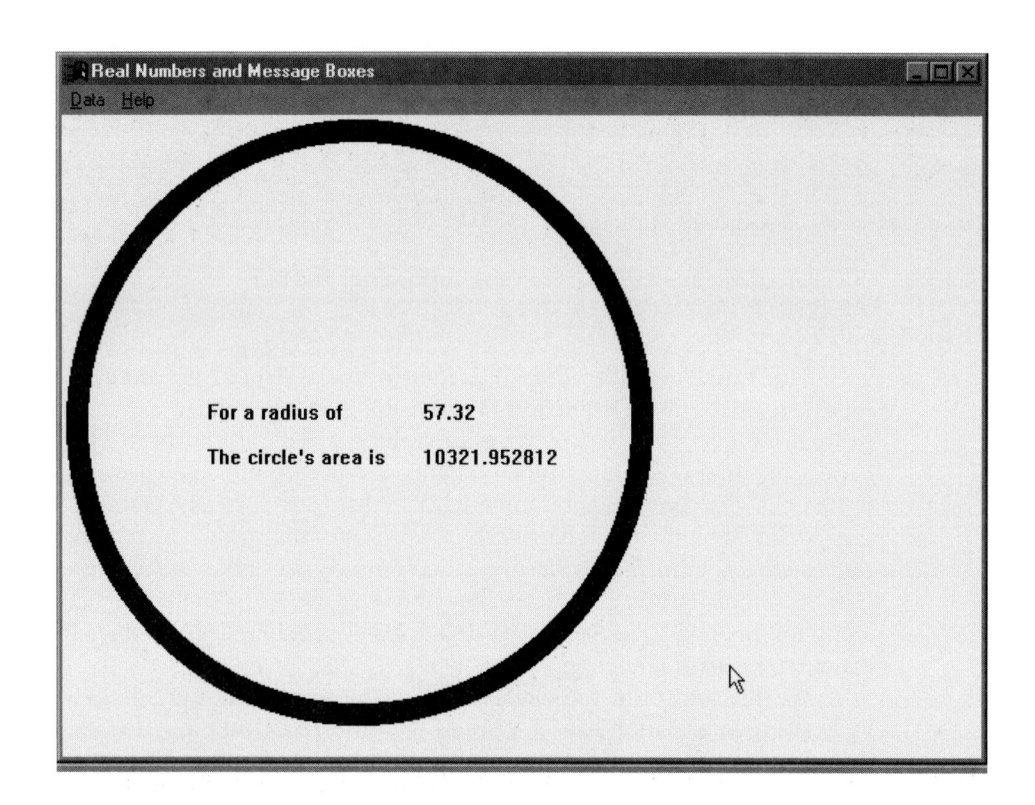

![Screenshot: Real Numbers and Message Boxes window showing a large circle with text "For a radius of 57.32" and "The circle's area is 10321.952812"]

Figure 11-17 *Calculating with real numbers under Windows.*

WHAT ABOUT THOSE MESSAGE BOXES? • Return to the section of RealMessgDlg.cpp code where the case statements appear. It is that portion of code containing the **MessageBox()** functions. Notice that the **MessageBox()** function uses a handle, a string, a caption, and an assortment of types. The *type* is the fourth parameter and can have several values, coupled with logical ORs. Each message box type starts with *MB_*, as you can see in the following listing.

```
MB_ABORTRETRYIGNORE
MB_APPLMODAL
MB_DEFBUTTON1
MB_DEFBUTTON2
MB_DEFBUTTON3
MB_DEFMASK
MB_ICONASTERISK
MB_ICONEXCLAMATION
```

```
MB_ICONHAND
MB_ICONINFORMATION or MB_ICONASTERISK
MB_ICONMASK
MB_ICONQUESTION
MB_ICONSTOP or MB_ICONHAND
MB_NOFOCUS
MB_OK
MB_OKCANCEL
MB_RETRYCANCEL
MB_SYSTEMMODAL
MB_TASKMODAL
MB_TYPEMASK
MB_YESNO
MB_YESNOCANCEL
```

Most message box types are self-explanatory, but if you need additional information, use your compiler's on-line Help.

Figure 11–18 shows the screen output for one message box.

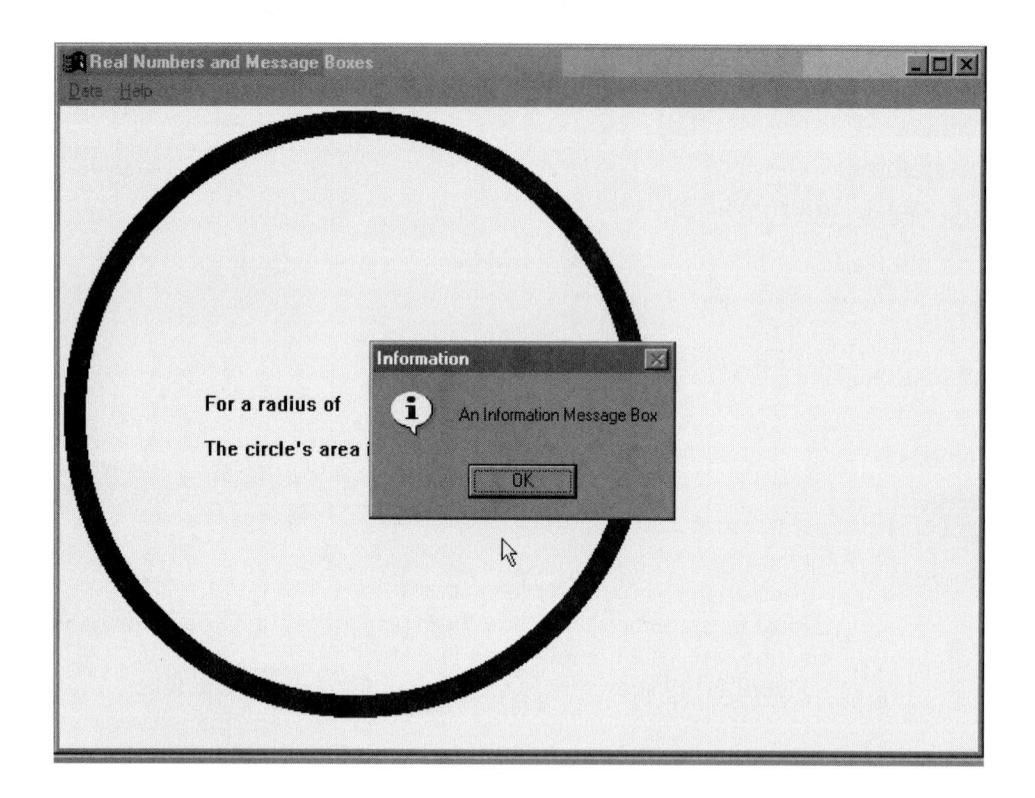

Figure 11-18   *Message boxes are a simple form of dialog box.*

A message box could also be used as a quick and easy About dialog box. If this is all that is needed, you can completely bypass the Resource Editor!

Get Ready

Dialog box resources really give Windows applications a lot of interactive power. However, there are additional resources such as toolbars, tab controls, folders, common controls, etc., that we haven't discussed yet. Just wait until you get to Chapter 12!

TWELVE

Special Controls and Dialog Boxes

Microsoft Windows offers a variety of special controls and resources. At one time it was easy to divide controls, for example, into categories such as standard controls, common controls, and custom controls. Now, the boundaries between these types have blurred a little.

Standard controls such as scroll bars, push buttons, radio buttons, and so on have been available as long as Windows has been on the market. They have always been the easiest controls to access and implement because the control itself was completely designed and implemented, in terms of functions, by Microsoft. Many of these controls were discussed in the previous chapter.

There is another group of controls called *common controls*. Common controls were not typically part of the toolbox of tools available to the resource designer. As such, their implementation was somewhat more difficult. For example, pick up a copy of a Windows programming book for Windows 95 and you'll see that common controls are created with a call to a **Create.....()** function. The layout and placement of the control within a dialog box was done outside of the graphical environment. Not a friendly approach to resource design! However, with the release of Windows 95, a new emphasis was placed on the use of this group of controls. It might not come as a surprise to you that with the release of Windows 98 and the latest version of the Visual C++ compiler, many common controls (they are still called by that name) have migrated to the Toolbox in the resource editor. This group contains slider, spinner button, progress, date time picker, and calendar controls. The migration of the control to the Toolbox of the graphical environment means easier implementation because the control can be dragged, dropped, and sized as you examine the results visually. It also means that you won't have to use a **Create...()** function to manually create, place, and size each common control. We'll investigate several common controls in this chapter. Once you learn the technique for implementing a common control, a common control of your choice won't be difficult to use either.

The third group of controls is the custom control, better known as an *ActiveX* control. This type of control is the hardest to design, implement, and use. You, the programmer, are responsible for the graphical design of the control and the implementation of all functions and parameters related to the use of the control. Trust us—if you are a newcomer to the Windows environment, wait a while before tackling custom controls.

There is an additional type of resource that doesn't have anything directly to do with controls. It is the common dialog box. In the last chapter, you learned how to design your own dialog boxes. No doubt you found the design, control placement, and implementation time-consuming. Well, the good news is that there are a group of predefined dialog boxes that save you design time and provide a consistent look across multiple applications. These common dialog boxes, designed by Microsoft, include the common font, color, and file dialog boxes.

In this chapter, you will learn how to implement several common controls and common dialog boxes. If you follow the steps in each section, you'll soon be able to implement any common control or common dialog box provided by Windows.

Toolbars and Tooltips

The toolbar.cpp application, discussed in this section, shows you how to add toolbar and tooltip resources to your programs.

The use of toolbars and their associated tooltips began to appear in applications several years ago. With the advent of Windows NT and 95, the popularity of toolbars and tooltips increased even more. When you click on your Visual C++ compiler's Insert|Resource menu selection, you'll learn that toolbars are treated as resources. They are grouped with bitmaps, menus, and dialog boxes. As such, they do not appear in the Resource Editor's Toolbox. To implement our toolbar and tooltip application, we'll use the **CreateToolbarEx()** function.

Our toolbar project will create an application that will allow us to resize a graphics object in the window. That, of course, is something we already learned to do in an earlier chapter. What is new, however, is that we'll also create a toolbar of twelve colors. They can be selected with the mouse and will immediately change the background color of the window. Of course, we'll also support the background color change with standard menu and keyboard accelerators. The toolbar will also support tooltips. If the user points to one of the 12 colored icons and waits a moment, a tooltip will pop up with the name of the color.

Toolbar Bitmaps

Each toolbar button can use a bitmapped image. The bitmapped image and its size are specified when the **CreateToolbarEx()** function is called. It is assumed that all bitmapped images in the toolbar are the same size. The default image size for each button's bitmap is 16 x 15 pixels. The size of each image can be changed by using the TB_SETBITMAPSIZE message. However, this must be done before adding any images.

Each bitmapped image has a zero-based index value. The first image is assigned a zero, with each subsequent image being assigned. It is the images index value that is used to associate it with a particular toolbar button.

The toolbar for this example is actually a bitmapped image created in the Resource Editor. This bitmap is made up of twelve 16 x 16 pixel bitmaps placed side to side. The image is named *toolbar.bmp*. Figure 12–1 shows a portion of the toolbar bitmap while it was being constructed.

You'll see how this bitmap is used in the next few sections as we look at the program code for the application.

The resource.h Header File

This project uses a resource.h header file that is generated by the Resource Editor upon the completion of all of the project's resources. Here is an edited portion of the header file showing the unique ID values created by us for various menu items.

```
//{{NO_DEPENDENCIES}}
// Microsoft Developer Studio generated include file.
// Used by Toolbar.rc
//

// toolbar information
//
#define IDTB_BITMAP     101
#define IDTB_TOOLBAR    201

#define IDM_SMALL       501
#define IDM_MEDIUM      502
#define IDM_LARGE       503

#define IDM_BLACK       601
#define IDM_WHITE       602
#define IDM_RED         603
#define IDM_ORANGE      604
#define IDM_YELLOW      605
#define IDM_GREEN       606
```

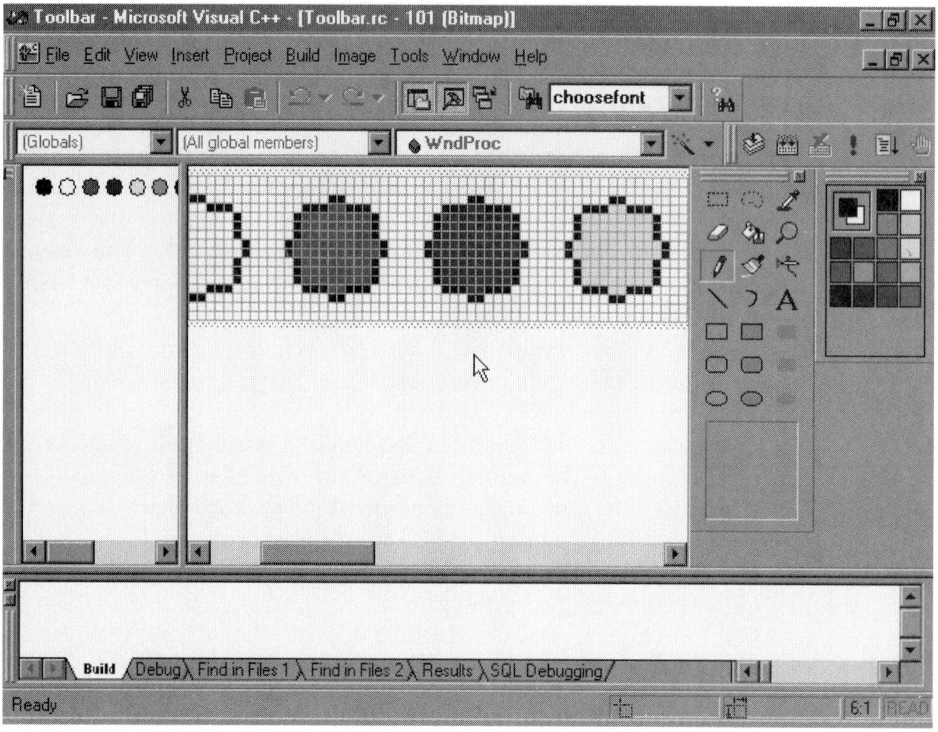

Figure 12-1 *A toolbar bitmap image under construction in the bitmap editor.*

```
#define  IDM_BLUE      607
#define  IDM_MAGENTA   608
#define  IDM_LTGREEN   609
#define  IDM_LTBLUE    610
#define  IDM_LTRED     611
#define  IDM_LTGRAY    612
   .
   .
   .
```

The first two ID values are unique to the toolbar implementation. The first ID value is for the toolbar bitmap and the second ID value for the toolbar itself. The remaining ID values are for menu items that allow the user to select an object size or background color as a menu option.

The toolbar.rc Resource Script File

The resource script file, toolbar.rc, includes descriptions for the applications menu and accelerator descriptions as well as tools for toolbar ID with the bitmap.

```
//Microsoft Developer Studio generated resource script.
//
#include "resource.h"
      .
      .
      .
/////////////////////////////////////////////////////////
//
// Bitmap
//

101      BITMAP   MOVABLE PURE   "toolbar.bmp"

/////////////////////////////////////////////////////////
//
// Menu
//

ALTERATION MENU DISCARDABLE
BEGIN
   POPUP "&Rectangle_Size"
   BEGIN
      MENUITEM "&small",          501
      MENUITEM "&Medium",         502
      MENUITEM "&LARGE",          503
   END
   POPUP "Ba&ckground_Colors"
   BEGIN
      MENUITEM "BLAC&K\tF1",      601
      MENUITEM "&WHITE\tF2",      602
      MENUITEM "&RED\tF3",        603
      MENUITEM "&ORANGE\tF4",     604
      MENUITEM "&YELLOW\tF5",     605
      MENUITEM "GREE&N\tF6",      606
      MENUITEM "&BLUE\tF7",       607
      MENUITEM "&MAGENTA\tF8",    608
      MENUITEM SEPARATOR
      MENUITEM "Lt GR&EEN\tF9",   609
      MENUITEM "Lt BL&UE\tF10",   610
      MENUITEM "Lt RE&D\tF11",    611
      MENUITEM "Lt GR&AY\tF12",   612
   END
END
END
```

```
//////////////////////////////////////////////////////
//
// Accelerator
//

ALTERATION ACCELERATORS MOVABLE PURE
BEGIN
    VK_F1,      601,        VIRTKEY
    VK_F2,      602,        VIRTKEY
    VK_F3,      603,        VIRTKEY
    VK_F4,      604,        VIRTKEY
    VK_F5,      605,        VIRTKEY
    VK_F6,      606,        VIRTKEY
    VK_F7,      607,        VIRTKEY
    VK_F8,      608,        VIRTKEY
    VK_F9,      609,        VIRTKEY
    VK_F10,     610,        VIRTKEY
    VK_F11,     611,        VIRTKEY
    VK_F12,     612,        VIRTKEY
END
         .
         .
         .
```

Well, except for the reference to the bitmapped image, there is no information in the toolbar.rc resource script file concerning the toolbar itself. What you did find in the file was a text description of the graphically designed menu and keyboard accelerators. We'll have to wait for the toolbar description in the source code file, named *toolbar.cpp*. After all, the toolbar for this application will be created and placed with a call to the **CreateToolbarEx()** function!

The toolbar.cpp Source Code File

The following is a complete listing for the toolbar.cpp source code file. As you examine this file, see if you can detect what code was added to support the toolbar and tooltip resources.

```
//
// Toolbar.cpp
// This application shows how to
// create a toolbar along with tooltips.
// The toolbar is used to change background colors.
// Copyright (c) William H. Murray and Chris H. Pappas, 1999
//

#include <windows.h>
#include "commctrl.h"
#include "resource.h"
```

Toolbars and Tooltips 439

```c
#define TOTALBUTTONS 12

char szProgName[]="ProgName";
char szApplName[]="Alteration";
static WORD wSize=30;
static WORD wColor;
static HWND hTBWnd;
static HACCEL hAccel;

TBBUTTON TBButtons[TOTALBUTTONS];

LRESULT CALLBACK WndProc(HWND,UINT,WPARAM,LPARAM);
void DefToolbar();

int WINAPI WinMain(HINSTANCE hInst,HINSTANCE hPreInst,
                   LPSTR lpszCmdLine,int nCmdShow)
{
  HWND hWnd;
  MSG lpMsg;
  WNDCLASS wcApp;
  if (!hPreInst) {
    wcApp.lpszClassName=szProgName;
    wcApp.hInstance    =hInst;
    wcApp.lpfnWndProc  =WndProc;
    wcApp.hCursor      =LoadCursor(NULL,IDC_ARROW);
    wcApp.hIcon        =0;
    wcApp.lpszMenuName =szApplName;
    wcApp.hbrBackground=(HBRUSH) GetStockObject(WHITE_BRUSH);
    wcApp.style        =CS_HREDRAW|CS_VREDRAW;
    wcApp.cbClsExtra   =0;
    wcApp.cbWndExtra   =0;
    if (!RegisterClass (&wcApp))
      return 0;
  }
  hWnd=CreateWindow(szProgName,"A Toolbar with Tooltips",
                    WS_OVERLAPPEDWINDOW,CW_USEDEFAULT,
                    CW_USEDEFAULT,CW_USEDEFAULT,
                    CW_USEDEFAULT,(HWND)NULL,(HMENU)NULL,
                    hInst,(LPSTR)NULL);
  hAccel=LoadAccelerators(hInst,szApplName);

  DefToolbar();
  hTBWnd = CreateToolbarEx(hWnd,WS_VISIBLE|WS_CHILD|WS_BORDER
                           |TBSTYLE_TOOLTIPS, IDTB_TOOLBAR,
                           TOTALBUTTONS,hInst,IDTB_BITMAP,
                           TBButtons,TOTALBUTTONS,0,0,16,16,
                           sizeof(TBBUTTON));

  ShowWindow(hWnd,nCmdShow);
  UpdateWindow(hWnd);
```

```
    while (GetMessage(&lpMsg,0,0,0)) {
      if (!TranslateAccelerator(hWnd,hAccel,&lpMsg)) {
        TranslateMessage(&lpMsg);
        DispatchMessage(&lpMsg);
      }
    }
    return(lpMsg.wParam);
}

LRESULT CALLBACK WndProc(HWND hWnd,UINT messg,
                         WPARAM wParam,LPARAM lParam)
{
  HDC hdc;
  PAINTSTRUCT ps;
  LPTOOLTIPTEXT TTStr;
  HMENU hmenu;
  static int xClientView,yClientView;
  static int wColorValue[12][3]={0,0,0,          //BLACK
                                 255,255,255,    //WHITE
                                 255,0,0,        //RED
                                 255,96,0,       //ORANGE
                                 255,255,0,      //YELLOW
                                 0,255,0,        //GREEN
                                 0,0,255,        //BLUE
                                 255,0,255,      //MAGENTA
                                 128,255,0,      //LT GREEN
                                 0,255,255,      //LT BLUE
                                 255,0,159,      //LT RED
                                 180,180,180};   //LT GRAY

    switch (messg) {
      case WM_COMMAND:
        switch (LOWORD(wParam)) {
          case IDM_SMALL:
            wSize=20;
            break;
          case IDM_MEDIUM:
            wSize=70;
            break;
          case IDM_LARGE:
            wSize=110;
            break;
          case IDM_BLACK:
          case IDM_WHITE:
          case IDM_RED:
          case IDM_ORANGE:
          case IDM_YELLOW:
          case IDM_GREEN:
          case IDM_BLUE:
          case IDM_MAGENTA:
```

```
      case IDM_LTGREEN:
      case IDM_LTBLUE:
      case IDM_LTRED:
      case IDM_LTGRAY:
        hmenu=GetMenu(hWnd);
        CheckMenuItem(hmenu,wColor,MF_UNCHECKED);
        wColor=LOWORD(wParam);
        CheckMenuItem(hmenu,wColor,MF_CHECKED);
        SetClassLong(hWnd,GCL_HBRBACKGROUND,
                  (LONG) CreateSolidBrush(RGB
                  (wColorValue[wColor-IDM_BLACK][0],
                  wColorValue[wColor-IDM_BLACK][1],
                  wColorValue[wColor-IDM_BLACK][2])));
        break;
      default:
        break;
    }
    InvalidateRect(hWnd,NULL,TRUE);
    break;

  case WM_SIZE:
    xClientView=LOWORD(lParam);
    yClientView=HIWORD(lParam);
    break;

  case WM_NOTIFY:
    TTStr=(LPTOOLTIPTEXT) lParam;
    if(TTStr->hdr.code==TTN_NEEDTEXT)
      switch(TTStr->hdr.idFrom) {
        case IDM_BLACK:
          TTStr->lpszText="Black";
          break;
        case IDM_WHITE:
          TTStr->lpszText="White";
          break;
        case IDM_RED:
          TTStr->lpszText="Red";
          break;
        case IDM_ORANGE:
          TTStr->lpszText="Orange";
          break;
        case IDM_YELLOW:
          TTStr->lpszText="Yellow";
          break;
        case IDM_GREEN:
          TTStr->lpszText="Green";
          break;
        case IDM_BLUE:
          TTStr->lpszText="Blue";
          break;
```

```
            case IDM_MAGENTA:
              TTStr->lpszText="Magenta";
              break;
            case IDM_LTGREEN:
              TTStr->lpszText="Light Green";
              break;
            case IDM_LTBLUE:
              TTStr->lpszText="Light Blue";
              break;
            case IDM_LTRED:
              TTStr->lpszText="Light Red";
              break;
            case IDM_LTGRAY:
              TTStr->lpszText="Light Gray";
              break;
          }
       break;

    case WM_PAINT:
       hdc=BeginPaint(hWnd,&ps);

       SetMapMode(hdc,MM_ISOTROPIC);
       SetWindowExtEx(hdc,500,500,NULL);
       SetViewportExtEx(hdc,xClientView,-yClientView,NULL);
       SetViewportOrgEx(hdc,xClientView/2,yClientView/2,NULL);

       Rectangle(hdc,-(wSize*2),-wSize,
                 wSize*2,wSize);
       TextOut(hdc,-(wSize*2),(wSize*2)-10,
               "Surround Your Rectangle",23);

       ShowWindow(hTBWnd,SW_SHOW);
       UpdateWindow(hTBWnd);

       ValidateRect(hWnd,NULL);
       EndPaint(hWnd,&ps);
       break;

    case WM_DESTROY:
       PostQuitMessage(0);
       break;

    default:
       return(DefWindowProc(hWnd,messg,wParam,lParam));
  }
  return(0);
}

void DefToolbar()
{
```

```
TBButtons[0].iBitmap=0;
TBButtons[0].idCommand=IDM_BLACK;
TBButtons[0].fsState=TBSTATE_ENABLED;
TBButtons[0].fsStyle=TBSTYLE_BUTTON;
TBButtons[0].dwData=0L;
TBButtons[0].iString=0;

TBButtons[1].iBitmap=1;
TBButtons[1].idCommand=IDM_WHITE;
TBButtons[1].fsState=TBSTATE_ENABLED;
TBButtons[1].fsStyle=TBSTYLE_BUTTON;
TBButtons[1].dwData=0L;
TBButtons[1].iString=0;

TBButtons[2].iBitmap=2;
TBButtons[2].idCommand=IDM_RED;
TBButtons[2].fsState=TBSTATE_ENABLED;
TBButtons[2].fsStyle=TBSTYLE_BUTTON;
TBButtons[2].dwData=0L;
TBButtons[2].iString=0;

TBButtons[3].iBitmap=3;
TBButtons[3].idCommand=IDM_ORANGE;
TBButtons[3].fsState=TBSTATE_ENABLED;
TBButtons[3].fsStyle=TBSTYLE_BUTTON;
TBButtons[3].dwData=0L;
TBButtons[3].iString=0;

TBButtons[4].iBitmap=4;
TBButtons[4].idCommand=IDM_YELLOW;
TBButtons[4].fsState=TBSTATE_ENABLED;
TBButtons[4].fsStyle=TBSTYLE_BUTTON;
TBButtons[4].dwData=0L;
TBButtons[4].iString=0;

TBButtons[5].iBitmap=5;
TBButtons[5].idCommand=IDM_GREEN;
TBButtons[5].fsState=TBSTATE_ENABLED;
TBButtons[5].fsStyle=TBSTYLE_BUTTON;
TBButtons[5].dwData=0L;
TBButtons[5].iString=0;

TBButtons[6].iBitmap=6;
TBButtons[6].idCommand=IDM_BLUE;
TBButtons[6].fsState=TBSTATE_ENABLED;
TBButtons[6].fsStyle=TBSTYLE_BUTTON;
TBButtons[6].dwData=0L;
TBButtons[6].iString=0;

TBButtons[7].iBitmap=7;
```

```
    TBButtons[7].idCommand=IDM_MAGENTA;
    TBButtons[7].fsState=TBSTATE_ENABLED;
    TBButtons[7].fsStyle=TBSTYLE_BUTTON;
    TBButtons[7].dwData=0L;
    TBButtons[7].iString=0;

    TBButtons[8].iBitmap=8;
    TBButtons[8].idCommand=IDM_LTGREEN;
    TBButtons[8].fsState=TBSTATE_ENABLED;
    TBButtons[8].fsStyle=TBSTYLE_BUTTON;
    TBButtons[8].dwData=0L;
    TBButtons[8].iString=0;

    TBButtons[9].iBitmap=9;
    TBButtons[9].idCommand=IDM_LTBLUE;
    TBButtons[9].fsState=TBSTATE_ENABLED;
    TBButtons[9].fsStyle=TBSTYLE_BUTTON;
    TBButtons[9].dwData=0L;
    TBButtons[9].iString=0;

    TBButtons[10].iBitmap=10;
    TBButtons[10].idCommand=IDM_LTRED;
    TBButtons[10].fsState=TBSTATE_ENABLED;
    TBButtons[10].fsStyle=TBSTYLE_BUTTON;
    TBButtons[10].dwData=0L;
    TBButtons[10].iString=0;

    TBButtons[11].iBitmap=11;
    TBButtons[11].idCommand=IDM_LTGRAY;
    TBButtons[11].fsState=TBSTATE_ENABLED;
    TBButtons[11].fsStyle=TBSTYLE_BUTTON;
    TBButtons[11].dwData=0L;
    TBButtons[11].iString=0;
}
```

Wow, is that a long listing! Be sure when you're creating applications of the length that you take the time to enter your code accurately. We've all seen error message reports at compile time reporting 300 errors in a new application. Later, we've discovered that all 300 errors were the result of leaving out one set of closing brackets on a function.

When you are building applications that use common controls, be sure to add the library to your linker's library list. For our applications, this will be comctl32.lib. Figure 12–2 shows where this can be placed.

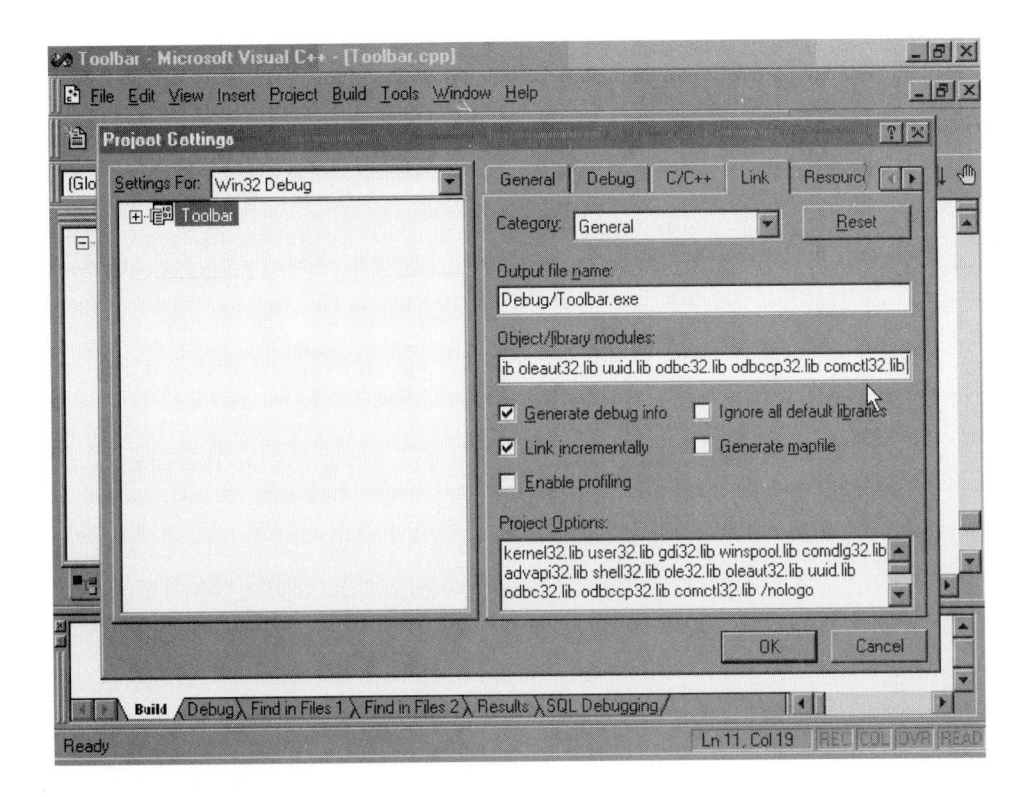

Figure 12-2 *Be sure to add comctl32.lib to the linker's library list.*

Failure to add the comctl32.lib library will lead to unpredictable error messages when you attempt to build the project.

UNIQUE SOURCE CODE

The majority of the code used in this application is similar to the code used in previous chapters. However, there is one unique twist that we'll examine in this section. The toolbar's bitmapped image is basically laid on top of the application's window. This is done by treating it as a child window of the parent window. The child window is described with a call to the **CreateToolbarEx()** function.

```
DefToolbar();
hTBWnd = CreateToolbarEx(hWnd,WS_VISIBLE|WS_CHILD|WS_BORDER
               |TBSTYLE_TOOLTIPS,IDTB_TOOLBAR,
               TOTALBUTTONS,hInst,IDTB_BITMAP,
               TBButtons,TOTALBUTTONS,0,0,16,16,
               sizeof(TBBUTTON));
```

In this example, the toolbar will be a visible child with a border. This is achieved by using the WS_VISIBLE, WS_CHILD, and WS_BORDER window styles. It will include tooltips that are identified with the IDTB_TOOLBAR ID parameter. The total number of toolbar buttons (in this example, each button is a bitmapped image) is given by TOTALBUTTONS. This value was set to 12. IDTB_BITMAP is the module instance identifying the file containing the bitmap resource. TBButtons holds the address for the toolbar array containing the descriptions of the 12 toolbar buttons. The initial position (0,0) and size (16,16) of the first button must be specified. The last parameter returns the size of the TBButton array structure.

You might have noticed that there is only one class-specific style associated with **CreateToolbarEx()** function. The TBSTYLE_TOOLTIPS style allows the **CreateToolbarEx()** function to creates a tooltip control. The tooltip control is a small pop-up window with a line of text used to describe the toolbar button. Each tooltip is hidden and pops up when the user leaves the mouse cursor over the button for approximately a second. The tooltip is then drawn near the cursor.

A toolbar's tooltips are processed when a WM_NOTIFY message is received by the application. Here is a portion of the required code.

```
case WM_NOTIFY:
  TTStr=(LPTOOLTIPTEXT) lParam;
    if(TTStr->hdr.code==TTN_NEEDTEXT)
      switch(TTStr->hdr.idFrom) {
        case IDM_BLACK:
          TTStr->lpszText="Black";
          break;
        case IDM_WHITE:
          TTStr->lpszText="White";
          break;
        case IDM_RED:
          TTStr->lpszText="Red";
          break;
        case IDM_ORANGE:
          TTStr->lpszText="Orange";
          break;
             .
             .
             .
        case IDM_LTRED:
          TTStr->lpszText="Light Red";
          break;
        case IDM_LTGRAY:
          TTStr->lpszText="Light Gray";
          break;
      }
      break;
```

Toolbars and Tooltips 447

A switch-case statement handles the WM_NOTIFY messages generated for each color. TT STR is the tooltip string to be placed in the tooltip box.

Each toolbar button is described in the **DefToolbar()** function. Twelve buttons require 12 similar but different descriptions. Here is a portion of that function.

```
void DefToolbar()
{
  TBButtons[0].iBitmap=0;
  TBButtons[0].idCommand=IDM_BLACK;
  TBButtons[0].fsState=TBSTATE_ENABLED;
  TBButtons[0].fsStyle=TBSTYLE_BUTTON;
  TBButtons[0].dwData=0L;
  TBButtons[0].iString=0;

  TBButtons[1].iBitmap=1;
  TBButtons[1].idCommand=IDM_WHITE;
  TBButtons[1].fsState=TBSTATE_ENABLED;
  TBButtons[1].fsStyle=TBSTYLE_BUTTON;
  TBButtons[1].dwData=0L;
  TBButtons[1].iString=0;

  TBButtons[2].iBitmap=2;
  TBButtons[2].idCommand=IDM_RED;
  TBButtons[2].fsState=TBSTATE_ENABLED;
  TBButtons[2].fsStyle=TBSTYLE_BUTTON;
  TBButtons[2].dwData=0L;
  TBButtons[2].iString=0;

  TBButtons[3].iBitmap=3;
  TBButtons[3].idCommand=IDM_ORANGE;
  TBButtons[3].fsState=TBSTATE_ENABLED;
  TBButtons[3].fsStyle=TBSTYLE_BUTTON;
  TBButtons[3].dwData=0L;
  TBButtons[3].iString=0;
     .
     .
     .
  TBButtons[10].iBitmap=10;
  TBButtons[10].idCommand=IDM_LTRED;
  TBButtons[10].fsState=TBSTATE_ENABLED;
  TBButtons[10].fsStyle=TBSTYLE_BUTTON;
  TBButtons[10].dwData=0L;
  TBButtons[10].iString=0;

  TBButtons[11].iBitmap=11;
  TBButtons[11].idCommand=IDM_LTGRAY;
  TBButtons[11].fsState=TBSTATE_ENABLED;
  TBButtons[11].fsStyle=TBSTYLE_BUTTON;
  TBButtons[11].dwData=0L;
```

```
    TBButtons[11].iString=0;
}
```

The first entry in the array, TBButtons[0].iBitmap, specifies which of the 12 bitmaps to use for the first button position. TBButtons[0].idCommand gives the ID value for the color to be associated with this button. Then TBButtons[0].fsState=TBSTATE_ENABLED enables this bitmapped image. Next, TBButtons[0].fsStyle=TBSTYLE_BUTTON specifies a toolbar button style. The TBButtons[0].dwData array element specifies any data associated with the toolbar button, and TBButtons[0].iString is a string value.

If you are ready to do a little digging for more information on toolbars and tooltips, take advantage of your Visual C++ compiler's Help facility. There is plenty of detail and information for creating some really unique toolbars.

Figure 12–3 shows the toolbar project in action.

If you have the time and are up to the challenge, why not replace this toolbar with a toolbar that would allow you to select the size of the graphics object instead of the background color?

Investigating the Spin and Progress Bar Common Controls

Spin and progress controls are very popular common controls. We're sure you have encountered each many times as you have used various Windows applications. The project for this section is named *SpecCont*. This project is designed to show you how to implement both a spin control and progress control within a standard dialog box.

A Spin or Up-Down Control

A spin control allows the user to increment or decrement values with the click of an up or down button. Spin controls are often referred to as *up and down controls*. Frequently, an edit box is used in conjunction with a spin control. When the spin control bonds with another control, it forms a relationship where the associated control is called a *buddy*. If the autobuddy feature is set via the control's property features, the edit box will automatically be selected if it is the first edit box control, in tab order, before the spin button.

When spin controls are created, they are specified with a group of constants that determine their style. This group of constants can be found in the commctrl.h header file. Table 12.1 shows the various style constants for spin controls and gives a brief description of their purpose.

Investigating the Spin and Progress Bar Common Controls

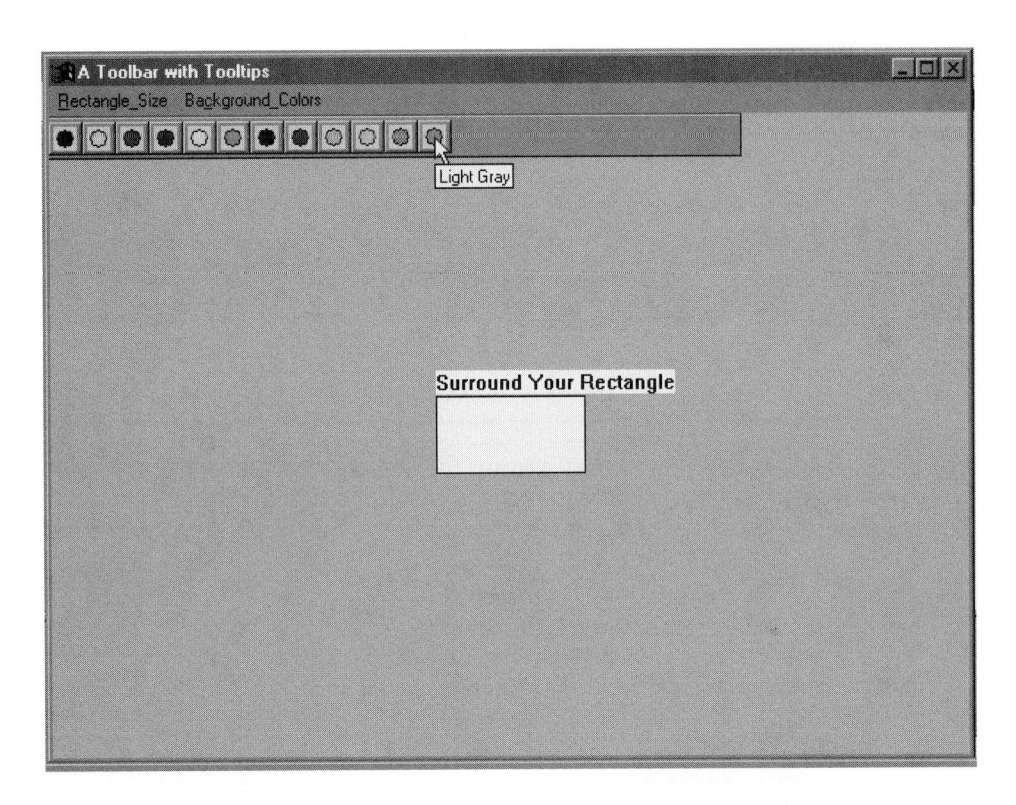

Figure 12-3 *A toolbar and tooltip are visible in the toolbar project.*

Table 12.1 Spin (Up-Down) Control Style Constants.

Style Constant	Description
UDS_WRAP	Wraps to the opposite limit if either the minimum or maximum limit is to be exceeded.
UDS_SETBUDDYINT	Issues a call to the **SetDlgItemInt()** function to update the buddy control.
UDS_ALIGNRIGHT	Aligns the spin control on the right edge of the buddy control.
UDS_ALIGNLEFT	Aligns the spin control on the left edge of the buddy control.
UDS_AUTOBUDDY	Identifies the buddy control as the previously defined control.

Table 12.1 Spin (Up-Down) Control Style Constants. (Continued)

Style Constant	Description
UDS_ARROWKEYS	Intercepts the up/down arrow keys in the buddy control.
UDS_HORZ	Draws the spin buttons side by side instead of one over the other
UDS_NOTHOUSANDS	Directs that a separator will not be inserted between groups of three digits.
UDS_HOTTRACK	Allows the control to be hottracked via the mouse.

UDS_ styles are used during the design phase as the control is being created. The Resource Editor will automatically assign UDS_ style constants to a spin control based upon user-selected properties when the control is being created. UDS_ styles can be ORed together. You'll see UDS_ style constants in the resource script file for this project.

To manage the spin control under program operation, UDM_ messages can be sent to the control. Table 12.2 shows UDM_ message constants and provides a brief description of each.

Table 12.2 Spin (Up-Down) Control Message Constants.

Message Constant	Description	wParam	lParam
UDM_SETRANGE	Sets the range (upper and lower) of the control. (16-bit value). The default is 0 to 100.	0	MAKELONG (nUpper, nLower)
UDM_GETRANGE	Gets the range of the control.	0	0
UDM_SETPOS	Sets the initial position of the control. The default is 0.	0	MAKELONG (nPosition, 0)
UDM_GETPOS	Gets the position of the control.	0	0

Table 12.2 Spin (Up-Down) Control Message Constants. (Continued)

Message Constant	Description	wParam	lParam
UDM_SETBUDDY	Provides the handle for the buddy control.	handle to buddy control	0
UDM_GETBUDDY	Gets the handle of the buddy control.	0	0
UDM_SETACCEL	Sets the accelerators for the control.	number of accelerators	pointer to array of accelerators
UDM_GETACCEL	Gets the accelerators for the control.	number of accelerators	pointer to array to hold accelerator values.
UDM_SETBASE	Sets the base value for the control (decimal or hexadecimal).	base value	0
UDM_GETBASE	Gets the base value for the control.	0	0
UDM_SETRANGE32	Provides an extended range (32 bits) for the control's range (-0x7FFFFFFF to +- 0x7FFFFFFF).	low 16 bits	high 16 bits
UDM_GETRANGE32	Gets the extended range for the control.	return value	0

Messages are usually sent to the spin control with the **SendDlgItemMessage()** function. You'll see several calls to this function in the SpecCont.cpp source code file.

Figure 12–4 shows a spin control placed near an edit box control in the Resource Editor.

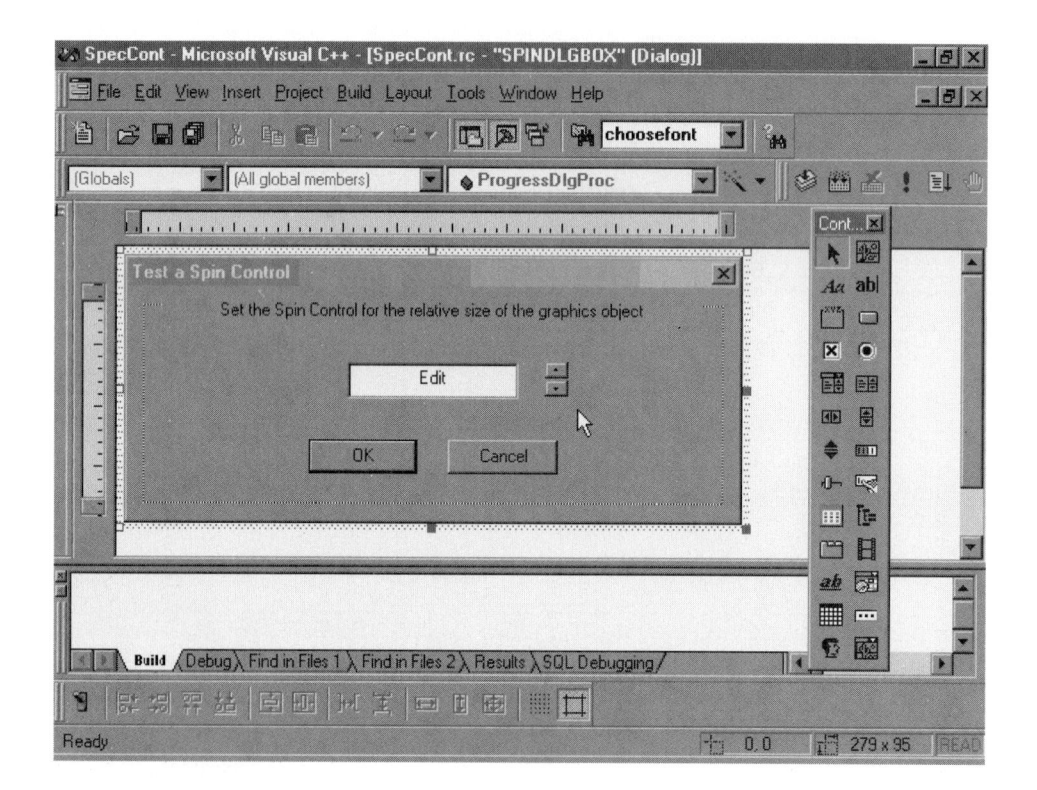

452 Chapter 12 • Special Controls and Dialog Boxes

Figure 12-4 *A spin control is placed near an edit box control in the dialog box.*

Figure 12–5 shows some of the spin control properties that were set during the design phase of this dialog box.

You'll see how these property choices are reflected in the resource script file.

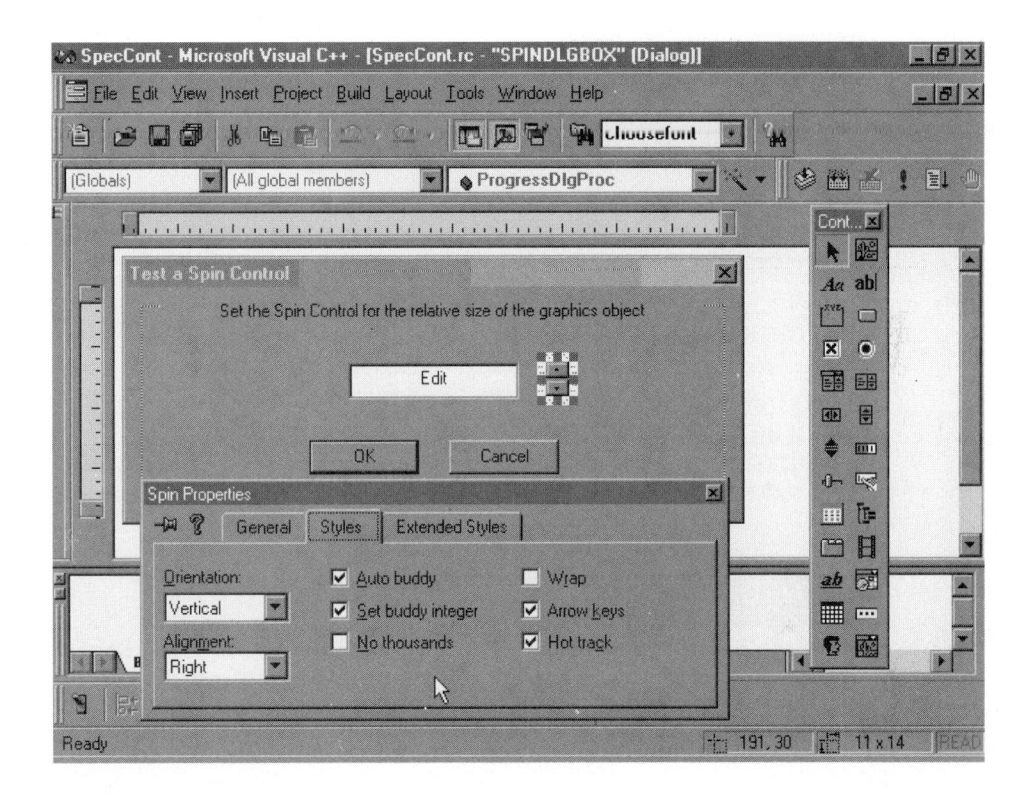

Investigating the Spin and Progress Bar Common Controls **453**

Figure 12-5 *Several spin control properties are set.*

A Progress Control

A progress control is a small window used by an application to indicate the progress of a lengthy operation. You've seen progress controls used in conjunction with setup or installation programs when a large number of files are being copied. The range and current position of the progress control can be set initially. Then the position can be advanced at a predefined step. Frequently, a progress control will include text that indicates either a percentage of the entire range or as the value of the current position.

A progress control uses the system's highlight color to show the progress of an operation. The default range for a progress control is from 0 to 100. The default step or increment is 10. All values can be redefined.

When progress controls are created, they are specified with a group of constants that determine their style. This group of constants can be found in the commctrl.h header file. Table 12.3 shows the various style constants for progress bar controls and gives a brief description of their purpose.

Table 12.3 Progress Control Style Constants.

Style Constant	Description
PBS_SMOOTH	Draws a single continuous bar instead of smaller rectangular bars.
PBS_VERTICAL	Draws the control vertically instead of horizontally.

PBS_ styles are used during the design phase as the control is being created. The Resource Editor will automatically assign PBS_ style constants to a progress control based upon user selected properties when the control is being created. PBS_ styles can be ORed together. Look for PBS_ style constants in the resource script file for this project.

Messages manage progress controls while under program operation. Table 12.4 shows PBM_ message constants and provides a brief description of each.

Table 12.4 Progress Control Message Constants.

Message Constant	Description	wParam	lParam
PBM_SETRANGE	Sets the range (minimum and maximum) for the control.	0	MAKELONG(nMinimum, nMaximum)
PBM_SETPOS	Advances to a new position.	new position	0
PBM_DELTAPOS	Advances position of the control by the given increment size.	increment size	0
PBM_SETSTEP	Sets the step increment size.	increment size	0
PBM_STEPIT	Advances position of the control by the step size.	0	0
PBM_SETRANGE32	Provides an extended 32-bit range of values.	low 16 bits	high 16 bits
PBM_GETRANGE	Gets the range of the control.	return value	0

Investigating the Spin and Progress Bar Common Controls

Table 12.4	Progress Control Message Constants. (Continued)		
Message Constant	**Description**	**wParam**	**lParam**
PBM_GETPOS	Gets the control's current position.	0	0
PBM_SETBARCOLOR	Sets bar color.	0	color value
PBM_SETBKCOLOR	Sets background color.	0	color value

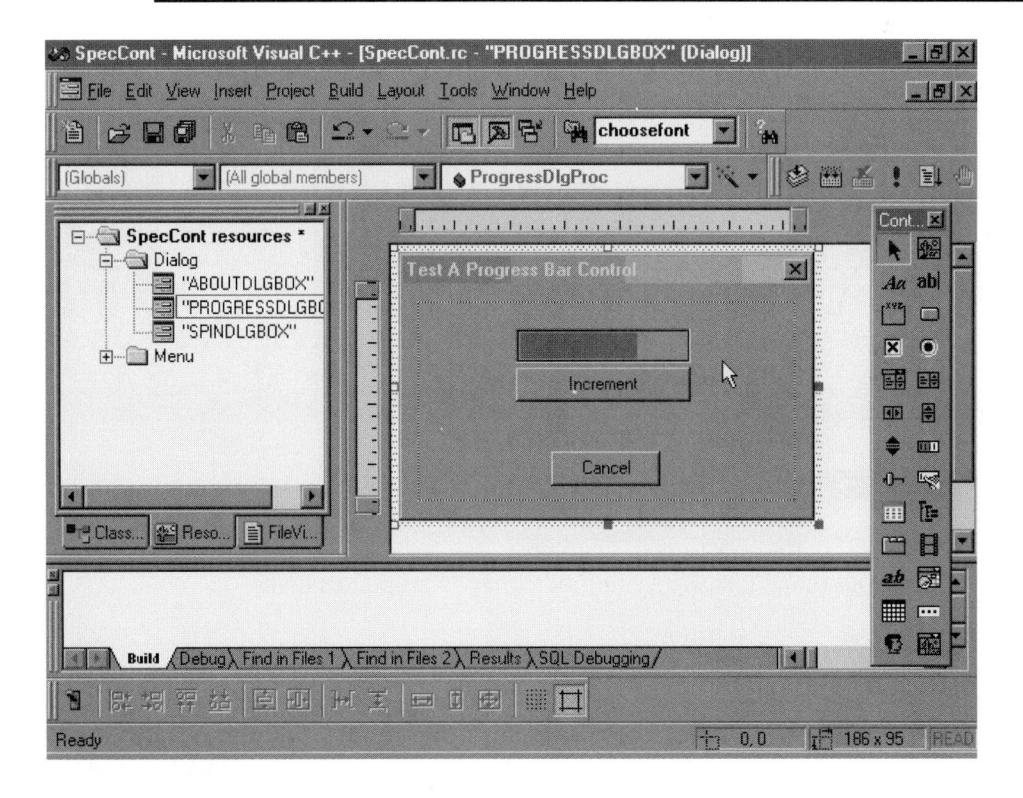

Figure 12-6 *A progress control is placed in a dialog box.*

Messages are usually sent to the progress control with the **SendDlgItemMessage()** function.

Figure 12-6 shows a progress control placed in a dialog box while in the Resource Editor.

Figure 12-7 shows progress bar properties that can be set during the design phase of the dialog box.

Chapter 12 • Special Controls and Dialog Boxes

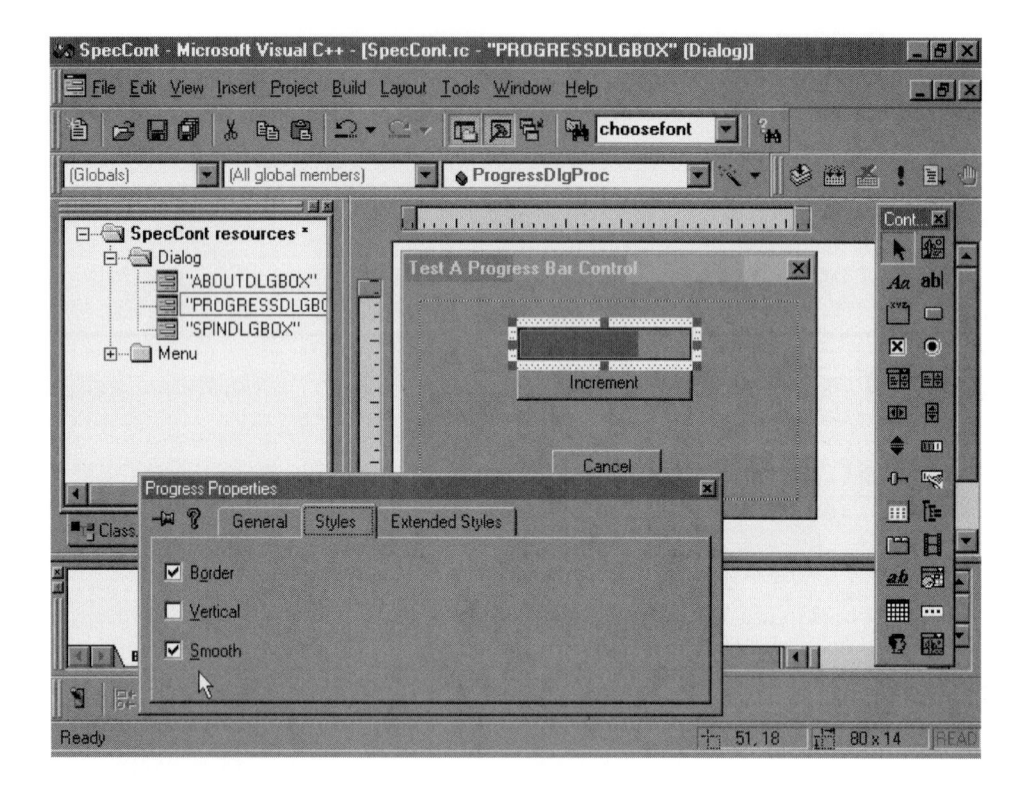

Figure 12-7 *Several progress control properties are set.*

Be sure to pay attention to the resource script file. You'll see how the Resource Editor specifies the control's properties there.

Project Code

The SpecCont project uses several files in addition to the project file. The resource script file contains the constants selected by the Resource Editor for the menu, dialog box, and control IDs. The following listing is an edited version of the resource.h header file for this project.

```
//{{NO_DEPENDENCIES}}
// Microsoft Developer Studio generated include file.
// Used by SpecCont.rc
//
#define IDD_DIALOG1                     101
#define IDC_INTEGER                     1000
#define IDC_SPIN1                       1013
#define IDC_PROGRESS1                   1014
#define IDC_INCREMENT                   1015
#define ID_CONTROLS_PROGRESS            40001
```

```
#define ID_CONTROLS_INT                 40002
#define ID_HELP_ABOUT                   40003
#define ID_HELP_EXIT                    40004
       .
       .
       .
```

The resource script file, SpecCont.rc, contains the description of the project's menu and three dialog boxes.

```
//Microsoft Developer Studio generated resource script.
//
#include "resource.h"
     .
     .
     .

/////////////////////////////////////////////////////////
//
// Dialog
//
ABOUTDLGBOX DIALOG DISCARDABLE  0, 0, 186, 90
STYLE DS_MODALFRAME | WS_POPUP | WS_CAPTION | WS_SYSMENU
CAPTION "About Dialog Box"
FONT 8, "MS Sans Serif"
BEGIN
   DEFPUSHBUTTON    "OK",IDOK,71,68,50,14
   CTEXT            "Working with Special Controls",
                    IDC_STATIC,15,10,151,10
   CTEXT            "by",IDC_STATIC,80,25,30,10
   CTEXT            "William H. Murray and Chris H. Pappas",
                    IDC_STATIC,12,43,160,10
END

PROGRESSDLGBOX DIALOGEX 0, 0, 186, 95
STYLE DS_MODALFRAME | WS_POPUP | WS_CAPTION | WS_SYSMENU
CAPTION "Test A Progress Bar Control"
FONT 8, "MS Sans Serif"
BEGIN
   PUSHBUTTON       "Cancel",IDCANCEL,67,68,50,14
   CONTROL          "Progress1",IDC_PROGRESS1,
                    "msctls_progress32",PBS_SMOOTH |
                    WS_BORDER,51,18,80,14,WS_EX_CLIENTEDGE
   PUSHBUTTON       "Increment",IDC_INCREMENT,51,34,80,14
END

SPINDLGBOX DIALOG DISCARDABLE  0, 0, 279, 95
STYLE DS_MODALFRAME | WS_POPUP | WS_CAPTION | WS_SYSMENU
CAPTION "Test a Spin Control"
FONT 8, "MS Sans Serif"
BEGIN
   DEFPUSHBUTTON    "OK",IDOK,83,62,50,14
```

```
    PUSHBUTTON        "Cancel",IDCANCEL,147,62,50,14
    CTEXT             "Set the Spin Control for the relative
                      size of the graphics object",
                      IDC_STATIC,15,5,248,12
    EDITTEXT          IDC_INTEGER,101,31,78,15,
                      ES_CENTER | ES_AUTOHSCROLL
    CONTROL           "Spin1",IDC_SPIN1,"msctls_updown32",
                      UDS_SETBUDDYINT | UDS_ALIGNRIGHT |
                      UDS_AUTOBUDDY | UDS_ARROWKEYS |
                      UDS_HOTTRACK,191,30,11,14
END
        .
        .
        .
//////////////////////////////////////////////////////////
//
// Menu
//
CONTROLMENU MENU DISCARDABLE
BEGIN
    POPUP "&Controls"
    BEGIN
        MENUITEM "&Progress Bar Control...",  ID_CONTROLS_PROGRESS
        MENUITEM "&Spin Control...",          ID_CONTROLS_INT
    END
    POPUP "&Help"
    BEGIN
        MENUITEM "&About...",                 ID_HELP_ABOUT
        MENUITEM "&Exit",                     ID_HELP_EXIT
    END
END
        .
        .
        .
```

Be sure to examine the UDS_ and PBS_ style constants contained in the SpecCont.rc script file for the PROGRESSDLGBOX and SPINDLGBOX descriptions. Remember, these style constants, along with all of the text in this file, are returned by the Resource Editor after the controls, menus, and dialog boxes are added in the graphical environment. The UDS_ and PBS_ constants are determined by the control styles selected by the designer.

The SpecCont.cpp source code file is provided in the next listing. There is some interesting code that should catch your attention immediately.

```
//
// SpecCont.cpp
// Application demonstrates how to use a few special
// controls for controlling a Windows application.
// Copyright (c) William H. Murray and Chris H. Pappas, 1999
//
```

```
#include <windows.h>
#include <commctrl.h>
#include "resource.h"

HINSTANCE hInst;

LRESULT CALLBACK WndProc(HWND,UINT,WPARAM,LPARAM);
BOOL CALLBACK AboutDlgProc(HWND,UINT,WPARAM,LPARAM);
BOOL CALLBACK ProgressDlgProc(HWND,UINT,WPARAM,LPARAM);
BOOL CALLBACK SpinDlgProc(HWND,UINT,WPARAM,LPARAM);

char szProgName[]="ProgName";
char szApplName[]="ControlMenu";
char screentext[20]="Testing Controls:";
int idelta;

int WINAPI WinMain(HINSTANCE hInst,HINSTANCE hPreInst,
                   LPSTR lpszCmdLine,int nCmdShow)
{
  HWND hWnd;
  MSG  lpMsg;
  WNDCLASS wcApp;

  wcApp.lpszClassName=szProgName;
  wcApp.hInstance    =hInst;
  wcApp.lpfnWndProc  =WndProc;
  wcApp.hCursor      =LoadCursor(NULL,IDC_ARROW);
  wcApp.hIcon        =0;
  wcApp.lpszMenuName =szApplName;
  wcApp.hbrBackground=(HBRUSH) GetStockObject(WHITE_BRUSH);
  wcApp.style        =CS_HREDRAW|CS_VREDRAW;
  wcApp.cbClsExtra   =0;
  wcApp.cbWndExtra   =0;
  if (!RegisterClass (&wcApp))
    return 0;

  hWnd=CreateWindow(szProgName,
                    "Working with Special Controls",
                    WS_OVERLAPPEDWINDOW,CW_USEDEFAULT,
                    CW_USEDEFAULT,CW_USEDEFAULT,
                    CW_USEDEFAULT,(HWND)NULL,(HMENU)NULL,
                    hInst,(LPSTR)NULL);
  ShowWindow(hWnd,nCmdShow);
  UpdateWindow(hWnd);
  while (GetMessage(&lpMsg,0,0,0)) {
    TranslateMessage(&lpMsg);
    DispatchMessage(&lpMsg);
  }
  return(lpMsg.wParam);
}
```

```c
// Process the Progress dialog box control selection
BOOL CALLBACK ProgressDlgProc(HWND hDlg,UINT messg,
                              WPARAM wParam,LPARAM lParam)
{
  INITCOMMONCONTROLSEX icex;
  icex.dwSize=sizeof(icex);
  // supported controls for this application
  icex.dwICC=ICC_PROGRESS_CLASS;
  // initialize use of controls
  InitCommonControlsEx(&icex);

  switch (messg) {
    case WM_INITDIALOG:
      // Set initial progress control range to 0-200
      SendDlgItemMessage(hDlg,IDC_PROGRESS1,PBM_SETRANGE,0,
                        (LPARAM) MAKELONG(0,200));
      // Set initial progress control position to 5
      SendDlgItemMessage(hDlg,IDC_PROGRESS1,PBM_SETPOS,
                        (WPARAM) 5,0);
      // Set progress control step size to 5
      SendDlgItemMessage(hDlg,IDC_PROGRESS1,PBM_SETSTEP,
                        (WPARAM) 5,0);
      // Set progress control bar color to green.
      SendDlgItemMessage(hDlg,IDC_PROGRESS1,PBM_SETBARCOLOR,
                        0,(LPARAM) RGB(0,255,0));
      // Set progress control background to yellow.
      SendDlgItemMessage(hDlg,IDC_PROGRESS1,PBM_SETBKCOLOR,
                        0,(LPARAM) RGB(255,255,0));
      break;

    case WM_COMMAND:
      switch (LOWORD(wParam)) {
        case IDC_INCREMENT:
          // Increment the progress bar by one step
          SendDlgItemMessage(hDlg,IDC_PROGRESS1,PBM_STEPIT,
                            0,0);
          break;
        case IDCANCEL:
          EndDialog(hDlg,FALSE);
          break;
        default:
          return FALSE;
      }
      break;
    default:
      return FALSE;
  }
  return TRUE;
}
```

Investigating the Spin and Progress Bar Common Controls

```
// Process the Spin dialog box control selection
BOOL CALLBACK SpinDlgProc(HWND hDlg,UINT messg,
                          WPARAM wParam,LPARAM lParam)
{
  INITCOMMONCONTROLSEX icex;
  icex.dwSize=sizeof(icex);
  // supported controls for this application
  icex.dwICC= ICC_UPDOWN_CLASS;
  // initialize use of controls
  InitCommonControlsEx(&icex);

  switch (messg) {
    case WM_INITDIALOG:
      // initialize spin control for edit control
      // which is already identified as an
      // autobuddy.
      // Set range of spin control to 0-200
      SendDlgItemMessage(hDlg,IDC_SPIN1,UDM_SETRANGE,0,
                         MAKELONG(200,0));
      // Set initial position of spin control to 100
      SendDlgItemMessage(hDlg,IDC_SPIN1,UDM_SETPOS,0,
                         MAKELONG(100,0));
      break;
    case WM_COMMAND:
      switch (LOWORD(wParam)) {
        case IDOK:
          // Get spin control data from edit box control
          idelta=GetDlgItemInt(hDlg,IDC_INTEGER,NULL,0);
          EndDialog(hDlg,TRUE);
          break;
        case IDCANCEL:
          EndDialog(hDlg,FALSE);
          break;
        default:
          return FALSE;
      }
      break;
    default:
      return FALSE;
  }
  return TRUE;
}

// Process the About dialog box control selection
BOOL CALLBACK AboutDlgProc(HWND hDlg,UINT messg,
                           WPARAM wParam,LPARAM lParam)
{
  switch (messg) {
    case WM_INITDIALOG:
      break;
```

```
      case WM_COMMAND:
        switch (LOWORD(wParam)) {
          case IDOK:
            EndDialog(hDlg,0);
            break;
          default:
            return FALSE;
        }
        break;
      default:
        return FALSE;
  }
  return TRUE;
}

LRESULT CALLBACK WndProc(HWND hWnd,UINT messg,
                         WPARAM wParam,LPARAM lParam)
{
  HDC hdc;
  PAINTSTRUCT ps;
  static HPEN hPen;

  switch (messg)
  {
    // Process the menu item selection
    case WM_COMMAND:
      switch (LOWORD(wParam)) {
        // Draw the Progress dialog box
        case ID_CONTROLS_PROGRESS:
          DialogBox(hInst,"ProgressDlgBox",hWnd,
                    (DLGPROC)ProgressDlgProc);
          InvalidateRect(hWnd,NULL,TRUE);
          UpdateWindow(hWnd);
          break;
        // Draw the Spin dialog box
        case ID_CONTROLS_INT:
          DialogBox(hInst,"SpinDlgBox",hWnd,
                    (DLGPROC)SpinDlgProc);
          InvalidateRect(hWnd,NULL,TRUE);
          UpdateWindow(hWnd);
          break;
        // Draw the About dialog box
        case ID_HELP_ABOUT:
          DialogBox(hInst,"AboutDlgBox",hWnd,
                    (DLGPROC)AboutDlgProc);
          break;
        // End the application
        case ID_HELP_EXIT:
          SendMessage(hWnd,WM_CLOSE,0,0L);
          break;
```

```
      default:
        break;
    }
    break;

  case WM_PAINT:
    hdc=BeginPaint(hWnd,&ps);

    // Create a yellow pen, 15 pixels wide
    hPen=CreatePen(PS_SOLID,15,RGB(255,255,0));
    SelectObject(hdc,hPen);

    // Draw a circle whose size is relative to
    // the value returned by the Spin Control.
    Ellipse(hdc,320-idelta,240-idelta,
            320+idelta,240+idelta);
    TextOut(hdc,100,100,screentext,strlen(screentext));

    ValidateRect(hWnd,NULL);
    EndPaint(hWnd,&ps);
    break;

  case WM_DESTROY:
    DeleteObject(hPen);
    PostQuitMessage(0);
    break;
  default:
    return(DefWindowProc(hWnd,messg,wParam,lParam));
    break;
  }
  return(0);
}
```

If you caught the reference to the INITCOMMONCONTROLSEX structure under the **ProgressDlgProc()** or **SpinDlgProc()** you discovered the really unique feature in this project. You'll learn about this structure and functions such as **InitCommonControlsEx()** in the next section of this chapter.

Unique Features

This application makes use of common controls that are dragged and dropped from the toolbar. As such, it is no longer necessary to use the **Create...()** function to create and place a common control. Common controls available in the Resource Editor's Toolbar can use the Comctl32.dll dynamic link library (DLL) in conjunction with the INITCOMMONCONTROLSEX structure and the **InitCommonControlEx()** function.

Imagine that you have created an application just like this one. You have created a dialog box with a spin control and a progress control. The question becomes, How do I communicate with these controls as I never created them directly? The answer is through the previously mentioned structure and function call.

The INITCOMMONCONTROLSEX structure is used in both the **ProgressDlgProc()** and the **SpinDlgProc()** of this application. The structure contains two members.

```
typedef struct tagINITCOMMONCONTROLSEX {
  DWORD dwSize;
  DWORD dwICC;
} INITCOMMONCONTROLSEX, *LPINITCOMMONCONTROLSEX;
```

The structure is used in conjunction with the **InitCommonControlsEx()** function to load common control classes from the Comctl32.dll DLL. Here the dwSize member holds the size of the structure in bytes. The dwICC member holds a set of flags used to indicate which common control classes are loaded from the DLL. Table 12.5 shows the flag constants and gives a brief description of each.

Table 12.5 INITCOMMONCONTROLSEX structure flag constants.

Flag Constant	Description
ICC_ANIMATE_CLASS	Loads the animate control class.
ICC_BAR_CLASSES	Loads the toolbar, status bar, tooltip, and trackbar control classes.
ICC_COOL_CLASSES	Loads the rebar control class.
ICC_DATE_CLASSES	Loads the date and time picker control class.
ICC_HOTKEY_CLASS	Loads the hot key control class.
ICC_INTERNET_CLASSES	Loads the IP address class.
ICC_LISTVIEW_CLASSES	Loads the list view and header control classes. Loads the list view and header control classes.
ICC_PAGESCROLLER_CLASS	Loads the pager control class.
ICC_PROGRESS_CLASS	Loads the progress bar control class.
ICC_TAB_CLASSES	Loads the tab and tooltip control classes.
ICC_TREEVIEW_CLASSES	Loads the tree view and tooltip control classes.
ICC_UPDOWN_CLASS	Loads the up-down control class.
ICC_USEREX_CLASSES	Loads the ComboBoxEx class.
ICC_WIN95_CLASSES	Loads the animate control, header, hot key, list view, progress bar, status bar, tab, toolbar, tooltip, trackbar, tree view, and up-down control classes.

The **InitCommonControlsEx()** function is used to register specific common control classes from the common control DLL. The function uses the lpInitCtrls parameter to point to the address of the INITCOMMONCONTROL-SEX structure containing information on which control classes will be registered. Multiple calls using this function produce cumulative control registrations.

As an example for our discussion, we'll look specifically at the **SpinDlgProc()** from the SpecCont.cpp source code file.

The first piece of code in **SpinDlgProc()** sets the size of the structure and registers the spin control (also known as an *up-down control*).

```
INITCOMMONCONTROLSEX icex;
  icex.dwSize=sizeof(icex);
  // supported controls for this application
  icex.dwICC= ICC_UPDOWN_CLASS;
  // initialize use of controls
  InitCommonControlsEx(&icex);
```

Remember that the control has already been created in the dialog box by dragging, dropping, and sizing it while in the Resource Editor. This process registers the control for use in the application.

Communication with a control is now carried out with calls to functions such as **SendDlgItemMessage()**. With this function, it is possible to initialize the control's range, step, and so on. Specifically, those values whose messages were shown earlier in Tables 12.2 and 12.4, starting with UDM_ and PBM_ for the controls in this application.

Here is how the range of the spin control is set to 0 to 200 with the **SendDlgItemMessage()** function.

```
 // Set range of spin control to 0-200
SendDlgItemMessage(hDlg,IDC_SPIN1,UDM_SETRANGE,0,
            MAKELONG(200,0));
```

The fourth and fifth parameters of the **SendDlgItemMessage()** refer to the wParam and lParam values shown earlier in Table 12.2. To set the range for the control, the handle of the dialog box containing the control (hDlg), the ID value for the spin control itself (IDC_SPIN1), the message (UDM_SETRANGE), and the values for wParam and lParam must be sent. The wParam value for this message is 0 and the lParam value is a **long**, formed by combining 200 and 0 into a **long** value.

That's all there is to it. See if you can figure out how the initial position is set to 100 (halfway between the 0 and 200 values in the range) with the following function call.

```
 // Set initial position of spin control to 100
SendDlgItemMessage(hDlg,IDC_SPIN1,UDM_SETPOS,0,
            MAKELONG(100,0));
```

When the spin control is in use, data can be returned with a call to the **GetDlgItemInt()** function.

```
case IDOK:
  // Get spin control data from edit box control
  idelta=GetDlgItemInt(hDlg,IDC_INTEGER,NULL,0);
  EndDialog(hDlg,TRUE);
  break;
     .
     .
     .
```

Wait a minute. What kind of trick is this? We just said that "spin control data can be obtained...," but then used a function call to get data from the edit box control. You know it's the edit box control because IDC_INTEGER is a constant associated with that control. What gives? Well, back when you designed the spin control, you specified that the edit box control was to be the autobuddy of the spin control. You did this in the Resource Editor by setting various properties for the spin control.

Here is a small portion of the SpecCont.rc resource script file.

```
CTEXT           "Set the Spin Control for the relative
                size of the graphics object",
                IDC_STATIC,15,5,248,12
EDITTEXT        IDC_INTEGER,101,31,78,15,
                ES_CENTER | ES_AUTOHSCROLL
CONTROL         "Spin1",IDC_SPIN1,"msctls_updown32",
                UDS_SETBUDDYINT | UDS_ALIGNRIGHT |
                UDS_AUTOBUDDY | UDS_ARROWKEYS |
                UDS_HOTTRACK,191,30,11,14
```

We're sure you can find the UDS_AUTOBUDDY constant in the previous listing. The question is, How is the association made? When UDS_AUTOBUDDY is used, the spin control is associated with the previously created edit box control. That means that if you wanted to create multiple spin controls with edit boxes set as their autobuddy, you would need to create an edit box control, then the spin control, then another edit box control, then the final spin control.

Figure 12–8 shows the spin control being used in the application's dialog box.

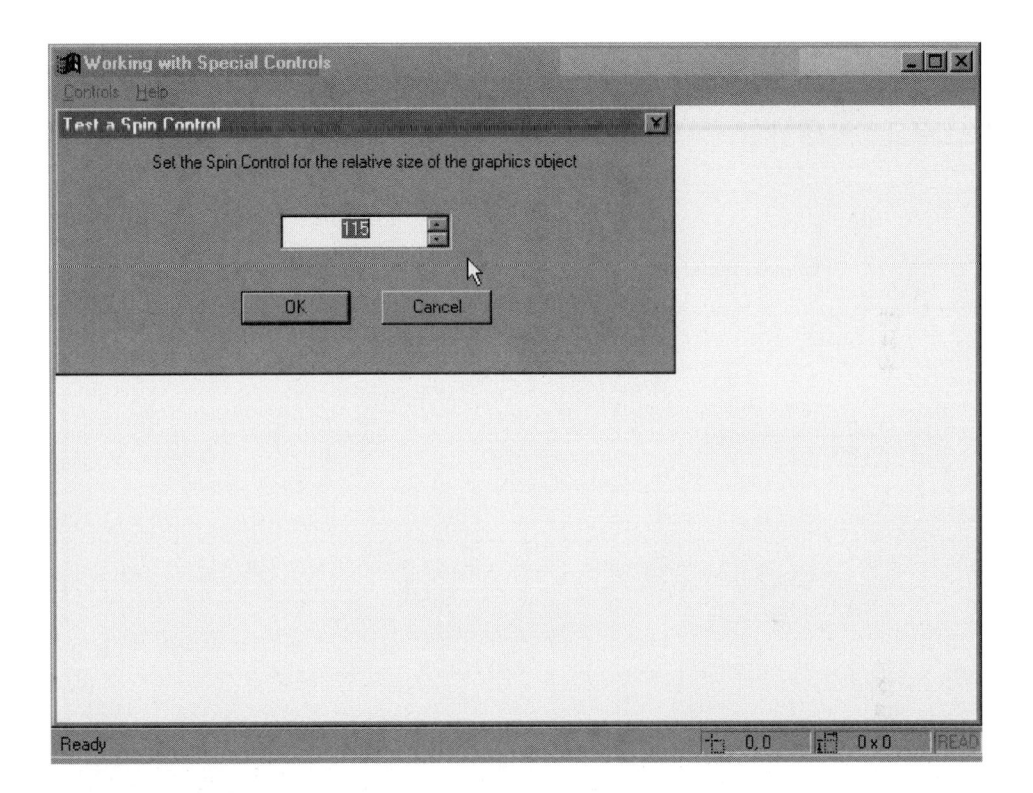

Investigating the Spin and Progress Bar Common Controls

Figure 12-8 *The spin control is associated with the edit box control.*

Compare Figure 12–8 to Figure 12–4. Who moved the spin control or the edit box control? The Resource Editor moved the two controls together because we also requested a UDS_ALIGNRIGHT property to be set. The Resource Editor then aligned the spin control on the right edge of the edit box control.

Lest we forget, the value being returned from the spin control is used to size a graphics shape in the window. Figure 12–9 shows the application's window after the spin control has been incremented to a specific value.

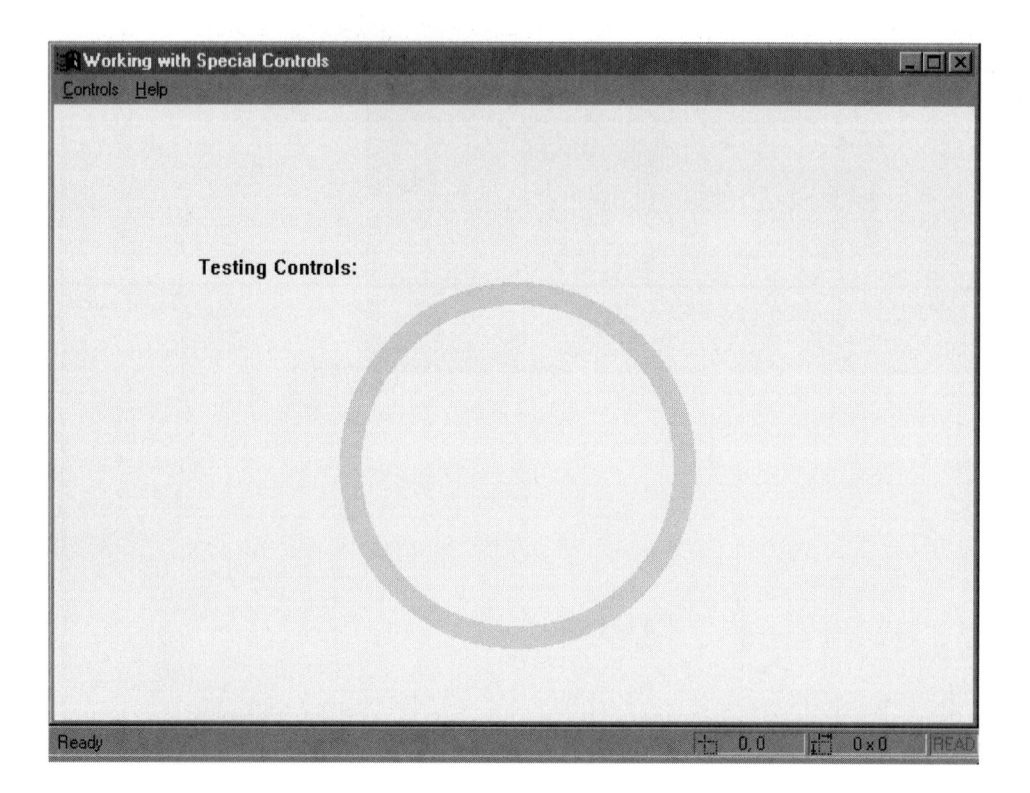

Figure 12-9 *The output to the window after the spin control has been set to a specific value.*

Figure 12–10 shows the progress bar after it has been incremented.

If you try this application, you'll notice that the color of the progress bar and the background color of the bar have been altered, in addition to the initializing of the bar's range and step values.

You'll find most of the common controls in the Toolbox just as easy to use. Remember to use the compiler's Help facilities and the information contained in the commctrl.h header file to help you with specific constants and functions.

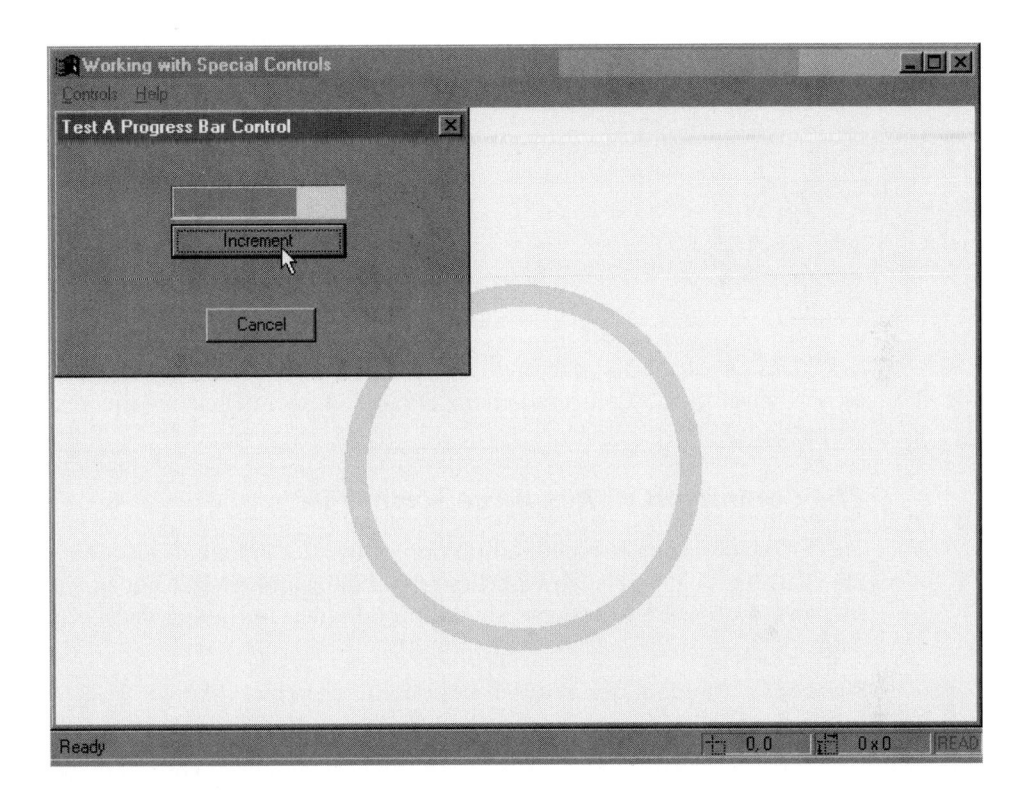

Figure 12-10 *The progress bar in another contol that you can experiment with.*

The Common Font Dialog Box

In the previous chapter, you learned how to design and implement your own dialog boxes. There is a group of predefined dialog boxes, called *common dialog boxes*, that can be used easily. By using common dialog boxes, the programmer saves design time. However, the user also wins. Common dialog boxes retain a consistent look and feel across any application.

In the following project, named *CommFont*, a common font dialog box will be used that will allow the selection of font resources in an application.

The resource.h Header File

Here is an edited portion of the resource.h header file used by the CommFont application. The ID values are generated by the Resource Editor after all resources for the application have been designed.

```
//{{NO_DEPENDENCIES}}
// Microsoft Developer Studio generated include file.
// Used by CommFont.rc
//
#define IDR_MENU1                       101
#define ID_HELP_ABOUT                   40001
#define ID_HELP_EXIT                    40002
#define ID_FONTSELECTOR_FONT            40003
      .
      .
      .
```

This application apparently uses a menu with one menu item identified as a "fontselecto." We'll learn more about this menu item in the resource script file.

The CommFont.rc Resource Script File

The following listing is an edited portion of the CommFont.rc resource script file. This file is generated by the Resource Editor and should not be entered by hand. Rather, each resource should be designed in the graphical environment.

```
//Microsoft Developer Studio generated resource script.
//
#include "resource.h"
      .
      .
/////////////////////////////////////////////////////////////
//
// Menu
//
FontMenu MENU DISCARDABLE
BEGIN
  POPUP "&Font-Selector"
  BEGIN
    MENUITEM "&Pick A Font",     ID_FONTSELECTOR_FONT
  END
  POPUP "&Help"
  BEGIN
    MENUITEM "&About...",        ID_HELP_ABOUT
    MENUITEM "&Exit",            ID_HELP_EXIT
  END
END
      .
      .
/////////////////////////////////////////////////////////////
//
```

```
// Dialog
//
AboutDlgBox DIALOG DISCARDABLE  0, 0, 186, 95
STYLE DS_MODALFRAME | WS_POPUP | WS_CAPTION | WS_SYSMENU
CAPTION "About Dialog Box"
FONT 8, "MS Sans Serif"
BEGIN
    DEFPUSHBUTTON   "OK",IDOK,69,62,50,14
    CTEXT           "Using the Common Font Dialog Box",
                    IDC_STATIC,15,14,155,12
    CTEXT           "by",IDC_STATIC,86,30,20,12
    CTEXT           "William H. Murray and Chris H. Pappas",
                    IDC_STATIC,24,47,138,9
END
     .
     .
     .
```

As you can see from this listing, the application will use a menu and an About dialog box, in addition to the common font dialog box. But wait—where was the description for the common dialog box? That's right—it's predefined and does not appear in the resource script file. Actually, the commdlg.h header file contains information on all of the common dialog boxes whose specifications are found in the comdlg32.lib library.

The CommFont.cpp Source Code

The following listing contains all of the source code for the CommFont.cpp application. Examine the code carefully and try and detect the code related directly to the common font dialog box implementation.

```
//
// CommFont.cpp
// This application illustrates how you can take
// advantage of the Common Font Dialog Box to
// define a font family, style, size and so on.
// Copyright (c) William H. Murray and Chris H. Pappas, 1999
//

#include <windows.h>
#include <commdlg.h>   // add common dialog box resources
#include "resource.h"
HINSTANCE hInst;

LRESULT CALLBACK WndProc(HWND,UINT,WPARAM,LPARAM);
BOOL CALLBACK AboutDlgProc(HWND,UINT,WPARAM,LPARAM);

char szProgName[]="ProgName";
```

```
char szApplName[]="FontMenu";

int WINAPI WinMain(HINSTANCE hInst,HINSTANCE hPreInst,
                   LPSTR lpszCmdLine,int nCmdShow)
{
  HWND hWnd;
  MSG  lpMsg;
  WNDCLASS wcApp;

  wcApp.lpszClassName=szProgName;
  wcApp.hInstance    =hInst;
  wcApp.lpfnWndProc  =WndProc;
  wcApp.hCursor      =LoadCursor(NULL,IDC_ARROW);
  wcApp.hIcon        =0;
  wcApp.lpszMenuName =szApplName;
  wcApp.hbrBackground=(HBRUSH) GetStockObject(WHITE_BRUSH);
  wcApp.style        =CS_HREDRAW|CS_VREDRAW;
  wcApp.cbClsExtra   =0;
  wcApp.cbWndExtra   =0;
  if (!RegisterClass (&wcApp))
    return 0;

  hWnd=CreateWindow(szProgName,"The Common Font Dialog Box",
                    WS_OVERLAPPEDWINDOW,CW_USEDEFAULT,
                    CW_USEDEFAULT,CW_USEDEFAULT,
                    CW_USEDEFAULT,(HWND)NULL,(HMENU)NULL,
                    hInst,(LPSTR)NULL);
  ShowWindow(hWnd,nCmdShow);
  UpdateWindow(hWnd);
  while (GetMessage(&lpMsg,0,0,0)) {
    TranslateMessage(&lpMsg);
    DispatchMessage(&lpMsg);
  }
  return(lpMsg.wParam);
}


// Process the About dialog box control selection
BOOL CALLBACK AboutDlgProc(HWND hDlg,UINT messg,
                           WPARAM wParam,LPARAM lParam)
{
  switch (messg) {
    case WM_INITDIALOG:
      break;
    case WM_COMMAND:
      switch (LOWORD(wParam)) {
        case IDOK:
          EndDialog(hDlg,0);
          break;
        default:
```

```
          return FALSE;
        }
        break;
      default:
        return FALSE;
  }
  return TRUE;
}

LRESULT CALLBACK WndProc(HWND hWnd,UINT messg,
                         WPARAM wParam,LPARAM lParam)
{
  HDC hdc;
  PAINTSTRUCT ps;
  static HPEN hNPen;
  static HFONT hNFont;
  static CHOOSEFONT cf;
  static LOGFONT lf;
  static iInc;

  switch (messg)
  {
    case WM_CREATE:
      //initial values for Common Font Dialog Box
      GetObject(GetStockObject(SYSTEM_FONT),
              sizeof(LOGFONT),(LPSTR) &lf);
      cf.Flags=CF_EFFECTS|CF_INITTOLOGFONTSTRUCT|
              CF_SCREENFONTS;
      cf.hwndOwner=hWnd;
      cf.lpLogFont=&lf;
      cf.lStructSize=sizeof(CHOOSEFONT);
      break;

    // Process the menu item selection
    case WM_COMMAND:
      switch (LOWORD(wParam)) {
        // Draw the Common Font Dialog Box
        case ID_FONTSELECTOR_FONT:
          if (ChooseFont(&cf))
            InvalidateRect(hWnd,NULL,TRUE);
          break;
        // Draw the About dialog box
        case ID_HELP_ABOUT:
          DialogBox(hInst,"AboutDlgBox",hWnd,
                  (DLGPROC)AboutDlgProc);
          break;
        // End the application
        case ID_HELP_EXIT:
          SendMessage(hWnd,WM_CLOSE,0,0L);
          break;
```

```
        default:
          break;
      }
      break;

    case WM_PAINT:
      hdc=BeginPaint(hWnd,&ps);

      // Create a font based on the Common
      // Font Dialog Box selection
      hNFont=CreateFontIndirect(&lf);
      SelectObject(hdc,hNFont);
      SetTextColor(hdc,cf.rgbColors);

      // Create a magenta pen
      hNPen=CreatePen(PS_SOLID,4,RGB(255,0,255));
      SelectObject(hdc,hNPen);

        // Draw some graphics to the window
        for (iInc=200; iInc>10; iInc-=20)
          Ellipse(hdc,320-iInc,300-iInc,320+iInc,300+iInc);

      // Draw some fancy text to the window
      // based upon the user's selection.
      TextOut(hdc,140,40,"Draw some fancy text",20);

      ValidateRect(hWnd,NULL);
      EndPaint(hWnd,&ps);
      break;

    case WM_DESTROY:
      DeleteObject(hNPen);
      PostQuitMessage(0);
      break;

    default:
      return(DefWindowProc(hWnd,messg,wParam,lParam));
      break;
  }
  return(0);
}
```

You should notice that **AboutDlgProc** is used to define the operation of the About box. However, what is *still* missing? That's correct, there is no description of the common font dialog box. As a matter of fact, you'll know nothing about the appearance of this dialog box until you successfully implement the code in your application! Well, that is unless you cheat and find it in your Visual C++ compiler's Help facilities!

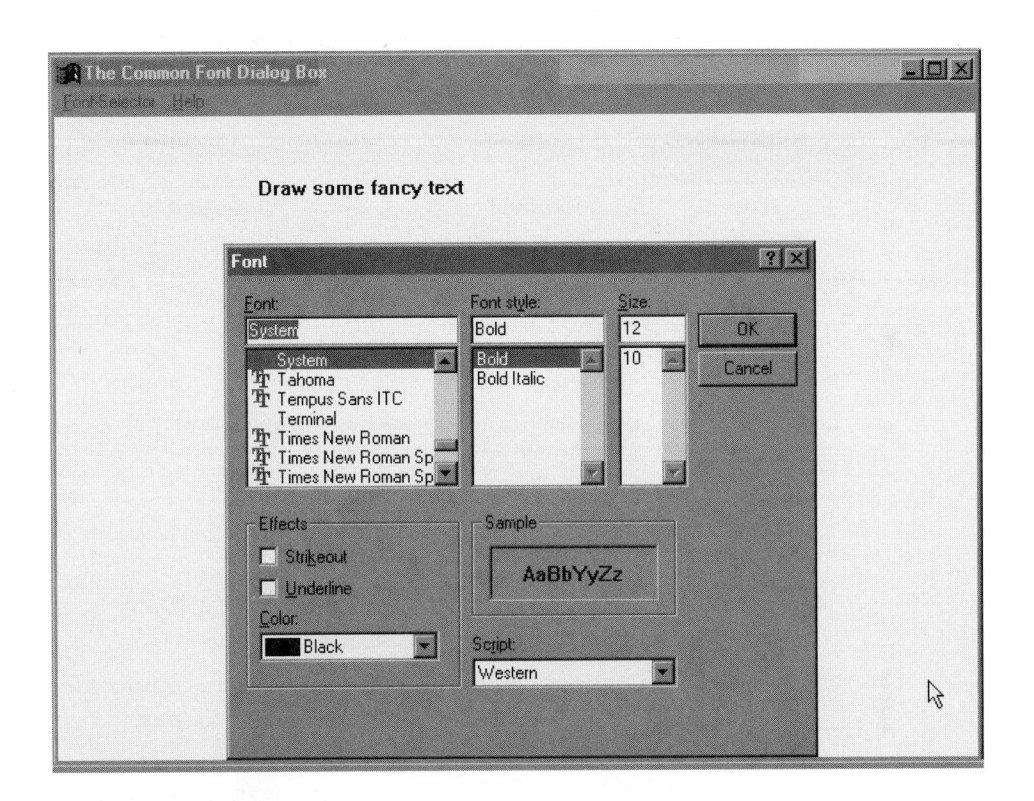

Figure 12-11   *A common font dialog box is used to select font resources.*

UNIQUE SOURCE CODE

As we have already mentioned, information concerning the common font dialog box, as well as information on all common dialog boxes, included in the commdlg.h header file. You should be able to locate this file in your compiler's include subdirectory. Examine the commdlg.h header file and notice the variety of common dialog boxes you can select. You may find that printing a copy of the commdlg.h header file is useful, but be warned—it is a very long document.

Figure 12–11 shows the initial common font dialog box.

The programming interface to the common font dialog box is through the use of the CHOOSEFONT structure and by calling the **ChooseFont()** function. You'll see in the WM_PAINT message handler that we use a tag name of *cf* and associate it with the CHOOSEFONT structure.

See if you can locate the following description of the **ChooseFont()** function in the commdlg.h header file:

```
BOOL CALLBACK ChooseFont(LPCHOOSEFONT);
```

The CHOOSEFONT structure allows a number of member values to be set or read, as shown in Table 12.6.

Table 12.6 CHOOSEFONT types, members, and descriptions.

Type	Member	Description
DWORD	lStructSize	structure size
HWND	hwndOwner	owner's window handle
HDC	hDC	printer DC or NULL
LPLOGFONT	lpLogFont	printer to a LOGFONT struct
int	iPointSize	10*size of font in points
DWORD	Flags	enumerates type flags
COLORREF	rgbColors	text color returned
LPARAM	lCustData	data passed to hook fn.
LPCFHOOKPROC	lpfnHook	printer to hook function
LPCSTR	lpTemplateName	custom template name
HINSTANCE	hInstance	instance handle of executable that contains custom dialog template
LPSTR	lpszStyle	style field returned here, must be LF_FACESIZE or larger
WORD	nFontType	same value reported to EnumFonts with extra FONTTYPE_ bits added
int	nSizeMin	minimum pt size allowed if CF_LIMITSIZE used
int	nSizeMax	max pt size allowed if CF_LIMITSIZE used

This application makes use of the **GetStockObject()** function to obtain the handle for the Windows SYSTEM_FONT. The **GetObject()** function uses the handle returned by **GetStockObject()**, along with the size of the LOGFONT structure and the address of the tag variable, *lf*, associated with the structure.

```
GetObject(GetStockObject(DEVICE_DEFAULT_FONT),
      sizeof(LOGFONT),(LPSTR) &lf);
```

WM_CREATE messages are responsible for initializing various members of the CHOOSEFONT structure.

```
cf.Flags=CF_EFFECTS|CF_INITTOLOGFONTSTRUCT|
```

```
                CF_SCREENFONTS;
cf.hwndOwner=hWnd;
cf.lpLogFont=&lf;
cf.lStructSize=sizeof(CHOOSEFONT);
```

The *cf.Flags* member allows various attributes to be applied by logically ORing terms together. For example, CF_EFFECTS allows the **ChooseFont()** function to enable strikeouts, underlines, and color effects. With CF_EFFECTS, it is possible to set the lfStrikOut, lfUnderline, and rgbColors members before calling the **ChooseFont()** function. CF_INITTOLOGFONTSTRUCT states that the LOGFONT structure, pointed to by *lpLogFont*, will initialize the dialog controls. The CF_SCREENFONTS parameter will force the common font dialog box to list just the screen fonts supported by the system. You'll find additional flags described in the Help facility of your Visual C++ compiler.

The *cf.hwndOwner* member value for this application is *hWnd*. The *cf.lpLogFont* member is set to *&lf*. Finally, the *cf.lStructSize* is set to the size of the CHOOSEFONT structure.

The application has initialized numerous values at this point but has not retrieved any font information for the application. Information is returned when a WM_COMMAND message is processed. If the *Pick a Font...* menu item is selected by the user, the **ChooseFont()** function will be called. Now it is possible to obtain the information on a user selected font, font size, font color, and so on.

Figure 12–12 shows one example of font items selected by a user.

When the user clicks on the Okay button, the information from the dialog box is returned to a CHOOSEFONT structure, *cf*. This information will not be utilized until a WM_PAINT message is received.

The values returned by the **ChooseFont()** function assume the default MM_TEXT mapping mode. The selected font is created for the application with a call to **CreateFontIndirect()** and selected with the **SelectObject()** function.

```
hNFont=CreateFontIndirect(&lf);
SelectObject(hdc,hNFont);
```

The color of the font displayed to the screen was set while in the dialog box. This information can now be retrieved and processed with a call to the **SetTextColor()** function.

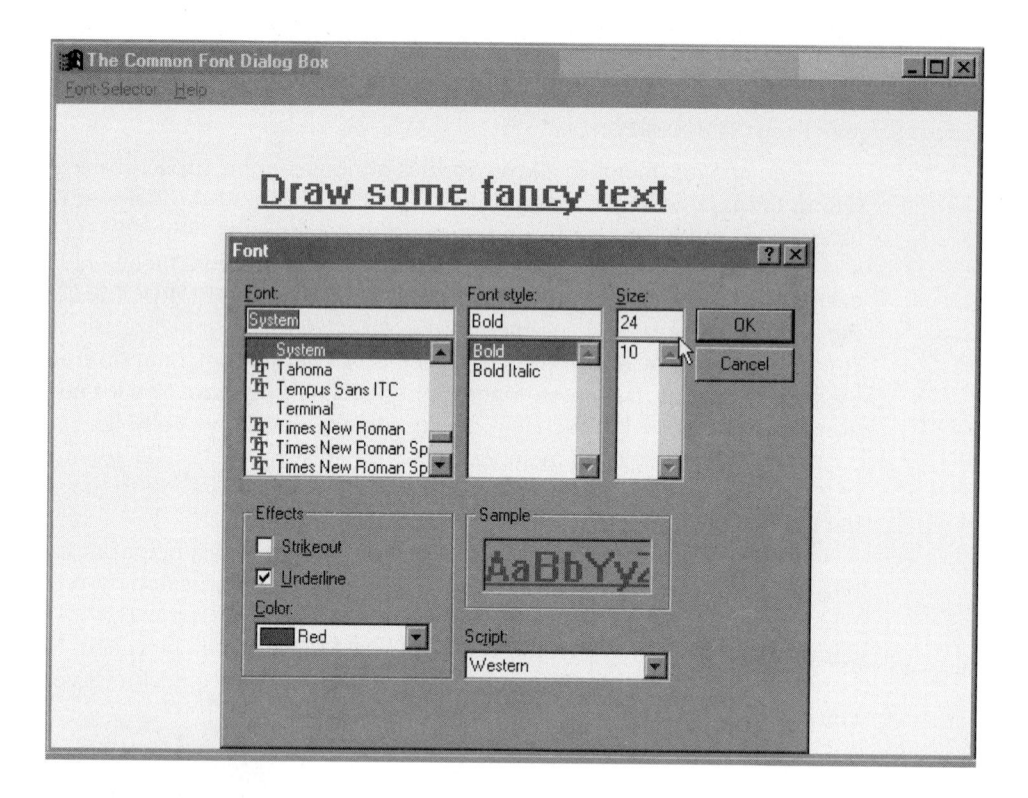

478 Chapter 12 • Special Controls and Dialog Boxes

Figure 12-12 *Various font parameters can be changed with the common font dialog box.*

```
SetTextColor(hdc,cf.rgbColors);
```

String information is then printed to the window with calls to the familiar **TextOut()** function. Figures 12–13 and 12–14 show additional screens produced with the CommFont application.

Now that you've seen how easy it is to use this dialog box, we're sure you'll want to include it in all of your applications involving fonts.

The Common Color Dialog Box

The CommColor project illustrates how it is possible to use a common color selection dialog box to allow users to select colors for pens or brushes. This dialog box is used in a manner similar to that of the common font dialog box discussed in the previous section.

The Common Color Dialog Box   **479**

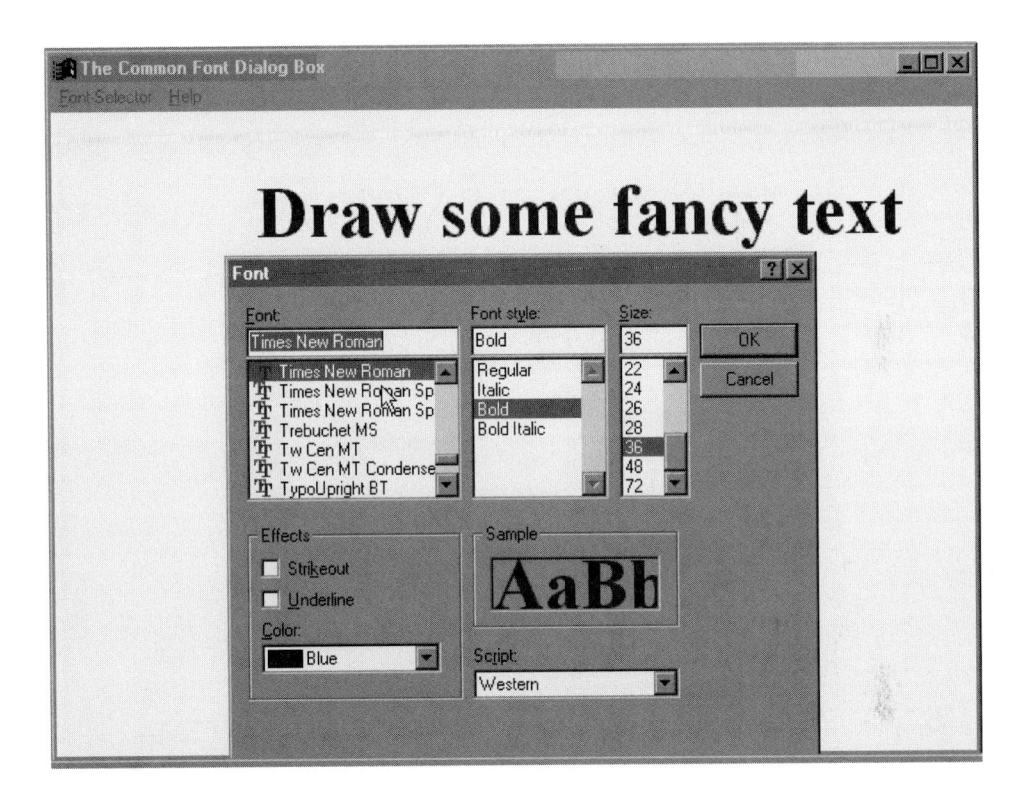

Figure 12-13 *Selecting and using a Times New Roman TrueType font.*

In addition to the project file, this application uses a resource.h header file, resource script file, and source code file. We'll look at important features in each of these files in the following sections.

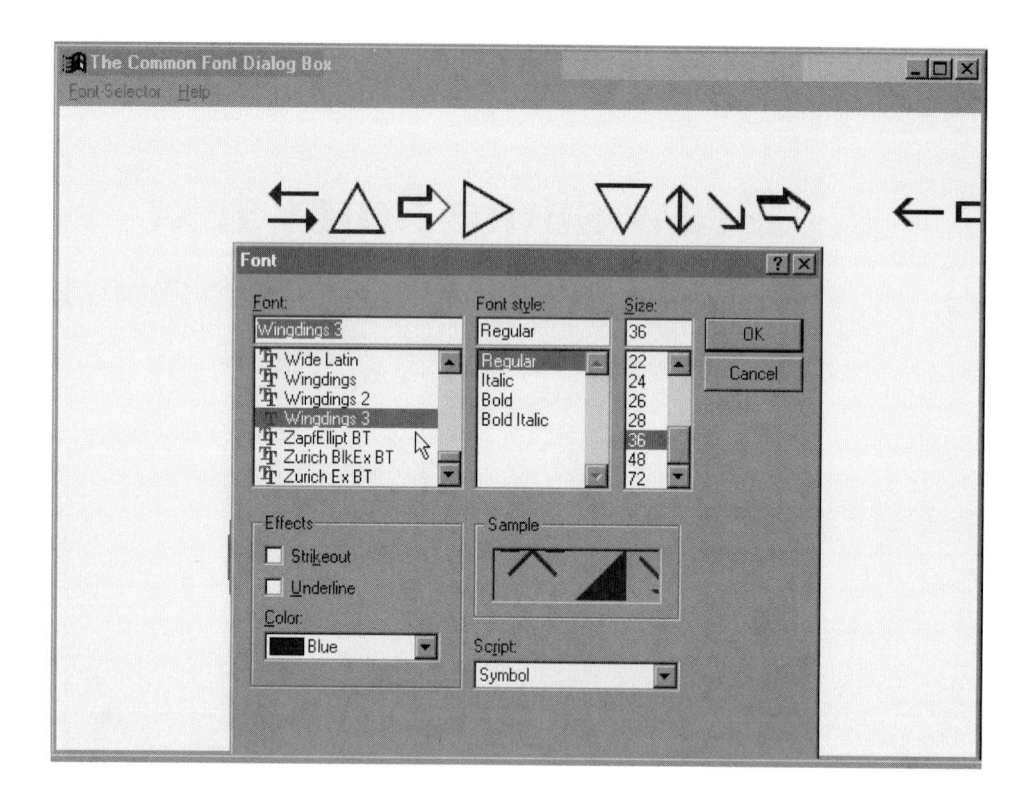

Figure 12-14 *Selecting unique font characteristics for a font.*

The resource.h Header File

The resource.h header file is generated by the Resource Editor. This file contains the ID values used to support the menu items used by the application's menu resource. Here is an edited version of that file, showing three unique ID values for this application.

```
//{{NO_DEPENDENCIES}}
// Microsoft Developer Studio generated include file.
// Used by CommColor.rc
//
#define ID_HELP_ABOUT                   40001
#define ID_HELP_EXIT                    40002
#define ID_COLORSELECTOR_COLOR          40003
     .
     .
     .
```

The ID values for the Help menu are becoming familiar items. The unique ID value used for the color selector menu item is named ID_COLORSELECTOR_COLOR. In the resource script file, discussed in the next section, you'll see how these ID values are used.

The CommColor.rc Resource Script File

The following listing is an edited portion of the CommColor.rc resource script file. Remember that resource script files are generated by the Resource Editor and should not be entered by hand. Each resource should be designed in the graphical environment, letting the Resource Editor generate all resource script code.

```
//Microsoft Developer Studio generated resource script.
//
#include "resource.h"
    .
    .
    .
/////////////////////////////////////////////////////////////
//
// Menu
//

ColorMenu MENU DISCARDABLE
BEGIN
  POPUP "&Color-Selector"
  BEGIN
    MENUITEM "&Pick A Color...",     ID_COLORSELECTOR_COLOR
  END
  POPUP "&Help"
  BEGIN
    MENUITEM "&About...",            ID_HELP_ABOUT
    MENUITEM "&Exit",                ID_HELP_EXIT
  END
END
    .
    .
    .
/////////////////////////////////////////////////////////////
//
// Dialog
//
AboutDlgBox DIALOG DISCARDABLE  0, 0, 186, 95
STYLE DS_MODALFRAME | WS_POPUP | WS_CAPTION | WS_SYSMENU
CAPTION "About Dialog Box"
FONT 8, "MS Sans Serif"
BEGIN
  DEFPUSHBUTTON   "OK",IDOK,69,67,50,14
  CTEXT           "Using the Common Color Dialog Box",
                  IDC_STATIC,17,17,150,13
  CTEXT           "by",IDC_STATIC,82,32,22,12
```

482 Chapter 12 • Special Controls and Dialog Boxes

```
    CTEXT          "William H. Murray and Chris H. Pappas",
                   IDC_STATIC,14,48,159,11
END
       .
       .
       .
```

This listing shows that the application will use a menu and an About dialog box in addition to the common color dialog box. But wait, just like the common font example, where is the description for the common color dialog box? You're right—because it is a predefined resource, it does not appear in the resource script file. You are also right if you concluded that the commdlg.h header file contains information on this dialog box and that its source code is part of the comdlg32.lib library file.

The CommColor.cpp Source Code

The following listing contains all of the source code for the CommColor.cpp application. Examine the code carefully and try and detect the code related directly to the common color dialog box implementation. You'll find this program is structurally similar to the CommFont project described in the previous section.

```
//
// CommColor.cpp
// This application illustrates how you can take
// advantage of the Common Color Dialog Box to
// define drawing or fill colors.
// Copyright (c) William H. Murray and Chris H. Pappas, 1999
//

#include <windows.h>
#include <commdlg.h>    // add common dialog box resources
#include "resource.h"

HINSTANCE hInst;

LRESULT CALLBACK WndProc(HWND,UINT,WPARAM,LPARAM);
BOOL CALLBACK AboutDlgProc(HWND,UINT,WPARAM,LPARAM);

char szProgName[]="ProgName";
char szApplName[]="ColorMenu";

int WINAPI WinMain(HINSTANCE hInst,HINSTANCE hPreInst,
                   LPSTR lpszCmdLine,int nCmdShow)
{
  HWND hWnd;
  MSG   lpMsg;
  WNDCLASS wcApp;
```

```
  wcApp.lpszClassName=szProgName;
  wcApp.hInstance    =hInst;
  wcApp.lpfnWndProc  =WndProc;
  wcApp.hCursor      =LoadCursor(NULL,IDC_ARROW);
  wcApp.hIcon        =0;
  wcApp.lpszMenuName =szApplName;
  wcApp.hbrBackground=(HBRUSH) GetStockObject(WHITE_BRUSH);
  wcApp.style        =CS_HREDRAW|CS_VREDRAW;
  wcApp.cbClsExtra   =0;
  wcApp.cbWndExtra   =0;
  if (!RegisterClass (&wcApp))
    return 0;

  hWnd=CreateWindow(szProgName,"The Common Color Dialog Box",
                    WS_OVERLAPPEDWINDOW,CW_USEDEFAULT,
                    CW_USEDEFAULT,CW_USEDEFAULT,
                    CW_USEDEFAULT,(HWND)NULL,(HMENU)NULL,
                    hInst,(LPSTR)NULL);
  ShowWindow(hWnd,nCmdShow);
  UpdateWindow(hWnd);
  while (GetMessage(&lpMsg,0,0,0)) {
    TranslateMessage(&lpMsg);
    DispatchMessage(&lpMsg);
  }
  return(lpMsg.wParam);
}


// Process the About dialog box control selection
BOOL CALLBACK AboutDlgProc(HWND hDlg,UINT messg,
                           WPARAM wParam,LPARAM lParam)
{
  switch (messg) {
    case WM_INITDIALOG:
      break;
    case WM_COMMAND:
      switch (LOWORD(wParam)) {
        case IDOK:
          EndDialog(hDlg,0);
          break;
        default:
          return FALSE;
      }
      break;
    default:
      return FALSE;
  }
  return TRUE;
}
```

484 Chapter 12 • Special Controls and Dialog Boxes

```c
LRESULT CALLBACK WndProc(HWND hWnd,UINT messg,
                        WPARAM wParam,LPARAM lParam)
{
  HDC hdc;
  PAINTSTRUCT ps;
  static HPEN hNPen;
  static CHOOSECOLOR ccs;
  static COLORREF rgbColor;
  static DWORD dCustomColors[16];
  static int xClientView,yClientView;
  static HWND hInst1;

  switch (messg)
  {
    case WM_CREATE:
      //initial values for common color dialog box
      ccs.lStructSize=sizeof(CHOOSECOLOR);
      ccs.hwndOwner=(HWND) hWnd;
      ccs.hInstance=(HWND) NULL;
      ccs.rgbResult=RGB(255,0,0);
      ccs.lpCustColors=dCustomColors;
      ccs.Flags=CC_RGBINIT|CC_FULLOPEN;
      ccs.lCustData=0L;
      ccs.lpfnHook=(LPCCHOOKPROC) NULL;
      ccs.lpTemplateName=(LPSTR) NULL;
      break;

    // Process the menu item selection
    case WM_COMMAND:
      switch (LOWORD(wParam)) {
        // Draw the Common Color Dialog Box
        case ID_COLORSELECTOR_COLOR:
          if (ChooseColor(&ccs)) {
            rgbColor=(COLORREF) ccs.rgbResult;
            InvalidateRect(hWnd,NULL,TRUE);
          }
          break;
        // Draw the About dialog box
        case ID_HELP_ABOUT:
          DialogBox(hInst,"AboutDlgBox",hWnd,
                   (DLGPROC)AboutDlgProc);
          break;
        // End the application
        case ID_HELP_EXIT:
          SendMessage(hWnd,WM_CLOSE,0,0L);
          break;
        default:
          break;
      }
      break;
```

```
    case WM_PAINT:
      hdc=BeginPaint(hWnd,&ps);

      // Create a pen based upon the color
      // selection from the Common Color
      // Dialog Box
      hNPen=CreatePen(PS_SOLID,16,rgbColor);
                   SelectObject(hdc,hNPen);

      // Draw four wide "colorful" lines
      MoveToEx(hdc,50,60,NULL);
      LineTo(hdc,500,400);

      MoveToEx(hdc,400,30,NULL);
      LineTo(hdc,70,400);

      MoveToEx(hdc,10,10,NULL);
      LineTo(hdc,40,100);

      MoveToEx(hdc,350,240,NULL);
      LineTo(hdc,600,200);

      // Draw some text to the window
      TextOut(hdc,140,80,"Draw some colorful lines",24);

      ValidateRect(hWnd,NULL);
      EndPaint(hWnd,&ps);
      break;

    case WM_DESTROY:
      DeleteObject(hNPen);
      PostQuitMessage(0);
      break;

    default:
      return(DefWindowProc(hWnd,messg,wParam,lParam));
      break;
  }
  return(0);
}
```

In the next section, you will learn about the unique features of the common color dialog box.

UNIQUE SOURCE CODE

As we have already mentioned, when discussing the common font dialog box project, the information concerning common dialog boxes is included in the

486 Chapter 12 • Special Controls and Dialog Boxes

commdlg.h header file. You should be able to locate this file in your compiler's include subdirectory. You might want to have that file opened on your computer as you continue in this section.

This application uses a menu item to enable the selection of the common color dialog box. As a matter of fact, the user can select the menu and chose a menu item to view an About dialog box, or the Color Selector dialog box, or to exit the application.

Figure 12–15 shows the common color dialog box that returns drawing color values to a CHOOSECOLOR structure.

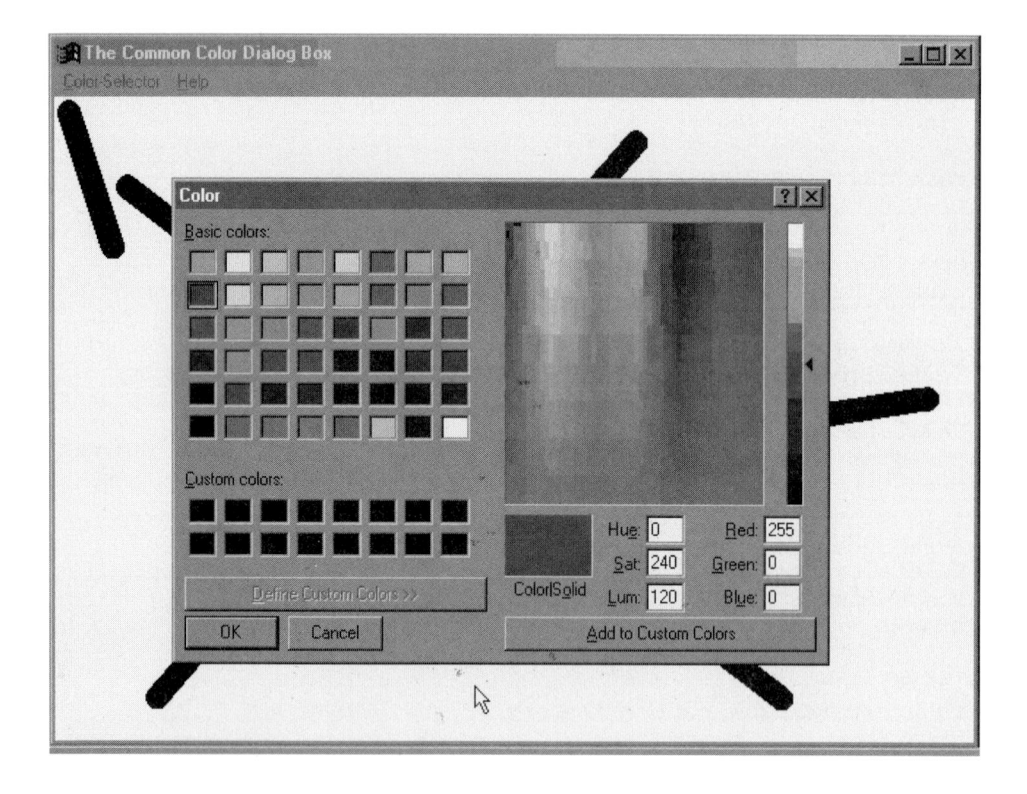

Figure 12-15 *Using the common color dialog box to select drawing colors.*

Information is passed to and from the common color dialog box with a call to the **ChooseColor()** function. The information that is passed is held in a CHOOSECOLOR structure as, shown:

```
typedef struct
{
  DWORD    lStructSize;
  HWND     hwndOwner;
```

The Common Color Dialog Box 487

```
  HWND      hInstance;
  DWORD     rgbResult;
  LPDWORD   lpCustColors;
  DWORD     Flags;
  DWORD     lCustData;
  LPCCHOOKPROC lpfnHook;
  LPSTR     lpTemplateName;
} CHOOSECOLOR;
typedef CHOOSECOLOR FAR *LPCHOOSECOLOR;
```

Here is a partial listing of the project's code to show how these structure values were initialized for this project.

```
//initial values for common color dialog box
  ccs.lStructSize=sizeof(CHOOSECOLOR);
  ccs.hwndOwner=(HWND) hWnd;
  ccs.hInstance=(HWND) NULL;
  ccs.rgbResult=RGB(255,0,0);
  ccs.lpCustColors=dCustomColors;
  ccs.Flags=CC_RGBINIT|CC_FULLOPEN;
  ccs.lCustData=0L;
  ccs.lpfnHook=(LPCCHOOKPROC) NULL;
  ccs.lpTemplateName=(LPSTR) NULL;
  break;
```

The CHOOSECOLOR structure is associated with the *ccs* tag. The structure is initialized when a WM_CREATE message is processed. The first member in the structure holds the size of the CHOOSECOLOR structure. The size is found with a call to the **sizeof()** function. The handle of the owner of the dialog box is hWnd. This value may also be set to NULL when there is no owner. The instance handle is the handle to a block of data describing a dialog template. It can be set to NULL, as it is here, when no template is identified in the lpTemplateName member (this member should also be NULL). A particular color can be identified as the default selection for the dialog box by initializing the rgbResult member. In this case, the color red is used. The lpCustColors member is a DWORD array that can hold up to 16 custom colors, if selected by the user. The Flags member can be any combination of the values, shown in Table 12.7, logically ORed together:

Table 12.7	Flags used in the CHOOSECOLOR structure.
Flag Constants	**Description**
CC_RGBINIT	The color specified will be the default color selection for the dialog box.
CC_FULLOPEN	Will display the entire dialog box and the custom color option.

Table 12.7 — Flags used in the CHOOSECOLOR structure. (Continued)

Flag Constants	Description
CC_PREVENTFULLOPEN	Will display the entire dialog box but not the custom color option.
CC_SHOWHELP	Displays the Help push button. When used, HwndOwner cannot be set to NULL.
CC_ENABLEHOOK	Enables the hook function.
CC_ENABLETEMPLATE	Creates a dialog box using a template specified with hInstance and lpTemplateName.
CC_ENABLETEMPLATE-HANDLE	When set, lpTemplateName is ignored, along with the hInstance used to identify a data block that describes a preloaded dialog box template.

The lCustData structure member passes data to the hook function identified by lpfnHook. The data is passed in the lParam field while processing a WM_INITDIALOG message. The lpfnHook member points to a function that processes messages intended for the dialog box only if CC_ENABLEHOOK is used by the Flags member.

When a new color is selected by the user, the value for the selected color will be returned to the application's rgbColor variable. This color information is extracted from the CHOOSECOLOR structure, via the rgbResult member, when an ID_COLORSELECTOR_COLOR message is processed.

```
case ID_COLORSELECTOR_COLOR:
  if (ChooseColor(&ccs)) {
    rgbColor=(COLORREF) ccs.rgbResult;
    InvalidateRect(hWnd,NULL,TRUE);
  }
  break;
```

This color is then used to specify a new pen color when WM_PAINT messages are processed.

```
// Create a pen based upon the color
// selection from the Common Color
// Dialog Box
hNPen=CreatePen(PS_SOLID,16,rgbColor);
SelectObject(hdc,hNPen);
```

Examine the source code listing once again and make sure you understand these particular pieces of code. Additional information on the **ChooseColor()** function and the CHOOSECOLOR structure can be found by using your Visual C++ compiler's Help facility. The remainder of the application is fairly straightforward. Several GDI graphics primitives are used to draw lines and to draw some text in the window to illustrate the color just selected.

```
// Draw four wide "colorful" lines
MoveToEx(hdc,50,60,NULL);
LineTo(hdc,500,400);

MoveToEx(hdc,400,30,NULL);
LineTo(hdc,70,400);

MoveToEx(hdc,10,10,NULL);
LineTo(hdc,40,100);

MoveToEx(hdc,350,240,NULL);
LineTo(hdc,600,200);

// Draw some text to the window
TextOut(hdc,140,80,"Draw some colorful lines",24);
```

Figure 12–16 shows the window after a pen color has been selected and the dialog box closed.

Figure 12–17 shows the common color dialog box during the selection of a new pen color.

You'll notice that the lines are drawn in a new color but that the text is printed in black. What alterations would you have to make to this code so that the text color also reflects the color just selected from the common color dialog box? (Hint: You just learned how to do this in the previous chapter!)

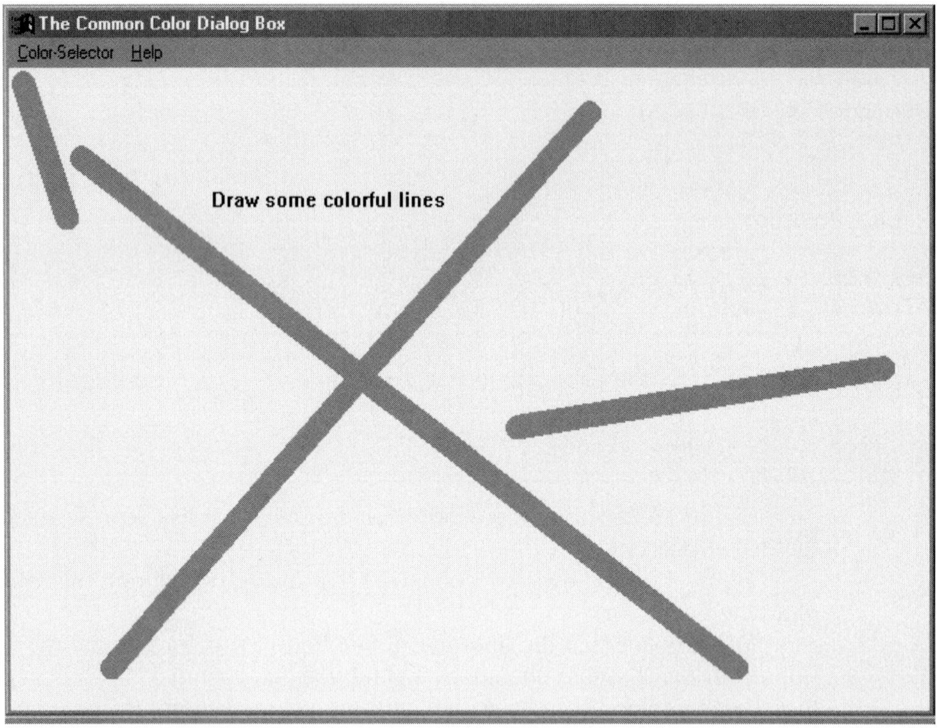

490 Chapter 12 • Special Controls and Dialog Boxes

Figure 12-16   *A typical window after a color selection has been made.*

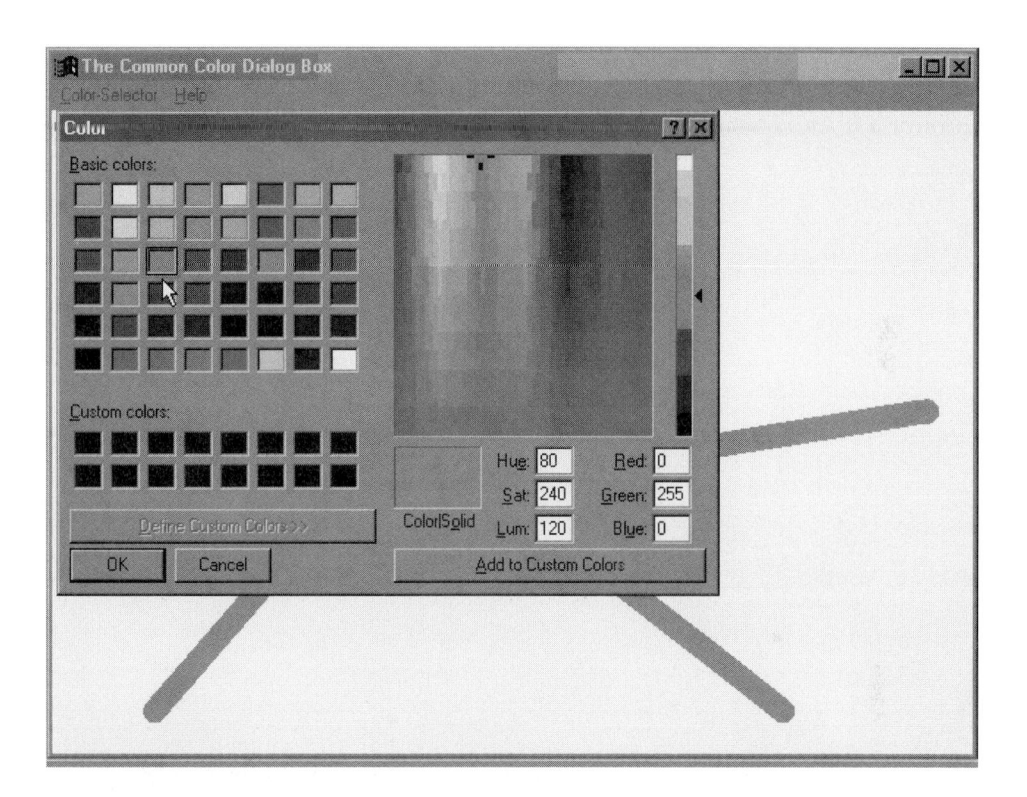

Figure 12-17 *A new pen color is selected from the common color dialog box.*

What's Coming?

In this chapter, you learned how to use special controls and dialog boxes. These common resources are easy to implement and give your applications a consistent look with other Windows applications. In the next chapter, we'll create more robust and complete applications that will allow the user to chart data in a variety of formats.

T H I R T E E N

Developing Complete Applications

In earlier chapters, you learned numerous techniques for drawing graphics device interface (GDI) graphics primitives, manipulating the window, creating fonts, icons, cursors, and so on. In this chapter, two complete applications will be developed—a pie chart and a bar chart. These applications encompass all of the features presented in those earlier chapters and give you a glimpse of how individual features can be used to build professional quality applications.

The pie and bar charts, and the programming concepts they teach, form the basis for developing many business and scientific graphs. Though each charting application is complete in itself, we want you to view both applications as models you can develop further. They are complete but just waiting for your individual touch. Study the code for each application and learn what it can do, then customize the code to suit your needs.

The Pie Chart

The pie chart project is the easiest to understand of the two charting applications. This particular pie chart project uses three dialog boxes for user input and two common dialog boxes similar to those used in Chapter 12. One of the data entry dialog boxes allows the user to specify a chart title, and another allows the user to enter up to 12 pie slice values and associated labels.

The pie slice values, entered by the user, are proportionally scaled to make up a 360-degree pie chart. Each pie slice is colored sequentially from a predefined table of color values. This color sequence is defined in the **Wnd-**

494   Chapter 13 •   Developing Complete Applications

Proc() callback function in the crColor[] array. When colors are specified in this manner, they tend to be device-dependent. What you see on the screen is not necessarily what you'll see on that new ink jet printer.

This project also uses a custom cursor. The cursor is created with the Resource Editor and saved as PieChart.cur. Figure 13–1 shows the cursor we designed for this project.

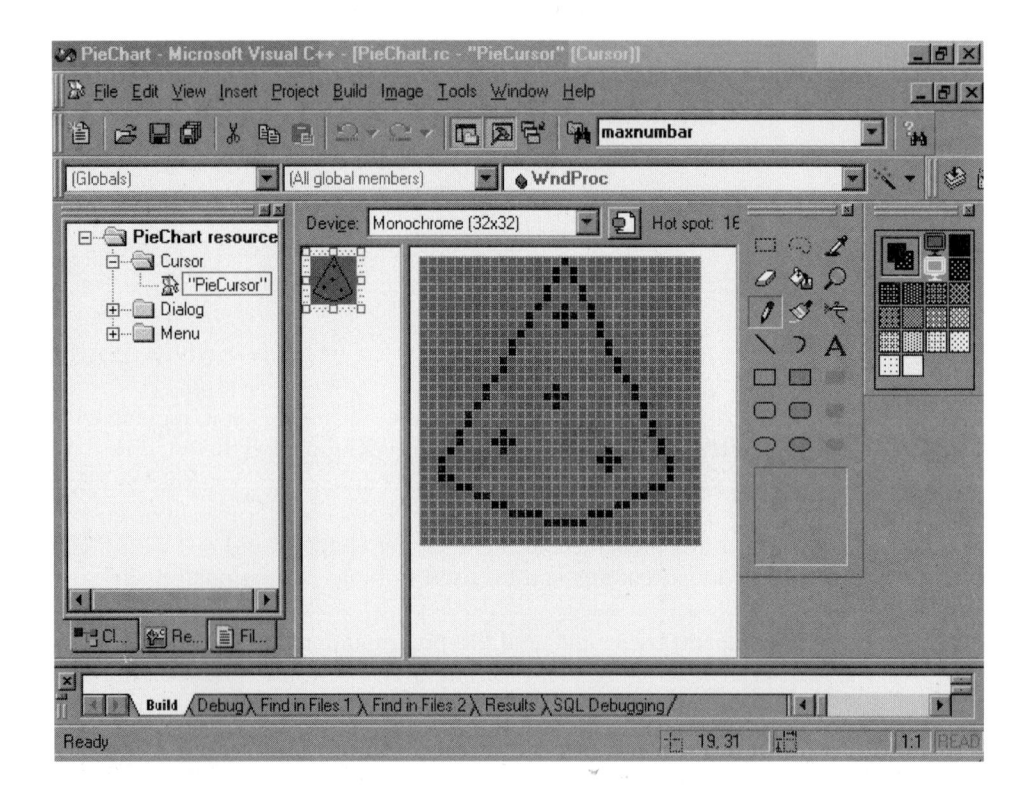

Figure 13-1   *A custom cursor is created for the pie chart project.*

The application builds and saves all of the application's resources in the PieChart.rc file. When you create and compile these resources, the Resource Editor will also create a resource.h header file containing appropriate ID values for each resource. Here is an edited portion of the resource.h header file used for this application.

```
//{{NO_DEPENDENCIES}}
// Microsoft Developer Studio generated include file.
// Used by PieChart.rc
//
#define IDR_MENU1                       101
#define IDD_DIALOG_ABOUT                102
```

```
#define IDD_DIALOG_TITLE              103
#define IDD_DIALOG_DATA               104
#define IDC_EDIT_TITLE                1000
#define IDC_EDIT_SLICE                1001
#define IDC_EDIT_LABEL                1002
#define ID_HELP_ABOUT                 40001
#define ID_PIEDATA_CHARTTITLE         40002
#define ID_PIEDATA_CHARTDATA          40003
#define ID_PIEDATA_EXIT               40004
#define ID_PIEDATA_BACKCOLOR          40005
#define ID_PIEDATA_TITLEFONT          40006
       .
       .
       .
```

Remember, you do not enter this code. The Resource Editor generates this file for you automatically as you define your project's menu, dialog box, and cursor resources.

The resource script file, named PieChart.rc, provides a text description for the menu and dialog box resources designed in the Resource Editor. Here is an edited version of the PieChart.rc file showing a menu and three dialog box descriptions.

```
//Microsoft Developer Studio generated resource script.
//
#include "resource.h"
       .
       .
       .
/////////////////////////////////////////////////////////////
//
// Menu
//
PieMenu MENU DISCARDABLE
BEGIN
  POPUP "&PieData"
  BEGIN
    MENUITEM "Chart &Title...",          ID_PIEDATA_CHARTTITLE
    MENUITEM "Chart Title &Font...",     ID_PIEDATA_TITLEFONT
    MENUITEM "Chart &Data...",           ID_PIEDATA_CHARTDATA
    MENUITEM "Chart &Background Color...",ID_PIEDATA_BACKCOLOR
    MENUITEM "&Exit",                    ID_PIEDATA_EXIT
  END
  POPUP "&Help"
  BEGIN
    MENUITEM "&About...",                ID_HELP_ABOUT
  END
END

/////////////////////////////////////////////////////////////
```

```
//
// Dialog
//
PieChartAbout DIALOG DISCARDABLE  0, 0, 186, 95
STYLE DS_MODALFRAME | WS_POPUP | WS_CAPTION | WS_SYSMENU
CAPTION "About Pie Chart Application"
FONT 8, "MS Sans Serif"
BEGIN
   DEFPUSHBUTTON "OK",IDOK,69,68,50,14
   CTEXT "Pie Chart Application",IDC_STATIC,7,13,172,11
   CTEXT "by",IDC_STATIC,85,28,16,10
   CTEXT "William H. Murray and Chris H. Pappas",IDC_STATIC,
         7,42,172,11
END

PieChartTitle DIALOG DISCARDABLE  0, 0, 186, 95
STYLE DS_MODALFRAME | WS_POPUP | WS_CAPTION | WS_SYSMENU
CAPTION "Pie Chart Title"
FONT 8, "MS Sans Serif"
BEGIN
   DEFPUSHBUTTON "OK",IDOK,34,68,50,14
   PUSHBUTTON "Cancel",IDCANCEL,107,68,50,14
   LTEXT "Enter a title for this Pie Chart:",IDC_STATIC,
         13,14,158,11
   EDITTEXT IDC_EDIT_TITLE,15,30,154,12,ES_AUTOHSCROLL
END

PieChartData DIALOG DISCARDABLE  0, 0, 272, 146
STYLE DS_MODALFRAME | WS_POPUP | WS_CAPTION | WS_SYSMENU
CAPTION "Pie Chart Data"
FONT 8, "MS Sans Serif"
BEGIN
   DEFPUSHBUTTON "OK",IDOK,66,114,50,14
   PUSHBUTTON "Cancel",IDCANCEL,161,113,50,14
   LTEXT "Enter pie slice sizes (separated by a comma):",
         IDC_STATIC,15,14,151,11
   EDITTEXT IDC_EDIT_SLICE,15,25,241,14,ES_AUTOHSCROLL
   LTEXT "Enter pie slice labels (separated by a comma):",
         IDC_STATIC,13,61,153,12
   EDITTEXT IDC_EDIT_LABEL,15,74,237,13,ES_AUTOHSCROLL
END
     .
     .
     .
/////////////////////////////////////////////////////////////
//
// Cursor
//
PieCursor CURSOR  DISCARDABLE "PieChart.cur"
     .
     .
     .
```

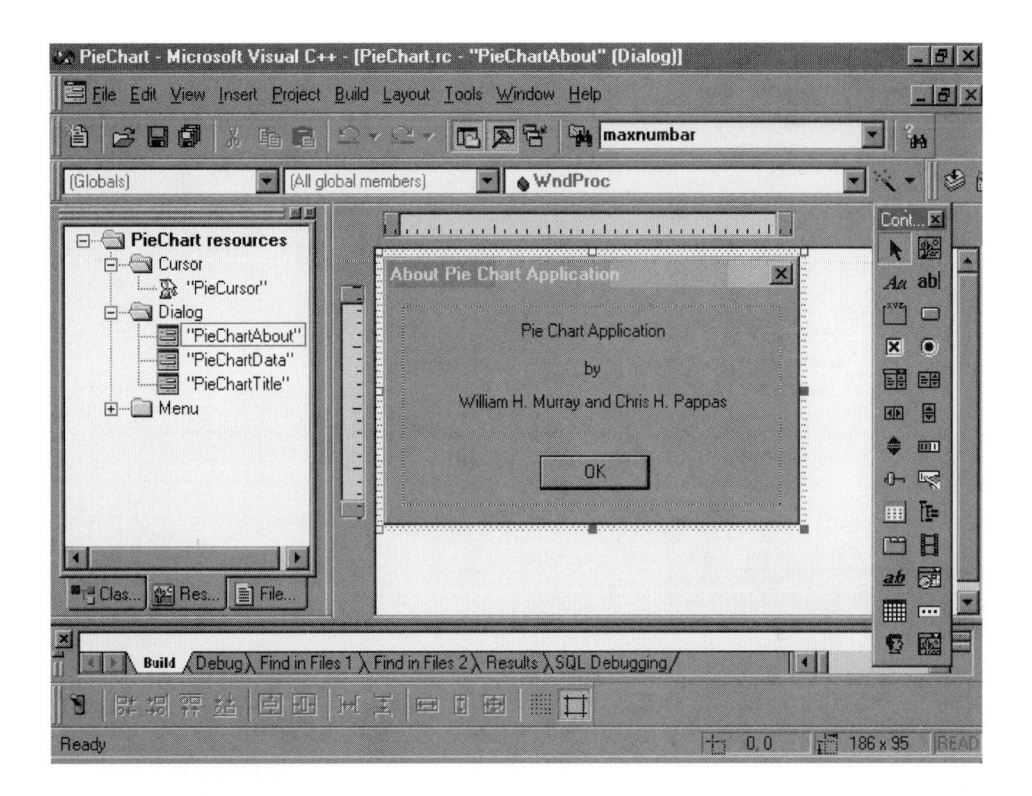

Figure 13-2 *The About dialog box for the pie chart project.*

Figure 13-2 shows the About dialog box, as it is being created, in the Resource Editor.

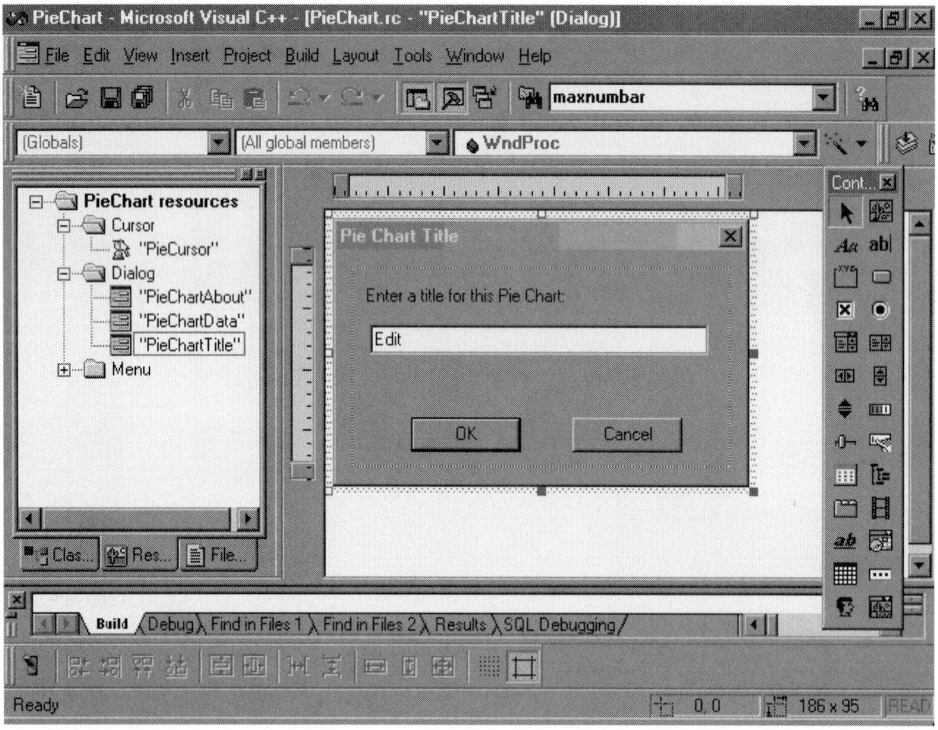

498 Chapter 13 • Developing Complete Applications

Figure 13-3 *The title entry dialog box for the pie chart project.*

Figure 13-3 shows the dialog box used to enter the title of the pie chart.

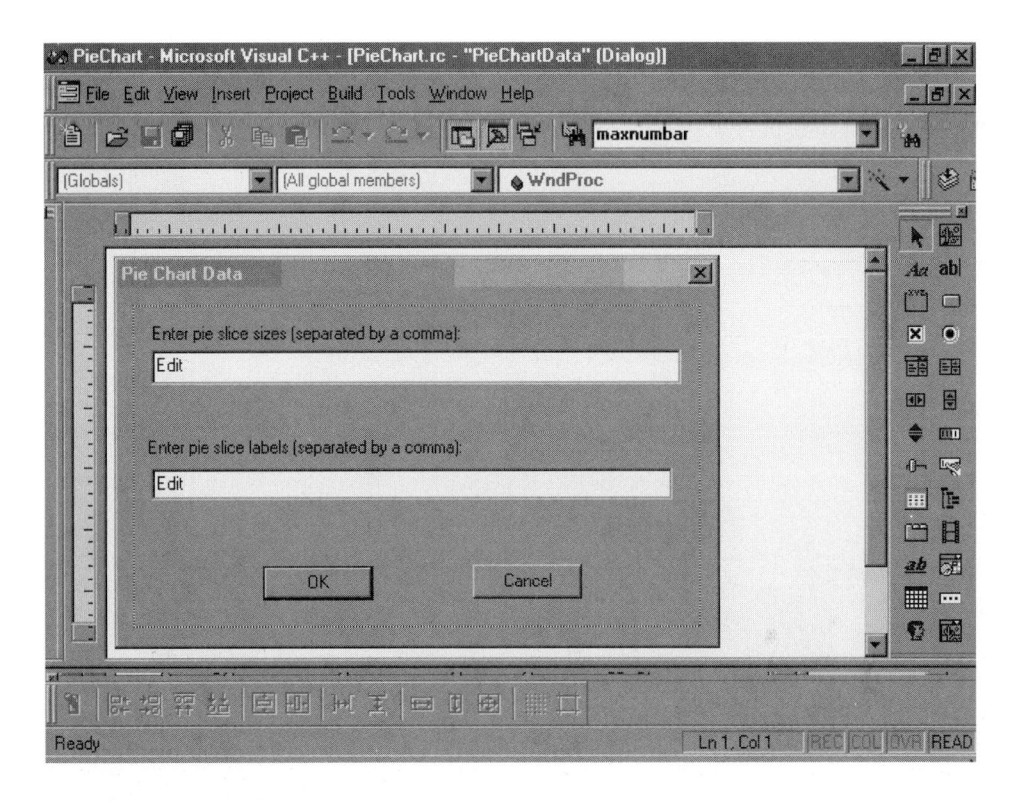

Figure 13-4 *The data entry dialog box for the pie chart project.*

Figure 13-4 shows the dialog box used to enter the pie slice sizes and pie slice labels.

As you know from your study of Chapter 12, the two common dialog boxes do not appear in the code of the PieChart.rc file, simply because you did not design them. However, in the final project, they will work seamlessly with the three dialog boxes you designed. Figure 13-5 shows the common font dialog box.

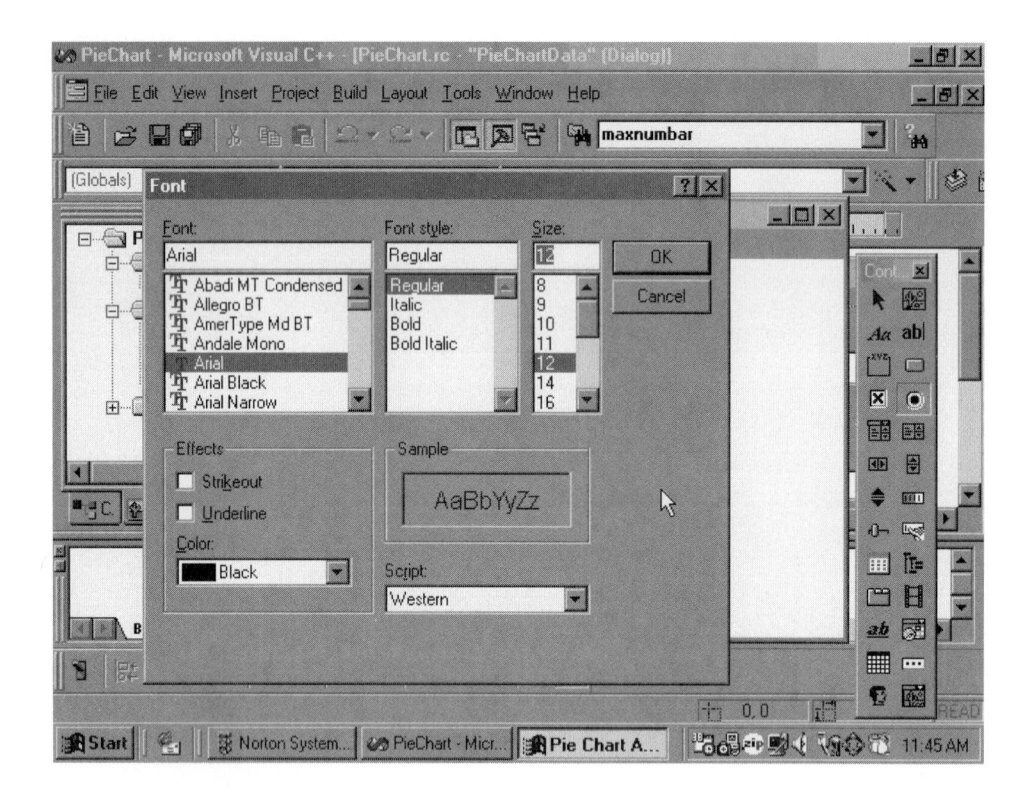

Figure 13-5 *The common font dialog box used in the pie chart project.*

    The common font dialog box will allow the user to select the font family, font size, and features such as font color for the pie chart's title.

    The common color dialog box, shown in Figure 13-6, allows the user to select a color from a palette of colors.

The Pie Chart **501**

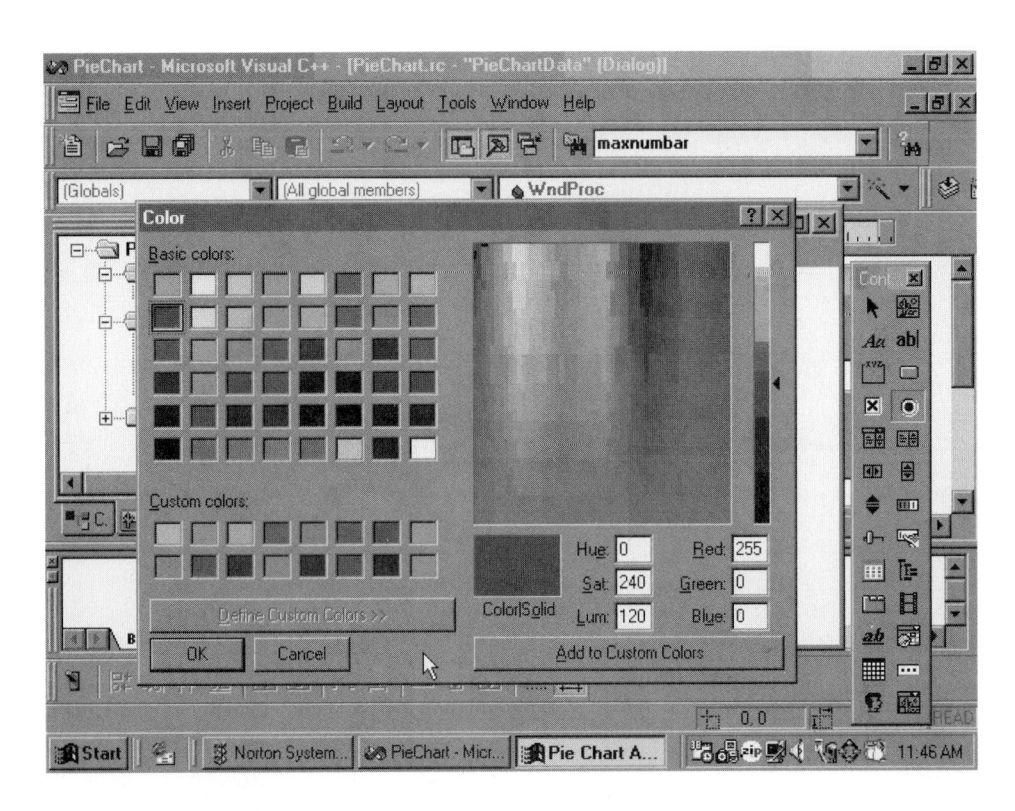

Figure 13-6 *The common color dialog box used in the pie chart project.*

In addition to the project, header, and resource script files for this project, we also need a source code file. The following source code listing, named PieChart.cpp, is created for this application. Though this listing is quite long, you should now be able to recognize many individual components within the listing and understand how they work together to complete the entire application.

```
//
// PieChart.cpp
// This project demonstrates a complete Windows
// application that plots a pie chart.
// This project illustrates how to change mapping
// modes, origins, viewports, uses several data
// entry dialog boxes and two common dialog boxes.
// Copyright (c) William H. Murray and Chris H. Pappas, 1999
//

#include <windows.h>
#include <commdlg.h>
#include <string.h>
```

Chapter 13 • Developing Complete Applications

```c
#include <math.h>
#include "resource.h"

#define radius        150
#define maxnumwedge    12
#define pi            3.14159265359

HINSTANCE hInst;

LRESULT CALLBACK WndProc(HWND,UINT,WPARAM,LPARAM);
BOOL CALLBACK AboutDlgProc(HWND,UINT,WPARAM,LPARAM);
BOOL CALLBACK ChartTitleDlgProc(HWND,UINT,WPARAM,LPARAM);
BOOL CALLBACK ChartDataDlgProc(HWND,UINT,WPARAM,LPARAM);

char szProgName[]="ProgName";
char szApplName[]="PieMenu";
char szCursorName[]="PieCursor";

// initial chart data
char szChartTitle[20]="Pie Chart Title";
char szDlgLabels[240]="#1,#2,#3,#4";
char szDlgWedge[120]="20,5,10,15";

int WINAPI WinMain(HINSTANCE hInst,HINSTANCE hPreInst,
                   LPSTR lpszCmdLine,int nCmdShow)
{
  HWND hWnd;
  MSG  lpMsg;
  WNDCLASS wcApp;

  wcApp.lpszClassName=szProgName;
  wcApp.hInstance     =hInst;
  wcApp.lpfnWndProc   =WndProc;
  wcApp.hCursor       =LoadCursor(hInst,szCursorName);
  wcApp.hIcon         =0;
  wcApp.lpszMenuName  =szApplName;
  wcApp.hbrBackground=(HBRUSH) GetStockObject(WHITE_BRUSH);
  wcApp.style         =CS_HREDRAW|CS_VREDRAW;
  wcApp.cbClsExtra    =0;
  wcApp.cbWndExtra    =0;
  if (!RegisterClass (&wcApp))
    return 0;

  hWnd=CreateWindow(szProgName,"Pie Chart Application",
                    WS_OVERLAPPEDWINDOW,CW_USEDEFAULT,
                    CW_USEDEFAULT,CW_USEDEFAULT,
                    CW_USEDEFAULT,(HWND)NULL,(HMENU)NULL,
                    hInst,(LPSTR)NULL);
  ShowWindow(hWnd,nCmdShow);
  UpdateWindow(hWnd);
```

```
  while (GetMessage(&lpMsg,0,0,0)) {
    TranslateMessage(&lpMsg);
    DispatchMessage(&lpMsg);
  }
  return(lpMsg.wParam);
}

// process the chart title dialog box
BOOL CALLBACK ChartTitleDlgProc(HWND hDlg,UINT messg,
                                WPARAM wParam,LPARAM lParam)
{
  switch (messg) {
    case WM_INITDIALOG:
      break;
    case WM_COMMAND:
      switch (LOWORD(wParam)) {
        case IDOK:
          // get the pie chart title
          GetDlgItemText(hDlg,IDC_EDIT_TITLE,
                         szChartTitle,20);
          EndDialog(hDlg,TRUE);
          break;
        case IDCANCEL:
          EndDialog(hDlg,FALSE);
          break;
        default:
          return FALSE;
      }
      break;
    default:
      return FALSE;
  }
  return TRUE;
}

// process the chart data dialog box
BOOL CALLBACK ChartDataDlgProc(HWND hDlg,UINT messg,
                               WPARAM wParam,LPARAM lParam)
{
  switch (messg) {
    case WM_INITDIALOG:
      break;
    case WM_COMMAND:
      switch (LOWORD(wParam)) {
        case IDOK:
          // get the pie chart slice data
          GetDlgItemText(hDlg,IDC_EDIT_SLICE,
                         szDlgWedge,120);
          // get the pie chart label data
          GetDlgItemText(hDlg,IDC_EDIT_LABEL,
```

```
                           szDlgLabels,240);
          EndDialog(hDlg,TRUE);
          break;
        case IDCANCEL:
          EndDialog(hDlg,FALSE);
          break;
        default:
          return FALSE;
      }
      break;
    default:
      return FALSE;
  }
  return TRUE;
}

// Process the About dialog box
BOOL CALLBACK AboutDlgProc(HWND hDlg,UINT messg,
                           WPARAM wParam,LPARAM lParam)
{
  switch (messg) {
    case WM_INITDIALOG:
      break;
    case WM_COMMAND:
      switch (LOWORD(wParam)) {
        case IDOK:
          EndDialog(hDlg,0);
          break;
        default:
          return FALSE;
      }
      break;
    default:
      return FALSE;
  }
  return TRUE;
}

LRESULT CALLBACK WndProc(HWND hWnd,UINT messg,
                         WPARAM wParam,LPARAM lParam)
{
  HDC hdc;
  PAINTSTRUCT ps;
  HGDIOBJ hOBrush,hNBrush;

  // chart font structures and variables
  HGDIOBJ hOFont,hNFont;
  static LOGFONT lf;
  static LOGFONT tlf;
  static CHOOSEFONT cf;
```

```
    // miscellaneous chart variables
    static int xClientView,yClientView;
    char *n,*p;
    char szSliceLabel[12][20];
    char szWedgeSize[120];
    char szChartLabels[240];
    UINT iTotalWedge[maxnumwedge+1];
    int iWedgeSize[maxnumwedge];
    int i,y1,y2,iNWedges;

    // common color dialog box structures
    // and variables
    static CHOOSECOLOR ccs;
    COLORREF rgbColor;
    DWORD dCustomColors[16];

    // color array for coloring pie slices
    COLORREF crColor[maxnumwedge]={0xFF0000L,0xFFFF00L,
                                   0x80FF00L,0x00FFFFL,
                                   0x0080C0L,0xFF00FFL,
                                   0x800000L,0xFF8000L,
                                   0x008000L,0x0000FFL,
                                   0x800080L,0x808080L};

    switch (messg)
    {
      //initial values for common font dialog box
      case WM_CREATE:
        // initialize common font dialog box values
        cf.Flags=CF_EFFECTS|CF_INITTOLOGFONTSTRUCT|
                 CF_SCREENFONTS;
        cf.hwndOwner=hWnd;
        cf.lpLogFont=&tlf;
        cf.iPointSize=20;
        cf.lStructSize=sizeof(CHOOSEFONT);

        // initialize common color dialog box values
        ccs.lStructSize=sizeof(CHOOSECOLOR);
        ccs.hwndOwner=(HWND) hWnd;
        ccs.hInstance=(HWND) NULL;
        ccs.rgbResult=RGB(255,0,0);
        ccs.lpCustColors=dCustomColors;
        ccs.Flags=CC_RGBINIT|CC_FULLOPEN;
        ccs.lCustData=0L;
        ccs.lpfnHook=(LPCCHOOKPROC) NULL;
        ccs.lpTemplateName=(LPSTR) NULL;
        break;

      // process the menu item selection
      case WM_COMMAND:
```

Chapter 13 • Developing Complete Applications

```
        switch (LOWORD(wParam)) {
          // draw the chart title text dialog box
          case ID_PIEDATA_CHARTTITLE:
            DialogBox(hInst,"PieChartTitle",hWnd,
                    (DLGPROC)ChartTitleDlgProc);
            InvalidateRect(hWnd,NULL,TRUE);
            UpdateWindow(hWnd);
            break;
          // draw the common font dialog box
          case ID_PIEDATA_TITLEFONT:
            if (ChooseFont(&cf))
              InvalidateRect(hWnd,NULL,TRUE);
            break;
          // draw the common color dialog box
          case ID_PIEDATA_BACKCOLOR:
            if (ChooseColor(&ccs)) {
              rgbColor=(COLORREF) ccs.rgbResult;
              SetClassLong(hWnd,GCL_HBRBACKGROUND,
                        (LONG) CreateSolidBrush(rgbColor));
              InvalidateRect(hWnd,NULL,TRUE);
            }
            break;
          // draw the chart data entry dialog box
          case ID_PIEDATA_CHARTDATA:
            DialogBox(hInst,"PieChartData",hWnd,
                    (DLGPROC)ChartDataDlgProc);
            InvalidateRect(hWnd,NULL,TRUE);
            UpdateWindow(hWnd);
            break;
          // end the application
          case ID_PIEDATA_EXIT:
            SendMessage(hWnd,WM_CLOSE,0,0L);
            break;
          // draw the About dialog box
          case ID_HELP_ABOUT:
            DialogBox(hInst,"PieChartAbout",hWnd,
                    (DLGPROC)AboutDlgProc);
            break;

          default:
            break;
        }
        break;

      case WM_SIZE:
        xClientView=LOWORD(lParam);
        yClientView=HIWORD(lParam);
        break;

      case WM_PAINT:
```

The Pie Chart

```
hdc=BeginPaint(hWnd,&ps);

// set mapping mode, extents and origin
SetMapMode(hdc,MM_ISOTROPIC);
SetWindowExtEx(hdc,500,500,NULL);
SetViewportExtEx(hdc,xClientView,
                 -yClientView,NULL);
SetViewportOrgEx(hdc,3*xClientView/8,
                 yClientView/2,NULL);

// get selected font data from common font
// dialog box
hNFont=CreateFontIndirect(&tlf);
hOFont=SelectObject(hdc,hNFont);
SetTextColor(hdc,cf.rgbColors);
TextOut(hdc,
        (-100-(strlen(szChartTitle)*tlf.lfWidth/2)),
        240,szChartTitle,strlen(szChartTitle));
DeleteObject(hOFont);

// make copy of size and label strings for repeating
strcpy(szWedgeSize,szDlgWedge);
strcpy(szChartLabels,szDlgLabels);

// parse the slice size data
iNWedges=0;
i=0;
n=szWedgeSize;
p=strtok(n,",");
while ((n != NULL)) {
  iWedgeSize[i]=atoi(n);
  p=strtok(NULL,",");
  n=p;
  iNWedges++;
  i++;
}

// check that maximum is not exceeded
if (iNWedges>12) iNWedges=12;

// parse the slice label data
i=0;
n=szChartLabels;
p=strtok(n,",");
while ((n != NULL)) {
  strcpy(szSliceLabel[i],n);
  p=strtok(NULL,",");
  n=p;
  i++;
}
```

Chapter 13 • Developing Complete Applications

```
      // scale the pie wedges
      iTotalWedge[0]=0;
      for (i=0;i<iNWedges;i++)
        iTotalWedge[i+1]=iTotalWedge[i]+iWedgeSize[i];

      // create a font for the chart labels
      lf.lfWeight=FW_NORMAL;
      lf.lfCharSet=ANSI_CHARSET;
      lf.lfPitchAndFamily=34;
      lf.lfHeight=xClientView/50;
      hNFont=CreateFontIndirect(&lf);
      hOFont=SelectObject(hdc,hNFont);

      // draw the pie chart and legend labels
      y1=-100;
      y2=y1+15;
      for(i=0;i<iNWedges;i++) {
        hNBrush=CreateSolidBrush(crColor[i]);
        hOBrush=SelectObject(hdc,hNBrush);
        Pie(hdc,-180,180,180,-180,
            (int) (radius*cos(2.0*pi*iTotalWedge[i]/
            iTotalWedge[iNWedges])),
            (int) (radius*sin(2.0*pi*iTotalWedge[i]/
            iTotalWedge[iNWedges])),
            (int) (radius*cos(2.0*pi*iTotalWedge[i+1]/
            iTotalWedge[iNWedges])),
            (int) (radius*sin(2.0*pi*iTotalWedge[i+1]/
            iTotalWedge[iNWedges])));
        DeleteObject(hOBrush);
        if ((strlen(szSliceLabel[0])>0) && (xClientView>300)) {
          Rectangle(hdc,190,y1,205,y2);
          TextOut(hdc,210,y2+2,szSliceLabel[i],
                  strlen(szSliceLabel[i]));
          y1=y2+5;
          y2+=20;
        }
      }
      DeleteObject(hOFont);

      ValidateRect(hWnd,NULL);
      EndPaint(hWnd,&ps);
      break;

    case WM_DESTROY:
      PostQuitMessage(0);
      break;
    default:
      return(DefWindowProc(hWnd,messg,wParam,lParam));
      break;
  }
}
```

```
    return(0);
}
```

We're sure you'll agree that there is a lot going on in this project. In the next section, we'll discuss those parts of the previous listing that are truly unique to this application.

Unique Coding Features

This PieChart.cpp application allows the user to create a pie chart with as many as 12 slices. Using two dialog boxes, the user enters the chart title, size of slices, and slice labels.

If you examine the PieChart.cpp file, shown earlier, you'll see the description of three dialog box procedures; **ChartTitleDlgProc()**, **ChartDataDlgProc()** and **AboutDlgProc()**. Remember that even though this project uses five dialog boxes, two of them are common dialog boxes, and they do not require a separate dialog procedure in the source code listing. The first new and really interesting piece of code occurs in **ChartDataDlgProc()** under the case IDOK statement. The other dialog boxes operate in a manner illustrated earlier in Chapter 11. Locate this code in the composite listing.

```
case IDOK:
  // get the pie chart slice data
  GetDlgItemText(hDlg,IDC_EDIT_SLICE,
                 szDlgWedge,120);
  // get the pie chart label data
  GetDlgItemText(hDlg,IDC_EDIT_LABEL,
                 szDlgLabels,240);
  EndDialog(hDlg,TRUE);
  break;
```

Upon entering data in this dialog box and clicking on the Okay button, the individual slice values are returned as a text string using the **GetDlgItemText()** function. The szDlgWedge string contains values representing the size of individual pie slices. This information will have to be parsed and converted to integer information in order to draw the pie chart. Label information is also entered as a text string. The szDlgLabels string will be parsed to return individual pie slice labels for the chart's legend.

The alternative to parsing a string of data would be to create 12 edit boxes for the slice values and 12 edit boxes for the label values. That creates a large and cluttered dialog box. We think you'll agree that this approach is simple and straightforward.

The real work in this project is handled by **WndProc()**. With the exception of the data gathering done by the five dialog boxes, all calculations, scaling, drawing, and so on are handled by this procedure. Various pieces of information and data are sent as messages and processed by the five case statements. Study this procedure in the PieChart.cpp listing and locate the WM_CREATE, WM_COMMAND, WM_SIZE, WM_PAINT, and WM_DESTROY message handlers. Let's examine the function of each of these message handlers separately.

WM_CREATE

The WM_CREATE message handler is often used to process and initialize project items during the creation of the window. This is the ideal place, in this project, to initialize the structure members for the two common dialog boxes. You can see upon examining this project code that the common font and common color dialog boxes will be used in the project. If you need more detailed information on the structure values used here, return to Chapter 12 for a more complete treatment.

WM_COMMAND

The WM_COMMAND message handler is used to process menu selection requests selected by the user. Figure 13–7 shows the first menu for the application.

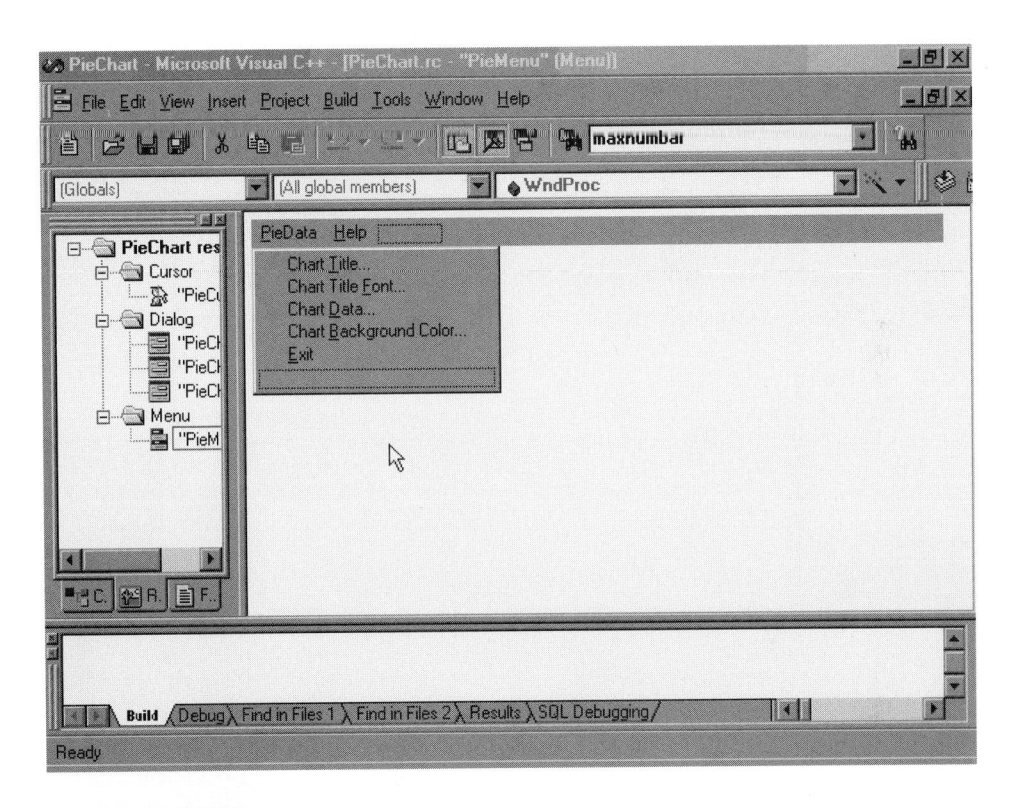

Figure 13-7 *This menu provides all of the data entry dialog boxes for the pie chart project.*

Figure 13–8 shows the second menu for the application.

In this application, each of the menu items are assigned appropriate ID values by the Resource Editor or programmer. For example, the menu item responsible for drawing the chart title dialog box uses the ID_PIEDATA_CHARTTITLE identification value. The ID_PIEDATA_TITLEFONT identification value is associated with the menu item that draws the common font dialog box that allows the user to select the font properties for the chart's title. The ID_PIEDATA_BACKCOLOR identification value is associated with the menu item that draws the common color dialog box, allowing the user to select a custom background color for the chart. The ID_PIEDATA_CHARTDATA identification value is associated with the menu item that draws the data entry dialog box responsible for obtaining the pie slice sizes and labels. The ID_PIEDATA_EXIT identification value is asso-

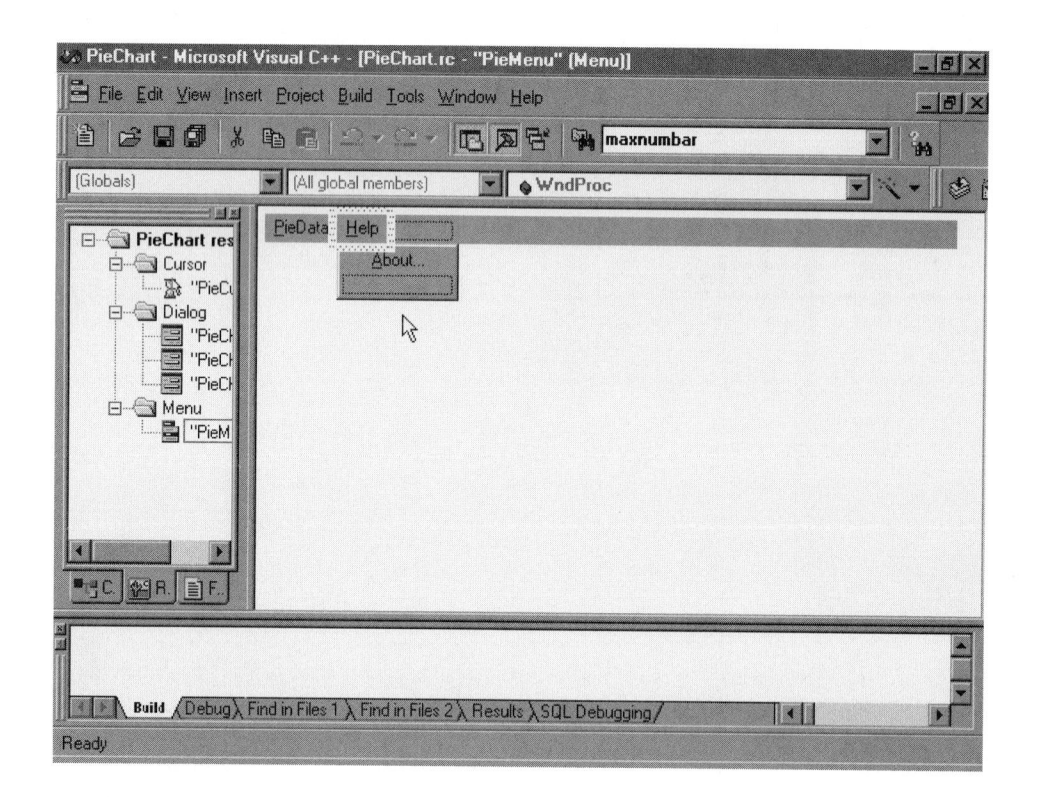

Figure 13-8 *This menu provides the route to the application's About dialog box.*

ciated with a menu item that simply ends the application. No dialog box is drawn in this instance. Finally, the ID_HELP_ABOUT identification value is associated with the second menu's About dialog box menu item. This menu item selection draws a standard About dialog box to the window.

You should be familiar with the operation of the WM_COMMAND message handler. This is basically the same style of code used in Chapters 11 and 12 to draw and process dialog box information.

WM_SIZE

The WM_SIZE message handler, in this application, is responsible for extracting the size of the application's window. As the window size is increased or decreased, this message handler will return the appropriate values to the xClientView and yClientView variables. The size of the application's window will be used to set the viewport extents and origin for the project.

WM_PAINT

The WM_SIZE message handler provides us with the application's window size. You have learned that this information is returned in the xClientView and yClientView variables. One of the first things accomplished by the WM_PAINT message handler is to set the mapping mode, extents, and origin.

```
// set mapping mode, extents and origin
SetMapMode(hdc,MM_ISOTROPIC);
SetWindowExtEx(hdc,500,500,NULL);
SetViewportExtEx(hdc,xClientView,
            -yClientView,NULL);
SetViewportOrgEx(hdc,3*xClientView/8,
            yClientView/2,NULL);
```

In this project, an MM_ISOTROPIC mapping mode is used. MM_ISOTROPIC mapping modes are useful when the horizontal and vertical drawing parameters are to be the same. In this example, the window's extent is set to 500 x 500. That means that regardless of the physical size of the window on the screen, there will always be 500 horizontal units and 500 vertical units. Obviously, the unit size changes as the physical screen size changes. The window's viewport is set to reflect the xClientView and the yClientView. In other words, the viewport is set so that the user views the entire window. The negative sign on the yClientView value makes the vertical coordinate system increase in size as you move from the bottom to the top of the window. Finally, the origin is altered, based on the window's size, so that the center of the pie chart is (0,0) rather than the corner of the window. The pie chart is centered vertically in the window and a little left of center to allow for the chart's legend values to be drawn.

The next portion of code draws the chart's title and includes any user-selected font values selected from the common font dialog box.

```
// get selected font data from common font
// dialog box
hNFont=CreateFontIndirect(&tlf);
hOFont=SelectObject(hdc,hNFont);
SetTextColor(hdc,cf.rgbColors);
TextOut(hdc,
      (-100-(strlen(szChartTitle)*tlf.lfWidth/2)),
       240,szChartTitle,strlen(szChartTitle));
DeleteObject(hOFont);
```

In this project, the **CreateFontIndirect()** function uses the values in a LOGFONT structure when creating a font. Information is returned from the common font dialog box to a CHOOSEFONT structure. You can see, for example, how the color of the font is set with a call to the **SetTextColor()** function. The default color for text is black. When the font's color is changed, it will remain that color unless it is changed again. We decided in this project that if the user changes the color of the title, we will allow all of the application's fonts to be drawn in the same color. So you won't see another call to the **SetTextColor()** function, and all text will be drawn with the text color returned by the common font dialog box.

The **TextOut()** function is responsible for drawing the actual chart title to the window. The second parameter used in this function is an attempt to center the chart title, regardless of its length. Centering is difficult when proportional fonts are used. This is because a series of 'w's, for example, take up much more space than the same number of 'i's. The normal approach is to determine the average width of the font's characters and hope that the string employs enough characters so that their average width matches the average width returned by the lfWidth parameter. If that is true, you have centered the string, if it is not, the string will not be centered.

The next portion of new code involves two parsing routines. Because both are similar in structure, we'll examine the parsing routine that parses a string into integer values for each pie slice. Recall that the dialog box returns the pie slice size data as a string. Each value in the returned string is separated by a comma. Those values can be separated (parsed) with the following routine.

```
// parse the slice size data
iNWedges=0;
i=0;
n=szWedgeSize;
p=strtok(n,",");
while ((n != NULL)) {
   iWedgeSize[i]=atoi(n);
   p=strtok(NULL,",");
   n=p;
   iNWedges++;
   i++;
}
```

There are many ways to parse a string. We like to use the **strtok()** function instead of writing our own parsing routine. When used correctly, this function will save you hours of work. If the function is used incorrectly, it will cost you hours of work!

The **strtok()** function is used to parse one string, in this case n, with characters found in another string. For this project, we'll assume that a comma delimiter is used to separate the numbers. The string to be parsed is identified only the first time the function is called. For all other calls to the **strtok()** function, a NULL value is used.

The **strtok()** function is called within a **while** loop. The string will be parsed until a NULL value is returned, marking the end of the string. Here is the catch for using this function correctly. The string pointer must be updated with each pass through the loop or the scan for the next comma will begin at the start of the string! Some programming gymnastics are used to accomplish this, but the technique is easy enough to follow.

With each pass through the loop, the string information contained between delimiter values is converted to an integer number and stored in the iWedgeSize[] array. The conversion from string to integer value is achieved with the **atoi()** function.

We know the number of pie wedges from the parsing routine. The number of wedges is held in the iNWedges variable.

```
// scale the pie wedges
iTotalWedge[0]=0;
for (i=0;i<iNWedges;i++)
  iTotalWedge[i+1]=iTotalWedge[i]+iWedgeSize[i];
```

A progressive total on wedge values is returned to the iTotalWedge[] array. These values will help determine where one pie slice ends and the next begins. For example, if the user enters 5, 20, 35, and 40 for wedge sizes in the dialog box, iTotalWedge[] would contain the values 0, 5, 25, 60, and 100.

The values contained in iTotalWedge[] are used to calculate the beginning and ending angles for each pie wedge. The **Pie()** function accepts nine parameters. The first parameter is the handle and the next four parameters are used to represent the coordinates of the bounding rectangle. For this project, those values are set to -180, 180, 180 and –180. Recall that the origin has been set to the center of the pie chart. The remaining four parameters for the **Pie()** function are used to designate the starting X-Y pair and the ending X-Y pair for the pie arc. To calculate X values, the **cos()** function is used; to calculate Y values, the **sin()** function is used. For example, the first X position is determined by multiplying the radius of the pie by the cosine of 2*pi*iTotalWedge[0]. The 2*pi value is needed in the conversion of degrees to radians. The Y value is found with the **sin()** function in the same way. Those two points serve as the starting coordinates for the first slice. The ending coordinates are found by using the same equations but with the next value in the iTotalWedge[] array.

To make all slices proportional and fit a 360-degree pie, each coordinate point is divided by the grand total of all individual slices. This total, as you learned earlier, is the last number contained in iTotalWedge[]. Observe how this calculation is achieved in the next piece of code.

```
// draw the pie chart and legend labels
y1=-100;
y2=y1+15;
for(i=0;i<iNWedges;i++) {
  hNBrush=CreateSolidBrush(crColor[i]);
  hOBrush=SelectObject(hdc,hNBrush);
  Pie(hdc,-180,180,180,-180,
      (int) (radius*cos(2.0*pi*iTotalWedge[i]/
      iTotalWedge[iNWedges])),
      (int) (radius*sin(2.0*pi*iTotalWedge[i]/
      iTotalWedge[iNWedges])),
      (int) (radius*cos(2.0*pi*iTotalWedge[i+1]/
```

```
          iTotalWedge[iNWedges])),
          (int) (radius*sin(2.0*pi*iTotalWedge[i+1]/
          iTotalWedge[iNWedges])));
          .
          .
          .
```

Yes, this is a messy equation. However, if the equation is set up properly, it will function perfectly. Notice that the **for** loop is used to include drawing and filling each pie slice with the proper color. The **for** loop will index through all iNWedge values.

If pie slice label values exist and if the window size is large enough to permit drawing a legend, the following piece of code will draw each legend value using a small rectangle filled with a color that matches each pie slice. To the right of each rectangle is the label entered in the data entry dialog box. A legend permits each pie slice to be clearly identified.

```
if ((strlen(szSliceLabel[0])>0) && (xClientView>300)) {
  Rectangle(hdc,190,y1,205,y2);
  TextOut(hdc,210,y2+2,szSliceLabel[i],
          strlen(szSliceLabel[i]));
  y1=y2+5;
  y2+=20;
  }
```

Remember to include the math.h header file as this application requires the use of trigonometric functions. Figure 13–9 shows the default pie chart for this project.

Figure 13–10 shows a pie chart created with user-entered data.

Remember, don't believe everything you see plotted in a chart!

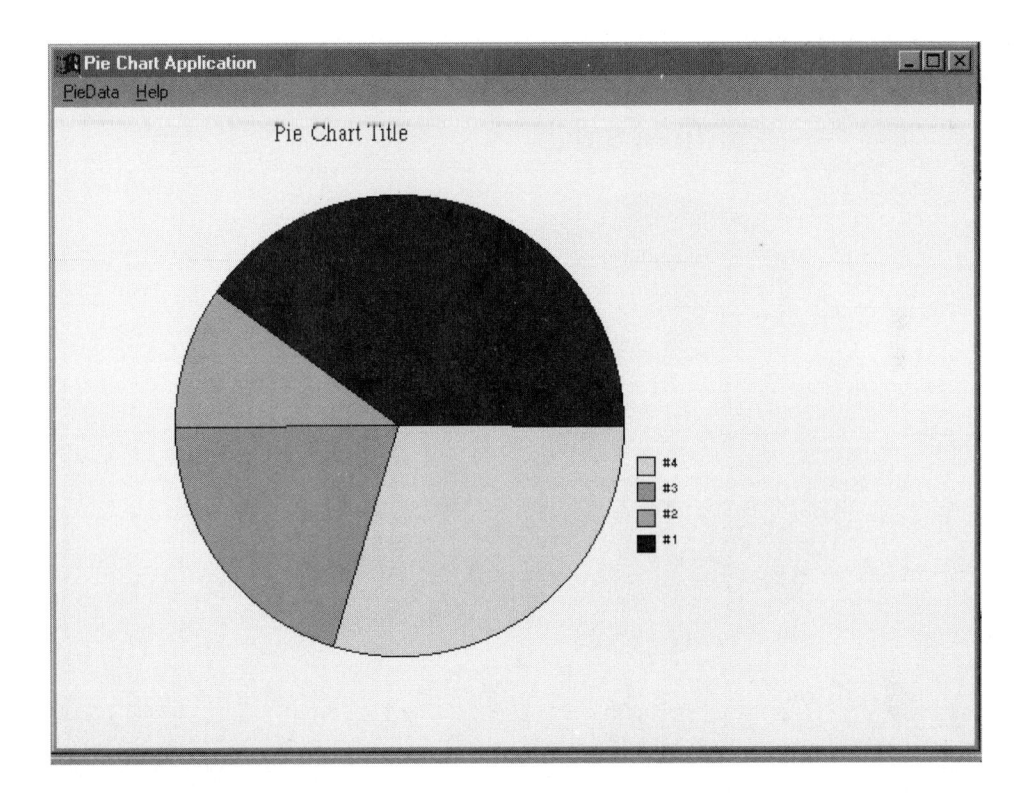

Figure 13-9 *The default pie chart for the pie chart project.*

WM_DESTROY

Finally, the WM_DESTROY message handler is responsible for exiting the application when the proper message is received.

The Bar Chart

The bar chart application, BarChart.cpp, closely parallels the pie chart application discussed in the previous project. The bar chart project allows the user to enter up to 12 bar heights using a dialog box, legend labels, axis labels, and a chart title. The bar widths are scaled so that the final figure will fill the entire horizontal axis, regardless of the number of bars. Thus, three bars or 12 bars will produce a horizontal plot of the same size. Obviously, the bar widths change to accommodate the number of bars. The vertical heights

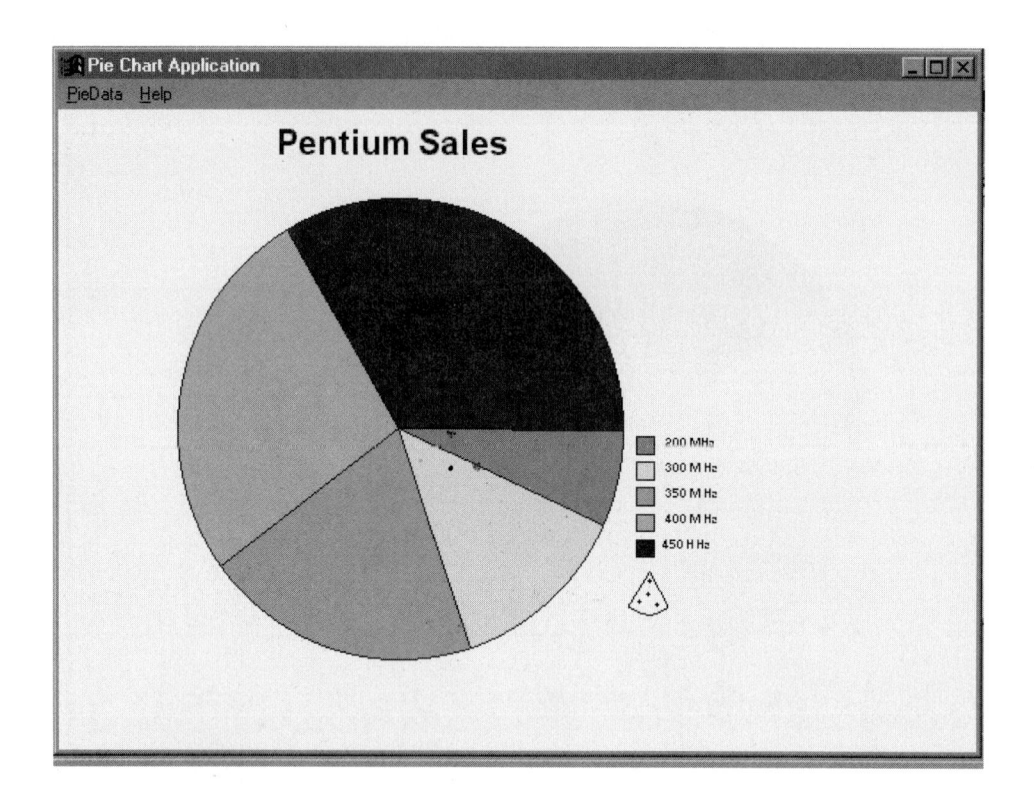

Figure 13-10 A custom pie chart for user-entered data.

of the bars are also scaled. The value for the largest bar is scaled to the maximum value of the Y axis, with all other values drawn in proportion to this value. Using this form of automatic scaling, the chart can plot a wide range of data values without the need for changing plotting ranges and so on. The bars are colored in a sequential manner similar to that used for the pie chart, with color values being selected from an array of predefined colors.

This project uses a custom cursor. The cursor is created with the Resource Editor and saved as BarChart.cur. Figure 13–11 shows the cursor we designed for the bar chart project.

The application builds and saves all of the application's resources in the BarChart.rc file. When you create and compile these resources, the Resource Editor will also create a resource.h header file containing appropriate ID

The Bar Chart

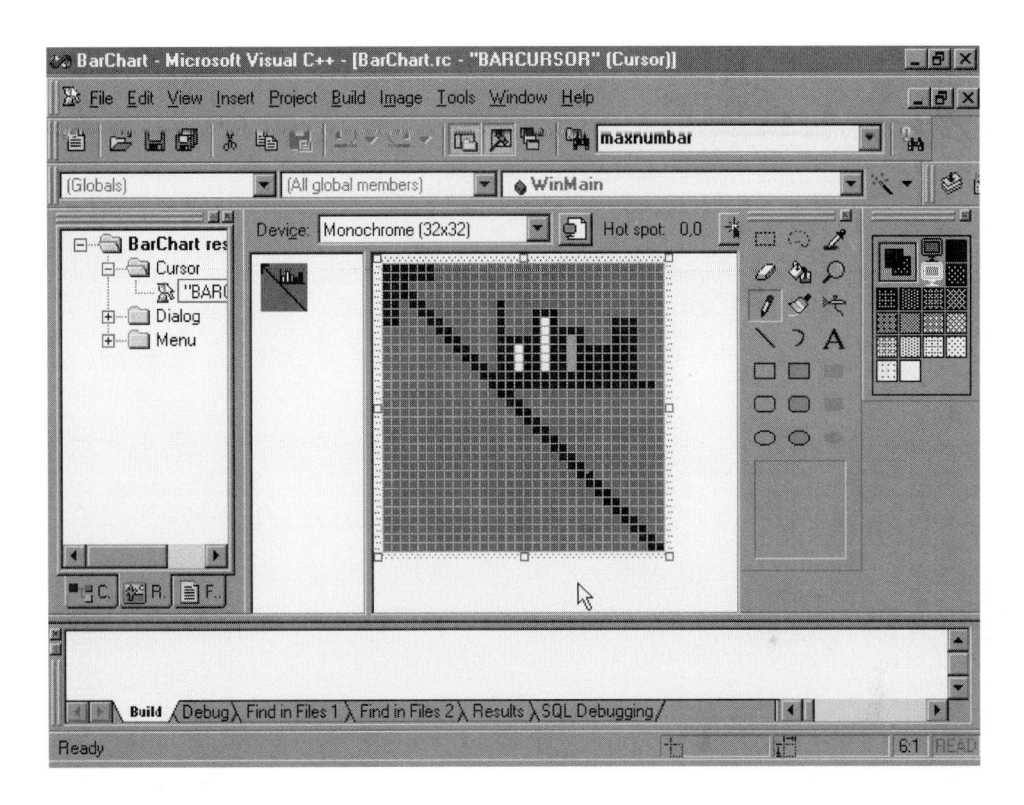

Figure 13-11 *A custom cursor is created for the bar chart project.*

value for each resource. Here is an edited portion of the resource.h header file used for this application.

```
//{{NO_DEPENDENCIES}}
// Microsoft Developer Studio generated include file.
// Used by BarChart.rc
//
#define IDR_MENU1                       101
#define IDD_DIALOG1                     102
#define IDC_EDIT_BAR                    1001
#define IDC_EDIT_LABEL                  1003
#define ID_BARDATA_XLABEL               1004
#define ID_BARDATA_YLABEL               1005
#define ID_PIEDATA_CHARTTITLE           40001
#define ID_BARDATA_CHARTTITLE           40002
#define ID_BARDATA_CHARTDATA            40003
#define ID_BARDATA_BACKCOLOR            40004
#define ID_BARDATA_EXIT                 40005
#define ID_HELP_ABOUT                   40006
#define ID_BARDATA_TITLEFONT            40007
```

520 Chapter 13 • Developing Complete Applications

Do not enter this code directly, remember that the Resource Editor generates this file for you automatically as you define your project's menu, dialog box, and cursor resources. You can see by examining the resource.h header file that approximately the same number of ID values is required by this application as for the pie chart project.

The resource script file, named *BarChart.rc*, provides a text description for the menu and dialog box resources designed in the Resource Editor. Here is an edited version of the BarChart.rc file showing a menu and three dialog box descriptions.

```
//Microsoft Developer Studio generated resource script.
//
#include "resource.h"
   .
   .
   .
/////////////////////////////////////////////////////////////////
//
// Menu
//
BARMENU MENU DISCARDABLE
BEGIN
  POPUP "&BarData"
  BEGIN
    MENUITEM "Chart &Title...",        ID_BARDATA_CHARTTITLE
    MENUITEM "Chart Title &Font...",   ID_BARDATA_TITLEFONT
    MENUITEM "Chart &Data...",         ID_BARDATA_CHARTDATA
    MENUITEM "Chart &Background Color...",
       ID_BARDATA_BACKCOLOR
    MENUITEM "&Exit",                  ID_BARDATA_EXIT
  END
  POPUP "&Help"
  BEGIN
    MENUITEM "&About...",              ID_HELP_ABOUT
  END
END
   .
   .
   .
/////////////////////////////////////////////////////////////////
//
// Dialog
//
BARCHARTABOUT DIALOG DISCARDABLE  0, 0, 186, 95
STYLE DS_MODALFRAME | WS_POPUP | WS_CAPTION | WS_SYSMENU
CAPTION "About Bar Chart Application"
FONT 8, "MS Sans Serif"
BEGIN
  DEFPUSHBUTTON    "OK",IDOK,67,68,50,14
```

```
    CTEXT               "Bar Chart Application",IDC_STATIC,
                        30,14,125,12
    CTEXT               "by",IDC_STATIC,81,28,22,11
    CTEXT               "William H. Murray and Chris H. Pappas",
                        IDC_STATIC,18,43,146,11
END

BARCHARTTITLE DIALOG DISCARDABLE  0, 0, 218, 130
STYLE DS_MODALFRAME | WS_POPUP | WS_CAPTION | WS_SYSMENU
CAPTION "Bar Chart Title"
FONT 8, "MS Sans Serif"
BEGIN
    DEFPUSHBUTTON    "OK",IDOK,33,103,50,14
    PUSHBUTTON       "Cancel",IDCANCEL,127,103,50,14
    LTEXT            "Enter a title for this Bar Chart:",
                     IDC_STATIC,15,15,188,14
    EDITTEXT         ID_BARDATA_CHARTTITLE,15,33,183,12,
                     ES_AUTOHSCROLL
    LTEXT            "X axis label:",IDC_STATIC,17,58,58,13
    EDITTEXT         ID_BARDATA_XLABEL,105,56,92,13,
                     ES_AUTOHSCROLL
    LTEXT            "Y axis label:",IDC_STATIC,17,80,55,12
    EDITTEXT         ID_BARDATA_YLABEL,105,79,91,12,
                     ES_AUTOHSCROLL
END

BARCHARTDATA DIALOG DISCARDABLE  0, 0, 230, 158
STYLE DS_MODALFRAME | WS_POPUP | WS_CAPTION | WS_SYSMENU
CAPTION "Bar Chart Data"
FONT 8, "MS Sans Serif"
BEGIN
    DEFPUSHBUTTON    "OK",IDOK,35,121,50,14
    PUSHBUTTON       "Cancel",IDCANCEL,149,122,50,14
    LTEXT            "Enter bar sizes (separated by a comma):",
                     IDC_STATIC,16,18,132,11
    EDITTEXT         IDC_EDIT_BAR,13,32,204,16,ES_AUTOHSCROLL
    LTEXT            "Enter bar labels (separated by a comma):",
                     IDC_STATIC,15,65,136,15
    EDITTEXT         IDC_EDIT_LABEL,13,81,202,15,ES_AUTOHSCROLL
END
        .
        .
        .
//////////////////////////////////////////////////////
//
// Cursor
//
BARCURSOR    CURSOR   DISCARDABLE      "BarChart.cur"
        .
        .
        .
```

522 Chapter 13 • Developing Complete Applications

As you examine the BarChart.rc resource script file, notice how similar the data entry dialog box descriptions are to those of the pie chart application.

Figure 13–12 shows the About dialog box, as it is being created, in the Resource Editor.

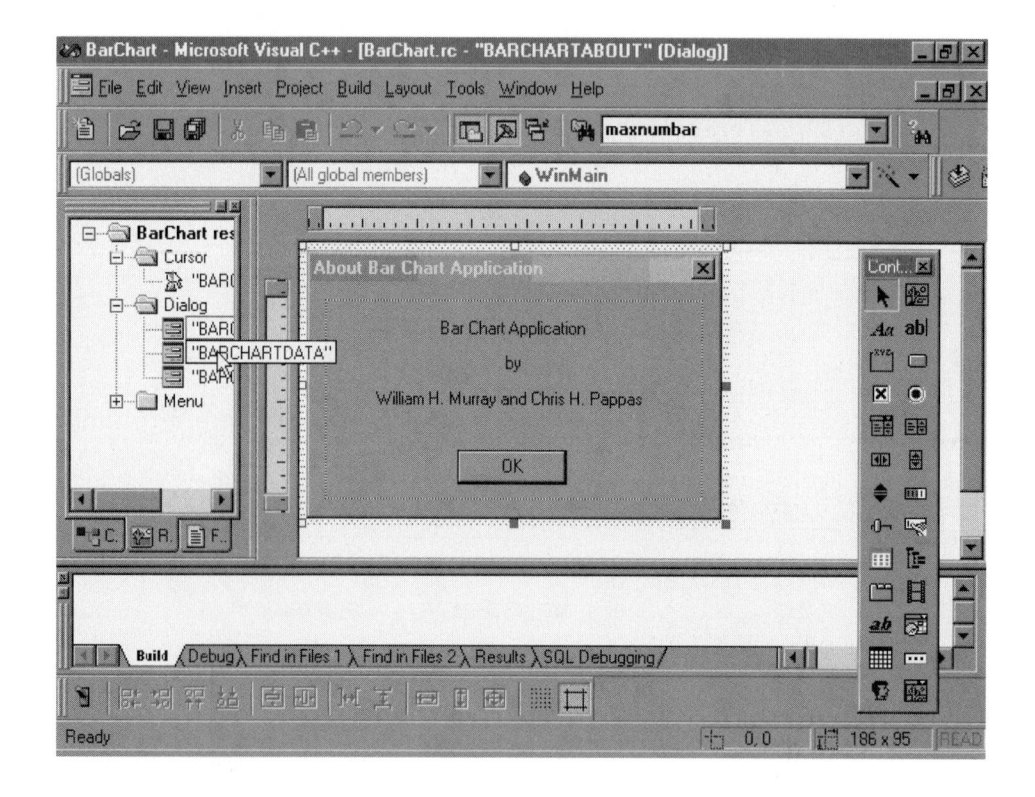

Figure 13–12 *The About dialog box for the bar chart project.*

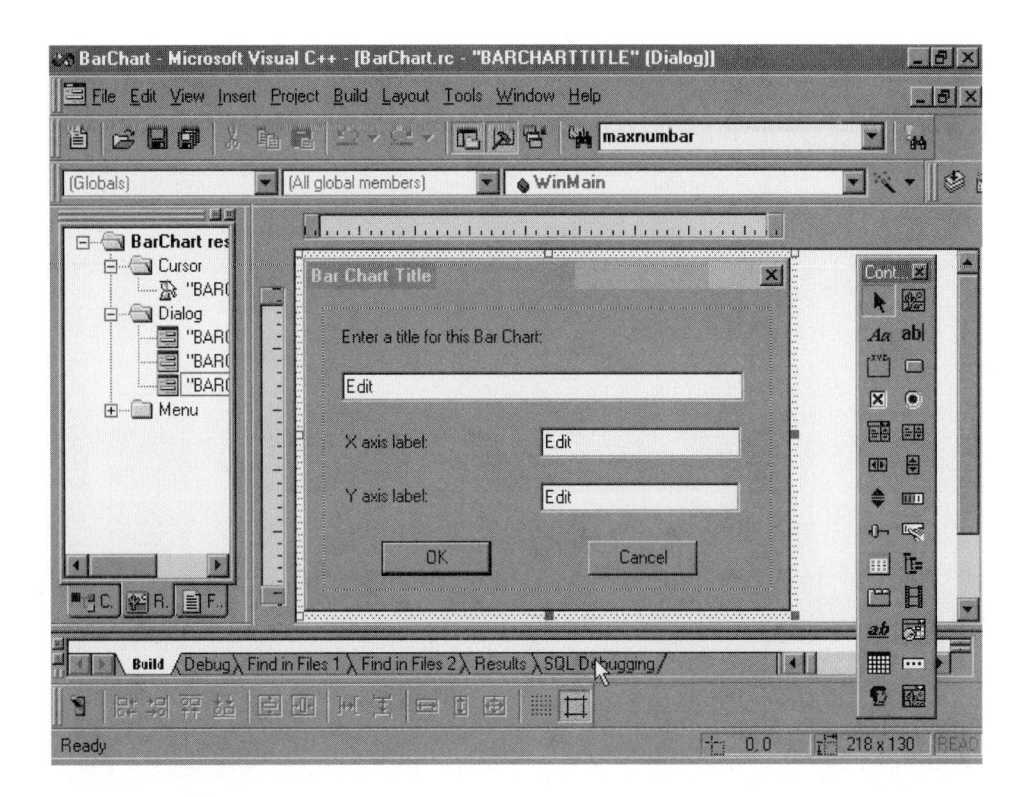

Figure 13-13   *The title and axis label dialog box for the bar chart project.*

Figure 13–13 shows the dialog box used to enter the title and axis labels for the pie chart.

Figure 13–14 shows the dialog box used to enter the bar height values and legend labels for the project.

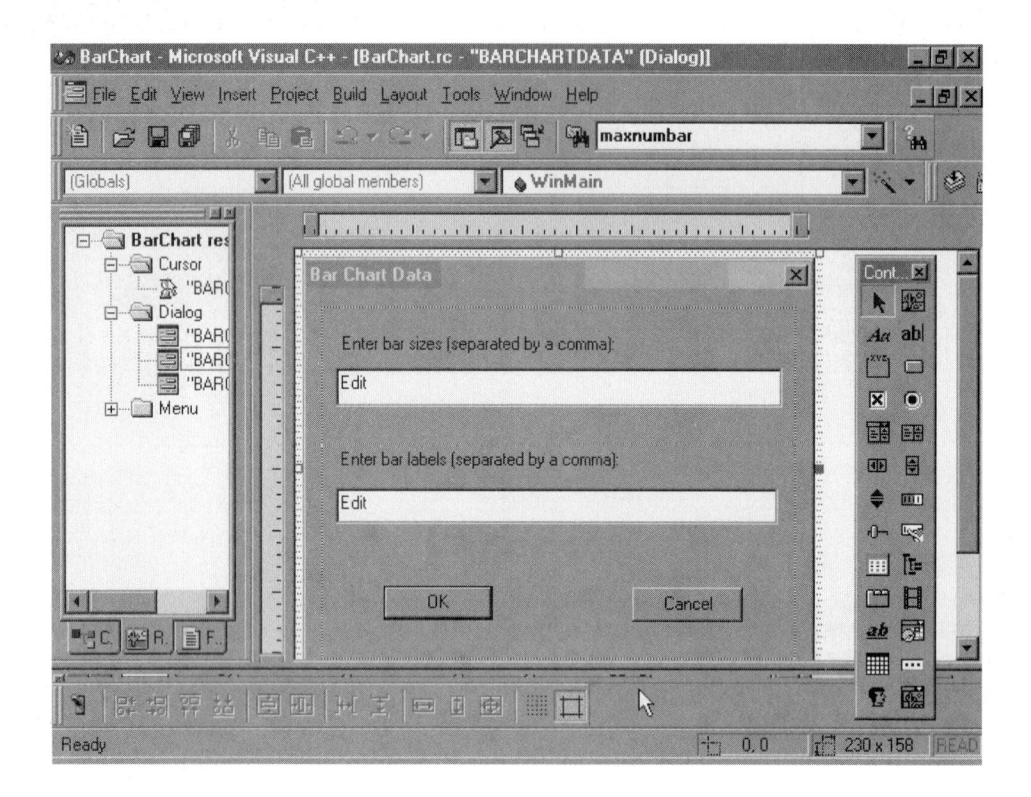

524 Chapter 13 • Developing Complete Applications

Figure 13-14 *The data entry dialog box for the bar chart project.*

Like the pie chart project, this project uses two common dialog boxes. As you have learned, the two common dialog box descriptions do not appear in the code of the BarChart.rc file because you did not design them. Figure 13–15 shows the common font dialog box.

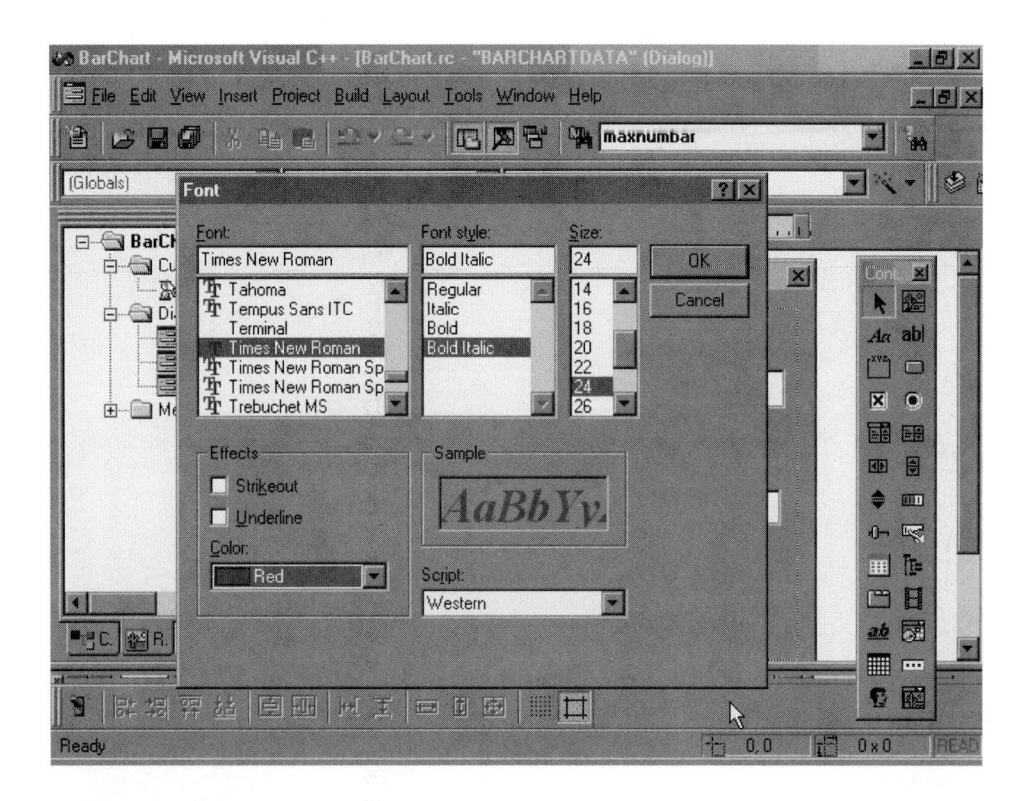

Figure 13-15 *The common font dialog box used in the bar chart project.*

The common font dialog box will allow the user to select the font family, font size, and features such as font color for the bar chart's title.

The common color dialog box, shown in Figure 13-16, allows the user to select a color from a palette of colors.

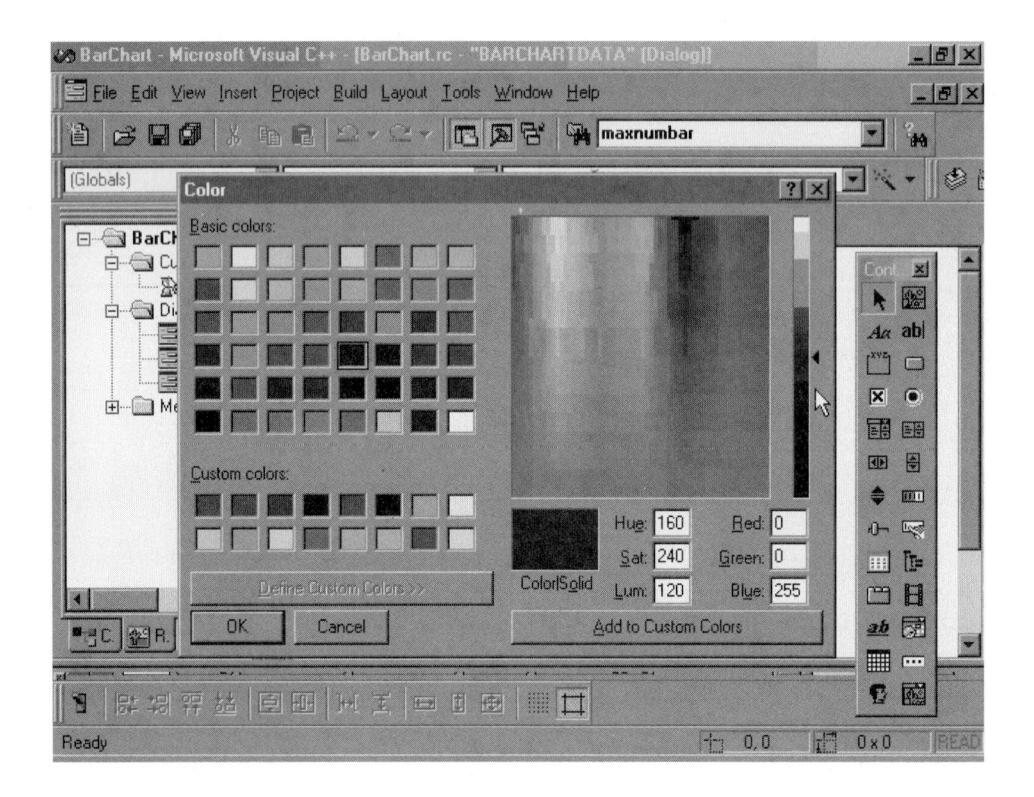

526 Chapter 13 • Developing Complete Applications

Figure 13-16 *The common color dialog box used in the bar chart project.*

This project needs a source code file in addition to the project, header, and resource script files. The following source code listing, named *BarChart.cpp*, is created for this application. As you examine this listing, notice the large number of similarities to the PieChart.cpp source code file.

```
//
// BarChart.cpp
// This project demonstrates a complete Windows
// application that plots a bar chart.
// This project illustrates how to change mapping
// modes, origins, viewports, uses several data
// entry dialog boxes and two common dialog boxes.
// Copyright (c) William H. Murray and Chris H. Pappas, 1999
//
#include <windows.h>
#include <commdlg.h>
#include <string.h>
#include "resource.h"

#define maxnumbar 12
```

```
HINSTANCE hInst;

LRESULT CALLBACK WndProc(HWND,UINT,WPARAM,LPARAM);
BOOL CALLBACK AboutDlgProc(HWND,UINT,WPARAM,LPARAM);
BOOL CALLBACK ChartTitleDlgProc(HWND,UINT,WPARAM,LPARAM);
BOOL CALLBACK ChartDataDlgProc(HWND,UINT,WPARAM,LPARAM);

char szProgName[]="ProgName";
char szApplName[]="BarMenu";
char szCursorName[]="BarCursor";

// initial chart data
char szChartTitle[20]="Bar Chart Title";
char szXLabel[20]="x-axis label";
char szYLabel[20]="y-axis label";
char szDlgLabels[240]="#1,#2,#3,#4";
char szDlgBar[120]="20,5,10,15";

int WINAPI WinMain(HINSTANCE hInst,HINSTANCE hPreInst,
                   LPSTR lpszCmdLine,int nCmdShow)
{
  HWND hWnd;
  MSG  lpMsg;
  WNDCLASS wcApp;

  wcApp.lpszClassName=szProgName;
  wcApp.hInstance     =hInst;
  wcApp.lpfnWndProc   =WndProc;
  wcApp.hCursor       =LoadCursor(hInst,szCursorName);
  wcApp.hIcon         =0;
  wcApp.lpszMenuName  =szApplName;
  wcApp.hbrBackground=(HBRUSH) GetStockObject(WHITE_BRUSH);
  wcApp.style         =CS_HREDRAW|CS_VREDRAW;
  wcApp.cbClsExtra    =0;
  wcApp.cbWndExtra    =0;
  if (!RegisterClass (&wcApp))
    return 0;

  hWnd=CreateWindow(szProgName,"Bar Chart Application",
                    WS_OVERLAPPEDWINDOW,CW_USEDEFAULT,
                    CW_USEDEFAULT,CW_USEDEFAULT,
                    CW_USEDEFAULT,(HWND)NULL,(HMENU)NULL,
                    hInst,(LPSTR)NULL);
  ShowWindow(hWnd,nCmdShow);
  UpdateWindow(hWnd);
  while (GetMessage(&lpMsg,0,0,0)) {
    TranslateMessage(&lpMsg);
    DispatchMessage(&lpMsg);
  }
  return(lpMsg.wParam);
```

```c
}

// process the chart title dialog box
BOOL CALLBACK ChartTitleDlgProc(HWND hDlg,UINT messg,
                                WPARAM wParam,LPARAM lParam)
{
  switch (messg) {
    case WM_INITDIALOG:
      break;
    case WM_COMMAND:
      switch (LOWORD(wParam)) {
        case IDOK:
          // get the bar chart title
          GetDlgItemText(hDlg,ID_BARDATA_CHARTTITLE,
                         szChartTitle,20);
          GetDlgItemText(hDlg,ID_BARDATA_XLABEL,
                         szXLabel,20);
          GetDlgItemText(hDlg,ID_BARDATA_XLABEL,
                         szXLabel,20);
          GetDlgItemText(hDlg,ID_BARDATA_YLABEL,
                         szYLabel,20);
          EndDialog(hDlg,TRUE);
          break;
        case IDCANCEL:
          EndDialog(hDlg,FALSE);
          break;
        default:
          return FALSE;
      }
      break;
    default:
      return FALSE;
  }
  return TRUE;
}

// process the chart data dialog box
BOOL CALLBACK ChartDataDlgProc(HWND hDlg,UINT messg,
                               WPARAM wParam,LPARAM lParam)
{
  switch (messg) {
    case WM_INITDIALOG:
      break;
    case WM_COMMAND:
      switch (LOWORD(wParam)) {
        case IDOK:
          // get the bar chart bar size data
          GetDlgItemText(hDlg,IDC_EDIT_BAR,szDlgBar,120);
          // get the bar chart label data
          GetDlgItemText(hDlg,IDC_EDIT_LABEL,
```

```
                         szDlgLabels,240);
          EndDialog(hDlg,TRUE);
          break;
        case IDCANCEL:
          EndDialog(hDlg,FALSE);
          break;
        default:
          return FALSE;
      }
      break;
    default:
      return FALSE;
  }
  return TRUE;
}

// process the About dialog box
BOOL CALLBACK AboutDlgProc(HWND hDlg,UINT messg,
                           WPARAM wParam,LPARAM lParam)
{
  switch (messg) {
    case WM_INITDIALOG:
      break;
    case WM_COMMAND:
      switch (LOWORD(wParam)) {
        case IDOK:
          EndDialog(hDlg,0);
          break;
        default:
          return FALSE;
      }
      break;
    default:
      return FALSE;
  }
  return TRUE;
}

LRESULT CALLBACK WndProc(HWND hWnd,UINT messg,
                         WPARAM wParam,LPARAM lParam)
{
  HDC hdc;
  PAINTSTRUCT ps;
  HGDIOBJ hOBrush,hNBrush;

  // chart font structures and handles
  HGDIOBJ hOFont,hNFont;
  static LOGFONT lf;
  static LOGFONT tlf;
  static CHOOSEFONT cf;
```

Chapter 13 • Developing Complete Applications

```c
// miscellaneous chart variables
char *n,*p;
char szBarLabel[12][20];
char szBarSize[120];
char sbuffer[10],*strptr;
static char szChartLabels[240];
int iBarSize[maxnumbar];
int ilenMaxLabel;
int x1,x2,y1,y2,z1,z2;
int i,iNBars,iBarWidth,iBarMax;
static int xClientView,yClientView;
float fBarSizeScaled[maxnumbar];

// common color dialog box structures
// and variables
static CHOOSECOLOR ccs;
COLORREF rgbColor;
DWORD dCustomColors[16];

// color array for coloring bars
COLORREF crColor[maxnumbar]={0xFF0000L,0xFFFF00L,
                             0x80FF00L,0x00FFFFL,
                             0x0080C0L,0xFF00FFL,
                             0x800000L,0xFF8000L,
                             0x008000L,0x0000FFL,
                             0x800080L,0x808080L};

switch (messg)
{
  //initial values for common font dialog box
  case WM_CREATE:
    // initialize common font dialog box values
    cf.Flags=CF_EFFECTS|CF_INITTOLOGFONTSTRUCT|
             CF_SCREENFONTS;
    cf.hwndOwner=hWnd;
    cf.lpLogFont=&tlf;
    cf.iPointSize=20;
    cf.lStructSize=sizeof(CHOOSEFONT);

    // initialize common color dialog box values
    ccs.lStructSize=sizeof(CHOOSECOLOR);
    ccs.hwndOwner=(HWND) hWnd;
    ccs.hInstance=(HWND) NULL;
    ccs.rgbResult=RGB(0,0,255);
    ccs.lpCustColors=dCustomColors;
    ccs.Flags=CC_RGBINIT|CC_FULLOPEN;
    ccs.lCustData=0L;
    ccs.lpfnHook=(LPCCHOOKPROC) NULL;
    ccs.lpTemplateName=(LPSTR) NULL;
    break;
```

```
// process the menu item selection
case WM_COMMAND:
  switch (LOWORD(wParam)) {
    // draw the chart title text dialog box
    case ID_BARDATA_CHARTTITLE:
      DialogBox(hInst,"BarChartTitle",hWnd,
                (DLGPROC)ChartTitleDlgProc);
      InvalidateRect(hWnd,NULL,TRUE);
      UpdateWindow(hWnd);
      break;
    // draw the common font dialog box
    case ID_BARDATA_TITLEFONT:
      if (ChooseFont(&cf))
        InvalidateRect(hWnd,NULL,TRUE);
      break;
    // draw the common color dialog box
    case ID_BARDATA_BACKCOLOR:
      if (ChooseColor(&ccs)) {
        rgbColor=(COLORREF) ccs.rgbResult;
        SetClassLong(hWnd,GCL_HBRBACKGROUND,
                    (LONG) CreateSolidBrush(rgbColor));
        InvalidateRect(hWnd,NULL,TRUE);
      }
      break;
    // draw the chart data entry dialog box
    case ID_BARDATA_CHARTDATA:
      DialogBox(hInst,"BarChartData",hWnd,
                (DLGPROC)ChartDataDlgProc);
      InvalidateRect(hWnd,NULL,TRUE);
      UpdateWindow(hWnd);
      break;
    // end the application
    case ID_BARDATA_EXIT:
      SendMessage(hWnd,WM_CLOSE,0,0L);
      break;
    // draw the About dialog box
    case ID_HELP_ABOUT:
      DialogBox(hInst,"BarChartAbout",hWnd,
                (DLGPROC)AboutDlgProc);
      break;
    default:
      break;
  }
  break;

case WM_SIZE:
  xClientView=LOWORD(lParam);
  yClientView=HIWORD(lParam);
  break;
```

Chapter 13 • Developing Complete Applications

```
case WM_PAINT:
  hdc=BeginPaint(hWnd,&ps);

  // set mapping mode, extents and origin
  SetMapMode(hdc,MM_ISOTROPIC);
  SetWindowExtEx(hdc,640,480,NULL);
  SetViewportExtEx(hdc,xClientView,yClientView,NULL);
  SetViewportOrgEx(hdc,0,0,NULL);

  // get selected font data from common
  // font dialog box and draw the chart title
  hNFont=CreateFontIndirect(&tlf);
  hOFont=SelectObject(hdc,hNFont);
  SetTextColor(hdc,cf.rgbColors);
  TextOut(hdc,300-(strlen(szChartTitle)*tlf.lfWidth/2),
          15,szChartTitle,strlen(szChartTitle));
  SelectObject(hdc,hOFont);
  DeleteObject(hNFont);

  // make copy of size and label strings for repeating
  strcpy(szBarSize,szDlgBar);
  strcpy(szChartLabels,szDlgLabels);

  // parse the bar size data
  iNBars=0;
  i=0;
  n=szBarSize;
  p=strtok(n,",");
  while ((n != NULL)) {
    iBarSize[i]=atoi(n);
    p=strtok(NULL,",");
    n=p;
    iNBars++;
    i++;
  }

  // check that maximum is not exceeded
  if (iNBars>maxnumbar) iNBars=maxnumbar;

  // parse the bar label data
  i=0;
  n=szChartLabels;
  p=strtok(n,",");
  while ((n != NULL)) {
    strcpy(szBarLabel[i],n);
    p=strtok(NULL,",");
    n=p;
    i++;
  }
```

The Bar Chart

```
// calculate width of each bar on chart
iBarWidth=400/iNBars;

// find bar in array with maximum height
iBarMax=iBarSize[0];
for(i=0;i<iNBars;i++)
  if (iBarMax<iBarSize[i]) iBarMax=iBarSize[i];

// convert maximum y value to a string
strptr=_itoa(iBarMax,sbuffer,10);
ilenMaxLabel=strlen(sbuffer);

// scale bars in array.  highest bar = 270
for (i=0;i<iNBars;i++)
  fBarSizeScaled[i]=(float) (iBarSize[i]*270.0/iBarMax);

// create a font for drawing labels
hNFont=CreateFont(8+(yClientView/45),0,0,0,FW_NORMAL,
                  FALSE,FALSE,FALSE,
                  OEM_CHARSET,
                  OUT_DEFAULT_PRECIS,
                  CLIP_DEFAULT_PRECIS,
                  DEFAULT_QUALITY,
                  34,"Arial");
hOFont=SelectObject(hdc,hNFont);

// draw coordinate axis
MoveToEx(hdc,99,49,NULL);
LineTo(hdc,99,350);
LineTo(hdc,510,350);
MoveToEx(hdc,99,350,NULL);
x1=100;
y1=350;
x2=x1+iBarWidth;

// draw each bar
z1=100;
z2=z1+15;
for(i=0;i<iNBars;i++) {
  hNBrush=CreateSolidBrush(crColor[i]);
  hOBrush=SelectObject(hdc,hNBrush);
  y2=350-(int) fBarSizeScaled[i];
  Rectangle(hdc,x1,y1,x2,y2);
  x1=x2;
  x2+=iBarWidth;
  SelectObject(hdc,hNBrush);
  DeleteObject(hNBrush);

  // if window is large enough draw legend labels
  if ((strlen(szBarLabel[0])!=0)&&(xClientView>300)) {
```

```
              hNBrush=CreateSolidBrush(crColor[i]);
              hOBrush=SelectObject(hdc,hNBrush);
              Rectangle(hdc,550,z1,565,z2);
              TextOut(hdc,570,z1-5,szBarLabel[i],
                      strlen(szBarLabel[i]));
              z1=z2+5;
              z2+=20;
              SelectObject(hdc,hNBrush);
              DeleteObject(hNBrush);
            }
          }

          // draw horizontal axis label and
          // chart maximum
          TextOut(hdc,(300-(strlen(szXLabel)*10/2)),
                  365,szXLabel,strlen(szXLabel));
          TextOut(hdc,(90-ilenMaxLabel*12),
                  70,strptr,ilenMaxLabel);
          SelectObject(hdc,hOFont);
          DeleteObject(hNFont);

          // create a font for vertical axis label with
          // escapement and orientation set to 90 degrees
          hNFont=CreateFont(8+(yClientView/45),0,900,900,
                            FW_BOLD,FALSE,FALSE,FALSE,
                            OEM_CHARSET,OUT_DEFAULT_PRECIS,
                            CLIP_DEFAULT_PRECIS,
                            DEFAULT_QUALITY,
                            34,"Arial");
          hOFont=SelectObject(hdc,hNFont);
          TextOut(hdc,50,200+(strlen(szYLabel)*10/2),
                  szYLabel,strlen(szYLabel));
          SelectObject(hdc,hOFont);
          DeleteObject(hNFont);

          ValidateRect(hWnd,NULL);
          EndPaint(hWnd,&ps);
          break;

      case WM_DESTROY:
        PostQuitMessage(0);
        break;
      default:
        return(DefWindowProc(hWnd,messg,wParam,lParam));
        break;
    }
    return(0);
}
```

This project is on the same complexity level as is the pie chart project. In the next section, we'll discuss those parts of the previous listing that are unique to this application.

Unique Coding Features

This BarChart.cpp application allows the user to create a bar chart with as many as 12 bars. The chart title, axis labels, bar heights, and legend labels are entered by the user with the aid of two dialog boxes.

If you examine the previous listing for the BarChart.cpp source code file, you'll see the description of three dialog box procedures: **ChartTitleDlgProc()**, **ChartDataDlgProc()**, and **AboutDlgProc()**. If you compare these procedures with their counterparts in the pie chart project, you'll see structurally that they are quite similar. For that reason, we will not repeat the discussion of how each of these procedures operated. For a complete explanation, just return to the pie chart project. Remember that even though this project uses five dialog boxes, two of them are common dialog boxes, and they do not require a separate dialog procedure in the source code listing.

The **WndProc()** procedure handles most of the work in this project, such as calculations, scaling, drawing, and so on. Five **case** statements are used to route messages to the proper message handlers. Examine the **WndProc()** portion of code and locate the WM_CREATE, WM_COMMAND, WM_SIZE, WM_PAINT, and WM_DESTROY message handlers. In the next sections we'll discuss the purpose of each of these message handlers.

WM_CREATE

As you have already learned, the WM_CREATE message handler is frequently used to process and initialize project items during the creation of the window. Notice that the common font and common color dialog boxes are initialized here. If you need to refresh you understanding, remember that these common dialog box structures were discussed in Chapter 12.

WM_COMMAND

The WM_COMMAND message handler is used to process menu selection requests selected by the user. Figure 13–17 shows the first menu for the application.

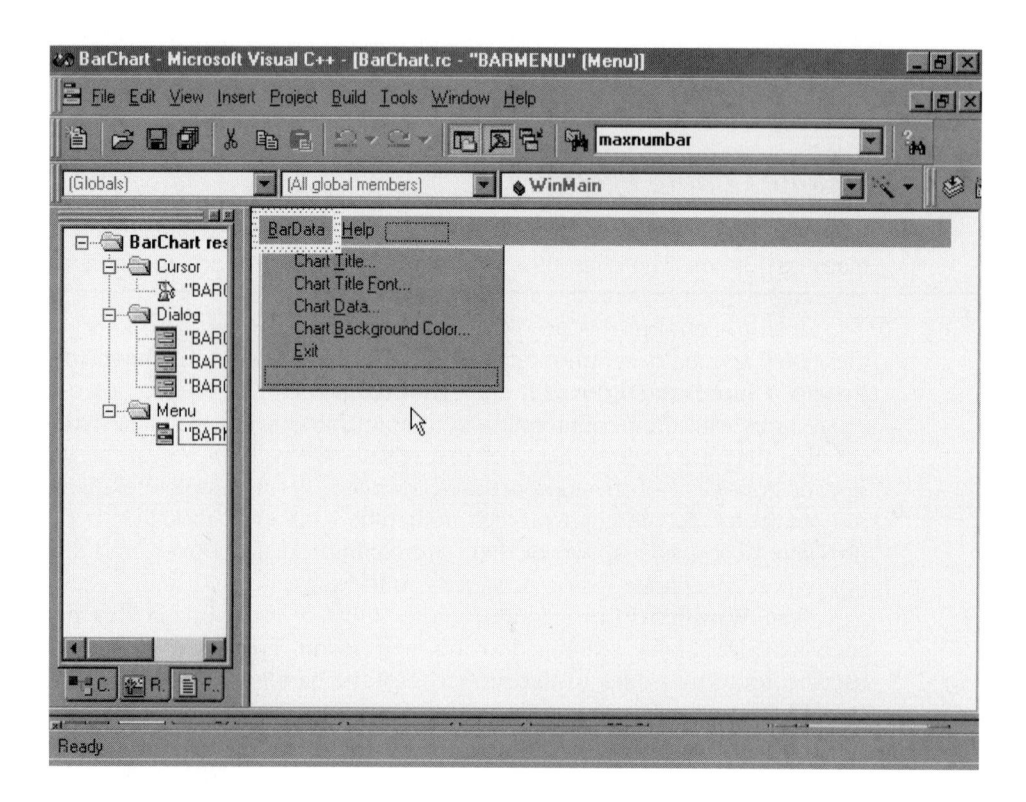

536 Chapter 13 • Developing Complete Applications

Figure 13–17 *This menu provides all of the data entry dialog boxes for the bar chart project.*

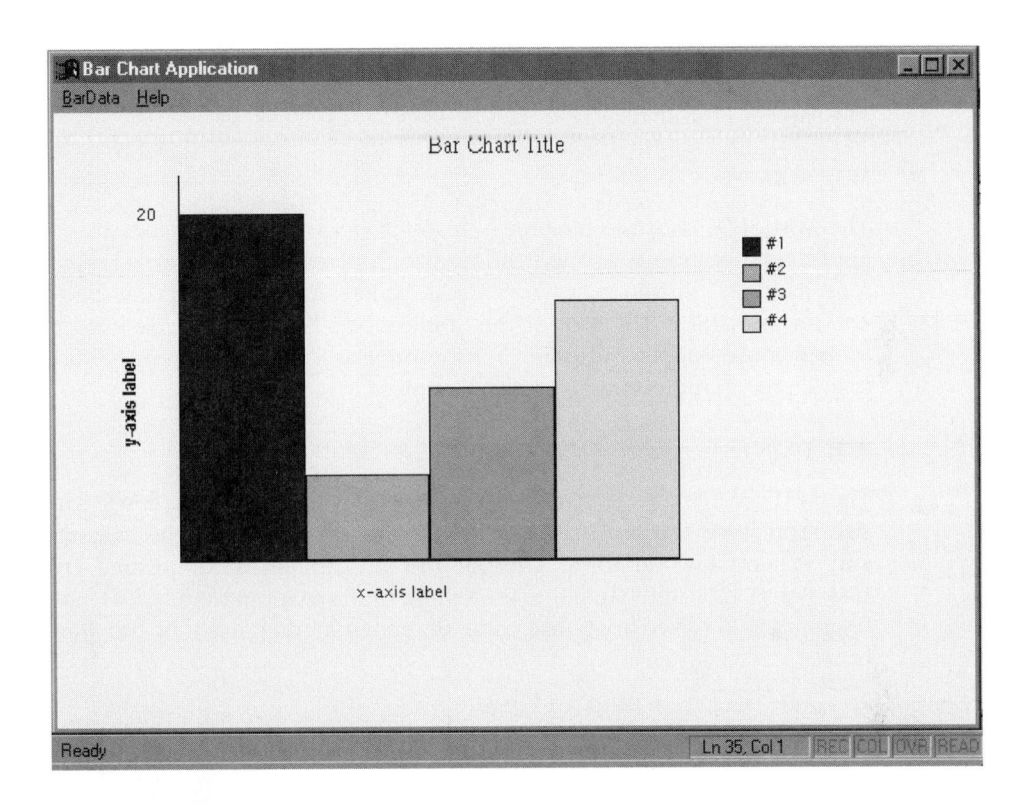

Figure 13–18 *This menu provides the route to the application's About dialog box.*

Figure 13–18 shows the second menu for the application.

In this application, each of the menu items are assigned appropriate ID values by the Resource Editor or programmer. For example, the menu item responsible for drawing the chart title and axis label dialog box uses the ID_BARDATA_CHARTTITLE identification value. The ID_BARDATA_TITLEFONT identification value is associated with the menu item that draws the common font dialog box that allows the user to select the font properties for the chart's title. The ID_BARDATA_BACKCOLOR identification value is associated with the menu item that draws the common color dialog box, allowing the user to select a custom background color for the chart. The ID_BARDATA_CHARTDATA identification value is associated with the menu item that draws the data entry dialog box responsible for obtaining the bar sizes and legend labels. The ID_BARDATA_EXIT identification value is associated with a menu item that simply ends the application. No dialog box is drawn in this instance. Finally, the ID_HELP_ABOUT identification value is associated with the second menu's About dialog box menu item. This menu item selection draws a standard About dialog box to the window.

The operation of the WM_COMMAND message handler is essentially the same as it was for the pie chart application and those applications discussed in Chapters 11 and 12.

WM_SIZE

The WM_SIZE message handler is responsible for extracting the size of the application's window. As the window size is increased or decreased, this message handler will return the appropriate values to the xClientView and yClientView variables. The size of the application's window will be used to set the viewport extents and origin for the project. This will eventually allow us to scale the graphics drawn to the window.

WM_PAINT

The WM_SIZE message handler provides us with the application's window size. You have learned that this information is returned in the xClientView and yClientView variables. One of the first things accomplished by the WM_PAINT message handler is the setting of the mapping mode, extents, and origin. You'll notice that this code differs from that used in the PieChart project.

```
// set mapping mode, extents and origin
SetMapMode(hdc,MM_ISOTROPIC);
SetWindowExtEx(hdc,640,480,NULL);
SetViewportExtEx(hdc,xClientView,yClientView,NULL);
SetViewportOrgEx(hdc,0,0,NULL);
```

Here the MM_ISOTROPIC mapping mode is used because the horizontal and vertical drawing parameters are to be the same. The window's extent is set to 640 x 480. That means that, regardless of the physical size of the window on the screen, there will always be 640 horizontal units and 480 vertical units. Obviously, the unit size changes as the physical screen size changes. The window's viewport is set to reflect the xClientView and the yClientView. In other words, the viewport is set so that the user views the entire window. Finally, the origin is placed at the upper left corner of the window. In this project, we are not offsetting the origin for the chart. The bar chart is drawn in the window a little left of center to allow for the chart's legend values to be drawn.

The next portion of code draws the chart's title and includes any user-selected font values selected from the common font dialog box.

```
// get selected font data from common
// font dialog box and draw the chart title
hNFont=CreateFontIndirect(&tlf);
hOFont=SelectObject(hdc,hNFont);
SetTextColor(hdc,cf.rgbColors);
TextOut(hdc,300-(strlen(szChartTitle)*tlf.lfWidth/2),
```

```
          15,szChartTitle,strlen(szChartTitle));
SelectObject(hdc,hOFont);
DeleteObject(hNFont);
```

The **CreateFontIndirect()** function uses the values in a LOGFONT structure when creating a font. Information is returned from the common font dialog box to a CHOOSEFONT structure. You can see, for example, how the color of the font is set with a call to the **SetTextColor()** function. Recall that the default color for text is black. When the font's drawing color is changed, it will remain that color until it is changed again. The **TextOut()** function is responsible for drawing the actual chart title to the window. The second parameter used in this function is an attempt to center the chart title, regardless of its length. Centering is difficult when proportional fonts are used. Remember that a series of 'w's, take up much more space than the same number of 'i's.

The parsing routines for this project are the same as those used for the pie chart project. If you need to refresh your memory on how they work, just return to the previous example.

Let's examine how the chart is actually constructed. Because there are 400 data points available horizontally, the width of each bar, iBarWidth, can be calculated by dividing 400 by iNBars.

```
iBarWidth=400/iNBars;
```

The largest bar value needs to be found. This can be done by scanning the array and saving the largest value in iBarMax.

```
// find bar in array with maximum height
iBarMax=iBarSize[0];
for(i=0;i<iNBars;i++)
  if (iBarMax<iBarSize[i]) iBarMax=iBarSize[i];
```

We'll also need to convert this maximum value to a string and reference it as *strptr* so that we can draw the maximum Y value in the final chart.

```
// convert maximum y value to a string
strptr=_itoa(iBarMax,sbuffer,10);
ilenMaxLabel=strlen(sbuffer);
```

All remaining bars in the chart are scaled to the bar with the maximum height. These scaled height values are saved in a new array, fBarSizeScaled[]. The maximum vertical height for bars is defined as 270.

```
// scale bars in array. highest bar = 270
for (i=0;i<iNBars;i++)
  fBarSizeScaled[i]=(float) (iBarSize[i]*(270.0/iBarMax));
```

Now move down to the code contained under WM_PAINT. Notice that the MM_ISOTROPIC mapping mode is used in this example, too. This was done so that, when the graph is minimized, the icon produced will be a miniature bar graph of your current data.

540 Chapter 13 • Developing Complete Applications

The section of code devoted to printing labels actually creates two fonts. The first is a variable-pitch Roman font for printing horizontal labels; the second is the same font rotated 90 degrees for plotting the vertical Y label. You might want to return to Chapter 9 for a review of how **CreateFont()** utilizes its parameters.

Finally, the X-Y coordinate axes are drawn in black, and the bars are plotted.

```
// Draw Coordinate Axis
MoveToEx(hdc,99,49,NULL);
LineTo(hdc,99,350);
LineTo(hdc,500,350);
MoveToEx(hdc,99,350,NULL);
x1=100;
y1=350;
x2=x1+iBarWidth;
```

The **CreateFont()** function is used to create a font for drawing legend labels. Legend labels will be drawn at the same time each bar is drawn to the chart. Next, the coordinate axes are drawn with calls to the **MoveToEx()** and **LineTo()** functions.

Note that individual bars are drawn by first subtracting the bar size from 350. This is necessary, because the origin for the chart is in the upper left corner of the window. The **Rectangle()** function is used to draw each bar and to fill it with the current color. For each pass through the **for** loop, the *x1* value will be set to the *x2* value of the previous bar, and *x2* will be incremented by the bar width, iBarWidth.

```
// draw each bar
z1=100;
z2=z1+15;
for(i=0;i<iNBars;i++) {
  hNBrush=CreateSolidBrush(crColor[i]);
  hOBrush=SelectObject(hdc,hNBrush);
  y2=350-(int) fBarSizeScaled[i];
  Rectangle(hdc,x1,y1,x2,y2);
  x1=x2;
  x2+=iBarWidth;
  SelectObject(hdc,hNBrush);
  DeleteObject(hNBrush);
```

The legend rectangles and text will be drawn only if the client window is large enough. If the window has been sized below 300 pixels or if there are no legend values, the legend drawing routine is skipped.

```
// if window is large enough draw legend labels
if ((strlen(szBarLabel[0])!=0)&&(xClientView>300)) {
  hNBrush=CreateSolidBrush(crColor[i]);
  hOBrush=SelectObject(hdc,hNBrush);
  Rectangle(hdc,550,z1,565,z2);
```

```
    TextOut(hdc,570,z1-5,szBarLabel[i],
            strlen(szBarLabel[i]));
    z1=z2+5;
    z2+=20;
    SelectObject(hdc,hNBrush);
    DeleteObject(hNBrush);
}
```

The chart axis labels are drawn next. The only twist to doing this is that the vertical axis label is drawn in a rotated manner. To accomplish this, the orientation and escapement are changed when the font is created.

```
// create a font for vertical axis label with
// escapement and orientation set to 90 degrees
hNFont=CreateFont(8+(yClientView/45),0,900,900,
                  FW_BOLD,FALSE,FALSE,FALSE,
                  OEM_CHARSET,OUT_DEFAULT_PRECIS,
                  CLIP_DEFAULT_PRECIS,
                  DEFAULT_QUALITY,
                  34,"Arial");
hOFont=SelectObject(hdc,hNFont);
TextOut(hdc,50,200+(strlen(szYLabel)*10/2),
        szYLabel,strlen(szYLabel));
SelectObject(hdc,hOFont);
DeleteObject(hNFont);
```

Remember that the 900 that you see twice in this function call represents 90.0 degrees.

Now, let's see what the actual chart looks like. Figure 13–19 shows the default bar chart for the project.

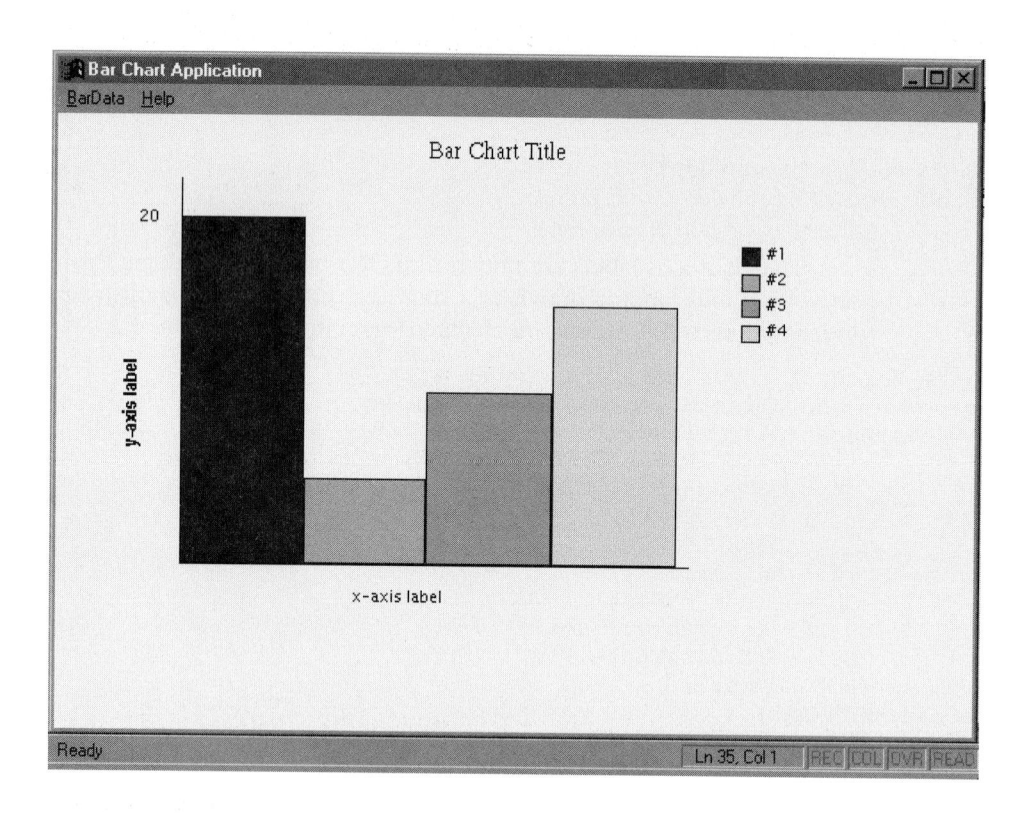

Figure 13-19 *The default bar chart drawn with the bar chart project.*

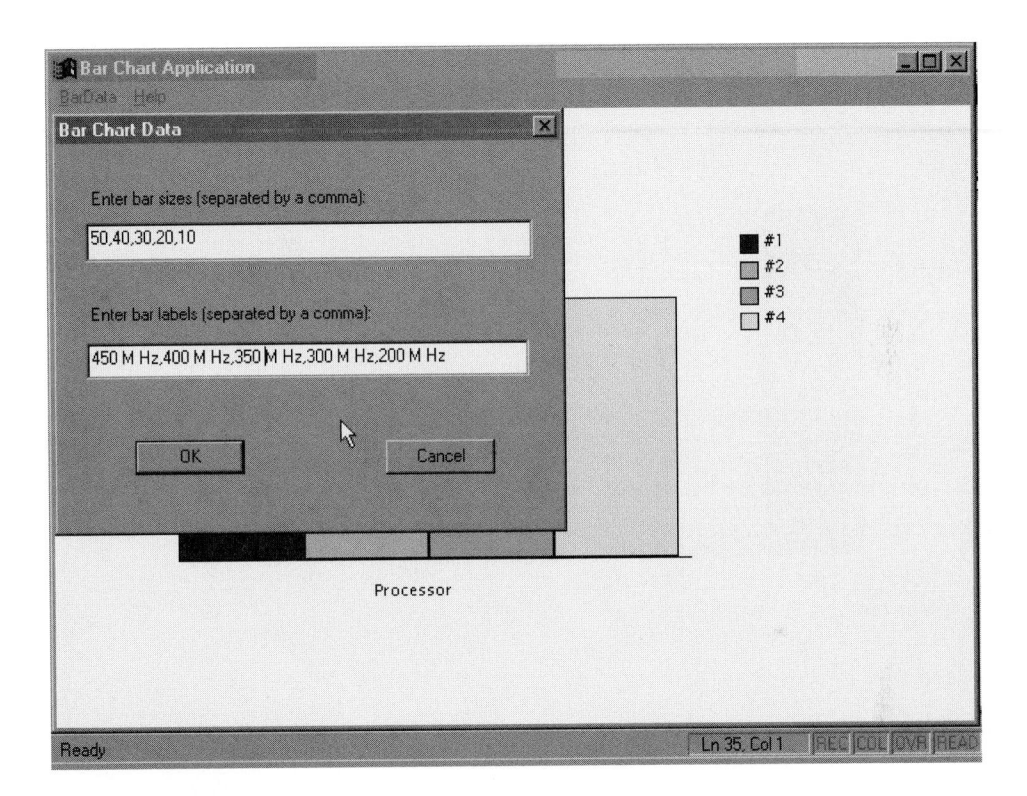

Figure 13-20 *The data entry dialog box with some unique data values.*

Figure 13–20 shows user-entered data being entered in the data entry dialog box.

Figure 13–21 shows the bar chart of the custom data just entered in the dialog box.

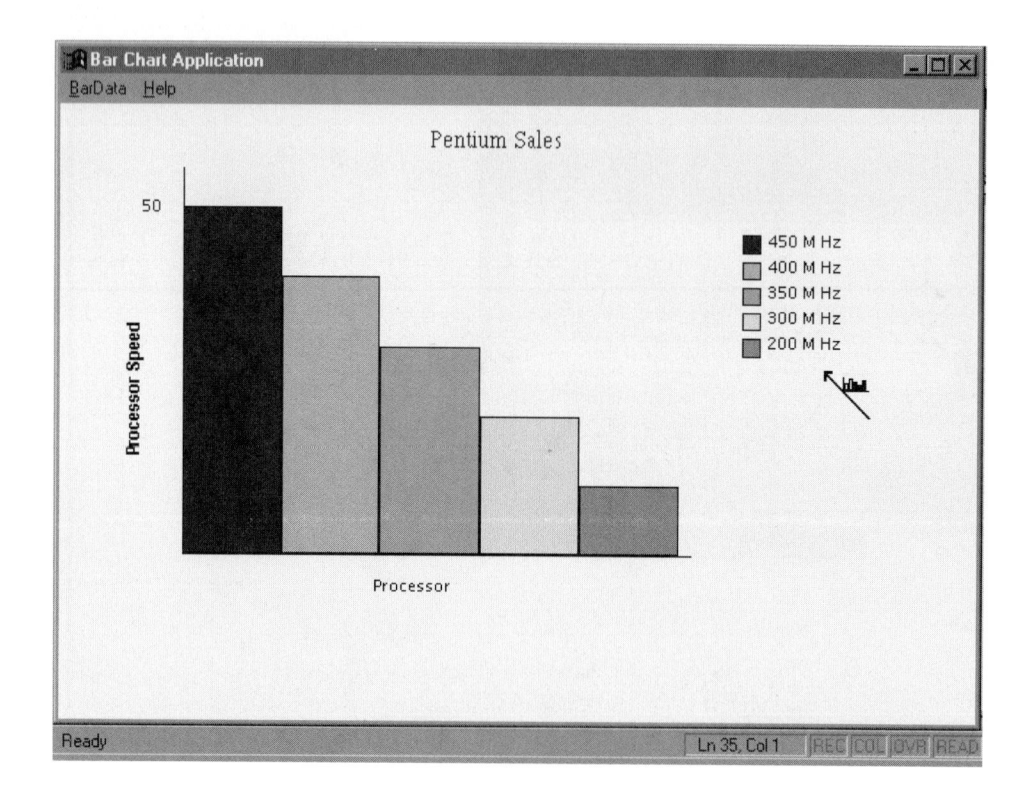

Figure 13-21 *A custom bar chart is drawn with new data.*

WM_DESTROY

The last message handler is WM_DESTROY. This message handler is responsible for exiting the application when the proper message is received.

Charting Variations

Are you having fun with charts? Here is a little challenge. Why not alter the pie chart project so that you can specify an "exploded" pie wedge for the largest slice. Or you might want to alter the bar chart project so that it draws a three-dimensional bar chart.

In additional to charting data, you'll find that professional presentations also use animation to enhance applications. In the next chapter, you will see how you can add simple animation effects to an application.

FOURTEEN

Sketching, Animation, and Video

In Chapters 1 through 12, you learned all of the fundamentals required to develop professional-quality Windows applications. However, we're sure you know there are still a lot of bells and whistles that can be included in applications. This chapter will explore a segment of Windows programs that are simply fun to use. For example, no book on Windows programming would be complete without a sketching application. Our mouse sketching version will allow you to apply your creative talents to the window's canvas and to use many components from previous chapters. The animation example represents another interesting facet of graphics programming that can be applied to your Windows applications. Finally, we'll look at an application that will show you how to create a simple video player. After all, you have already learned how to incorporate multimedia sound! The video player application will show you how to insert the necessary code into an application that will allow you to play video clips on command.

A Mouse Sketching Application

The mouse sketching application uses the mouse as a drawing instrument. As you move the mouse about, you'll be dragging a "paintbrush" about on the screen. Colors in the painter's palette will be selected with the use of the common color dialog box, which you learned about in Chapter 12. If you have artistic talent, you'll be amazed by the bright colors of the high-resolution screen and equally impressed by the various sketching tricks you can perform with the mouse.

This project is named *Sketch*. You'll find that menu selections lead you to appropriate dialog boxes, pen widths, and other painting options. The sketch application uses a menu that will allow you to select colors and pen widths for painting. Once you build this application, you might want to expand its capabilities by adding various shapes, such as circles, ellipses, boxes, and so on to the basic menu.

The Sketch Files

The Sketch project uses several files. The resource.h header file is created by the Resource Editor once all of the menu and dialog boxes are added to the project.

Here is an edited portion of the resource.h header file used for the Sketch project.

```
//{{NO_DEPENDENCIES}}
// Microsoft Developer Studio generated include file.
// Used by Sketch.rc
//
#define ID_OPTIONS_CLEAR        40001
#define ID_OPTIONS_EXIT         40002
#define ID_PEN_TWO              40004
#define ID_PEN_FIVE             40005
#define ID_PEN_TEN              40006
#define ID_PEN_THIRTY           40007
#define ID_PEN_SIXTY            40008
#define ID_HELP_ABOUT           40009
#define ID_OPTIONS_COLORS       40010
      .
      .
      .
```

This header file contains the ID values used by the menus items and dialog boxes for the Sketch project.

The resource script file, Sketch.rc, describes the resources for the project. These were designed in the graphical Resource Editor and translated to a text file.

Here is an edited portion of the resource script file, Sketch.rc.

```
//Microsoft Developer Studio generated resource script.
//
#include "resource.h"
      .
      .
      .
/////////////////////////////////////////////////////////////
//
```

```
// Menu
//
SKETCHMENU MENU DISCARDABLE
BEGIN
  POPUP "&Options"
  BEGIN
    MENUITEM "&Colors...",      ID_OPTIONS_COLORS
    MENUITEM "&Wipe Slate",     ID_OPTIONS_CLEAR
    MENUITEM "&Exit",           ID_OPTIONS_EXIT
  END
  POPUP "&Pen-Widths"
  BEGIN
    MENUITEM "&2",              ID_PEN_TWO
    MENUITEM "&5",              ID_PEN_FIVE
    MENUITEM "&10",             ID_PEN_TEN
    MENUITEM "&30",             ID_PEN_THIRTY
    MENUITEM "&60",             ID_PEN_SIXTY
  END
  POPUP "&Help"
  BEGIN
    MENUITEM "&About...",       ID_HELP_ABOUT
  END
END

/////////////////////////////////////////////////////////
//
// Dialog
//
ABOUTDLGBOX DIALOG DISCARDABLE  0, 0, 186, 108
STYLE DS_MODALFRAME | WS_POPUP | WS_CAPTION | WS_SYSMENU
CAPTION "About Mouse Sketching"
FONT 8, "MS Sans Serif"
BEGIN
  DEFPUSHBUTTON "OK",IDOK,67,80,50,14
  CTEXT "Mouse Sketching Application",
        IDC_STATIC,15,14,156,12
  CTEXT "by",IDC_STATIC,76,31,33,12
  CTEXT "William H. Murray and Chris H. Pappas",
        IDC_STATIC,15,51,158,16
END
      .
      .
      .
/////////////////////////////////////////////////////////
//
// Icon
//
// Icon with lowest ID value placed first to ensure
// application icon remains consistent on all systems.
SketchIcon    ICON    DISCARDABLE     "Sketch.ico"
```

548 Chapter 14 • Sketching, Animation, and Video

```
//////////////////////////////////////////////////////////
//
// Cursor
//
SketchCursor    CURSOR    DISCARDABLE        "Sketch.cur"
       .
       .
       .
```

Examine the resource script file and see whether you can identify each menu item, dialog box, icon, and cursor resource.

Figure 14–1 shows the Options menu for the Sketch project.

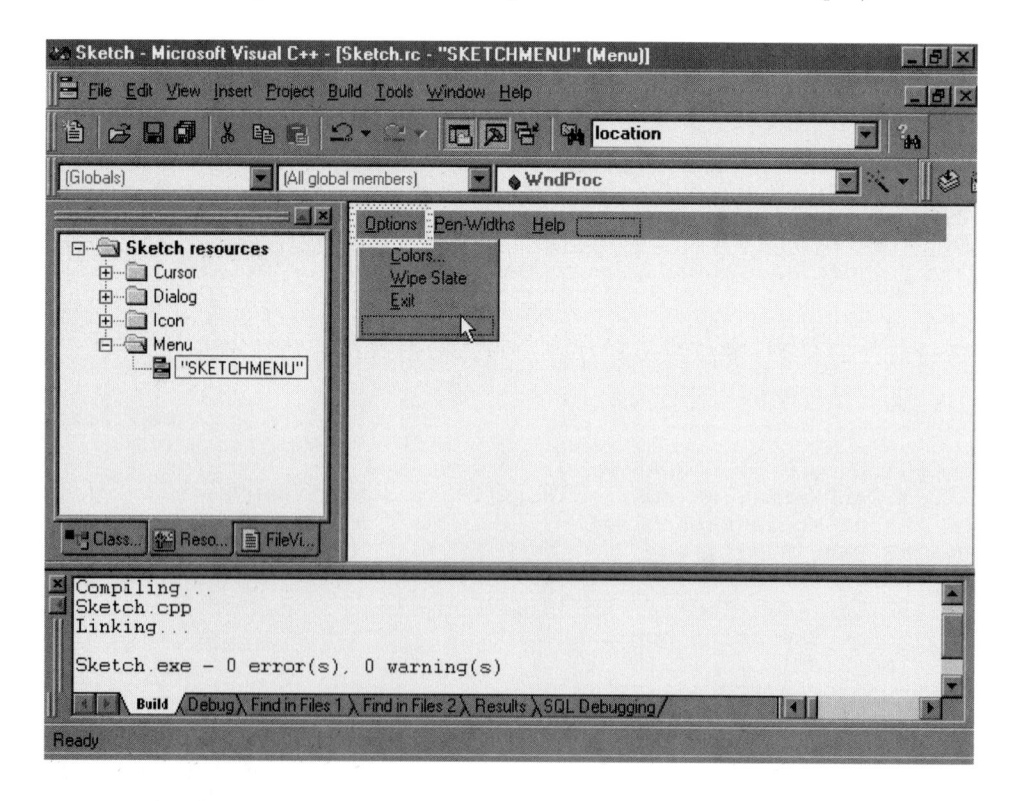

Figure 14-1 *The Options menu uses three menu items.*

The menu items provided by the Options menu allow the user to select the drawing color, a new canvas, or a quick exit from the application. The Pen-Widths menu, shown in Figure 14–2, allows the user to select one of several predefined pen widths for drawing.

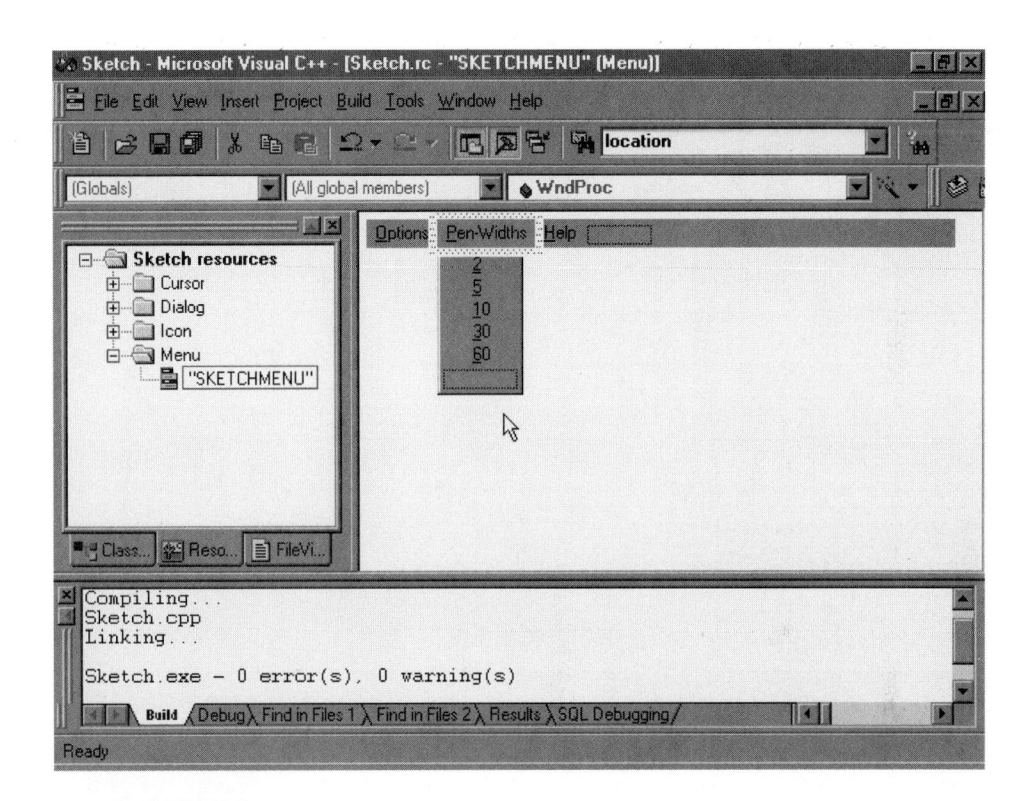

A Mouse Sketching Application **549**

Figure 14-2 *The Pen-Widths menu allows the user to select the width of the drawing pen.*

The Help menu leads the user to an About dialog box for the project. The Help menu is shown in Figure 14–3.

550 Chapter 14 • Sketching, Animation, and Video

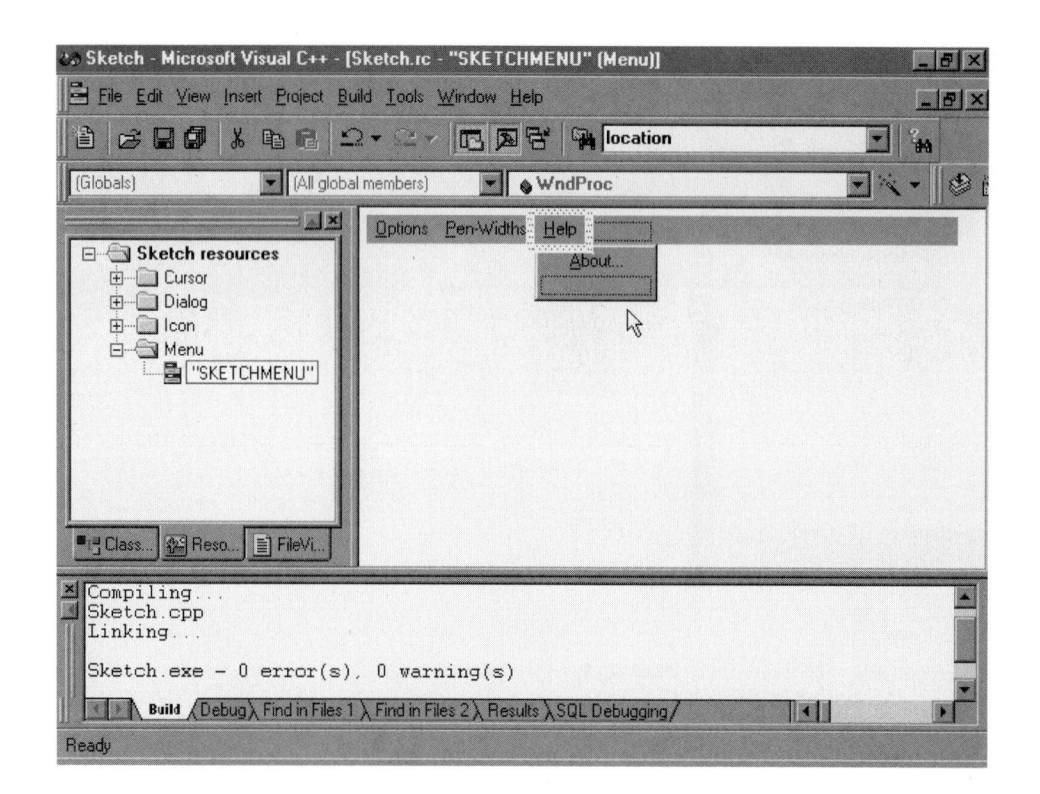

Figure 14-3 *The Help menu allows the user to open an About dialog box.*

You have seen the common color dialog box in previous chapters, and the About dialog box is also similar to previous examples. Note that this project uses a custom cursor and icon. The icon is designed in the Resource Editor and saved as Sketch.ico. Figure 14-4 shows the icon for this project while being designed in the Resource Editor.

A Mouse Sketching Application **551**

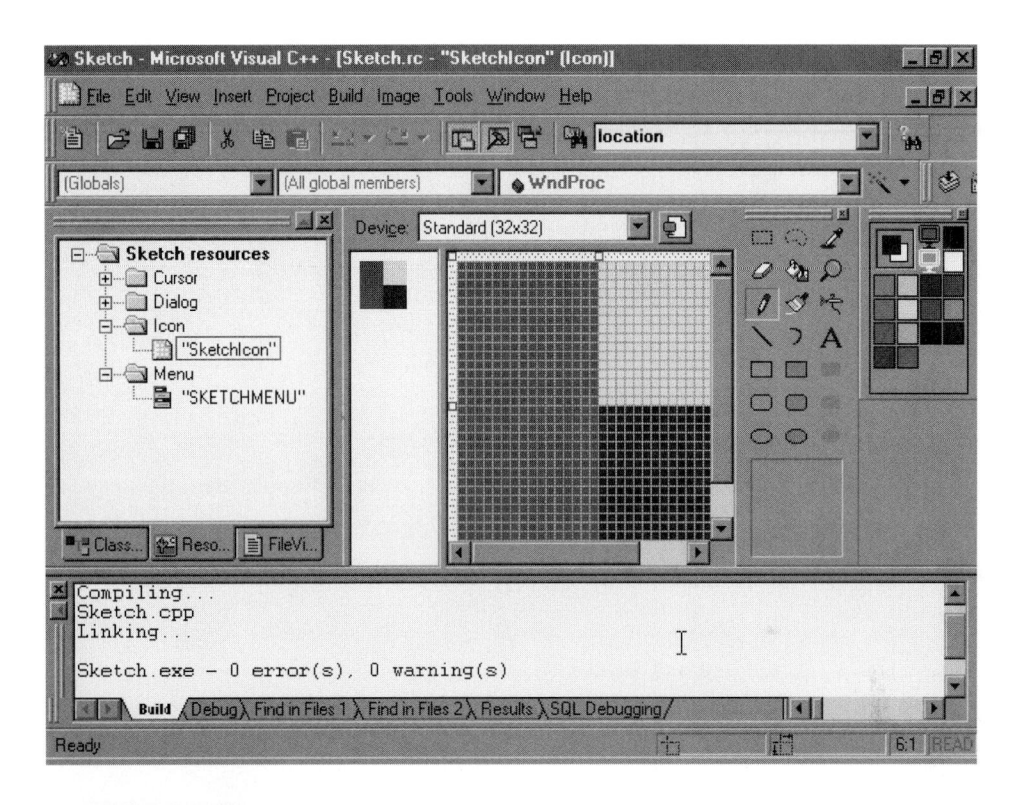

Figure 14–4 *The icon used in the Sketch project is designed in the Resource Editor.*

The cursor for the project is also designed in the Resource Editor. The cursor is saved in a file named *Sketch.cur*. Figure 14–5 shows the cursor we designed for the project.

552 Chapter 14 • Sketching, Animation, and Video

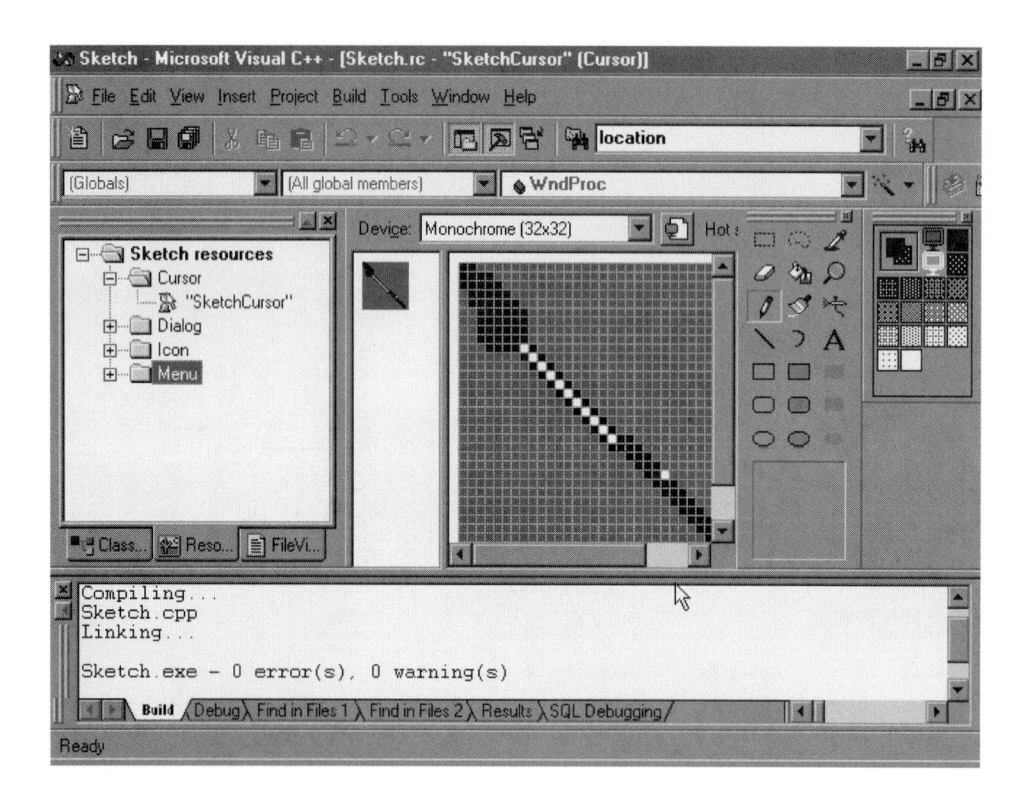

Figure 14-5 The cursor used in the Sketch project while being designed in the Resource Editor.

The source code for this application is named *Sketch.cpp*. As you study the source code listing, take note of where the calls are for multimedia sound. This resource is not included in the resource script file discussed earlier.

```
//
// Sketch.cpp
// This application allows the user to use the mouse to
// sketch drawings in the window. Colors are selected
// from the common color dialog box and pen widths from
// a menu of predefined pens. A multimedia sound file
// plays when the pen hits the canvas.
// Copyright (c) William H. Murray and Chris H. Pappas, 1999
//

#include <windows.h>
#include <mmsystem.h>  // add multimedia resources
#include <commdlg.h>   // add common dialog box resources
#include "resource.h"
```

```c
HINSTANCE hInst;

LRESULT CALLBACK WndProc(HWND,UINT,WPARAM,LPARAM);
BOOL CALLBACK AboutDlgProc(HWND,UINT,WPARAM,LPARAM);

char szProgName[]="ProgName";           // app name
char szApplName[]="SketchMenu";         // menu name
char szCursorName[]="SketchCursor";     // cursor name
char szIconName[]="SketchIcon";         // icon name
char szWaveName[]="Sketch.wav";         // sound file
BOOL bDrawtrail;
POINT omouselocat,nmouselocat;

int WINAPI WinMain(HINSTANCE hInst,HINSTANCE hPreInst,
                   LPSTR lpszCmdLine,int nCmdShow)
{
  HWND hWnd;
  MSG  lpMsg;
  WNDCLASS wcApp;

  wcApp.lpszClassName=szProgName;
  wcApp.hInstance    =hInst;
  wcApp.lpfnWndProc  =WndProc;
  wcApp.hCursor      =LoadCursor(hInst,szCursorName);
  wcApp.hIcon        =LoadIcon(hInst,szIconName);
  wcApp.lpszMenuName =szApplName;
  wcApp.hbrBackground=(HBRUSH) GetStockObject(WHITE_BRUSH);
  wcApp.style        =CS_HREDRAW|CS_VREDRAW;
  wcApp.cbClsExtra   =0;
  wcApp.cbWndExtra   =0;
  if (!RegisterClass (&wcApp))
    return 0;

  hWnd=CreateWindow(szProgName,"Mouse Sketching Application",
                    WS_OVERLAPPEDWINDOW,CW_USEDEFAULT,
                    CW_USEDEFAULT,CW_USEDEFAULT,
                    CW_USEDEFAULT,(HWND)NULL,(HMENU)NULL,
                    hInst,(LPSTR)NULL);
  ShowWindow(hWnd,nCmdShow);
  UpdateWindow(hWnd);
  while (GetMessage(&lpMsg,0,0,0)) {
    TranslateMessage(&lpMsg);
    DispatchMessage(&lpMsg);
  }
  return(lpMsg.wParam);
}
// Process the About dialog box control selection
BOOL CALLBACK AboutDlgProc(HWND hDlg,UINT messg,
                           WPARAM wParam,LPARAM lParam)
{
```

554   Chapter 14 • Sketching, Animation, and Video

```
   switch (messg) {
     case WM_INITDIALOG:
       break;
     case WM_COMMAND:
       switch (LOWORD(wParam)) {
         case IDOK:
           EndDialog(hDlg,0);
           break;
         default:
           return FALSE;
       }
       break;
     default:
       return FALSE;
   }
   return TRUE;
}

LRESULT CALLBACK WndProc(HWND hWnd,UINT messg,
                         WPARAM wParam,LPARAM lParam)
{
  HDC hdc;
  PAINTSTRUCT ps;
  static HPEN hOPen,hNPen;
  static CHOOSECOLOR ccs;
  static DWORD dCustomColors[16];
  static COLORREF colorshade=0;
  static int penwidth=2;
  static POINT pt;

  switch (messg)
  {
    case WM_CREATE:
      // initial values for common color dialog box
      ccs.lStructSize=sizeof(CHOOSECOLOR);
      ccs.hwndOwner=(HWND) hWnd;
      ccs.hInstance=(HWND) NULL;
      ccs.rgbResult=RGB(0,0,255);
      ccs.lpCustColors=dCustomColors;
      ccs.Flags=CC_RGBINIT|CC_FULLOPEN;
      ccs.lCustData=0L;
      ccs.lpfnHook=(LPCCHOOKPROC) NULL;
      ccs.lpTemplateName=(LPSTR) NULL;
      break;

    case WM_COMMAND:
      // process menu item selections
      switch (LOWORD(wParam)) {
        case ID_OPTIONS_COLORS:
          if (ChooseColor(&ccs)) {
```

```
          colorshade=(COLORREF) ccs.rgbResult;
        }
        break;
      case ID_OPTIONS_CLEAR:
        colorshade=PALETTERGB(0xFF,0xFF,0xFF);
        InvalidateRect(hWnd,NULL,TRUE);
        break;
      case ID_OPTIONS_EXIT:
        SendMessage(hWnd,WM_CLOSE,0,0L);
        break;
      case ID_PEN_TWO:
        penwidth=2;
        break;
      case ID_PEN_FIVE:
        penwidth=5;
        break;
      case ID_PEN_TEN:
        penwidth=10;
        break;
      case ID_PEN_THIRTY:
        penwidth=30;
        break;
      case ID_PEN_SIXTY:
        penwidth=60;
        break;
      case ID_HELP_ABOUT:
        DialogBox((HINSTANCE) GetModuleHandle(NULL),
                  "AboutDlgBox",hWnd,
                  AboutDlgProc);
        break;
      default:
        break;
    }
    break;

  case WM_LBUTTONDOWN:
    // when mouse button is down - draw
    nmouselocat.x=LOWORD(lParam);
    nmouselocat.y=HIWORD(lParam);
    omouselocat=nmouselocat;
    SetCapture(hWnd);
    bDrawtrail=TRUE;
    sndPlaySound(szWaveName,SND_ASYNC);
    break;

  case WM_MOUSEMOVE:
    // follow that mouse
    if (bDrawtrail) {
      omouselocat=nmouselocat;
      nmouselocat.x=LOWORD(lParam);
```

```
            nmouselocat.y=HIWORD(lParam);
            InvalidateRect(hWnd,NULL,FALSE);
            UpdateWindow(hWnd);
          }
          break;

      case WM_LBUTTONUP:
          // when mouse button is up - do not draw
          ReleaseCapture();
          bDrawtrail=FALSE;
          break;

      case WM_PAINT:
          hdc=BeginPaint(hWnd,&ps);

          hNPen=CreatePen(PS_SOLID,penwidth,colorshade);
          hOPen=(HPEN) SelectObject(hdc,hNPen);
          MoveToEx(hdc,omouselocat.x,omouselocat.y,NULL);
          LineTo(hdc,nmouselocat.x,nmouselocat.y);
          SelectObject(hdc,hOPen);
          DeleteObject(hNPen);

          ValidateRect(hWnd,NULL);
          EndPaint(hWnd,&ps);
          break;

      case WM_DESTROY:
          PostQuitMessage(0);
          break;

      default:
          return(DefWindowProc(hWnd,messg,wParam,lParam));
          break;
    }
    return(0);
}
```

Remember when you build this application that it is necessary to specify the winmm.lib library in the list of compiler linker libraries. The winmm.lib library provides the necessary multimedia capabilities to drive your sound card.

The Sketch.cpp Application Code

The Sketch.cpp source code file contains additional information on multimedia parameters and return values. Information on these functions can be found in the mmsystem.h header file. If you haven't printed a copy of this header file while studying an earlier chapter, why not print a copy of the file now? It should be found in your Visual C++ compiler's include subdirectory.

A Mouse Sketching Application

The sound wave file for this application is named *Sketch.wav*. There are other sources for wave files. You can create your own unique sounds with the sound board installed in your computer and save them in a wave format. You'll also find that there are probably a large number of wave files already installed on your computer. Just search your disk for *.wav. Notice, too, that an include statement for the multimedia resources is provided in the application file. This statement provides mmsystem.h header information.

In earlier chapters, you learned how to manipulate menu items and dialog box resources, so we won't discuss them again. However, there are some interesting aspects of this application that we should mention. The main action takes place in several case statements in the WndProc procedure.

Menu options are processed under WM_COMMAND. Additional case statements allow the variable colorshade to be set to the correct color value by calling the common color dialog box and returning the appropriate color information. The penwidth variable is used to change the pen width of the drawing instrument. Both of these values are used by the **CreatePen()** function to create a new pen width and color. The **LineTo()** function uses the current nmouselocation information to complete a straight line. The user marks the starting point of the line with a click of the left mouse button. If that button is held down, points are marked repeatedly, creating a smoothly flowing line as the mouse is moved across the canvas. Because the line lengths will be short line segments, curves and other shapes can be created easily.

The WM_LBUTTONDOWN message handler receives a message when the user clicks the left mouse button. When this occurs, the mouse coordinate information is passed through the lParam parameter. This information is used to create the coordinates for the **MoveToEx()** function. When the user clicks the left mouse button it effectively moves the cursor to the current mouse position on the screen. The left button must be clicked to set the bDrawtrail flag to TRUE.

The sound board will produce a unique sound when the left mouse button is clicked. This is easy to do with a simple call to the **sndPlaySound()** function. The parameters for the **sndPlaySound()** function are discussed next. Here is the function's syntax:

```
BOOL sndPlaySound(lpszSoundName, wFlags)
```

The name of the sound resource to play is identified by (LPCSTR) lpsz-SoundName. In the present example, this sound has been associated with szWave. The UINT wFlags parameter gives options for playing the sound. For example, if the parameter is set to SND_SYNC, the resource is played asynchronously. In other words, the function does not return until the sound ends. If the parameter is set to SND_ASYNC, the resource will be played synchronously. This mode will allow the function to return immediately after starting the sound. The SND_NODEFAULT value is used for cases where the sound resource might not be found. In these cases, the flag permits the function to return silently, without playing the default sound. Use SND_MEMORY to point to an in-memory sound waveform. Use SND_LOOP and SND_ASYNC to play a sound resource over and over until the function is called again with the sound resource set to NULL. Use SND_NOSTOP to return FALSE without playing the sound. The **BOOL** return value is TRUE if the sound is played; otherwise, it is FALSE.

The paintbrush, which is actually a drawing pen, reflects the user's mouse movements. The WM_MOUSEMOVE message handler intercepts mouse movement information and, if bDrawtrail is TRUE, records the mouse coordinates once again. If bDrawtrail is FALSE (that is, if the left mouse button isn't down), no call is made to invalidate the rectangle and update the window. However, if the flag is TRUE, both the **InvalidateRect()** and **UpdateWindow()** functions are called. The mouse coordinates are passed to the global variable nmouselocation. When the left mouse button is released during the drawing cycle, the WM_LBUTTONUP message handler intercepts the message and sets the bDrawtrail variable to FALSE. With the bDrawtrail variable set to FALSE, the mouse may be moved about on the mouse pad without doing any drawing on the canvas.

If you have ever painted with water colors or oils, you know the kind of trouble you can get into. Just imagine what you can do with an electronic painting program! This application provides the supplies you'll need to get started. Just add your own talents and you'll be creating masterpieces under Windows.

Figures 14–6 shows the painting attempt of a user selected at random. Of course, we didn't do this drawing!

Figure 14-6 *Being creative with the sketch application.*

Flying Saucer Animation Application

An animation effect can be created with a simple draw, erase, move, and redraw mechanism. In this case, a simple figure is drawn on the screen and allowed to remain there for a set time. Next, the figure is erased. In the cases where figures are created with graphics device interface (GDI) graphics primitives or are small bitmapped images, this can be accomplished by redrawing the figure in the background color, clearing a rectangular portion around the figure, or clearing the entire screen. The coordinates for the figure are then shifted to the left, right, up, down, or a combination of both by a small number of pixels, and the figure is redrawn. If the timing is right, you will get the sense of motion as you view the window.

Bitmaps often produce smoother animation results because the bitmapped image can be drawn previously and stored in memory. In contrast, images made from GDI graphics primitives must be drawn in real time. By using a bitmap to reproduce small figures, the constant draw-erase-redraw cycle time can be eliminated. This technique helps eliminate an annoying flicker that results from the delay. Perhaps you have already noticed how pointers and other icons seem to slide effortlessly across the screen as you move the mouse? This motion suggests that a bitmap can actually float over the drawing surface.

For our example, the **BitBlt()** function, that you studied in Chapter 9, will be used to move a bitmapped image about on the screen. The bitmap will erase its tracks as long as the image contains a border surrounding the pattern that is the same color as the background of the window.

If the bitmapped image remains the same throughout the application it is static. Even though the figure or bitmap was moved about on the screen, there was no animation within the bitmap. The image itself can be made to move by making the bitmapped image dynamic. This can be done, once the new position has been achieved, by quickly drawing several images of the same figure at that location. The figures drawn at the same location have only subtle changes from each previous figure. When these figures are viewed quickly, the perception of movement is achieved. Hollywood studios have made millions of dollars using this simple concept.

For the Saucer project, a tiny flying saucer bitmap is created with an alien inside the ship. Four slight variations of the saucer bitmap will give the illusion that the alien is moving its arms and that flames are shooting out of the bottom of the ship. During the sequence, the saucer's lights change colors, too.

Figures 14–7–14–10 show the bitmapped images in the Resource Editor as they are being designed.

Flying Saucer Animation Application 561

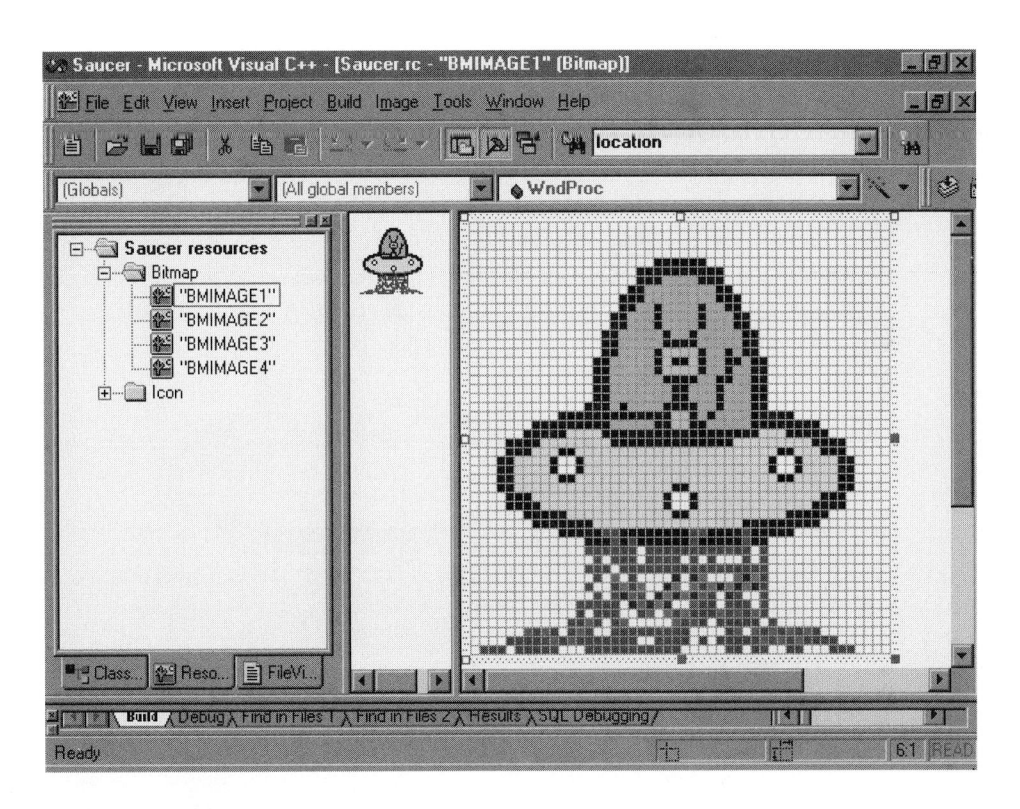

Figure 14-7 *bmp1.bmp is the first image of the ship and alien.*

562 Chapter 14 • Sketching, Animation, and Video

Figure 14-8 bmp2.bmp is the second image of the ship and alien.

Flying Saucer Animation Application 563

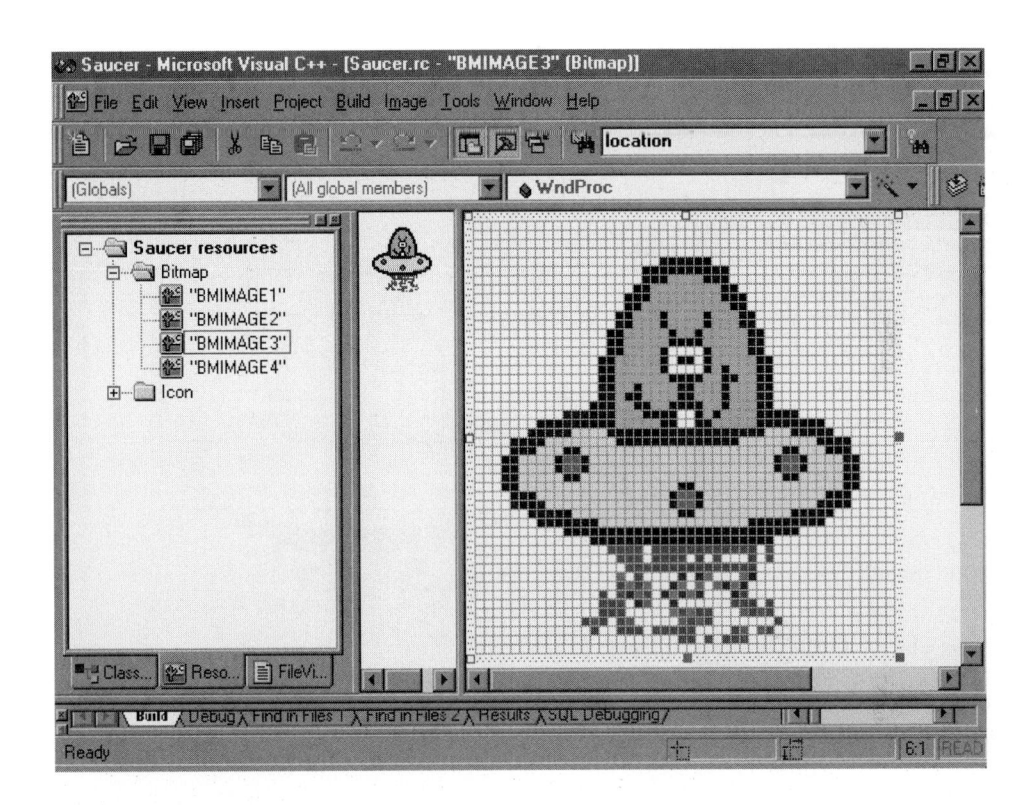

Figure 14-9 *bmp3.bmp is the third image of the ship and alien.*

564 Chapter 14 • Sketching, Animation, and Video

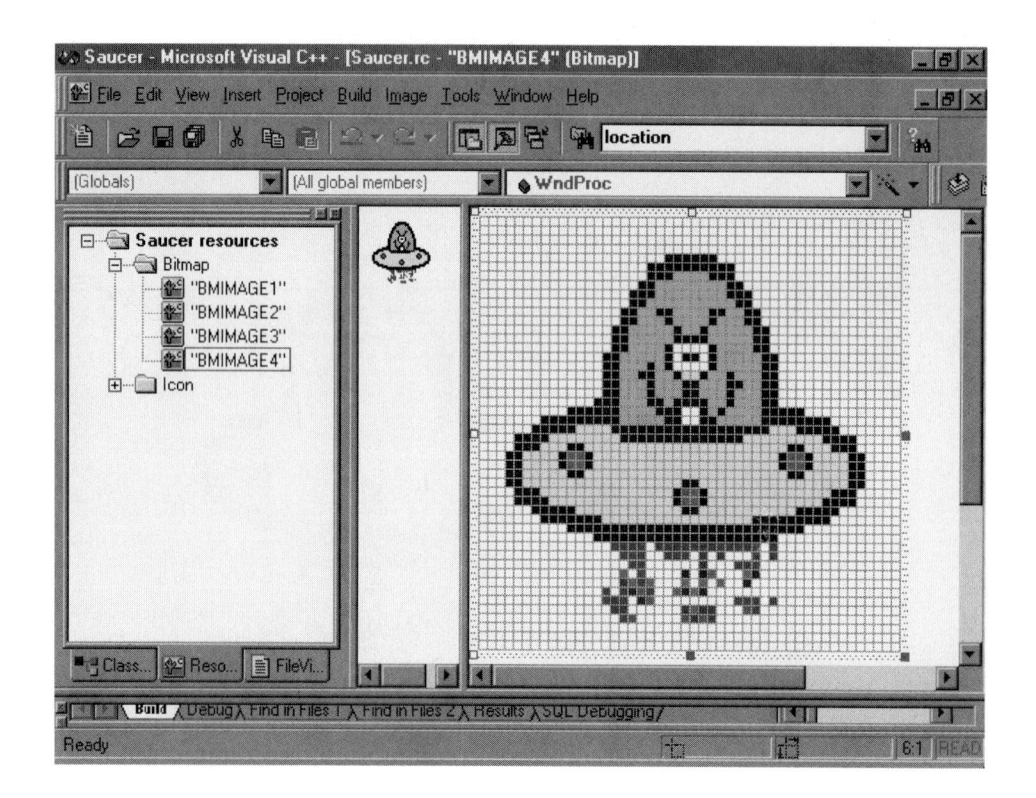

Figure 14-10 *bmp4.bmp is the fourth image of the ship and alien.*

The Saucer project also requires two sound resource files named *mm1.wav* and *mm2.wav*. You can create your own wave files with the Windows sound recorder or use any prerecorded wave file you desire.

This project will require the bitmapped images just mentioned and the wave files for the various sounds. When you create the bitmapped images, they should be saved in four separate files named *bmp1.bmp, bmp2.bmp, bmp3.bmp,* and *bmp4.bmp*. The resource.h header file is generated by the Resource Editor and would normally contain ID values associated with a project. In this example, there are no additional ID values associated with our resources, so that file will be ignored for purposes of discussion.

The Saucer.rc resource script file is used to identify the bitmap resources and a unique icon for the project. Here is an edited portion of the resource script file.

```
//////////////////////////////////////////////////////////
//
// Bitmap
//
BMImage1       BITMAP    DISCARDABLE     "Bmp1.bmp"
```

```
BMImage2    BITMAP   DISCARDABLE    "Bmp2.bmp"
BMImage3    BITMAP   DISCARDABLE    "Bmp3.bmp"
BMImage4    BITMAP   DISCARDABLE    "Bmp4.bmp"
        .
        .
        .
//////////////////////////////////////////////////////
//
// Icon
//
// Icon with lowest ID value placed first to
// ensure application icon
// remains consistent on all systems.
SaucerIcon  ICON     DISCARDABLE    "Saucer.ico"
```

The next listing is the Saucer.cpp source code for the project. As you examine the source code file, try and find where the **Sleep()** function is used.

```
//
// Saucer.cpp
// A Windows Application that demonstrates simple
// animation techniques with a bitmapped image.
// Copyright (c) William H. Murray and Chris H. Pappas, 1999
//

#include <windows.h>
#include <mmsystem.h>

LRESULT CALLBACK WndProc(HWND,UINT,WPARAM,LPARAM);

char szProgName[]="ProgName";
char szIconName[]="SaucerIcon";
char szBMName1[]="BMImage1";
char szBMName2[]="BMImage2";
char szBMName3[]="BMImage3";
char szBMName4[]="BMImage4";

HBITMAP hBitmap1,hBitmap2;
HBITMAP hBitmap3,hBitmap4;
int iDelay,iTimer,xPos,yPos;
int xPosInit,yPosInit,xStep,yStep;

int WINAPI WinMain(HINSTANCE hInst,HINSTANCE hPreInst,
                   LPSTR lpszCmdLine,int nCmdShow)
{
  HWND hWnd;
  MSG  lpMsg;
  WNDCLASS wcApp;

  wcApp.lpszClassName=szProgName;
  wcApp.hInstance      =hInst;
```

566 Chapter 14 • Sketching, Animation, and Video

```
   wcApp.lpfnWndProc   =WndProc;
   wcApp.hCursor       =LoadCursor(NULL,IDC_ARROW);
   wcApp.hIcon         =LoadIcon(hInst,szIconName);
   wcApp.lpszMenuName  =0;
   wcApp.hbrBackground=(HBRUSH) GetStockObject(WHITE_BRUSH);
   wcApp.style         =CS_HREDRAW|CS_VREDRAW;
   wcApp.cbClsExtra    =0;
   wcApp.cbWndExtra    =0;
   if (!RegisterClass (&wcApp))
     return 0;

   hWnd=CreateWindow(szProgName,"Flying Saucer Application",
                     WS_OVERLAPPEDWINDOW,CW_USEDEFAULT,
                     CW_USEDEFAULT,CW_USEDEFAULT,
                     CW_USEDEFAULT,(HWND)NULL,(HMENU)NULL,
                     hInst,(LPSTR)NULL);
   ShowWindow(hWnd,nCmdShow);
   UpdateWindow(hWnd);

   // load all saucer bitmaps
   hBitmap1=LoadBitmap(hInst,szBMName1);
   hBitmap2=LoadBitmap(hInst,szBMName2);
   hBitmap3=LoadBitmap(hInst,szBMName3);
   hBitmap4=LoadBitmap(hInst,szBMName4);

   while (GetMessage(&lpMsg,0,0,0)) {
     TranslateMessage(&lpMsg);
     DispatchMessage(&lpMsg);
   }
   return(lpMsg.wParam);
}

LRESULT CALLBACK WndProc(HWND hWnd,UINT messg,
                         WPARAM wParam,LPARAM lParam)
{
   HDC hdc;
   HDC hmdc;
   RECT rcWnd;
   static BITMAP bm;

   switch (messg)
   {
     case WM_CREATE:
       // initial values for timer #1
       // and positions
       iDelay=10;
       xPosInit=100;
       yPosInit=100;
       xStep=2;
       yStep=2;
```

```
      xPos=xPosInit;
      yPos=yPosInit;
      iTimer=SetTimer(hWnd,1,iDelay,NULL);
      break;

    case WM_TIMER:
      // with each timer tick, draw each
      // of four bitmapped images
      hdc=GetDC(hWnd);
      GetClientRect(hWnd,&rcWnd);
      hmdc=CreateCompatibleDC(hdc);
      xPos+=xStep;
      yPos+=yStep;

      // draw image 1
      SelectObject(hmdc,hBitmap1);
      GetObject(hBitmap1,sizeof(bm),(LPSTR) &bm);
      BitBlt(hdc,xPos,yPos,bm.bmWidth,bm.bmHeight,
             hmdc,0,0,SRCCOPY);
      Sleep(iDelay);

      // draw image 2
      SelectObject(hmdc,hBitmap2);
      GetObject(hBitmap2,sizeof(bm),(LPSTR) &bm);
      BitBlt(hdc,xPos,yPos,bm.bmWidth,bm.bmHeight,
             hmdc,0,0,SRCCOPY);
      Sleep(iDelay);

      // draw image 3
      SelectObject(hmdc,hBitmap3);
      GetObject(hBitmap3,sizeof(bm),(LPSTR) &bm);
      BitBlt(hdc,xPos,yPos,bm.bmWidth,bm.bmHeight,
             hmdc,0,0,SRCCOPY);
      Sleep(iDelay);

      // draw image 4
      SelectObject(hmdc,hBitmap4);
      GetObject(hBitmap4,sizeof(bm),(LPSTR) &bm);
      BitBlt(hdc,xPos,yPos,bm.bmWidth,bm.bmHeight,
             hmdc,0,0,SRCCOPY);
      Sleep(iDelay);

      // examine left and right window edges
      if((xPos+bm.bmWidth > rcWnd.right) ||
         (xPos < rcWnd.left)) {
        xStep=-xStep;
        sndPlaySound("mm1.wav",SND_ASYNC);
      }

      // examine top and bottom window edges
```

```
            if((yPos+bm.bmHeight > rcWnd.bottom) ||
               (yPos < rcWnd.top)) {
              yStep=-yStep;
              sndPlaySound("mm2.wav",SND_ASYNC);
            }

            ReleaseDC(hWnd,hdc);
            DeleteDC(hmdc);
            break;

        case WM_DESTROY:
            if (hBitmap1) DeleteObject(hBitmap1);
            if (hBitmap2) DeleteObject(hBitmap2);
            if (hBitmap3) DeleteObject(hBitmap3);
            if (hBitmap4) DeleteObject(hBitmap4);
            if(iTimer) KillTimer(hWnd,1);
            sndPlaySound(NULL,0);
            PostQuitMessage(0);
            break;

        default:
            return(DefWindowProc(hWnd,messg,wParam,lParam));
            break;
    }
    return(0);
}
```

Remember to add the winmm.lib to the Visual C++ linker's library list during the build operation. This library provides the routines that will allow the two multimedia sounds for this application.

As you study the Saucer.cpp source code, notice that provisions have been made for two-dimensional movement. The ship and alien can bounce off of the top, bottom, right side, or left side of the window. With each timer message, a sequence of four bitmapped images is drawn, with a short time delay inserted between each. Here is a small piece of that code.

```
// draw image 1
SelectObject(hmdc,hBitmap1);
GetObject(hBitmap1,sizeof(bm),(LPSTR) &bm);
BitBlt(hdc,xPos,yPos,bm.bmWidth,bm.bmHeight,
       hmdc,0,0,SRCCOPY);
Sleep(iDelay);

// draw image 2
SelectObject(hmdc,hBitmap2);
GetObject(hBitmap2,sizeof(bm),(LPSTR) &bm);
BitBlt(hdc,xPos,yPos,bm.bmWidth,bm.bmHeight,
       hmdc,0,0,SRCCOPY);
Sleep(iDelay);
```

The four bitmapped images are identified with handles; hBitmap1, hBitmap2, hBitmap3, and hBitmap4. The creature's arms were moved to a different position in each of the four figures. A flaming exhaust and flashing lights add additional dramatic action to this image. A 10-millisecond delay is inserted between each drawing, using the **Sleep()** function, to allow the eye to see the image before it is erased. Once all four images have been drawn, the entire ship is moved to a new position.

Animation of the saucer is achieved in two dimensions. Here is the code responsible for moving the ship and alien about on the screen.

```
// examine left and right window edges
if((xPos+bm.bmWidth > rcWnd.right) ||
   (xPos < rcWnd.left)) {
  xStep=-xStep;
  sndPlaySound("mm1.wav",SND_ASYNC);
  }

// examine top and bottom window edges
if((yPos+bm.bmHeight > rcWnd.bottom) ||
   (yPos < rcWnd.top)) {
  yStep=-yStep;
  sndPlaySound("mm2.wav",SND_ASYNC);
  }
```

One **if** statement controls the left-to-right motion and another controls the up-and-down motion. With each timer tick, a new screen position is specified. These two statements check the values of the horizontal movement and vertical movement to make sure that the new screen positions fit within the boundaries of the window's bounding rectangle. If they do, everything is fine. If they don't, it means a collision has occurred between the bitmapped image and a boundary. When this happens, the direction of movement is reversed by changing the sign of the xStep or yStep increment.

Figure 14–11 shows the application in action. The hapless little alien seems to be screaming "Let me out before I hit another wall!"

Figure 14-11   *Here are the saucer and the alien flying about the window.*

This application was designed to play two different sounds. One sound is used for top and bottom collisions, and another is for side-to-side collisions.

A Video Player Application

You have already learned that it is relatively easy to add multimedia sounds to a project. You will be astonished to find out that it is almost as easy to add video playback features to your project, too. That is, as long as you are happy with the default playback window!

The Video project discussed next will allow you to play back any AVI video file. You can create your own AVI files with a video capture board, download an AVI file from the Internet, or search for an AVI file that might already exist on your system. It doesn't matter what the source of the AVI file is—the Video project will play it back for you.

This project also introduces you to the common file dialog box. In Chapter 12, you learned how to use the common font and color dialog boxes to produce a consistent look across applications. The common file dialog box will allow you to add file loading and saving capabilities to your projects.

Here is an edited portion of the resource.h header file created by the Resource Editor for this project.

```
//{{NO_DEPENDENCIES}}
// Microsoft Developer Studio generated include file.
// Used by Video.rc
//
#define ID_SELECT_FILE          40001
#define ID_SELECT_EXIT          40002
#define ID_HELP_ABOUT           40003
#define IDC_STATIC              -1
    .
    .
    .
```

The ID values shown in the resource.h header file are for two simple menus that will allow access to the common file dialog box, an About dialog box, and a menu exit option.

The resource script file, video.rc, gives the description for the menu and About dialog box used in this example.

```
//Microsoft Developer Studio generated resource script.
//
#include "resource.h"
    .
    .
    .
/////////////////////////////////////////////////////////////
//
// Menu
//
FileMenu MENU DISCARDABLE
BEGIN
    POPUP "&Select"
    BEGIN
        MENUITEM "&File...",        ID_SELECT_FILE
        MENUITEM "&Exit",           ID_SELECT_EXIT
    END
    POPUP "&Help"
    BEGIN
        MENUITEM "&About...",       ID_HELP_ABOUT
    END
END
    .
    .
    .
/////////////////////////////////////////////////////////////
//
```

Chapter 14 • Sketching, Animation, and Video

```
// Dialog
//
AboutDlgBox DIALOG DISCARDABLE  0, 0, 186, 106
STYLE DS_MODALFRAME | WS_POPUP | WS_CAPTION | WS_SYSMENU
CAPTION "About AVI Video Player"
FONT 8, "MS Sans Serif"
BEGIN
   DEFPUSHBUTTON   "OK",IDOK,68,79,50,14
   CTEXT     "AVI Video Player",IDC_STATIC,15,13,158,13
   CTEXT     "by",IDC_STATIC,81,30,28,13
   CTEXT     "William H. Murray and Chris H. Pappas",
             IDC_STATIC,16,50,154,14
END
       .
       .
       .
```

Remember that the description of the common file dialog box will not show up in the resource script file as it is predefined in the comctl32.lib.

Here is the Video.cpp source code listing used for this project. We'll take a closer look at the important elements shortly.

```
//
// Video.cpp
// This application demonstrates how to create a simple
// AVI video player..
// Copyright (c) William H. Murray and Chris H. Pappas, 1999
//

#include <windows.h>
#include <commdlg.h>
#include <vfw.h>
#include <mmsystem.h>   // multimedia header
#include <string.h>
#include "resource.h"

HINSTANCE hInst;

LRESULT CALLBACK WndProc(HWND,UINT,WPARAM,LPARAM);
BOOL CALLBACK AboutDlgProc(HWND,UINT,WPARAM,LPARAM);

char szProgName[]="ProgName";
char szApplName[]="FileMenu";
char buffer[80]="";

int WINAPI WinMain(HINSTANCE hInst,HINSTANCE hPreInst,
                   LPSTR lpszCmdLine,int nCmdShow)
{
  HWND hWnd;
  MSG  lpMsg;
  WNDCLASS wcApp;
```

```
  wcApp.lpszClassName=szProgName;
  wcApp.hInstance     =hInst;
  wcApp.lpfnWndProc   =WndProc;
  wcApp.hCursor       =LoadCursor(NULL,IDC_ARROW);
  wcApp.hIcon         =0;
  wcApp.lpszMenuName  =szApplName;
  wcApp.hbrBackground=(HBRUSH) GetStockObject(WHITE_BRUSH);
  wcApp.style         =CS_HREDRAW|CS_VREDRAW;
  wcApp.cbClsExtra    =0;
  wcApp.cbWndExtra    =0;
  if (!RegisterClass (&wcApp))
    return 0;

  hWnd=CreateWindow(szProgName,"Live Video",
                    WS_OVERLAPPEDWINDOW,0,0,
                    639,479,(HWND)NULL,(HMENU)NULL,
                    hInst,(LPSTR)NULL);
  ShowWindow(hWnd,nCmdShow);
  UpdateWindow(hWnd);
  while (GetMessage(&lpMsg,0,0,0)) {
    TranslateMessage(&lpMsg);
    DispatchMessage(&lpMsg);
  }
  return(lpMsg.wParam);
}

// Process the About dialog box control selection
BOOL CALLBACK AboutDlgProc(HWND hDlg,UINT messg,
                           WPARAM wParam,LPARAM lParam)
{
  switch (messg) {
    case WM_INITDIALOG:
    break;
    case WM_COMMAND:
      switch (LOWORD(wParam)) {
        case IDOK:
          EndDialog(hDlg,0);
          break;
        default:
          return FALSE;
      }
      break;
    default:
      return FALSE;
  }
  return TRUE;
}
LRESULT CALLBACK WndProc(HWND hWnd,UINT messg,
                         WPARAM wParam,LPARAM lParam)
{
```

Chapter 14 • Sketching, Animation, and Video

```
   static WNDCLASS cwcApp;
   static HWND hChild1;
   static OPENFILENAME of;
   UINT    wDeviceID;
   DWORD   dwReturn;
   MCI_OPEN_PARMS mciOpenParms;
   MCI_PLAY_PARMS mciPlayParms;

   switch (messg)
   {
     // Process the menu item selection
     case WM_COMMAND:
       switch (LOWORD(wParam)) {
         // select the common file dialog box
         case ID_SELECT_FILE:
           of.lStructSize      = sizeof (OPENFILENAME);
           of.hwndOwner        = NULL;
           of.hInstance        = hInst;
           of.lpstrFilter      = "AVI\000 *.avi\000\000";
           of.lpstrCustomFilter = NULL;
           of.nMaxCustFilter   = 0;
           of.nFilterIndex     = 0;
           of.lpstrFile        = buffer;
           of.nMaxFile         = MAX_PATH;
           of.lpstrFileTitle   = NULL;
           of.nMaxFileTitle    = 0;
           of.lpstrInitialDir  = "c:\\";
           of.lpstrTitle       = NULL;
           of.Flags            = OFN_HIDEREADONLY;
           of.nFileOffset      = 0;
           of.nFileExtension   = 0;
           of.lpstrDefExt      = NULL;
           of.lCustData        = 0;
           of.lpfnHook         = NULL;
           of.lpTemplateName   = NULL;
           if (!GetOpenFileName (&of)) return 0L;

           mciOpenParms.lpstrDeviceType="AVIVideo";
           mciOpenParms.dwCallback=(DWORD) hWnd;
           mciOpenParms.lpstrElementName=buffer;
           dwReturn=mciSendCommand(0,MCI_OPEN,MCI_OPEN_TYPE|
                         MCI_OPEN_ELEMENT,
                         (DWORD)(LPVOID)&mciOpenParms);

           wDeviceID=mciOpenParms.wDeviceID;

           dwReturn=mciSendCommand(wDeviceID,MCI_PLAY,
                         MCI_NOTIFY,
                         (DWORD)(LPVOID)&mciPlayParms);
```

```
              if (dwReturn = 0 )
                 wDeviceID=mciSendCommand(wDeviceID,MCI_CLOSE,0,
                                     (DWORD)(LPVOID) NULL);

              InvalidateRect(hWnd,NULL,TRUE);
              break;
           // exit the application
           case ID_SELECT_EXIT:
              SendMessage(hWnd,WM_CLOSE,0,0L);
              break;
           // draw the About dialog box
           case ID_HELP_ABOUT:
              DialogBox(hInst,"AboutDlgBox",hWnd,
                       (DLGPROC)AboutDlgProc);
              break;
           default:
              break;
         }
      break;

      case WM_DESTROY:
         PostQuitMessage(0);
         break;
      default:
         return(DefWindowProc(hWnd,messg,wParam,lParam));
         break;
   }
   return(0);
}
```

Remember that you'll need to include comctl32.lib, winmm.lib, and vfw.lib in the Visual C++ linker's library list when you build the project. Figure 14–12 shows a portion of an AVI file during playback.

576 Chapter 14 • Sketching, Animation, and Video

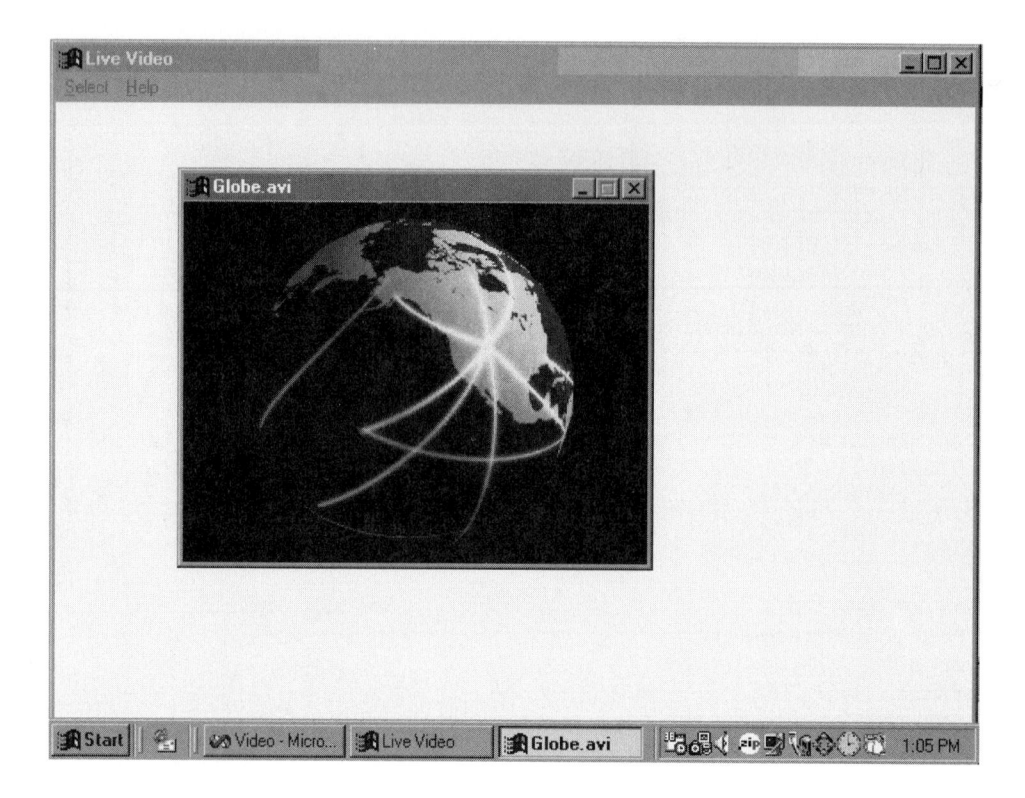

Figure 14–12 *AVI video clips can be played back with the Video.cpp application.*

In the next sections, we'll look at important source code elements and see how they affect the operation of this project.

The Common File Selection Dialog Box

When the user selects the File... menu item, the common file selection dialog box will appear. This dialog box is used to identify the video source that the user wishes to play. Figure 14–3 shows this common file dialog box.

A Video Player Application

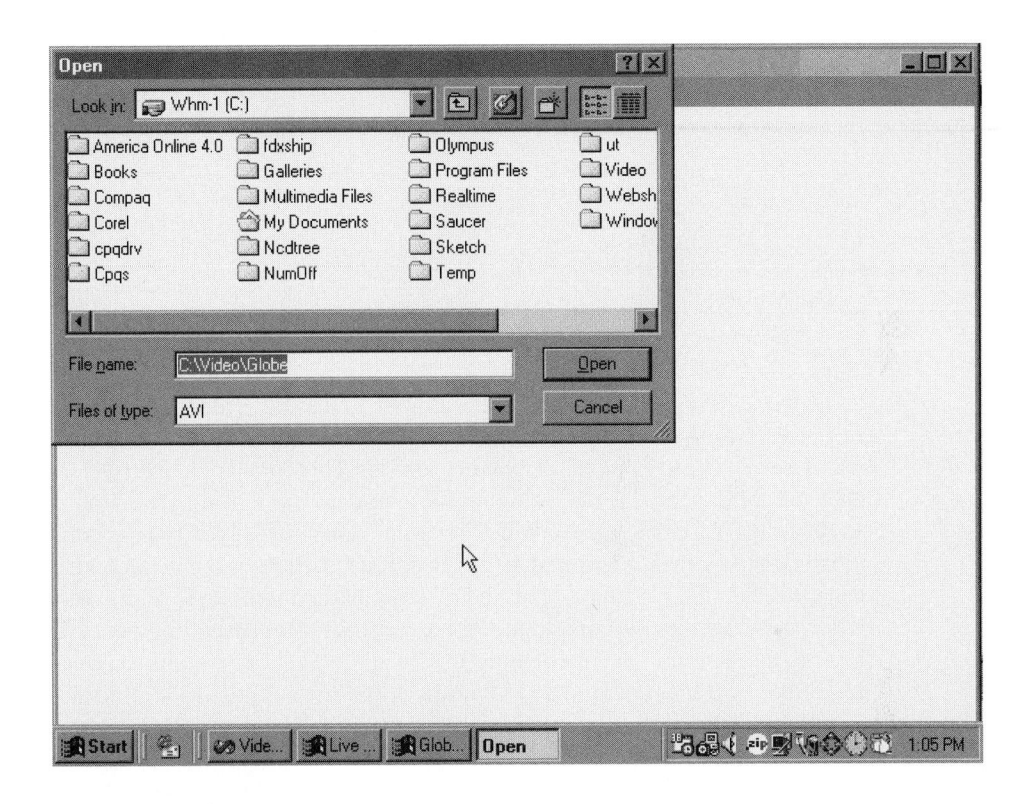

[Screenshot of Open file dialog]

Figure 14-13 *The common file dialog box is used to select AVI files.*

When an AVI file has been selected by the user, information is returned and processed under the IDM_FILE message handler. This information is placed in an OPENFILENAME structure. Here is a portion of that code showing various OPENFILENAME structure members. Remember that this portion of code has nothing to do with video playback. All we're doing is getting file information from the common file dialog box and placing it in a data structure.

```
of.lStructSize       = sizeof (OPENFILENAME);
of.hwndOwner         = NULL;
of.hInstance         = hInst;
of.lpstrFilter       = "AVI\000 *.avi\000\000";
of.lpstrCustomFilter = NULL;
of.nMaxCustFilter    = 0;
of.nFilterIndex      = 0;
of.lpstrFile         = buffer;
of.nMaxFile          = MAX_PATH;
of.lpstrFileTitle    = NULL;
of.nMaxFileTitle     = 0;
```

```
of.lpstrInitialDir  = "c:\\";
of.lpstrTitle       = NULL;
of.Flags            = OFN_HIDEREADONLY;
of.nFileOffset      = 0;
of.nFileExtension   = 0;
of.lpstrDefExt      = NULL;
of.lCustData        = 0;
of.lpfnHook         = NULL;
of.lpTemplateName   = NULL;
if (!GetOpenFileName (&of)) return 0L;
```

The file information is returned to an OPENFILENAME structure using a tag name of *of* for this application.

Here, the lStructSize structure member gives the length of the structure (in bytes). The hwndOwner member gives the window that owns the dialog box. Use a NULL value if no owner exists. The hInstance member is the instance handle for the dialog template given by the lpTemplateName member. The lpstrFilter member is a pointer to a buffer that holds pairs of null-terminated filter strings. The first string describes a filter and the second string describes the filter pattern. The lpstrCustomFilter member is a pointer to a buffer that contains two user-defined filter strings. The first string gives the filter and the second the filter pattern. The nMaxCustFilter member gives the size of the buffer (in characters) given by lpstrCustomFilter. nFilterIndex gives an index in the buffer pointed to by lpstrFilter. The lpstrFile member is a pointer to a buffer that holds a file name used to initialize the file name edit control. The nMaxFile member gives the size of the buffer pointed to by lpstrFile, in characters. The lpstrFileTitle member is a pointer to a buffer that holds the title of the file selected. The nMaxFileTitle member gives the maximum length of the string that can be copied to the lpstrFileTitle buffer. The lpstrInitialDir member is a pointer to a string that gives the initial file directory. Use a NULL value to allow the current directory to be used as the initial directory. The lpstrTitle member is a pointer to a string for the title bar. If a NULL value is used, a default title is selected. The Flags member represents the dialog box creation flags and can be any of the values shown in Table 14.1.

Table 14.1 OPENFILENAME flags and descriptions.

Flag	Descriptions
OFN_ALLOWMULTISELECT	Allows multiple selections.
OFN_CREATEPROMPT	Asks to create a file that does not exist.
OFN_ENABLEHOOK	Enables the hook function.
OFN_ENABLETEMPLATE	Creates the dialog box using the dialog box template.
OFN_ENABLETEMPLATEHANDLE	Identifies a data block containing a preloaded dialog box template.

Table 14.1 OPENFILENAME flags and descriptions. (Continued)

Flag	Descriptions
OFN_EXTENSIONDIFFERENT	Allows the user a different file extension than given by lpstrDefExt.
OFN_FILEMUSTEXIST	Only existing file names are allowed.
OFN_HIDEREADONLY	Hides the Read Only check box.
OFN_NOCHANGEDIR	The current directory is used.
OFN_NONETWORKBUTTON	Hides and disables the network button.
OFN_NOREADONLYRETURN	The Read Only check box is not checked nor is the file in a write-protected directory.
OFN_NOTESTFILECREATE	The file is not created before closing the dialog box.
OFN_NOVALIDATE	Invalid characters are permitted in the file name.
OFN_OVERWRITEPROMPT	If the file exists, the Save As dialog box will generate a message box.
OFN_PATHMUSTEXIST	Only valid paths and file names are permitted.
OFN_READONLY	The Read Only check box is initially checked.
OFN_SHAREAWARE	A network-sharing violation causes a failure.

Additionally, the lpfnhook member responds to the flags shown in Table 14.2.

Table 14.2 OPENFILENAME ipfnhook member flags and descriptions.

Flag	Descriptions
OFN_SHAREFALLTHROUGH	The file name is returned by the dialog box.
OFN_SHARENOWARN	No further action is taken.
OFN_SHAREWARN	The user receives a standard warning message.
OFN_SHOWHELP	The dialog box will show the Help button.

In this project, the nFileOffset member gives a zero-based offset from the beginning of the path to the file name in the string. This file name is pointed to by lpstrFile. The nFileExtension member is a zero-based offset measured from the beginning of the path to the file name extension. Again, the string is lpstrFile. For example, if lpstrFile points to the following string, c:\win98\media\skiing.avi, this member contains the value 22. The lpstrDefExt member is a pointer to a buffer that holds the default file extension.

580 Chapter 14 • Sketching, Animation, and Video

The lCustData member gives application-defined data from the operating system. This data is then used by the hook function, pointed to by lpfnHook. The lpfnHook member points to a hook function that processes messages being sent to the dialog box. The lpTemplateName member is a pointer to a null-terminated string naming the substitution dialog box template.

Data can subsequently be retrieved from this structure for use by the Video project.

The Code for Playing AVI Files

High-level media control interface (mci) functions can be used to add video capabilities to an application. Only three mci function calls are necessary to add a video clip playback to your program. This application will use the file name of the AVI file entered in the common file dialog box and will play the video clip in the default playback window.

Each of the three mci function calls uses parameter values that are previously loaded into a predefined structure indicating the desired operation. For this project, we'll need to perform three operations: open, play, and close an AVI file.

To open an AVI file, the MCI_OPEN_PARMS structure is used. Here is the syntax for this structure.

```
typedef struct {
  DWORD       dwCallback;
  MCIDEVICEID wDeviceID;
  LPCTSTR     lpstrDeviceType;
  LPCTSTR     lpstrElementName;
  LPCTSTR     lpstrAlias;
} MCI_OPEN_PARMS;
```

In this structure the dwCallback member identifies a window handle used for the MCI_NOTIFY flag. The wDeviceID member holds the device identifier. This identifier is returned to the user. The lpstrDeviceType member is a pointer to the name or constant identifier of the device type. The lpstrElementName member is a pointer to the device-element name. The device-element name is usually a path. The lpstrAlias member is a pointer to a device alias. The use of this parameter is optional.

For the project, the following values were passed to this structure through a call to the **mciSendCommand()** function.

```
mciOpenParms.lpstrDeviceType="AVIVideo";
mciOpenParms.dwCallback=(DWORD) hWnd;
mciOpenParms.lpstrElementName=buffer;
dwReturn=mciSendCommand(0,MCI_OPEN,MCI_OPEN_TYPE|
                MCI_OPEN_ELEMENT,
                (DWORD)(LPVOID)&mciOpenParms);
```

The syntax for the **mciSendCommand()** function is given next.

```
MCIERROR mciSendCommand(MCIDEVICEID IDDevice,
                UINT uMsg,
                DWORD fdwCommand,
                DWORD dwParam);
```

The IDDevice parameter gives the device identifier. The uMsg parameter gives the command message. The fdwCommand parameter gives the flags for the command message, and dwParam serves as a pointer to a structure containing parameters for the command message.

To play the AVI file, another structure is used; MCI_PLAY_PARMS. Here is the syntax for this structure:

```
typedef struct {
  DWORD    dwCallback,
  DWORD    dwFrom,
  DWORD    dwTo
} MCI_PLAY_PARMS;
```

Here, the dwCallback member provides the window handle used for the MCI_NOTIFY flag. The dwFrom member gives the position to play from, and dwTo gives the position to play to.

For our example, the device ID, *wDeviceID*, was returned from the previous function call.

```
wDeviceID=mciOpenParms.wDeviceID;
dwReturn=mciSendCommand(wDeviceID,MCI_PLAY,
                MCI_NOTIFY,
                (DWORD)(LPVOID)&mciPlayParms);
```

Notice that because the dwFrom and dwTo structure members are not specified, the entire file will be played back.

The third function call, **mciSendCommand()**, is called to close the device and release the ID value.

```
if (dwReturn = 0 )
  wDeviceID=mciSendCommand(wDeviceID,MCI_CLOSE,0,
                (DWORD)(LPVOID) NULL);
```

This example has taught you the basics for including video playback capabilities in your application. Why not expand this example and use a dialog box, as a child window, with play, fast forward, reverse, and stop controls?

Experiment and Have Fun

The programming concepts presented in this chapter have been a combination of old and new ideas. By this time, you should be quite comfortable working with the Windows platform, menus, dialog boxes, and so on. The new ideas introduced in this chapter include the integration of the mouse into the Windows environment, the continued work with bitmaps as they apply to animation, and the patching of multimedia video and sounds into your application code.

Experiment with each of the projects in this chapter and add your own special touches. In the next chapter, you'll learn how to create screen saver applications that use many of the building blocks discussed in Chapters 1 through 14.

F I F T E E N

Building Screen Saver Applications

Windows has a built-in screen saver facility that is easy to manage. The screen saver is accessed through the Screen Saver folder of the Display dialog box present in the Windows Control Panel. If you open this panel, you will find many screen saver applications that are provided with Windows. The files for these screen savers are usually found in the Windows/System subdirectory. The screen saver files in this subdirectory have .scr file extensions.

What is special about a screen saver application? Screen saver applications are very similar to the Windows applications you have been writing to this point. Most screen saver applications include the following characteristics:

- They monitor keyboard keys, mouse buttons, and mouse movement for activity.
- If there is no activity for a preset period of time, they will pop up a topmost window.
- The top-most window is usually full screen and frequently uses a black background. Some type of graphics or iconic image then moves about the topmost window to indicate screen blanking.

The knowledge you have gained in your study of the previous chapters will provide all of the programming skills necessary to develop great screen saver applications. In this chapter, you will learn how to use a special Microsoft library designed for screen saver developers. This library, scrnsave.lib, will allow you to build 32-bit screen saver applications easily.

A Screen Saver Application

Microsoft anticipated that many Visual C++ programmers would like to develop their own screen saver applications. The Visual C++ compiler provides an easy-to-use screen saver interface through the scrnsave.lib library. The functions for this library are prototyped in the scrnsave.h header file. It would probably be a good idea for you to print a copy of this header file for your use. To make use of the scrnsave.lib library, the windows.h file must precede the scrnsave.h header file in the application's code.

Screen Saver Components

All screen savers are required to have a *Description* string. This string can contain a maximum of 25 characters and provides the information for the Screen Saver folder of the Display dialog box present in the Windows Control Panel. Screen saver passwords are now handled by the log-on process. If the registry value is nonzero, the user will be asked for the Login password before they are allowed to exit the screen saver. In the screen saver we are about to build, all password data and dialog boxes have been removed. The screen saver must have another string, *szAppName*, declared globally to hold the name of the screen saver.

Here is an edited portion of the scrnsave.h header file:

```
//
// scrnsave.h      Windows NT 3.1 screensaver defines and
//                 definitions.
//                 Version 1.0
//                 NOTE: windows.h must be #included first
// MANDATORY string required in .RC file
// This string should contain a less than 25 char
// name/description of the screen saver.  This string is
// what will be seen by the user in the Control
// Panel's Desktop applet screen saver listbox.
//

#define IDS_DESCRIPTION            1

// Icon resource ID.
// This should be the first icon used and must have this
// resource number. This is needed as the first icon in
// the file will be grabbed
//
#define ID_APP                     100
#define DLG_SCRNSAVECONFIGURE      2003

#define idsIsPassword              1000
#define idsIniFile                 1001
#define idsScreenSaver             1002
```

```
#define idsPassword            1003
#define idsDifferentPW         1004
#define idsChangePW            1005
#define idsBadOldPW            1006
#define idsAppName             1007
#define idsNoHelpMemory        1008
#define idsHelpFile            1009
#define idsDefKeyword          1010
     .
     .
     .
#ifdef UNICODE
LRESULT WINAPI ScreenSaverProcW(HWND hWnd,UINT message,
                                WPARAM wParam,
                                LPARAM lParam);
#define   ScreenSaverProc ScreenSaverProcW
#else
LRESULT WINAPI ScreenSaverProc(HWND hWnd,UINT message,
                               WPARAM wParam,
                               LPARAM lParam);
#endif
     .
     .
     .
LRESULT WINAPI DefScreenSaverProc(HWND hWnd,UINT msg,
                                  WPARAM wParam,
                                  LPARAM lParam);
     .
     .
     .
BOOL WINAPI ScreenSaverConfigureDialog(HWND hDlg,
                                       UINT message,
                                       WPARAM wParam,
                                       LPARAM lParam);
     .
     .
     .
BOOL WINAPI RegisterDialogClasses(HANDLE hInst);
     .
     .
     .
#define WS_GT (WS_GROUP | WS_TABSTOP)

#define MAXFILELEN          13
#define TITLEBARNAMELEN     40
#define APPNAMEBUFFERLEN    40
#define BUFFLEN             255
// The following globals are defined in scrnsave.lib
extern HINSTANCE hMainInstance;
```

```
extern HWND    hMainWindow;
extern BOOL    fChildPreview;
extern TCHAR   szName[TITLEBARNAMELEN];
extern TCHAR   szAppName[APPNAMEBUFFERLEN];
extern TCHAR   szIniFile[MAXFILELEN];
extern TCHAR   szScreenSaver[22];
extern TCHAR   szHelpFile[MAXFILELEN];
extern TCHAR   szNoHelpMemory[BUFFLEN];
extern UINT    MyHelpMessage;

// OPTIONAL - for Win98
#define SCRM_VERIFYPW    WM_APP
    .
    .
    .
void WINAPI ScreenSaverChangePassword(HWND hParent );
    .
    .
    .
```

By taking advantage of the various procedures prototyped in scrnsave.h and found in the scrnsave.lib, programmers can eliminate the redundancy of writing the same code over and over again. Additionally, by using these functions the finished screen saver application will be consistent with other screen saver applications developed with this library.

In the next section, you will learn how to build a simple but neat screen saver application using the scrnsave.lib functions. This application will use the animated flying saucer from Chapter 14. The bitmapped image of the flying saucer will move about the darkened window in two dimensions. Each time the alien and the ship bump into a screen edge, a multimedia sound effect will be played. You can, of course, substitute your own bitmapped images and sound files and produce screen savers with moving pumpkins, faces, or whatever you like.

The ScrSav Screen Saver Project

To create this screen saver project, the application must be built with the files shown in this section. The executable file, ScrSav.exe, is renamed ScrSav.scr and copied to the Windows/System subdirectory. The new screen saver will then appear in the list of optional screen savers in the screen saver list box.

This project uses four bitmapped images (Bmp1.bmp, Bmp2.bmp, Bmp3.bmp, and Bmp4.bmp), two sound files (mm1.wav and mm2.wav), two header files (ScrSav.h and resource.h), a resource script file (ScrSav.rc) and a C++ source code file (ScrSav.cpp). The only requirement for the bitmapped images is that they be the same size. The bitmapped images should also be created with a black background.

A Screen Saver Application

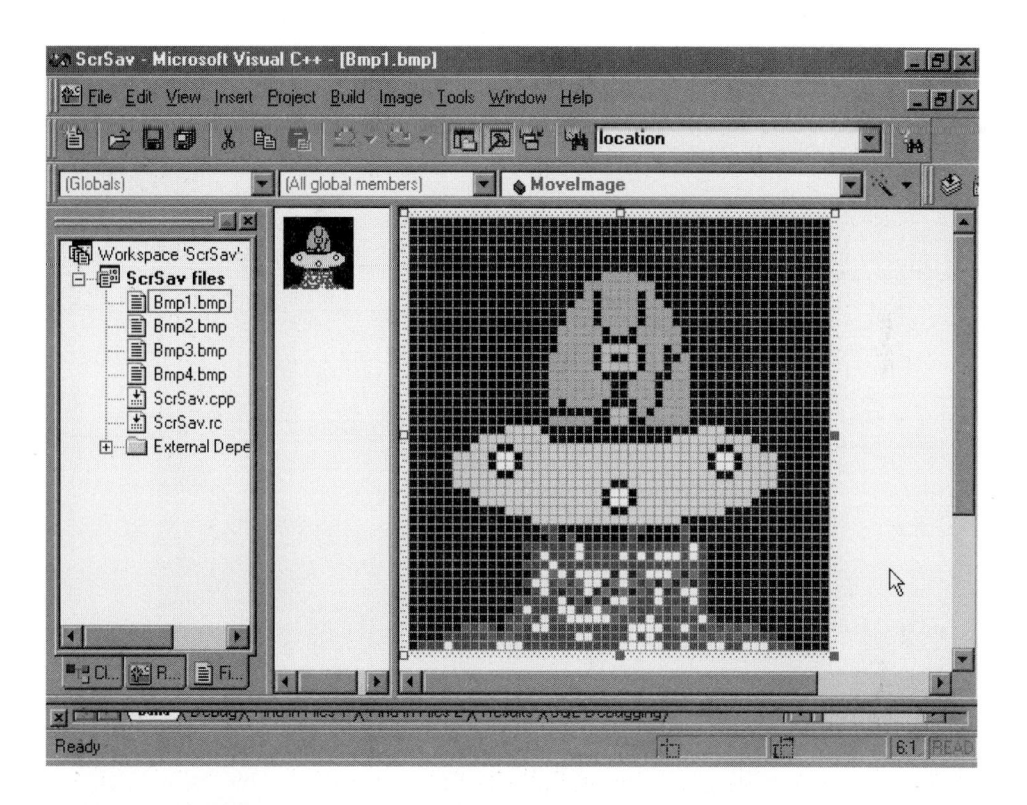

Figure 15-1 *The alien and ship used for bitmap one.*

Figures 15-1-15-4 show the images of the alien and saucer while they are in the Resource Editor.

These images are almost identical to the bitmaps used in Chapter 14. The main difference is that the background is filled with a black brush.

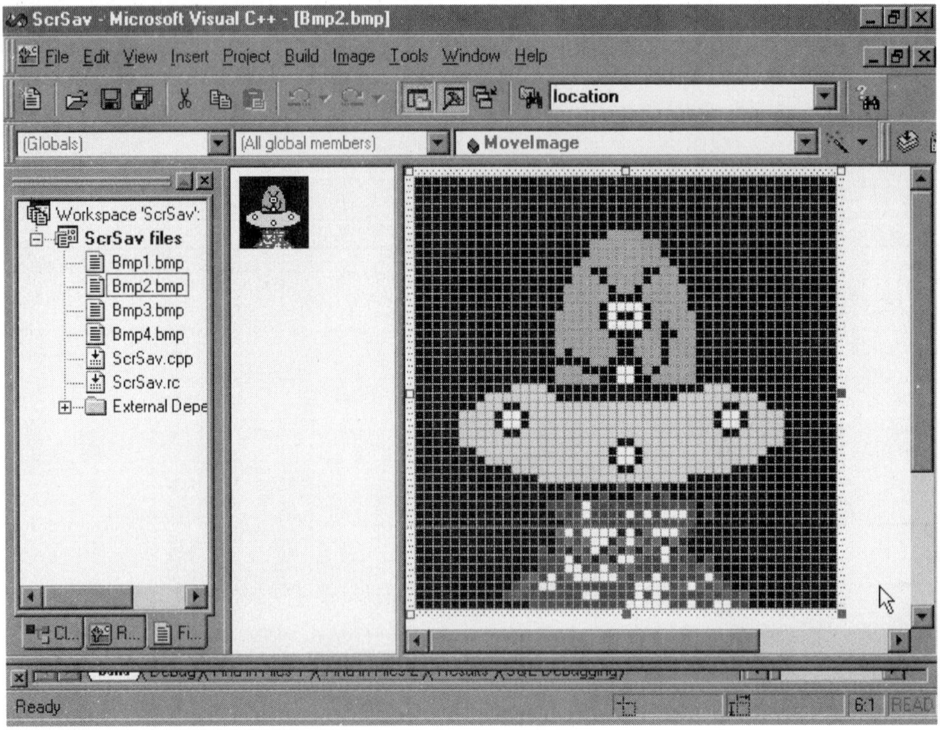

588 Chapter 15 • Building Screen Saver Applications

Figure 15-2 *The alien and ship used for bitmap two.*

A Screen Saver Application **589**

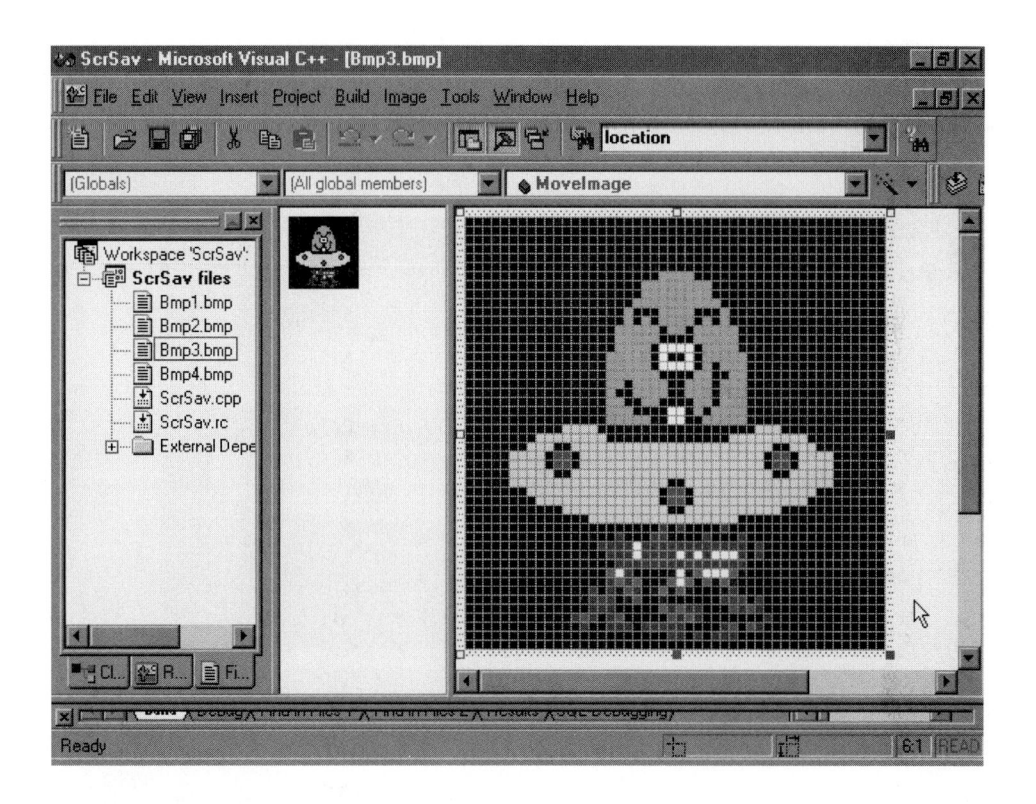

Figure 15-3 *The alien and ship used for bitmap three.*

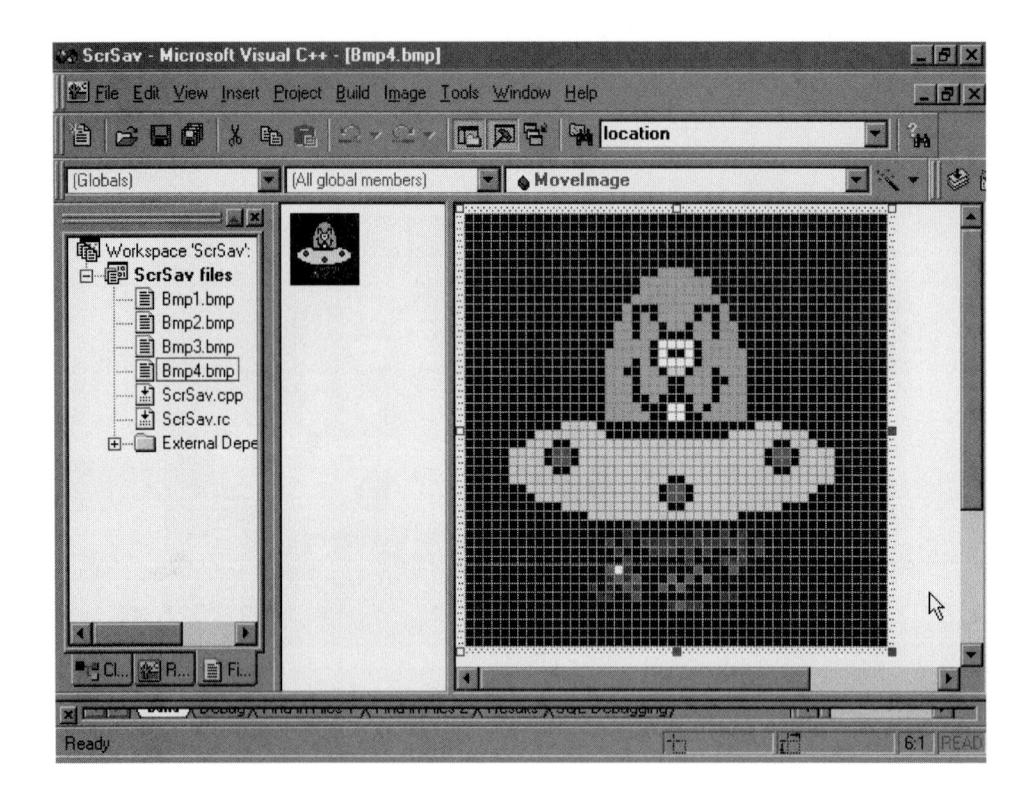

Chapter 15 • Building Screen Saver Applications

Figure 15-4 *The alien and ship used for bitmap four.*

You can use predefined sound files found on your computer, files downloaded from the Internet, or files created with the Windows Sound Recorder.

As you study the files in the next listings, notice how similar they are when compared with the Windows applications you have studied in earlier chapters. Also, try to detect the subtle differences that exist.

Here is the ScrSav.h header file:

```
#include <windows.h>
#include <scrnsave.h>

#define ID_TIMER      100
#define IDS_NAME      200

TCHAR szName[TITLEBARNAMELEN];
TCHAR szAppName[APPNAMEBUFFERLEN];
TCHAR szScreenSaver[22];
```

The ScrSav.h header file references the windows.h and scrnsave.h header files and provides ID information and string variables used by the scrnsave.lib functions.

A Screen Saver Application **591**

The resource.h header file is created automatically by the Resource Editor as various resources are added to the resource script file. You'll add the bitmapped images to the resource script file, but there will be no unique ID information added to the resource.h header file, so we'll skip a discussion of that file.

Here is an edited portion of the ScrSav.rc resource script file:

```
//Microsoft Developer Studio generated resource script.
//
#include "resource.h"
      .
      .
      .
/////////////////////////////////////////////////////////////
//
// Bitmap
//
BMImage1      BITMAP    DISCARDABLE      "Bmp1.bmp"
BMImage2      BITMAP    DISCARDABLE      "Bmp2.bmp"
BMImage3      BITMAP    DISCARDABLE      "Bmp3.bmp"
BMImage4      BITMAP    DISCARDABLE      "Bmp4.bmp"
```

As you might have guessed, the real work in this application takes place in the ScrSav source code file. Here is the ScrSav.cpp file.

```
//
//   ScrSav.cpp
//   A Visual C++ Screen Saver Project
//   This application attaches to specific Visual C++ files
//   designed for creating 32-bit screen saver applications.
//   Copyright (c) Chris H. Pappas and William H. Murray, 1999
//

#include <windows.h>
#include <scrnsave.h>
#include "ScrSav.h"

LRESULT WINAPI ScreenSaverProc(HWND,UINT,WPARAM,LPARAM);
BOOL WINAPI ScreenSaverConfigureDialog(HWND,UINT,WPARAM,LPARAM);
BOOL WINAPI RegisterDialogClasses(HANDLE);
void vLoadStrings(VOID);
void MoveImage(HWND hWnd);
void GetIniSettings(void);

char szBMName1[]="BMImage1";
char szBMName2[]="BMImage2";
char szBMName3[]="BMImage3";
char szBMName4[]="BMImage4";

HBITMAP hBitmap1,hBitmap2;   // bitmap handles
HBITMAP hBitmap3,hBitmap4;
```

Chapter 15 • Building Screen Saver Applications

```c
int xPos;                   // X position
int yPos;                   // Y position
int xPosInit;               // init X position
int yPosInit;               // init Y position
int xStep;                  // X step size
int yStep;                  // Y step size
int iDelay;                 // image delay
int iTimer;                 // speed control for image

// main entry point for screen saver messages.
LRESULT WINAPI ScreenSaverProc(HWND hWnd,UINT messg,
                               WPARAM wParam,LPARAM lParam)
{
  RECT rc;
  switch (messg)
  {
    case WM_CREATE:
      // load screen saver strings
      vLoadStrings();
      // get initial settings for image
      GetIniSettings();
      // load all four bitmapped images
      hBitmap1=LoadBitmap(hMainInstance,szBMName1);
      hBitmap2=LoadBitmap(hMainInstance,szBMName2);
      hBitmap3=LoadBitmap(hMainInstance,szBMName3);
      hBitmap4=LoadBitmap(hMainInstance,szBMName4);
      // start system timer
      iTimer=SetTimer(hWnd,ID_TIMER,iDelay,NULL);
      // make init positions current positions
      xPos=xPosInit;
      yPos=yPosInit;
      break;

    case WM_TIMER:
      MoveImage(hWnd);
    break;

    case WM_DESTROY:
      // when finished, delete bitmaps
      if (hBitmap1) DeleteObject(hBitmap1);
      if (hBitmap2) DeleteObject(hBitmap2);
      if (hBitmap3) DeleteObject(hBitmap3);
      if (hBitmap4) DeleteObject(hBitmap4);
      // destroy the system timer
      KillTimer(hWnd,ID_TIMER);
      sndPlaySound(NULL,0);
    break;

    case WM_ERASEBKGND:
      // prepare for erasing whole screen
```

```
      GetClientRect(hWnd,&rc);
      FillRect((HDC)wParam,&rc,
             (HBRUSH) GetStockObject(BLACK_BRUSH));
      return 0L;

    default:
      break;
  }
  return (DefScreenSaverProc(hWnd,messg,wParam,lParam));
}

// Register the window
BOOL WINAPI RegisterDialogClasses(HANDLE hInst) {
  return TRUE;
}

void vLoadStrings(VOID) {
  LoadString(hMainInstance,idsAppName,szAppName,
            APPNAMEBUFFERLEN);
  LoadString(hMainInstance,IDS_NAME,szName,TITLEBARNAMELEN);
  LoadString(hMainInstance,idsScreenSaver,szScreenSaver,22);
  LoadString(hMainInstance,IDS_DESCRIPTION,"Saucer",6);
}

// Screen saver interface
BOOL WINAPI ScreenSaverConfigureDialog(HWND hDlg,
                                      UINT messg,
                                      WPARAM wParam,
                                      LPARAM lParam) {
  return FALSE;
}

static void GetIniSettings() {
  xPosInit=320;
  yPosInit=240;
  xStep=2;
  yStep=2;
  xPos=xPosInit;
  yPos=yPosInit;
  iDelay=40;
}

static void MoveImage(HWND hWnd) {
  HDC hdc, hmdc;
  BITMAP bm;
  RECT rcWnd;
  static RECT rcFill;

  GetClientRect(hWnd,&rcWnd);
  GetObject(hBitmap1,sizeof(bm),(LPSTR)&bm);
```

594 Chapter 15 • Building Screen Saver Applications

```c
xPos+=xStep;
yPos+=yStep;

hdc=GetDC(hWnd);
hmdc=CreateCompatibleDC(hdc);

// draw image 1
SelectObject(hmdc,hBitmap1);
GetObject(hBitmap1,sizeof(bm),(LPSTR) &bm);
BitBlt(hdc,xPos,yPos,bm.bmWidth,bm.bmHeight,
       hmdc,0,0,SRCCOPY);
Sleep(iDelay);

// draw image 2
SelectObject(hmdc,hBitmap2);
GetObject(hBitmap2,sizeof(bm),(LPSTR) &bm);
BitBlt(hdc,xPos,yPos,bm.bmWidth,bm.bmHeight,
       hmdc,0,0,SRCCOPY);
Sleep(iDelay);

// draw image 3
SelectObject(hmdc,hBitmap3);
GetObject(hBitmap3,sizeof(bm),(LPSTR) &bm);
BitBlt(hdc,xPos,yPos,bm.bmWidth,bm.bmHeight,
       hmdc,0,0,SRCCOPY);
Sleep(iDelay);

// draw image 4
SelectObject(hmdc,hBitmap4);
GetObject(hBitmap4,sizeof(bm),(LPSTR) &bm);
BitBlt(hdc,xPos,yPos,bm.bmWidth,bm.bmHeight,
       hmdc,0,0,SRCCOPY);
Sleep(iDelay);

// examine left and right window edges
if((xPos+bm.bmWidth > rcWnd.right) ||
   (xPos < rcWnd.left)) {
  xStep=-xStep;
  sndPlaySound("c:\\ScrSav\\mm1.wav",SND_ASYNC);
}

// examine top and bottom window edges
if((yPos+bm.bmHeight > rcWnd.bottom) ||
   (yPos < rcWnd.top)) {
  yStep=-yStep;
  sndPlaySound("c:\\ScrSav\\mm2.wav",SND_ASYNC);
}

// do some erasing on the screen
rcFill.left=xPos;
```

A Screen Saver Application   595

```
    rcFill.right=xPos+bm.bmWidth;
    rcFill.bottom=yPos;
    rcFill.top=yPos+bm.bmHeight;
    FillRect(hdc,&rcFill,(HBRUSH) GetStockObject(BLACK_BRUSH));
    DeleteDC(hmdc);
    ReleaseDC(hWnd,hdc);
}
```

In this project, two function calls link the application with Microsoft's screen saver code:

```
// Register the window
BOOL WINAPI RegisterDialogClasses(HANDLE hInst) {
  return TRUE;
}

// Screen saver interface
BOOL APIENTRY ScreenSaverConfigureDialog(HWND hDlg,
                                         UINT messg,
                                         WPARAM wParam,
                                         LPARAM lParam) {
  return FALSE;
}
```

Examine the source code, find these functions, and satisfy yourself that all other functions are defined within the application or are functions you have already used to build normal Windows applications. In the next section, we'll examine this code in more detail.

SOURCE CODE DETAILS

The **ScreenSaverProc()** is responsible for initially loading the bitmaps, creating a system timer, calling the **MoveImage()** function, deleting the bitmap resources, destroying the system timer, and erasing the background information in the window.

The bitmapped images are drawn to the screen and moved in the traditional animation manner. Compare this code with the code for the animation example in Chapter 14.

```
GetClientRect(hWnd,&rcWnd);
GetObject(hBitmap1,sizeof(bm),(LPSTR)&bm);
xPos+=xStep;
yPos+=yStep;

hdc=GetDC(hWnd);
hmdc=CreateCompatibleDC(hdc);
// draw image 1
SelectObject(hmdc,hBitmap1);
GetObject(hBitmap1,sizeof(bm),(LPSTR) &bm);
BitBlt(hdc,xPos,yPos,bm.bmWidth,bm.bmHeight,
       hmdc,0,0,SRCCOPY);
```

```
Sleep(iDelay);

// draw image 2
SelectObject(hmdc,hBitmap2);
GetObject(hBitmap2,sizeof(bm),(LPSTR) &bm);
BitBlt(hdc,xPos,yPos,bm.bmWidth,bm.bmHeight,
       hmdc,0,0,SRCCOPY);
Sleep(iDelay);
   .
   .
   .
```

You'll find this code identical to the code used in Chapter 14 for moving an object in two dimensions.

A conditional **if** statement plays a sound when the alien and ship bump into the left or right edge of the window. Here is the code that handles the horizontal motion.

```
// examine left and right window edges
if((xPos+bm.bmWidth > rcWnd.right) ||
   (xPos < rcWnd.left)) {
  xStep=-xStep;
  sndPlaySound("c:\\ScrSav\\mm1.wav",SND_ASYNC);
}
```

If you examine the entire source code listing, you'll see that the code for top and bottom collisions is similar. Notice that the sound file is "hard wired" into the application. When the application is executed, it will look for the mm1.wav file in the C:\ScrSav subdirectory. If the file is not there, Windows will substitute a default wave file.

Screen savers usually use a black background or one that constantly changes to make sure individual screen pixels are not "burned" by being turned on too long.

BUILDING THE APPLICATION

Screen saver projects require a little more attention to detail than do normal Windows applications. Here are the steps necessary to create a successful screen saver:

1. Create and enter all of the files previously shown and save them in a project named *ScrSav*.
2. Design four bitmapped images and two sound resources. Save them as bitmap and wave files, respectively.
3. Use the Visual C++ compiler's Project menu, select the Settings... menu item to open the Project settings dialog box. Change the Project Settings for the C/C++ Folder and Linker Folder Options to include the options, libraries, and specifications shown respectively in Figures 15-5 and 15-6.

A Screen Saver Application

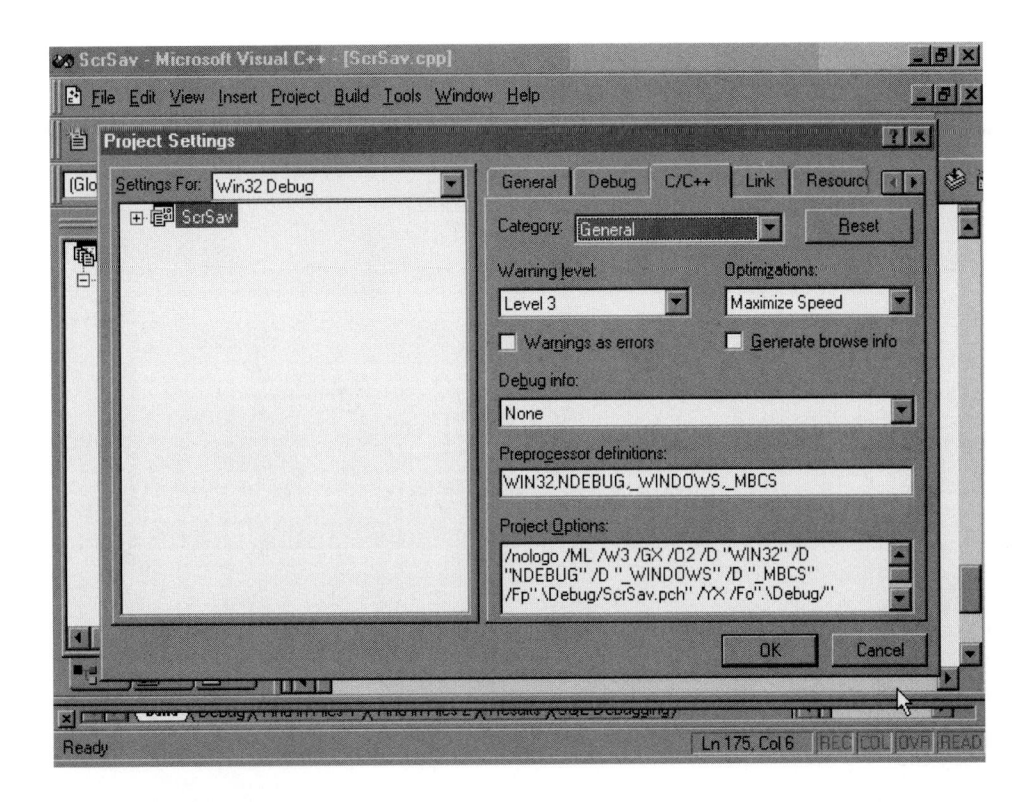

Figure 15-5 *C/C++ compiler options for screen saver projects.*

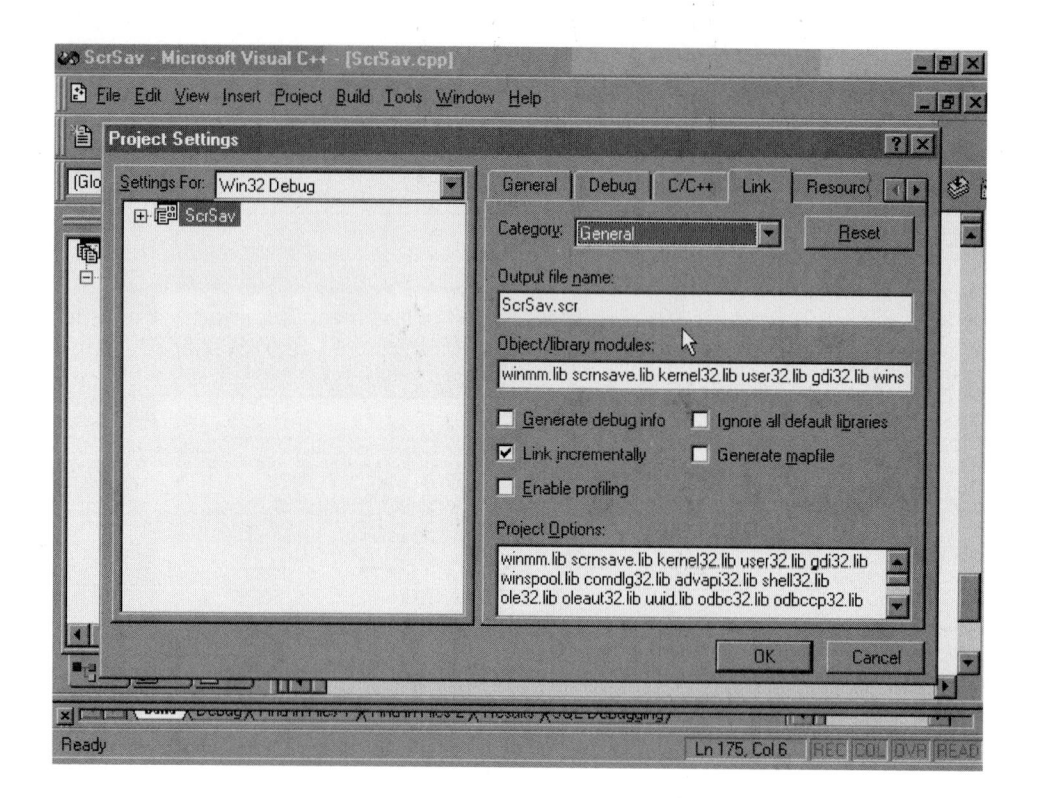

Chapter 15 • Building Screen Saver Applications

Figure 15-6 *Linker options for screen saver projects.*

In particular, make sure the C/C++ compiler options contain the following Project Options.

```
/nologo /ML /W3 /GX /O2 /D "WIN32" /D "NDEBUG"
/D "_WINDOWS" /D "_MBCS" /Fp".\Debug/ScrSav.pch"
/YX /Fo".\Debug/" /Fd".\Debug/" /FD /c
```

Then make sure the Project Options for the linker include the following:

```
winmm.lib scrnsave.lib kernel32.lib user32.lib gdi32.lib
winspool.lib comdlg32.lib advapi32.lib shell32.lib
ole32.lib oleaut32.lib uuid.lib odbc32.lib odbccp32.lib
/nologo /subsystem:windows /incremental:yes
/pdb:".\ScrSav_/ScrSav.pdb" /machine:I386 /out:"ScrSav.scr"
```

Notice, in particular, the inclusion of the winmm.lib and scrnsave.lib libraries in this listing.

Once you have specified these items, the build operation should go smoothly. Remember to change the name of the executable file from *ScrSav.exe* to *ScrSav.scr* and to move this file to the Windows/System subdirectory. If this isn't done, you won't find the new screen saver listed in the available screen saver list.

Is There More?

Of course! But you have all of the tools necessary to build neat Windows projects right now. The question becomes, How far do you want to go?

In the next chapter, we're going to discuss another approach to Windows programming. Rather than the traditional procedure-oriented approach used throughout this book, we'll introduce you to some of the concepts used in an object-oriented approach. If you are ready for the challenge, the Microsoft Foundation Class (MFC) library provides much of the functionality of procedure-oriented coding wrapped in an object-oriented environment.

SIXTEEN

What's Next?

This book is designed for programmers wishing to expand their knowledge into the world of Windows programming. The book has been geared to the traditional procedure-oriented programming approach using Windows-supplied functions that are contained in a message-based system. The Windows application program interface (API) has been the center of these discussions.

There is, however, an entirely different programming approach to Windows that involves object-oriented programming. If you are familiar with the use of C++ objects, you may want to consider the use of the Microsoft Foundation Library (MFC) for creating projects. The advantages of the MFC do not really become apparent until project sizes increase well beyond those projects illustrated in this book. For large projects, though, the use of reusable objects becomes a real advantage.

The use of objects in Visual C++ Windows programming is not for the faint-hearted. You must have a thorough understanding of object-oriented programming. In this chapter, we'll examine the advantages of the MFC and introduce you to simple MFC projects.

A Look at the Microsoft Foundation Class Library

The Microsoft Visual C++ compiler provides a class library containing a new set of tools for the development of C++ and C++ Windows applications. The MFC library is used exclusively for Windows 98 and Windows NT project development and offers class support for all Windows programming needs, including control bars, property sheets, OLE, and so on.

In this chapter, you'll learn terms, definitions, and techniques that are common across all MFC versions.

Why Do I Need the MFC Library?

The MFC provides easy-to-use objects for the programmer. Windows, from its very inception, has followed many principles of object-oriented programming design within the framework of a non-object-oriented language such as C. Many of these pseudo-object-oriented features were discussed in the initial chapters of this book. The use of Windows and the C++ language opens the whole world of object-oriented programming to the developer. The MFC development team has designed a comprehensive implementation of the Windows API. This C++ library encapsulates the most important data structures and API function calls within a group of reusable classes. This is one of the reasons we think it is so important to first understand the procedure-oriented approach to Windows programming.

Class libraries such as the MFC offer many advantages over the traditional function libraries used by C programmers, especially for large projects. These advantages include:

- Class libraries often reduce code size.
- Classes appear to be natural extensions of the language.
- Code and data can be encapsulation within the class definition.
- Function and variable name collisions are eliminated.
- Inheritance is permitted.

By using the MFC, you'll discover that code size has been reduced. For simple applications, this reduction is typically over 50%. A reduction in code size allows you, the developer, to spend less time writing redundant code and more time developing specific application code.

DESIGN CONSIDERATIONS

The MFC team set rigorous design principles that had to be followed in the implementation of the MFC. These principles and guidelines include the following:

- Create a class library (MFC) that will easily migrate to new platforms, such as Windows 95, 98, and the various versions of NT.
- Permit the mixing of traditional functions calls with the use of the MFC library.
- Balance power and efficiency in the design of class libraries.
- Make the transition from API function calls to the MFC as simple as possible.
- Use the power of C++ without overwhelming the programmer.

The MFC team felt that good code design had to start with the MFC library itself. The MFC classes had to be designed to be small in size but fast in execution time. The results were simple classes with execution speeds close to those of the API function libraries of traditional Windows programs.

When the MFC team originally started, Windows 95 and NT were on the horizon. The team designed the original class library to be dynamic rather than static. With a dynamic architecture, the MFC classes could be scaled to the growing Windows environment we now have. As a result, the MFC library is fully integrated across all Windows platforms, including Windows 3.x, 95, 98, and the various versions of NT.

CObject

All class libraries have a root parent class. Subsequent child classes are derived from the parent class. Microsoft uses a few classes as parent classes. Additional classes are then derived from the parent classes. **CObject** is one parent class used extensively in developing Windows applications. The MFC header files located in the Visual C++ compiler's mfc/include subdirectory provide a wealth of information on defined MFC classes.

Let's take a brief look at **CObject**, which is prototyped in the MFC afx.h header file. This code has been edited for clarity:

```
//////////////////////////////////////////////////////////
// class CObject is the root of all compliant objects
    .
    .
    .
public:
    // Object model (types, destruction, allocation)
    virtual CRuntimeClass* GetRuntimeClass() const;
    // virtual destructors are necessary
    virtual ~CObject();

    // Diagnostic allocations
    void* PASCAL operator new(size_t nSize);
    void* PASCAL operator new(size_t, void* p);
    void PASCAL operator delete(void* p);
    .
    .
    .
    // Disable the copy constructor and assignment by
    // default so you will get compiler errors instead
    // of unexpected behavior if you pass objects
    // by value or assign objects.
protected:
    CObject();
private:
    // no implementation
    CObject(const CObject& objectSrc);
    void operator=(const CObject& objectSrc);
```

```cpp
// Attributes
public:
   BOOL IsSerializable() const;
   BOOL IsKindOf(const CRuntimeClass* pClass) const;

// Overridables
   virtual void Serialize(CArchive& ar);
      .
      .
      .
   // Diagnostic Support
   virtual void AssertValid() const;
   virtual void Dump(CDumpContext& dc) const;
```

Examine the components that make up the CObject class definition in the previous listing. **CObject**, which is typical of most class objects, is divided into public, protected, and private parts. **CObject** also provides normal and dynamic type checking and serialization. Dynamic type checking allows the type of object to be determined at run time. The state of the object can be saved to a storage medium, such as a disk, through a concept called *persistence*. Object persistence allows object member functions to be persistent also permitting retrieval of object data.

If CObject serves as a parent class, child classes such as CGdiObject can be derived from it. Here is an edited portion of the **CGdiObject** class definition also prototyped in the MFC afxwin.h header file.

```cpp
class CGdiObject : public CObject
{
   DECLARE_DYNCREATE(CGdiObject)
      .
      .
      .
public:
   HGDIOBJ m_hObject;
   HGDIOBJ GetSafeHandle() const;
   static CGdiObject* PASCAL FromHandle(HGDIOBJ hObject);
   static void PASCAL DeleteTempMap();
   BOOL Attach(HGDIOBJ hObject);
   HGDIOBJ Detach();
   CGdiObject();
   BOOL DeleteObject();
   int GetObject(int nCount, LPVOID lpObject) const;
   BOOL CreateStockObject(int nIndex);
   BOOL UnrealizeObject();
      .
      .
      .
public:
   virtual ~CGdiObject();
      .
```

```
    .
    .
  virtual void Dump(CDumpContext& dc) const;
  virtual void AssertValid() const;
};
```

The CGdiObject and its methods (member functions) allow drawing items such as stock and custom pens, brushes, and fonts. These are the same graphics device interface (GDI) objects you accessed through normal API function calls when writing procedure-oriented applications.

Microsoft has provided complete documentation for the MFC library to allow the utmost in programming flexibility and customization. However, for the beginner, it is not even necessary to know how the various classes are defined to use them efficiently.

For example, in traditional procedure-oriented Windows applications, the **DeleteObject()** function is frequently used. Here is an example.

```
DeleteObject(hBRUSH);   /*hBRUSH is the brush handle*/
```

If you are writing a C++ object-oriented application using the MFC library, the same results will be achieved by accessing the member function with the following syntax:

```
newbrush.DeleteObject(); //newbrush is current brush
```

As you can see, switching between procedure-oriented Windows function calls and object-oriented class library objects can be intuitive. Microsoft has used this approach in developing all Windows classes, making the transition from traditional function calls to MFC library objects very easy.

IMPORTANT PARENT CLASSES

Table 16.1 provides a list of important and frequently used MFC classes. All of the classes shown in this table are derived from CObject.

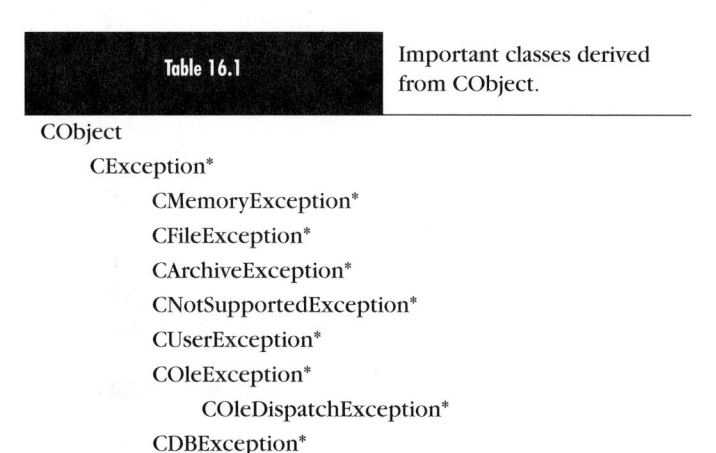

Table 16.1 Important classes derived from CObject.

CObject
    CException*
        CMemoryException*
        CFileException*
        CArchiveException*
        CNotSupportedException*
        CUserException*
        COleException*
            COleDispatchException*
        CDBException*

Table 16.1 Important classes derived from CObject. (Continued)

CFile*
- CStdioFile*
- CMemFile*
- COleStreamFile*

CDC*
- CClientDC*
- CWindowDC*
- CPaintDC*
- CMetaFileDC*

CGdiObject*
- CPen*
- CBrush*
- CFont*
- CBitmap*
- CPalette*
- CRgn*

CMenu*
CArray
CByteArray*
CWordArray*
CDWordArray*
CPtrArray*
CObArray*
CStringArray*
CUIntArray*
CList

A Look at the Microsoft Foundation Class Library

Table 16.1 Important classes derived from CObject. (Continued)

CPtrList*
CObList*
CStringList*
CMap
CMapWordToPtr*
CMapPtrToWord*
CMapPtrToPtr*
CMapWordToOb*
CMapStringToPtr*
CMapStringToOb*
CMapStringToString*
CDatabase*
CRecordSet*
CLongBinary*
CCmdTarget
  CWinThread
    CWinApp
  CDocTemplate
    CSingleDocTemplate
    CMultiDocTemplate
  COleObjectFactory
    COleTemplateServer
  COleDataSource
  COleDropSource
  COleDropTarget
  COleMessageFilter
  CDocument
    COleDocument
      COleLinkingDoc
        COleServerDoc
  CDocItem
    COleClientItem
    COleServerItem

Table 16.1 Important classes derived from CObject. (Continued)

CWnd
  CFrameWnd
    CMDIChildWnd
    CMDIFrameWnd
    CMiniFrameWnd
    COleIPFrameWnd
  CControlBar
    CToolBar
    CStatusBar
    CDialogBar
    COleResizeBar
  CSplitterWnd
  CPropertySheet
  CDialog
    COleDialog
      COleInsertDialog
      COleChangeIconDialog
      COlePasteSpecialDialog
      COleConvertDialog
      COleBusyDialog
      COleLinksDialog
      COleUpdateDialog
    CFileDialog
    CColorDialog
    CFontDialog
    CPrintDialog
    CFindReplaceDialog
    CPropertyPage
    CView
      CScrollView
        CFormView
          CRecordView
  CEditView
  CStatic
  CButton
    CBitmapButton

A Look at the Microsoft Foundation Class Library

Table 16.1	Important classes derived from CObject. (Continued)

CListBox
CComboBox
CScrollBar
CEdit

Table 16.2 provides a listing of those classes that provide Run-time Object Model Support.

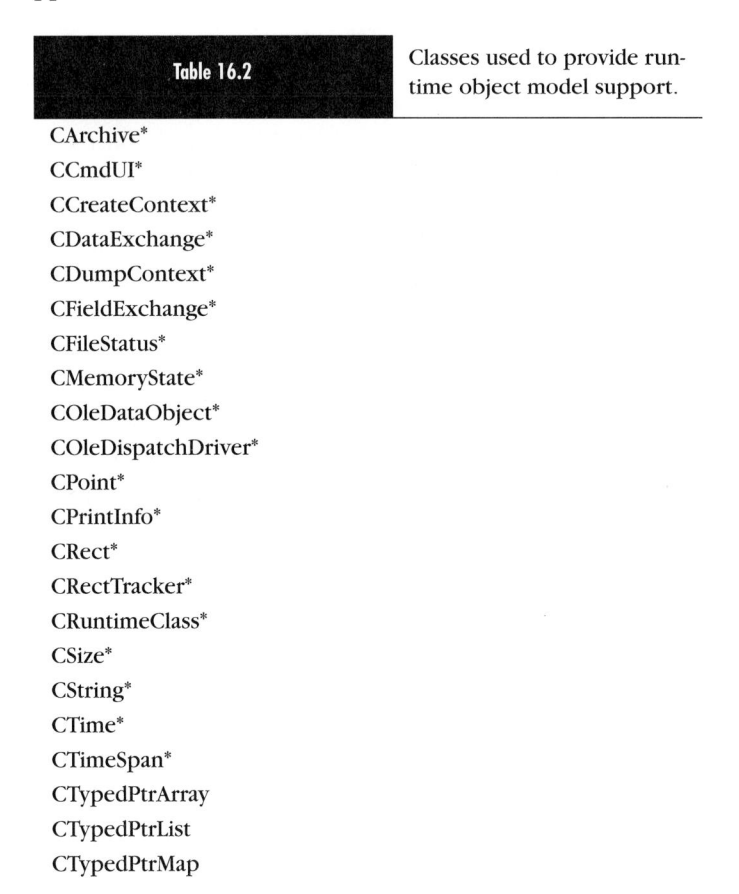

Table 16.2	Classes used to provide run-time object model support.

CArchive*
CCmdUI*
CCreateContext*
CDataExchange*
CDumpContext*
CFieldExchange*
CFileStatus*
CMemoryState*
COleDataObject*
COleDispatchDriver*
CPoint*
CPrintInfo*
CRect*
CRectTracker*
CRuntimeClass*
CSize*
CString*
CTime*
CTimeSpan*
CTypedPtrArray
CTypedPtrList
CTypedPtrMap

It might be a good idea to put a bookmark at this spot. These tables will help you as you continue to study various MFC classes in this chapter.

MFC Programming Concepts

Before writing a complete MFC program, let's examine the code necessary for simply establishing a window on the screen. When you use the power of the MFC, don't be surprised by the overall length of the application code when compared with an equivalent procedure-oriented application.

This section examines the *simplest* possible Windows application, *Easy.cpp*. This application will create a window and place a title in its title bar area.

Creating a Window

Start a new 32-bit C++ application in Visual C++ as you have been doing throughout the book. Name this project *Easy*. Create a new, empty, source code file named *Easy.cpp* for the project. Add the following code to this file instead of using the procedure-oriented template code we have used in earlier chapters.

```
//
// Easy.cpp
// The simplest MFC code required to establish a
// window on the screen.
// Copyright (c) William H. Murray and Chris H. Pappas, 1999
//

#include <afxwin.h>

class CTheApp : public CWinApp
{
public:
  virtual BOOL InitInstance();
};

class CMainWnd : public CFrameWnd
{
public:
  CMainWnd()
  {
    Create(NULL,"A Simple MFC Application",
           WS_OVERLAPPEDWINDOW,rectDefault,NULL,NULL);
  }
};

BOOL CTheApp::InitInstance()
{
  m_pMainWnd=new CMainWnd();
  m_pMainWnd->ShowWindow(m_nCmdShow);
  m_pMainWnd->UpdateWindow();
```

MFC Programming Concepts

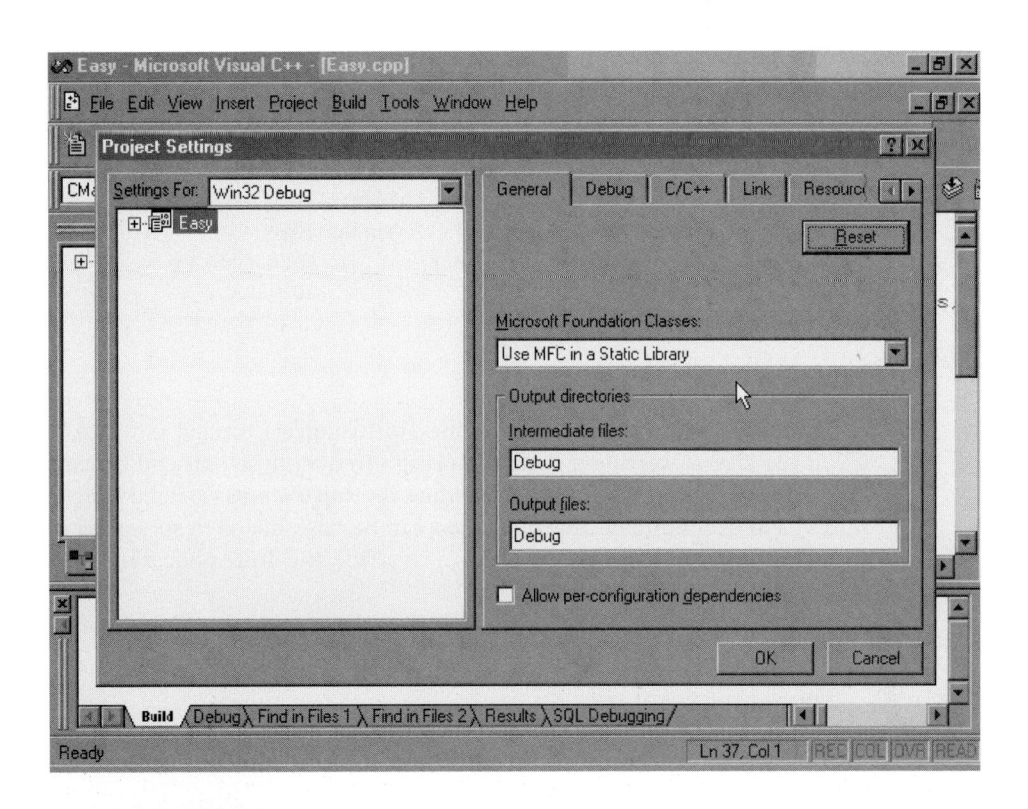

Figure 16-1

The MFC library is induced in the build options for this application.

```
    return TRUE;
}

CTheApp TheApp;
```

Once this code is entered, you can build the application from the integrated environment. Make sure to set the compiler option to include the MFC library, as shown in Figure 16-1.

In the following sections, we'll examine how each piece of code works in establishing the window on the screen.

USING THE AFXWIN.H HEADER FILE

The afxwin.h header file is the gateway to Windows programming with the MFC library. Like the windows.h header file used for procedure-oriented applications, this header file calls all subsequent header files required by the MFC. Using one header file also aids in creating precompiled header files. Precompiled header files save time when repeated compilation is being done during application development.

CTHEAPP FROM CWINAPP

This application starts by deriving the CTheApp class. This is our class definition, and it is based on (derived from) the MFC CWinApp class.

```
class CTheApp : public CWinApp
{
public:
  virtual BOOL InitInstance();
};
```

The CTheApp class overrides the **InitInstance()** method provided by the CWinApp class. Overriding methods occurs frequently when child classes are derived from parent classes. By overriding the **InitInstance()** method, the initialization and execution of the application can be customized to suite your needs. In the CWinApp class, it is possible to override the **InitApplication()**, **ExitInstance()**, and **OnIdle()** methods.

Here is a portion of the CWinApp class description found in the MFC afxwin.h header file.

```
class CWinApp : public CObject
{
  DECLARE_DYNAMIC(CWinApp)
public:
  CWinApp(const char* pszAppName=NULL);
  void SetCurrentHandles();
       .
       .
       .
  const char* m_pszAppName;
  HANDLE m_hInstance;
  HANDLE m_hPrevInstance;
  LPSTR m_lpCmdLine;
  int m_nCMDShow;
       .
       .
       .
  CWnd* m_pMainWnd;
       .
       .
       .
  HCURSOR LoadCursor(LPSTR lpCursorName);
  HCURSOR LoadCursor(WORD nIDCursor);
  HCURSOR LoadStandardCursor(LPSTR lpCursorName);
  HCURSOR LoadOEMCursor(WORD nIDCursor);

  HICON LoadIcon(LPSTR lpIconName);
```

MFC Programming Concepts 613

```
  HICON LoadIcon(WORD nIDIcon);
  HICON LoadStandardIcon(LPSTR lpIconName);
  HICON LoadOEMIcon(WORD nIDIcon);
     .
     .
     .
  BOOL PumpMessage();
     .
     .
     .
  virtual BOOL InitApplication();
  virtual BOOL InitInstance();
     .
     .
     .
  virtual int Run();
     .
     .
     .
  virtual BOOL PreTranslateMessage(MSG* pMsg);
  virtual BOOL OnIdle(LONG lCount);
  virtual int ExitInstance();
protected:
  MSG m_msgCur;
};
```

The **CWinApp** class is responsible for establishing and implementing the Windows message loop. Message loops are a familiar part of every procedure-oriented application. This action, alone, eliminates many lines of repetitive code that you've seen in every procedure-oriented application in this book.

THE CFRAMEWND CLASS

The application's window is established by the CMainWnd class. The CMainWnd class is derived from the CFrameWnd base class.

```
class CMainWnd : public CFrameWnd
{
public:
  CMainWnd()
  {
    Create(NULL, "A Simple MFC Application",
           WS_OVERLAPPEDWINDOW, rectDefault, NULL, NULL);
  }
};
```

The constructor for the **CMainWnd()** class calls the **Create()** method to establish initial window parameters. In this application, the window's style and caption are provided as parameters.

Here is an edited portion of the CFrameWnd class found in the MFC afx-win.h header file.

```
class CFrameWnd : public CWnd
{
  DECLARE_DYNAMIC(CFrameWnd)
    .
    .
    .
protected:
  HANDLE m_hAccelTable;
    .
    .
    .
public:
  static const CRect rectDefault;
    .
    .
    .
  CFrameWnd();
    .
    .
    .
  BOOL LoadAccelTable(const char FAR* lpAccelTableName);
  BOOL Create(const char FAR* lpClassName,
              const char FAR* lpWindowName,
              DWORD dwStyle = WS_OVERLAPPEDWINDOW,
              const RECT& rect = rectDefault,
              const CWnd* pParentWnd = NULL,
              const char FAR* lpMenuName = NULL);
    .
    .
    .
public:
  virtual ~CFrameWnd();
  virtual CFrameWnd* GetParentFrame();
  virtual CFrameWnd* GetChildFrame();
    .
    .
    .
protected:
  virtual BOOL PreTranslateMessage(MSG* pMsg);
};
```

The first parameter used in the **Create**() method allows a class name to be given in compliance with the traditional Windows API **RegisterClass**() function. Normally, this parameter is set to NULL in the applications you develop, and a class name will not be required.

USING MEMBER FUNCTIONS

Remember that the CTheApp-derived class object overrode the **InitInstance()** method provided by the parent class, CWinApp. Here is the code that shows how this application implements a new **InitInstance()** method.

```
BOOL CTheApp::InitInstance()
{
  m_pMainWnd=new CMainWnd();
  m_pMainWnd->ShowWindow(m_nCmdShow);
  m_pMainWnd->UpdateWindow();
  return TRUE;
}
```

The *new* operator is used to invoke the constructor **CMainWnd**, discussed in the previous section. The m_pMainWnd member variable (*m_* indicates a member variable) holds the location for the application's main window. The **ShowWindow()** method is required to display the window on the screen. The parameter m_nCmdShow is initialized by the application's constructor. **UpdateWindow()** displays and paints the window being sent to the screen.

THE CONSTRUCTOR

The last portion of program code is used to invoke the application's constructor at the startup of the application.

```
CTheApp TheApp;
```

The application code for this example is very simple and very straightforward. The application merely establishes a window; but it does not permit you to draw anything in the window at this time.

Executing the MFC Application

Figure 16-2 shows a window similar to the one that will appear on your screen. Though the application doesn't draw anything in the client area of the window, it does give the application a new title!

Figure 16-2 *Using the MFC to create a window.*

Though this code forms the foundation for most MFC projects, there are still a few missing pieces. In the next section, we've provided a complete MFC application that can be used as a template for all MFC applications that you may wish to experiment with.

A Complete MFC Application

In Chapter 2, we created a procedure-oriented template named *swt.cpp*. This application, or template, was then used as the backbone of all application development in this book. In this section, we'll create a similar template for the MFC object-oriented environment. This template project will be named *Swt-MFC*. The application simply prints a message in the window's client area and draws a few GDI graphics shapes.

The project will use a header file that contains information on how our application's classes were derived from the MFC library classes. This is a style of coding that is encouraged by Microsoft. Here is code for the SwtMFC.h header file.

```
class CMainWnd : public CFrameWnd
{
public:
  CMainWnd();
  afx_msg void OnPaint();
  DECLARE_MESSAGE_MAP();
};

class CSwtMFCApp : public CWinApp
{
public:
  BOOL InitInstance();
};
```

The C++ source code file is straightforward. As you examine the SwtMFC.cpp file pay particular attention to the length of the listing.

```
//
//   SwtMFC.cpp
//   A Simple Windows Template using the MFC library.
//   This code can serve as a template for the development
//   of other simple MFC applications.
//   Copyright (c) William H. Murray and Chris H. Pappas, 1999
//

#include <afxwin.h>
#include "SwtMFC.h"

CSwtMFCApp theApp;

CMainWnd::CMainWnd()
{
  Create(NULL,"A MFC Windows Programming Template",
         WS_OVERLAPPEDWINDOW,rectDefault,NULL,NULL);
}

void CMainWnd::OnPaint()
{
  CPaintDC dc(this);
  // draw text
  dc.TextOut(180,200,"Using the MFC Library",21);
  // draw a rectangle
  dc.Rectangle(10,10,100,150);
  // draw an ellipse
  dc.Ellipse(200,10,400,50);
  // draw a circle
  dc.Ellipse(10,250,210,450);
  // draw a diagonal line
```

```
  dc.MoveTo(300,300);
  dc.LineTo(450,420);
}

BEGIN_MESSAGE_MAP(CMainWnd,CFrameWnd)
  ON_WM_PAINT()
END_MESSAGE_MAP()

BOOL CSwtMFCApp::InitInstance()
{
  m_pMainWnd=new CMainWnd();
  m_pMainWnd->ShowWindow(m_nCmdShow);
  m_pMainWnd->UpdateWindow();

  return TRUE;
}
```

In the previous source code listing, you can examine all of the code necessary to produce this working template application. The next sections examine the programming details unique to the SwtMFC project.

The SwtMFC.h Header File

The SwtMFC.h header file is used to separate and identify the class definitions that are unique to the application. In the Easy project, shown earlier, these classes were part of the body of the application. Putting them in a separate header file is a matter of style, one encouraged by Microsoft as applications get larger and larger.

As you examine the header file, notice that the CMainWnd class contains a member function declaration named **OnPaint**() and a message map. For methods (member functions) such as **OnPaint** (), the *afx_msg* keyword is used instead of virtual. The **OnPaint**() method is a member of the CWnd class that the CMainWnd class overrides. This, in turn, allows the client area of the window to be altered.

> **note** This is why the Easy project couldn't draw in the client area! The **OnPaint()** method is automatically called when a WM_PAINT message is sent to a CMain Wnd object.

DECLARE_MESSAGE_MAP is used in virtually all MFC Windows applications. This line states that the class overrides the handling of certain messages. Microsoft uses message maps, instead of virtual functions, because they are more space efficient.

The Application File

The majority of this application's code is the same as that shown in the Easy project. The real difference is the inclusion of the **OnPaint()** message handler. Examine this unique piece of code.

```
void CMainWnd::OnPaint()
{
  CPaintDC dc(this);
  // draw text
  dc.TextOut(180,200,"Using the MFC Library",21);
  // draw a rectangle
  dc.Rectangle(10,10,100,150);
  // draw an ellipse
  dc.Ellipse(200,10,400,50);
  // draw a circle
  dc.Ellipse(10,250,210,450);
  // draw a diagonal line
  dc.MoveTo(300,300);
  dc.LineTo(450,420);
}
```

A device context is created for handling WM_PAINT messages. Now any Windows GDI functions that are encapsulated in the device context can be used to draw in the client area. When the **OnPaint()** method has ended, the destructor for CPaintDC is called automatically.

This application uses a fairly short message map, as you can see in the following code segment.

```
BEGIN_MESSAGE_MAP(CMainWnd,CFrameWnd)
  ON_WM_PAINT()
END_MESSAGE_MAP()
```

Two classes are identified by BEGIN_MESSAGE_MAP: CMainWnd and CFrameWnd. CMainWnd is the target class, and CFrameWnd is derived from the CWnd class. The **ON_WM_PAINT()** function processes all WM_PAINT messages and directs them to the **OnPaint()** method just discussed.

One of the biggest advantages of using message maps is the elimination of many switch/case statements that are so typical of procedure-oriented Windows applications.

Running the SwtMFC Project

When you create this project, name it *SwtMFC*. The header file is added by selecting the option shown in Figure 16-3.

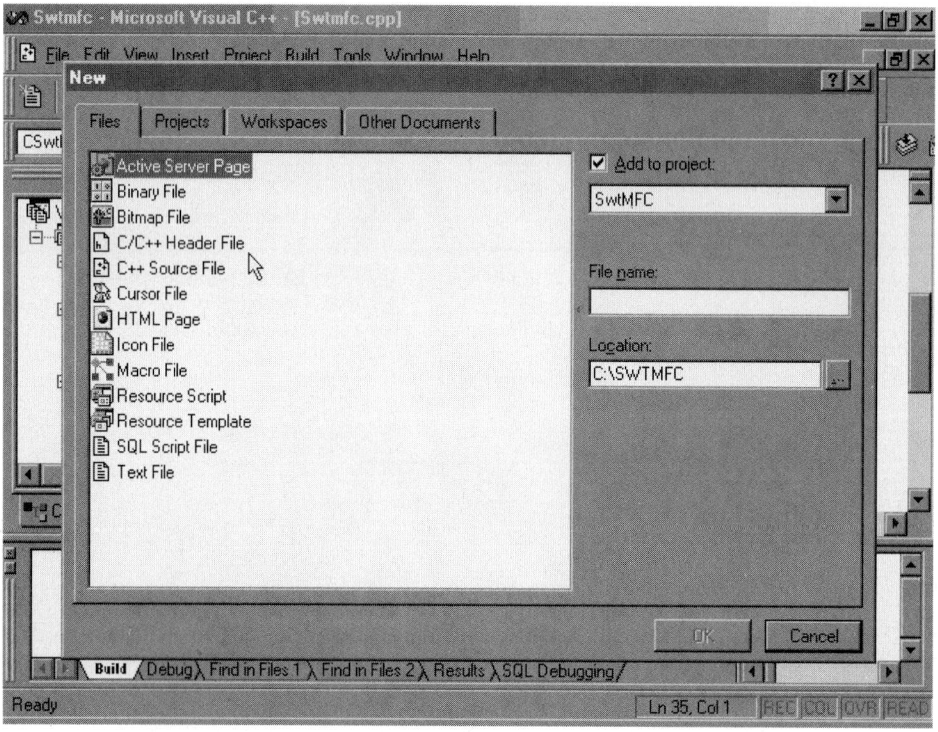

Chapter 16 • What's Next?

Figure 16-3 *Use this option to add a header file to the SwtMFC project.*

A Complete MFC Application **621**

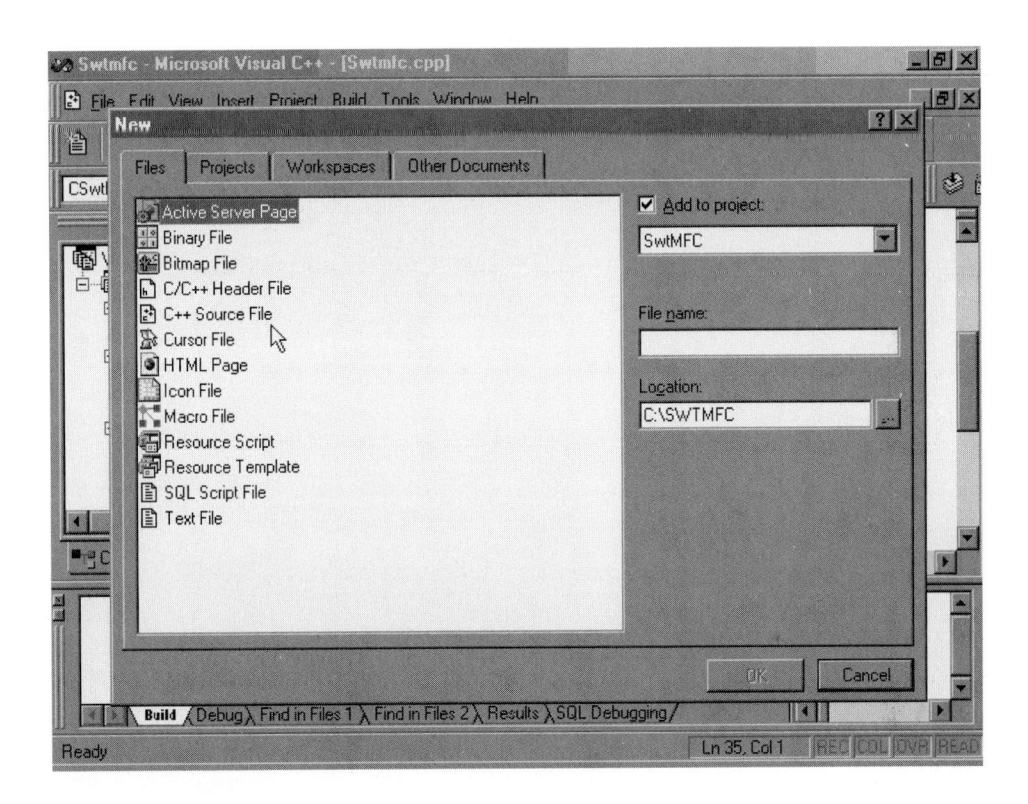

Figure 16–4 *Use this option to add a source code file to the SwtMFC project.*

The source code file can be added by using the option shown in Figure 16-4.

Chapter 16 • What's Next?

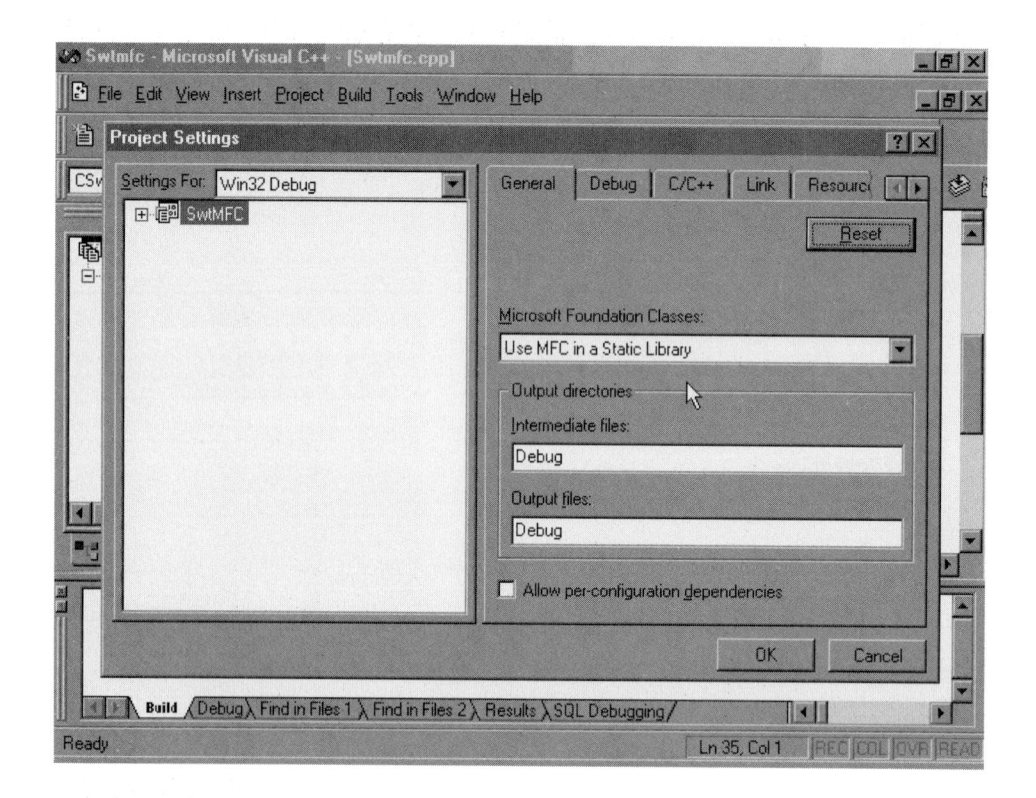

Figure 16-5 *Include the static MFC library as part of this project's build options.*

The SwtMFC project is built as a normal 32-bit application, but remember to set the build option to include the static MFC library, as shown in Figure 16-5.

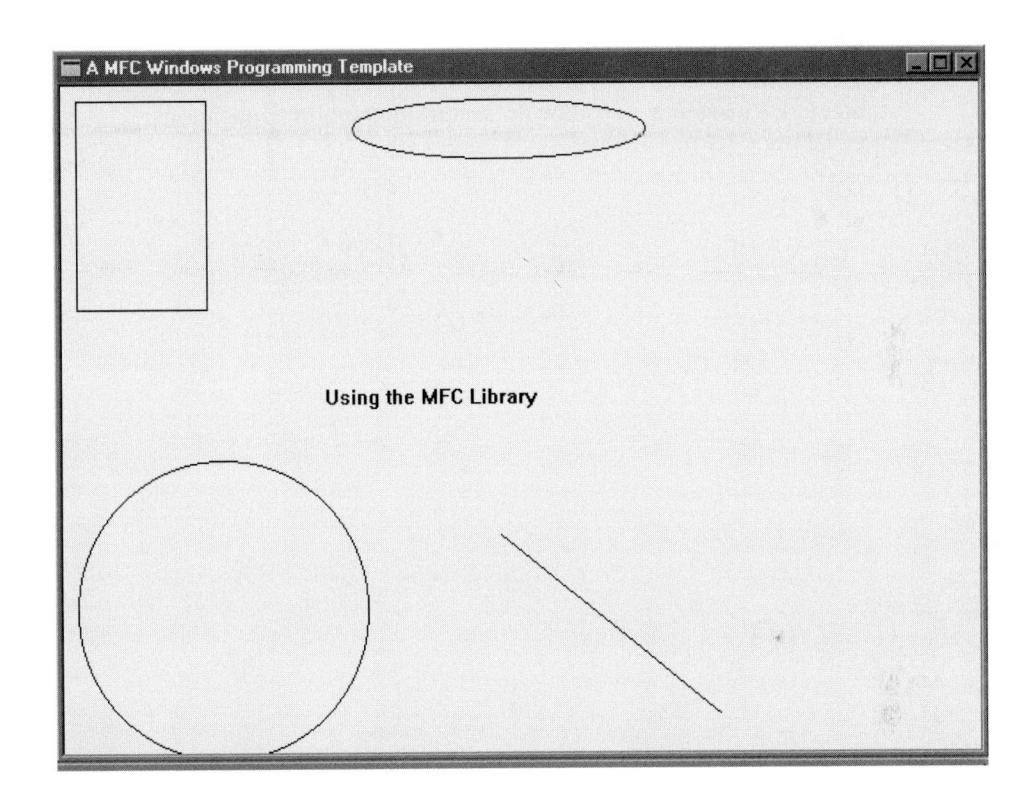

Figure 16-6 *SwtMFC is a template for all future MFC applications.*

Once all of the code is in place, build and execute the application. The screen should be similar to the one shown in Figure 16-6.

If you want to experiment with other GDI primitives, just add or remove them at will.

What's Really Next?

Not everything on a topic can be included in one book. No, not even in those monster 1,200-page complete references that bend the bookshelves at your favorite book store. If you've mastered the material in this book and want to continue your study of object-oriented Windows code, we suggest that you locate another book published by Prentice-Hall to complement the material presented in this book. Yes, there is still more! How about adding project resources such as menus, dialog boxes, icons, cursors, bitmaps, and so on?

The use of reusable classes is one of main drawing cards for simplified design and application maintenance with the MFC. If you continue your study of Windows programming with objects, you'll find that many additional features of the MFC library will help you develop applications ranging from simple interactive programs to robust presentation graphics applications.

INDEX

Symbols

#define, 32
& (ampersand), 326
.ani, 283
.cur, 283
.dsp, 52
.dsw, 52
.idb, 86
.ilk, 85
.obj, 85
.opt, 84
.pch, 85
.pdb, 85-86
.plg, 84
.wav (finding on system), 291-292
\\, 371
\t (tab stop), 338
__cdecl, 31
_afx_no_xxx, 85
_BRUSH (table of colors), 128-129
_gcvt(), 428-429
_itoa(), 139, 533, 539
| (OR), 66
16-bit nonpreemptive, 2-3
16x16 icons, 268
32-bit,
    addressing, 11
    heap, 11
    preemptive multitasking, 2-3
32x32 icons, 268
64-bit address, 14

A

about box example, 394-401
accelerated graphics port (AGP), 16
accelerators, 338-345
ACCELERATORS, 343-344, 353
accessing Windows environment, 89-141
active (application), 4
ActiveX control, 434
actual coordinates, 91
add icon to project, 267
adding
    project files, 45-48
    sound, 287-300
addressing (32-bit), 11
AFXWIN.H header file, 611-612
AGP (accelerated graphics port), 16
alarms, 121
Alpha systems, 12
ALT, 5
America Online (AOL), 292
ampersand (&), 336
AND, 162
ANSI fonts, 239
ANSI_CHARSET, 508
AnsiToOem(), 239
AOL (America Online), 292
application,
    message queue, 29
    writing simple Windows, 37-87
arbitrary units, 134
Arc(), 151-152, 163
ArcTo(), 151-152
argument (variable - function), 31
ASCII, 70
aspect ratio, 144
asynchronous message, 29
atof(), 427-429
atoi(), 507, 515, 532
autobuddy, 466
automatic leading and kerning, 239

B

background (changing color), 125-130
background.cpp, 125-128
bar chart, 168-175, 517-544
bars (drawing), 173
basetsd.h, 81
BEGIN, 342-343, 346
BeginPaint(), 79-81, 149
binding (delayed), 9

BitBlt(), 143, 175-187, 302-318, 560, 567, 594
    table raster operations, 179
bitmap objects, 25
BITMAP, 184, 304-307, 316, 324-327, 566
bitmapped image,
    manipulating, 175-187
    retrieval, 184-186
bitmaps, 30, 124, 301-328
    examples, 309-328
    functions, 302-309
    GDI bitmapped image, 309-312
    monochrome to color, 307
    photographic bitmapped image, 320-328
    raster operation codes, 303
    scanned bitmapped image, 312-320
    stretch mode parameters, 308
BM_, 28
BOOL, 152
border, 19
Borland, 37-38
BRUSH (table of colors), 128-129
brush, 30, 158-161
    color changing, 173
    objects, 26
BS_ (brush styles),
    controls, 96
    SOLID, 159
    styles, 102-103
    table of, 160
BS_AUTORADIOBUTTON, 404
buddy (control), 448
build, 53-55
button control, 390

626   Index

C

C/C++, 5
callback, 122
CALLBACK, 59
calling convention, 31
CANCEL, 115
CAPTION, 386, 396
caret, 23, 30
    objects, 23
cbClsExtra, 64
CBS_ (table of COMBOBOX styles), 107-108
cbSize, 200
cbWndExtra, 64
CC_ (table of), 146-147
CC_FULLOPEN, 484, 505, 530
CC_RGBINIT, 484, 530
cf.cpp, 245-250
CF_EFFECTS, 473, 505, 530
CF_INITTOLOGFONTSTRUCT, 473, 505, 530
CF_SCREENFONTS, 473, 505, 530
cfi.cpp, 250-255
CFrameWnd, 610, 617, 613-615
CGdiObject, 604
changing,
    background color, 125-130
    font program, 242-257
    mapping mode, 130-136
    pen, brush color, 173
    text color, 161, 173-174
    viewport and window extents, 93
    window (SetClassWord()), 114
character,
    cell, 237
    height, 202
characteristics (font table of), 237
chart (bar - simple), 168-175
check box control, 115, 390
CHECKED, 344
CheckMenuItem(), 356, 360, 441
CheckRadioButton(), 405-4098
CHOOSECOLOR, 484-489, 505, 530, 554
    flag constants, 487-488

CHOOSEFONT, 475-477, 504, 513, 529
    types and members, 476
choosing initial window parameters, 94
Chord(), 152, 163
circles, 148
ClassView, 82
client area coordinates, 21, 91-92
clienttoScreen(), 92
CLIP_ (table of), 233
ClipCursor(), 284
CObject, 603-609
    derived classes (table of), 605-609
color changing,
    background, 125-130
    text, 173-174
COLOR_ (table of), 65
COLORREF, 157-159, 161, 505, 530, 554
colors (changing text), 161
combo box control, 391
COMBOBOX control, 98
commdlg.h (common dialog header file), 471, 475, 482, 501, 526, 552, 572
comment block, 57
common,
    color dialog box, 478-492
    controls, 433
    font dialog box, 469-478
    user interface, 4
commonly used controls, 114
comparison of Windows, 14-16
complete applications, 493-544
    bar chart, 517-544
    pie chart, 493-517
concepts (Windows), 1-36
Console API, 12
constants,
    font, 232-234
    scroll bar - table of, 191
control,
    box, 19
    classes (table of), 95-99

    message timing, 136-141
    panel (sound), 288-290
control buddy, 448
CONTROL, 404
controls (dialog box), 389-392
coordinate system, 11, 90-94, 172
cos(), 508, 515
count.cpp, 254-257
CP_ (table of), 145
CPaintDC, 617
crash management, 13
create an About dialog box, 392-393
Create(), 610, 613, 617
CreateCompatibleDC(), 186, 305, 318-319, 326-327, 567, 594
CreateDC(), 93
CreateFont(), 242, 245, 247-249, 533-534
    parameters (table of), 243-244
CreateFontIndirect(), 242, 244-245, 250, 474-477, 508, 513, 532-538
CreateHatchBrush(), 173
CreateIcon(), 261
CreateIconFromResource(), 260-261
CreateIconFromResourceEx(), 261
CreateIconIndirect(), 261, 274
CreatePen(), 173, 398, 407
CreateSolidBrush(), 179, 310-311, 356, 508
CreateToolbarEx(), 434-435, 438-440, 445-448
CreateWindow(), 199, 208
    parameters, 94-95
    understanding, 68
creating a window with MFC, 610-611
CS_ (table of), 63
CS_HREDRAW, 66
CS_VREDRAW, 66
CTEXT, 396, 403, 414, 423
CTRL, 5
Ctrl+F5 (execute program), 55
cursor, 30
    .cpp, 278-285
    .cur, 279

Index

and icons, 259-300
custom and standard,
    276-285
objects, 23
resource editor, 275
special functions, 281-
    285
Windows standard
    table of, 277-278
custom,
    and standard cursors,
        276-285
    control, 391
    or standard icons?,
        261-262
CW_USEDEFAULT, 68, 172
CWinApp, 610, 612-613, 617

D

date time picker control, 391
DDE (dynamic data exchange),
    28
debug,
    file entries, 84-86
    release, 52
    subdirectory, 52
default,
    mapping mode, 148
    pixel mapping mode,
        144
DECLARE_MESSAGE_MAP(),
    617
DEFPUSHBUTTON, 387, 396,
    403, 413
DefWindowProc(), 81
delayed binding, 9
DeleteDC(), 186, 306, 318-319,
    326-327, 568
DeleteObject(), 159, 161, 256,
    399
DestroyIcon(), 275
developing Windows pro-
    grams, 34
device,
    context handle, 149-
        150
    context, 92
    coordinates, 92
    driver, 7
    drivers, 143
    independence, 7
    independent, 144
    units, 91

DEVICE_DEFAULT_FONT, 476
dialog boxes, 24, 30, 381-432
    about box example,
        394-401
    controls, 389-392
    create an about box,
        392-393
    message boxes, 430-
        432
    radio button example,
        401-408
    real number example,
        421-430
    resource editor, 386-
        389
    shape dialog exam-
        ple, 408-411
    text and integer exam-
        ple, 411-421
    variety of inputs, 394
    what is a, 385-386
DIALOG, 386, 396, 403
DialogBox(), 398-400, 406-
    407, 417, 427, 462, 531
DISCARDABLE, 30, 264, 316,
    324, 346
dispatch message, 30
DispatchMessage(),69-70, 359,
    440
display (graphics), 143
distributed computing, 13
DLGPROC, 398
DLLs, 5
document-centric, 2
DrawIcon(), 261, 274
DrawIconEx(), 274
drawing,
    bars, 173
    functions, 90
    mode selection, 162
    primitives, 143-187
DrawText(), 219-222
drivers, 7
DS_MODALFRAME, 386, 396
DT_ (table of), 145, 220-221
DWORD, 364
dynamic,
    data exchange (DDE),
        28
    linking, 9

E

edit box,

control, 391
    what is, 116
EDITTEXT, 387, 413
elements (key Windows), 3-9
Ellipse(), 135, 138, 152-153,
    163, 187, 228, 349-352, 357,
    407-410, 617
END, 342, 346
EndDialog(), 398-400, 405-408,
    416-417, 426, 472
EndPaint(), 80, 150
environment (GDI), 144-148
ES_ (table of EDIT controls),
    96-97, 104-105
ES_AUTOHSCROLL, 387
executable (generating), 53-55
executing a program -
    Ctrl+F5(first), 55-57
EXECUTIVE, 27
extents (window changing),
    93, 134
ExtractIcon(), 261

F

families (font), 241-242
FAR PASCAL, 60
FF_ (table of), 233
FIFO (first in first out), 29
file-format-transparent, 1
files (adding to project), 45-48
FileView, 82
FillRect(), 593-595
filters (message), 70
final release, 52
FindClose(), 376-379
FindFirstFile(), 376-378
finding sound resources, 287-
    293
FindNextFile(), 376-379
first in first out (FIFO), 29
fixed fonts, 239
flying saucer animation appli-
    cation, 559-570
fMask, 200
font, 30, 201, 231-257
    ANSI, 239
    basics, 238-241
    characteristics (table
        of), 237
    constants, 232-234
    families, 241-242
    logical vs. physical,
        240

mapping penalty weights (table of), 241
objects, 24
OEM, 239
printer, 242
scheme for mapping, 240-241
system default, 242
FONT, 386, 396
for, 311, 379, 516
format (standard message), 27-28
functions,
    special cursor, 281-285
    special icon, 273-275
    standard Windows, 31
    variable argument, 31
fuSound, 297
FW_ (table of), 232
FW_NORMAL, 508

G

G2 security, 13
GCL_HBRBACKGROUND, 129, 356, 441
GDI,
    bitmapped image, 309-312
    drawing primitives, 150-187
    environment, 144-148
    improvements, 12
    tools and techniques, 158-161
generating executable, 53-55
GetClassLong(), 125
GetClientRect(), 567, 592-593
GetCurrentDirectory(), 364, 370
GetDC(), 92, 373, 567, 592
GetDeviceCaps(), 144-148
GetDiskFreeSpaceEx(), 364, 368-370
GetDlgItemInt(), 411, 416, 420, 461, 465
GetDlgItemText(), 411, 416, 419, 426-428, 503-509, 528
GetLocalTime(), 365, 369
GetMapMode(), 91
GetMenu(), 356, 359-360, 441
GetMessage(), 69-70

GetObject(), 305-306, 318-319, 326-327, 473, 476
GetPixel(), 157
GetScrollInfo(), 199
GetStockObject(),66, 128, 158-159, 473, 476
GetTextMetrics(), 201, 373, 378
getting started, 16-18
GetUpdateRect(), 80
GetVersion(), 364, 370
GetWindowDC(), 93
graph1.cpp (primitives - GDI), 163-168
graph2.cpp (bar chart), 169-172
graph3.cpp (Bitblt()), 176-178
graph4.cpp (BitBlt()), 182-184
graphics (scrolling), 223-229
Graphics Device,
    drawing primitives, 143-187
    interface (GDI - defined), 143
graphics primitives, 143
Graphics User Interface (GUI), 8
graphics.cpp, 223-228
GRAYED, 344
group box control, 391
HAL (hardware abstraction layer), 10
handle, 59-60
    device context, 149-150
    memory device context (hmdc), 304
hardware,
  abstraction layer (HAL), 10
  independence, 6-8
  indifferent, 1
  portability, 10

H

HBITMAP, 319, 565, 591
hbrBackground, 65, 128
HBRUSH, 160, 310
hCursor, 65
heap (32-bit), 11
HELP, 344
HFONT, 473
HGDIOBJ, 504, 529
hIcon, 64
hIconSm, 67

HIGH_PRIORITY_CLASS, 30
high-resolution graphics, 124
hinst, 61
hInstance, 64
HIWORD, 133, 349
hmdc (handle memory device context), 304
HMENU, 356
hNFont, 247
hOFont, 247
horizontal scroll bar, 20-21
hot,
    key, 339
    spot, 276
HPEN, 158, 398, 406, 473
hPreInst, 61
HS_ (table of), 160
hungarian style, 32-33
HWND, 59
hWnd, 62

I

ICC_ (INITCOMMONCONTROLSEX structure flag constants), 464
ICC_PROGRESS_CLASS, 460
ICC_UPDOWN_CLASS, 461, 465
icon, 30
    adding to project, 267
    and cursors, 259-300
    functions (special), 273-275
    large, 262-263
    objects, 23
    recommended size, color, 261
    resource editor, 259-263
    size, 260-261
    standard or custom, 261-262
    standard Windows table of, 262
ICON, 264
icon.cpp, 262-267
icon98.cpp, 269-273
ICONINFO, 274
IDC_ (table of), 277, 282-283
IDC_ARROW, 66
IDI_ERROR, 272
IDLE_PRIORITY_CLASS, 30
if, 569, 596

Index 629

image, 301-302
    bitmapped - manipulating, 175-187
    retrieval, 184-186
INACTIVE, 344
Information on Installed Devices, 144-148
INITCOMMONCONTROLSEX structure flag constants (ICC_), 464
InitCommonControlsEx(), 460-465
    flag constants, 464
INITCOMMONCONTROLSEX, 460-461, 465
initial window parameters, 94
initiating message-loop, 60
InitInstance(), 610, 617
input message, 5
instance, 59
Internet (sound resources finding), 292-294
InvalidateRect(), 80, 140, 203-204, 210, 256, 349-352, 378, 417
InvalidateRgn(), 80
itoa(), 256-257

K

kerning, 239
key codes (table of virtual), 117-120
key elements of Windows, 3-9
keyboard input, 115
keywords (menu), 344-345
KillTimer(), 121, 568, 592, 617

L

large and small icons, 268-273
LB_, 28
LBS_,
    table of LISTBOX controls, 97
    table of LISTBOX styles, 105-107
LC_ (table of), 147
leading, 239
lfHeight, 252
lfPitchAndFamily, 238
LineTo(), 153, 163, 168, 398, 407-409
LINK, 85
linker, 34

linking (dynamic), 9
list box control, 391
    what is, 115-116
LoadAccelerators, 355, 359, 439
LoadBitmap(), 185, 304-305, 317, 325, 566
LoadCursor(), 66, 280-283
LoadCursorFromFile(), 283-284
LoadIcon(), 261, 271, 273-274
LoadImage(), 274
LoadString(), 593
loan application, 211-217
loan.cpp, 211-217
LOGFONT, 232, 473, 476, 504, 513, 529
LOGFONTA, 236-238, 245
LOGFONTW, 237
logical,
    font, 252
    units, 90, 134
    versus physical fonts, 240
look (The - creating), 19
loop (standard message), 29-30
LOWORD, 133, 349, 356
LPARAM, 27, 59
*lpCursorName*s (table of), 282-283
lpfnWndProc, 63-64
lpLogFont, 244
lpMsg, 62
lpMsg, 69-70
lpszCmdLine, 61
lpszSound, 297
lpszSoundName, 297
LPTOOLTIPTEXT, 441, 446
lpwcx, 67
LRESULT CALLBACK, 79
LTEXT, 387, 413, 423
LTGRAY_BRUSH, 129, 160
LYCOS, 293

M

mainframe computer, 13
makefiles, 86
MAKELONG, 461
making sound resources, 294-300
mapper.cpp (change map mode), 130-136
mapping fonts, 240-241
mapping mode, 91
    changing, 130-136

default pixel, 144
MaskBlt(), 302
maximize box, 20
MB_ICONEXCLAMATION, 427
MB_ICONQUESTION, 427
MB_ICONSTOP
MCI_OPEN_PARMS, 574
MCI_PLAY_PARMS, 574
mciOpenParms(), 574
mciSendCommand(), 574, 580-581
member functions, 615
memory, 11
    allocation, 123
    management, 5, 122-125
    protection, 13-14
menu bar, 21
menu, 329-380
    accelerators, 338-345
    concepts, 330-338
    designing menus, 330-338
    examples, 345-380
    keywords, 344-345
    pathway to dialog boxes, 329
    virtual key, 340-344
    what is a menu?, 330
MENU, 342, 346, 353, 403
MENUBREAK, 344
MENUITEM, 342, 346, 353, 403
message, 5
    box, 24, 30, 430-432
    box constants, 430-431
    communication via, 26-30
    control with timer, 136-141
    filters, 70
    format (standard), 27-28
    loop, 29-30, 69-70
    processing, 29
    queue, 27
    system, 6
    type, 28
    who sends, 28
    Windows - table of, 72-79
message-based communication, 6
MessageBox(), 208, 427-430

Index

MF_CHECKED, 356, 441
MF_UNCHECKED, 356, 441
MFC,
    application SwtMFC.cpp, 616-624
    constructor, 615
    Microsoft Foundation Class, 37
    programming concepts (easy.cpp), 610-616
    why use?, 602-603
Microsoft Foundation Class Library, 601-624
    why use the MFC, 602-603
    CObject, 603-609
    complete MFC application SwtMFC.cpp, 616-624
    application code, 619
    SwtMFC header file, 618
    testing the application, 619-624
    programming concepts (easy.cpp), 610-616
    AFXWIN.H header file, 611-612
    CFrameWnd, 613-615
    constructor, 615
    creating a window, 610-611
    CWinApp, 612-613
    member functions, 615
    testing a simple application, 615
Microsoft Windows 95/98/NT, 1, 3
millimeters, 93
minimize box, 20
MIPS (symmetric multiprocessing), 3
MM_ (table of), 91
MM_ANSIOTROPIC, 93
MM_HIENGLISH, 93
MM_ISOTROPIC, 93, 134, 173, 352, 538
MM_LOENGLISH, 92
MM_TEXT, 90, 144, 158, 167
mmsystem.h (sound header file), 552, 572

monochrome to color (bitmaps), 307
month calendar control, 391
mortgage application, 211-217
mouse, 5
    input, 115
    sketching application, 545-559
MoveTo(), 618
MoveToEx(), 153-154, 156, 163, 168, 398, 407-409
MSG (struct typedef), 62
multimedia sound (adding), 287-300
multiprocessing, 12
multitasking operating systems, 4-5
multithread, 12

N

naming conventions (Windows, table of), 32-33
nCmdShow, 61, 68
Network API, 12
new,
    project (starting), 40-53
    technologies, 16
NEWTEXTMETRIC, 232, 234-235
NEWTEXTMETRICA, 235, 238
NMAKE, 52
NOINVERT, 343-344, 353
nonrelocatable objects, 125
non-TrueType, 240
NORMAL_PRIORITY_CLASS, 30
NOT, 162
NULL, 61
NUM LOCK, 5

O

object,
    classes, 21-22
    model, 2-3
    oriented technology, 22-23
OCR_ (table of), 283-284
OEM fonts, 239
OemToAnsi(), 239
OK, 115
OnPaint(), 618-619
open system architecture, 13

OPENFILENAME, 574, 577-580
    flags, 578-579
    lpfnhook flags, 579
OR, 162
orientation, 91
origin, 91
    shifting, 135
OS/2, 1, 3
ostrstream(), 219
OUT_ (table of), 233
OWL (Object Windows Library), 37-38
OWNERDRAW, 345

P

paint, 29
PAINTSTRUCT, 79, 149, 310, 326, 356
PALETTERGB, 555
pane (Workspace), 82
PBM_ (progress control message constants), 454-455
PBM_SETBARCOLOR, 460
PBM_SETBKCOLOR, 460
PBM_SETPOS, 460
PBM_SETRANGE, 460
PBM_SETSTEP, 460
PBM_STEPIT, 460
PBS_ (progress control styles), 454
PC_ (table of), 147
pen, 30, 158-159
    color changing, 173
    objects, 25
persistence, 604
photographic bitmapped image, 320-328
physical,
    address, 14
    units, 91
    versus logical fonts, 240
pie,
    chart application, 493-517
    wedges, 148
Pie(), 154-155, 163, 508, 515
pixels, 92
platform independence, 10
PlgBlt(), 302
plotter, 143
plug-and-play, 8
point (type font), 231

Index

POINT, 155, 554
Polygon(), 155, 163
Polyline(), 156, 163, 168
PolylineTo(), 156-157
POPUP, 342, 345-346, 353, 403
position,
    screen output, 189
    scroll bar, 192
preemptive multitasking, 4-5
primitives (drawing - GDI), 143-187
printer, 143
    fonts, 242
privilege level, 14
processing messages, 29
ProgName[], 60
program,
    database, 85
    developing Windows, 34
    message queue, 27
    writing simple Windows, 37-87
progress control, 391, 448-469
    message constants (PBM_), 454-455
    styles (PBS_), 454
project,
    adding files, 45-48
    adding icon resource, 267
    files, 84-86
    new starting, 40-53
proportionally spaced fonts, 239
PS_ (table of), 158
push-button control (what is), 115
PUSHBUTTON, 387, 413
pushing parameters, 31

Q

queue-based input, 5-6
quit, 29

R

R2_ (table of), 162
R2-COPYPEN, 162
radio button,
    control, 392
    dialog box example, 401-408
    what is, 115

range (scroll bar), 192
raster,
    fonts, 240
    operation codes, 303
    table BitBlt(), 179
RC_ (table of), 146
rcPaint, 149
read-only, 30
real number dialog box example, 421-430
REALTIME_PRIORITY_CLASS, 30
reasons for developing Windows apps. 1-3
rebuild all, 53-55, 83
recording (sound), 295-296
RECT, 149-150, 566
Rectangle(), 157, 163, 168, 180, 187, 223, 310-311, 407-412, 617
rectangle, 135
reducing,
    number of objects in memory, 124
    object size, 124
RegisterClass(), 59
    understanding, 66-67
RegisterClassEx(), 67, 261, 271
registering window, 60
ReleaseCapture(), 556
ReleaseDC(), 374, 568
relocatable objects, 125
remote procedure call (RPC), 12
required,
    software, 17
    system, 17
    Window function, 71-79
resource compiler, 34
resource editor, 34, 386-389
    icon, 259-263, 275
resources,
    sound, 287-300
    standard Windows, 30-31
retrieval (image), 184-186
reusable dynamic link libraries (DLL), 8-9
RGB(), 159, 161
RISC, 3
RoundRect(), 157, 163

RPC (remote procedure call), 12
RTEXT, 414

S

SB_ (table of), 191, 202
SB_LINEDOWN, 191
SB_LINELEFT, 203
SB_LINERIGHT, 203
SB_PAGEDOWN, 191
SB_PAGERIGHT, 203
SB_RIGHT, 191
SB_THUMBTRACK, 201, 203
SBS_,
    table of SCROLLBAR controls, 98
    table of SCROLLBAR styles, 108-109
scalability, 12-13
scaled axes, 134
scan code, 5
scanned bitmapped image, 312-320
screen,
    coordinate system, 92
    output (position of), 189
    saver application (scrsav), 586-599
    saver components, 584-586
screen-saver, 583-600
    components, 584-586
    scrsav project, 586-599
ScreenToclient(), 92
scrnsave.h (screen saver header file), 584-586, 591
scrnsave.lib (screen saver library), 583
scroll bar,
    adding to application, 193-199
    constants, 191
    control, 392
    position, 192
    range, 192
    types, 192
    understanding control, 190-229
    what is, 116
scroll.cpp, 193-199
SCROLLBAR control, 98
SCROLLINFO, 200, 372

scrolling,
    graphics, 223-229
    table, 211-217
ScrollwindowEx(), 203, 209, 375
security, 13
selection,
    check list, 115
    group items, 115
SelectObject(), 158-160, 173, 186, 305, 310, 318-319, 326-327
SendDlgItemMessage(), 115, 451, 455, 460-461, 465
sending messages, 28
SendMessage(), 398-400, 406, 418, 427, 462
SEPARATOR, 342, 344, 353
serifs, 231
SetBkColor(), 174
SetBkMode(), 161
SetCapture(), 555
SetClassLong(), 114, 356, 360, 441, 506, 531
SetClassWord(), 114
SetCurrentDirectory(), 376-378
SetCursor(), 284
SetCursorPos(), 284
SetMapMode(), 91-93, 349-352, 357, 442, 505, 513, 532-538
SetPixel(), 157, 163
SetROP2(), 162
SetScrollInfo(), 199, 202, 209, 374-375
SetStretchBltMode(), 302-328
SetTextColor(), 161, 168, 173, 474, 477, 513, 532-539
SetTimer(), 121, 139, 208, 567, 592
SetViewportExt(), 134
SetViewportExtEx(), 349-352, 357, 442, 505, 513, 532-538
SetViewportOrgEx(), 135, 349-352, 357, 442, 505, 513, 532-538
SetWindowExt(), 134
SetWindowExtEx(),93, 134-135, 349-352, 357, 442, 505, 513, 532-538
shape dialog box example, 408-411

shapes (drawing variety), 163-168
shareable objects, 124
shared,
    memory, 11
    resource, 5
shell,
    large, 260
    small, 260
SHIFT, 5
ShowCursor(), 285
showing a window, 68-69
ShowWindow(), 68-69, 112-113, 610, 615, 618
SIF_ (table of), 200
simple, applications using GDI tools and techniques, 163-187
    understanding template, 57-87
    windows template (swt.cpp), 37-87
sin(), 508, 515
size (icons), 260-261
sizeof(), 272
sketching, animation and video, 545-582
    flying saucer animation application, 559-570
    mouse sketching application, 545-559
    video player application, 570-582
Sleep(), 565-567, 594
slider control, 392
small and large icons, 268-273
SND_ASYNC, 297, 567
SND_LOOP, 297
SND_MEMORY, 297
SND_NODEFAULT, 297
SND_NOSTOP, 297
SND_SYNC, 297
sndPlaySound(), 297-300, 555-557, 567, 592-594 .
software,
    indifferent, 1
    required, 17
sound,
    adding, 287-300
    control panel, 288-290
    finding, making, 287-293
    recorder, 295-296

special controls and dialog boxes, 433-492
    common color dialog box, 478-492
    common font dialog box, 469-478
    spin and progress controls, 448-469
    toolbars and tooltips, 434-448
special,
    cursor functions, 281-285
    icon functions, 273-275
spin control, 392, 448-469
    message constants (UDM_), 450-451
    styles (UDS_), 449-450
sprintf(), 364, 369, 379
SRCCOPY, 307, 319
SS_,
    table of STATIC controls, 99
    table of STATIC styles, 109-110
stack, 31
standard,
    and custom cursors, 276-285
    message format, 27-28
    message loop, 29-30
    or custom icons, 261-262
    Windows functions, 31
    Windows resources, 30-31
starting new project, 40-53
static control (what is), 114-115
STATIC control, 98
static text control, 392
static, 140
stdafx.h, 85
stdlib.h, 139
strcpy(), 375-376, 532
stretch mode parameters for bitmaps, 308
StretchBlt(), 302, 306-309, 319-320, 326
strlen(), 508, 533
strtok(), 507, 514, 532
style, 63
SVGA, 144

Index 633

SW_ (table of window states), 61-62, 112-113
SW_SHOWMAXIMIZED, 61, 69
SW_SHOWMINIMIZED, 61, 69
SW_SHOWMINNOACTIVE, 69
SW_SHOWNORMAL, 61, 68
switch-case, 351
swt.cpp, 37-87
    understanding code, 57-87
    WNDCLASS wcApp, 65-66
symbolic constants, 27
symmetric multiprocessing, 12
synchronous message, 29
system,
    font, 242
    large, 260
    menu, 19
    message queue, 27-29
    queue, 5
    requirements, 17
    small, 260
    timer, 204-211
    timer (using), 136-141
    timer (what is), 120-122
SYSTEM_FONT, 473
SYSTEMTIME, 367-369
systimer.cpp (timer message control), 136-139
szCursorName, 280
szIconName, 266
szProgName, 68

T

tab,
    control, 392
    stop (\t), 338
table (scrolling), 211-217
tape backup, 12
TB_SETBITMAPSIZE, 435
TBBUTTON, 439
TBSTATE_ENABLED, 443-444, 447-448
TBSTYLE_BUTTON, 443-444, 447-448
TBSTYLE_TOOLTIPS, 439, 445
TC_ (table of), 147
technologies (new), 16
template (swt.cpp), 37-87
terminate box, 20
terminology (Windows), 1-36

text,
    changing color, 161, 173-174
    and integer dialog box example, 411-421
TEXTMETRIC, 201, 232, 372, 378
TEXTMETRICA, 235
TEXTMETRICS, 228
TextOut(),90-93, 173, 204, 256-257, 310-311, 349-352, 365, 379, 429, 532, 617
thumb, 190
thunks, 11
ticker.cpp, 204-207
ticker-tape message, 207
timer, 5-6, 29
    using system, 136-141
title bar, 19
tmAscent, 235
tmAveCharWidth, 235
tmDescent, 235
tmDigitizedAspectX, 238
tmDigitizedAspectY, 238
tmExternalLeading, 238
tmHeight, 235
tmInternalLeading, 235, 238
tmOverhang, 238
TMPF_ (table of), 233
toolbars, 434-448
tooltips, 434-448
TranslateAccelerators(), 359, 440
TranslateMessage(), 69-70, 359, 440
TrueType, 238-241, 252
    fonts, 240
    names (table of), 250
TTN_NEEDTEXT, 441, 446
type (of scroll bar), 192
typedef, 32
typeface, 231

U

UDM_ (spin control message constants), 450-451
UDM_SETPOS, 461
UDM_SETRANGE, 461
UDS_ (spin control styles), 449-450
UINT, 59
ULARGE_INTEGER, 364, 368
understanding,

    Simple Windows Template (swt.cpp), 57-87
    Windows Concepts, 1-36
UNICODE, 237
United States Dept. of Defense, 13
universal serial bus (USB), 16
UNIX, 1, 3, 10
update window contents (timer), 121
UpdateWindow(), 68-69, 203-204, 210, 256, 417, 610, 615, 618
updating a window, 68-69
upward compatibility, 3
USB (universal serial bus), 16
USER, 27
user-defined units, 93

V

variable argument functions, 31
variety of inputs for dialog boxes, 394
vector fonts, 240
version features (table - 15), 14-16
vertical scroll bar, 20
vfw.h (video header file), 572
VGA, 148, 167
video player application, 570-582
viewport, 92-93, 135
VIRTKEY, 343-344, 353
virtual,
    address space, 14, 122
    key (table of), 117-120, 340-344
    key code, 5
    machine, 26
    memory, 11-14
Visual C/C++ compiler, 34
visual interface, 2
Visual Studio (starting), 38-39
VK_, 353

W

wave.cpp, 298-300
wcApp, 62
what is a dialog box?, 385-386
while, 514
WHITE_BRUSH, 129

634   Index

whole window coordinate system, 92
width (font), 239
WIN.INI, 283
Win16 versus Win32, 9-10
Win32, 4
    application (project-type), 42
    based, 60
    table of, 10-12
WIN32_FIND_DATA, 372, 379
WINAPI, 31, 60
window,
    control (taking of), 189-230
    handle, 27
    showing, 68-69
    updating, 68-69
Windows,
    3.x, 9-10
    background color, 125-130
    details, 89-141
    messages (table), 72-79
    NT, 2
    NT security, 13

version comparison, 14-16
versus windows, 18
windows.h, 32
WinMain(), 59-62
    return value, 70
    swt.cpp, 66-67
wizards, 16
WM_, 28
    message table, 72-79
WM_CHAR, 70
WM_CREATE, 32, 201
WM_DESTROY, 81, 121
WM_HSCROLL, 203, 209, 228
WM_KEYDOWN, 70
WM_KEYUP, 70
WM_PAINT, 69, 79-81, 140, 204, 210, 219, 228, 247, 252
WM_QUIT, 60, 70
WM_SIZE, 133, 201
WM_TIMER, 121, 140, 207, 209, 256
WM_VSCROLL, 203, 209, 228
WNDCLASS (struct typedef), 63, 267, 272
WNDCLASSEX, 67-261, 271-272
WndProc() (understanding), 59, 71-79, 209, 218, 228

work area, 21
workspace pane, 82
workspace, 52
WPARAM, 27, 59
writing (Windows apps.), 37-87
WS_ (styles - table of window), 99-102
WS_CAPTION, 386, 396
WS_EX_ (table of extended styles), 111-112
WS_HSCROLL, 200
WS_OVERLAPPEDWINDOW, 68
WS_POPUP, 386, 396
WS_SYSMENU, 386, 396
WS_VSCROLL, 200
www.lycos.com, 292-293

X

x-axis, 134
xClientView, 133
XGA, 144
XOR, 162

Y

y-axis, 134
yClientView, 133

PRENTICE HALL
Professional Technical Reference
Tomorrow's Solutions for Today's Professionals.

Keep Up-to-Date with PH PTR Online!

We strive to stay on the cutting-edge of what's happening in professional computer science and engineering. Here's a bit of what you'll find when you stop by **www.phptr.com**:

Special interest areas offering our latest books, book series, software, features of the month, related links and other useful information to help you get the job done.

Deals, deals, deals! Come to our promotions section for the latest bargains offered to you exclusively from our retailers.

Need to find a bookstore? Chances are, there's a bookseller near you that carries a broad selection of PTR titles. Locate a Magnet bookstore near you at www.phptr.com.

What's New at PH PTR? We don't just publish books for the professional community, we're a part of it. Check out our convention schedule, join an author chat, get the latest reviews and press releases on topics of interest to you.

Subscribe Today! **Join PH PTR's monthly email newsletter!**

Want to be kept up-to-date on your area of interest? Choose a targeted category on our website, and we'll keep you informed of the latest PH PTR products, author events, reviews and conferences in your interest area.

Visit our mailroom to subscribe today! **http://www.phptr.com/mail_lists**